The
SECRET
SEX LIVES
of
FAMOUS
PEOPLE

The
SECRET
SEX LIVES
of
FAMOUS
PEOPLE

Irving Wallace
Amy Wallace
David Wallechinsky
Sylvia Wallace

DORSET PRESS
New York

A Cresset Press Book,
an imprint of Random House UK Ltd,
20 Vauxhall Bridge Road, London SW1V 2SA

First published in 1981 as
The Intimate Sex Lives of Famous People
This edition published in 1993

This edition distributed by Dorset Press,
a division of Marboro Books Corp.
1993 Dorset Press

Cover photograph: Reed International Books Ltd/Vernon Morgan

ISBN 1–56619–161–0

Printed and bound in Great Britain by
Mackays of Chatham PLC, Chatham, Kent

Executive Editor:
Carol Orsag
Intimate Lives Managing Editor:
Vicki Scott
Associate Editor:
Elizebethe Kempthorne
Senior Staff Researchers:
Helen Ginsburg
Anita Taylor
Loreen Leo
Linda Schallan
Torene Svitil
Claudia Peirce
Assistant Staff Researchers:
Diane Brown Shepard
Kristine H. Johnson
Karen Pedersen
Sue Ann Power
Editorial Aides:
Linda Laucella
Lee Clayton
Joanne Maloney
Patricia Begalla
Photograph Editor:
Danny Biederman
Foreign Researchers:
Dr Primo Povolato (Italy)
Dr L. Alonso Tejada (Spain)
Copy Editor:
Wayne Lawson
Lists for this edition devised by
Alexis Lykiard

Contributors

The initials of contributor(s) appear at the end of each entry.
When 'Eds.' is used, it means that the material has been
contributed by the authors and staff of *The Secret
Sex Lives of Famous People*.

A.E.	Ann Elwood	K.P.	Karen Pedersen
A.K.	Aaron Kass	L.A.B.	Laurie A. Brannen
A.L.G.	Alan L. Gansberg	L.K.S.	Laurie K. Strand
A.S.M.	Anthony S. Maulucci	L.L.	Loreen Leo
A.W.	Amy Wallace	L.S.	Linda Schallan
B.B.	Barbara Bedway	M.B.T.	Marguerite B. Thompson
B.J.	Burr Jerger	M.J.T.	Michael J. Toohey
C.D.	Carol Dunlap	M.O.	Marty Olmstead
C.H.S.	Charles H. Salzberg	M.S.	Michael Sheeter
C.L.W.	Craig L. Wittler	M.W.	Mark Wheeler
C.O.	Carol Orsag	N.C.S.	Nancy C. Sorel
D.M.L.	Deci M. Lowry	P.A.R.	Patricia A. Ryan
D.R.	Dan Riley	R.G.P.	Roberta G. Peters
D.W.	David Wallechinsky	R.J.F.	Rodger J. Fadness
E.K.	Elizebethe Kempthorne	R.J.R.	R. John Rapsys
E.Z.	Ernest Zebrowski	R.K.R.	R. Kent Rasmussen
F.C.	Flora Chavez	R.M.	Robert McGarvey
G.A.M.	Greg A. Mitchell	R.S.F.	Robert S. Fenster
I.W.	Irving Wallace	R.W.S.	Roy W. Sorrels
J.A.M.	Joshua A. Martin	S.L.W.	Sandra L. Weiss
J.E.	John Eastman	S.W.	Sylvia Wallace
J.H.	Jannika Hurwitt	V.S.	Vicki Scott
J.M.	Josef Marc	W.A.D.	William A. DeGregorio
J.M.B.E.	John M. B. Edwards	W.A.H.	William A. Henkin
J.M.M.	John M. Moran	W.K.	Walter Kempthorne
J.Z.	John Zebrowski	W.L.	William Lawren

The way in which people make love
may tell us more about them than
any searching analysis could.
                    Maurice Nadeau,
        editor of *Les Lettres Nouvelles*

Sexual Characteristics
Cross references after entries refer to these lists

1 *Hanging on: late virginity losers*

Catherine II
Isadora Duncan
Havelock Ellis
Johann Wolfgang von
  Goethe

Victor Hugo
D. H. Lawrence
Bertrand Russell
Ruth St Denis
Marie Stopes

Mao Tse-tung
Mark Twain
H. G. Wells
Mary Wollstonecraft
Virginia Woolf

2 *Early to bed: precocious sex and loss of virginity*

Pope Alexander VI
Gabriele D'Annunzio
Josephine Baker
Natalie Barney
John Barrymore
Simon Bolivar
Lord Byron
Cleopatra
Mahatma Gandhi

Jean Harlow
Jimi Hendrix
Ninon de Lenclos
Louis XIV
Amedeo Modigliani
Marilyn Monroe
Aristotle Onassis
La Belle Otero
Cora Pearl

Eva Perón
Édith Piaf
Rainer Maria Rilke
Jean Jacques
  Rousseau
Harriette Wilson
Thomas Wolfe

3 *Men who enjoyed girls 16 years old or younger*

John Barrymore
Lewis Carroll
  (platonic)
Casanova
Charlie Chaplin
William Douglas

Errol Flynn
Paul Gauguin
Johann Wolfgang von
  Goethe
Howard Hughes
Samuel Pepys

Elvis Presley
John Ruskin
  (platonic)
Marquis de Sade
Mark Twain
  (platonic)

4 *Outsize organs*

Charlie Chaplin
Charles II
Gary Cooper

Jimi Hendrix
Guy de Maupassant
Aristotle Onassis

Grigori Rasputin
Henri de
  Toulouse-Lautrec

5 *Minute members*

Napoleon Bonaparte
Frédéric Chopin
Edward VIII

Farouk I
F. Scott Fitzgerald
Ernest Hemingway

Waslaw Nijinsky
Rainer Maria Rilke

6 Weird quirks

Natalie Barney
(men's clothes)
Colette (men's clothes)
Havelock Ellis
(urination voyeur)
André Gide
(deformity fetish)

Jean Harlow (dyed
pubic hair)
Marilyn Monroe
(dyed pubic
hair)
Adelina Patti (liked a
midget)

Jean Jacques
Rousseau
(exhibitionist,
inanimate objects)
Algernon Swinburne
(corporal
punishment)

7 Fetishes

James Boswell
(arborophilia)
Robert Burns
(graphomania)
Havelock Ellis
(algolagnia)
Clark Gable
(cleanliness)
Mahatma Gandhi
(sleeping naked)
André Gide
(deformity)

Adolf Hitler
(coprophilia)
Howard Hughes
(cleanliness; body
hair)
Victor Hugo (feet)
James Joyce
(graphomania;
underwear)
Martin Luther
(coprophilia)

Yukio Mishima
(white gloves;
armpit hair; sweat)
Algernon Swinburne
(babies)
Henri de
Toulouse-Lautrec
(unexpected
erogenous zones)

8 'Do you take these women?' A bird – or two – in the bush, as well as in the hand Sir (Bigamists, polygamists, etc.)

Honoré de Balzac
James Boswell
Sir Richard Burton
Claude Debussy
Alexandre Dumas
    père
Farouk I
William Faulkner
W. C. Fields
F. Scott Fitzgerald
Errol Flynn

Paul Gauguin
Henry VIII
Victor Hugo
Lillie Langtry
Jack London
W. Somerset
    Maugham
Adah Isaacs Menken
Mongkut
Lola Montez
Benito Mussolini

Horatio, Lord Nelson
Pablo Picasso
Ezra Pound
Bertrand Russell
Lillian Russell
Leopold Stokowski
Rudolph Valentino
H. G. Wells
Alma Mahler Werfel
Brigham Young
Emile Zola

9 Troilism and ménages à trois

Honoré de Balzac
Natalie Barney
Casanova
Paul Gauguin

George Gershwin
Jack Johnson
Janis Joplin
John F. Kennedy

Nikolai Lenin
Guy de Maupassant
Edna St Vincent
    Millay

Friedrich Nietzsche
Elvis Presley
Grigori Rasputin

Jean Jacques
   Rousseau
Bertrand Russell

Marquis de Sade
Mary Wollstonecraft
Brigham Young

10 Open marriages

Colette
Amelia Earhart
Havelock Ellis
William Faulkner
Errol Flynn
Victor Hugo
Carl Gustav Jung

Lillie Langtry
Charles Laughton
Edna St Vincent
   Millay
Pablo Picasso
Ezra Pound
Grigori Rasputin

Bertrand Russell
Ruth St Denis
Jean-Paul Sartre
Marie Stopes
H. G. Wells

11 Orgiasts

Pope Alexander VI
Gabriele D'Annunzio
Honoré de Balzac
Natalie Barney
John Barrymore
Sarah Bernhardt
James Boswell
Clara Bow
Robert Burns
Sir Richard Burton
Lord Byron
Casanova
Catherine II
Charlie Chaplin
Cleopatra

Gary Cooper
Joan Crawford
Fëdor Dostoevski
Alexandre Dumas
   père
Isadora Duncan
Farouk I
Errol Flynn
Clark Gable
Paul Gauguin
Johann Wolfgang von
   Goethe
Jimi Hendrix
Victor Hugo
Janis Joplin

Edmund Kean
John F. Kennedy
Lillie Langtry
Guy de Maupassant
Amedeo Modigliani
Philippe I, Duc
   d'Orléans
Elvis Presley
Grigori Rasputin
'Babe' Ruth
Marquis de Sade
Stendhal
Leo Tolstoi

12 Male homosexuals

André Gide
Christopher
   Isherwood
Charles Laughton
T. E. Lawrence
W. Somerset
   Maugham

Yukio Mishima
Waslaw Nijinsky
Philippe I, Duc
   d'Orléans
Pëtr Ilich
   Tchaikovsky

William Tilden Jr
Paul Verlaine
Oscar Wilde

13 Lesbians

Natalie Barney
Rosa Bonheur

Emily Dickinson (?)
Gertrude Stein

14 Bisexuals

Gabriele D'Annunzio
Napoleon Bonaparte
Robert Burns
Sir Richard Burton
Lord Byron
Casanova
Colette
James Dean
George Eliot
Frederick II
Sigmund Freud
André Gide

Billie Holliday
Janis Joplin
D. H. Lawrence
W. Somerset
  Maugham
Edna St Vincent
  Millay
Yukio Mishima
Waslaw Nijinsky
Philippe I,
  Duc d'Orléans

Marquis de Sade
George Sand
Bessie Smith
Algernon Swinburne
Vincent Van Gogh
Paul Verlaine
Oscar Wilde
Mary Wollstonecraft
Virginia Woolf
Voltaire

15 Mother-fixated

Honoré de Balzac
J. M. Barrie
Johannes Brahms
James Dean
Sigmund Freud

J. Edgar Hoover
D. H. Lawrence
Yukio Mishima
Sir Isaac Newton
Stendhal

August Strindberg
Pëtr Ilich
  Tchaikovsky
Paul Verlaine
William Tilden

16 Interfered with when young

Hans Christian
  Andersen
John Barrymore
Lord Byron
Billie Holliday

Carl Gustav Jung
D. H. Lawrence
La Belle Otero
Philippe I, Duc
  d'Orléans

Leo Tolstoi
Virginia Woolf
Emile Zola

17 Sex trials and famous scandals

Alexander II
Gabriele D'Annunzio
J. M. Barrie
John Barrymore
Clara Bow
Robert Burns
Lord Byron
Enrico Caruso
Charlie Chaplin
Joan Crawford
Father Divine
Alexandre Dumas
  père
Edward VII
Edward VIII
Errol Flynn

André Gide
Maxim Gorki
Jean Harlow
Howard Hughes
Edmund Kean
Lillie Langtry
D. H. Lawrence
Jack London
Louis XIV
General Douglas
  MacArthur
Mata Hari
W. Somerset
  Maugham
Aimee Semple
  McPherson

Adah Isaacs Menken
Lola Montez
Horatio, Lord Nelson
Rembrandt van Rijn
John Ruskin
Lillian Russell
'Babe' Ruth
Marquis de Sade
George Sand
Marie Stopes
William Tilden Jr
Paul Verlaine
H. G. Wells
Oscar Wilde
Brigham Young
Emile Zola

18 *Venereal disease*

Cesare Borgia
James Boswell
Lord Byron
Casanova
Frédéric Chopin
Alexandre Dumas
  père
Paul Gauguin
Francisco de Goya

Henry VIII
James Joyce
Edmund Kean
W. Somerset
  Maugham
Guy de Maupassant
Adah Isaacs Menken
Lola Montez
Benito Mussolini

Friedrich Nietzsche
Marquis de Sade
Arthur Schopenhauer
Stendhal
Henri de
  Toulouse-Lautrec
Vincent Van Gogh
Paul Verlaine
Oscar Wilde

19 *You get what you pay for: prostitutes, ordinary and exotic*

Kitty Fisher
Billie Holliday
Ninon de Lenclos

Mata Hari
Adah Isaacs Menken
La Belle Otero

Cora Pearl
Eva Perón
Harriette Wilson

20 *They paid for what they got: clients*

Pope Alexander VI
Gabriele D'Annunzio
Honoré de Balzac
John Barrymore
Napoleon Bonaparte
James Boswell
Johannes Brahms
Sir Richard Burton
Lord Byron
Casanova
Charlie Chaplin
Charles II
Fëdor Dostoevski
Alexandre Dumas
  père
Edward VII
Duke Ellington
F. Scott Fitzgerald
Errol Flynn
Clark Gable
Paul Gauguin

George Gershwin
André Gide
William Gladstone
Francisco de Goya
Ernest Hemingway
Victor Hugo
Christopher
  Isherwood
James Joyce
John F. Kennedy
Charles Laughton
Jack Laughton
Jack London
Louis XV
W. Somerset
  Maugham
Guy de Maupassant
Yukio Mishima
Amedeo Modigliani
Benito Mussolini
Napoleon III

Friedrich Nietzsche
Waslaw Nijinsky
Elvis Presley
Grigori Rasputin
Jean Jacques
  Rousseau
Peter Paul Rubens
Marquis de Sade
Jean-Paul Sartre
Bessie Smith
Stendhal
Algernon Swinburne
Leo Tolstoi
Henri de
  Toulouse-Lautrec
Vincent Van Gogh
Paul Verlaine
H. G. Wells
Oscar Wilde
Thomas Wolfe

21 *Prodigious progenitors*

Pope Alexander VI
James Boswell

Robert Burns
Charlie Chaplin

Charles II
Charles Dickens

Alexandre Dumas
père
Sigmund Freud
Mahatma Gandhi
Paul Gauguin
William Gladstone
Francisco de Goya
Victor Hugo
Carl Gustav Jung
Robert E. Lee

Louis XIV
Louis XV
Martin Luther
María Luisa
Karl Marx
Mongkut
Wolfgang Amadeus
Mozart
Napoleon III
Rembrandt van Rijn

Franklin D.
Roosevelt
Jean Jacques
Rousseau
Peter Paul Rubens
August Strindberg
Leo Tolstoi
Mao Tse-tung
Victoria
Brigham Young

22 Numbers game: great lovers and satyrs

Pope Alexander VI
Gabriele D'Annunzio
Honoré de Balzac
Natalie Barney
John Barrymore
Sarah Bernhardt
Napoleon Bonaparte
Pauline Bonaparte
Simon Bolivar
James Boswell
Clara Bow
Robert Burns
Lord Byron
Casanova
Catherine II
Charlie Chaplin
Charles II
Alexandre Dumas
père
Edward VII
Duke Ellington

Errol Flynn
Paul Gauguin
George Gershwin
Jimi Hendrix
Howard Hughes
Victor Hugo
Janis Joplin
John F. Kennedy
Aly Khan
Lillie Langtry
Ninon de Lenclos
Franz Liszt
Jack London
Louis XIV
Louis XV
María Luisa
Guy de Maupassant
Edna St Vincent
Millay
Amedeo Modigliani
Mongkut

Marilyn Monroe
Napoleon III
Aristotle Onassis
La Belle Otero
Cora Pearl
Édith Piaf
Pablo Picasso
Elvis Presley
Grigori Rasputin
Bertrand Russell
'Babe' Ruth
Marquis de Sade
Ruth St Denis
Leopold Stokowski
Henri de
Toulouse-Lautrec
Duke of Wellington
H. G. Wells
Alma Mahler Werfel
Thomas Wolfe
Harriette Wilson

23 Macho chauvinists

Gabriele D'Annunzio
Juan Belmonte
Cesare Borgia
Charles II
Alexandre Dumas
père
Edward VII
Errol Flynn
Clark Gable
Ernest Hemingway
Henry VIII

John F. Kennedy
Jack London
Louis XIV
Louis XV
General Douglas
MacArthur
Guy de Maupassant
Benito Mussolini
Aristotle Onassis
Pablo Picasso
Elvis Presley

Grigori Rasputin
'Babe' Ruth
Marquis de Sade
Arthur Schopenhauer
Leo Tolstoi
Richard Wagner
Duke of Wellington
Thomas Wolfe
Brigham Young

24 Sex with partners twenty years (or more) older

Honoré de Balzac
Clara Bow
Maria Callas
Casanova
Edward VII
Jean Harlow

Henry VIII
Ninon de Lenclos
Mata Hari
Marilyn Monroe
Friedrich Nietzsche
Waslaw Nijinsky

La Belle Otero
Eva Perón
Marquis de Sade
Thomas Wolfe

25 Sex with partners twenty years (or more) younger

Alexander II
Honoré de Balzac
Natalie Barney
John Barrymore
Sarah Bernhardt
Enrico Caruso
Casanova
Catherine II
Charlie Chaplin
Colette
Charles Dickens
Fëdor Dostoevski
Alexandre Dumas
 père
Edward VII
George Eliot
William Faulkner
W. C. Fields
Henry Ford

Paul Gauguin
André Gide
Johann Wolfgang von
 Goethe
Francisco de Goya
Henry VIII
Adolf Hitler
Howard Hughes
Victor Hugo
Christopher
 Isherwood
T. E. Lawrence
Franz Liszt
Mata Hari
W. Somerset
 Maugham
Yukio Mishima
Aristotle Onassis
Adelina Patti

Édith Piaf
Pablo Picasso
Elvis Presley
Peter Paul Rubens
Bertrand Russell
Marquis de Sade
George Sand
Jean-Paul Sartre
Ruth St Denis
Leopold Stokowski
August Strindberg
Richard Wagner
Duke of Wellington
H. G. Wells
Oscar Wilde
Brigham Young
Emile Zola

26 Old-age potency – busy after 70

Gabriele D'Annunzio
Natalie Barney
Sarah Bernhardt
Charlie Chaplin
Colette
William Douglas
Havelock Ellis
Benjamin Franklin

Johann Wolfgang von
 Goethe
Victor Hugo
Ninon de Lenclos
Franz Liszt
Louis XIV
W. Somerset
 Maugham

Pablo Picasso
Bertrand Russell
Leopold Stokowski
Leo Tolstoi
Duke of Wellington
H. G. Wells
Alma Mahler Werfel
Brigham Young

27 Kiss and tell

Gabriele D'Annunzio
Alexandre Dumas
 père

Clark Gable
Ernest Hemingway
Janis Joplin

John F. Kennedy
Jack London

General Douglas   Guy de Maupassant   Marquis de Sade
  MacArthur   Benito Mussolini   Oscar Wilde

28 Overrated or disappointing lovers
Edward VIII   George Gershwin
Clark Gable   Ernest Hemingway

29 Low sex drives, possible virgins and virgins
Hans Christian   Frédéric Chopin   Nikolai Lenin
  Andersen   Emily Dickinson   Sir Isaac Newton
J. M. Barrie   Elizabeth I   John Ruskin
Lewis Carroll   J. Edgar Hoover   William Tilden

30 Chronic impotence
Napoleon Bonaparte   W. C. Fields (due to   John Ruskin
  (after 42)   alcohol)
Havelock Ellis   D. H. Lawrence

31 Endurance and staying power
John Barrymore   Edward VII   Guy de Maupassant
James Boswell   Errol Flynn   Pablo Picasso
Charlie Chaplin   Jimi Hendrix   Grigori Rasputin
Gary Cooper   Victor Hugo   'Babe' Ruth
Fëdor Dostoevski   Aly Khan
Alexandre Dumas   Louis XIV
  père   Louis XV

32 Holier than thou: religious people interested in sex
Pope Alexander VI   Mahatma Gandhi   Aimee Semple
Cesare Borgia   William Gladstone   McPherson
Father Divine   Martin Luther   Grigori Rasputin
Mary Baker Eddy   Carry Nation   Brigham Young

33 In the interests of science: work before pleasure
Alexander   Albert Einstein   Edward Jenner
  Graham Bell   Henry Ford   Louis Pasteur

34 Here's looking at you: voyeurs

Pope Alexander VI
Lord Byron
Casanova
Charlie Chaplin
Farouk I

Errol Flynn
William Gladstone
Maxim Gorki
Victor Hugo
Martin Luther

Elvis Presley
Marquis de Sade
Bessie Smith
Stendhal

35 Creators or readers of erotica

Gabriele D'Annunzio
Alexander II
Robert Burns
Sir Richard Burton
Casanova
Charlie Chaplin
Colette
Alexandre Dumas
    père

Farouk I
William Faulkner
Paul Gauguin
William Gladstone
Adolf Hitler
J. Edgar Hoover
James Joyce
D. H. Lawrence
T. E. Lawrence

Karl Marx
Samuel Pepys
Rembrandt van Rijn
Rainer Maria Rilke
Marquis de Sade
Algernon Swinburne
Mark Twain
Paul Verlaine
Emile Zola

36 Fans of flagellation

Sir Richard Burton
Fëdor Dostoevski
William Gladstone
T. E. Lawrence

Grigori Rasputin
Jean Jacques
    Rousseau

Marquis de Sade
Algernon Swinburne

37 Masochists and sadists

Fëdor Dostoevski
Adolf Hitler
James Joyce
D. H. Lawrence
T. E. Lawrence

Yukio Mishima
Amedeo Modigliani
Benito Mussolini
Jean Jacques
    Rousseau

Marquis de Sade
Algernon Swinburne
Paul Verlaine

38 Uncontrollable appetites: food fetishists

Pope Alexander VI
Honoré de Balzac
Alexander
    Graham Bell

Casanova
Edward VII
Farouk I
Henry VIII

Lillian Russell
Thomas Wolfe

39 Interracial couplings

Josephine Baker
Rupert Brooke
Sir Richard Burton
Casanova

Father Divine
Alexandre Dumas
    père
Paul Gauguin

André Gide
Ernest Hemingway
Jimi Hendrix
Billie Holliday

Jack Johnson
T. E. Lawrence

General Douglas
   MacArthur
Yukio Mishima

Friedrich Nietzsche
Brigham Young

40 *Incest*

Pope Alexander VI
John Barrymore
James Boswell
Lord Byron

Casanova
Cleopatra
Colette
Benito Mussolini

Friedrich Nietzsche
   (unproved)
Marquis de Sade
H. G. Wells

41 *Their majesties' pleasure: royal playthings*

Josephine Baker
Sarah Bernhardt
Lillie Langtry

Mata Hari
Lola Montez
Virginia Oldoini

La Belle Otero
Cora Pearl
Richard Wagner

42 *Caught in the act: busy entertainers*

Josephine Baker
John Barrymore
Sarah Bernhardt
Clara Bow
Maria Callas
Enrico Caruso
Charlie Chaplin
Colette
Gary Cooper
Joan Crawford
James Dean

Duke Ellington
Errol Flynn
Clark Gable
David Garrick
George Gershwin
Jean Harlow
Jimi Hendrix
Billie Holliday
Janis Joplin
Lillie Langtry
Charles Laughton

Mata Hari
Adah Isaacs Menken
Marilyn Monroe
La Belle Otero
Nicolò Paganini
Adelina Patti
Édith Piaf
Elvis Presley
Lillian Russell
Bessie Smith
Rudolph Valentino

43 *Curious locations*

Josephine Baker
   (train)
Natalie Barney
   (fields, theatre
   boxes)
James Boswell
   (outdoors)
Gary Cooper (on
   beaches, in groves)

Clark Gable (in a
   duck blind)
Victor Hugo (secret
   rooms)
John F. Kennedy
   (cupboard)
Ninon de Lenclos
   (doorway)
Jack London (train)

Benito Mussolini
   (window-seats,
   staircases)
La Belle Otero (in a
   balloon)
Grigori Rasputin (any
   convenient place)

44 Nudists and strippers

Gabriele D'Annunzio
Josephine Baker
Joan Crawford
Isadora Duncan
Havelock Ellis
Mahatma Gandhi

John F. Kennedy
Martin Luther
Mata Hari
Amedeo Modigliani
Marilyn Monroe

Cora Pearl
Grigori Rasputin
Rainer Maria Rilke
Jean Jacques
  Rousseau

45 Clean and unclean

Honoré de Balzac (U)
Pauline Bonaparte (C)
Casanova (C)

Clark Gable (C)
Howard Hughes (C)
Martin Luther (U)

Marilyn Monroe (U)
Benito Mussolini (U)

46 The keepers and the kept: gigolos and squires

Gabriele D'Annunzio
Honoré de Balzac
Sarah Bernhardt
Casanova
Catherine II
Colette
James Dean
Kitty Fisher
Howard Hughes

Lillie Langtry
Charles Laughton
D. H. Lawrence
Ninon de Lenclos
General Douglas
  MacArthur
W. Somerset
  Maugham
Adah Isaacs Menken

La Belle Otero
Cora Pearl
Eva Perón
Jean Jacques
  Rousseau
Rudolph Valentino
Oscar Wilde
Harriette Wilson

47 Getting a kick out of it: foot fetishists

Fëdor Dostoevski

F. Scott Fitzgerald

Victor Hugo

48 Boys will be girls: children brought up as or dressed in clothing of opposite sex

Ernest Hemingway
Philippe I, Duc
  d'Orléans

Rainer Maria Rilke
William Tilden
Oscar Wilde

Thomas Wolfe

49 Bottom fetishists and coprophiliacs

Napoleon Bonaparte
Enrico Caruso
Havelock Ellis
Adolf Hitler
James Joyce

Carl Gustav Jung
Martin Luther
Wolfgang Amadeus
  Mozart
Samuel Pepys

Elvis Presley
Jean Jacques
  Rousseau
Mark Twain

Foreplay

To the making of sex books there is no end. Countless books have been written about the biology and anatomy of sex, on polls surveying sexual behaviour, histories of sexual mores through the ages and cases of sexual aberrations. On this infinite shelf there is only one gaping omission. No one has as yet written a comprehensive volume that reveals the sexual behaviour of well-known, famous, distinguished men and women in world history.

This is one reason we decided to write *The Secret Sex Lives of Famous People*.

We were curious to see the lives of great people of the distant or immediate past made complete. Too many biographers omitted, glossed over, or did not delve into, the sex lives of their subjects. They presented incomplete people, a crucial part of their lives airbrushed away. We wanted to see the missing facets of these famous or infamous personalities, to understand better that powerful force which so inevitably affected their psyches and work. From time to time, researching for *The People's Almanac* and *The Book of Lists*, we would stumble upon a long-suppressed piece of intimate information about a US president, a European queen, a scientific genius, an artist, that deepened our knowledge of that person. As these facts continued to surface, we began to believe they deserved a book of their own.

Maurice Nadeau, editor of *Les Lettres Nouvelles*, once said that the function of literature is to explore the human heart and every manifestation of being. 'The way in which people make love,' he added, 'may tell us more about them than any searching analysis could. It, too, reveals a form of truth which is interesting because it is usually concealed.'

Like H. L. Mencken, we believe it is better to know than to be ignorant. We hoped that readers unfamiliar with famous people of the past but captivated by their love lives would be stimulated enough to search out the rest of their histories, their successes and failures, in the otherwise definitive biographies available.

In undertaking this book, we knew that there would be those who felt strongly that the sex life of the celebrated was not a fit subject for general readers. But sex is part of us all. As the late Justice William O. Douglas of the US Supreme Court put it, 'The idea of using censors to bar thoughts of sex is dangerous. A person without sex thoughts is abnormal.'

1

Our first problem when writing this book was the plethora of interesting people to write about. To contain our information in one volume, we had to make a representative selection from the major fields of human endeavour. We drew upon the worlds of art, music, literature, business, religion, films, government. We rejected the temptation to include people noted just for their sexual activity. Some of the latter are here, certainly, but the majority of names included were not known for their sexual behaviour; they are here because they are famous – a few because they are infamous – and because their sex lives have until now been overlooked or concealed. Of course, Casanova and Lord Byron and Marilyn Monroe, all associated with sex, are here. But here also are James Boswell, Leo Tolstoi and Martin Luther, Enrico Caruso, Virginia Woolf and Albert Einstein – none of whom is identified in most people's minds with sex.

In our researches it was illuminating to learn that every imaginable type of sex was practised by our more illustrious predecessors, and that a handful of the most famous remained chaste throughout their lives.

Readers may wonder how we were able to obtain information about an area of human behaviour so long hidden, kept secret and private. The search for facts was difficult and challenging. Twenty people in the USA – the authors included – and six specialized researchers in England, France, Italy and Spain delved into the past, into every obscure recess of history, for relevant information. We naturally read biographies, from 1500 to 1980, and constantly had excerpts from foreign language biographies translated. Most valuable were autobiographies of the famous and memoirs by their lovers, friends, enemies. Even more valuable was the correspondence of the famous. We pored over rare pamphlets, studying old periodicals and newspapers on microfilm. We leafed through legal transcripts, documents recounting cases that involved people like Gabriele D'Annunzio, Clara Bow, Errol Flynn and Charles Chaplin. Diaries, journals, recorded divorce actions and medical reports provided much revealing material. For twentieth-century information, we interviewed mates, children and confidants of the great.

No week of research was without its surprises. Discoveries of unusual and unexpected couplings abounded – Jack Johnson had an affair with Mata Hari, Eva Perón with Aristotle Onassis, Milton Berle with Aimee Semple McPherson, Edith Piaf with John Garfield. Other matings were equally astonishing – Adelina

2

Patti with a midget, innumerable eminent men with their land-ladies, Friedrich Nietzsche with his sister, General Douglas MacArthur with his Eurasian mistress, James Boswell with Jean Jacques Rousseau's wife, Albert Einstein with his cousin.

More surprises lay in store. To celebrate the start of their love affair, Lady Caroline Lamb sent Lord Byron some of her pubic hair. While they adored him, Clark Gable's bed partners called him a poor lover. The same applied to the Duke of Windsor. Victor Hugo and his wife were virgins on their bridal night – during which he had intercourse with her nine times. Marie Curie was involved in a scandal with a married man. Napoleon Bonaparte and the Duke of Wellington had more than Waterloo in common – they both slept with the same French actress, Mademoiselle George (whose vote, incidentally, went to the Iron Duke). Samuel Pepys recorded his sexual adventures in his diary in an early form of shorthand. Brigham Young was an aphrodisiac user. John Ruskin died a virgin....

In writing this book, we have tried to be honest and frank, yet have made every effort to handle the varieties of sexual behaviour with delicacy. In our own use of language, we have tried not to give offence. But when our subjects wished to use explicit language we allowed them to speak for themselves.

We hope you will find this book enlightening and entertaining. After you have read it, we would like to hear from you. We want to know whether or not you enjoyed it and we would also appreciate any suggestions you have to make. We plan another book of new Sex Lives soon, and you can help us decide which people should be included in the next volume. Also, we want you to share with us any intimate information you have about famous people. If you can send us facts we do not already possess and give us the source of this information, we will happily pay you for your material if we use it in our next book. Please send your comments and suggestions to the following address:

Intimate Lives Editor,
PO Box 49699,
Los Angeles,
California 90049,
USA

IRVING WALLACE
AMY WALLACE
DAVID WALLECHINSKY
SYLVIA WALLACE

♣ Alexander II
17 April 1818 to 1 March 1881

Often called the 'Czar Liberator' after his Edict of Emancipation freed the serfs in 1861, Alexander II was indeed liberal compared to his oppressive, autocratic predecessors. However, the numerous reforms instituted during his reign resulted more from the need to placate growing revolutionary unrest than from any humanitarian initiative.

Despite his renowned heritage – Catherine the Great was his great grandmother – Alexander was indolent, weak-willed and only averagely intelligent. He was also attractive: '. . . tall with a fine figure, a pleasing . . . countenance . . . fine blue eyes . . . a pretty mouth . . . good-natured, natural and merry,' according to Queen Victoria. In 1855 36-year-old Alexander succeeded his father. During his twenty-six-year reign the czar was dependent on feminine guidance, turning continually to his wife, aunt and mistresses for advice. Despite having no overall plan or vision, he effected great social changes. Since these modern reforms often did not harmonize with feudal policies, Alexander had enemies on both left and right. He lived in constant fear of assassination but, as a fortune-teller had predicted, he survived seven such attempts before a terrorist's bomb blew him to pieces.

Alexander indulged his fickle nature in his youth, but proved his constancy in later years. At 20, he was sent on a grand tour of Europe, primarily to cool a romance with Olga Kalinovskaya, a young and beautiful Polish commoner elevated to the post of lady-in-waiting at the imperial court. On this tour he met Princess Maria of Hesse-Darmstadt, and claimed he had found his perfect bride. His parents protested that her royal birth was questionable, but Alexander stood firm, preferring to renounce the throne before Maria. While arrangements were being made for their wedding in Russia, Alexander travelled to England, where he met his cousin Victoria. She was 20 and had been queen for just one year. The two young sovereigns found each other very attractive.

5

For a few idyllic spring days they cherished their infatuation. They talked affectionately, danced and dined, watching the stunned reactions of their courtiers. Their romance was politically impossible, so Alexander left, promising never to forget her. After a brief vacillation, during which Alexander threatened to take up with Olga again, he and 17-year-old Princess Maria were married on 16 April 1841. In the following years, eight children were born to them. Maria's beauty faded early, she developed a consuming interest in the Russian Orthodox Church, and Alexander grew bored with her. In 1848, a son resulted from his renewed affair with Olga Kalinovskaya. A few years later his interest turned to other ladies of the court, including Princess Alexandra Dolgoruki, his wife's lady-in-waiting. This young 'tigress' was, however, as devoted to her mistress as she was flirtatious with Alexander. Maria and the princess formed an alliance of their own – to encourage Alexander's social reforms.

Though most of his affairs were short-lived, in 1862 the czar fell prey to a grand passion which lasted until the day he died. He was swept off his feet by 16-year-old Catherine Dolgoruki, distantly related to Princess Alexandra. Catherine was fresh, charming and startlingly beautiful. Alexander was deeply enough in love to wait years before consummating their relationship. He courted her, becoming a trusted friend as well as ardent suitor, and, in 1866, when she was barely out of her teens, they at last made love. Three or four days a week Catherine would come secretly to a room on the ground floor of the Winter Palace at St Petersburg, letting herself in with a key. Their trysts became known eventually, and the affair turned into a national scandal. A member of the royal family called Catherine a 'scheming adventuress', and even the common people called her a 'hussy'. Declaring Catherine his 'wife before God', Alexander remained devoted and spent his free hours composing love letters, sometimes several a day, in French. By 1872, she had borne him the first of their four children. In 1878, he feared for the safety of this second family and moved Catherine into the Winter Palace, in rooms directly above those of Maria, who was dying of tuberculosis. Maria was able to hear the sounds of Catherine and Alexander's children at play, and she confessed that this hurt her terribly. She died in 1880. Alexander waited the required minimum forty days before marrying Catherine on 6 July in a secret ceremony. Resentment of Catherine only increased after the marriage. Her children in the palace were an affront to the czar's heirs by Maria and, when Alexander became ill from exhaustion, the doctor suspected 'excesses in sexual relations' were sapping the strength needed for affairs of state.

Indeed, the letters Alexander and Catherine exchanged speak of a tender yet torrential passion undimmed by the passage of fifteen years. Her letters recall moments 'When we clenched each other like cats and plunged in ecstasy to the verge of madness'. He wrote, 'I am still all saturated with our delirious bingerles [a word they used to describe the lovemaking] a little while ago. It was so good I wanted to cry out....' They preferred to make love on a hard couch, covered in coarse blue cloth, and the use of a bed was cause for comment in their correspondence. Even on the day he died, he had, in a moment of high-spirited lust, taken her 'roughly' on the blue couch. The next time she saw him, he was carried into the palace, his body torn apart by a bomb thrown in the street. At his funeral, she placed a long lock of her hair in the casket and, when she left Russia for Paris, she took with her one of his shattered fingers as a memento.

Alexander had had a private collection of erotica. Among his favourites were his own pencil drawings of Catherine in the nude.

A.K. and K.P. (Lists 25, 35)

♣ Pope Alexander VI
1 January 1431 to 18 August 1503

Scion of Spain's powerful Borgia family, Rodrigo was the protégé of his uncle, Alonso de Borgia, Bishop of Valencia. Uncle Alonso supervised Rodrigo's education and, after becoming Pope Calixtus III, elevated his 25-year-old nephew into the College of Cardinals. Young Rodrigo so enjoyed the trappings of wealth and power that he scandalized the Church and embarrassed his uncle, even in those free-wheeling days. Rodrigo himself was unembarrassed by the vast number of children – mostly out of wedlock – that he sired during his career as churchman. A fully accurate roster of his offspring cannot be compiled.

Rodrigo's own (bought) tenure as Pope Alexander VI began in 1492. Once installed, he and his son Cesare commenced a campaign of diplomacy, assassination and treachery that brought the whole of northern Italy under Borgia control. Rodrigo and Cesare outflanked and routed the powerful Orsini and Colonna families, and successfully resisted the reform movement of the Dominican

7

monk Savonarola, whom they burned at the stake as a heretic. Folklore has made much of the Borgias' reliance upon poison as a political tool, painting Rodrigo's daughter Lucrezia as a specialist in its use, but there is no evidence that she poisoned anybody. Her duty was to marry anyone Rodrigo told her to, whether she felt like it or not. As for poison, the Borgias used it sparingly, preferring instead a straightforward strangling or bludgeoning carried out by hired thugs. Although intrigue was Rodrigo's lifeblood, he was given to spasms of repentance, usually short-lived. He was a foremost practitioner of simony – the buying and selling of religious favours. For 24,000 gold pieces Rodrigo once sold a nobleman permission to commit incest with his sister. Rodrigo was a great patron of the arts. He coaxed Michaelangelo to undertake the rebuilding of St Peter's, and supported many other Renaissance artists in projects intended to glorify his reign. Still, towards the end of his life, it was popularly thought that he had made a pact with the devil.

He is said to have been a handsome youth, tall and robust, with penetrating eyes. His contemporaries called him an irresistible conqueror. But, then, who would have dared resist? One of his mistresses, Giulia Farnese, was 16 and already married when he became her lover. The Romans sarcastically called her the 'bride of Christ'. Another woman, Vannozza dei Cattanei, bore Rodrigo at least four children before he became pope. Three of those – Lucrezia, Cesare and Giovanni – followed in their father's footsteps. Lucrezia may have been sexually available to both Rodrigo and Cesare, among others, and to this day historians debate whether her child was the issue of her father or her brother. The family's notorious preference for sexy entertainments kept the clan's blood boiling and tended to obscure such hair-splitting.

At 29, Rodrigo was rebuked by Pope Pius II for appearing at an orgy in his cardinal's robes; Rodrigo delighted in sponsoring entertainments featuring nude and nubile dancers. It was not unusual for him to obstruct the solemn high mass. During one mass, he brought giggling women up to the altar, and on another occasion he carelessly trampled the sacred host underfoot. He would celebrate at any excuse, bringing a rowdy crew of prostitutes into the papal apartments. During festivals, an average of twenty-five courtesans a night was provided for the pope's entertainment. Discretion was never Rodrigo's strong point, and he used to scandalize Christendom with his travelling arrangements – often including scantily clad dancing girls.

One of the pope's banquets was chronicled by his master of ceremonies – Burchard, Bishop of Ostia – who wrote in his *Diarium Romanum*, '. . . fifty reputable whores, not common but the kind called courtesans, supped [at the Vatican] . . . and after supper they danced about with the servants and others in that place, first in their clothes and then nude . . . candelabra with lighted candles were set on the floor and chestnuts were strewn about and the naked courtesans on hands and feet gathered them up, wriggling in and out among the candelabra. . . . Then all those present in the hall were carnally treated in public. . . .' The pope, Cesare, and Lucrezia gave prizes to the men who copulated most times with the prostitutes.

Unlike a previous pope, Sixtus IV, Rodrigo was heterosexual. But legend persists that Rodrigo and Cesare imprisoned and raped the most beautiful young man in Italy. Proof is lacking, however, since the victim was found in the Tiber with a stone round his neck before he could talk. Existing evidence indicates that Rodrigo preferred women. In addition to the army of courtesans constantly at his command, Rodrigo maintained a private harem, and his sons Giovanni and Cesare vied with each other for the pope's favour by sending him exotic beauties for his collection. At one point, Giovanni outmanoeuvred his brother by supplying a Spanish beauty who moved Rodrigo to ecstasy. Cesare, jealous of his brother's secular glory, had Giovanni stabbed and thrown in the Tiber. The murder of his favourite son caused the pope such distress that he briefly reformed. But this reformation turned into merely a rest period, and soon he was back to his decadent ways.

M.J.T. (Lists 2, 11, 20, 21, 22, 32, 34, 38, 40)

❧ Hans Christian Andersen
2 April 1805 to 4 August 1875

Andersen's only ambition was to become a *Digter* – a creative writer held in highest esteem. To this end, he wrote poetry, plays, novels, travel books – and fairy tales, which brought him worldwide recognition. Altogether he wrote 156 tales that have been translated into over 100 languages.

As a youth, Andersen worked in a cloth factory where he was often embarrassed by the workmen's bawdy stories and dirty jokes. Gifted with a fine soprano voice, he loved to sing in the shop – until the day when the workmen pulled off his pants to see if he was a girl. At 14 – dressed like a beggar and carrying one small bundle of clothes – Hans set out for Copenhagen in search of a future. He was a tall, delicate man with brown hair, small blue eyes, and a sharp nose that dominated his face. His arms and legs were disproportionately long for his body, and his feet were gigantic. When he travelled, strangers would stop and point, calling him 'stork' and 'lamp-post'. At his best, Andersen was simple, sincere, affectionate and witty, at his worst, vain, irritable, snobbish and peculiar. His fits of depression and hypochondria were compounded by his many phobias. Andersen was so scared of dying in a fire that he always packed a rope in his suitcase when he travelled – to be used should be need to slide to safety. Terrified of being buried alive, he asked friends to cut one of his arteries before ever putting him into a coffin. When in poor health, he sometimes left a note at his bedside. It read, 'I only seem dead.' Andersen became one of the most sought-after writers in the world and the honoured guest of royalty throughout Europe. He lived his last years in Copenhagen – alone in an apartment – but spent almost every night with various friends. He died of cancer of the liver.

Andersen never had a sexual experience with a woman or a man, but did have normal physical desires. In Naples in 1834, he wrote in his diary, 'Tremendous feeling of sensual desire and internal battle. . . . I am still innocent, but my blood is burning. . . . I'm half ill. Happy is he who is married, who is engaged to be married.'

Although he tried hard, the highly emotional, sentimental *Digter* was not able to capture any of the women he chose as a mate.

There were three important women in Andersen's life, but he was totally incapable of arousing passion in any of them. First was Riborg Voigt, the 24-year-old sister of a school friend. Andersen, only a year younger than Riborg, was totally taken by her lovely face and lively manner. Had Andersen been forceful and decisive, he could have won her, but he wasn't, and Riborg's sense of honour toward her fiancé prevailed. When Andersen died many years later, he was wearing a small leather bag around his neck. In it was a letter from Riborg – possibly a farewell letter she had written to him. It was, however, immediately destroyed – unread – as Andersen had instructed.

Next came 18-year-old Louise Collin, daughter of his patron,

10

Jonas Collin. In the beginning, Andersen only wanted sympathy to help get him over the break with Riborg. Gradually, he began to notice Louise's almond-shaped blue eyes, fair skin and silky blonde hair. He was in love again; she was not interested. To stop his amorous letters, Louise told Andersen that any correspondence from him had to be reviewed by her older, married sister (a common practice in those days). Shortly afterwards, Louise became engaged to a young lawyer.

Jenny Lind waltzed into Andersen's life in 1843. In Copenhagen for a singing engagement, the 'Swedish Nightingale' was a tall, striking figure with auburn hair and large grey eyes. Andersen showered her with poems and gifts. In 1846, he travelled to Berlin, hoping to spend Christmas Day with her. When he received no invitation, he sat alone in a hotel room, close to tears. Jenny's only terms of endearment for Andersen were 'brother' and 'friend'. He was devastated when she married in 1852.

Andersen had very close friendships with three men: Edvard Collin (son of Jonas Collin), the hereditary Duke of Weimar (whom he met during a trip to Germany in 1844), and Danish ballet dancer Harald Scharff. His 'love letters' – particularly to Collin who was definitely heterosexual – might almost suggest that Andersen was a latent homosexual, but he was simply a hopeless eccentric who was starving for deep affection and praise. His only sexual outlet was masturbation, an act which caused him enormous guilt. On excursions to Paris in the 1860s, the elderly Andersen sometimes visited a brothel. While there, he enjoyed polite conversations with naked prostitutes. When anyone suggested that he was doing more than just talking, he was shocked and disgusted.

C.O. (Lists 16, 29)

♣ Gabriele D'Annunzio
12 March 1863 to 1 March 1938

A controversial poet and politician during the Fascist era, D'Annunzio laced his works so heavily with vivid descriptions of sex and death that author Henry James labelled them 'vulgar'. The eccentric writer (who was also Italy's greatest First World War flying ace) will perhaps be best remembered as one of the founders of realism in Italian fiction. By the time he graduated from the Cicognini College in Prato, D'Annunzio, son of the

11

wealthy Mayor of Pescara, had published his first volume of poetry and earned a scandalous reputation as a Don Juan. Women found the handsome, muscular, 5 foot 6 inch poet irresistible, and he engaged in hundreds of affairs during his lifetime, often using them as story lines for his novels.

In 1883, he settled down long enough to marry Maria Gallese, daughter of the Duke di Gallese. Despite the fact that D'Annunzio continued his illicit affairs, Maria bore him three sons in the next four years. D'Annunzio spent frivolously – on clothes, servants, and other women – until his lavish life-style forced him into bankruptcy. In 1910, he fled to France to escape creditors.

When the First World War erupted, D'Annunzio returned to Italy. In 1915, he enlisted as an aviator and gained recognition and rank – he commanded the air squad at Venice – after flying a number of dangerous missions. His heroics cost him his left eye when he was permanently blinded by an enemy bullet. Undaunted, he led a troop of 12,000 *Arditi* into the city of Fiume in 1919, conquered it, and ruled the Italian town as a dictator for two years. In reward for his vociferous support of Musssolini's Fascist government, D'Annunzio was named Prince of Monte Nevoso in 1924. Surrounded by 100 servants, separated from his family, D'Annunzio lived out his final years at his elegant Vittoriale estate. Obsessed with making his death as memorable as his life, he claimed he would like to be blown from a cannon, or die by having his body dissolved in acid. Undramatically, he died of a cerebral haemorrhage, while sitting at his desk, eleven days before his 75th birthday.

D'Annunzio, who considered himself a 'high priest of erotica', was a sex maniac whose life and writings were guided by women. By the age of 7 he had fallen in love for the first time. At 12, he was in trouble at school for trying to guide the hands of a nun who was fitting his uniform towards his 'private parts'. When he had turned 16 D'Annunzio had his first woman – a Florentine prostitute – after pawning a watch to pay her fee. His reputation as a womanizer did not prevent his marriage to Maria Hardouin di Gallese. Her father, the Duke di Gallese, despised D'Annunzio, but Maria ignored her father's threats of boycotting the wedding and severing all family ties. The 20-year-old author married his 19-year-old bride, in a sad sombre ceremony, on 28 July 1883. No one knew that the willowy blonde-haired Maria was already three months pregnant. D'Annunzio, repelled by his wife's pregnant body, took to sleeping with other women, but still treated Maria to an 'intoxicating night' from time to time. He left her in 1887, and before Maria died she had earned the title *madone des tantes* (madonna of the fairies) for having charmed a number of male homosexuals.

Though D'Annunzio viewed women as enemies, was rarely compassionate, had eyes which Sarah Bernhardt described as 'little blobs of shit', and was bald by 23, women dreamed of making love to him. Ladies were willing to risk their wealth, marriage and reputation for him, although he was well known as 'a fickle lover whose passions were swift and changing'. D'Annunzio's tastes knew no boundaries: he was susceptible to the beauty of young boys, and engaged in an affair with a lesbian mistress, whom he taught 'the parting of the legs'. Even in his old age, the author's sexual prowess did not wane. He paid people to visit neighbouring villages and bring him women 'whose novelty would stimulate his fancy'.

Of his handful of long-lasting affairs, many ended tragically. His romance with the religious Countess Mancini caused her such severe guilt that she went mad and was institutionalized in an asylum. Likewise, his relationship with Marchesa Alessandra di Rudini Carlotti, daughter of an Italian prime minister, ended in ruin. A 'sinner of love', who desired to repent for her frenzied lovemaking, the marchesa abandoned her children, became a nun and died the mother superior of a convent in Savoy.

D'Annunzio was instantly awed by Barbara Leoni's goddess-like beauty when they first met at a concert in 1887. They shared a passionately intense love, and met at secret hideaways as often as they could. She confessed to him, 'You have had a virgin in me.' He kept one of Barbara's hairs in a locket and, throughout their five-year affair, while making love, D'Annunzio would cover her body with rose petals.

But as she lay nude in bed asleep, he would sit alongside her jotting down details of their lovemaking bouts and noting the contours of her body for future use in *The Innocent*.

In 1891, D'Annunzio kindled an affair with 30-year-old Countess Maria Anguissola Gravina Cruyllas di Ramacca, wife of a Neapolitan nobleman. The statuesque woman was driven mad by jealousy and she squandered a fortune in a futile attempt to retain D'Annunzio's love. They were charged with, and found guilty of, committing adultery, and were sentenced to five months in prison. Their sentences were later suspended, however, and D'Annunzio went on to father two children by the countess

13

during the course of their affair. When their son, Dante Gabriele, was born, the countess threatened to kill the baby unless D'Annunzio remained loyal. He refused to do so, instead showering his affections on the actress Eleanora Duse.

D'Annunzio's affair with Duse, a woman four years his senior, was the zenith of his romantic career. For 'La Duse', who also had had many lovers, D'Annunzio was the consuming passion of her life. Starting in 1895, they lived together, on and off, for nine years. She not only demanded little of him, but gave him her money, inspiration, companionship and advice. In return, he wrote plays in which Duse performed.

During the good days, they drank strange brews together from a virgin's skull and on one birthday she sent him a dozen telegrams, one every hour. But, in 1900, Duse was stunned by the release of a novel written by D'Annunzio which detailed their affair intimately. According to *The Flame of Life*, D'Annunzio had eventually tired of his 42-year-old lover because her body had grown old and her breasts (to D'Annunzio a woman's most important asset) had begun to droop. They parted company in 1904, and after Duse died D'Annunzio claimed he could communicate with her spirit by biting into a pomegranate while standing in front of a statue of a buddha.

        A.K. (Lists 2, 11, 14, 17, 20, 22, 26, 27, 35, 44, 46)

♣ Josephine Baker
3 June 1906 to 12 April 1975

In the 1920s and 1930s, dancer/singer Josephine Baker became the first black female entertainer to star in the Folies Bergère, as well as the first American black woman to achieve international renown. Dancing the Charleston, wearing only a blue and red ring of feathers around her hips, she took Paris by storm.

Her mother, Carrie Smith, told Josephine that her father was a Spaniard whose family had forbidden him to marry a black woman. As an infant, Josephine was sent to live with her grandmother. She had an affinity for music and on Saturdays joined in with the scratch neighbourhood band. By the time Josephine returned to her mother, Carrie was married and had three more children. They lived in a one-room shack in the poorest section of St Louis. As the oldest child, Josephine Baker did domestic work for white families. She never forgot the cruelties she sometimes encountered, but also remembered the kindness of one family, the Masons, who took her to the theatre for the first time and encouraged her to build her own makeshift theatre in their basement. When Josephine told Mrs Mason that Mr Mason sometimes came into her room at night and stood beside her bed, staring down at her and breathing heavily, she was sacked. While job-hunting, 13-year-old Josephine applied for work at the Booker T. Washington Theatre. That evening she left St Louis as singer Bessie Smith's maid. On Bessie's advice, she became a chorus girl at New York's Cotton Club. In 1925, Baker went to Paris as part of *La Revue Nègre*. Asked to dance at the Folies Bergère, she prepared for opening night by holding bowls of cracked ice against her bosom to make her breasts firm and pointed. In her debut, she wore only a belt of bananas. Her wildly daring image was reflected a thousand times as she danced before a background of mirrors. Improvising, Baker sang, and closed her act by leaping into a banana tree, spreading its leaves, crossing her eyes, and waving to the thunderous applause. To the French, this was the epitome of *le jazz hot*. Overnight, Josephine became a sensation and the reigning queen of the Folies.

With the advent of the Second World War Baker joined the French Resistance, delivering to the Allies the original copy of an Italian–German codebook. Baker's marriage to a Jewish businessman, Jean Léon, brought her to the attention of the Gestapo. They decided to kill her. When Hermann Goering invited her to dinner, her fish course contained cyanide. Forewarned, Baker excused herself from the table as soon as the fish was served, saying she had to go to the bathroom. There she intended to drop herself down the laundry chute into the arms of Resistance members below. Before she could leave the table, however, Goering – gun in hand – ordered her to eat the fish. She did so, dizzily stumbled to the bathroom, lowered herself into the laundry chute, and slid downward. Resistance members broke her fall and rushed her to an underground clinic, where her stomach was quickly pumped. After being near death for a month, she slowly recovered. Word was put out that she had died in Morocco. The poisoning episode caused her to lose all her hair (she wore wigs from then on), and her courage won her the Croix de Guerre, the Rosette of the Resistance and the Legion of Honour. After the war, Baker returned to the stage. Also, to prove universal brotherhood was possible, she adopted eleven children of different races and religions – some coming from places as diverse as Korea, Algeria and Israel.

Although Josephine Baker had considerable sexual experience as an adolescent, it was mostly transitory. Her more serious affairs began when she moved to Paris at the age of 19. She fell in love with a fair-haired, handsome Frenchman named Marcel, who set her up in a luxurious apartment on the Champs Elysées which she called her 'marble palace'. Marcel appeared every evening and brought live gifts with him – white mice with pink noses, a parrot, a miniature monkey. At last, Baker asked him when they would be married. He said marriage was impossible because she was black and a public dancer. The next day she walked out on her palace and menagerie.

Baker's first distinguished admirer was a Moroccan desert leader she called the 'Sheik of Araby'. He came backstage at the Folies to meet her, sent her a tame panther wearing a diamond necklace, and took both Baker and panther to dinner. But she decided that having sex with him was impossible. He was short and chubby, and she was tall. 'The problem,' she said, 'was that when I was young I used to like to do it standing up and, if I had ever done it with him, he would have been jabbing me in the knees.'

In 1929, Crown Prince Adolf, the future King Gustav VI of Sweden, entranced by Baker, visited her dressing room and invited her to his country. Although Baker knew the prince was married, she sent him a one-word telegram later that night: 'When?' The next morning she had his reply: 'Tonight.' That evening Baker boarded the prince's private *wagon-lit* railway carriage with its gold interior and silk and Aubusson carpets. In her sleeping quarters, there was a swan-shaped bed covered with satin sheets that would highlight the contours of her dusky body. She had just settled into bed as the prince arrived. When she complained of being cold, the prince warmed her heart by fastening a three-strand diamond bracelet to her arm. While grateful, she told the prince that her other arm was still cold. He roared with laughter and gave her another bracelet. He joined her in bed and, as they embraced, the train began moving. They allowed the undulating movements of the railway carriage to set the tempo of their lovemaking. 'He was a real fox,' Baker said afterwards. 'He was my cream and I was his coffee, and when you poured us together it was something!' They spent a warm wintry month together in his isolated summer palace, making love indoors and playing like children in the snow outside. On the last night of their idyll, she wore a floor-length sable coat he had given her as she danced a silent waltz with him. They never met again.

Josephine was introduced to Count 'Pepito' Abatino, an Italian administrator at a cabaret and they tangoed. Baker was impressed. She let Abatino become her lover and manager. They never married, but Baker always presented him as her husband. He was a jealous lover as well as a tough manager, sometimes locking her in her room to force her to work on dance routines. The affair lasted ten years, and ended in New York when Baker decided she wanted to be free. Next, Baker fell in love with French businessman Jean Léon. They were married in November 1937. He wanted a home in the country, and they leased Les Milandes, a chateau that became her dream house. He also wanted children. Baker became pregnant but miscarried, losing not only the baby but Léon as well. The judge who dissolved their marriage in 1939 said, 'They were two strangers who never really met.'

It took Baker five years to find another love. Earlier, in 1933, she had met Jo Bouillon, a French orchestra leader, when he came backstage at the Folies to ask her for an autographed picture. They met again in October 1944. She had gone to Bouillon to urge him to work for the Free French, and, on 3 June 1947, they were married. During their marriage, Baker purchased the chateau she had once leased, Les Milandes, and turned it into a resort. She incurred huge debts, placing tremendous pressure on the relationship with her husband. Her marriage to Bouillon lasted thirteen years.

In her last years, Josephine Baker gave more and more time to her adopted children and to her growing struggle against racism, especially in the USA, where many of her bookings had been cancelled. Ironically, it was following a triumphant tour of the USA that Baker died of a heart attack in Paris at the age of 68.

F.C. (Lists 2, 39, 41, 42, 43, 44)

✺ Honoré de Balzac
20 May 1799 to 18 August 1850

Balzac had a miserable childhood in Tours with an indifferent mother. She sent him off to boarding school and soon gave birth to a 'love child' whom she openly preferred. After completing law studies at the Sorbonne and working for three years as a law clerk, in 1819 Balzac locked himself in an attic and started his writing career. It would be another ten years before he established his reputation. In the interim, he was a hack writer, launched a short-lived printing concern, and speculated in a Sardinian silver-mining operation which drove him to debt. Throughout his life he remained imprudent about money.

Inspired by a desire to be the Napoleon of novelists – near his desk was a marble bust of the late emperor – Balzac began his typical working day at midnight. Dressed in a monastic white robe, he would write, quickly wearing out goose-quill pens, and pausing only to drink several dozen cups of coffee in the next sixteen hours. One could not write, he believed, without quantities of black coffee. Between books, he would reach other extremes, eating orgiastically and engaging in multiple love affairs as he charted a course through high society. His reputation as a novelist who 'understood' women grew, and so did the number of his female admirers. Portraits do not reveal him to be especially attractive; he stood 5 feet 3 inches and was grossly overweight. He wore even the best clothes badly, had dirty nails and picked his nose in public. For his charm to shine through, however, he had only to speak; all of his conversation sparkled with vitality and wit. A lover of worthless and often useless antiques, he collected canes with handles of gold, silver and turquoise. Inside one handle, he claimed, was the nude portrait of a 'secret mistress'. On his deathbed, he is said to have cried, 'Send for Bianchon!' – a doctor he created in *La Comédie Humaine*. To the end, Balzac was different: of all the great writers to have died of drink, he was probably the only one for whom the fatal brew was coffee.

'A woman is a well-served table,' Balzac observed, 'that one sees with different eyes before and after the meal.' By all accounts Balzac devoured his lovers as voraciously as he enjoyed a good dinner. Young girls bored him. He preferred mature women, and said at the start of virtually every affair, 'I never had a mother. I never knew a mother's love.' Despite his bizarre appearance, he had no trouble finding willing women, and he was a virtuoso at juggling his numerous affairs. (It is surprising that he had time for such dalliances, given his immense literary output.) Some of the 12,000 letters he received from female admirers contained explicit propositions, many of which he accepted. He often struck a responsive chord with his sympathetic delineations of unappreciated matrons. A biographer refers to Balzac's virile and experimental bedroom manner. Apparently he had been instructed by many courtesans over the years. 'He slept with aristocrats, courtesans and trollops indiscriminately,' wrote Gerson, 'displaying in his love life the same dazzling diversification that appeared in his writing. His yearning for romance, like all of his other appetites, was insatiable.' Considering his indifference to fidelity, it is noteworthy that he also had at least two very tender and enduring affairs.

Balzac boasted of his chastity during his early days of writing, but at 23 was introduced to sexual passion by Laure de Berny, a 45-year-old grandmother. Madame de Berny was the archetypal 'Balzacian' – a lonely older woman. Their relationship lasted fifteen years. Balzac also found time to carry on with a wealthy widow, the blonde Duchesse d'Abrantes. He met her in 1825, when she was 40; he set his sights on making love to this woman, who had slept with Prince Metternich. Another of her charms was her fortune – and she paid some of his mounting debts. His two reigning passions – women and fame – were in part fuelled by a desire for the money they could provide. He became increasingly promiscuous with age, and maintained the energy required for his demanding double life as lover and artist.

In 1832, however, he suffered rejection at the hands of the Marquise de Castries, one of the most beautiful aristocrats in France. She was perhaps the first woman of note who simply could not overcome the revulsion she felt at his appearance. Balzac got his revenge by ridiculing her in his novel *La Duchesse de Langeais*. The episode left him feeling vulnerable and depressed; he was 33, and his debts were mounting. Madame de Berny was old and he felt the need for a protectress more than ever. Then he received an intriguing letter from the Ukraine signed 'The Stranger'. Balzac replied and discovered the writer, Evelina Hanska, was married to a baron. The following year Balzac and Evelina secretly met in Switzerland; they found each other plumper than they had hoped, but they fell in love. For years they conducted a passionate correspondence. Evelina promised to marry him when her elderly husband died. Occasionally they would meet in various European cities for lovemaking that was, as he described it, 'honey and fire'. Balzac did not deny himself the attentions of other women, however, and throughout this time he dallied with 24-year-old Marie Louise du Fresnay, who bore him a child. She passed the infant off as her husband's. He also had a two-month affair with the most 'divinely beautiful' woman he had ever seen, the notoriously promiscuous Lady Ellenborough. Another affair – with Frances Sarah Lovell, the reputedly 'highly sexed' wife of Count Guidoboni-Visconti – lasted five years. She affectionately called him 'Bally', paid many of his debts, and bore him a child. Throughout all this philandering, Balzac kept up his association with various prostitutes, sometimes two at a time. In 1841, Evelina Hanska's husband died, and Balzac – troubled by his coffee-assaulted stomach – was finally willing to settle down. But Evelina, now pregnant with Balzac's child, refused to marry him. The child was stillborn. Balzac moved in with another mistress, Louise Breugnol, and his health began to fail. When he was near death, Evelina took pity on him and, seventeen years after they first met, they married. Balzac died five months later with his wife asleep in the next room.

'It is easier,' he said, 'to be a lover than a husband, for the same reason that it is more difficult to show a ready wit all day long than to say a good thing occasionally.'

G.A.M. (Lists 8, 9, 11, 15, 20, 22, 23, 24, 25, 38, 45, 46)

♣ Natalie Barney
31 October 1876 to 12 February 1972

The leading lesbian of her time, Barney was a writer of epigrams, memoirs and poetry, but she was most widely known for her affairs and intrigues with beautiful, brilliant and famous women, and for her salon, where an international cultural elite met for more than sixty years.

Known as *l'Amazone* (the Amazon) because of Rémy de Gourmont's immortalization of her in his *Lettres à l'Amazone*, Natalie was raised in Cincinnati. She had an early predilection for all things French, and could speak the language perfectly as a child. Born into the 'fabulous Barney fortune' (her grandparents on both sides were industrial magnates), Natalie was able to make trips abroad at an early age, and at 11 was placed in a French boarding school, where she realized she was a lesbian: 'My only books/Were women's looks.' Back in America, she was whisked around high-society circles in Washington, until she was free to settle in Paris. At 32, she bought the townhouse at 20 rue Jacob (the street on which courtesan Ninon de Lenclos had lived two centuries earlier), which was to become the most famous literary salon of her time. Known for its cucumber sandwiches and chocolate cakes, it boasted such regulars as Anatole France, Valéry, Gide, Gertrude Stein and Ezra Pound. Once Mata Hari arrived, completely naked, on a bejewelled white horse. Though some of her writing was favourably received, Natalie was much like her friend Oscar Wilde, who said, 'I've put my genius into my life; I've put only my talent into my works.' Radclyffe Hall's *The Well of Loneliness*, Liane de Pougy's *Idylle Sapphique* and most of Renée Vivien's poetry were some of the literary works Natalie inspired. Composed, wilful and independent, Natalie Barney saw her life as a series of love affairs. Having learned to masturbate in the bath, she was a sensualist at an early age. As she put it, 'Yes, at 12, I knew exactly what I liked and I firmly decided not to let myself be diverted from my tastes.' Though not conventionally beautiful, she was bewitching, with long, untamed blonde hair, small breasts and piercing blue eyes. She wore long flowing gowns, usually white. Many men courted her assiduously, but Barney remained a 'friend of men, lover of women'. She enjoyed feminine women, once remarking, 'Why try to resemble our enemies?' She would have sex at any time, and often in unusual places or circumstances; in fields and streams, in theatre boxes, or with two women at a time, and she had an unquenchable thirst for conquest. Sometimes when lovers tired of Natalie's unfaithfulness, they would try to resist her: they rarely succeeded. As one ex-lover, who had sworn off lesbianism and married, said after seeing Natalie, '[For a few minutes] I committed the delicious sin of abandoning myself to her caresses. . . .' The Amazon was notoriously good at what she did.

Barney's liaisons numbered over forty, not including countless casual affairs. She had her first physical relationship when she was 16, and had several others before her first famous affair when, at 22, she courted and won the fabulously beautiful Liane de Pougy. Liane was the most famous courtesan of the period, and the women had a passionate affair in between Liane's liaisons with princes and other nobility. Years later, when Liane had married a prince, she only allowed Natalie to caress her above the waist. Later Natalie was to say that Liane had been her 'greatest sensual pleasure', whereas Liane, turning pious, called Natalie her 'greatest sin'. During one of Liane's absences, Natalie met and fell in love with Renée Vivien, a brilliant poet who was morbidly obsessed with the idea of death. Renée could not tolerate Natalie's faithlessness and eventually refused to see her any more, whereupon Natalie resorted to such pranks as dressing in white and having herself delivered to Renée's door in a white satin coffin. Renée came to ignore such dramatics, and died a few years later of what Colette termed 'voluntary consumption' (she weighed 65 pounds), and Natalie gained her reputation as a femme fatale.

After Renée Vivien, Natalie took a host of other lovers, who sometimes stayed simultaneously at 20 rue Jacob. Her greatest problem was keeping peace within the harem. Dolly Wilde, who in both looks and wit resembled her uncle Oscar, would shut herself away with drugs and alcohol when Natalie betrayed her – once she slit her wrists and was nursed by Natalie's maid. In better spirits, Dolly enlivened Natalie's salons with such remarks as, 'Oh, Natalie, you forgot to put the hermaphrodites in the bushes.' Dolly was ousted, however, when Romaine Brooks – an American painter living in Paris – jealously ordered Natalie to get rid of Dolly. When Romaine spoke, Natalie obeyed.

Romaine was Natalie's longest and most serious relationship. They met as both neared their forties, and remained together – living sometimes apart, sometimes in adjoining houses – for over fifty years. But, even as an octogenarian, Natalie had a wandering eye. At 82, she met and seduced a 58-year-old woman who was formerly the heterosexual wife of a retired ambassador. Romaine tolerated this liaison for eleven years, and then the embittered woman of 94 refused ever to see Natalie again, breaking Natalie's heart. Romaine died two years later, and two years later Natalie followed suit. Natalie's funeral, like all her salons, was on a Friday.

J.H. (Lists 2, 6, 9, 11, 13, 22, 25, 26, 43)

♣ J. M. Barrie
9 May 1860 to 19 June 1937

The creator of Peter Pan, J. M. Barrie was a literary giant in his lifetime but his life was peppered with the tragic deaths of those he loved. The first occurred when Barrie was 6, growing up in the little Scottish village of Kirriemuir. His father was a hand-loom weaver, and he and his wife Margaret had nine children. Margaret's favourite, David, was 13 when he died after a skating accident. His death plunged her into a black depression. Little Jamie Barrie did all he could to cheer his mother, and tried to be so much like his brother 'that even my mother should not see the difference'. Once, he even put on the dead boy's clothes and imitated his whistle, hoping to fool his mother with his disguise.

As Barrie grew up, his dream of becoming a writer materialized and by 25 he was a London journalist. Success came quickly, as he turned to novels and plays, churning out a prodigious amount of work. Soon the shy little playwright (he was barely 5 feet tall) had become immensely wealthy and famous. In addition to his work, Barrie amused himself with his cricket team, the Alahak-barries (*'Allah akbar'* is Arabic for 'Heaven help us'), made up of noted writers and artists such as A. Conan Doyle and P. G. Wodehouse. Barrie's primary pleasure, however, was in his numerous friendships with children. Despite these diversions, his personal life was usually troubled. His mother died, one of his sisters died, and another sister's fiancé died falling off the horse Barrie had given him as a wedding present. These tragedies contributed to Barrie's lifelong reserve. Only children felt comfortable with the tiny man with the deep, rumbling Scottish voice. His behaviour often intimidated adults, for he would lapse into silences that went unbroken for hours and he swung regularly from dark depression to charming gaiety. One of Barrie's better traits was his unstinting generosity. He gave abundantly to friends and strangers in need, often anonymously. Barrie died at the age of 77, finally worn down by emotional duress and by the physical ailments which had long troubled him – coughs (he was forever puffing on his pipe), colds, headaches and insomnia. His last words were, 'I can't sleep.'

Barrie had one of the most profound cases of mother-fixation ever recorded. When he was 36, he wrote a book called *Margaret Ogilvy*, a sentimental memoir of his mother. The book was so personal and adoring that one critic called it 'a positive act of indecency'. In addition to being obsessed by his mother, Barrie was woefully self-conscious about his height, and this strongly affected his attitude towards women. When he was 18, he made these notes in his notebook (in which he often wrote in the third person):

'He is very young-looking – trial of his life is always thought a boy.'

'Greatest horror – dream I am married – wake up shrieking.'

'Grow up & have to give up marbles – awful thought.'

Barrie wrote of being crushed that women found him 'quite harmless', and summed up his misery in this outpouring: 'Six feet three inches.... If I had really grown to this it would have made a great difference in my life. I would not have bothered turning out reels of printed matter. My one aim would have been to become a favourite of the ladies which between you and me has always been my sorrowful ambition. The things I could have said to them if my legs had been longer. Read that with a bitter cry. . . .'

Barrie liked actresses, but did little in the way of pursuing them. In 1892, he was looking for a second leading lady for his new play, *Walker, London* – he wanted a woman who was 'young, quite charming . . . and able to flirt'. He gave the part to 29-year-old Mary Ansell, who met all the requirements. Mary and Barrie began to see a great deal of each other. There are two versions of what ensued. According to one, Barrie, after keeping Mary anxiously waiting, finally proposed. He then fell seriously ill with pneumonia – a matter of national concern – and Mary rushed to his side and nursed him back to health. According to the other version, she refused to marry him many times. When he fell ill, she went to him at his mother's behest, and they were married on what was expected to be his deathbed. The wedding took place on 9 July 1894. What followed on the honeymoon is a matter of speculation. It has been much rumoured that Barrie was completely impotent – he was jokingly labelled 'the boy who couldn't go up' – but no one knows for sure. One biographer states that Mary told her friends that the marriage was never consummated. In Andrew Birkin's biography, *J. M. Barrie and The Lost Boys*, Mary is said to have confided to a friend that she and her husband had 'normal marital relations' in the early days of their marriage. John Middleton Murry, a friend of Mary's, said Barrie was guilty of 'unmentionable sex behaviour toward Mary'. Wherever the truth lies, it does not point to sexual harmony between the Barries. Nevertheless, the couple settled down to married life, and Mary turned her frustrated maternal instincts towards Porthos, their big brown-and-white St Bernard, the model for 'Nana' in *Peter Pan*. While Mary tried to amuse herself with clothes and house-hunting, Barrie plunged into his work, which he never discussed with his wife. He remained silent for hours in her company and rarely spent any time with her.

During a stroll in London's Kensington Gardens, Barrie met two handsome, charming little boys wearing red berets, out walking with their nurse. They were 5-year-old George Davies and his 4-year-old brother Jack, the sons of Arthur Llewelyn Davies, a good-looking, struggling young barrister, and his enchanting wife Sylvia, sister of Gerald du Maurier and daughter of author George du Maurier. Sylvia had another boy, Peter, and would soon add two more to her brood – Michael and Nico. Thus began the truly great love affair in J. M. Barrie's life. Barrie 'adopted' the Davieses. He visited them daily, brought them presents, flirted sweetly with Sylvia (whom he worshipped), and entertained the boys with the stories of fairies and pirate adventures that were to become *Peter Pan*. Years later, Barrie told the boys, 'I made Peter by rubbing the five of you violently together, as savages with two sticks produce a flame.' Barrie's 'adoption' disgruntled Arthur Davies, but he remained a gentleman. What could he do? Barrie, as he had written of himself, was 'quite harmless', and the boys loved 'Uncle Jim'. What Mary Barrie felt about all this can be imagined. To add to the irony, Barrie was working on a novel, *Tommy and Grizel*, and had decided to switch the model for Grizel from Mary to Sylvia. In 1903 Arthur died of a terrible disease of the jaw, having been disfigured by facial operations. Barrie was at his side throughout the ordeal, and at the courageous Sylvia's side as well. It was understood that Barrie would assume financial responsibility for the family.

Two years later, as Barrie sat working at his desk in his summer cottage, a second blow fell. The gardener informed him that Mary Barrie (now in her forties) was having an affair with Gilbert Cannan, a 24-year-old barrister and writer and a friend of the Barries. A stupefied Barrie confronted Mary, who denied nothing and asked for a divorce. In a letter to her friend H. G. Wells, she wrote, 'He seems to have developed the most ardent passion for me now that he has lost me; that frightens me.' In 1909, the couple divorced. Barrie was shattered. In an attempt to keep publicity from further upsetting the miserable playwright, a petition signed by Henry James, H. G. Wells and Arthur Pinero, among others, was prepared asking the press to treat the matter discreetly. Barrie found solace only in his work, and in the Davies family. But one year later, in 1910, Sylvia died. The 50-year-old Barrie legally adopted the five boys – George and Peter were at Eton, Jack was in the navy, and Michael and Nico were 10 and 6 respectively. All the boys felt well loved by 'Uncle Jim', though George and Michael were the favourites. Michael, particularly, had much in common with Barrie – he was sensitive, poetic and brilliant. In 1914, George went to war in France; in March, 1915, he was killed. Barrie's grief was terrible. But an even greater grief was waiting. In May, 1921, Michael died. He drowned with a friend in a pool at Oxford. He could not swim, and was terrified of water – it was thought by many to be a suicide. It was the cruellest blow Barrie had ever received. He never fully recovered.

A year after Michael's death, Barrie wrote to Michael's Oxford tutor, '. . .what happened was in a way the end of me.'

The question has often been asked: 'Was Barrie homosexually in love with the boys?' It is a difficult question to answer – J. M. Barrie was not a simple man. In many ways his love for the boys was an odd mixture of a father's, a mother's and a lover's. Nico, the last Davies boy alive, does not feel it was a sexual love. He said, 'Of all the men I have ever known, Barrie was the wittiest, and the best company. He was also the least interested in sex. He was a darling man. He was an innocent; which is why he could write *Peter Pan*.'

A.W. (Lists 15, 17, 29)

♣ John Barrymore
15 February 1882 to 29 May 1942

Son of Maurice Barrymore and brother of Ethel and Lionel Barrymore, Jack was a member of the most distinguished family of actors to appear on the American stage. Although he conquered the legitimate theatre with his good looks, his career was a duel between his awesome talents and his inexorable drive toward self-destruction. Inherently lazy and an alcoholic since the age of 14, Jack chose the stage as the easiest way of making a living. He had been fired from a job as a caricaturist on a New York newspaper because of his heavy drinking, so he joined an acting troupe on its way to Australia. Before departing, he managed to sleep through the great San Francisco earthquake of 1906. Soldiers pressed him into clearing rubble, causing his uncle to remark, 'It took a calamity of nature to get him out of bed and the US army to make him go to work.'

He returned to America a polished light comedian and was soon the toast of Broadway. The young matinee idol was kept busy trying to support his profligate life-style and, though he despised the repetition of stage acting, his characterizations of Richard III and Hamlet are still regarded as classics. He made fifteen films before following his drinking buddies, Ben Hecht, Gene Fowler and W. C. Fields, from New York to Hollywood. At his peak he was earning the unheard-of sum of a minimum of $76,250 per picture and was nationally acclaimed as the 'Great Lover'. However, he hated his pretty-boy image and never missed an opportunity to act in grotesque make-up, relishing roles

26

like Svengali, Mr Hyde and Captain Ahab.

Barrymore was notoriously witty. While attending the funeral of a friend, he was about to depart with the other mourners when he saw a doddering old man lingering behind, staring down into the grave. Barrymore sidled up to the old fellow, leaned over and whispered, 'I guess it hardly pays to go home.' When he met Louella Parsons at a social function, he commented in a voice loud enough to be heard by the entire room, 'She's a quaint old udder, isn't she?' He described another woman as looking 'exactly like a dental filling'. Barrymore was equally well known for his superhuman drinking and carousing, which aged him rapidly. In 1935, in an attempt to dry out, he took his daughter Diana on a cruise on his yacht. All alcoholic drink was removed from the boat before it sailed. Yet Barrymore was drunk during the entire voyage. He had found a means of secretly siphoning off alcohol from the yacht's engine cooling system. By the end of his life, the once great actor was reduced to a pitiful series of self-mocking roles which reflected his tarnished reputation – that of a lecherous old drunkard. A friend summed up Barrymore's life by observing, 'Nobody can run downhill as fast as a thoroughbred.' He lived voraciously until his death from premature old age at 60.

At 15, Jack lost his virginity to his stepmother, who seduced him. After that, he was to make love to countless women, but he never really trusted any of them. His first romantic scandal solidified this feeling. He had been sleeping with 16-year-old show-girl Evelyn Nesbit, the girlfriend of society architect Stanford White. Evelyn's parents discovered the affair and hastily married her off to Harry K. Thaw, a psychotic millionaire. Thaw publicly murdered White out of jealousy, and Barrymore was forced to hide out for months until the case blew over.

In 1910, Jack married debutante Katherine Harris. Blonde, shapely, cultured and intelligent, Katherine married against her parents' wishes, yet she was the envy of her peers. However, Jack's accelerating career, coupled with his impromptu drinking binges, ended their marriage in 1917. On the rebound, he met and married Blanche Thomas, who led suffragette marches and wrote poetry under the pen name Michael Strange. The couple startled New Yorkers of the day with their unisex attire – matching outfits of black velvet. His time with Michael Strange was marked with fights and sonnets, and the birth of a daughter, Diana. When he divorced the poetess in 1928, he renounced all rights to their infant daughter and headed west.

27

In Hollywood, his lust seemed insatiable. Although most star-lets succumbed to his charm, he struck out with a young Southern actress named Tallulah Bankhead. One afternoon he invited her to his backstage dressing room and, as Tallulah recal-led, started making 'little animal noises' as he led her to his casting couch. She refused to have sex with him and escaped intact. He was far more successful with 17-year-old Mary Astor, who would appear in his suite on Sundays, accompanied by her mother. After sending the mother outside on the veranda to enjoy the sun, he would take Mary into his bedroom.

Soon the golden-haired bit-part player Dolores Costello caught his eye, and he chose her as his leading lady in *The Sea Beast*. When Michael Strange saw the love scenes in the film, she said bitterly, 'That's not acting. He's in love with the girl.' She was right. Barrymore dropped Michael flat for Dolores and conceded, 'I'm just a son of a bitch.' He made Dolores his protégée and married her, but was insecure in the relationship. In a rage of jealousy, he snatched her away from a party when he saw her dancing with David O. Selznick, took her home and lectured her until daybreak. He accused her of plotting an affair with Selznick and insisted that all married women were constantly unfaithful. On another occasion, he physically ejected her obstetrician from the house, claiming she was infatuated with the doctor. Maybe she was; after she divorced Jack she married him.

In later years, Barrymore was drawn to exotic prostitutes. When he visited India in search of a guru, he wound up in a Calcutta whorehouse which he described as a 'pelvic palace'. He was delighted by the 'gentle music that went directly to the scrotum and cuddled there,' and he stayed on for a month. 'And so I never met my saint,' he explained. 'I met only dancing girls and singing girls, all of them devout students of the *Kamasutra*, which teaches that there are thirty-nine different postures for the worship of Dingledangle – the god of love.' His sojourn in Calcutta was followed by a visit to a brothel in Madras, where he enjoyed himself so much that he rented the establishment exclu-sively for himself for an entire week.

His last wife, Elaine Barrie, married the wreckage of the once-great actor in 1936. She met him when she was a sophomore at Hunter College and spent the next year chasing him across the country. The day before their wedding he told his cronies, 'Gentlemen, you are talking to a man who is about to go over Niagara Falls in a barrel.' On their wedding night he was insanely

28

jealous because she was such a good lover. He demanded to know exactly how, when and where she had learned her skills. Later he said of Elaine, 'That little filly made a racehorse out of me again.' Elaine made a banned film called *How to Undress in Front of Your Husband*, starring 'Mrs John Barrymore.' Then, aware that he was nearly washed-up in films, Elaine took her husband on the road in a play called *Dear Children*. People flocked to see the great Barrymore, a sick old man, humiliate himself. He vomited on stage and urinated in public – once in a hotel lobby sandbox and another time in a socialite's private lift. Aware that he was dying, he faced the end with his own brand of gallantry. When a priest entered his hospital room with an extremely ugly nurse and asked, 'Anything to confess, my son?' Barrymore replied, 'Yes, father. I confess having carnal thoughts.' Astonished, the priest asked, 'About whom?' Barrymore pointed at the ugly nurse. 'About her,' he said.

The night that Barrymore died, his long-time friend Gene Fowler and Gene's son Will held vigil by his body at Pierce's Funeral Home. The only person who came to pay him homage was an old prostitute, who knelt in silent prayer – and then disappeared into the dark.

John Barrymore had earned over $3 million in his day. When his estate was auctioned off after he died, he was still $75,000 in debt.

M.S. and Eds. (Lists 2, 3, 11, 16, 17, 20, 22, 25, 31, 40, 42, 51)

❧ Alexander Graham Bell
3 March 1847 to 2 August 1922

The telephone, Bell's most famous invention, made him wealthy. Most of his work was directed at improving communication for the deaf; Bell lectured extensively, and taught many deaf pupils to speak. One of his prodigies was Helen Keller. It was not surprising, then, that Bell developed a romantic interest in one of his students, Mabel Hubbard. She was only 15 when Bell started teaching her to speak. On Mabel's 18th birthday, Thanksgiving Day, they were engaged. Thanksgiving always remained a special holiday for them. A year and a half later, Bell's lecturing had earned him enough to convince Mabel's parents that the time was right for marriage. Mabel wrote to her mother, 'Every day I see something new in him to love and admire.' In another, more practical, note, she added, 'I am beginning to learn that my happiness in life will depend on how well I can feed him.' This was a rather prophetic remark, since Bell weighed up to 250 pounds in later years – 85 pounds more than on their wedding day.

After marrying in 1877, the couple honeymooned in Niagara Falls. Business trips often separated the Bells and Alexander wrote in a letter, 'I *dread* absence from you . . . Let us lay it down as a principle of our lives, that we shall be together.' But Bell's working hours were a source of some conflict – he always worked at night, usually retiring at 4.00 a.m. 'Our worst quarrels have been about that,' Mabel noted in her journal. Then she added 'No, the front rank belongs to . . . getting up in the morning, but this follows close behind.' Bell tried unsuccessfully several times to change his schedule to please her. Mabel bore two daughters, Elsie May and Marian; two sons died in infancy. The Bells grieved deeply over these deaths, but Mabel tried to be philosophical. She wrote of her sons, 'I have had them and my whole life is the happier for this consciousness.'

Teacher and student enjoyed forty-five happy years of marriage. On 2 August 1922, Bell was near death after a long illness. He roused from sleep to smile at Mabel, by his side. 'Don't leave me,' she begged him, and his fingers spelled out for her the sign for 'no'. With this last silent message, the inventor of the telephone passed away peacefully.

A.W. and J.M. (Lists 33, 38)

♣ Jack Benny
14 February 1894 to 27 December 1973

American comedian Jack Benny was known to millions as a violin-playing miser. He was star of vaudeville, radio, television, stage and screen. Benny (born Benjamin Kubelsky) had a number of romances, but only one true love – Sadie Marks. Jack first met Sadie when she was 12. Zeppo Marx, one of the Marx brothers, brought Jack to her family's house for a Passover meal, and to meet Sadie and her sisters, who were, said Zeppo, 'very cute numbers'. Jack and Sadie did not hit it off. Four years later, in 1926, they met again. This second meeting also failed to impress Sadie, but the next day Jack appeared at the shop where she worked. Jack came to within hearing distance of the customers and said, 'Pardon me, miss, can you tell me where the men's room is?' Another inauspicious encounter. But Jack kept coming back to the store just to stand and stare at Sadie.

They were married in Illinois in 1927. When the rabbi pronounced them man and wife, Sadie called her parents to tell them she had married Jack. When her mother said, 'Your father and I wish you every happiness – but I don't think it will work out,' Sadie promptly fainted. It took half an hour to revive her. The bride spent much of her wedding night watching her husband perform in *The Great Temptations*. She was so tired she fell asleep during the show. Sadie said, 'I'm quite sure I was not in love with Jack Benny when I married him. I'm convinced he was not really in love with me, either. At the beginning, we had nothing in common except our sense of humour, and the fact that, when I was little, I had studied the violin. . . . On the night he proposed to me, Jack was newly rejected from a four-year love affair. When I accepted, I was wearing another boy's engagement ring. What we had together – our great love for each other – came gradually over that first year. I was a teenage bride. Jack was 33. I didn't know what being in love was all about.'

Sadie began to work with Jack onstage, and changed her name to Mary Livingstone. She remembers some of the mishaps of their first year together. One night she was backstage when a chorus girl pulled a prank, not knowing Mary was there. The girl had painted one of her breasts with lipstick to look like a pig. She pulled out the breast, and yelled, 'Oink, oink,' hoping to get a laugh out of Jack. Benny had trouble convincing Mary it was a joke. As the newlyweds travelled from town to town, Jack received a steady stream of phone calls from old girlfriends. He was always polite, saying, 'I'm sorry – I can't make it tonight.' When Mary would ask, 'Why didn't you tell her you were married?' he would reply, 'Gee, Mary, I guess I forgot.' After Jack 'forgot' one too many times, Mary scratched his cheek with her fingernails. Benny had to go onstage holding one hand over the side of his face. Perhaps that was where the famous Benny 'hand on cheek' gesture originated.

Mary had one more spurt of jealousy in 1942, while Benny was working on a movie with Ann Sheridan. Impulsively, Mary invited Ann to a party she and Jack were giving. Mary approached Ann and told her, 'Miss Sheridan, I don't know whether you like Jack or he likes you. . . . But you *are* making a picture together . . . and I wanted to remind you of something. Jack wouldn't give my little finger for your *whole body*! Now,

31

have a good time. . . .'

The Bennys' one separation occurred in San Francisco after a fight over a loud necktie of Jack's. Mary (then Sadie) said, 'If you don't take that tie off, I'm leaving you and going home to my folks in Los Angeles.' Jack refused, and Mary left. After a week of silence, Jack sent Mary the tie with a note which read, 'I thought you'd like to give this tie to the Salvation Army. All my love, Jack.' Mary returned on the next train, and she presented him with a beautifully wrapped gift – the tie.

Near the end of his life, Jack Benny told this joke in some of his stage appearances: 'Mary and I have been married forty-seven years, and not once have we ever had an argument serious enough to mention the word "divorce" . . . "murder", yes, but "divorce", never.' Mary and Jack had forty-eight happy years together. Mary never removed her wedding ring. When she acted the role of a single woman, she covered it with tape. Jack even gave her presents on *his* birthday. Mary said, 'With him, I found complete and total fulfilment . . . He adored me. I adored him. . . . I always will.'

A.W. and J.M.

❧ Sarah Bernhardt
22/3 October 1844 to 26 March 1923

Sarah Bernhardt gained international acclaim with her roles in Victor Hugo's *Ruy Blas*, Racine's *Phèdre*, and the younger Dumas's *La Dame aux Camélias*. Her acting was characterized by an emotional intensity which inspired poets and critics alike to sing her praises. Fellow actress Ellen Terry described her as 'a miracle'.

The daughter of a beautiful, unmarried milliner-turned-courtesan, Sarah was ignored by her mother. A sickly child, she suffered from tuberculosis and was not expected to live to adulthood. When she was 16 she hoped to become a nun. However, her mother's current lover, the Duc de Morny – half-brother of Napoleon III – decided that Sarah should be trained as an actress. He used his influence to enrol her first in the Conservatoire – the French government's acting school – and two years later in the Comédie Française. She was forced to leave the Comédie in 1863 after she slapped another actress in a fit of anger. Emotionally unpredictable, extremely thin, and with a head of unruly, fair, curly hair, she scored her first major triumph at the Odéon Theatre in *Kean*, a play by Dumas *père*. Success followed success for the 'nicely polished skeleton', and in 1880 she formed her own company and toured the world with her productions. Despite her increasing fame, Sarah continued to be plagued with stage fright. Her nervous agitation, combined with the emotional demands of her performance, would often cause her to faint after the last curtain fell. Nor was she ever free of her tubercular ailment, being frequently afflicted with spells during which she coughed blood. Although frail, her will-power was remarkable. She required little sleep and was said to have the energy of ten people. Even after her leg was amputated in 1915, she kept to her demanding schedule until shortly before her death aged 78 in her Paris home.

Reputed to have had thousands of affairs, the 'Divine Sarah' herself proclaimed, 'I have been one of the great lovers of my century.' (Originally, her mother had considered grooming Sarah as a courtesan, but the independent girl was temperamentally unsuited for that 'lucrative form of slavery'.) Her initial affair, at 18, was with the Count de Kératry, but the first man who truly won her heart was Henri, Prince de Ligne. By Henri, the 20-year-old Sarah had a son, Maurice, whom many considered the real love of her life. While still in her twenties she became the toast of Europe, and her admirers included Gustave Doré, Victor Hugo, Edmond Rostand, Oscar Wilde and Emile Zola. She was always attracted to men of talent, and she expected them to pay tribute to her in their art. Although Sarah flung herself into her affairs with curiosity and passion, she rarely abandoned herself to them. Perhaps her childhood partly accounted for her caution. She once recalled, 'My mother's house was always full of men, and the more I saw of them, the less I liked them.' None the less, the actress who moved in 'a halo of glory' had a magnetic effect on both men and women, and she was adored by royalty. In a pamphlet entitled 'The Love of Sarah Bernhardt', the far-fetched allegation was made that she had seduced all the European heads of state, including the pope himself. There is evidence that she did indeed have 'special relationships' with the Prince of Wales (later Edward VII) and Prince Napoleon, nephew of Napoleon I, to whom she had been introduced by George Sand. As for the other leaders of Europe, although she may not have occupied their beds, it is clear that she won their hearts. She was showered with gifts from Emperor Franz Josef of Austria, King Alfonso of

Spain and King Umberto of Italy. King Christian IX of Denmark lent her his yacht, and the Archduke Frederick allowed her to use his chateau.

Her leading men usually became her lovers, these affairs often lasting only as long as the show ran. Once captivated by the Bernhardt charm, however, her conquests stayed on as friends. Foremost among these friend–lovers were Philippe Garnier, who appeared in *Théodora*, and Pierre Berton, who played opposite her in *Fédora* and *La Tosca*. She and Berton were said to generate enough electricity 'to light the streets of London'. Perhaps her best pairing, both romantically and theatrically, was with the magnificent Jean Mounet-Sully. One of the most talented of all French tragic actors, he shared the spotlight with Sarah in *Ruy Blas*, *Phèdre* and *Hernani*. She and Sully were referred to as '*le couple*', and the joint appearance of their names on the theatre marquee ensured a box-office success.

As she grew older, she continued to have affairs with her leading men. When 66, while on tour in the USA, Sarah established a four-year liaison with Dutch-born Lou Tellegen, an untalented blond Hercules at least thirty-five years her junior. In his autobiography, *Women Have Been Kind*, he acknowledged that the time he had spent as her leading man had been 'the most glorious four years of my life'.

Her only marriage, in 1882, was to the outrageously handsome but dissolute Aristides Jacques Damala, a Greek diplomat–playboy eleven years her junior. Described as a cross between Casanova and the Marquis de Sade, he flaunted his infidelities and seemed to take particular pleasure in humiliating her in public. They separated within a year, but during the last months of his life she nursed him devotedly. He died in 1889, ravaged by morphine and cocaine.

Among Sarah Bernhardt's many eccentricities was her well-publicized satin-lined rosewood coffin. Given the doctors' verdict that she did not have long to live, the teenage Sarah entreated her mother to buy her this coffin so that she would not be consigned to 'an ugly bier'. She sometimes slept in it, and she had herself photographed in it more than once. In her book *The Memoirs of Sarah Barnum* – a thinly disguised, obscene 'biography' of Sarah Bernhardt – actress Marie Colombier claimed Sarah 'demanded that her intimate friends should keep her company in the narrow box. Some of them hesitated, because this funereal furniture killed their desires.'

Shortly before the First World War, author Octave Mirbeau asked Sarah Bernhardt when she intended to give up love. She responded, 'When I draw my last breath. I hope to live as I have always lived. The strength of my energy and vitality lies entirely in their subservience to my destiny as a woman.'

Eds. (Lists 11, 22, 25, 26, 41, 42, 46)

♣ Simón Bolívar
24 July 1783 to 17 December 1830

Six Latin American countries – Venezuela, Colombia, Ecuador, Peru, Bolivia and Panama – owe their independence from Spanish rule to Bolívar, the Venezuelan-born son of Spanish aristocrats, who was orphaned at 9. Under the care of an uncle, he was tutored by Simón Ródriguez, a disciple of Rousseau, and was indoctrinated with eighteenth-century liberalism. An unruly child, he was sent as a youth to study in Europe. The 16-year-old Bolívar was a zealous student and, learning about the great European rationalists, he became convinced that South America was ripe for independence.

The instability in Spain, caused by Napoleon's invasion, enabled political leaders in the Spanish colonies to foment a rebellion. Bolívar was a participant in this rebellion, and also served as emissary to Great Britain. Returning to his home, he became leader in the ultimate liberation movement and marched his victorious armies as far south as what is now the Bolivia–Argentine border. Eventually, Bolívar was caught between squabbling local factions in the new republic and fell out of favour. He died in Colombia in 1830, poor and despised, after his exile from Venezuela, one of the countries he had helped to free.

Bolívar was a voracious lover, but rarely became emotionally involved with his sex partners. His sexual awakening came early in his teens. At 12, while living with his uncle in Caracas, he became involved with his attractive female cousins, the Aristiguietas, consummating his relationship with many of the girls. Later in life, he was to refer to them as 'beautiful girls of happy and independent natures'. His reputation as a 'catch' grew rapidly, and one story – probably apocryphal – asserts that Bolívar had a love affair with Queen Maria Luisa of Spain, then 50: Few women of that day would forgo a chance to be intimate

35

with Bolívar, who had a slim body, a broad chest and a sensual mouth.

In 1802, Bolívar married Maria Teresa de Toro, three years his senior, in Madrid. His charming bride died of yellow fever less than a year later, deeply influencing Bolívar, who repeatedly insisted that, if Teresa had not died, he would never have dedicated himself to the independence movement. He vowed never to marry again.

In 1804, Bolívar went to Paris, where he was 'sheltered' by a distant cousin, Fanny du Villars. Although married to one of Napoleon's generals, the middle-aged Fanny taught her young lover how to be a gentleman. It was rumoured that Simon fathered her second child, but Bolívar never acknowledged parentage and details of the life of Fanny's son are obscure.

A man of many moods, he hated to be alone, and, in fact, needed the company of women. His lovers remained true. One French girl, Anita Lenoit, was seduced in a hammock during a lull in fighting. She refused all other suitors after her affair with Bolívar, waiting seventeen years in the hope he would return.

Wherever his armies went, Bolívar was never without female companions. It has been said that he once risked capture by the Spanish, refusing to move until his current mistress could join him. While with one woman, he was writing to another. Many of the cities of South America were filled with his happy conquests – in Lima, Quito and elsewhere, the list was endless – including Josefina Núñez, Janette Hart and Isabel Soublette. However, only once did a woman other than his wife capture his emotions. On 16 June 1822, during a victory parade through Quito, in present-day Ecuador, a pretty married 24-year-old aimed a laurel wreath at 'the Liberator's' feet. When it hit him on the side of the face, Bolívar angrily turned towards the horrified Manuela Saenz, whose dark beauty instantly transformed his indignation into forgiveness. That evening they danced together for hours before quietly disappearing from the ball to enjoy the first of many trysts. Manuela was sterile, free to make love without fear of consequences. Bolívar was in the initial stages of tuberculosis – and he found sex relieved some symptoms of the disease, such as itching in the genitals. Although Bolívar had other women after meeting Manuela, she was different and not easily forgotten after one night of love. Bolívar's most romantic letters were addressed to her. Manuela replied, 'Marriage pledges one to nothing,' and spurned her wealthy English husband to follow Bolívar to Bogota, accompanied by her devoted mulatto slave, Jonatas. Perhaps it was Jonatas's constant presence or her habit of dressing as a soldier (except when she donned a skirt to perform lewd dances) that started the gossip that she and her mistress were lovers. But gossip was stilled in 1828, when Manuela saved Bolívar's life by devising an escape plan for him and diverting his would-be assassins. After that, they openly lived together, and Manuela was honoured as 'the Liberatress'. Though they never married, the fiery relationship between Bolívar and Manuela Saenz lasted until his death, even when worsening tuberculosis brought his sex life to an end.

A.L.G. and Eds. (Lists 2, 22)

♣ Napoleon Bonaparte
15 August 1769 to 5 May 1821

A relatively obscure artillery officer in his early military career, Napoleon won distinction – and a general's rank – by capturing Toulon (1793) from British forces aiding the French royalists. Called to Paris in 1795, his ruthless suppression of a rebel mob saved the new republic and he was given command of French armies in Italy. There, in battles against the Austrian armies, Napoleon's victories made him a national hero. Returning secretly to Paris after his Egyptian campaign (1799), Bonaparte took advantage of the directory's internal dissention and executed a coup d'état. The consulate was created and – as first consul – Napoleon became master of France at 30. He set up a military dictatorship, camouflaged by a constitution that gave him unlimited political power. Continental Europe fell under his domination during the ensuing Napoleonic Wars. His efforts to exclude British goods by boycott caused Spain to revolt and other nations joined in. A disastrous Russian campaign (1812) and a crushing defeat at Leipzig (1814) led to a forced abdication and his banishment to Elba. Although Bonaparte escaped briefly to wage the 'Hundred Days' struggle, his effort to regain the French throne ended in his defeat by the Duke of Wellington at Waterloo (1815). Exile for life on St Helena followed.

During his two official marriages, Napoleon also made love to a dozen known mistresses. Another twenty were said to have shared his bed before he was sent into exile. By his own admission, Napoleon lost his virginity at 18, to a prostitute he had picked up on a Parisian boulevard. This commercial experience did little to overcome the future emperor's timidity towards women. In 1795, eager to wed, he courted his first real love, his sister-in-law Eugénie Désirée Clary, hoping that his brother Joseph – who had married Eugénie's older sister – would smooth the way. Joseph's effort failed, and Napoleon withdrew the marriage proposal abruptly, possibly fearing he would be impotent with the young beauty destined to become Sweden's queen. Thereafter, he shifted his wooing to more mature women, making firm offers to at least five. Two were old enough to be his grandmother and mother, respectively: Mademoiselle de Montansier (aged 60), and Madame Permon (aged 40). Both were shocked to learn that he was serious.

His frantic search for a suitable wife finally ended when Count Paul Barras, seeking to rid himself of his expensive and ageing Creole mistress Joséphine de Beauharnais, arranged for the two to meet. Relying on the count's assurance that the match would have great benefits both monetarily and socially, Napoleon married the '28-year-old'. (She knocked four years off her age on the marriage certificate – and he added two – to make the gap between them less obvious.) On their marriage night, engaged in vigorous intercourse, the bridegroom suddenly uttered a shriek as Joséphine's pet pug, Fortuné, joined the act. Believing his mistress was being attacked, the dog had jumped on the bed and then bitten *le petit général* on his bare left calf. Two days later, the wounded warrior cut the honeymoon short and left for Italy, freeing the insatiable Joséphine – who rarely slept alone – to resume her liaisons with standby lovers. Irked by Joséphine's constant unfaithfulness – a contemporary once smirked that the empress seemed to believe '. . . far-sighted nature had placed the wherewithal to pay her bills beneath her navel . . .' – Napoleon took Pauline Fourès as his new mistress during the Egyptian campaign of 1798. He became smitten with the 20-year-old blonde, who had disguised her boyish figure in male attire to be with her soldier husband. The cuckolded lieutenant was cunningly sent back to Paris with dispatches and Pauline moved into a house near Napoleon's Cairo headquarters. Nicknamed 'Our Lady of the Orient' and 'Madame la Générale', she heightened the general's passion by wearing plumed hats, gold-braided coats and skintight white pantaloons that pandered to his buttock fetish. (A lifelong connoisseur of bottoms, he had once fondly described Joséphine's rump as 'the prettiest little backside imaginable'.) The notorious affair was

38

spiked by the British, who captured the ship on which Lieutenant Fourès had sailed and maliciously returned him to Egyptian soil to play the role of outraged husband.

For Napoleon's casual romps, Duroc, his chief aide-de-camp and intimate confidant for fifteen years, served as pimp. The over-nighters were brought to a bedroom adjacent to Napoleon's study in the Tuileries. Duroc admitted the girls secretly and gave orders for them to strip and slip beneath the bedcovers, to be ready for instant sex once Bonaparte's work was over. Some intrigues of longer duration, like those with ladies-in-waiting Eléonore Denuelle and Marie Antoinette Dûchatel, were deliberately arranged by conniving members of Napoleon's family, eager to sponsor any mistress who could prove the hated Joséphine to be barren. They succeeded with Denuelle: in 1806, she gave birth to a son, Léon, and Napoleon proudly claimed credit as the father. Although Bonaparte preferred to keep his trysts secret, the affair with Mademoiselle Georges (real name: Marguérite Weymer, later called the 'Whale' because of a huge gain in weight) erupted publicly, to his great embarrassment. An erotic book surfaced with illustrations showing his mistress engaged in graphic homosexual acts with her lesbian lover Raucort.

Napoleon's favourite partner, Marie Walewska, was an unsolicited 'gift' from her fellow Poles, who needed France's might to achieve independence for their homeland. The liaison began unevenly. Taken to Napoleon's private apartments in Warsaw, the nervous young countess fainted when he became sexually aggressive. Undeterred, Napoleon raped her. Regaining consciousness, she quickly forgave him, and the affair flourished for over three years. Her quiet charm and devotion captivated the emperor, and Marie may have been the only woman he ever really loved. In 1810, she gave him his second son, Alexander, further proving that he was not impotent. Meanwhile, the problem of producing legally acceptable offspring became of even greater concern. In 1809, after his tempestuous marriage to Joséphine failed to result in an heir, Napoleon reluctantly annulled the union. Out of political necessity, he chose as his second wife Marie Louise of Austria, an 18-year-old virgin so sheltered during childhood that all male animals were kept from her view. After checking over her prolific ancestors like a farmer seeking a prize brood mare, the heirless emperor concluded that she had '. . . the kind of womb I want to marry'. Marie Louise proved true to her breeding and presented Napoleon with a son a year after their marriage in 1810. Both wives were showered by thousands of love letters whose flaming prose included phrases like 'I kiss your breasts, and lower down, much lower down!' or 'I kiss the little black forest. . . .'

Napoleon not only tolerated homosexuality among his associates; he also refused to permit punitive legislation against its practice. His habit of caressing his soldiers intimately while tweaking noses or pulling ears hinted strongly at his own homosexuality. Aides were often chosen for their youth and effeminate behaviour. To one, Napoleon himself gave the nickname 'Miss Sainte Croix'. Another, the baron Gaspard Gourgard, was the emperor's personal orderly for six years. Gourgard was furiously jealous of any who dared pay undue personal attention to 'Her Majesty', his affectionate name for his master. After he reached the age of 42, the question of Napoleon's true gender did not matter. He became impotent, fulfilling Joséphine's derisive charge of earlier years that 'Bon-a-parte est Bon-à-rien', or 'Bonaparte is good-for-nothing.'

Napoleon's known loss of sexual potency, combined with a pronounced lemon-yellow cast to his skin in his last years, hinted at a progressively fatal malfunctioning of the endocrine glands. The medical examination and autopsy performed by Dr Antommarchi, witnessed by several English doctors, provided further evidence that his pituitary, thyroid, renal and gonad glands were rapidly failing and almost certainly tumorous. A huge gastric ulcer and extensive calcium deposits throughout the urinary system were found to be the primary causes for his lifelong indigestion and painful urination. The urethral obstruction was probably responsible for his complaint of being afflicted by *le chaud pisse* ('burning urine'). The ulcer was seen to be cancerous, although it had not yet spread elsewhere in the body. Napoleon's penis had shrunk to one inch in length and both testicles were minuscule, showing an advanced case of hypogonadism. The body hair was almost non-existent, and the pubis was feminine in appearance. Glandular changes had produced softly rounded, creamy-textured breasts that many women would have envied, and had reduced his hands and feet to an abnormally small size. Napoleon's final height, as recorded in the autopsy, was 5 feet 2 inches, perhaps reduced several inches because of the ravages of his multiple ailments.

W.K. (Lists 5, 14, 20, 22, 30, 49)

✤ Napoleon Bonaparte III

20 August 1808 to 9 January 1873

The third son of Louis Bonaparte – the eccentric if not insane king of Holland – Napoleon III was raised by his mother, Hortense de Beauharnais Bonaparte, whose bedroom escapades and infidelities were legendary. Consumed with the ambition to restore Napoleonic rule and gain glory for France, Louis Napoleon tried unsuccessfully to overthrow the French government in 1836 and 1840. After the second attempt, he was arrested and imprisoned for six years before escaping to England. The revolution of 1848, which toppled the French government, set the stage for Louis Napoleon's return to Paris and his subsequent election to the presidency of the new French Republic. Four years later, he overthrew the republican government and proclaimed himself Emperor Napoleon III. During his eighteen-year reign, he initiated social reforms and economic programmes aimed at modernization. However, he also involved France in a series of costly wars, the last of which, the Franco-Prussian, lost him his throne when France went down to total defeat. He died three years later while living in Great Britain, hopeful until the end of a triumphant return to France.

Almost as strong as his political ambitions were Napoleon's sexual urges. From an early age he had a ceaseless string of lovers by whom he fathered a legion of children. Asked once why he ran from one bed to the next, he replied, 'I need my little amusements.' Napoleon's style was reportedly quite simple and crude. One mistress, the Marquise Taisey-Chatenoy, described a session with the emperor. With mauve silk pyjamas covering his long torso and short legs, the large-nosed, plain-looking Napoleon came to her chambers and immediately engaged in intercourse. During the session the wax on his moustache melted, allowing its pointed ends to droop. After a brief period of heavy breathing, Napoleon concluded his business and departed, leaving the marquise emotionally and physically unsatisfied.

In his twenties, Louis Napoleon proposed to a cousin, the Princess Mathilde Bonaparte, but any hopes of marriage were dashed by his abortive attempts to seize power in France. During his subsequent confinement in the fortress of Ham, he pleaded for feminine company and was allowed visits from Alexandrine Vergeot, a voluptuous 20-year-old officially employed as an ironer of officers' clothes and unofficially known as 'bedmaker to

41

State Prisoner No. 1'. During his six years there she bore him two sons.

Once out of prison, he gained a reputation as an avid romancer who wooed both respectable and less respectable ladies. The French tragedienne Rachel was one of his mistresses. He may have had an affair with Cora Pearl, a notorious courtesan who recorded the names of more than 1000 lovers in her diary, and later he was intimate with the beautiful Italian courtesan Giulia Beneni, known as 'La Barucci'. Proud of her conquest, La Barucci kept in her salon a silver goblet on a velvet-covered stand which bore the initial 'N' and the imperial crown.

By far the most important courtesan who figured in Napoleon's life was Elizabeth Howard, an English beauty whom he called 'my landlady'. He lived with Howard in London from 1846 to 1848. Although accused of being a cold-blooded schemer, she footed the bills during their two years together and also financed his coup d'état in 1848. When Napoleon III married, Howard was duly rewarded with over five million francs and the title of Comtesse de Beauregard.

In 1853, he selected the Spanish aristocrat Eugénie de Montijo, the libertine emperor's sexual opposite, as his bride. It seems that every time he tried to seduce the beautiful, auburn-haired virgin, who was eighteen years his junior, she told him the only way into her bed was through marriage. A devout Catholic, Eugénie considered sex unimportant except as a means of procreation. To friends she confided that sex was 'disgusting', and added, 'Men are worth nothing at all.' (It has been suggested that, in view of her fierce attachment to her sister Paca, Eugénie had lesbian tendencies, and it is certainly true that she was a woman of contradictions.) The Princess Mathilde scornfully remarked that Eugénie 'belonged in a cloister', but Eugénie could also be a seductive tease, and enjoyed telling risqué stories which shocked Napoleon. After the birth of their son in 1855 – which nearly caused her death – sex between them virtually ended. However, Eugénie was still jealous of those who did sleep with her husband. In a rage, she once accused him of having sex with the 'scum of the earth' just to embarrass her.

Indeed, Napoleon was so blatant about his affairs that a French senator in a speech once remarked, 'The emperor is not suffi-ciently careful in his intercourse with the fair sex. Out of sheer consideration for the country, His Majesty ought not to place himself in the power of this or that adventuress.' In 1855, Prime

42

Minister Cavour of Sardinia dispatched a beautiful 19-year-old noblewoman, the Countess di Castiglione, to seduce Napoleon and enlist his aid in the struggle to unify Italy. She was successful. After the countess had been banished from Paris, Napoleon replaced her with Madame Walewska, the Florentine-born wife of his foreign minister. She was a model of discretion – and quickly won Eugénie's affection.

Napoleon's last important mistress was Marguérite Bellanger, a robust young country woman whose simplicity delighted the emperor. By this time, however, he was in frail health, and Eugénie – convinced the rigours of a new affair would kill him – persuaded Marguérite to put an end to the relationship.

During Napoleon's final years, he and Eugénie had a reconciliation. It brought great comfort to a man who had been 'tortured by the flesh' all his life.

R.J.F. (Lists 20, 21, 22)

♣ Pauline Bonaparte
20 October 1780 to 9 June 1825

Pauline Bonaparte interests history mainly because she was Napoleon's favourite sister, one of the classical beauties of her time, an unremitting nymphomaniac, and the model for Antonio Canova's most popular sculpture. Pauline came from Ajaccio, Corsica, the sixth of her parents' thirteen children. When she was 12, her family moved to Toulon, France. As her older brother moved up in the world, she was transformed from peasant to princess. When Napoleon graduated from general to emperor, his pet sister, Pauline, also stood in the limelight of Parisian society. Men constantly pursued her. According to the French dramatist Arnault, 'She was an extraordinary combination of perfect physical beauty and the strangest moral laxity. If she was the loveliest creature one had ever seen, she was also the most frivolous.' Of her, Countess Anna Potocka wrote: 'With the finest and most regular features imaginable she combined a most shapely figure, admired (alas!) too often.'

Pauline loved fornication and luxury. She owned 600 dresses, priceless jewels, and travelled in a carriage drawn by six horses. In a time when most French women did not bathe frequently, Pauline made a fetish of cleanliness because her body was constantly exposed. She bathed every morning in a bath filled with 20 litres of milk mixed with hot water. After disrobing, she got her young black servant, Paul, to carry her to the bath. When onlookers were scandalized, Pauline said, 'But why not? A Negro is not a man. Or are you shocked because he is unmarried?' To remedy this, she married Paul off to one of her white kitchen maids – and he continued to carry her to the bath. To immortalize her perfect body, Pauline commissioned Antonio Canova, the Italian sculptor, whose previous subjects included Pope Clement XIV and Napoleon, to sculpt her in marble as a nude Venus. Afterwards, when someone asked how she could pose naked, she answered, 'It was not cold. There was a fire in the studio.' When Napoleon fell, Pauline was the only one of his siblings to join him in exile – for four months – on the isle of Elba.

At 15, she fell in love with 40-year-old Louis Fréron, an intelligent but unscrupulous political adventurer who was called the 'king of the dandies'. Napoleon had ambivalent feelings about the match, but their mother, Letizia, was certain Fréron was wrong for her daughter and he was sent away. Fréron removed, Pauline began to flirt with most of Napoleon's general staff. Napoleon therefore sought a husband for Pauline. He found an army comrade, Victor Leclerc – blond, clean-cut, serious and the son of a wealthy miller. Napoleon handed him Pauline *and* a promotion to brigadier general. Pauline and Leclerc were married in June 1797. While she had no great passion for Leclerc, he satisfied her in bed and that was enough. The next year, when she was 17, Pauline bore her husband a son, whom Napoleon named Dermide. In 1801, when the rich French colony of Saint Domingue – now Haiti – in the Caribbean was threatened by the Spanish, the English, and soon by the independence-minded Toussaint L'Ouverture, Napoleon sent Leclerc at the head of 25,000 troops to restore order. Pauline was forced to accompany her husband. Just as she was beginning to enjoy the social amenities of Haiti, her husband died from yellow fever in 1802.

Back in Paris, Pauline's mourning was short-lived. But then Napoleon found her a second husband, 28-year-old Prince Camillo Borghese, an attractive, dark-haired, empty-headed elegant Italian who owned one of the world's biggest diamond collections and countless properties including the art-laden Villa Borghese in Rome. Pauline was not very interested in Borghese, but she liked the wealth and the title he brought. From the wedding night on, their sexual union was a disaster. What ruined their coupling for Pauline, as one biographer put it, was that Prince

Borghese 'somewhat disappointingly had a very small penis. Pauline, whose nymphomania was periodic but intense, scorned all but very large ones.' Disgusted, Pauline wrote an uncle, 'I'd far rather have remained Leclerc's widow with an income of only 20,000 francs than be married to a eunuch.'

After that, she separated herself from Prince Borghese and went on a hunt for men of the proper proportions. By 1806, she had found what she wanted in Paris. A tall, muscular, society painter, Louis Philippe Auguste de Forbin was 30 and mightily endowed. Pauline made him her royal chamberlain and copulated with him endlessly. This excessive fornicating began to affect Pauline's health and, at the urging of her doctors and mother, Forbin left to enlist in the French army. Long after, he became director of the Louvre. Despite her physical exhaustion, Pauline's sexual activity rarely abated in the next fifteen years. In Nice, she took up with a mild-mannered young musician, Félix Blangini. She hired him to 'conduct her orchestra'; they enjoyed many duets in her bed. In 1810, she tried out an aide to Napoleon's chief of staff, a sensual lady's man of 25. Her affair with Colonel Armand Jules de Canouville was passionate and wild, and to nip any potential scandal Napoleon had the colonel transferred to Danzig. In 1812, he was killed near Moscow, a locket containing a miniature of Pauline pressed against his chest. For days, Pauline sobbed with grief. Finally, she distracted herself with other affairs, including a loveless one with the celebrated actor François Talma. After Waterloo, and St Helena, she had a brief reconciliation with Prince Borghese, and in the Villa Borghese, mirror in hand, she died of cancer at 44. Her last wish was that her coffin should not stand open at her funeral, but that the Canova nude be brought out of storage to represent her.

Pauline Bonaparte's case was an unusual one – that of a woman suffering from excessive sexual intercourse. The problem first appeared during her mating with Forbin. In contrast to Prince Borghese's 'very small penis', Forbin possessed a huge organ of copulation. This organ was so often inside Pauline that she suffered acute vaginal distress. Her unhealthy state, said one biographer, 'was based on nothing but undue friction, mostly brought on by M. de Forbin, who was endowed with a usable gigantism and very hard to get rid of'. When Pauline's vaginal distress worsened, her doctor called in France's leading gynaecologist, Dr Jean-Noël Hallé, to have a look at her. Hallé did so twice and then wrote the following memorandum to Pauline's physician: 'Her general appearance indicates ... exhaustion. The womb was still sensitive, but somewhat less so; and the ligaments still exhibited signs of the painful inflammation for which we prescribed baths last Thursday. The present condition of the uterus is caused by a constant and habitual excitation of that organ; if this does not cease, an exceedingly dangerous situation may result. That is the source of her trouble, and I hinted at its causes when speaking to the Princess last Thursday. I blamed the internal douches, and spoke in a general way of possible causes of an irritation of the womb.... The douche and its tube cannot always be held responsible. One is bound to assume a continuous cause for such exhaustion in the case of a young and beautiful woman living apart from her husband. If there is anyone who shares the fault for these indulgences, this person would not accuse himself. We would be blamed for seeing nothing and permitting everything. I've no wish to pass for a fool nor be accused of base and stupid complacency. But quite apart from that, there is the necessity of saving this unfortunate young woman....'

The doctors acted. Forbin was sent away. And Pauline rested – but not for long. Soon the inflammation reappeared, as it would continue to do for the rest of her life.

I.W. (Lists 22, 45)

♣ Rosa Bonheur
16 March 1822 to 25 May 1899

By the late 1840s, Rosa Bonheur had established a brilliant reputation in France and abroad for her paintings of animals. Her work is appreciated for its detail, bold sense of movement and effective use of light. One of the most celebrated canvases she exhibited, *The Horse Fair*, acquired by Cornelius Vanderbilt, now hangs in the Metropolitan Museum of Art in New York. Probably the world's most famous woman animal painter, Rosa was also the first female artist to be given the cross of the French Legion of Honour. Her personal life – which included a fondness for pet lions, men's clothing, cigarette smoking, and a lifelong woman companion – made her notorious. Raised as a feminist by her father, Rosa cropped her hair and wore trousers and smocks, a uniform which she adopted for comfort and efficiency. These clothes also provided a disguise for going where women were not readily accepted – such as the slaughterhouses in which she researched animal anatomy.

Although Rosa enjoyed a close friendship with minor artist Paul Chardin, she did not develop any sexual relationships with men. When a friend teased her for socializing 'unchaperoned' with a group of men, she retorted, 'Oh, my dear sir, if you knew how little I care for your sex, you wouldn't get any ideas in your head. The fact is, in the way of males, I like only the bulls I paint.' Her passions were animals, painting and her companion of more than forty years, Nathalie Micas. The two women had met as teenagers, when Nathalie's parents brought her to the studio of Rosa's artist father for a sitting. The girls grew close in their twenties. After that, they rarely parted. Nathalie was an amateur veterinarian, who dressed gaudily and spoke pompously. But she did have an endearing sentimental nature. She also painted cats (rather badly), and Rosa lovingly touched up her canvases and encouraged her to continue painting.

Nathalie and her mother, who lived with the two women, freed Rosa from housework and business matters and kept others from interrupting her while she worked. As Princess Stirby, a friend of Rosa's, wrote, 'Rosa Bonheur could never have remained the celebrated artist she was without someone beside her. . . .' When Nathalie died in 1889, Rosa cried out, 'What will become of me?' She lost interest in art and wrote letters lamenting the loss of her 'friend'.

Rosa's loneliness was quelled a few years later, when the American painter Anna Klumpke came to paint her portrait. Rosa demanded that Anna stay on, forsake her own career, and write Rosa's biography. Anna agreed. Rosa died at 77 and was buried beside Nathalie Micas in a vault which eventually included Anna Klumpke.

A.W. and J.M. (List 13)

♣ Cesare Borgia
c.1476 to 12 March 1507

Borgia, the model for Machiavelli's *The Prince*, was intelligent, handsome, virile, athletic, at times charming, and utterly without scruple. The single good deed attributed to him was the founding of a hospital ward as a sort of retirement home for prostitutes too old or sick to work. Born probably in Rome of Spanish heritage, the son of Cardinal Rodrigo Borgia (later Pope Alexander VI) and

47

his mistress Vannozza dei Catanei, Cesare Borgia was legitimized by papal decree in 1480. When his father bribed his way into the papacy in 1492, Cesare's future was secure. The next year he was made a cardinal, but left the Church to enter into a politically profitable marriage. In 1499, he tried to win control of the Romagna, while his father still held the Vatican and the Church purse strings. Opponents, like his brother-in-law, the Duke of Bisceglie, he murdered. Cesare seemed on the verge of consolidating all of the Romagna when his father died suddenly in 1502. Seriously ill himself, Cesare was unable to cope with the sudden turn of events and failed to block the election of Pope Julius II, an old foe of the Borgias. Arrested, Cesare escaped from custody twice and ultimately sought refuge with another brother-in-law, the King of Navarre. In 1507, Cesare rode into an ambush near Viana and was run through with lances twenty-five times. Stripped of its armour, his bloody body was found naked except for a stone carefully placed atop the genitals by one of the attackers.

For Cesare Borgia, women were exclusively sex objects. There is no record of his ever having truly loved a woman, despite many affairs. His sexual behaviour was scandalous even for Renaissance Italy. Rumours persisted of an incestuous relationship with his sister Lucrezia. On 30 October 1501, he threw a party where – while he, his sister, the pontiff and others looked on – fifty naked courtesans slithered across a lamplit floor gathering strewn nuts. Prizes were awarded to men able to fornicate most often with the prostitutes that evening. In another event, four stallions were turned loose on two mares as Cesare, Lucrezia and the pope merrily watched the horses scramble and fight for mounting rights.

In 1496, while still a cardinal, Cesare began an affair with Sancia, sensuous 22-year-old bride of his brother Jofre, then about 15. Soon after, Cesare decided that, to further his interests and to perpetuate the House of Borgia, he must resign as cardinal and marry. He announced his intention in August 1498, having decided to take as wife Carlotta of Aragon, daughter of King Frederick of Naples. To this end his father secured the help of King Louis XII of France, who promised to encourage Carlotta to accept Cesare's proposal in exchange for a papal annulment of his own marriage so that he could wed Anne of Brittany. With all arrangements made, Cesare set out for France to claim his bride. But Carlotta refused to marry him. Her father was privately against the match and, besides, she was in love with a Breton nobleman. So, King Louis offered as substitute Charlotte d'Albret, the beautiful daughter of the Duke of Guyenne, then aged 17. Cesare accepted. The marriage took place on 12 May 1499. The couple consummated the union with a vengeance – twice that afternoon and six more times in the evening. But the wedding night was not all bliss for Cesare, thanks to a practical joker who substituted laxatives for some other pills Cesare had requested from the apothecary. According to Charlotte's attendants, who monitored events that night from the keyhole, Cesare spent nearly as much time on the toilet as he did with the bride. The couple remained together just four months before Borgia left for battle in Italy. They never saw each other again. Nor did Borgia see the daughter Charlotte bore him several months later. Named Luisa, she was his only legitimate offspring. Upon hearing of her husband's death, Charlotte – then 25 – went into mourning and continued to dress in black until her own death seven years later.

Predictably, Borgia cheated on his wife. In 1500, he captured the Romagnan stronghold of Forli and, with it, Caterina Sforza, 37, dubbed the 'virago' for her bravery in battle, unremitting defence of her lands and people, and fearless defiance of her captors. She had even tried to murder the pope long-distance by sending him surrender papers carefully contaminated with plague germs. Borgia raped her, and further humiliated the defeated Caterina by publicly telling his officers that she had defended her fortress better than her virtue. The same year as he captured Sforza, Borgia also took up with a beautiful, rich courtesan from Florence named Fiametta de' Michelis. Far from being an uneducated whore, she spoke Latin fluently, played the lyre, sang, and quoted Greek poetry. She died in 1512.

Of all his affairs, none generated so much controversy as that with Dorotea Malatesta Caracciolo, wife of a Venetian army officer. In 1501, Borgia apparently had her kidnapped while she was en route to her husband. The subsequent criticism against the Borgias prompted Cesare to deny any knowledge of the kidnapping and to shift the blame on to one of his own officers. For two years Dorotea remained incommunicado, subject to the sexual whims of Cesare Borgia. She was later transferred to a convent, from which she was released in 1504, free to join her husband at last.

From Cesare's many extramarital affairs just two children, both born at the dawn of the sixteenth century, are known by name: a son called Gerolamo, who married the daughter of the Lord of Capri in 1537 and who reportedly inherited the ruthless character of his father; and a daughter christened Camilla Lucrezia, who, ironically, became a nun in 1516 and led a saintly life until her death in 1573. Their mother or mothers are unknown.

Syphilis, first contracted in 1497, left Cesare with periodic groin pains and facial blotches, which he often hid behind a mask.

W.A.D. (Lists 18, 23, 32)

♣ James Boswell
29 October 1740 to 19 May 1795

The discovery of Boswell's papers in the 1920s made him the 'best self-documented man in all history'. His mother was a Calvinist, his father a stern Whig. He grew up in Scotland on the family estate, abnormally afraid of sin and hellfire. Throughout his life, he suffered from episodic depression. At 16, he was laid low by a 'terrible Hypochondria' and became a Methodist vegetarian, which, like a later fling with Catholicism, did not last. After he graduated from the University of Edinburgh at 18, his father insisted he study law; Boswell capitulated, and began his practice in Edinburgh in 1766. Meanwhile, he pursued a literary career and spent as much time in London as he could. In London, in 1763, he met Dr Johnson – then 53 while Boswell was only 22 – in the back room of a bookshop.

Boswell hunted throughout Europe for a dowried wife, recording the yearly income of various women in his journal along with their other attributes. But, in 1769, he married his penniless first cousin, Margaret Montgomerie; he suddenly realized he loved her while he was on his way to court an Irish heiress. Margaret was a buxom, witty, patient woman with beautiful eyes. Her life with Boswell was stormy. Grand gestures, hedged with prudence, were typical of him, and he would promise 'from henceforth I shall be a perfect man; at least I hope so'. In 1789, his wife died of tuberculosis, leaving him to raise five children who adored him in spite of his failings. His last decade was spent in public disgrace and private remorse because of his dissolute life.

The story of Boswell's sex life is littered with innumerable whores, several mistresses, countless partners in casual sex, and many rich ladies unsuccessfully pursued with marriage in mind. Even in the context of his time, he was a male chauvinist, with a

50

great need for women, yet he considered the opposite sex inferior. The urge to copulate came over him strongly in times of heightened emotion: in church he laid 'plans for having a woman' while having 'the most sincere feelings of religion'; after seeing a notice of his mother's death in a newspaper, he assuaged his shock in a Paris brothel. He was likely to hunt for prostitutes after drinking, and often had more than one in a night. One evening, he got drunk toasting a woman he was courting, then spent the rest of the night with a 'whore worthy of Boswell if Boswell must have a whore'. His treatment of whores was often abominable. When a prostitute in a park complained loudly that the sixpence he had offered her was not enough for her services, Boswell told the crowd that had gathered that he was an officer on half-pay and could afford no more. He then forced himself on her and 'abused her in blackguard style' – his euphemism for rape. Intercourse was best for him when hurried, while standing up, and in public places – in parks and dark spots, and once on a bridge accompanied by the sound of the water gurgling below. Though often filled with remorse, he also bragged of dipping 'my machine into the Canal' and performing 'most manfully'. He claimed that 'licentious love' made him 'humane, polite, generous' (generous, that is, with compliments – but not financial rewards – to prostitutes who performed well). After his marriage, he was faithful to Margaret for nearly three years, but she was often 'averse to hymeneal rites', so he told her he 'must have a concubine', and she agreed. He called his practice of having many woman 'Asiatic multiplicity', and kept it up until the end of his life.

In his pubescent years, his partners were trees, which he assaulted by masturbating against their trunks, something he thought of as a 'small sin'. But, by 13, he so feared the 'larger sin' of fornication that he briefly considered self-castration. He put that thought behind him when he discovered that women were attracted to him. Though short and somewhat fleshy, he was handsome, with black hair and eyes, and a lively expression. It was a prostitute, Sally Forrester, who introduced him to the 'melting and transporting rites of love'. She was only one in a long line of whores, many of whom infected and reinfected him with gonorrhoea from the age of 19 onwards. His short-term affairs included those with the high-born, like Girolama Piccolomini, whom he met in Siena in 1765. Though she was infatuated with him, he courted another while pursuing her – he would send a valet out with a letter for Girolama in one pocket and a letter for his second *signorina* in another. Even though their affair didn't last long, she wrote to him after he returned to England. The women with whom he had affairs included: a pregnant soldier's wife who came to his rooms in Berlin selling chocolate (with her it was 'in a minute – over'); Annie Cunninghame, his wife's orphaned, teenaged niece from whom he 'snatched a little romping pleasure'; Thérèse Le Vasseur, Jean Jacques Rousseau's mistress, as he was escorting her to meet Rousseau in England; and Peggy Doig, a servant girl, who bore him a son who died in infancy.

In 1762, he planned on a 'winter's safe copulation' with Mrs Anne Lewis, his first 'real' mistress. They consummated their love at the Black Lion Inn, where he performed with vigour – five climaxes in one night – at a total cost, he boasted, of only 18s. for bed and food. It was no bargain, as he discovered six days later. 'Too, too plain was Signor Gonorrhoea.' In a fury, he wrote to her demanding repayment of a small loan, and the affair was over. His affair with a Mrs Dodds, a lady 'admirably formed for amorous dalliance' who was 'quite a rompish girl', though 'ill-bred', lasted longer. She had a daughter by him who died in infancy.

The upshot of his relationships was not *always* seduction. Off and on, for six years, he pursued Zélide (Isabella van Tuyll), a Dutch aristocrat and writer. 'She is much my superior. One does not like that.' She refused his conditional marriage proposals – he demanded the right to approve whatever she wrote. They insulted each other with exquisite hostility – he suggested she turn to embroidery rather than speculate about metaphysics; she called him 'a fatuous fool' with 'the arrogant rigidity of an old Cato'. Rigidity was something Boswell seldom worried about, but it was with Margaret, his 'valuable spouse', that he suffered at least one bout of impotence. He recorded only five such incidents in his entire diary. Margaret hated these logs in which he chronicled his sexual escapades using a Greek-letter code which, unfortunately for her, she could decipher.

In *Boswell's Clap and Other Essays*, using Boswell's detailed journals, Dr William B. Ober has compiled a comprehensive medical chart of Boswell's nineteen bouts of urethritis due to gonorrhoea, from his first infection at 19 to his last at 50. Though Boswell often used 'armour' (condoms made of dried animal intestines), his sexual drives were such that he constantly took chances. By the time he was 22, when he suffered his third infection, he recognized the symptoms and described them as 'an unaccountable alarm of unexpected evil; a little heat in the members of my body sacred to Cupid, very like a symptom of that distemper with which Venus, when cross, takes it into her head to plague her votaries'. He also suffered from prostatitis, epididymitis and crab lice. And he suffered through the treatments as well – irrigation of the urinary tract with medicines, bloodletting, cauterization of the sores: there was even a medicine called Kennedy's Lisbon Diet Drink (a concoction of sarsaparilla, sassafras, licorice and guaiac wood). Boswell died at 54 from complications arising from his gonorrhoea.

A.E. (Lists 7, 8, 11, 18, 20, 21, 22, 31, 40, 43)

♣ Clara Bow
6 August 1905 to 27 September 1965

Clara Bow personified the Roaring Twenties on film, with forty-eight films to her credit by the age of 25. In 1927, she was receiving 40,000 fan letters a week. Clara's was the classic Hollywood story – from obscurity at 19 to reigning sex goddess of her time, collecting the obligatory emotional scars along the way. Father Robert was often either unemployed or footloose; Mother Sarah was bitter. She would stick Clara in the closet of their Brooklyn tenement while prostituting herself for food and rent money. Once, when she learned that Clara and her father were submitting a picture of Clara for a magazine beauty contest, she crept into Clara's bedroom with a knife, vowing that her daughter wouldn't live to be one of those whores strutting in front of cameras for the pleasure of men. Luckily Clara escaped into the bathroom that night, and subsequently won the contest and an entrée into Hollywood which eventually led to her signing with Paramount. She became one of the studio's biggest stars, earning $7,500 a week. And, thanks to the insomnia which resulted from her mother's late-night threat on her life, she was able to assume a life-style that reinforced her screen image. She used to speed up and down Sunset Boulevard in an open convertible accompanied by a couple of chows to match her hennaed hair. She would run up incredible gambling bills in Las Vegas, and she was scandalous in her personal affairs. In 1931, those affairs ruined her, when she sued Daisy DeVoe, her private secretary, for embezzling $16,000. During the trial, the judge would not permit Daisy to discuss Clara Bow's sexual escapades – so Daisy sold her exposé to Bernard MacFadden's New York *Evening Graphic* (incidentally,

53

the authors of this book scoured the USA for a copy of the exposé issue, but no copy was available anywhere). Daisy was found guilty and sent to jail for a year, but word got out about Clara's private life and damaged her career.

In her heyday, Clara reputedly made love to Gilbert Roland, Victor Fleming, Gary Cooper, John Gilbert, Eddie Cantor, Bela Lugosi and the entire USC football team. She met Roland, Paramount's Latin lover, during the filming of *The Plastic Age*. He was the first man she ever cared about, she said, but this wasn't enough for the temperamental Roland, who went into fits of jealousy at Clara's continued interest in other men. When he proposed marriage as remedy for his insecurity, she dismissed the proposal, saying that no man would ever own her. Thus she set the pattern for most of her relationships with men. She would love them, but never enough to satisfy their egos. Director Victor Fleming was twenty years older than Clara and had vast experience with women, but neither fact helped him cope with her, especially when he learned that, after they finished having sex together, she would head off for a session with another, usually younger, man. Most notable amongst these was Gary Cooper, who had a bit part in *It* and was dubbed the 'It Boy' for his involvement with Clara, the quintessential 'It Girl'. In later years, Coop tried to dismiss the relationship as publicity, but Clara told delicious stories of his bathing her and her dogs in the morning and making love to her all night with the sexual equipment of a horse. And, speaking of horses, there was the Thundering Herd, the University of Southern California's football team, whom Clara entertained on a regular basis at her Beverly Hills home. Those with a vested interest in the Trojan sports programme have always maintained that the post-game get-togethers at Clara's place were nothing more than good clean fun, but neighbours and 'friends' told tales of nude football games on the front lawn and all-night orgies. The legend grew that Clara introduced the team concept to lovemaking by taking on more than a single player at a time. Whatever the truth of the stories, a sign was eventually posted in the Trojan locker room making Clara Bow off limits.

Clara took a brief fancy to Robert Savage, a millionaire's son who played football for Yale. Unlike most of Clara's other lovers, who merely went off and brooded when they found out that they weren't number one, Savage tried to kill himself by slashing his wrists and letting the blood flow on to an autographed picture of Clara. Clara exclaimed, 'Jesus Christ, he's got to be kidding. Men don't slash their wrists, they use a gun!'

Broadway showman Harry Richman did not become a Hollywood immortal like some of Clara's other lovers, although he tried – by flaunting their relationship. He boasted that she was the only woman who could ever keep up with him sexually. She gave him a ring worth $2000. He gave her a child (which she aborted), put detectives on her tail when he was out of town, and even followed her himself to see where she went after their nights together. Needless to say, they did not live happily ever after.

She might happily have married William Earl Pearson, a Texas doctor who performed an emergency appendectomy on her during the filming of *Dangerous Curves*. She loved him enough to try monogamy for a while, presenting him with a $4000 watch, but, when he returned to his wife in Texas, Clara was left with nothing but an alienation-of-affections suit that was filed against her and later settled out of court.

There had been actors, athletes, stuntmen, airmen and guys off the street, but finally there was Rex Bell, a cowboy actor and staunch Republican who twice became lieutenant governor of Nevada during the 1950s. Clara married Bell in 1931 and he saw her through the Daisy DeVoe trial, a failed comeback in the early 1930s and a series of emotional breakdowns. Because of her instability, she lived apart from Bell and their two sons, seeking help in various sanatoriums. In 1961, the 59-year-old Bell died of a heart attack. Clara succumbed to death four years later while watching television with a nurse/companion in her Los Angeles home.

D.R. (Lists 11, 17, 22, 24, 42)

♣ Johannes Brahms
7 May 1833 to 3 April 1897

Raised in the poverty-stricken, red-light district of Hamburg, Brahms's early environment affected his personality and love life. At an early age, he played the piano in taverns in order to earn money, and most of his audiences consisted of prostitutes and their clients. His mother, a plain, lame woman, was seventeen years older than his father, a timid orchestral musician; she lavished her affections on her young son. Maintaining an unnaturally strong attachment to her until her death in 1865, Brahms cried out over her grave, 'I no longer have a mother!

I must marry!' This was not to be. An infinitely kind man who secretly supported struggling musicians when able, Brahms was also temperamental and singularly lacking in tact and social graces. Although he enjoyed bawdy nights of beer drinking and folk songs, his music tended to reflect his darker side. While serving as a conductor in Vienna, his programme was invariably so serious that people joked, 'When Brahms is really in high spirits, he gets them to sing "The Grave is My Joy".' His first few recitals brought him little public attention. But, after his initial concert tour, aged 20, he met composer Robert Schumann in Düsseldorf. Schumann was so impressed by Brahms's compositions that he recommended publication. Schumann also wrote about Brahms for a music magazine. His article created a sensation; the young composer's fame and reputation began to spread throughout Europe. Eventually, Brahms adopted Vienna as his home, producing four symphonies and the famous *German Requiem*.

As a lover, Brahms led a double life – he fell in love with numerous respectable women (always singers or musicians), but slept only with prostitutes. One possible exception was Clara Schumann, the charming and beautiful wife of Robert Schumann. When Schumann suffered a nervous breakdown and was confined to a mental institution, Brahms stayed at Clara's side. Her appeal as a mother figure (she had seven children) was combined with that of friend and musical adviser (she was an accomplished pianist). His feelings for her quickly grew, as their correspondence shows. During Schumann's confinement, the conflict Brahms felt between his friendship for Schumann and his passion for Clara made him so miserable that he gave only occasional concerts. When Schumann died after two years in the mental institution, however, the couple shied away from further romantic involvement. They remained close friends for the rest of their lives, and Brahms rarely published any music without Clara's approval.

Brahms's other affairs went much the same way. Unable to resist a comely figure or a beautiful voice, he had at least seven major, unconsummated, relationships, but always bolted before exchanging marriage vows, and he remained single. A fellow bachelor once remarked, 'Brahms would not have confided to his best friend the real reason why he never married.' His early exposure to the 'singing girls' of Hamburg had certainly left its mark. He occasionally burst into tirades against women and, in an attempt to explain his behaviour to a friend, spoke of his early encounters with tavern prostitutes: 'These half-clad girls, to make the men still wilder, used to take me on their laps between dances, and kiss and caress and excite me. This was my first impression of the love of women. And you expect *me* to honour them as you do!' Always courteous to prostitutes, who found him an eager, if awkward, lover, his caustic side was more likely to surface with society women. In his relationships with women, Brahms liked to do the wooing and was deterred if the object of his affection displayed any initiative.

While he longed for domestic happiness and often complained of having missed the best part of life, Brahms continued to fall in love well into his fifties, only to end the affairs before they threatened his bachelorhood.

J.H. (Lists 15, 20)

♣ Rupert Brooke
3 August 1887 to 23 April 1915

The son of a Rugby housemaster, Brooke grew up in a very proper British atmosphere and was educated accordingly. However, like so many others of his generation, he began questioning the legacy of the Victorians while a student at King's College, Cambridge. He developed an antipathy towards organized religion and was attracted to socialism, becoming president of the Fabian Society. No matter where he was, Brooke's charisma gained him friends – both male and female. He was considered more stunning in appearance than actually handsome, with thick, auburn-red hair, a golden gleam to his skin, expressive lips and piercing eyes. Brooke suffered from delicate mental health – he had a major breakdown a year after the death of his father in 1910 – yet he joined the Royal Navy at the outbreak of the First World War. He died of septicemia at Skiros, Greece, in April 1915, and was buried there.

Rupert Brooke was a prolific letter writer, so we are privy to his loves, feelings, attitudes and activities during his short life. He enjoyed a sensuous, free life-style, although sometimes the conventional Englishman re-emerged from behind the anti-establishment façade. For the most part, the attractive, open Brooke found love and sex where and when he needed it, and raised eyebrows by reporting on his findings. Writing to friends about a Bacchus-Fest in Germany in 1910, he said, 'I took off my clothes and went . . . the young lay round in couples, huggin' and kissin'. I roamed round, wondering if I couldn't, once, be even as they, as the animals. I found a round damp young sculptress. . . . We curled passionate limbs round each other in a perfunctory manner and lay in a corner, sipping each other and beer in polite alternation.' The women he preferred were usually young and artistic or slightly older than he and worldly.

When he was 19, Brooke was invited to a party for the Fabian politician Sydney Olivier, and promptly fell in love with Olivier's 15-year-old daughter Noël. Four years later, he declared he would marry her, but Noël went to medical school, Brooke travelled to Germany, and the union never took place. They corresponded for the rest of Brooke's life, but were never lovers.

Katharine Cox – the darling of the avant-garde painters of London, even though she was neither beautiful nor witty – is probably the person with whom Brooke had his most torrid love affair. 'Ka', as she was called, was one of his closest friends for many years, and went to Germany to live with Brooke after his breakdown. Brooke used to write about her 'passionate lips', but he knew that she was really in love with painter Henry Lamb. Ka, for her part, was willing to sacrifice her own happiness because she thought Brooke needed her more than Lamb did. Brooke was irritated that Ka would give herself to him without a full, romantic love and their affair ended, but he respected her and left his manuscripts to her when he died.

Other liaisons in his active life included a literary relationship with Virginia Stephen (later Woolf), with whom he used to swim 'quite naked' at Grantchester; a secretive encounter with the Marchesa Capponi, a mysterious international society woman cryptically referred to in Brooke's letters as the 'Lady of the Chateau'; and a highly amorous period with Taatamata, reportedly the daughter of a village chief on Tahiti. Brooke wrote one of his best poems, 'Tiare Tahiti', for her, yet the only memento that he kept of this period in his life was a crumpled photograph of the bare-breasted Taatamata.

Of all his women, his favourite was seemingly the young actress Cathleen Nesbitt, to whom he wrote volumes of letters. 'If you don't know that you're the most beautiful thing in the world,' Brooke wrote, 'either you're imbecile, or else, something's wrong with your mirror.' No one can say whether Brooke would have married Nesbitt had he lived. Her beauty and goodness perhaps were compromised in his eyes by her stage career; he resented it, and had pointedly written, 'I loathe women acting in public.'

Brooke's letters speak earnestly of a desire to marry, but he never did. His romantic view of sex gave women freedom to be passionate, as he believed was their nature. But he also felt that independence was not natural; it did nothing to enhance a woman's charms. Although his quest was fired by lust and longing, he never found his ideal woman.

A.L.G. (List 39)

✤ Robert Burns
25 January 1759 to 21 July 1796

Scotland's national poet earned his greatest acclaim for his first published volume, *Poems, Chiefly in the Scottish Dialect*, but one of his collections of songs, *The Merry Muses of Caledonia*, which contains his bawdiest lyrics, was not published for the general public in uncensored form until 1965.

Robert Burns was the oldest of seven children born to William and Agnes Burns, who leased a small farm in Ayrshire. Robert received most of his formal education from John Murdoch, a tutor hired by the local farmers, who encouraged him to study literature. At 22, Robert left home for Irvine to study to be a flax-dresser, but was forced to return after his patron's shop burned down. His father died two years later, and Robert and his brother Gilbert moved to a new farm at Mossgiel. He earned a local reputation for his poetry and, in 1786, arranged for *Poems* to be printed in Kilmarnock. Near the end of the year, the young poet set out for Edinburgh, where he received honour, praise and 100 guineas for the copyright to his popular book. He made several tours of the Scottish countryside, working on the two collections of traditional songs, without pay, considering it a duty to his country. By then he had a wife and several children (legitimate and illegitimate) to support, and the family farm was close to failure. So, in September 1789, he accepted a position with the excise service as a tax inspector. He did well at this job, but these years were marred by rumours of his drinking and controversies over his support of the French Revolution. He continued to write poetry until he died of rheumatic fever in 1796.

Robert Burns was 5 feet 10 inches tall and well built. His most striking feature was his wide, deep-set eyes, which gave a look of innocence to the 'peasant poet'. Burns's legendary drinking habits have been refuted by most biographers, but his sexual reputation is well substantiated by personal letters, legal records of paternity suits, and his poems. To Burns, love and poetry were inseparable. Consequently, many poems chronicled his experiences, relationships and rejections. At 15, his first love, by his own account, was Nelly Kirkpatrick, his partner in the traditional harvest festivities, and the subject of the first poem he ever wrote, 'Handsome Nell'. Their relationship was innocent, and his affection mostly unrequited, as with his later courtship of Alison Begbie. He wrote Alison a series of romantic, but very proper, love letters, leading to a proposal of marriage, followed by a polite acknowledgement of her rejection. But, during a brief stay in Irvine, he became friends with a sailor, Richard Brown, who encouraged him towards looser ways and, in Burns's words, 'did me mischief'.

Rural society in Scotland was sexually quite open, and marriage usually occurred after the woman became pregnant. Both common-law and trial marriages were frequent. And even the Church would forgive fornication for a small fine and the acceptance of a rebuke before the congregation. However, it was not until after his father's death that Robert dared to make love to Elizabeth Paton, a servant girl working for his mother. Their relationship was short, passionate and fruitful – a daughter was born in May 1785. He wrote a poem to mark the occasion, 'Welcome to a Bastart Wean'. The child was named Elizabeth. (In his lifetime, Burns had three daughters out of wedlock, each by a different woman, and all were called Elizabeth.) Miss Paton did not demand marriage but, after *Poems* was published, she sought and won 'a certain sum', then disappeared from Burns's life, leaving behind their little girl. Another of his poems, 'The Fornicator', chronicled the whole affair, including the rebuke he received in church:

> *Before the Congregation wide,*
> *I passed the muster fairly,*
> *My handsome Betsy by my side,*
> *We gat our ditty rarely;*
> *But my downcast eye by chance did spy*
> *What made my lips to water,*
> *Those limbs so clean where I, between,*
> *Commenc'd a Fornicator. . . .*

The poet blithely went on to his next affair. Jean Armour, six
years younger than Burns – and probably one of the most beautiful women in his life – was well aware of the reputation he had
already earned. In February 1786, she informed him that she was
pregnant, and they signed a document recognizing each other as
man and wife. But Jean's father, a master mason, preferred an
illegitimate grandchild to an impoverished son-in-law. He got a
lawyer to destroy the signed document and sent Jean to live with
relatives. Feeling quite betrayed, Burns made plans to leave
Scotland for Jamaica with another woman, Mary Campbell. Little
is known about 'Highland Mary', except that Burns considered
her the personification of innocence and purity. That may have
been a poor judgement, since there is evidence that she was the
same Mary Campbell who had been mistress to several notable
Scotsmen of the time. She was pregnant by Burns, but died
suddenly, possibly in childbirth, and Burns turned his attention
to his poems which had just been published.

During the months spent in Edinburgh and in touring the
Scottish countryside, Robert Burns had a wide assortment of
relationships with women whose social statuses varied sharply.
He had a long and loving correspondence with Mrs Frances
Dunlop, a widow with thirteen children, to whom he confided his
other affairs. He proposed marriage to Margaret Chalmers
(daughter of a gentleman farmer), who turned him down in
favour of a banker. A brief encounter in Edinburgh with May
Cameron, a servant girl, resulted in another paternity claim, and
his second daughter Elizabeth. However, his most unusual relationship was that with Agnes Maclehose, of Edinburgh, whose
husband lived in Jamaica. He wrenched his knee before he was to
meet Mrs Maclehose and their rendezvous had to be postponed.
Instead, she wrote to him, and their correspondence turned very
romantic. They even gave each other mythical names. He was
'Sylvander', she was 'Clarinda'. But, after Robert was back on his
feet, Clarinda would allow the relationship to go no further, so he
sought out a servant girl, Jenny Clow, who bore him a son. Jenny
later made a claim for support, contacting a surprised Robert
Burns through Mrs Maclehose.

Meanwhile, Burns was reunited with Jean Armour. He briefly
visited her home during his first tour, in June 1787, and found
that Mr Armour had changed his opinion of the newly successful
poet. In fact, he locked Robert and Jean in her bedroom that
night, to ensure 'a happy reunion'. When Burns returned again

the next spring, Jean was nine months pregnant and in a foul mood. He wrote to a friend that he cheered her up with vigorous lovemaking 'till she rejoiced with joy unspeakable and full of glory'. Then the author of the poem 'Nine Inch Will Please a Lady' commented, 'O, what a peacemaker is a guid weel-willy pintle! It is the mediator, the guarantee, the umpire, the bond of union, the solemn league and covenant ... the sword of mercy, the philosopher's stone, the horn of plenty, and the Tree of Life between Man and Woman. . . .' That same day, Jean gave birth to twins, both of whom died in infancy, but Robert and Jean married a month later. They had four more children. But neither married life nor his position with the excise service could fully control Burns's passions. In 1791, there was another paternity claim, from Anne Park, the barmaid at a local inn. Jean was totally understanding and ended up raising the child, the third Elizabeth. Burns was a frequent guest of the area's richer families, including the Riddells of Woodley Park. Mrs Maria Riddell was one of his most fervent admirers, and there were rumours that their relationship was extremely intimate. One evening near Christmas 1793, Burns attended a party at Woodley Park. Everyone was drinking heavily, and someone suggested that they amuse themselves with a mock 'Rape of the Sabine Women'. Burns went after Mrs Riddell with more enthusiasm and realism than the other guests could accept and, for the first time in his life, Robert Burns had compromised himself with a woman whose status was higher than his.

Toward marriage, he was totally practical and unsentimental. 'To have a woman to lye with when one pleases, without running any risk of the cursed expense of bastards. . . . These are solid views of matrimony.' In his short lifetime, Robert Burns successfully broke all of his own rules.

C.L.W. (Lists 7, 11, 14, 17, 21, 22, 35)

♣ Sir Richard Burton

19 March 1821 to 20 October 1890

Explorer, linguist and anthropologist, Sir Richard Burton had a thirst for adventure and a disregard for sexual convention, which made him one of the most controversial figures in Victorian England.

Burton was born in Devonshire, the son of an Irishman and an

English girl. The elder Burton's lack of success kept the family on the move throughout Richard's childhood. Growing up in France and Italy with a great deal of freedom, Richard and his brother Edward educated themselves on the streets, where Richard early showed both a great talent for languages – 'one of them pornography', it was later said – and a taste for seamy adventures. Sent to Oxford in 1840, he was expelled two years later, at which time he became an ensign in the Bombay Infantry. He was so fascinated by exotic India that he stayed there for eight years. He learned at least nine more languages, immersing himself in Muslim and Hindu culture, and living like a native. Recalled because his investigation of homosexual brothels resulted in an outcry, he proceeded to write four books on India while living in France with his mother and sister. In 1853, he travelled to the Middle East, disguising himself as a Muslim so he could secretly enter Mecca. From 1857 to 1859 he explored central Africa with John Speke, and the two men became the first Europeans to discover Lake Tanganyika. Burton then travelled across the USA by stagecoach to Salt Lake City, where he observed the Mormon colony with great interest. He married Isabel Arundell in 1861, and spent the next four years as consul on the West African island of Fernando Po. By 1865, he was off to Brazil, which he hated. He escaped Brazil when he was appointed consul in Damascus. As a result of his own political indiscretions and Isabel's misplaced missionary zeal, he was dismissed in 1871, and he left his beloved Middle East for Trieste. There he lived comfortably until his death, having gained financial success with his translation of *The Arabian Nights*. To the end of his life, Burton held that nothing could be called obscene because tastes and taboos differed throughout the world. Burton liked the story about a group of Englishmen who went to visit a Muslim sultan in the desert. As the Englishmen watched, the sultan's wife tumbled off her camel. In doing so, her dress slipped up and her private parts were revealed to all. 'Was the sultan embarrassed?' asked Burton. 'Oh, quite the opposite – he was pleased – because his wife had kept her face covered during her accident.'

Although Burton was a virtual encyclopedia of sexual knowledge, there is little evidence that he applied this expertise to his personal life. 'I'm no hot amorist,' he once admitted. Despite his posturing and satanic appearance, his life was full of overtones of homosexuality, impotence and castration complexes. As a young man, he seems to have enjoyed a riotous sex life – orgies with the prostitutes of Naples, a 'roistering and rackety life' among the women of Bombay – and he once attempted to kidnap and seduce a nun. (But, even with his Hindu *bubu* [mistress], who was skilled at prolonging the act of love, he complained she 'cannot be satisfied . . . with less than twenty minutes.') On the other hand, when Sir Charles Napier sent him to investigate a homosexual brothel in Karachi, Burton's report was so detailed and graphic as to smack of participation.

It was in his relationship with his wife that Burton's sexual vagueness was most apparent. It took five years of courtship – during which time Burton made protracted trips to observe sexual customs in East Africa and Utah – before the couple became engaged. Believing celibacy to be 'an unmitigated evil' and polygamy the 'instinctive law of nature', Burton admitted to a fascination with Brigham Young's Mormons which disturbed Isabel. None the less, she finally snared him, later saying, 'I wish I were a man: if I were I would be Richard Burton. But, as I am a woman, I would be Richard Burton's wife.' Although before her marriage Isabel had promised herself to 'keep up the honeymoon romance, whether at home or in the desert', the newlyweds' bliss was short-lived. Apparently sublimating his sexual drive in his constant quest for adventure, Burton never seems to have generated much passion for his wife. What little lust he felt after his marriage was shared not with Isabel but with cronies such as Monckton Milnes, an eccentric who had a world-famous library of the best collection of erotica in England. Always particularly intrigued by flagellation and sexual mutilation, Burton found ready material in Milnes's library. Regardless of her frustrations as his wife, Isabel admired Burton, participating vicariously in his adventures and in his fame. At the same time, it was important to her to tame the man who claimed to have committed 'every sin in the Decalogue'.

After his initiation at the hands of the prostitutes of Naples, Burton's first real affair was with the unnamed Hindu woman whom he kept as *bubu*. Soon afterwards, he met a beautiful Persian girl in a caravan near Karachi, and the memory of this girl remained with him for the rest of his life. After his return from India in 1849, he fell in love with his cousin Elizabeth Stisted, but her parents would not allow a marriage. At the time he met Isabel he was carrying on 'a very serious flirtation' with another cousin, Louisa. Although he was reticent about his involvements with native women, he did write that the Wagogo women of East

Africa were 'well-disposed towards strangers of fair complexion, apparently with the permission of their husbands'.

In his sixteen-volume translation of *The Arabian Nights*, he presented much of the vast amount of material he had collected over the years on such subjects as childbirth, circumcision, defloration, hermaphroditism, castration, birth control and aphrodisiacs (including recipes for hashish). Although some reviewers considered *The Arabian Nights* a marvel of psychological insight presented in an incomparable literary style, others called it 'garbage of the brothels'. Singled out for special indignation was the collection's 'Terminal Essay', in which Burton dealt with sex education for women and devoted over 18,000 words to a study of homosexuality. A 'household edition' of *The Arabian Nights* – throughout which Isabel had judiciously substituted 'assistant wife' for 'concubine' – sold dismally, but the unexpurgated work netted Burton 10,000 guineas – the first appreciable sum he had ever received for any of his writings. He reflected, 'Now that I know the tastes of England, we need never be without money.'

The 'tastes of England' were not Isabel's, and Burton's pornographic works were a constant source of anguish to her. After *The Arabian Nights*, he embarked upon yet another scandalous project, which he called 'the crown of my life': the translation of *The Perfumed Garden*, a sixteenth-century Arabian sex manual. Burton confided to a friend, 'It will be a marvellous repertory of Eastern wisdom; how Eunuchs are made, and are married; what they do in marriage; female circumcision, the Fellahs copulating with crocodiles, etc. . . .' It was nearing completion when he died.

As executor of his estate, Isabel was in an agony of indecision about *The Perfumed Garden*. Her inner turmoil was ended when Richard suddenly appeared to her in a vision and clearly instructed her to burn the book. Thus, although she had been offered 6000 guineas for it, she burned the manuscript page by page, saying that to have accepted the offer would have been equivalent to selling her soul for thirty pieces of silver. More important than the destruction of *The Perfumed Garden* was the tossing into the fire of Burton's diaries, which spanned forty years. Posterity will not forgive her.

When Burton was living in India, he once set up house for some forty monkeys in order to study their 'language'. The 'prettiest' of the apes Burton called his 'wife', adorning her with pearls and seating her by his side at the table.

Dr F. Grenfell Baker, Burton's private physician, reported that Burton told him that his testicles had been severely damaged in an unspecified 'accident' in East Africa, and that he had been sterile thereafter.

W.L. (Lists 8, 11, 14, 20, 35, 36, 39, 51)

♣ Lord Byron
22 January 1788 to 19 April 1824

Young Byron – a lord by the age of 10 – was influenced adversely by an unstable mother and a foot so crippled that he once begged a doctor to amputate it. Nevertheless, he became an excellent long-distance swimmer, easily lasting for five miles or more. This exercise did not end his constant battle against obesity, and at 17 he entered Cambridge University weighing almost 16 stone, although he was only 5 feet 8 inches tall. To maintain his weight at a reasonable level in adult life, Byron fasted frequently, took drugs and kept to a fairly steady diet of hard biscuits plus a little rice, washed down by soda water or diluted wine. Occasionally gorging on meat and potatoes when he could no longer resist the temptation prompted an immediate digestive upset and added rolls of fat to his middle. Byron hoped that his lifelong Spartan regime would also '. . . cool his passions' but it didn't. In 1809, he sailed with John Cam Hobhouse for a two-year 'grand tour' of Europe. Upon his return, Byron published *Childe Harold's Pilgrimage*, a fictionalized narrative of the trip in Spenserian stanzas, and the poem brought instant fame. He followed the success quickly with a series of Graeco-Turkish tales (*The Bride of Abydos*, *The Corsair*, *The Siege of Corinth*, and others) that enhanced his reputation further. Driven from England by public reaction to his sex life, Byron made his way to Italy. He continued to write brilliantly, producing *Manfred* (1817) and *Beppo* (1818) along with *Don Juan* (1818–24). Intrigued by Balkan politics, Byron slipped into Greece to fight against its Turkish masters but died of malaria at Missolonghi. His death fulfilled a fortune teller's prophecy, made to his mother in 1801, that he would die in his thirty-seventh year.

Byron was sexually initiated at the age of 9 by the family nurse, May Gray. For three years, the devout, bible-quoting Scottish girl seized every chance to creep into the child's bed and 'play tricks with his person'. Arousing the boy physically by every

66

variation she could think of, May also allowed him to watch while she made love with her uninhibited lovers. Thus primed, Byron – eager for continued stimulation – moved with ease into sexual activities during his four years at Harrow.

There he preferred the company of young boys: the Earl of Clare, the Duke of Dorset, among many others. Although he may have been bisexual, the thought of having sex with adult males repelled him. One such proposition from 23-year-old Lord Grey de Ruthyn, tendered while Byron was visiting on holiday from Harrow, sent the future poet fleeing in terror. In 1805, at Cambridge, Byron fell in love with choirboy John Edleston, who gave him a heart-shaped cornelian to seal their friendship. Byron combined three years of intermittent studies with an orgiastic existence in London, staging bacchanalian revelries that nearly killed him. Living on laudanum, he cavorted nightly with prostitutes while maintaining at least two mistresses, one of whom he dressed in boy's clothing and passed off as a cousin. The deception ended when 'the young gentleman miscarried in a certain family hotel in Bond Street, to the indescribable horror of the chambermaids'.

Leaving England for a Continental tour in 1809, Byron spent almost two years travelling through Greece, Albania and Asia Minor. In Turkey, he was fascinated that the major physical difference seemed to be 'that we have foreskins and they none', and that 'in England the vices in fashion are whoring and drinking; in Turkey, sodomy and smoking. We prefer a girl and a bottle, they a pipe and pathic.' The publication of *Childe Harold* in March 1812 brought Byron into contact with the amoral Lady Caroline Lamb, the 27-year-old wife of William Lamb, who later became Lord Melbourne, Prime Minister of England. After meeting Byron, she wrote in her journal that he was 'mad, bad and dangerous to know'. Her slender, boyish figure met Byron's standards and they were soon lovers. A notorious exhibitionist and outspoken eccentric, 'Caro' – as Byron fondly called her – proved a unique sex partner. In August, Byron opened an envelope to find a thatch of Caro's curly black pubic hair and a long note. 'I cut the hair too close,' she wrote, 'and it bled. Do you not the same.' She asked for a like gift, admonishing him to be careful when handling the scissors. Amused, Byron complied but soon tired of her. With the help of his friend Lady Melbourne – who was also Caro's mother-in-law – he broke off the affair in December. Caro burned Byron's effigy, vowed revenge and bided her time. Fleeing from Caro's fury, he moved in with Jane Elizabeth Scott, the 40-year-old wife of Edward Harley, Earl of Oxford. Happily servicing Lady Jane until the following June, Byron was the latest in a series of lovers she had enjoyed during her marriage. (The Oxford children were known as the 'Harleian Miscellany' because of their uncertain paternity.)

In July 1813, Byron flouted the ultimate sexual taboo – incest – by seducing his married half-sister, Augusta Leigh. Reared separately, the two children born to Captain 'Mad Jack' Byron rediscovered each other with an intense passion. Nine months and two weeks later, Augusta gave birth to a daughter, Medora, and a proud Byron left little doubt as to the father. Referring to the belief held in the Middle Ages that incestuous intercourse produced monsters, he wrote to Lady Melbourne, 'it is not an ape and, if it is, that must be my fault'. To silence the malicious gossip that the affair had created, Byron married Annabella Milbanke, a prim and scholarly heiress who believed she could reform him. Their one-year marriage was a disaster. Byron became almost psychotic, taunting her for months with embellished stories of his past orgies. He suffered continual nightmares, awakening at the slightest body contact with Annabella, screaming, 'Don't touch me!' or crying out, 'Good God, I am surely in hell!' only dimly aware of the red damask curtains around the huge four-poster and the flickering tapers he kept burning in the bedroom. Since Byron felt 'a woman should never be seen eating or drinking', Annabella took her meals alone. In December, after the birth of her daughter Augusta Ada, a fearful Lady Byron filed and sued for a legal separation. The ensuing scandal feasted upon rumours about Byron's sexual perversions: he'd made love to the aging Lady Melbourne at *her* request. . . . He'd sodomized his terrified wife in the final month of her pregnancy. . . . He'd attempted to rape Lady Oxford's 13-year-old daughter. . . . The sensational charges, viciously helped along by a vengeful Lady Caroline bent on Byron's ruin, led to such drastic ostracism that he was forced to leave England for good on 25 April 1816, his reputation in shreds. But, in his last month before leaving, Byron 'put it about' – his own term for copulating – one last time, with Claire Clairmont, the plain 17-year-old stepdaughter of free-love advocate William Godwin. Attracted by Byron's notoriety, Claire brazenly propositioned him in a series of letters. Drawn by her persistent suggestions that he use her body at his earliest convenience, Byron finally gave in a week before departure. Their brief coupling produced Allegra, born the following January.

Once an expatriate in Venice, Byron resumed his sexual excesses in earnest. He found rooms near St Mark's Square, and immediately took his landlord's wife, dark-eyed Marianna Segati, as his next mistress. Almost simultaneously, he acquired a second partner, the Junoesque baker's wife Margarita Cogni, 'La Fornarina'. The fiery Amazon's explosive jealousy forced Byron to schedule his other assignations very carefully. Although very religious – she crossed herself every time prayer bells rang, even when making love with Byron – Margarita would have stabbed any rival. In 1818, Byron broke with Marianna and rented the Palazzo Mocenigo. The palace doubled as a personal brothel for Byron, populated by a harem of mistresses and streetwalkers. For a time, his gentle tigress Margarita – secure in her role as the poet's primary mistress – served as housekeeper, but her tantrums proved too much for Byron. When asked to leave, she threatened him with a knife and stabbed his hand. She then threw herself into the canal. Finally convinced Byron no longer wanted her, she returned to her husband.

Later, Byron estimated that almost half of his annual expenses had gone for purchased sex with at least 200 women. 'Perhaps more,' he wrote, 'for I have not lately kept the count.' The orgies were not without additional cost: Byron was plagued by gonorrhoea, the 'curse of Venus'.

In April 1818, tiring of endless promiscuity and growing fat, Byron met Teresa Guiccoli, a 19-year-old countess trapped in a marriage of convenience. He became her *cavaliere servente*, fulfilling the role of official public escort as allowed by Italian custom for such marriages. Privately, the two fell genuinely in love. Byron cut down sharply on his sexual prowling, writing to friends that he had 'not had a whore this half year', and had confined himself 'to the strictest adultery'. At Count Guiccoli's invitation, Byron moved in, thereby simplifying the affair. Eventually, however, Guiccoli tired of the arrangement, and after an emotional confrontation Teresa was granted a separation. Ironically, the four-year affair domesticized Byron almost completely, and he wistfully pictured himself as a living example of conjugal happiness. Teresa and Byron lived together until July 1823, when he left for Greece.

W.K. (Lists 2, 11, 14, 16, 17, 18, 20, 22, 34, 40)

♣ Maria Callas

3 December 1923 to 16 September 1977

Maria Callas was born in Manhattan, the daughter of two Greek immigrants, Georges and Evangelia Kalogeropoulos. Her father changed the family name to Callas when he opened a drugstore in the city. The Callases already had a daughter – Jackie – when Maria was born, and had hoped for a son. Consequently, Maria never felt wanted, possibly with justification.

An overweight, myopic child, she was shy and unpopular. In 1929, her father lost his drugstore at the beginning of the Depression and her mother, realizing that both Jackie and Maria had musical ability, set out to find them fame. When Maria was 13, Evangelia took her daughters back to Greece. The Callas women were in Greece during the Second World War, and they became friendly with some Italian army officers. Maria would delight them by singing arias from Italian operas; in turn, the officers taught her their native tongue. During the war, she also acquired some formal musical training, studying with the well-known soprano Elvira de Hidalgo, but her career did not really start until her triumphant performance in *La Gioconda* at Verona in 1947. Throughout the 1950s her success was constant. Slimmed to 9 stone 9 pounds by the time she was an international star, Maria Callas was relatively tall – 5 feet 7 inches – and prone to fragile health. Nevertheless, she had one of the most penetrating voices of modern opera.

Despite the publicity her private life received, Callas was involved with only two men in her adult life. While singing in Verona in 1947, she met Giovanni Battista Meneghini, an Italian industrialist and opera patron thirty years her senior, who was not put off by the fact that she then weighed 16 stone 6 pounds. She later remarked, 'I knew he was *it* five minutes after I first met him. . . . If Battista had wanted, I would have abandoned my career without regrets, because in a woman's life love is more important than artistic triumph.' But both families opposed their marriage plans. Meneghini's feared he would immerse himself in operatic matters and neglect the family business, while Maria's mother was upset by the age difference and because Meneghini was not a Greek. With no family members in attendance, the pair married in 1949, in Verona. Maria's new husband immediately took over her career. Under his tutelage, the overweight bride quickly grew trim and learned to dress with style. Her debut at

La Scala – the famous Milanese opera house – in 1950 was a triumph. Meneghini would not let his wife bear children because it might harm her career, but their marriage seemed to be on smooth ground until a fateful sea cruise in 1959. That cruise was aboard Aristotle Onassis's yacht *Christina*. The Meneghinis boarded with Onassis, his wife Tina, and Sir Winston and Lady Churchill. Throughout the two and a half week voyage, Maria vented her hot temper on her husband. Meanwhile she and Onassis grew closer, often taking trips to the Mediterranean ports, leaving the others behind. By the end of the cruise, both the Meneghini marriage and the Onassis union were destroyed. Maria and Meneghini separated a month later, he claiming, 'I created Callas and she repaid my love by stabbing me in the back.' She alternated between public statements such as a shrill 'To hell with him', and a more subdued 'The breaking of my marriage is my greatest admission of failure.' Tina Onassis divorced Ari; however, it was not Callas who was named as co-respondent, but Jeanne Rhinelander, a Riviera socialite with whom Ari had had an affair much earlier.

Callas had met Onassis before; he was the uncle of one of her classmates. He admired her talent, but fell asleep when she sang. Maria tolerated this, however. After Callas was freed from Meneghini in 1966, she and Ari discussed marriage, but two years later Onassis married Jacqueline Kennedy instead. Afterwards Callas's temper cooled, and she and Onassis resumed their relationship, creating quite a splash in the newspapers when they were photographed kissing under a beach umbrella. Looking back on her years with Onassis, Callas once commented, 'We were doomed, but oh how rich we were. . . .'

Callas's last years were lonely. She had more or less abandoned her singing career, and she had also rejected Meneghini's offer of reconciliation after Onassis's death in 1975. Callas died in September 1977, still a legendary opera figure and an object of public interest.

A.L.G. (Lists 24, 42)

♧ Carol II
15 October 1893 to 4 April 1953

Abdication seemed to be a family tradition for the Romanian branch of the Hohenzollerns. Carol's father, King Ferdinand I, had abandoned the throne to live with a commoner, but eventually regained his crown after a state marriage to Carol's mother, Queen Marie. Another family tradition was marital infidelity. Ferdinand was a notorious womanizer, but Queen Marie had even more love affairs. When she was 57, her affair with a young officer prompted her son Carol to have the man stationed at a remote outpost. Marie protested by throwing a tantrum in front of Carol and his advisers, and the officer was returned to her arms. The people of Romania were fond of Carol, the first of their rulers actually born in the country. He spoke their language and attended their church. His greatest fault was being too much in love. The flamboyant ruler gave up the throne for love and died, exiled, in Portugal.

The Romanians viewed Carol as a Casanova. According to Madame Lupescu's biographer, Alice-Leone Moats, the stories of Carol's great virility were part of a publicity campaign begun by his secretary to endear the king to his subjects. Tales were spread of the king's powers as a lover. Although people whispered that Carol's manhood compared favourably to the Eiffel Tower, he was, in fact, timid, weak and easily dominated by women.

During Carol's youth, many of his liaisons were arranged by his mother, as a way of controlling him. Still, Carol scored on his own occasionally, since little effort was required by a future king. He used women and discarded them immediately, which pleased his mother. However, when 'Zizi' Lambrino, one of the queen's handmaidens, played hard to get, Carol fell in love with her. The royal family arranged active military service for Carol and hoped the passion would fade. But Carol left his post to elope with Zizi. Under threat of arrest for desertion, he agreed to an annulment, but continued to see Zizi, and in 1920 she gave birth to his son. Marie and Ferdinand were determined that Carol should have a suitable wife, so, in 1921, Carol entered into an acceptable marriage with Princess Helen of Greece. She soon bore him a son, Crown Prince Michael, but it was well known that the royal couple had no physical relations after the heir's birth. Helen and Carol had agreed that he was to keep his 'sentimental' freedom and be permitted love affairs. Helen allowed women, even Zizi

Lambrino for a time, to consort with her husband at the palace. Sometimes he attended parties elsewhere, such as at the bachelor residence of Tautu, a playboy sea captain. In 1923, Tautu first set Carol up with Magda Lupescu, the divorced daughter of a Jewish pharmacist. Magda had a reputation as a manhunter, but resisted Carol's advances at Tautu's party, which intrigued Carol even more. Later, attempting to nip this potentially disastrous romance in the bud, Tautu rushed into his bedroom and emerged carrying a nightgown, which he flung into Lupescu's face, shouting, 'Get out of here, you [whore], and take your dirty rags with you!' But the ruse did not work – after a moment, Lupescu countered by saying, 'Is there no gentleman here to protect the honour of a helpless woman?' Carol gave her his arm, and they left together.

The red-head was seen by Ferdinand and Marie as a grave threat to the monarchy. Carol would not listen to their counsel, whereupon Ferdinand blackmailed Lupescu into leaving Romania by hinting that the country's Jews might otherwise be slaughtered by anti-Semites. In 1925, she fled to Paris, leaving Carol heartbroken. Before long, he joined 'Bibi' (his pet name for her) and renounced the throne of Romania 'for ever'. The lovers enjoyed the high life in Paris. The forgotten Zizi hounded Carol for financial support and sued him in the French courts. She lost her battle. Helen divorced Carol in 1928, a year after the death of Ferdinand. But a coup d'état against the ruling regency of Prince Michael installed Carol on the throne in 1930. He double-crossed his followers by bringing Lupescu into the country, and she was soon widely hated and feared because of her influence upon the king. A stronger or wiser monarch would have been more discreet: Carol never hid the fact that he cohabited with Lupescu – a serious political error. She often contradicted him and dressed him down in public for his awkwardness. She also beat him and was once seen brandishing a pistol, chasing the naked king down a palace corridor. He was becoming a figure of fun. There was no doubt as to who really wore the ermine breeches in Romania.

In 1937, Carol, at Lupescu's prompting, proclaimed himself dictator, but three years later was caught in a three-way squeeze with the Nazis, the Soviets and the Romanian Iron Guard fascists. He resettled the crown on 18-year-old Michael and fled the country with Lupescu. They took with them most of the funds for the planned Romanian air force. As the royal train neared the border, they were very nearly intercepted by irate Iron Guards, who passionately wanted Lupescu dead. Finally, the locomotive ran through the border blockade.... Thus rid of government duties, they enjoyed the good life in Spain, Cuba, Mexico, Brazil, eventually settling in Portugal. In 1947, Lupescu feigned a terminal illness and Carol married her on her 'deathbed'. When she miraculously recovered they held a second wedding ceremony at home. They spent their last years together as fixtures of high society, Lupescu entertaining guests with bawdy anecdotes and, as always, Carol laughing the loudest, crowing at the company, 'Is she not witty? Is she not amusing?' He died of a heart attack in 1953; Lupescu outlived him by twenty-four years, dying at her home in Portugal in 1977, aged 81.

M.S.

♣ Lewis Carroll
27 January 1832 to 14 January 1898

Under the name of Lewis Carroll, mathematician Charles Lutwidge Dodgson wrote the two best-known children's stories in the world: *Alice's Adventures in Wonderland* and *Through the Looking-Glass*.

The eldest son in a family of eleven children – seven of them girls – he showed early interest in the three subjects which would dominate his career: mathematics, writing and divinity. He entered Christ Church, Oxford, at the age of 18 and stayed there for the rest of his life, teaching mathematics and logic and serving as a deacon. He maintained his health and youthful appearance well into his sixties. He was shy and stammered, although this impediment disappeared in the presence of children. He preferred the company of little girls and enjoyed taking them out and entertaining them with fantastic stories. On one such excursion, on 4 July 1862, Dodgson, inspired by 10-year-old Alice Liddell, created the tale that became known as *Alice's Adventures in Wonderland*. Published three years later, it brought its author more fame than was considered proper for an Oxford don.

Lewis Carroll liked little girls. Although he undoubtedly died a virgin, he had over 100 small girlfriends. He didn't care for young boys: 'To me they are not an attractive race of beings.' To one correspondent he wrote, 'I am fond of children (except boys).' At first he recruited his companions from the children of his friends, but later expanded his horizons and discovered new child friends on trains, or beaches, or while out walking. He became a connoisseur, preferring girls to be upper-class, fair of face and figure, and intelligent and energetic. He got on well with all girls up to the age of 10, although he thought 12-year-olds were the most physically attractive. Puberty ruined everything, and nine out of ten of his child friends disappeared from his life by the time they were 16. Gertrude Chataway, one of the few who remained close to Carroll into adulthood, explained it thus: 'Many girls when grown up do not like to be treated as if they were still 10 years old. Personally I found that habit of his very refreshing.' Carroll was an early amateur photographer and, naturally, his best subjects were little girls. He often posed them in costumes, but his favourite costume was none at all. Apparently this hobby of photographing naked, pre-pubescent girls (though always with their mothers' permission) led to gossip, because in 1880 he suddenly gave up photography.

In the late 1880s, he took to inviting girls to stay with him at his summer quarters in Eastbourne and he loosened his age restrictions a bit. In a letter to Gertrude Chataway, when he was 59, Carroll wrote, 'Five years ago ... I ventured to invite a little girl of 10, who was lent me without the least demur. The next year I had one of 12 staying here for a week. The next year I invited one of 14, quite expecting a refusal.... To my surprise, and delight, her mother simply wrote "Irene may come to you for a week, or a fortnight...." After taking her back, I boldly invited an elder sister of hers, aged 18. She came quite readily. I've had another 18-year-old since, and feel quite reckless now, as to ages.'

It has been speculated that Lewis Carroll proposed marriage to Alice Liddell, but there is no proof of this, although Alice's mother did angrily destroy all the letters which Carroll had written to her daughter. It has also been suggested that he had an affair with the actress Ellen Terry, whom he first admired on the stage when she was 8 and he was 24. They did become lifelong friends, but in her autobiography she dismissed talk of a romantic involvement with the comment, 'He was as fond of me as he could be of anyone over the age of 10.'

Indeed, Carroll was very concerned about the proper age to kiss a girl. He wrote to one mother, 'Are they [your daughters] kissable? ... With girls under 14, I don't think it necessary to ask the question: but I guess Margery to be *over* 14, and, in such cases, with new friends, I usually ask the mother's leave'. But he also wrote (tongue-in-cheek or no), 'If you limit your actions in life to things that *nobody* can possibly find fault with, you will not do much.'

D.W. (Lists 3, 29)

♣ Enrico Caruso
25 February 1873 to 2 August 1921

Generally credited with being the first singer to recognize the value of the phonograph as a means of recording one's voice for posterity and making a great deal of money while doing it, Enrico Caruso was one of the most popular opera singers the world has ever known.

Born in the slums of Naples to a family with twenty-one children, young Enrico escaped a life of poverty because, while singing in the church choir, he realized his voice was golden; young suitors were willing to pay him to serenade their sweethearts. Tutored by the great singers of Italy, Caruso achieved an unequalled prominence in both England and America. He enjoyed an opulent life, and spent a fortune surrounding himself and his loved ones with luxury. A man of tremendous appetites, Caruso risked losing his voice by smoking two packs of Egyptian cigarettes a day (but sought to protect his throat by wearing anchovies around his neck). In later life, he suffered from a variety of physical afflictions, but continued to sing until he succumbed to pleurisy.

A dumpy little man with a barrel chest and an absurd waxed moustache, Caruso enchanted women with the magic of his voice. Early in his career, he was betrothed to the daughter of an opera theatre manager. At the last moment he broke the engagement and fled with a ballerina, an elderly opera director's mistress, for a brief but torrid fling.

Attracted to older women, Caruso fell in love with Ada Giachetti, a voluptuous opera singer ten years his senior. Responding to her young lover's passion, Ada sacrificed her own singing career to care for him. In turn, Caruso turned down countless offers of liaisons from his female fans, although his constant flirtations drove Ada wild with jealousy. Their affair, marked by numerous separations and mutual accusations of infidelity, lasted for eleven years. They had two sons out of wedlock. Caruso's jealousy was finally justified when Ada ran away with their young chauffeur. Shocked but still in love with Ada, Caruso suffered a nervous breakdown that nearly cost him his career. Then, seeking revenge, Caruso plunged into a brief, turbulent affair with Ada's younger sister. When this tactic did not bring Ada back, Caruso threw himself into a series of casual romances with opera groupies. Ada responded by suing Caruso for 'stealing' her jewellery, but she settled out of court for a monthly allowance.

Then, at the age of 45, Caruso shocked the opera world by marrying Dorothy Benjamin, a quiet, prim woman, twenty years his junior. The product of an old New England family, Dorothy was not a music lover. Her father immediately disinherited her, and friends of the passionate singer thought he would soon wear her out in bed. But Dorothy bore Caruso a daughter, and they remained devoted for the rest of their lives. Frequently Caruso exhorted her to 'become very fatty so no one else will look at you'.

Caruso made headlines in 1906 when he was arrested in New York City for pinching a strange woman's bottom while strolling through Central Park Zoo. In what became known as the Monkey House Scandal, Caruso was attacked by the press as an 'Italian pervert' intent on seducing innocent American women. At the trial a mystery witness, dramatically veiled in white, testified that Caruso had fondled her at the Metropolitan Opera House. A deputy police commissioner claimed that he had built up a file on Caruso as a frequent molester of women. Caruso was convicted and fined, despite the fact that the arresting policeman had often been accused of filing trumped-up charges and had been best man at the wedding of the 'victim' – 30-year-old Hannah Graham of the Bronx – who refused to take the stand. Caruso steadfastly maintained he had been framed by enemies in the operatic world trying to sabotage his popularity with the American public. Caruso's friends pointed out that the singer had just returned from a tour of Latin America, where pinching women in public was considered a casual sport for the elite, and suggested that Caruso simply forgot where he was.

Worried that the Monkey House Scandal would ruin his career, Caruso hid from the press, but finally returned to the New York stage, greeted by wild applause from enthusiastic opera lovers who cared more about his voice than his peccadilloes.

R.S.F. (Lists 17, 25, 42, 49)

❧ Giovanni Jacopo Casanova
2 April 1725 to 4 June 1798

Casanova's name has gone down in history as a synonym for a great lover. He was also a compulsive gambler, a writer, a prac- titioner of the occult, and an inveterate traveller, who lived and loved by his wits. 'I was not born a nobleman – I achieved nobility,' declared Casanova, who was sensitive about his ante- cedents. His mother was a promiscuous young Venetian actress, Zanetta Farussi, who married a dancer named Casanova; his father, he believed, was Michele Grimani of the patrician theatri- cal family. He was raised by his grandmother, boarding as a student at the University of Padua, from which he received a doctorate of laws at 17. After being expelled from a seminary for alleged homosexual activity, Casanova eventually made his way into the Venetian army.

At 21, having acquired a knowledge of homeopathy and the occult, Casanova nursed back to health an ageing Venetian aris- tocrat named Matteo Bragadin, who adopted him in gratitude. Incarcerated in the Leads Prison, Venice, for various peccadilloes – many of them sexual – Casanova escaped to spend the next eighteen years wandering over Europe. He served briefly as organizer of the French state lottery; translated the *Iliad* and wrote prolifically, including a prophetic novel in five volumes. He visited Voltaire in Switzerland, fought a duel with a Polish count, interviewed Russia's Catherine the Great (about calendar reform), and affected the title Chevalier de Seingalt.

Returning to Venice in 1774, Casanova served the Inquisition as a spy and bureaucrat for seven years, until he was exiled for writing a satire on the Venetian ruling classes. He ended his life as librarian to Count Von Waldstein in the chateau of Dux in Bohemia.

Casanova was tall, dark, powerfully built and witty, and his sexual conquests were legion. 'There was not a woman in the world who could resist constant attentions,' he claimed. A Machiavelli of sexual intrigue, he would court, cajole, scheme, insult and threaten until he got his way; rebuffed, his ardour would only increase. Continence caused illness, he thought – though indulgence resulted in at least eleven attacks of venereal disease. (Perhaps on this account, but also because he was sympathetic to the woman's risk of pregnancy, he was familiar with the use of a 'protective covering' as well as a contraceptive diaphragm made of half a lemon, the citric acid acting as a spermicide.) A vigorous sexual athlete, he refers casually to 'running my sixth race', and more. In his prime, he was capable of having sex anywhere, with anyone, and in any position, with particular reference to the positions described by sixteenth-century satirist Aretino.

Unlike a Don Juan with a constant need to prove his virility, Casanova was a connoisseur who 'enjoyed the sexual encounter as much for the pleasure it afforded him as for the satisfaction obtained in the seduction process itself, and in the mystique of the adventure'. Gourmand as well, Casanova celebrated women with all his senses. 'The odour of those I loved was always fragrant to my nostrils,' he wrote. And of course he had a highly developed sense of taste. One of his specialities was the oyster orgy, which involved passing the savoury aphrodisiacs from mouth to mouth, retrieving them with his lips should they happen to fall between 'alabaster spheres . . .'. Above all, Casanova was an incurable romantic who constantly fell in love. 'Without love this great business is a vile thing,' he believed. He was forever rescuing damsels in distress, then extricating himself with difficulty. He considered marriage 'the tomb of love', preferring instead the 'inexpressible charm of stolen pleasures'. He described these pleasures in exquisite and occasionally fictional detail in the twelve-volume *Histoire de Ma Vie*.

Sexual awakening came, when Casanova was 11 or so, at the hands of Bettina Gozzi – his landlord's sister – who, while washing him, touched his thighs suggestively. His first complete sexual experience, six or seven years later, involved two young nymphets, Nanetta and Marta Savorgnan. Conspiring to introduce himself into their bed, he lulled them into a deceptive sense of security by feigning sleep. Gradually he uncurled first one girl, then the other, slowly moving toward his ultimate object. After washing together, the three aroused themselves to such a state of sexual intoxication that they spent the remainder of the night 'in ever-varied skirmishes'.

'With a female friend,' Casanova discovered, 'the weakness of the one brings about the fall of the other.' The pattern later repeated itself with Helena and Hedwig, cousins in Geneva. Having pierced their maidenheads and bathed them (an activity that always delighted him), Casanova found his ardour renewed by their curious hands, which aroused him to fill 'their cup of happiness for several hours, changing from one to the other five or six times before I . . . reached the paroxysm of consummation'. Even then, one of the girls was delighted on kissing his 'pistol', as Casanova occasionally referred to his member, to prompt yet another eruption.

In his youth, Casanova became obsessed with what he mistakenly believed to be a *castrato*, one of the young boys playing women's roles on the Italian stage. 'Bellino' turned out to be Teresa, a 16-year-old girl with whom he had an affair. Later, unwilling to forgo any new sexual experiences, he indulged in more than one homosexual encounter. Bragadin, Casanova's adoptive father, may have been a pederast. And in Russia Casanova exchanged 'tokens of the tenderest friendship, and swore eternal love', while with the beautiful androgynous Lieutenant Lunin.

'C.C.' (Casanova usually concealed the identity of his lovers) was a 15-year-old who, relieved of her virginity by Casanova, was locked up by her father in the convent at Murano. While visiting her there, Casanova caught the eye of Mother 'M.M.', a beautiful young nun with a very catholic libido, who proposed an assignation at her lover's casino. Their first coupling was staged for the voyeuristic pleasure of M.M.'s lover, Abbé François de Bernis, France's ambassador to Venice, who was observing them from a hidden chamber. On another occasion, C.C. was persuaded to join M.M. and Casanova. M.M. and C.C. began by exploring 'the mysteries of Sappho'. Then 'all three of us,' Casanova wrote, 'intoxicated by desire . . . and transported by continual furies, played havoc with everything visible and palpable . . . freely devouring whatever we saw and finding that we had all become of the same sex in all the trios which we performed.'

Another nun, also referred to as M.M., later seduced a 12-year-old boarder at a French convent for Casanova's pleasure. By demonstrating the manual technique of verifying virginity, Casanova aroused the child to perform fellatio. She 'sucked the quintessence of my soul and my heart,' Casanova related in his memoirs. The entire encounter took place through the grating which separated the nuns from the visitors.

'I have never been able to understand how a father could tenderly love his charming daughter without having slept with her at least once,' wrote Casanova, having discovered the pleasures of incest. He had fallen in love with Leonilda, the mistress of a homosexually-inclined duke, only to find that she was his daughter by Lucrezia with whom he had enjoyed copulating marathons seventeen years earlier. Leonilda personally observed her parents' reenactment of her conception, undressing ('saying that as her father I was entitled to see all my handiwork'), and even taking part somewhat in their lovemaking. The relationship between father and daughter was consummated, nine years later, when Leonilda was married to an impotent old marquis and Casanova fathered her son.

Casanova had a sense of humour about sex, as evidenced by his affair with 'Mlle X.C.V.' (Giustiniana Wynne). Since the lady was already pregnant, his motives were initially honourable – to help her obtain an abortion. All else having failed, he tried a cure from cabbalistic literature: the 'aroph of Paracelsus', a concoction which was to be applied to the mouth of the uterus, by means of an object six to seven inches in length, when the subject was in a state of sexual arousal. Casanova was convulsed with laughter when the moment arrived, but soon recovered enough to achieve repeated penetration, if not the abortion.

Casanova's most elaborate episode of sexual charlatanry involved the widowed Marquise d'Urfé, a rich eccentric whose consuming passion was to be reborn as a male child. He proposed first to impregnate personally an 'angelic virgin' with a son, into whom the marquise would breathe her soul. But the 'virgin' proved to be something of a trollop, and Casanova was forced to consider the necessity of procreating with the elderly marquise. This would of course require aid and inspiration from a 'divine spirit' in the person of Marcoline, actually a lesbian nymphomaniac. Marcoline arrived dressed all in green, with a note in invisible ink introducing her as a water sprite, adept at certain ceremonial ablutions. The marquise failed to bear the desired male child, but she was good for about two years' worth of pocket money. Casanova's other conquests included the mayoress of Cologne; a nun, a lock of whose pubic hair he kept for remembrance; a black woman, out of curiosity; an actress with two humps on her back and an erotically irregular vulva. Eager to explore all the combinations and permutations of sexual pleasure, he assembled more than one harem of nubile young seamstresses. Most of his women were of the demimonde or lower classes, with a few exceptions. Perhaps Casanova's most rewarding affair was with a well-bred, well-educated Frenchwoman named Henriette, his equal in adventure and hedonism. They spent three months together before she returned to her home. Years later, Casanova

81

found himself in the same hotel room in Geneva, on the window of which she had scratched with a diamond her fateful farewell message: *Tu oublieras aussi Henriette* – 'You will also forget Henriette.'

Exhausted by his prodigious endeavours, Casanova's sexual potency began to flag before he reached 40. In London in 1763, he resorted to advertising for a companion, was driven to distraction by an unwilling beauty, and drained of his cash by five mercenary Hanoverian sisters. He began to revisit the same cities, repeating his old conquests. Back in Venice there was an uneducated seamstress, Francesca Buschini, who remained faithful to him for years. Otherwise, he was forced to frequent the women who could be had by anyone, for a price.

And during his thirteen years as a librarian in Bohemia, there were probably no women at all. There were only the pleasures of eating ('since he could no longer be a god in the gardens,' a contemporary wrote, 'he had become a wolf at the table'), of writing, and of reading – which prompted an aphorism on his favourite subject: 'Woman is like a book which, be it good or bad, must begin to please with its title page.' Needless to say, even though he was impotent during his final years, Casanova was 'always curious to read new ones'.

Casanova's memoirs, a manuscript of 4545 pages, covered his sex life to the summer of 1774 when he was 49. He probably enjoyed very little sex after that, even though he lived to the age of 73. The unexpurgated English version of these memoirs was published in twelve volumes between 1966 and 1971. We were curious to know just how much sex Casanova enjoyed, what kind of sex he had, and what kind of partners he engaged. To our knowledge, no one had ever undertaken a statistical study of Casanova's sexual activity. We decided to do so. We assigned seven trained researchers to comb the twelve volumes of Casanova's *History of My Life*. Computing the results, there was one major surprise. Casanova had one tenth the number of sex partners claimed by Sarah Bernhardt, Guy de Maupassant, Elvis Presley, Aleister Crowley, Ninon de Lenclos and others. It became clear that Casanova was not interested in being the world's busiest lover. He was interested in the quality of each encounter. The figures on Casanova represent a bare minimum. Sometimes he would speak of coupling with 'several' partners, and not knowing their exact number we had no way of including them in our count. Certainly, he must have had affairs with fifty or more partins in addition to those listed. Here then is the countdown on Casanova in love:

Number of women he had sex with: 132 plus
(Tallies below do not match total since Casanova chose not to describe all the women he made love to.)

Nationality of his loves:

Italian	47	Spanish	2
French	19	Polish	2
Swiss	10	Dutch	1
German	8	Russian	1
English	5	African	1
Greek	2	Portuguese	1

Ages of his loves:

11–15 years old	22
16–20 years old	29
21–29 years old	15
30–39 years old	5

The youngest he had sex with was 11 years old; the oldest, over 50.

The kinds of women he made love to:

Female servants	24
Wealthy women or gentlewomen	18
Royalty	15
Prostitutes	11 known plus many more
Actresses	7
Dancers	6
Peasants	6
Courtesans	4
Singers	3
Nuns	2
Theologian	1
Slave	1

Marital status of his women:

Single	85
Married	11
Widowed	5

Women's hair colours:

Dark	12
Blonde	8
Brown	2

Types of seduction:

Mutual agreement	36
He seduced her	33
She seduced him	12
She refused him	16

His style:

Sexual intercourse	52	Anal	1
Fellatio	5	Premature ejaculation	3
Cunnilingus	2	Impotent	7
Sexual intercourse fellatio and cunnilingus	4	'Love in the Albanian Fashion'	1

Masturbation:

He masturbates her	10
She masturbates him	5
He masturbates himself	2
They masturbate each other	1

General exotica:

Virgins he deflowered	31 plus
Two women at once	12 sets
Orgy	1
Most times with one woman in twenty-four hour period	12
Shortest time engaged in sexual intercourse	15 minutes
Longest time engaged in sexual intercourse	7 hours
Most orgasms given to one woman in one erection	14

C.D. and Eds. (Lists 3, 9, 11, 14, 18, 20, 22, 24, 25, 34, 35, 38, 39, 40, 45, 46, 52)

Virginia Oldoini, Countess di Castiglione
22 March 1837 to 28 November 1899

Regarded in the courts of Turin, Paris and London as the most beautiful woman of her time, the countess was a secret agent in France representing those who supported the unification of Italy.

Born in Florence, 'Nicchia' Oldoini was the product of a noble but uncaring father and an ailing mother. She was raised in luxury in a Florentine palace by her grandfather, a renowned jurist and scholar. As Nicchia matured, she acquired the looks of a goddess. At 18, she was chosen by her cousin, Premier Camillo Benso di Cavour, and King Victor Emmanuel II of Sardinia, to represent their cause in France, to bring together the small states of Italy into one nation. This they could not do alone. Austria controlled northern Italy. King Victor Emmanuel II and Cavour needed the help of France. And to obtain this they sent the Countess di Castiglione to seduce Napoleon III, Emperor of France. The countess fulfilled her mission. Her dazzling beauty made her the sensation of Paris. She was partially responsible for encouraging Napoleon's army to go to war against the Austrians in Italy. By 1861, with the help of Garibaldi, Italy was one nation and Victor Emmanuel II was king.

The young Countess di Castiglione was clever and witty, but basically cold, arrogant, egocentric and spoiled. Despite her endless sexual activity, she did not enjoy sex for its own sake, but as a means of humbling men. Few men could resist her beauty. She had rich brown hair, slanted blue eyes, parted lips ('like an opening crimson flower'), a dimpled chin, a perfect body ('faultless in its symmetry'). Attending the Empress Eugénie's prim crinoline court and elsewhere, the countess used her state of undress as a lure. At a ball given by the Count Walewski, France's new foreign minister, Nicchia appeared attired as the Queen of Hearts, a strip of gauze across her breasts with two hearts to hide her nipples, and a transparent skirt with a heart sewn on to cover her vagina. But her pubic hair could clearly be seen, provoking Empress Eugénie to remark acidly, 'Countess, your heart seems a little low.'

Nicchia began her amatory career at 16. Her first lover was an Italian naval officer, Marquis Ambrogio Doria. Shortly afterwards, she took his brothers, Andrea and Marcello, to bed, and started a diary, with her sexual activities kept carefully in code: 'B – a kiss; BX – beyond a kiss; F – everything!' Her family was worried about 'F' and decided to marry her. Then an eligible young nobleman, searching for a bride and advised to have a look at Nicchia, arrived. Conte Francesco Verasis di Castiglione was an aide to King Victor Emmanuel II. Her family forced her to marry the count in January 1854. She thought him a weakling, and told everyone, 'I am married to an imbecile.' She slept with him until they had a child, Georges, and then refused to share his bed again. Bored, she frittered away the count's fortune and put him two million francs in debt. By now, Premier Cavour had discovered that his cousin, the new countess, could be most useful if she were able to seduce Napoleon III. He outlined his scheme to King Victor Emmanuel II. The king had to be convinced of Nicchia's wonders. He tried her out in bed and pronounced her satisfactory. Leaving behind her bankrupt husband and infant child, the countess went to Paris in 1855. (She did not see her husband again for twelve years, when she returned to Italy for the wedding of the king's son.) When she was invited to a fancy-dress ball at the Tuileries at the age of 18, the countess's entrance was memorable. In a low-cut, tight gown, she was the centre of attention. Guards, ushers and servants fell back to make way for her. Some male guests clambered on tables to see her. Johann Strauss, conducting a waltz, stopped. Emperor Napoleon III, in conversation with the British ambassador, abruptly excused himself, and asked her for the next dance.

After that, Louis Napoleon wooed the countess. He gave a house in the rue de la Pompe, a 100,000 franc emerald and a 442,000 franc pearl necklace. He visited her house almost nightly. The countess was flirtatious, but played hard to get. After months of courting, Louis Napoleon invited her to Compiègne, his chateau outside Paris. During a play one evening, she excused herself to the emperor and empress, pleading a headache. Afterwards, the solicitous emperor visited her room and found her in bed wearing a fashionable batiste and lace nightgown. He slipped into bed with her. Previously the emperor had complained to his physician that sexual intercourse no longer 'contributed to [his] sound sleep'. But that night he slept soundly. They made love regularly for over a year. She became known as 'the woman with the cunt of imperial gold'. In court circles it was believed that she had presented Louis Napoleon with a son, who grew up to be the well-known Paris dentist Dr Hugenschmidt. Gradually the imperial ardour cooled. He told one friend, 'She talks about herself too much. She has bandied about our relationship. She allows herself to be seen in bed by all and sundry wearing monogrammed underwear that I had sent her.' One night, in 1859, an Italian tried to assassinate Louis Napoleon in her bedroom. A bodyguard saved the emperor. Days later, the Countess di Castiglione was deported from France.

Back in Italy, the countess wrote to King Victor Emmanuel II,

'If you want me, call me.' The king replied, 'I want you.' He set her up as his mistress in the Pitti Palace in Florence, and gave her a pension of 12,000 francs a year. After two years, and the intercession of French friends, Louis Napoleon allowed her to return to Paris. No longer his official mistress, she became what he called one of his 'little diversions'; this was not enough for her, and she began to entertain other men. The only qualifications required were noble birth or wealth. She slept with the French foreign minister, Prince Henri de la Tour d'Auvergne, over a period of four years. But other lovers overlapped. A senior member of the richest family in the world, 70-year-old Baron James de Rothschild, fell in love with her. A lady friend advised, 'Try to keep alive the passion of the old baron, maybe you will profit richly by it. Make available "the beautiful little thing".' The countess finally had sex with the old baron, and then gave herself to his three sons. Her most incredible coupling was with the eccentric British millionaire, the fourth Marquis of Hertford. He wrote to her, 'Give me one night of love, without excluding any erotic refinements, in exchange for a million francs.' The price for one night of her favours amused the countess. She accepted, unaware that Hertford was a stallion. Once in her bed, he made love to her the entire night. After he left, she was a wreck, unable to get up for three days.

Nicchia's husband had once warned her, 'The day will come when your fatal beauty will have disappeared and the flatterers will be rarer.' The countess dreaded this. At 40, she took a ground-floor flat in the Place Vendôme, shuttered the windows, covered all mirrors. She admitted no friends or relatives, dabbled in spiritualism, and taught her pet dogs, Kasino and Sandouga, to waltz. She never went out in daylight and took her dogs walking only at night. She sat alone in her untidy dark rooms with her memories, deluding herself she was ill and impoverished. She was neither. One night she was found dead of cerebral apoplexy, rats gnawing at her body. At her instructions, she was buried wearing the grey batiste and lace nightgown she had worn at Compiègne the night she gave herself to the emperor, with her two pet dogs stuffed and placed at her feet in the coffin.

I.W. (List 41)

❧ Catherine II, Empress of Russia
21 April 1729 to 6 November 1796

Married at 16 to her 17-year-old cousin Peter, the reigning Empress of Russia's nephew and heir, Catherine was under notice to produce children. (The Empress Elizabeth was herself childless.) Unfortunately, Peter was crazy, impotent and sterile. Catherine contemplated suicide, then sought escape in voracious reading and long strenuous hours on horseback. After nearly ten years of marriage, she gave birth to a son – probably by her first lover, Sergei Saltykov, a young Russian nobleman. Since Peter was growing crazier and more unpopular each day, Catherine's own chances of succession looked hopeless too; moreover, Peter was threatening to divorce her. She decided to plot a coup d'état. In June 1762, Peter had been emperor just six months and was absent planning an insane war against Denmark. Catherine donned a lieutenant's uniform, rode into St Petersburg (then the Russian capital), at the head of a detachment of imperial guards, and had herself proclaimed empress. Peter, shattered by the news, was quickly arrested and murdered. Catherine's chief accomplices had been her lover Count Grigori Orlov and his two brothers, all officers in the Horse Guards. In the course of her long reign, she broke the power of the clergy, put down a major rebellion, reorganized the civil service, forced the Ukrainian peasants into serfdom, and added more than 200,000 square miles to Russian territory – at the expense of the 95 per cent of the population that worked the land.

Catherine before marriage was innocently sensual; at night, she masturbated with a pillow between her legs. To her bridegroom, however, bed was where one played with toys. At 23 she was still a virgin. One stormy night on an island in the Baltic Sea, her lady-in-waiting, probably on the empress's instructions, left Catherine alone with Saltykov, a hardened young seducer. He promised her rapture, and she was not disappointed. The affair with Saltykov unleashed Catherine's sexuality. After two miscarriages, Catherine again became pregnant; she was ordered to take life easy. No sooner had her son Paul been born than the empress snatched him away. Catherine lay unattended in a draughty room while Russia celebrated. Her second child, also officially Peter's, died soon after the actual father, a young Polish nobleman employed by the British ambassador, was sent home in disgrace. Peter was overheard muttering, 'I don't know how it is that my wife becomes pregnant.' Catherine's three remaining children, all boys, were fathered by Grigori Orlov. They were born in secret, Catherine's hoopskirts having successfully concealed each pregnancy. The first birth occurred while Peter was still alive. In order to lure Peter away from the palace as she went into labour, Catherine's faithful servant burned down his own house. (Peter never could resist a good fire.) The other two children, brought up for a while in the homes of servants, were not introduced into the court nursery until nobody could be certain whose they were. These manoeuvres were necessary because Catherine, not wanting to end the Romanov dynasty, refused to marry Grigori. He retaliated by making the court his harem. Nevertheless, Catherine stayed faithful to him for fourteen years, turning him out only when he seduced his 13-year-old cousin.

Catherine was now 43. Her thick brown hair, expressive blue eyes, and small, sensual mouth had lost none of their appeal, while her figure was more voluptuous than in her youth. One of her protégés and original supporters, Grigori Potëmkin, a cavalry officer, had already declared his loyalty to her and then retired to a monastery (he had once studied to be a priest). Potëmkin was canny enough not to return to secular life until Catherine promised to appoint him her official favourite. But first the current favourite had to be dismissed. For two years thereafter the empress and her 35-year-old lover enjoyed a tumultuous affair, filled with quarrels and reconciliations. When the sexual passion died, Potëmkin, willing to give up Catherine but not his influence at court, convinced her that her favourites could be replaced as easily as any other servants. To make sure they were, he added, he would select them himself. Amazingly, the new system worked quite well until Catherine was 60. A potential favourite was first examined by Catherine's personal physician for signs of venereal disease. If pronounced healthy, he was then given a different kind of 'physical' – his virility was tested by a lady-in-waiting appointed for that purpose. The next stage, if he reached it, was installation in the favourite's special apartment, located directly below Catherine's and connected to it by a private staircase. There he would find a large monetary gift. Repeat performances with the empress brought additional rewards and honours, while his main job remained that of her adjutant general and 'emperor of the night'. On dismissal, he might receive anything from additional money to an estate complete with 4000 peasants. In this way Catherine ran through thirteen men and a great deal of public money in sixteen years. Growing old at last, the 60-year-old empress succumbed to the wiles of 22-year-old Platon Zubov, an officer of the Horse Guards, whom Potëmkin disapproved of because he was too ambitious. Zubov was her main sexual interest until her death at 67. Contrary to the rumour that she died attempting intercourse with a horse, Catherine succumbed two days after suffering a massive stroke.

Peter's impotence seems to have been due to an operable malformation of the penis. One story is that Saltykov and friends, having got Peter drunk persuaded him to undergo corrective surgery and so become accountable for Catherine's pregnancies. But we do not know whether Peter ever had sex with her, though he did begin having mistresses. Polish Count Stanislas Poniatowski, Catherine's second lover, was caught leaving her country retreat in disguise. When Peter accused him of having intercourse with Catherine, he indignantly denied it, whereupon Peter dragged her out of bed. Later he forced the lovers to join him and his mistress at supper. In 1764, Catherine had Poniatowski made King of Poland but when – like Stanislas II – he proved unable to control the Polish nationalists, she wiped the country off the map, annexing part of it and giving the rest to Prussia and Austria.

Grigori Orlov, a baby-faced colossus, flourished on physical danger but went to pieces as a courtier. He became a political liability to Catherine after mishandling some important peace negotiations with the Turks; his sexual exploits, however, had already become more than Catherine could stand. He died mad, haunted by Peter's ghost, though it was his brother Aleksei who had planned the murder. Of Aleksei Vasilchikov, Grigori's amiable replacement, Catherine wrote to Potëmkin: 'If that fool had stayed with me another year and you had not come ... it is quite likely that I should have grown used to him.' Potëmkin was a pot-bellied, hypocritical, one-eyed boor who guzzled huge midnight snacks in the palace sauna after frolicking there with Catherine in the steam. Perhaps he and Catherine were secretly married; she certainly called him 'husband' in her letters.

There is less to be said about Potëmkin's handpicked successors. All were handsome guards officers in their twenties – and none lasted long. The gentle Aleksandr Lanskoy, Catherine's favourite of favourites, died from diptheria after undermining his health with aphrodisiacs. Ivan Rimksi-Korsakov – grandfather of the composer – disgraced himself by returning to the 'virility tester', Countess Bruce, for additional 'tests'. The countess was subsequently replaced by an older woman. Aleksandr Dmitriev-Mamonov was allowed to resign in order to marry a very pregnant court lady; Catherine sulked for three days, then gave them a generous wedding present. Most of the royal favourites enjoyed successful careers in later life.

J.M.B.E. (Lists 1, 11, 22, 25, 46)

♣ Charlie Chaplin
16 April 1889 to 25 December 1977

The king of silent screen comedies, Charles Spencer Chaplin made eighty films and gained international fame with his portrayal of the pathetic yet humorous little tramp in such classics as *The Kid* (1920), *The Gold Rush* (1925), *City Lights* (1931) and *Modern Times* (1936). He was knighted in 1975 for his achievements.

Chaplin learned to sing and dance at an early age by watching his mother, Hannah, perform in the music halls of his native London. His alcoholic father left the family shortly after Charlie's birth and, because Hannah was often confined to mental institutions, Chaplin spent his childhood – when not on the street – in a series of orphanages and workhouses. As an adolescent, he earned a living by working as a lather boy in a barber's shop, a music-hall janitor, and a bit-part vaudeville performer. Chaplin's film career began in December 1913, after he had gone on a tour of America with the Fred Karno Company, a British vaudeville troupe. He was spotted by producer Mack Sennett, who signed him to appear in Keystone Films' one-reelers for $150 a week. Chaplin's salary increased with his popularity – in one year he earned $1 million for eight films. He had made sixty-nine films by the end of 1920, but his output dwindled as he began to control the screenwriting, directing and producing of his films – the moody perfectionist often shot up to fifty times more film footage than necessary. *The Great Dictator*, released during the Second World War, caused some politicians and journalists to believe that Chaplin was a leftist, because in it he made an impassioned plea for the launching of a second front in Europe in order to aid the Russians. His *Monsieur Verdoux* (1947), was vehemently attacked by censors and conservatives for its view of contemporary society. (*Monsieur Verdoux* was picketed against, banned in Memphis, and withdrawn from cinemas.) Chaplin left the USA in 1952, purportedly to take an extended vacation, but apparently aware that his re-entry would be challenged. Unable to return to America, he took residency in Switzerland, declaring himself a 'citizen of the world'. But he returned to the USA once in 1972, to receive an honorary academy award, and won another Oscar in 1973 for his 1952 score of *Limelight*.

Though a 'workaholic', Chaplin made time for sex 'between pictures' or, as he crudely put it, in 'that hour when [I am] bored'. When he did make the time, he preferred young girls; the result was four marriages (three to women 18 years of age or younger), eleven children and a harem of mistresses. Calling himself the 'Eighth Wonder of the World' and proud of his Hollywood reputation for having an oversized appendage, Chaplin relished the prospect of deflowering budding virgins. 'The most beautiful form of human life,' he once averred, 'is the very young girl just starting to bloom.' His first pubescent protégée was 14-year-old Mildred Harris, whom Chaplin took under his wing in 1916. He promised her a career in pictures, but Mildred was soon pregnant with Chaplin's child. Although he believed marriage would interfere with his work, there was no escaping the fury of Mildred's mother, and the couple married on 23 October 1918. Mildred's pregnancy turned out to be a false alarm. Though Chaplin grew fond of her, Mildred's mind, he said, was 'cluttered with pink-ribboned foolishness'. About a year after their marriage, she gave birth to a severely deformed son who lived only three days. As the child died, so did the marriage. They were divorced in 1920.

Chaplin loved hiring star-struck starlets to double as his leading lady both on screen and in bed. Lita Grey, for instance, first grabbed Chaplin's attention in 1914. She was only 6 years old. By the time she turned 12, Lita was prancing around Chaplin's studio under the lovelorn eye of her domineering director. For the next three years he groomed her for her first romantic fling and finally, in 1923, during the filming of *The Gold Rush*, Chaplin attempted to molest Lita in his hotel room. 'He kissed my mouth and neck and his fingers darted over my alarmed body,' Lita wrote in her autobiography. 'His body writhed furiously against mine, and suddenly some of my fright gave way to revulsion.' But over the next few months he coddled and charmed her. They were often seen together in the company of Thelma Morgan Converse (later known as Lady Furness) – whom he used as a 'chaperone' so that he could date Lita without arousing the suspicions of her mother. Eventually, on the tile floor of his steam bath, he took Lita's virginity.

Chaplin was well aware of his sex appeal. Once, when Lita remarked that he could probably have any one of a hundred girls in two minutes, Chaplin quickly corrected her. 'A hundred?' he said. 'No, a thousand. But I want to be naughty with you, not with them.' Months, however, passed before Lita experienced her first orgasm. Her constant pleas with Charlie to use contraceptives went unheeded – he felt rubbers were 'aesthetically hideous'. It was no surprise, then, when Lita became pregnant in 1924. She was 16 years old; he was 35. Chaplin shuddered at the news, suggesting she have an abortion. Lita refused. When Chaplin offered her $20,000 to marry some other man, Lita refused again. Threatened with a paternity suit and a charge of statutory rape, Chaplin agreed to marriage. On the ride from Mexico to Los Angeles after their 24 November 1924 wedding, Chaplin suggested to his pregnant wife that she commit suicide by throwing herself off the train. Yet, despite his hostility, Chaplin managed to separate sex from affection, claiming he could make love to Lita even though he detested her.

Two years and two children later, Lita filed for divorce. Her forty-two page legal complaint was made public and sold on the streets for a quarter of a dollar a copy. It exposed intimate details of their marriage: Chaplin had no fewer than five mistresses during their two-year marriage; he threatened her with a loaded revolver more than once; he wanted to engage in a ménage à trois and expressed a longing to make love to her in front of an audience; and throughout their marriage he belittled her because she refused to perform fellatio on him – she said it was perverted; he insisted 'all married people do it'.

Chaplin's third marriage is masked in mystery. He met actress Paulette Goddard when she was 20. Some journalists claim he married the starlet in April 1934, while at sea on his yacht, *Panacea*. Supposedly, he paid the skipper to tear the telltale page from the ship's logbook. While many sceptics insist the couple never married, Chaplin gave 1936 as the year of their marriage. Though she played stepmother to Chaplin's sons – Charles Jr and Syd – for a time, wedded bliss was once again undermined by the demands of film-making.

In 1941, Chaplin met 22-year-old Joan Barry when she came to his studio for a screen test. This time it was Chaplin who was

93

pursued, at first quite willingly. But he tried to call a halt when she began coming to his home at any hour, bathing in the sprinklers, breaking windows and threatening suicide. When she finally decided she didn't want to be an actress after all, he gladly paid her fare back to New York. But, in May of 1943, she returned to Los Angeles, broke into his home and, as a consequence, spent thirty days in jail. At the time of her arrest, she was three months pregnant. In the meantime, Chaplin met Oona O'Neill, the 17-year-old daughter of the playwright Eugene O'Neill. While Chaplin's sons engaged in a friendly rivalry for Oona's affections, their father easily out-distanced them. In June 1943, she became his fourth and final wife. Chaplin's marriage did not prevent Joan Barry from slapping him with a paternity suit. And, because Chaplin had given her money which she used for travelling back and forth across state lines, the federal government indicted him on morals charges. After Miss Barry's child was born in October 1943, a blood test proved that Chaplin was not the father. During the trial, the prosecuting lawyer referred to Chaplin as 'a runt of a Svengali' and a 'lecherous hound'. While on the stand, the 55-year-old actor was questioned about his virility and was forced to admit that he was still quite sexually potent. In April 1944, Chaplin was acquitted; none the less, he was ordered to pay child maintenance.

Persecuted by the US press and politicians as a 'debaucher' and a 'leftist', he and Oona settled down in Vevey, Switzerland, to a life of domestic happiness and serenity. 'If I had known Oona or a girl like her long ago, I would never have had any problems with women. All my life I have been waiting for her without even realizing it,' he said. By the time he died, Chaplin had fathered eight more children – the last one when he was in his early 70s.

Chaplin prided himself on bedding prominent women. Among his conquests were Clare Sheridan, cousin of Winston Churchill; actresses Mabel Normand, Edna Purviance, Pola Negri and Marion Davies, the starlet who carried on a long-lasting affair with William Randolph Hearst; and Peggy Hopkins Joyce, a *Ziegfeld* girl who became one of the wealthiest women in the world by marrying five millionaires. She and Chaplin were sometimes seen swimming nude off the island of Catalina.

In the early days of his career, he sometimes joined his vaudeville chums on their outings to brothels. When he was 20 and visiting Paris, he was so shocked at the price charged by a superior courtesan that he abandoned her on the journey to her apartment. This human sex-machine who, as a prelude to sex, recited erotic passages from *Fanny Hill* and *Lady Chatterley's Lover*, was good for as many as six 'bouts' in succession with scarcely five minutes' rest in between. Chaplain also practised voyeurism – he erected a high-power telescope in his house that gave him a bird's eye view of John Barrymore's bedroom.

He said 'No art can be learned at once. And lovemaking is a sublime art that needs practice if it's to be true and significant.'
A.K. and V.S. (Lists 3, 4, 11, 17, 20, 21, 22, 25, 26, 31, 35, 41)

❧ Charles II
29 May 1630 to 6 February 1685

Charles's first adviser and tutor, the Earl of Newcastle, told the teenage prince he would learn more from men than from books. The lessons the boy learned during the tumultuous, dangerous years of his teens and twenties were lessons of intrigue, political manoeuvring, and other necessary skills to survive as an exiled, uncrowned king. In 1646, during the civil war, Prince Charles took his father's advice and fled, first to the Scilly Isles, and then to Jersey and France. While in exile in 1649, he learned that his father had been beheaded by Oliver Cromwell's forces. Years of waiting and plotting were rewarded when, in 1660, he returned to take advantage of the struggle between Cromwell's successors. Britain welcomed him back. He was crowned, and married Catherine of Braganza, the daughter of the King of Portugal. The queen was never able to bear children, but Charles steadfastly refused to divorce her. He was a shrewd politician, a charming man loved by most of his subjects, and much interested in horse racing, fishing and naval matters, and he was even tolerant of rival religions.

The Puritans chose to represent Charles as a sexual monster, but another picture of the 'Merry Monarch' has emerged. The man did indeed enjoy sex enormously – he was good at it, pursued it vigorously and, as a handsome man and king, was never short of willing partners. His standards were high, however; he did not bed every available woman. And, despite his energetic extra-marital sex life, he was always attentive to Catherine, who quickly learned that forbearance and tact were the best means of exerting influence on her husband. Although they had no heir, it was not through lack of trying. They made love regularly, and Catherine was said to have suffered two miscarriages in her futile attempt to provide him with legitimate offspring. Charles's code of sexual ethics was summed up in his belief that God would never damn a man for 'allowing himself a little pleasure'. He lived up to his code, allowing himself more than a little, yet not causing intentional harm to any of his partners. Where other powerful men discarded their mistresses, Charles pensioned his off with an income and title and did the same for their children. He loved what might be called elaborate sexual games – dramas incorporating more or less consciously arranged role playing, with Charles himself as the central character. He loved to see women dressed as men – a taste which did not hint at all at homosexuality but sprang rather from the many 'breeches parts' written into Restoration plays, roles intended to allow shapely young actresses to scamper about the stage in tight-fitting breeches rather than skirts. As part of the game playing, he was in a position to indulge in the creation of complex sexual 'menus'. Two mistresses at the same time, for example, in separate residences, one of whom was an insatiable, sensual libertine, and the other a coy virgin playing with dolls and whetting the king's appetite but refusing to satisfy it. Or an elegant lady and a saucy actress. Charles's sex life seems to have been one in which there was never a dull moment. When boredom did threaten, the king relied on Will Chiffinch, his trusted private messenger, to arrange for the secret nocturnal visits of nameless but highly attractive wenches.

As a young man of 15, he was introduced to sex by his former governess, Mrs Wyndham, after which he indulged in an early taste for older women. Eventually his partners got younger, and his sexuality more adventurous; in his later years he tended to seek more settled relationships, usually one at a time in what might be called 'serial monogamy'. Although he once exclaimed, 'Odd's fish, I am an ugly fellow!' upon examining a quite realistic portrait, women found his tall, strong frame and dark sensual visage exciting. He loved his reputation as a sexual animal. The king was often called 'Old Rowley', after a famous stallion, prodigiously endowed and in great demand as a stud. While passing through the halls of his palace one day, Charles heard a young woman singing a satirical ballad entitled 'Old Rowley, the King'. He immediately knocked on the door of her apartment, and when she asked who was there he replied, 'Old Rowley himself, madam.' According to the poet Rochester: 'Nor are his high Desires above his Strength;/His sceptre and his p----k are of a length,/And she that plays with one may sway the other. . . .'

Nell Gwynne's rise to fortune was a storybook affair. Her father was an inveterate ne'er-do-well who breathed his last in a debtors' prison. Her mother was an alcoholic whose contribution to her daughter's future was to get her a job as a barmaid in her bawdy house. Sweet saucy Nell became one of the first English-speaking actresses in history (since before that only pre-adolescent boys had played women's roles) and therefore one of the first to use her antics on stage to catch the eye, and other more private parts, of a king. Her king was Charles II, although she called him her 'Charles the Third' because she had already had two lovers named Charles before him. Witty, playful, coarse, sweet and vulgar in turn, stimulating Charles with mock coyness and then satisfying him with her own very real sexuality, she was a perfect mistress to the king. Another of her charms was her perfect pair of calves and thighs, which she bared on stage. The common people loved Nell because she was one of them, a 'girl of the London streets' made good. One afternoon as she rode along in the carriage Charles had given her, she was suddenly the target of the jeers and curses of the unwashed rabble. Her carriage had been mistaken for that of Charles's other mistress, the elegant, haughty and strikingly beautiful Louise de Kéroualle who, because she was French and Catholic, some suspected of being a spy for King Louis. Nell poked her head out of the carriage window, smiled winningly, and cried out, 'Pray, good people, be civil! I am the *Protestant* whore!' The people were delighted. It also pleased king and people that Nell did not care to enter into politics. As an anonymous poet of the period put it:

> *Hard by Pall Mall lives a wench call'd Nell*
> *King Charles the Second he kept her.*
> *She hath got a trick to handle his prick*
> *But never lays hands on his sceptre.*
> *All matters of state from her soul she does hate,*
> *And leave to the politic bitches.*
> *The whore's in the right, for 'tis her delight*
> *To be scratching just where it itches.*

Charles revelled in the contrast between saucy Nell and cultured Louise. He also enjoyed the contrast between two of his other playmates: shy, demure, virginal Frances Stuart – who apparently never gave in to Charles although she was much pursued –

and rapacious, voluptuous, sexually insatiable Barbara Palmer (also known as Lady Castlemayne), of whom diarist Samuel Pepys wrote, 'My Lady Castlemayne rules him, who hath all the tricks of Aretin that are to be practised to give pleasure – in which he is too able, having a large ----, but that which is the unhappiness is that, as the Italian proverb says, "A man with an erection is in no need of advice."'

The rest of Charles's partners fall into two categories: those such as Moll Davis and Catherine Pegge whom he publicly acknowledged and by whom he had a dozen children, and the many fleeting passions which produced numerous unacknowledged children. As the Duke of Buckingham put it, a king is supposed to be the father of his people, and Charles certainly was father to a good many of them.

R.W.S. (Lists 20, 21, 22, 34)

♣ Frédéric François Chopin
1 March 1810 to 17 October 1849

Chopin was a musical prodigy who gave his first concert at 8 and became a local celebrity in his early teens. Warsaw then was a musical backwater, and Chopin's father, a French-born high-school teacher, had little money. In 1830, Chopin left Poland for ever to seek his fortune as a travelling virtuoso, though he lacked the physical strength to give public concerts. He settled in Paris, becoming piano teacher to rich men's wives, composer of best-selling sheet music and recitalist to the elite; a gifted mimic, he was also popular at fashionable parties. The social round wore him down and he contracted tuberculosis. The 1848 revolution drove his pupils out of Paris and forced him, despite his coughing blood, to play for his supper in the stately homes of England and Scotland. He returned to Paris a total invalid and died there after months of suffering.

Most women were as charmed by Chopin's romantic looks as by his music. Chopin was drawn to women, but not often sexually; their adoration reminded him of his mother and sisters. In his late teens, he pestered a male friend, Tytus Woyciechowski, with girlish notes. He was obsessed with kissing the reluctant Tytus's lips. 'Give me your mouth,' Chopin wrote, and once, while waiting for lunch, he said, 'In a while, the semolina! But for now, your mouth!' With girls he showed no such verve. Imagin-

98

ing himself in love with a fellow music student, Constantia Gladkowska, he could not bring himself to write her a letter. Constantia married someone else and was amazed to learn years later what she had meant to Chopin.

The temptations of Paris did not appeal to Chopin, but he appears to have caught a mild dose of venereal disease from a woman named Teressa. Perhaps this confirmed his distaste for sex. Still, ever since his death, there have been rumours – supported, it seems, by a cache of erotic letters – of an affair between him and one of his first pupils, the musical and sexually liberated Countess Delfina Potocka. 'I would like again to plop something down your little hole in D flat major' (a black key between two white keys), he wrote in one of the alleged letters, of which only a photocopy remains. (The document may have been faked by its 'discoverer', Pauline Czernicka, who committed suicide in 1949.)

Chopin always wanted a family life of his own. In 1836 he proposed to Maria Wodzinska, the pretty and musically accomplished daughter of a Polish count, and she accepted him, but the countess, disturbed by his evident poor health, made them keep their engagement secret. Chopin ignored the countess's pleas to take better care of himself, and soon Maria's letters stopped. Unwilling or unable to protest at this rejection, he abandoned all hopes of marriage.

Then he met the free-living novelist George Sand (q.v.), who admired him and pursued him. Chopin was not immediately attracted to her, declaring to a friend, 'What a repellent woman that Sand is. Is she really a woman? I am very much inclined to doubt it.' Eventually he did succumb to her advances but, despite Chopin's complaints that abstinence was killing him, she appears to have broken off sexual relations after the first year or two of their nine-year association. His bedroom performance, she let it be known, was corpselike, and he showed little interest in lovemaking. Preoccupied with raising two children, she was prepared to make him the third. Chopin enjoyed his part-time family, especially little Solange, the daughter. As she grew up, she took to flirting with him, calling him 'no-sex Chopin'. When, in his absence, Sand married Solange off to a rascally sculptor known for his suggestive nudes, Chopin was aghast. In a violent quarrel between Sand and Solange's husband, Chopin was tricked by Solange – a pathological liar – into siding against her mother, who then broke off with him. Chopin's conscious feelings for Solange remained paternal.

The last woman who seriously tried to attract him was his wealthy pupil and financial saviour Jane Stirling, of whom he remarked, 'I would as soon marry death.'

J.M.B.E. (Lists 5, 18, 29)

♣ Cleopatra
69 to 30 BC

Cleopatra was a Macedonian Greek descended from Ptolemy, Alexander the Great's general who ruled Egypt upon Alexander's death. An intellectual, she was the first member of the royal family who bothered to learn the Egyptian language, and was also fluent in other tongues. Educated in Hellenistic as well as Egyptian traditions, she was considered culturally superior to some of the greatest statesmen of Rome. With a long hooked nose and a large mouth, Cleopatra was not especially beautiful, but her body was slender and well proportioned and she was a mistress of the cosmetic arts. She was an enchantress of whom it was said that the sweetness of her melodic voice resembled the sound of a lyre.

Historians have recorded that Cleopatra staged weeks of nightly orgies, at which those in attendance engaged in various forms of debauchery. The lascivious atmosphere of her court during her love affair with Roman leader Mark Antony showed how she played to his notorious taste for obscene jokes and sexually provocative conversation. For his entertainment, she kept a *cinaedus*, or performer of lewd dances, at court. Cleopatra and Antony visisted the pleasure resorts outside Alexandria, and they formed a dining club, the Inimitables, where guests participated in lewd theatricals. One Roman guest played Glaucus the sea god, dancing and crawling on his knees, his naked body painted blue. The orgies led to scandals about Cleopatra's personal sex life. Rumours spread that she promiscuously indulged in fellatio; some Greeks called her Meriochane, which means 'she who gapes wide for ten thousand men'. According to one account, she was supposed to have fellated 100 Roman noblemen in a single night. The idea that Cleopatra was a harlot was developed by her enemies, one of whom, King Herod of Judea, claimed that she attempted to seduce him. His assertion is probably false, because Cleopatra's principal aim was to keep in the good graces of her lover, Antony, a formidable political ally.

In accordance with the Egyptian custom of marriage between

royal siblings, Cleopatra was married to two younger brothers: first to Ptolemy XIII in 51 BC, when she was 18, and shortly after his death in 47 BC to the 12-year-old Ptolemy XIV. There was no physical consummation of these marriages, which were arranged only because a male co-monarch was necessary for her to be queen. Although some sources maintain that Cleopatra began her sex life at the age of 12, it is possible that she took her first lover nine years later, choosing the 52-year-old dictator of Rome, Julius Caesar. Fleeing her country amidst a power struggle with her brothers and sisters, the 21-year-old queen presented herself to Caesar at his palace in Alexandria, smuggled past guards in a carpet or a roll of bedding. She quickly captivated the notorious womanizer and their love affair began, thus ensuring her political position. Although Caesar was already married, an Egyptian marriage possibly took place between Caesar and Cleopatra, and he soon brought her and their son Caesarion to Rome, installing them in one of his homes. He publicly proclaimed her influence over him by placing a statue of her in the temple of Venus, thus arousing Rome's anger by deifying a foreigner. Because Caesar had no legitimate son, the possibility of an Egyptian successor caused much resentment towards the queen, and she was often referred to as a whore in the bawdy songs sung by Caesar's soldiers.

Upon Caesar's murder, Cleopatra returned to Egypt where she learned of the emergence of a new Roman leader. Determined to seduce this Antony, Cleopatra sailed to Tarsus in an opulent barge with purple sails, silver oars and a poop deck of gold. The music of lutes and flutes announced the arrival of the queen dressed as Venus and surrounded by attendants dressed as Cupids and the Graces. For several days, she staged elaborate banquets and bestowed expensive gifts upon the soldier–statesman and his officers. By the time a power struggle with Caesar's nephew, Octavian, forced Antony back to Rome, she had conceived twins by him. Several years later he left his new wife Octavia – sister of Octavian – and returned to Cleopatra's side. The rupture in his relations with Octavian led to two years of war which culminated in Antony and Cleopatra's defeat at Actium. After Octavian's forces reached Egypt, Cleopatra fled to her mausoleum, barricading herself inside with three attendants. Antony received a report that she had committed suicide, and in his grief he stabbed himself. Mortally wounded, he was informed that she was still alive and was transported to her mausoleum, where he died in her

arms. Cleopatra was soon captured by Octavian: for once her
seductive powers proved unsuccessful. She took her own life
upon learning that she was to be paraded in the streets of Rome
upon Octavian's triumphant return.

L.A.B. (Lists 2, 11, 40)

♣ Colette
28 January 1873 to 3 August 1954

One of the most celebrated of French authors, Sidonie Gabrielle
Claudine Colette wrote seventy-three books – fiction, non-fiction
and a mixture of the two – about the sorrows and delights of love.
In her life, as in her art, she gave a new dimension to two of
France's most enduring sexual archetypes, the schoolgirl seduc-
tress and the ageing coquette.

Colette grew up in the country, the adored youngest child of a
fiercely possessive mother and a vaguely literary retired army
captain. She was a singular child, a tomboy who went by her
family surname and communed intimately with the flowers and
animals in her own private enchanted garden. At 20, an ingenu-
ous provincial with braided hair falling below her knees, she
married Henry Gauthier-Villars, a 35-year-old writer and friend
of the family. 'Willy,' as he was known, added his young bride to
his collection of mistresses, ghostwriters and pornographic postcards in decadent fin-de-siècle Paris. At Willy's urging, Colette
began to fill notebooks with vicariously erotic stories about the
adventures of a young girl. The four Claudine novels, published
from 1900 to 1903, enjoyed a great vogue, giving rise to a whole
line of 'Claudine' products and to a cult of the precocious schoolgirl, innocent yet alluring. Rebelling against her literary bondage
to Willy, who signed his name to his wife's first six books, Colette
began publishing voluptuous nature stories using the name
'Colette Willy' until 1906, and then simply 'Colette'. (She could
describe a vegetable as if it were a love object, it was said.) She
took up mime, divorcing Willy in 1906 to tour in mildly erotic
mime melodramas. She also contributed articles to *Le Matin*, a
leading French newspaper. The editor, Henri de Jouvenel,
fathered her only child (a girl) and became her second husband –
in that order. This marriage also ended in divorce, but while it
lasted Colette achieved her greatest fame with *Chéri* (1920), the
sexual tragedy of a young gigolo and an ageing coquette, followed

by *The Ripening Seed* (1923), a classic tale of adolescent sexual initiation. Married yet again in 1925, Colette enjoyed both fame and an active old age, raising the coquette to the rank of patriotic heroine with the publication of *Gigi* in 1945, when she was 72.

Colette's first husband, Willy, was constantly unfaithful to her. Once she followed him to an assignation, and found him fornicating with Lotte Kinceler, a foul-mouthed, hunchbacked dwarf. Sometimes he 'brought his other coquettes to Colette's apartment where they would finger her things and speak smut'. Willy tried to promote a liaison between his young wife, who described herself as 'sexually impartial', and one of his mistresses. At the time, Colette was more comfortable with Willy's male young homosexual secretaries. But, as she became disillusioned with Willy, whose bulbous eyes and drooping cheeks reminded her of Queen Victoria, she took refuge in her somewhat exhibitionistic career in mime and music-hall dancing. She also found comfort in the company of an aristocratic lesbian – Missy, the former Marquise de Belboeuf, a descendant of Napoleon, with whom she lived for six years after leaving Willy.

Full-bodied and feline in her thirties, with sloe eyes and a mop of curly hair, Colette appeared in the mime theatre seductively draped like an odalisque. One play required her to bare her breasts, which created 'a luscious thrill of sensation' in the audience. Sensation turned to scandal when, miming a ballet in which 'a mummy awakes from eternal sleep, undoes its bandages and, near nude, dances its ancient loves', she ardently embraced her 'prince' – who was in fact Missy, the choreographer of the ballet. Colette and Missy de Belboeuf, who looked and dressed like a man in daily life, enjoyed what was then known as 'a loving friendship'. Colette, who also appeared in a dinner jacket at the famous Sapphic banquets of the day and wore an ankle bracelet engraved 'I belong to Missy', described her friend's love as maternal and possessive. She wrote of Missy, 'You will give me sensual pleasure, leaning over me, your eyes full of maternal anxiety, searching through your passionate friend for the child you never had.' Colette had numerous lesbian loves, one of the most colourful being Natalie Barney, an American expatriate in Paris known for her Friday salons and her affairs with other women. On one occasion, Colette sent Barney a message reading, 'Natalie, my husband kisses your hands, and I the rest.'

After entering the world of journalism, Colette began a whirlwind affair with the aggressive, virile Henry de Jouvenel. (Fond of pet names, she called him 'Sidi the Pasha'.) The affair ended in marriage when Colette, nearly 40, became pregnant. Jealousy blooms 'like a dark carnation,' she wrote, with reference to her husband's chronic infidelity. De Jouvenel complained, for his part, about his wife's preoccupation with 'love, adultery, and half-incestuous relationships'. The latter was rumoured when Colette took off on a Swiss winter vacation with her 19-year-old stepson, Bertrand de Jouvenel – after her separation from his father.

It was only during the autumn of her womanhood, as Colette called it, that she was able to reconcile her fierce need for independence with both a desire for possession and a penchant for handsome young men. Colette was 52 when she met Maurice Goudeket, then 35, who later became her third husband. Whether writing in bed, surrounded by cats and cushions, or basking in the warm sunshine of St Tropez, she enjoyed with Goudeket a loving companionship which renewed her creative energy and enabled her to remain vigorously active well into old age.

'The seduction emanating from a person of uncertain or dissimulated sex is powerful,' wrote Colette, who refused to distinguish between normal and abnormal sexuality.

C.D. (Lists 6, 10, 14, 25, 26, 35, 40, 42, 46)

❧ Gary Cooper
7 May 1901 to 13 May 1961

Cooper won the Oscar for Best Actor in 1941 for *Sergeant York* and another in 1952 for *High Noon*. Nominated for the award three more times, in 1961 he received an honorary Oscar 'for his many memorable screen performances' in ninety-five pictures.

Despite his screen persona as an American Everyman, he was hardly unworldly. He was educated in England, safaried in Africa, and conquered women everywhere. Despite his art school background, he failed to sell any of his political cartoons, but his riding experience, gained on the family ranch in Montana, did land him a job as a film stuntman in the early twenties. However, he soon grew tired of falling off horses (sometimes as both cowboy and Indian in the same picture), and hired agent Nan Collins to help him get feature roles. She changed his name from Frank to Gary after her home town in Indiana, and he starred in *The*

Winning of Barbara Worth soon afterwards, in 1926. Paramount signed him to a contract, and unprecedented popularity followed, wavering only in 1944, when fans objected to his one political venture – a scathing anti-Roosevelt broadcast during the Dewey campaign, and in 1957, when the critics castigated him for playing the lover of 18-year-old Audrey Hepburn in *Love in the Afternoon*. He was 56 at the time and immediately went out for a facelift. In 1959, two years before his death from spinal cancer, he was converted to Roman Catholicism.

'Yup' and 'Nope' weren't his only trademarks. When asked why she was leaving New York for Hollywood, Tallulah Bankhead said for the money and 'to fuck that divine Gary Cooper'. Making love to Gary Cooper became as popular a pursuit among Hollywood's leading ladies as getting their prints enshrined in front of Grauman's Chinese Theatre. Director Howard Hawks commented on Cooper's technique, 'If I ever saw him with a good-looking girl and he was kind of dragging his feet over the ground and being very shy and looking down, I'd say, "Oh-oh, the snake's gonna strike again." He found that the little bashful boy approach was very successful.' Helen Hayes said she would have left her husband for Coop if he had only given the word during their filming of *A Farewell to Arms*. When John Gilbert found out that his own Marlene Dietrich was in love with Cooper, he went off the wagon and drank steadily until his death – the day after Cooper was named her co-star in *Desire*. And Warner Brothers held up release of *Saratoga Trunk* for two years in the forties, fearing that the smouldering relationship between Coop and co-star Ingrid Bergman would result in a double divorce that would kill the picture at the box office. Said Bergman, 'Every woman who knew him fell in love with Gary.'

Coop's wife Rocky, née Veronica Balfe, was a New York debutante and would-be actress whom Coop married in 1933, saying he was 'delighted to be rescued from his career as a playboy'. The couple omitted the word 'obey' from their wedding ceremony and allowed each other plenty of space thereafter – once even arriving at a ski resort separately, staying in separate rooms, skiing briefly together, and then departing separately.

The first lover of note in Coop's life was Clara Bow, his co-star in *It* in 1927. Clara rated her lovers, and gave Coop rave reviews on his magnificent endowments, boasting to Hedda Hopper that he was 'hung like a horse and could go all night'. They liked to make love outdoors, on beaches or in walnut groves. Clara told friends that Gary let her take her dog into the bathtub whenever he gave her a bath. Rumour had it that Cooper proposed marriage to Clara, which soured her feelings towards him. In the end, Cooper dismissed their relationship as a creation of the studio publicity department.

There was no denying his affair with actress Lupe Velez, the 'Mexican Spitfire'. She was the girlfriend of singer Russ Columbo when she and Coop first met for *Wolf Song* in 1929. Twenty-four hours later they were found in Coop's bed together. A friend told biographer Hector Arce of his embarrassment on being trapped in a naked Cooper's dressing room while Coop and Lupe tantalized each other over the phone with talk of the forthcoming night's activities and Coop developed an unabashed erection. The relationship was often characterized by screaming and violent fights which scarred Cooper physically and emotionally. Pressure from his mother and the studio finally broke up the relationship, leaving Coop with a nervous breakdown and only 10 stone 8 pounds on his 6 foot frame.

During a 'long walk' through Europe to clear his head, he met Contessa Dorothy di Frasso, an American who had married into Roman nobility. She helped Coop become a sophisticate and returned to Hollywood with him, where she became famous for throwing lavish parties and haunting film sets where he worked. The younger, beautiful Veronica Balfe soon eclipsed her in Coop's affections, and the contessa faded off to Palm Springs and an affair with gangster Bugsy Siegel.

Patricia Neal was 23 when Coop met her during filming of *The Fountainhead* in 1949. They fell in love, and he sought a legal separation from Rocky in 1950. He took Miss Neal to Havana in hopes of gaining the approval of his friend Ernest Hemingway, but neither Papa nor anyone else was willing to sanction the break-up of his seventeen-year marriage. As for Rocky, her Catholicism wouldn't permit her to consider divorce and her pedigree wouldn't permit her to wallow in self-pity. She continued to live her life to the fullest and, before the separation became final in May 1951, Cooper and Miss Neal had parted – she for a psychoanalyst and he for two more trivial liaisons before a reconciliation with Rocky and their daughter Maria.

D.R. (Lists 4, 11, 31, 42, 43)

106

♣ Joan Crawford
23 March 1906 to 10 May 1977

During her forty-year career as an actress, Joan Crawford appeared in over eighty films and was one of the screen's longest reigning stars. An emotional performance in *Mildred Pierce* earned her the 1945 Academy Award for Best Actress. Besides appearing in such memorable films as *The Women*, *Strange Cargo*, *Humoresque* and *Whatever Happened to Baby Jane?*, she served on the board of directors of the Pepsi-Cola company.

Crawford was permanently embittered by her battered, poverty-stricken childhood. Her real name was Lucille LeSueur, and she was born in San Antonio, Texas. When Lucille's father deserted the family, her mother found her jobs in Kansas City boarding schools. In one, the 12-year-old girl suffered severe beatings whenever she failed to perform her duties. Pudgy, buxom and rather bland, she stormed New York in 1924 and took to the stage as a dancer. Described by F. Scott Fitzgerald as 'the best example of the flapper', Lucille was dancing on Broadway when MGM studios discovered her and signed her to a five-year contract. On New Year's Day in 1925 she moved to Los Angeles. Through a combination of stringent dieting and extensive dental surgery, she created a new image and was transformed into 'Joan Crawford', a screen name coined for her in a fan magazine contest sponsored by MGM. By the end of 1927, the 5 foot 4 inch starlet had become a flamboyant off-screen personality. She changed her hair colour weekly, danced in revealing short skirts, and cavorted about town with a male harem of handsome escorts. During her tumultuous Hollywood career, she was alternately labelled 'First Queen of the Movies' and 'Box-Office Poison'. Survival as a star was her paramount aim and everything else – husbands, lovers and children – was secondary. She seemed to love her fans more than her family and kept in close touch with 1500 of them right up to May 1977, when she died from stomach cancer.

Joan was married four times and each marriage lasted four years. Every time she changed husbands she also changed the name of her Brentwood estate and installed new toilet seats. Her first fling was with Douglas Fairbanks Jr, charming scion of the royal Fairbanks family of Hollywood. Popularly referred to as 'the Prince and Cinderella', the couple married in June 1929, despite strong opposition from Joan's new in-laws. The elder Fairbanks and his then wife Mary Pickford boycotted the wedding, claiming that 23-year-old Joan was too old for 20-year-old Doug Jr. The marriage, which for two years was ideal, ended in a shambles. Joan and 'Dodo', as she called her husband, dreamed of having children. But the fiery Miss Pickford apparently warned, 'If you ever dare to make me a grandmother, I'll kill you.' The marriage died shortly after Joan had had a miscarriage – which she later admitted was really an abortion.

Before her 1933 divorce, Joan plunged into a love affair with actor Clark Gable. He too was married, but Joan enjoyed his company enough to carry on an intermittent affair with him until his death in 1960. Although she called Gable 'a magnetic man with more sheer male magic than anyone in the world', she later confessed that he was an unsatisfactory lovemaker, contradicting his screen image as a virile leading man. In fact, she was often faced with ploys which he devised to discourage sexual encounters between them. Realizing that marriage to Gable was unlikely, Joan showered her affections on actor Franchot Tone, a wealthy, cultured easterner. And, although she had claimed she would never marry again, the 29-year-old Joan and 30-year-old Tone married in October 1935. This marriage was shaky from the start, but Joan believed it might be saved if they had children. After suffering two miscarriages, she was informed that she could not bear children. When she caught Tone in bed with another actress, she decided that she had no further need of him anyway, and divorced him in 1939. While her relationship with Tone was disintegrating, she had a brief affair with Spencer Tracy. But his interest in her was fleeting. During a rehearsal, Joan betrayed her nervousness and botched her lines. Tracy lashed out at her, 'For crissake, Joan, can't you read the lines? I thought you were supposed to be a pro.' The wounded Crawford fled in tears, and the affair was over.

Now Joan centred her efforts on adopting a child. Despite her status as a single parent, in 1939 she began adoption proceedings for a baby girl she named Joan Crawford Jr. Months later, Joan changed the child's name to Christina. But having a child around did not fill the void. Lonely and love-starved, the 36-year-old actress married handsome, muscular, 6 foot 1 inch supporting actor Phillip Terry in 1942. She had known Terry, who was three years her junior, only six weeks and, by her own admission, she never loved him. Their marriage became so mechanical that the daily schedule Joan drew up for herself, and issued to staff members, always included a specific time allotted for sex –

usually an hour and a half in the late afternoon earmarked as 'time with Phillip'. During this period, she adopted a second child – a boy – and named him Phillip Terry Jr. Following Joan's 1946 divorce from Terry, the boy was re-named Christopher Crawford.

With another failed marriage behind her, Joan made her children the focal point of her frustration. Stories of extreme child abuse were well known to horrified journalists, but anyone who dared to publish them could count on his or her career being smashed by MGM's publicity department. The rumours didn't prevent her adoption of infants Cathy and Cynthia in 1947. Joan always referred to the girls as being twins even though they came from different families, were born a month apart, and in no way looked alike.

Joan's behaviour became increasingly eccentric and unpredictable. She started drinking heavily and often greeted her dates wearing little more than lingerie. She went out with numerous men, including young actors like Rock Hudson and George Nader, and was named as the other woman in two divorce suits. But, even though her emotional life was a mess, she continued to keep her body in excellent condition. Before her filming of *Torch Song*, the 50-year-old actress appeared at director Charles Walters's home wearing nothing but a housecoat. Flinging open the coat, she told him. 'I think you should see what you have to work with.' Walters was impressed.

Joan's final marriage took place in May 1955. Her fourth husband, Alfred Steele, was the dynamic president of Pepsi-Cola. Until he died of a heart attack in 1959, they circled the globe together promoting Pepsi. Despite her happiness in the role of corporate wife, Joan's feelings for Steele have often been called into question. Soon Joan described her 54-year-old bespectacled husband as being too fat and hard of hearing. Yet it appears that, for the first time, she really felt loved. Towards the end of her life, she confided to interviewer Roy Newquist in *Conversations with Joan Crawford*, 'A pillow is a lousy substitute for someone who really cares. And when it comes right down to it, aside from Alfred and the twins, I don't think I came across anyone who really cared.'

After achieving stardom, Crawford refused to go in front of the film cameras during her period, complaining that she didn't photograph well then. There was a time, however, when whe was willing to go to any extreme to appear on the screen. During her peak in popularity, stories began surfacing that, years before, while still known as Lucille LeSueur, Joan Crawford had made a series of sex films bearing such exploitative titles as *Velvet Lips* and *The Casting Couch*. Joan allegedly spent $100,000 buying up every copy of these films in order to destroy them. She learned later that one collector still harboured some prints, and shortly afterwards a mysterious fire swept through his home, burning to a crisp not only the sex films but the sleeping collector. Years afterwards, rumour had it that a complete set of Crawford's sex films had turned up in the private collection of a Prague munitions king.

A.K. (Lists 17, 42, 44)

♣ James Dean
8 February 1931 to 30 September 1955

Few film actors, in life or death, have been worshipped the way James Dean was after he died at the age of 24. He had major roles in only three films: *East of Eden*, *Rebel Without A Cause* and *Giant*. Humphrey Bogart said of him, 'Dean died at just the right time. He left behind a legend. If he had lived, he'd never have been able to live up to his publicity.' Andy Warhol called him 'the damaged but beautiful soul of our time'. And an entire generation of teenagers saw themselves in Dean as they had seen themselves in no other star. One publicist summed it up when he said, 'I though Dean was a legend, but I was wrong. . . . He's a religion.'

Dean's happy, healthy childhood in Fairmont, Indiana, and in Los Angeles, was marred when his mother died of cancer. He was 9 years old, and his father sent him back to Indiana, where he was raised on a farm by a kindly aunt and uncle. Despite his blond, boyish good looks, the sex-symbol-to-be was small, near-sighted, and spoke haltingly. Later, when he embarked on an acting career, he bounced back and forth between New York and Hollywood. Dean's personality was so intense that he made an indelible, and sometimes unfavourable, impression on almost everyone he met. He see-sawed wildly from clowning and joking to morbid, sullen depressions. Jimmy threw his energy into one activity after another. He studied dance, played the bongos, learned to sculpt, wrote poetry, dabbled in art, read constantly, and won trophies racing sports cars. When he turned this energy on his greatest passion, acting, the results were remarkable.

But it was Dean's death that was truly exceptional. On 30 September 1955, he was driving his $7000, silver, aluminium-bodied Porsche 550 Spyder to a race in Salinas, California. At 5.45 p.m., he died in a collision with a car driven by Donald Turnupseed. The end of Dean's life was only the beginning of a rabid death cult. It was bigger than Valentino's and bigger than Marilyn Monroe's. Teenagers paid 50c. to sit behind the wheel of the crushed Spyder. They bought chewing-gum wrappers supposedly peeled from gum chewed by Dean. In the three years following his death, the studio received more mail addressed to him than to any living star – hundreds of thousands of fans writing to him as if he were still alive. A magazine offering Dean's words 'from the other side' sold 500,000 copies. Dean's death mask was displayed in Princeton University along with Beethoven's.

The great debate over Jimmy Dean's sex life is whether he was gay, straight or bisexual. Actually, though he dabbled with both women and men, he was somewhat ambivalent sexually. One friend went so far as to say that he didn't think Dean enjoyed sex – that he only wanted to be mothered. Another said that he was basically asexual in his needs and drives – acting and car racing came first. The crushing loss of his mother seems to have infused him with a kind of little-boy quality that both women and men found very attractive. His favourite seduction technique, which he claimed never failed him, was to curl up with his head in a woman's lap and let her cuddle him. 'All women want to mother you. Give them a chance to and before you know it you're home free.' He discovered by the time he was 21 that he scored most successfully with older women. Sometimes he would date a girl for sex alone, and just as often he would date a girl repeatedly without ever making advances. As with every other aspect of his life, he was capable of yo-yo emotions and behaviour. When he was courting a girl, he would take her on a hair-raising motorcyle ride as a kind of initiation rite. He often went on such rides with his very close friend Eartha Kitt, who called him 'Jamie'. As with Kitt, he enjoyed an intimate, but platonic, relationship with singer Judy Collins. Naturally, as the god of a death cult that fed on hysterical teenage worship, he inspired some weird rumours about his sex practices. The rumour that he was a masochist who enjoyed being burned with cigarettes, and was dubbed the 'Human Ashtray', is completely false. Also, the fabled pornographic photos of a young man – allegedly Jimmy – sitting nude in a tree with a huge erection show no evidence of really being Dean. The rumours of his bisexuality, although greatly exaggerated, do have a basis. He probably did a bit of hustling in his early Hollywood days, when practically starving, calling his gay dates 'free meal tickets'. For a time, he was 'kept' by Rogers Brackett, a Hollywood ex-producer – but this was probably the only real affair he had with a man. Mostly what he did with men he did dispassionately – for the experience, for the money, or for the connections, until he found out the latter didn't work. He told a friend, 'I've had my cock sucked by five of the big names in Hollywood, and I think it's pretty funny because I wanted more than anything to get some *little* part, something to *do*, and they'd invite me for fancy dinners. . . .' When asked if he was gay, he replied, 'Well, I'm certainly not going through life with one hand tied behind my back.'

His first major love affair was with Elizabeth 'Dizzy' Sheridan, with whom he lived happily for a while in New York. Their relationship was a close and private one, and Dizzy remembers Jimmy as 'gentle'. Eventually they drifted apart, and he began what was to be a long-term love affair with the thin, highly-strung young actress, Barbara Glenn, whom he affectionately called 'my neurotic little shit'. After he moved to California, Barbara finally told him she was marrying someone else. He took the news badly.

The great love of Dean's life was petite, demure Italian actress Pier Angeli. The main impediment to their union was Pier's mother, who disapproved because of Jimmy's delinquent image, and because he wasn't a Catholic. To please Pier, Jimmy got regular haircuts, wore suits occasionally, and even considered becoming a Catholic. Pier and Jimmy discussed marriage, and quarrelled about it. When an interviewer asked him whether 'wedding bells would be heard,' he replied, 'You mean with Miss Pizza? Look, I'm just too neurotic.' Dean finally did ask her to marry him in New York, where he was going for a television show. Pier said it would break her mother's heart if they eloped. So she stayed behind and, while Dean was away, she announced her engagement to singer Vic Damone. It broke Jimmy's heart. Dean told a friend that he had beaten Pier up a few nights before her wedding, and there is a persistent story that he sat outside the church on his motorcycle during the ceremony, revving it up. Some time later, Pier visited Jimmy, to tell him she was going to have a baby. He cried after she left, and two days later he was dead. Pier Angeli's marriage to Damone was a flop, as was her second marriage, and her life ended after a drug overdose. She never got over Jimmy's magic, likening the two of them to Romeo and Juliet, and saying he was the only man she had ever loved. She said in an interview, 'I never loved either of my husbands the way I loved Jimmy,' admitting that when she lay in bed next to them she wished they were Dean.

Dean's last important romance was with the 19-year-old Ursula Andress, who had just been imported to America from Switzerland and was being billed as the 'female Marlon Brando'. At first she said, 'He nice but only boy.' As their relationship developed, Dean discovered that she was one of the few girls who wouldn't put up with his shenanigans. Dean even studied German 'so Ursula and I can fight better'. When she finally got fed up with his moods and left him, he was shocked.

A.W. (Lists 14, 15, 42, 46)

♣ Claude-Achille Debussy
22 August 1862 to 25 March 1918

Debussy was both intensely brilliant and emotional. While he gratified his whims when it came to women and expensive baubles, he could never quite enjoy happiness. Debussy was born in Saint-Germain-en-Laye, France, to a poor china-shop owner. He entered the Paris Conservatory of Music at 10 and studied there for eleven years. In 1884, his cantata *L'Enfant Prodigue* won him the coveted Grand Prix de Rome, which gave musicians three undisturbed years to work at the Villa Medici in Rome.

Debussy's country upbringing and uninterested attitude made him unpopular with his teachers and fellow musicians, so he made his few friends among the progressive painters and poets of his time. He never had money, never went to see a single performance of his own opera, and rejected the moderate degree of fame he received in his fifties (he hated to be called a professional musician). After he had endured several years of treatment and private suffering, cancer of the rectum killed him at 55.

Many women succumbed to Claude Debussy's genius and dark, brooding character; two wives and a mistress loved him deeply; two of his scorned women shot themselves. While studying at the conservatoire, 17-year-old Debussy took a summer job as music teacher to the children of Russian millionairess

113

Nadezhda von Meck, also Tchaikovsky's patroness. In his third summer with her, Debussy asked Madame von Meck for permission to marry her daughter and heiress, Sonia. Madame von Meck pointed out that he was obviously an unsuitable prospect for an heiress and dismissed him summarily. In disgrace, Debussy returned to Paris. Sex was not to be denied him however. His next job was as accompanist for an amateur singer whose husband could only suspect what was being taught in the private room provided for their rehearsals. While working for Madame Vasnier, Debussy won the Grand Prix de Rome but delayed moving to the Villa Medici for seven months. Vasnier, suspecting the affair between his wife and the 21-year-old musician, persuaded Debussy that the opportunity was too great to pass up. Debussy hated the Villa Medici and left after only two years. But, when he returned to Paris, his affair was quietly and amicably relegated to the past.

For the next two years Debussy had no fixed address – until he moved in with a pretty young blonde named Gabrielle Dupont, who worked at odd jobs to support him for the ten years they were together. Although Debussy was constantly unfaithful to 'Gaby', she stayed with him even while he was engaged to singer Thérèse Roger. That engagement was abruptly terminated when Thérèse and Debussy were performing in Brussels and she apparently learned of a one-night stand he had enjoyed there. Gaby's patience was remarkable, but it had its limits. Her affair with Debussy finally ended soon after an argument caused by a compromising note found in his coat pocket. Gaby shot herself, though not fatally. After her release from the hospital, she lived with Debussy for several more months, and he behaved as if the whole scene had never happened. Gaby became friendly with Rosalie 'Lily' Texier, a young, simple, dark-haired beauty, who was a dressmaker in a small Paris shop. She and Gaby often met in the coffee-houses, their friendship marred only by the way Gaby's composer lover mocked Lily's way of talking. But his ridicule soon turned to flattery, and Gaby was supplanted. Debussy and Lily were married in October 1899. They started married life without a sou, Debussy giving a piano lesson on their wedding day to pay for their breakfast.

Lily was absolutely devoted to Debussy, but youth, devotion and beauty were not enough. After four years of marriage, Debussy began seeing Emma Bardac, an amateur singer and the wife of a wealthy banker. On 14 July 1904, the composer went out for his morning walk and did not return. Weeks later, Lily heard from friends that Emma had deserted her husband for Debussy. On 13 October, Lily could stand it no longer and shot herself twice, once in the groin and once in the breast. She was found by Debussy, who had come home because she had sent him a suicide note. Lily recovered from her wounds but carried the bullet in her breast the rest of her life. Debussy was divorced from Lily on 2 August 1904, and Emma had his daughter in the autumn of 1905. When Emma's divorce was settled, in 1908, she and Debussy married. The marriage appeared to be happy, though some people unfairly accused Debussy of marrying for money. Emma was not young or beautiful, but was intelligent and cultured, and sustained Debussy as he aged and grew ill. He died in 1918 in Paris, while the city was under fire from German guns.

J.M. (List 8)

♣ Charles Dickens
7 February 1812 to 9 June 1870

One of Dickens's grandfathers was a domestic servant, the other an embezzler. His father, a clerk, made a good living, but was an extravagant spender who ended up in debtors' prison in 1824. Twelve-year-old Charles was forced to leave school and work in a factory. After working for some years as a newspaper reporter, Dickens began his first comic serial, *Pickwick Papers*, in 1836. Within months, he had become the most popular writer in England. For the next thirty years, a stream of enormously successful stories brought him popularity among rich and poor alike. Dickens was a witty conversationalist, always the centre of attention. In later life, he discovered it was more enjoyable, as well as more profitable, to give public readings of his works than write new ones. Dickens was a fantastic performer: his audiences invariably left the theatre in a state of emotional exhaustion. The intensity that he brought to these performances, which numbered over 470, is thought to have contributed to his early death at 58.

What we know of Charles Dickens's love life is coloured by the fact that, while letters written *by* him are well preserved (there are over 10,000, in fact), letters written *to* him are almost nonexistent. Acutely aware of his reputation as a symbol of wholesome family life, Dickens made an annual bonfire and burned private letters which he had received. When 17, he fell deeply in

115

love with Maria Beadnell, a flirtatious 18-year-old. Maria toyed with him capriciously until, after four years of agony, Dickens – his pride wounded – finally gave up the courtship. His experience of rejection was so strong that he learned to suppress emotion and many years later wrote that he was still 'chary of showing my affections, even to my children, except when they are very young'. Not surprisingly, when Dickens chose a woman to be his wife, he approached the relationship in a different manner. Dickens made it clear from the beginning that he expected the quiet Kate Hogarth to bear children and do what she was told. Ten children later, Kate was much fatter and submitted totally to his will. As the years went by, Dickens not only lost his affection for his wife, but came to resent and detest her. He engaged in numerous flirtations, usually with teenage girls, whom he found to be the essence of innocent perfection.

In fact, the most important woman in Charles Dickens's love life was not his wife, Kate, but her younger sister, Mary. When Charles and Kate married in 1836, 16-year-old Mary came to live with them. The three got along remarkably well. Mary was not as pretty as Kate, but she had a greater appreciation of literature, and Dickens enjoyed her companionship. Then, one Saturday night in May 1837, Kate, Mary and Charles returned from the theatre and bade one another good night. Then Charles heard a strangled cry from Mary's bedroom. Mary had had a heart attack. The next day she died peacefully in Dickens's arms at the age of 17. He removed a ring from her finger, put it on his own, and wore it for the rest of his life. For months he dreamed about Mary nightly. He saved her clothes, wished to be buried in her grave, and – a very rare occurrence – was unable to write for two months. No woman was able to compare in Dickens's mind and heart with Mary Hogarth. It was impossible to compete with the memory of someone frozen in time as a virginal, uncorrupted teenager.

However, if anyone had the potential to excite similar feelings in Dickens and to relieve him of the boredom of his marriage, it was his first love, Maria Beadnell, whose handwriting he recognized on a letter in 1855. Over twenty years after their youthful romance, she wrote to him. She was now Maria Winter, married with two daughters. Although she wrote that she was 'toothless, fat, old and ugly', Dickens's heart went immediately back to 1830. Once again, he wrote her passionate and suggestive letters and arranged for them to meet – alone. When the rendezvous finally took place, Dickens's wild fantasies plummeted earthwards. Maria had become fat and silly and bore a greater resemblance to his wife than to the Maria Beadnell of his youth. As soon as he saw her, Dickens began the irritating process of terminating their relationship.

Although Dickens spent much time in the company of many women, it is probable that he had only one sexual affair. Two years after the Maria Winter debacle, the 45-year-old Dickens met Ellen Ternan, an 18-year-old actress – the same age as his eldest daughter. Ellen was bright and intelligent. Kate became jealous of the time her husband spent with young 'Nelly', as Ellen was known. Less than a year later, a shocked public read Dickens's announcement of his separation from his wife of twenty-two years. Ironically, the separation announcement set off rumours that Dickens was having an affair – not with Ellen Ternan, but with another of Kate's sisters, Georgina Hogarth. She had moved into the Dickens household in 1842 when 15, and over the years she had supplanted her sister as head of the household, even taking over the responsibility of raising the children. Perhaps Georgina and Dickens did make love at some point, but there is no evidence to support this. Not only was Georgina not jealous of Ellen Ternan, but she had a genuine fondness for her.

During the last years of his life, Dickens spent much of his free time with Ellen and her family and supported them financially. It has been said that Dickens and Ellen had a child who died in infancy, but this is unproven. He did mention Ellen first in his will.

D.W. (List 25)

🍀 Emily Dickinson
10 December 1830 to 15 May 1886

Emily Dickinson grew up in high-minded gentility in the remote college town of Amherst, Massachusetts. Her father, whom she adored, was treasurer of Amherst College, a lawyer and a US congressman; her mother was nervous, sickly, and retiring. The Dickinsons were a closely knit family, remaining intact until Emily's parents died. Neither Emily nor her sister Lavinia married; when their brother Austin did, he simply moved next door.

Emily was plain and shy – 'small, like the wren,' – with little to distinguish her except her 'bold' red hair and 'eyes like the sherry

117

in the glass', as she wrote to Thomas Wentworth Higginson. When she returned home after a year at Mount Holyoke Female Seminary, she apparently enjoyed the customary dancing parties and the attentions of young beaux for a time. Gradually, however – amid rumours of thwarted love – she became a recluse, and wrote her own poems, which she bound into precious hand-sewn booklets. In 1862, she first sought the advice of Thomas Wentworth Higginson, a prominent literary figure who was to become her 'preceptor'. He continuously advised against publication.

During the last twenty years of her life, Emily scarcely left her childhood home. She began to dress exclusively in white and distilled her intense inner life into short poems which read like telegrams sent by the mind's eye. After her death from Bright's disease, her family found some 1800 poems and a wealth of correspondence. Published posthumously, her work included love poems and love letters from the 30-year-old poet to an anonymous 'master'. A mystery of the first order, the identity of this person has given rise to volumes of biographical, literary, even psychoanalytic detective work.

Whoever the 'master' was, it is known that, at the age of 48, Emily enjoyed a 'December romance' with 64-year-old Otis Lord, a distinguished jurist and lifelong friend of the family whose wife had just died. One biographer has even constructed a convincing case for Lord's being the elusive 'master', speculating that a secret passion may have blossomed fourteen years earlier when Emily was undergoing medical treatment in Cambridge and the judge was holding court nearby. The two never married – perhaps because their love was frowned upon by both families, or possibly because they had become too set in their separate ways. But Emily was in any case probably incapable of consummating her sexual passion, according to one psychoanalytic biographer. Suffering from an unresolved Oedipal conflict, an abnormally prolonged period of 'sexual latency', and an uncertain self-image as a woman due to her estrangement from her mother, she is said to have compensated by working out elaborate love fantasies in her writings. Finally, it has even been argued that Emily's 'master' was really a 'mistress'. Citing her ardent correspondence with her female friends and the occasional use of feminine pronouns and bisexual symbolism in her love poetry, proponents of this view hold that Emily was a lesbian and that her life was ruined by the restrictions of a heterosexual society.

C.D. (List 29)

118

♣ Walt Disney
5 December 1901 to 15 December 1966

Walter Elias Disney, in partnership with his brother Roy, produced hundreds of films, both short and feature-length, and created such characters as Mickey Mouse and Donald Duck. In 1955, Disneyland was opened, a huge amusement park near Los Angeles which became one of America's top tourist attractions.

In the early days of their career, Walt and Roy shared a one-room apartment in California. Living this close together, they frequently became irritated with one another. When they had a fight over Roy's cooking, Roy decided to send for his girlfriend and get married. The maid of honour at the wedding was Lillian Bounds, an ink-and-paint girl at the Disneys' studio. One evening when Walt gave Lillian a lift home from work, he said, 'I'm going to buy a new suit. When I get it, would it be all right if I called on you?' Lillian said it would be and Walt soon visited her in a grey-green, double-breasted suit. They began to meet regularly. Walt had always said he would never marry until he reached 25 and had $10,000 in the bank. But he didn't keep his word. The pair married in 1925, in Lillian's uncle's living room. Their first daughter, Diane Marie, was born in 1933, and a second daughter, Sharon Mae, followed in 1936. Walt's greatest pleasures were work, his family, and polo – he always preferred family life to socializing. Walt said, 'Let's face it – love is like everything else; if you don't have it, you can't give it'.

A.W. and J.H.

♣ Benjamin Disraeli
21 December 1804 to 19 April 1881

Disraeli twice became Queen Victoria's prime minister (1868 and 1874–80) and his policies eventually led to the founding of the present-day British Conservative party.

The youthful Disraeli, heavily in debt after stock-market losses and a disastrous publishing venture, became a writer out of sheer desperation. To call attention to his literary efforts, he set his black hair in ringlets and frequented the London salons of the 1830s in green velvet trousers, an embroidered, canary-yellow waistcoat, silver-buckled black shoes, and white wrist lace. Master of flattery and the witty, foppish reply, Disraeli entered the political arena in 1832. His unsavoury reputation – for extra-vagance and sexual encounters – caused four successive defeats before he finally sat in the House of Commons in 1837. During the next decade, Disraeli used his literary talent to promote his political, social and religious convictions. As his political career progressed, he abandoned his 'peacock' style of dress in favour of a dark suit, conservatively cut. Indispensable as a leader, yet distrusted by his colleagues, Disraeli was called both a man of genius and a self-serving opportunist during his long tenure in Parliament.

Disraeli's modus operandi was simple and direct: 'Talk to women as much as you can. . . . This is the way to gain fluency, because you need not care what you say, and had better not be sensible.' At 21, he had used the ploy to launch his novel *Vivian Grey* while having an affair with Mrs Sarah Austen, wife of a family friend. His bare-faced flattery so charmed the impression-able lady that she not only fell madly in love with the callow youth but also persuaded her gullible husband to loan the young Jew-turned-Christian large sums of money. To keep the author's identity secret (the novel's characters were thinly disguised and unflattering portraits of prominent society figures), Mrs Austen laboriously transcribed Disraeli's entire manuscript in her own distinctive handwriting before persuading a prominent publisher to buy it.

Seeking an *entrée* into London's drawing rooms in 1832, Dis-raeli used his mistress, Mrs Clara Bolton, a vivacious, party-giving doctor's wife with impressive literary and political con-nections. Within the year, he had exchanged her for the over-sexed and dazzling Lady Henrietta Sykes, a mother of four who fluttered obediently into his reach. Their passionate affair con-tinued for the next four years, aided conveniently by Henrietta's husband, Sir Francis, whose out-of-town grouse shooting was combined with an eye for a pretty ankle. Henrietta's initial wor-ries were forever banished when she caught her husband dallying with her lover's former mistress, Clara. A triumphant Henrietta secured Sir Francis's promise that their extramarital couplings would be mutually ignored. Disraeli moved in with Lady Sykes at her London residence, but her incessant sexual demands began to ruin his health. According to contemporary rumour, Disraeli struck a unique pact with Lord Lyndhurst, notorious womanizer and then leader of the Tory party. Lyndhurst – who fervently believed in platonic relationships 'after, but not before' sexual intercourse – was supposedly eager to take on the willing Henrietta and in return sponsored Disraeli's political career.

In 1839, Disraeli married Mary Anne Lewis, a wealthy widow twelve years older than he. His year-long courtship nearly ended in disaster when he demanded she become his wife. Indignant, she threw him out, but the resourceful suitor spent the night composing a masterly 1472-word plea for reconsideration. Tearfully, Mary Anne changed her mind, even though his letter candidly admitted that originally he had been solely interested in her money and devoid of all 'romantic feelings'. Surprisingly, their marriage became one of history's greatest love matches, lasting over thirty-three years. As Mrs Disraeli, she kept all of London in a continuous state of shock with her titillating double-entendres, while wearing outrageous costumes that defied the current fashion. But, even as she played the role of a flirtatious featherbrain, Mary Anne shrewdly kept her husband constantly in the public eye – an accomplishment which greatly helped Disraeli remain in office. She paid his enormous debts, cut his hair and mothered him through endless crises. Dying from stomach cancer (both thought they were concealing the fact from each other), she gave her beloved 'Dizzy' written permission to seek another mate after she was gone.

In 1873, a year after Mary Anne's death, Disraeli began his last affair, a bizarre romance with Lady Bradford. He chased her ardently for years, scribbling passionate notes daily while listening absentmindedly to boring speeches in Parliament. His cause was hopeless from the beginning: Lady Bradford was happily married, and a grandmother. In desperation, believing forlornly that the status of brother-in-law might allow closer contact with her, he even proposed formally to her 71-year-old sister, Lady Chesterfield. Tactfully, she turned him down.

His most famous witticism was when William Gladstone commented that Disraeli would '. . . probably die by the hangman's noose or a vile disease.' Disraeli replied, 'Sir, that depends upon whether I embrace your principles or your mistress.'

W.K.

121

♣ Father Divine

1877 to 10 September 1965

Although Father Divine, founder of the Peace Mission cult, carefully blurred the events of his early life, he was born George Baker, son – appropriately – of Joseph and Mary, Georgia share-croppers. This semi-official version conflicts with his own later account that he had been 'combusted' one day in 1900 on the corner of Seventh Avenue and 134th Street in Harlem. After serving his gospel apprenticeship in Baltimore, he returned to Georgia to promote himself as a 'Live Ever, Die Never' black evangelist, but intolerant officials arrested him as a public nuisance, booked him as 'John Doe, alias God' (he was already insisting on his divinity), and suggested he leave the state. With the statutory dozen disciples, he made his way to New York and set up on West 40th Street the first of many communal living arrangements, or 'heavens' as they came to be known. He found jobs for his little band and accepted their wages in return. Four years later, he moved them, now twenty-strong, to a house in Long Island. There his movement grew rapidly, especially after 1931 when his godly powers were 'proved' by the death (from a heart attack) of a local judge who four days before had sentenced Divine to six months in jail for disturbing the peace. During the Depression, thousands became 'angels'. Angelic requirements were: abstention from smoking, drinking, swearing, movies, cosmetics and sex; depositing all wages in the communal coffers; and a willingness to adore Father properly. In various heavenly annexes opened in Harlem, thousands feasted daily on fried chicken banquets that were absolutely free. In subsequent years, rural farms and urban hotels were acquired, all of which Divine visited regularly, descending from a chauffeur-driven Rolls-Royce or a Cadillac, although he claimed to own nothing himself and paid no income tax. When he died at Woodmont, his thirty-two-room chateau on Philadelphia's Main Line, aged almost 90, he was to his followers across the country truly 'God'.

The realistic Father Divine early accepted the fact that he was not the average woman's idea of a lover. Barely 5 feet tall, squat, bald, he suggested at best a dark-complexioned cupid. He was attracted to tall women; his two wives – Sister Peninah, later known as Mother Divine, who was black, and Edna Rose Ritchings, 'Sweet Angel', not only white but golden blonde as well – were considerably taller than he. Both were, however, wives in name only; the cult demanded unswerving celibacy from all. Men slept on one side of heaven, women on the other, and sex was strictly forbidden. The question was whether the Father applied the ban to himself – more than one angry and grudge-bearing deserter from the flock declared otherwise. Tales of seduction regularly surfaced. In 1937, 'Faithful Mary' broadcast an account of orgies in which young female converts ('Rosebuds', as they were known) were deflowered to such whispered phrases as 'Your body belongs to God' or 'Mary wasn't a virgin'. 'Faithful Mary' later retracted her statement, so the truth of such charges remains doubtful. More than one district attorney assigned a female undercover agent to pose as a new disciple and obtain conclusive evidence of immorality in the heavens, but none of these attempts was successful. Family court judges regularly branded the Father a 'homebreaker', but that was because of his habit of welcoming to his fold every unhappy wife who abandoned married life for the nearest heaven.

Why did Father Divine insist that married couples, too, abstain from sex? First, because he was determined to achieve racial equality and real integration in the Peace Mission. He was well aware that, in the twenties, thirties and forties, the slightest hint of inter-racial sexual impropriety would be disastrous: every heaven would have to close down. Better forbid sex entirely than risk that. True, his own second wife was white, but he had made it clear that 'Sweet Angel', who was 21 when he married her in his late 60s, was and would remain his 'spotless virgin bride', and apparently she did. Besides she was, he said, the reincarnated spirit of his first wife, Mother Divine. The notion of 'spotless virginity' fascinated the Father. His twenty-six secretaries – thirteen black, thirteen white, mostly young – were known as 'Father's Sweets', and were all supposedly virgins. He had been known to 'restore virginity' to a particularly attractive young convert with good typing and shorthand skills who otherwise would have been barred by an unfortunate indiscretion in her past. The second reason for the sex ban was simply Father Divine's own basic need to be father–husband–lover–God. Female angels, in particular, denied the release formerly provided by sex, tended to form passionate emotional attachments to him. A physical expression of that emotion, known as 'vibrating' and resembling an extraordinarily sensual ballet, was an approved sex substitute for those who required it. It allowed for a sublime spiritual climax, and sometimes orgasm. Father Divine would watch complacently.

N.C.S. (Lists 17, 32, 29)

♣ Fëdor Dostoevski

11 November 1821 to 9 February 1881

Short, frail and awkward, Dostoevski had such a strong tendency towards nervousness that his face and lips twitched in social situations. Nervous attacks in his teens developed into epilepsy in his twenties, and during one attack he damaged his right eye, causing it to become permanently distended and giving his eyes an asymmetrical appearance. In every way a passionate man, when Dostoevski became excited he worked himself up into a frenzy, gesticulated wildly and, some say, foamed at the mouth. Personal events intensified Dostoevski's preoccupation with sorrow and crime. When he was 13 his mother died of consumption, and five years later his drunken, miserly and lecherous father was killed by his serfs in an act of retribution. Soon afterwards, Dostoevski abandoned his career as a military engineer to become a writer, and at 25 his first novel, *Poor Folk*, was well received. Yet, a few years later, he was charged with revolutionary conspiracy for his involvement with a socialist circle, and placed before a firing squad. The death sentence was commuted at the last minute, and he was exiled to Siberia instead. It was ten years before he could return to St Petersburg (now Leningrad) and resume writing, and another seven years before he began producing his major works. Despite fragile health and a life fraught with tragedy, failed love affairs, and poverty, Dostoevski lived to be 59 and died a happily married man, having achieved creative and financial stability and recognition.

Called the 'Russian Marquis de Sade' by his contemporary Turgenev, Dostoevski did not have a major affair until he was 34, and did not find any semblance of sexual fulfilment until his mid-forties. His lack of romantic involvement in his twenties was probably due to a want of both self-confidence and opportunity; it is thought that he did sleep with prostitutes. After being transferred from hard labour to soldiering in Siberia, his sex life became more active. He dallied with several attractive young ladies before becoming involved with the pretty, soon-to-be-widowed Marya Isayeva, whom he later married. Dostoevski was as attracted by Marya's suffering (she was consumptive and her husband had been an alcoholic) as by her feminine virtues. He had a major epileptic fit on their honeymoon, which set the tone of their romantic life together – they were very unhappy and neither derived sexual satisfaction from the union. Marya died seven years later and Dostoevski continued an affair he had begun with Apollinariya Suslova. The proud, red-haired, fiery 'Polina' was an emancipated woman, twenty years his junior, with a formidable intellect and personality, but, after they had spent a year together, she merely teased Dostoevski, torturing him for several years before ending the affair. (Later it became evident that she was sadomasochistic and sexually cold.) The highly sexed Dostoevski began finding release in gambling, and his passion reached such a frenzy while travelling with Polina that he would pawn their valuables and beg his relatives for money. His gambling mania did not abate until his happy second marriage encouraged him to stop.

After Polina, Dostoevski was determined to marry a woman with whom he could establish some sort of domestic order and attempt to normalize, or at least stabilize, his sexual energies. Dostoevski was 45 when he married his 20-year-old stenographer, Anna Snitkina, who idolized him and wrote that she was 'prepared to spend the rest of my life on my knees to him'. Young and inexperienced, Anna found nothing strange in the extreme passion, and sometimes violence, of her husband's lovemaking, during which he could reach a blind frenzy similar to that he experienced in his epileptic fits, and after which he sometimes lay as rigid as a dead man. His erotic fantasies were highly diverse and sometimes involved corporal punishment, actual or simulated. Unfortunately, Anna obliterated the salacious details of Dostoevski's letters to her. However, by the time of their marriage, his penchant for violent and unusual forms of lovemaking was well known. The letters do show that Dostoevski enjoyed vast amounts of sexual pleasure with Anna, that a feverish physical longing would overcome him after a short separation, and that he continually had nightmares over the possibility that she was unfaithful. She never was. His passion was intensified by the awareness that his young, attractive wife found him sexually satisfying as well, and he often pleaded with her to speak more frankly on the subject. Dostoevski's love and lust for Anna not only did not abate but grew more intense during their fourteen years of marriage, and at 57 he was able to say that '[my] ecstasy and rapture are inexhaustible'.

Dostoevski was a foot fetishist. There is often mention in his letters to Anna of his longing for her feet: 'I go down on my knees before you and I kiss your dear feet a countless number of times. I imagine this every minute and I enjoy it. . . .' Anna had been a little diffident about the matter, and hence he insisted, 'I bear witness that I long to kiss every toe on your foot and you will see I shall achieve my purpose.' He was also obsessed with young girls. There was a rumour that Dostoevski had actually had sex with a little girl (presumably a child prostitute) when her governess brought the child to him in his bath. It is certainly true that in both his conversation and his novels the sexual fantasy of an older man who corrupts a young girl appears constantly; it was evidently much on his mind.

J.H. (Lists 11, 20, 25, 31, 36, 37, 47)

♣ William Douglas
16 December 1725 to 23 December 1810

'Old Q' was third Earl of March and fourth Duke of Queensberry. A gambler, sportsman and enthusiastic lecher, the duke was also a member of the notorious Friars of St Francis (or Hellfire Club), which scandalized a permissive England.

In some ways, William was an archetypal Scot: he saved his money, guarded his health, and never drank to excess. But Old Q did have his vices – gambling and fornicating. By 21, he had become an expert on horse racing, which he considered a science. In order to win a bet that a horse and carriage could travel 19 m.p.h., he designed a special vehicle of wood and whalebone, and fitted it out with silken harnesses. He once wagered that he could send a letter 50 miles in one hour, and won by having the message sewn inside a ball and hurled, man-to-man, cross-country. The duke frequently indulged himself with milk baths, in an era when any type of bath was a rarity. He ate slowly and took care to get enough sleep, a regimen he undertook to preserve his virility. His physician was paid for every day he kept the duke alive, with payment to cease upon his death. To everyone's satisfaction, the duke stayed virile, and the doctor stayed on the payroll, until the old man reluctantly died at age 85.

His amorous exploits and utter disregard for public opinion prompted William Wordsworth to call him 'degenerate Douglas', and Robert Burns also denounced Queensberry (when he had a forest on his own property cut down) as 'the worm that gnaw'd my bonnie trees'. Old Q was a lifelong bachelor who lived according to the precepts of the Hellfire Club: 'Do what you please.

Dare to despise convention.' Short, thin, and with a nose like a beak, the duke was not handsome, but managed to seduce women with single-minded attentiveness. It was said he could make a chambermaid feel like a duchess. Yet he never let the matrimonial hopes of high-born ladies interfere with his true mission in life – to bed as many young girls as possible. He preferred them slim, passionate, and about 15 years old. When possible, he liked them to be both virginal and clean but, being a realist, he knew these qualities were rare and didn't press the issue. However, in pursuing clean young girls, he beat the odds and managed to sidestep venereal disease. His hale and libidinous old age, free from syphilis, made him unique among the rakes of his time. Despite his scandalous reputation, Old Q might be considered positively wholesome compared to others in his circle. He was not a sadist like the Earl of Sandwich, nor a transvestite like the Chevalier d'Eon. He did not like public executions, young boys or experienced prostitutes, and Sir Francis Dashwood's Satanist orgies seemed to the duke an unduly complicated way of procuring sex partners. Like the later Queensberry – responsible for having Oscar Wilde jailed – Old Q had a conservative streak. Old Q was largely behind the prosecution of John Wilkes for his obscene *Essay on Woman*. Wilkes published this parody of Alexander Pope's *Essay on Man* for the private delight of the Hellfire Club members. But he lost his membership after he dressed a monkey up as Satan and set it loose during one of their Black Masses. Apparently the club members – not expecting to see the devil even though they had invoked his name – were scared out of their wits by the apparition. In revenge, Old Q and the Earl of Sandwich turned Wilkes in as the author of an 'obscene libel', and Wilkes was forced to flee the country for a time.

The duke's passion for nubile ballerinas and opera singers led him to patronize the arts. Teresina Tondino, a beautiful, dark-eyed Italian singer, fascinated the old paedophile with her baby talk and little-girl tantrums. When she left him, he consoled himself in the company of another Italian adolescent, Anna Zamparini, a singer and dancer. With his young mistresses, he would behave in both romantic and paternal fashion. He bought them expensive gifts and regularly professed his love, but was never faithful. The duke maintained a lifelong quest for the perfect female body. He held beauty contests in his boudoir. It is said that the closest he came to his ideal was the Countess Rena, who remained a friend even after their sexual relationship had ended.

He discovered he could gain access to the bedchamber of the Marchesa Fagniani, a former opera singer, by paying her husband's gambling debts. Whenever the marchesa showed reservations about the arrangement, the duke would take her husband gambling again and reaffirm the deal. After the marchesa gave birth to a baby girl, the child's paternity was disputed, since yet another party, the duke's friend George Selwyn, claimed to be the father.

At a ripe old age, he passed much of his time sitting on his balcony overlooking Piccadilly, ogling young girls. Eventually, his balcony became a popular symbol of sexual longevity. When his notorious lustful life finally ended, Old Q expired on a bed strewn with letters from over seventy female admirers.

M.S. (Lists 3, 26)

♣ Alexandre Dumas (*père*)
24 July 1802 to 5 December 1870

Dumas's paternal grandparents were a French nobleman and a black woman from Santo Domingo. His father, a general during the French Revolution, died when Alexandre was three years old, and from him he inherited vitality, fearlessness and great physical strength. Dumas's African ancestry was evident in his coarse hair and Creole accent; and a salon habitué who was crude enough to comment on the writer's heritage received the reply: 'My father was a mulatto, my grandmother was a negress, and my great-grandparents were monkeys. My pedigree begins where yours ends.'

Young Dumas received a scanty education from a priest in his home village of Villers-Cotterets near Soissons. At 20 he was employed in Paris as a clerk for the Duc d'Orléans, later King Louis Philippe. Dumas set up house with Catherine Labay, a dressmaker eight years his senior, who bore him a son in 1824. Alexandre Dumas *fils* was to become an author, like his father. In 1829, the elder Dumas scored his first great dramatic success and, by 1831, he was the darling of Paris and a Byronic hero in his own right. A lifelong pattern of mistresses, extravagance and superhuman work habits began to crystallize. Dumas was earning huge sums, but spent all he received. His estate, Monte-Cristo, was a carnival of starving artists, predatory actresses, playmates

128

of the moment and unclassified parasites. Dumas was a first-rate cook, an excellent hunter, and with age became a devoted father. He liked to boast that he had sired 500 illegitimate children, but the figure was somewhere closer to the three he acknowledged.

Dumas was a tireless satyr from the time he lost his virginity at 17 until his death at 68. His women described him as being like a 'force of nature'. Incapable of fidelity himself, he never demanded it of others, not even his wife. Once he caught her with his friend Roger de Beauvoir in her bedroom. It was a cold night and Dumas, although piqued, invited de Beauvoir to share their bed. At dawn, Dumas looked over the sleeping form of his wife and caught de Beauvoir's worried glance. 'Shall two old friends quarrel about a woman, even when she's a lawful wife?' Dumas asked, and shook de Beauvoir's hand.

In his later years, Dumas amused himself by presenting his many young lovers with ribald epigrams and obscene poems which he had written. When a lady was offended, he pointed out that 'all that comes from Daddy Dumas will fetch a good price some day'. A female visitor once surprised Dumas while he was 'at leisure'. The author's obese body was stuffed into crimson tights, while three naked girls cavorted around his chair. To Dumas's vast amusement, the woman turned and fled. However, the maestro found the infrequent visits of his disapproving son anything but a laughing matter, and he would run around the house frantically hiding women in closets whenever the younger Dumas was announced.

As time went on, father and son reached an understanding. How close they eventually became is illustrated by a conversation overheard by a group of mutual friends. 'You know, father,' said Dumas *fils*, 'it's a great bore, you always giving me your old mistresses to sleep with and your new boots to break in!' 'What are you complaining about?' his father replied. 'You should look on it as an honour. It proves you have a thick prick and a narrow foot.' Dumas did not believe in the sanctity of wedlock, and his one official marriage was the result of blackmail. Ida Ferrier – a small, rotund actress with whom the author was having an affair – got an accomplice to buy all Dumas's unpaid IOUs and gave him the choice of either marriage or debtors' prison. The Viscount of Chateaubriand, who was a witness at their wedding, is said to have stared at the sagging bosom of the bride and remarked to a guest, 'You see, my friend, everything I bless collapses.' The marriage itself collapsed about four years later, when Ida ran off

129

with an Italian nobleman. Dumas favoured actresses, and at one point three of his lovers found themselves in the awkward position of acting together in a Dumas play. However, Fanny Gordosa, a dark, passionate Italian, was more trying. Her first husband had become so overwhelmed by her enormous sexual appetite that he had forced her to wear wet towels around her middle in an effort to cool her off. Dumas unwrapped the lady, but found her habits of receiving visitors while perched on a chamber pot and chasing his other women out of the house intolerable. He finally sent Fanny away, pretending that he suspected her of 'playing duets' with her music teachers.

Dumas toured Garibaldi's Italy in the company of Emilie Cordier, whom he called the 'Admiral'. By day, he kept her dressed up as a sailor lad, thereby fooling nobody. The ruse proved impractical when Emilie became pregnant, and the 'Admiral' finally presented Dumas with a daughter, Micaella, whom he loved dearly. Much to his sorrow, Emilie refused to let Dumas acknowledge the child legally, and thus Micaella was deprived of her rightful share of her father's royalties when she came of age. The author had a brief affair with dancer Lola Montez, whose lurid stage performances shocked women, delighted men, and made Lola the reigning sex symbol of her day. She added Dumas to her string of famous lovers, spending only one or two nights with him, but doing it with unparallelled panache.

Even when Dumas was in his sixties, he remained a favourite subject of gossip. His final fling came with Adah Isaacs Menken, a Jewish girl from New Orleans, whom the world knew as the 'Naked Lady'. Adah's most famous stage role called for her to be bound, clad only in a sheer leotard, to the back of a galloping horse. Needless to say, she was everything Dumas asked for in a woman. Adah was an aspiring poet who boasted of her friendship with Bret Harte, Mark Twain and other authors. She cajoled Dumas into having his picture taken with her. The resultant photo, which shows vampish Adah draped all over the ageing Papa Dumas, circulated throughout Paris and went a long way towards destroying his waning prestige. It was his last great scandal. He died soon afterwards – unrepentant, but depressed by fears that his literary works were of no value.

It has been rumoured that Dumas died of the effects of advanced syphilis, contracted around the time of his affair with Lola Montez. Like many high-living men of his century, the author regarded the disease as an unfortunate adjunct to having a good time, a minor ailment that usually disappeared. According to one of his friends, Dumas 'continued his irregular mode of life until the very moment that disease paralysed both his brain and his limbs'. 'I need several mistresses', he had declared. 'If I had only one, she'd be dead inside eight days.'

M.S. (Lists 8, 11, 17, 18, 20, 21, 22, 25, 27, 31, 35, 39)

♣ Isadora Duncan
27 May 1878 to 14 September 1927

Isadora's unique dance-style was inspired by Greek and Italian art and based loosely upon the callisthenics system of François Delsarte, which coordinated voice with body gestures. In 1898, after her entire wardrobe was lost in New York City's disastrous Hotel Windsor fire, Isadora introduced an innovative twist at her next appearance – an improvised costume that left little to the imagination. One newspaper critic described it sarcastically as '...a species of surgical bandage of gauze and satin'. Undaunted, Isadora sailed for Europe where – in a diaphanous tunic of Liberty silk, adorned with colourful streamers – she became the barefoot dancing darling of the continent. Touring first with the Loie Fuller troupe, she was soon taken on by impresario Alexander Gross and booked for solo appearances in Budapest, Berlin, Vienna and other major capitals. A shocked but titillated audience arrived en masse to see the nearly nude nymph glide, pose and leap about the carpeted stage, to the accompaniment of, for example, *The Blue Danube* and Chopin's *Funeral March*.

A firm believer in free love, Isadora subsequently jolted her American fans by touring while obviously pregnant with her second child, although she had not bothered to marry the child's father. She remained the 'Pet of Society' for over two decades, but in a freak accident in 1913, her driverless car rolled backward down a slope, drowning her two children and their nurse in the muddy Seine. Professionally, as well as emotionally, Isadora never fully recovered. In 1922, her views on atheism and the Bolshevik Revolution brought further troubles. Coming to the USA from Moscow with her Russian husband, she infuriated Boston theatregoers by waving a red scarf at them from the stage. In Chicago, the tour earned the animosity of evangelist Billy Sunday. Playing upon the 'Red Menace' theme, he labelled her

'. . . that Bolshevik hussy who doesn't wear enough clothes to pad a crutch'. At Indianapolis, the mayor bluntly called Isadora a nude dancer whose appearance might earn a trip to jail by paddy wagon. Broke and disillusioned, Isadora returned to Europe. She eked out a twilight existence, shuttling between Paris and the Riviera, until a second freak car accident in 1927. Getting into a Bugatti, she tossed her trademark scarf about her throat, cheerily calling out, 'Farewell, my friends, I am going to glory!' The dangling scarf caught in the spokes of a rear wheel as the car started up, and her neck was instantly snapped.

Isadora kept her virginity until 25, but quickly made up for lost time. Her favours were dispensed initially to Oscar Beregi, a handsome Hungarian actor then appearing on the Budapest stage as Shakespeare's Romeo. Mutually smitten, they galloped off to the downy privacy of a peasant fourposter bed in the Danube countryside. The dark-eyed Magyar's all-day marathon left the dancer so exhausted that she admittedly limped around during her Urania Theatre recital that night. But the delighted Isadora rapidly booked Beregi again, especially after he promised that she '. . . finally would know what heaven was on earth'.

In December 1904, Isadora began a torrid liaison with theatrical designer Gordon Craig, the son of English actress Ellen Terry. This time, the nuptial bed was harder. For two wild weeks, the lovers copulated repeatedly on some old blankets spread over artificial rose petals strewn on the black, waxed floor of Craig's high-rise studio in Berlin. The non-stop orgy paused only for an occasional meal, ordered 'on credit' and delivered while 'Topsy' – Craig's name for Isadora – shivered outside on the narrow balcony. Her frantic manager had to cancel her shows while he searched police-station blotters, fearing abduction or worse. Eventually, he gave up and published a discreet newspaper notice which said, 'Fräulein Duncan has regrettably been taken seriously ill with tonsillitis.' Nine months later, the 'tonsillitis' was named Deirdre, Isadora's own contribution to the brood of six such 'free love' productions sired by Craig in his lifetime.

In 1906, Isadora became the mistress of Paris Singer, one of sewing-machine magnate Isaac Singer's twenty-three children. The playboy millionaire gave her seven years of luxury, along with her second love child, Patrick. The idyll ended with the drowning tragedy in 1913, and Isadora fled first to Italy, then France, where a willing sculptor fathered a third baby. The boy lived only an hour. At the close of the First World War, Isadora took on a new lover, pianist-composer Walter Rummel, her 'archangel'. He showed great talent, but an ageing and jealous Isadora called it quits in Greece when she suspected that his 'shining wings' were also being folded about a young dryad in her dance troupe.

In 1922, well past 40, she set aside her aversion to marriage long enough to become the wife of the Russian Revolution's poet laureate, Sergei Esenin, seventeen years her junior. The marriage was brief and disastrous. Esenin, half mad and alcoholic, left a trail of broken bottles and furniture on both sides of the Atlantic. His drunken antics in hotel corridors, and his distribution of her money and clothes to friends and relatives, proved too much for even the liberated Isadora. She coaxed him back to Moscow the next year and quietly went her own way.

W.K. (Lists 1, 11, 44)

♣ Amelia Earhart
b. 24 July 1898. Disappeared 2 July 1937

The Kansas-born Earhart, who led the way for women in aviation, is best remembered for her ill-fated attempt to fly around the world, following the path of the equator. She was 39 when she and her plane vanished near Howland Island in the central Pacific. Dubbed 'Lady Lindy' by the press because of her resemblance to Charles Lindbergh, she was tall with blue eyes, small breasts, and close-cropped hair. As a child, she had worn boys' gym suits and engaged in such unladylike pursuits as jumping over fences; as an adult, she delighted in wearing male flying gear. She charmed all with her characteristic grin, forthrightness and intelligence, but could also be stubborn and impulsive – traits that both made her success possible and probably cost her her life.

Earhart's first love was Samuel Chapman, a chemical engineer with a stern Yankee upbringing. He believed a wife should not work. But, famous after her successful Atlantic crossing in 1928, she broke off the engagement. It took courage, but in any case she had already met George Palmer Putnam, the son of the founder of a New York publishing house. Putnam had handled the publicity for her Atlantic voyage known as the *Friendship* flight and, afterwards, he became her personal adviser. He slowly insinuated himself into her life – eventually convincing her to write a book (which he would publish) about the flight. Though Putnam was married at first, for three years he pursued Amelia, proposing to her six times. Earhart still had reservations on their wedding day. On the morning of their marriage, Earhart made Putnam promise to 'let me go in a year if we find no happiness together'. Her declaration of independence also included, 'In our life together I shall not hold you to any medieval code of faithfulness to me, nor shall I consider myself bound to you similarly.'

Earhart retained her independence and her maiden name. Their marriage, which she described as a 'reasonable partnership', seems to have been only a natural extension of their business relationship and produced no children. Putnam offered the wealth and respectability to which she was accustomed, and she offered fame, which he could turn to commercial advantage. Earhart was 32; Putnam was 44 and thrice-divorced.

Amelia Earhart's record-breaking feats and promotion stunts kept her away from home. And 'Meely', as she was known to the boys around the hangar, liked to surround herself with dare-devil young men very different from her sedate husband. One of these young men was Paul Mantz, 31, a Hollywood stunt flier and the technical supervisor on her round-the-world flight. Another close friend was Fred Noonan, a tall, dark Irishman with a drink problem and enough adventures under his belt to satisfy Amelia's craving for excitement. Against the advice of her husband, who wanted her to fly solo for the publicity, she took Noonan along as navigator on her last adventure. Earhart's disappearance kindled many rumours about her love life. One story had Earhart in love with Noonan and living with him on an isolated Pacific island. Putnam repeatedly denied these rumours. Two years after she vanished, Putnam remarried.

S.L.W. (List 10)

❧ Mary Baker Eddy
16 July 1821 to 3 December 1910

Mary Morse Baker, founder of Christian Science, was the youngest of six children, whose father Mark was a pious, hard-working farmer. Mary was small, delicate and pretty, with wavy brown hair and blue eyes. A sickly child, she suffered from hysterical seizures and tantrums. As a result, she was treated by the family doctor with mesmerism and mental suggestion. Mary was a romantic child with a penchant for writing flowery verse; when adult, she fancied herself as an author.

In 1843, she married George Washington Glover, a building contractor, and they moved to Wilmington, North Carolina. There, after less than a year of marriage, Glover died of yellow fever and Mary, pregnant, was forced to move back to her father's home in New Hampshire. In 1844, she gave birth to her son, George Washington Glover II. Mary did not enjoy motherhood and, at the age of 6, George was sent off to Minnesota to live with foster parents. Mary did not see him again for twenty-three years. At home, Mary became a chronic invalid, having to be rocked to sleep in her father's arms. Her sister Abigail had a huge cradle constructed for her and neighbourhood boys often earned extra money by rocking Mary to sleep. In 1862, still suffering from extreme hysteria, Mary visited Phineas P. Quimby, a Maine faith-healer, and was at least temporarily cured. Much taken with Quimby's methods, she studied with him. When, in 1866, she fell on ice, and was again incapacitated, she was able to 'cure' herself by reading the bible. Her recovery eventually led to the development of her Christian Science Church. In 1875, she published *Science and Health* and, through the strength of her personality more than her book's merits, she gained adherents throughout New England. By the time of her death at 89, she had earned more than $400,000 in book royalties, and left behind a flourishing church.

Her first love, when she was 15, was Andrew Gault, a 21-year-old neighbour. Though Mary went so far as to write him her only love poem, Andrew married someone else. Her marriage to George Washington Glover ending tragically, she went into a mental and physical decline.

Nine years later, she married Dr Daniel Patterson, an itinerant dentist with a reputation as a philanderer. He was off on trips much of the time. Mary spent most of their married life as an invalid. Eventually Patterson left home for good in 1866, and Mary, deeply involved in her mental healing, took on several protégés including young Richard Kennedy, with whom she set up a profitable business. In 1873 she finally divorced Patterson on grounds of desertion, though later insisting it was because of adultery. Patterson sent Mary an allowance of $200 a year. In 1896, he died in a poorhouse.

In 1877, Mary married Asa Gilbert Eddy, a sewing-machine

salesman who became the first person to announce publicly that he was a Christian Scientist. On the marriage certificate, the 56-year-old Mrs Eddy gave her age as 40. A new husband seemed to aggravate Mary's various illnesses. She found Eddy increasingly irritating, but did not have to put up with him long. In 1882, Eddy died of organic heart disease.

But Mary was used to having a man nearby and, the same year as Eddy's death, a young machinist named Calvin Frye entered her life, serving as her steward, secretary, book-keeper and footman until her death. In 1888, she met Dr Ebenezer Johnson Foster, a homeopathic physician, and adopted him as her son. In her later years, all the men close to her seemed to have one thing in common: they were inferior to Mary and she could easily manipulate them. When she couldn't, she got rid of them by accusing them of being 'mesmerists'.

Mrs Eddy believed fervently in something she called 'Malicious Animal Magnetism' (MAM), which she thought her enemies were using to destroy her. (When her last husband, Gilbert, died, she insisted that the cause was arsenic poisoning at the hands of the 'mesmerists', by the use of MAM.) In order to protect herself, she created a select bodyguard of 'watchers' to ward off these attacks of mental mesmerism. As Mrs Eddy's stature grew she found it necessary to institute numerous lawsuits (all thrown out of court) against her enemies and their use of MAM. In fact, one of the reasons she took on Frye was his supposed efficacy as an 'anti-mesmerist'. Eventually, Mrs Eddy began to think herself infallible and became extremely autocratic. She preferred that her followers call her 'Mother', and she wrote about controlling the weather through mental processes. Continuing to suffer from bouts of hysteria, she took morphine to ease her physical pain. She advised complete celibacy as the only true spiritual state. Her last written words were, 'God is my life.'

C.H.S. (List 32)

🍀 Edward VII
9 November 1841 to 6 May 1910

The eldest son of Queen Victoria and Prince Consort Albert, 'Bertie', as Edward was called, had a bleak and lonely childhood. Hoping to turn him into a paragon of virtue, his parents separated him from other children. Victoria wanted her son to grow up as good as her 'beloved Albert', in spite of the fact that she believed that no one could be 'so great, so good, so faultless' as the prince consort. Bertie set about to prove that she was right. He completely rebelled against his parents' strict moral code, turned a deaf ear to his tutors' lectures on morality and ignored his father's memoranda on propriety. The pursuit of pleasure in all its forms became his life's goal. He was addicted to cigars before he turned 20. A man of gargantuan appetite, he ate several meals a day, sometimes consuming twelve courses in a sitting. He paid so much attention to clothes – he was a stickler for proper attire down to the last button – that even tea was a full-dress affair.

Bertie occupied himself with 'bachelor outings' (even after his marriage to Danish Princess Alexandra), which lasted several months of every year and consisted of visits to Paris, Bad Homburg and the Riviera, or hunting and shooting at his country estates. He was usually surrounded by his aristocratic friends of the 'Marlborough House set', forerunners of the modern jet set, who joined him for gambling parties or at the horse races at Ascot or Epsom. Bertie's own horses won the Derby three times. Because of Edward's life-style, Victoria would not allow him to assume any governmental responsibilities. He was merely the official host and tour guide for visiting dignitaries, and Victoria's stand-in at public ceremonies. When his 'eternal mother' finally died in 1901, he dropped the name Albert and was crowned Edward VII. He was 60 years old.

While serving with the British army in Ireland, 19-year-old Bertie lost his virginity when fellow officers smuggled actress Nellie Clifden into his bed. Albert passed away soon after hearing of his son's 'fall into sin'. It was decided that Bertie should marry immediately to remove him from further temptation. Victoria chose Princess Alexandra as her son's bride, and he accepted the selection. The beautiful princess and the stocky, handsome Prince of Wales were married in 1863. Alexandra bore five children over the next six years, and with marriage as a 'cover' Bertie played the field for over forty years. In spite of her husband's wanderings, Alix – as Alexandra was called by friends and family – always believed he loved her best and said that 'if he was a cowboy I should love him just the same'. In a sense he *was* a cowboy – he put his brand on women all across Europe. As prince and king, he took frequent trips to German spas, where he indulged himself with steam baths, colonic enemas and sex. French police recorded Edward's comings and goings from Parisian hotels and restaurants where he enjoyed the company of actresses, courtesans and noblewomen. At one Parisian dinner, a huge covered serving tray was set before the prince. When the lid was lifted, Bertie happily discovered he had been presented with the infamous and beautiful Cora Pearl, clad only in a sprig of parsley and a string of pearls. Giulia Barucci, who called herself the 'world's greatest whore', let her gown slide to the floor when she first met Bertie. He was pleased, but when her escort upbraided her she replied that she had only 'showed him the best I have – and for free'. He dallied with stage star Hortense Schneider, Moulin Rouge can-can dancer Louise Weber, known as 'La Goulue', actress Sarah Bernhardt and courtesan La Belle Otero.

Not all of the king's lovers were celebrities. He often cavorted at Le Chabanais, a Parisian brothel, where the chair upon which he sat with his lady of the evening became a conversation piece for the establishment's proprietor. It was said that King Edward, when he was a bit too rotund to enjoy the pleasures of the bed, would lounge in this chair and be fellated by a young woman. In spite of Bertie's tendency to stoutness, he was by all accounts very virile and had great sexual stamina. No woman ever gave him poor marks; he was a 'very perfect, gentle lover' said his mistress Daisy Brooke, Countess of Warwick. According to the Duke of Cambridge, Bertie had a special liking for young girls in his later years. Three young women he frolicked with became known as 'HRH's virgin band'. However, his favourites by far were married beauties. In general, their husbands were from his inner circle of friends and considered it their duty to be cuckolded by Bertie. His schedule usually consisted of visiting a woman's home in the afternoon while her husband was away, joining his regular mistress in the evening, and often meeting his latest actress friend later in the night. The Marlborough House set was usually sufficiently discreet, but the arrangement caused a nasty scandal at least once. When Lady Harriet Mordaunt had a child that was born blind, she believed that this was God's curse and confessed to her husband that she had 'done very wrong . . . with the Prince of Wales and others, often and in open day'. Bertie was forced to swear in court that he had not been her lover.

Bertie's lengthy affair with professional model Lillie Langtry cooled when scandal sheets started rumours that her husband was about to divorce her and name the Prince of Wales as correspondent. His five-year liaison with the 'Jersey Lily' began in 1877, and it was a very special one. She was independent, never subservient, and very different from Alix. Even Alix became fond of Lillie and spoke of her in glowing terms. The princess seldom became jealous of her husband's other women, knowing they posed no threat to her marriage, but she didn't take too kindly to an American actress named Miss Chamberlain, whom she disparaged as 'Miss Chamberpots'.

In the late 1880s, Bertie fell deeply in love with Daisy Brooke, the Countess of Warwick, a seductive beauty twenty years younger than he. Their relationship worried Alexandra more than any of her husband's other dalliances. Bertie and Daisy exchanged rings, and he addressed her as his 'little Daisy wife'. He became involved with her when her lover of the moment had had the nerve to make his own wife pregnant. Daisy was a volatile woman who couldn't stand such 'infidelity', but that didn't prevent her from taking the Prince of Wales into her own bed. Their affair lasted almost seven years, but he began to see less of her when, in spite of her wealth and privilege, she lectured him on the economic exploitation of the lower classes.

The king's last long-term mistress was Mrs Alice Keppel, who was his junior by thirty years. During Edward's twelve-year romance with her, both Mr Keppel and Alexandra fully accepted Mrs Keppel's role as second wife to Bertie. Mrs Keppel often called at Windsor Castle, where she became Alexandra's good friend, and Edward frequented the Keppel home and played with Keppel's two daughters. It was Alice Keppel whom Alexandra first notified when Bertie lay dying of bronchitis at 69. Bertie was, as Prime Minister Gladstone once wrote, 'kept in childhood beyond his time'.

R.J.F. and V.S. (Lists 17, 20, 22, 24, 25, 31, 38)

♣ Edward VIII

23 January 1894 to 28 May 1972

George V's eldest son, Edward (David to his friends) passed his youth preparing for kingship. But his childhood was not happy. His father, a strict disciplinarian, showed his children no affection. Edward preferred his mother, but their relationship was never close either and Queen Mary confessed to her intimates a distaste for raising children. Nor was Edward's youth auspicious. He completed his prescribed schooling, but did so lackadaisically. During the First World War he clamoured for a demanding military assignment, but his royal position made this impossible. After the war, however, Edward began to come into his own. Dispatched as an unofficial roving ambassador, Edward (as Prince of Wales) toured the globe and his unaffected bearing and abundant charm soon made him a universally popular figure. Even after his abdication, he retained his popularity, and his personal wealth (an estimated $15 million) allowed him to pursue a leisurely luxurious life as a resident of France, where he frequented the nightclubs upon which he doted and immersed himself in golf and gardening. A heavy smoker, he died of throat cancer in the arms of the woman he loved and for whom he had abdicated his throne. He was almost 78.

Edward's rank, wealth and charm guaranteed for the diminutive (5 foot 6 inch) and slender young man acclaim as the world's most eligible bachelor. He revelled in that role – and enjoyed the women it brought him. His affairs, or most of them, were brief. Only four women succeeded in engaging him in lengthy relationships. He met the first, Lady Coke, when he was 21. Although twelve years older and married, Lady Coke was deluged with Edward's love for three years. When in England, he strove always to be with her. When abroad, Edward's letters cascaded upon her home by the score. Whether Lady Coke reciprocated his ardour is unknown, but her marriage remained firmly intact throughout Edward's courtship.

Then Freda Ward came on the scene. Edward met Freda (who was married to a member of Parliament) in 1918 when an air raid drove the two strangers to seek shelter in a cellar. They conversed and, at the raid's end, Edward insisted that she join him at a party, where they danced for hours. That began their sixteen-year relationship during which Edward fell 'abjectly' in love, as friends put it, with the learned and witty Freda. He

140

underlined his devotion with telephone calls each morning and, whenever he was in London, they invariably met for the evening at 5.00 p.m. sharp. Occasional flings took Edward away from Frieda, but their relationship remained strong – and continued even after he met the beautiful Thelma Furness. The 24-year-old 'Toodles', Gloria Vanderbilt's twin sister, was married to Marmaduke, Lord Furness, a British shipping tycoon. Theirs was a marriage of convenience, destined to end in 1933 after seven years of mutual infidelity. Physical passion, not the intellectual conviviality he found with Freda, fuelled Edwards' intense five-year affair with Thelma. But, despite their selection of the teddy bear as an emblem of their love, their liaison was not a thoroughly happy one. Edward, Thelma later complained, suffered from chronic premature ejaculation. (One of Edward's friends further impunged his sexual prowess, saying, 'To put it bluntly, he had the smallest pecker I have ever seen.') But both Freda and Thelma slipped from Edward's life within months of his meeting Wallis Simpson, an American divorcée who, like her predecessors, was married when she met him. She entered Edward's life in 1931, when Thelma made the mistake of introducing her, as well as angering Edward by spending time with playboy Porfino Rubirosa. Wallis proceeded to take charge. She and Edward became inseparable. While not a beauty, Wallis's playfulness and interest in his work captivated Edward. He soon helped Wallis arrange a quick divorce and set his sights on marriage.

Edward was now king, however, and had vastly underestimated the royal family's opposition to Wallis – a woman his mother condemned as 'an adventuress' and whose two divorces smacked of scandal. Parliament, too, was unwilling to see Mrs Simpson become queen – a title that, barring a constitutional change, automatically went to the king's wife. As the crisis heightened, Edward confronted his options: Wallis or the throne had to go. In an emotional speech on BBC radio, Edward announced his decision to abdicate in favour of his younger brother, Albert. Six months later, Edward and Wallis married, despite continuing disapproval from the royal family and Parliament (the cabinet withheld from Wallis the title of 'Her Royal Highness', a slight that forever irked Edward). None the less, to all appearances, theirs was a storybook romance. Their opulent life filled the pages of every tabloid and, on a more private level, their love flourished too. Rare was the evening, even after many married years had passed, that Edward did not place a flower on Wallis's pillow.

141

But there were discordant undertones as well. Wallis was a hard-edged woman – 'If she happened to be hungry, she might have taken a bite out of you,' observed actress Lilli Palmer – and Edward was not spared. During one quarrel he exclaimed, 'Darling, are you going to send me to bed in tears again tonight?' Edward, for his part, upbraided Wallis only once – when rumours reached him that Jimmy Donahue, the couple's frequent nightclub companion and an heir to the Woolworth fortune, had become her lover. Happily, however, the rumours were false and Wallis assured him (truthfully) that Donahue was a homosexual, adding, 'His friends call me Queen of the Fairies.' Wallis dominated Edward's life and, for the man who once was king, it was exactly the way he wanted things to be.

R.M. (Lists 5, 17, 28)

❧ Albert Einstein
14 March 1879 to 18 April 1955

Despite the universal acclaim for his genius that was to come, Einstein's early school years in Germany proved inauspicious and his parents at first feared he was of below normal intelligence. In 1895, his application to Zurich's prestigious Polytechnic Academy was rejected. After a year of remedial schooling, Einstein was accepted. In 1900, he graduated, but his request for an academic appointment was denied and Einstein soon found it necessary to take a job as an examiner in the Swiss patent office in Bern. In 1905, he wrote 'A New Determination of Molecular Dimensions' and for this thesis the University of Zurich awarded him a Ph.D. That same year he published a paper on the special theory of relativity, and soon Einstein embarked on his career as a university professor. A few years after the 1916 publication of his work on the general theory of relativity, Einstein found himself a celebrity. Universities clamoured for him to join their faculties, fellow scientists sought his advice, and political and charitable groups competed for his support. But Einstein, true to his image as the genius lost in thought, restricted his non-scientific involvements to two causes that remained dear to him: pacifism and Zionism.

Einstein's love life, what is know of it, starts with his 1903 marriage to Mileva Maric, a mathematics student he met while both were university students in Zurich. Their marriage was ill-starred. For Einstein, physics came first; a wife ranked a distant second. Yet Einstein soon fathered two sons – Hans Albert and Edward and, in many respects, his marriage seemed stable. But Mileva's moods and introversion clashed with Einstein's vitality and humour. Finally, in 1914, Einstein accepted a position at the Prussian Academy of Sciences in Berlin. Mileva and the boys went to the capital but decided to holiday in Switzerland during the summer. When the eruption of the First World War prevented them from rejoining Einstein in Berlin, they stayed in Zurich. Einstein remained in Berlin and, during the war, made only a few trips to visit his family in Switzerland. After a final visit in 1916, Einstein confided to a friend that his decision never again to see Mileva was 'irrevocable'. She interfered, it seems, with his ability to concentrate on physics. In 1919 they were divorced, with Einstein confidently pledging to Mileva the proceeds of the Nobel Prize he anticipated. He won the prize in 1921 and promptly kept his promise. It is not known whether he fulfilled a second, more mysterious, promise: 'You will see,' he wrote to Mileva, 'that I will always remain true to you – in my way.'

Meanwhile, in Berlin, Einstein had been spending increasing amounts of time in the company of the daughter of his father's cousin, Elsa Lowenthal, widowed mother of two girls. Elsa and Einstein had known each other as children and corresponded sporadically for years. When, in 1917, Einstein fell seriously ill with stomach trouble, he had already moved in with Elsa, who nursed him back to health. After his recovery, Einstein stayed on and, within months of divorcing Mileva, he married his former 'nurse'. Although Einstein accepted her children as his own, all accounts point to his relationship with their mother as one primarily of convenience. She kept the material aspects of his life in order, taking responsibility for feeding and clothing him and maintaining his home. Once, asked what he gave in return, Einstein cryptically commented, 'My understanding'. After Elsa's death in 1936, Einstein – by then living in America – remained a widower, still close, in those years, to his elder son Hans Albert. He still ensured that his younger son Edward, who suffered from serious emotional disorders, received proper care in the institutions where he passed much of his adulthood.

R.M. (List 33)

♣ Dwight David Eisenhower
14 October 1890 to 28 March 1969

Supreme Allied Commander of the European Theatre in the Second World War, Eisenhower masterminded the Normandy invasion and liberated North Africa and Italy; it was to him that the Germans surrendered on 7 May 1945. He capped his career by serving two terms as President of the USA, from 1952 to 1960, but Eisenhower was raised in Abilene, Kansas, the son of a dairy worker. 'Ike', as he was called, entered West Point after working to help pay for a brother's college education, and graduated in 1915. While stationed in San Antonio, Texas, he met Mamie Geneva Doud, who was there with her parents, and they were married in 1916. One month later, Ike put his arms around his new wife and said, 'Mamie, there's one thing you must understand. My country comes first and always will. You come second.' The couple had two children, David, who died young, and John, born in 1923. As a professional officer, Eisenhower never remained in one post long; by the time he became president, he had moved thirty-four times, serving in Panama, France, the Philippines and elsewhere. But none of these assignments seems to have changed his provincial outlook – the French were always 'frogs' to Ike. In peacetime, his rise through the ranks was painfully slow – he was only a colonel at the outbreak of the Second World War. But his singular diplomatic gifts, including great skill at cards, won him rapid promotion during the war, with some assistance from friends like Generals George Marshall and Douglas MacArthur. Promoted for his ability to put strategic theory into action, Eisenhower always found time to play bridge and read pulp magazines. As general and president, he delegated as much work as he could.

His domestic life was far from tranquil – his wife Mamie, daughter of a wealthy Denver meat-packer, often refused to live in army housing at distant outposts. The death from scarlet fever of their beloved first son was a blow from which they never fully recovered; they drifted apart as Ike was shuffled from post to post. During the war their separation for over two years while Ike led the Allies to victory in Europe prompted bitter correspondence. After the war, there was less moving around. The marriage settled, and Ike became involved in civilian politics, seeking and winning two terms as president. In office, Ike steered a moderate conservative course, and tried to leave as much time as possible open for golf. When chipmunks disturbed his putting on the White House lawn, he had them box-trapped and carted away. He left the White House in 1960, retiring to his farm near Gettysburg, where he died nine years later after a heart attack, Mamie by his side.

When young, Ike had a reputation as a woman hater; wife Mamie once said this made him intriguing, adding that he was a 'bruiser' – well built and handsome. As a military hero during the war, he retained some of those qualities, and captivated Kay Summersby Morgan, an aristocratic young Irishwoman, his staff driver. 'His kisses absolutely unravelled me,' Summersby wrote afterwards. 'Hungry, strong, demanding.' Their affair, hotly denied by the Eisenhower family, was unconsummated because the general was impotent, according to Summersby's memoirs. After an attempt at lovemaking, the general reportedly confessed, 'It's too late.' On another occasion, Ike told her his marriage to Mamie 'killed something in me. Not all at once, but little by little. For years I never thought of making love, and when I did . . . I failed.' However, ghostwriter Sigrid Hedin says Summersby told her that Ike was not totally impotent, although Summersby had to teach him about lovemaking. But Kay loved him: 'I wanted to hold him . . . I wanted to lie on some grassy lawn and see those broad shoulders above me, feel that hard body against mine.' According to Harry Truman, Eisenhower wrote to General Marshall after the war, asking to be relieved of duty so he could divorce Mamie and marry Kay. Truman said Marshall sent a reply that, if Eisenhower ever did such a thing, Marshall would personally 'bust' him out of the army and make his life hell.

Eisenhower would not let romance ruin his political career. But the aborted affair haunted the general and his family for years, and would have surfaced in the 1952 election had Truman not destroyed the incriminating Marshall–Eisenhower correspondence. Ike and Mamie went on to share a king-sized, pink-ruffled bed during their White House years, though it was doubtful that this was pleasant for the general, who once changed his suite in Claridges because the bedroom was 'whorehouse pink'.

J.A.M.

♣ George Eliot

22 November 1819 to 22 December 1880

The daughter of an undistinguished estate agent, Mary Ann Evans – later to be known as George Eliot – was moulded by traditional, highly religious boarding schools. She decided early in life that her mission was to engage in good works. But she broke out of her religious cocoon when she returned home after her mother's death. Her subsequent association with free thinkers caused her to re-examine her beliefs and led to a family row when she stated she no longer wished to attend church. Upon her father's death in 1849, Eliot left Coventry for London, hoping to earn a living as a freelance writer. She moved in with publisher John Chapman and his family, but it soon became apparent that Chapman's interest extended beyond her literary efforts. The attraction was mutual, and the resulting tension within the household caused her to flee the city ten weeks after her arrival. But she returned a few months later to become an editor for the *Westminster Review*, which Chapman had recently acquired. It was while attending one of Chapman's parties that she met Herbert Spencer and, through him, George Henry Lewes, who was to become her lover and companion for more than twenty years.

Eliot's early romantic involvements were with self-absorbed, flirtatious men with whom she had no carnal initiations. She seemed destined for spinsterhood, since she was unattractive by the standards of the day – she had a large heavy nose, a dull complexion, and dark clinging hair. Yet her blue-grey eyes were charming and expressive. Henry James once wrote that George Eliot was 'magnificently ugly – deliciously hideous', and, although they were never romantically involved, he admitted, 'Behold me literally in love with this great horse-faced bluestocking.' James's sister Alice, described Eliot as 'a fungus of pendulous shape'.

While her two important affairs were to be with men, there was an aura of sexuality surrounding several of her intimate relationships with women. The most important of these was with Sara Hennell, a highly strung writer seven years older than Eliot. When Eliot couldn't decide whether or not to marry a young doctor, she longed for Sara's counsel. And yet, beginning in 1843, she wrote Sara seductive letters addressing her as 'Beloved Spouse'. At first they traded the 'husband' and 'wife' roles in their letters, until Eliot finally adopted the role of 'husband'.

In 1849, she was still writing to Sara: 'I have given you a sad excuse for flirtation, but I have not been beyond seas long enough to make it lawful for you to take a new husband – therefore I come back to you with all a husband's privileges and command you to love me. . . . I sometimes talk to you in my soul as lovingly as Solomon's Song.' In later years, Eliot's husband John Cross suppressed these passages.

Then she met George Henry Lewes, a writer who had achieved a moderate success. He was as ugly – and as charming – as Eliot. They fell in love, but Lewes could not divorce his adulterous wife since he had accepted all four children that had resulted from his wife's extramarital union as his own. According to law, he had thus forfeited the right to dissolve his marriage on grounds of infidelity. The free-spirited couple 'eloped' to Germany in 1854 when Eliot was 35, and upon returning to Britain they set up house together, living in an unmarried state until Lewes's death in 1878. Throughout this arrangement, Eliot considered herself as Mrs Lewes, but she was not foolish enough to expect to receive the privileges bestowed upon a married woman. For his part, Lewes convinced his beloved Eliot that she had all the makings of a great novelist. In return, she chose 'George' as part of her pseudonym and shared her earnings with him. The fact that her novels often dealt with illicit love – involving those who defy convention and are the underdogs of society – can be directly attributed to her life with Lewes. Apparently it was a very successful and sexually satisfying union. Lewes was a sensualist, and Eliot often said that many of her best ideas came after an enjoyable night as she lay in bed next to him. 'Mrs Lewes' practised birth control (of an unspecified form), and it was indicative of her liberal attitudes that she discussed the subject with friends.

Though George Eliot repeatedly disavowed any interest in legal marriage, in 1880 – less than two years after Lewes's death – she wed her banker, John Walter Cross, who was twenty years her junior. It is not clear why Eliot married Cross – perhaps it was because she needed a man in her life and he insisted upon marriage. Another reason may have been a passionate lesbian proposal from her friend Edith Simcox. While Lewes was alive, Edith had repressed her agonizing longing for Eliot. Edith's long-delayed confession of her love was met with overt resistance – Eliot lectured her that heterosexual love was what God had intended. And yet some part of Eliot was disturbed and tempted. The two women parted with a gentle kiss (and Edith with a broken heart). It was exactly a month after this incident that George Eliot decided to marry. She died seven months later.

A.L.G. and A.W. (Lists 14, 25)

❧ Elizabeth I
7 September 1533 to 24 March 1603

Elizabeth Tudor, the daughter of Henry VIII and Anne Boleyn, endured an emotionally battered childhood marked by the execution of both her mother and her stepmother, Catherine Howard. Ascending the throne in 1558, she strove to reconcile the country's fierce religious divisions and built the nation into a great sea and colonial power. She condemned both her cousin, Mary Queen of Scots, and Robert Devereaux, the Earl of Essex, to the block – but only after exhausting every other means of subduing them. Physically expressive with her intimates, she often caressed men and struck women; she laughed much and frequently wept. While she encouraged some personal familiarity, even flippancy, from her courtiers, she would not tolerate disrespect to the throne, and her chilling oath 'God's death, my lord!' usually preceded a royal temper that reduced many an arrogant knight to abject trembling. Though not beautiful, she was certainly attractive. Her slender medium stature, shapely hands, pale oval face and auburn hair were celebrated by poets of the time. Highly educated, she spoke five languages and was an expert rider and dancer. She thrived on flattery; even as she faded into a haggard, mirror-hating old woman with false red hair and plastered with cosmetics, she maintained her court of young studs, all competing to praise her physical charms. But her intelligence and razor-edged wit never faded, and English veneration for the 'Virgin Queen' crowned her with the aura of a surrogate Virgin Mary. She died at 69, apparently of an infection resulting from pyorrhea.

For thirty years, Elizabeth kept Englishmen and European courts wondering if, when and whom the queen would marry. Speculation persisted during most of her reign, and kept many a powerful man, both at home and abroad, on his best behaviour. Basically, she did not want to marry, and frequently said so. Yet she constantly invited men – young, athletic, handsome ones – to chase her. She loved the foreplay of passionate letters, ribald jokes, gifts, and at times it seemed she had half the princes of

Europe panting to share her bed and kingdom. She was an expert tease who always found excellent reasons to delay consummation. Strangely, few of her suitors learned her game, even after years of playing it. She loved their courtship and flattery, but had seen too much of what had happened to the royal wives in her own family. To her, a husband represented at best the sharing of her throne – at the worst, usurpation of her power.

Her first romance at 14 was with Lord Admiral Thomas Seymour, younger brother of England's Lord Protector and a handsome rake 'of much wit and very little judgement', as she later described him. Seymour habitually romped into her morning bedroom, where the couple played slap-and-tickle. It was expensive dalliance, eventually costing Seymour his head when his motives – to marry her and stage a palace coup – became known. Elizabeth, under suspicion as heir apparent and ill that summer, may have had a miscarriage. According to biographers, this was the only time in her life when a pregnancy might have passed undetected. Whatever trouble he caused, the dead Seymour became the favourite male prototype for her future romances – young, dashing and more brawn than brains.

English noblemen by the dozen courted Elizabeth after she became queen. These included Sir Christopher Hatton, Sir Walter Raleigh (who named colonial Virginia for her) and, most enduringly, Lord Robert Dudley. 'Sweet Robin,' she called him and nicknamed him 'My Eyes'. She tickled his neck during his solemn investiture as the Earl of Leicester, and he teased her openly about their wedding date. Though he was married to Amy Robsart, Dudley pursued Elizabeth with such ardour that their own marriage seemed likely. They visited each other's bedchambers, and rumours were rampant that 'Lord Robert did swyve [copulate with] the queen' and had fathered her child. But, after Amy's suspiciously timely death, Elizabeth dared not marry him since this might confirm that Dudley had poisoned his wife. Yet he stayed with her, a master intriguer who tried to steer her towards suitors he knew she could not marry. Their thirty-year affair flamed hot and cold, but not even his secret marriage to Lettice Knollys, which infuriated the queen, interfered for long. Yet, believing herself dying of smallpox in 1562, she swore, 'as God is my witness, nothing improper has ever passed between us'. Of all the men in her life, Dudley probably knew her best. And, when he died in 1588, she shut herself up for grief-stricken weeks and kept his last letter by her bedside until her own death.

149

At stake in her numerous foreign courtships was the balance of European power. Philip II of Spain, her former brother-in-law and a future enemy, pursued her; the Archdukes Ferdinand and Charles of Hapsburg, the Princes of Denmark and Sweden, Charles IX of France and his sulky homosexual brother, the Duke of Anjou, all sent proxies to woo her. She probably came closest to actual marriage when she was 49. The 27-year-old Duke of Alençon, the younger brother of the Duke of Anjou, was not much to look at, but charming, considered 'apt for the getting of children', and the only prince who actually came in person to see her. She called him her 'Frog', but she kept him, like the others, waiting too long (eleven years) and danced for joy when he finally died. Conveniently, the European courtiers who sought her Protestant hand were usually Catholic, so she always had an excuse for escape.

Her sex life became a favourite topic for gossip. In 1581, it was charged that Dudley 'hath five children by the queen', and that she never left long 'but to be delivered'. But foreign ambassadors inquired closely and often into her sexual morals, and none ever produced a shred of evidence for scandal. Elizabeth wanted her epitaph to declare that 'a queen, having reigned such a time, lived and died a virgin'. Was she really a virgin? The best contemporary sources indicate that, unlikely as it sounds, she was. A sexual liaison simply could not have been kept hidden. Was she a sexually normal woman? Lord Burghley, after thorough consultations with her doctors, concluded that she was 'very apt' for procreating children, and he recommended marital intercourse to cure her of 'such dolours and infirmities as all physicians do usually impute to womankind for lack of marriage'. A contradictory report came from Elizabeth's physician, Dr Huick, who advised her against marriage due to a 'womanish infirmity'. Playwright Ben Jonson, a contemporary, claimed she 'had a membrana on her, which made her uncapable of man, though of her delight she tryed many'. A current theory has been advanced by endocrinologist Dr Robert B. Greenblatt. He speculates that Elizabeth suffered from Rokitansky's syndrome, a congenital defect which produces a very shallow vaginal canal and an undeveloped uterus. This posthumous diagnosis could be true only if Elizabeth had never menstruated. A 1559 medical report written by Sir James Melville stated that 'she had few monthly periods or none'. This may be explained by another conjecture suggesting that Elizabeth suffered from anaemia, which started during puberty. In any case, sex for the queen was verbal and vicarious, and delightfully so. But no evidence exists that it ever went much further.

J.E. (List 29)

♣ Edward Kennedy (Duke) Ellington
29 April 1899 to 24 May 1974

Edward Kennedy Ellington was one of the foremost jazz composers, orchestra leaders and musicians of the twentieth century. Duke (a nickname given him by childhood friends due to his elegant dress and aristocratic manner) Ellington was born in Washington DC to middle-class parents. His father, James Edward, was a blueprint maker for the Department of the Navy and a sometime butler who occasionally worked in the White House. His family was devoutly religious and young Ellington was spoiled by his mother Daisy, to whom he was devoted throughout her life. Ellington showed an early talent in art and won a poster contest sponsored by the National Association for the Advancement of Colored People. Subsequently, he was offered an art scholarship, but Ellington, who had taught himself to play the piano by imitating ragtime piano rolls on the family's player piano, was more interested in music and chose to pursue that as a career. He formed a band and played at various functions in Washington, before finally travelling to New York, and becoming the mainstay of nightspots like the Cotton Club in Harlem. Soon he and his band were touring the country to great acclaim. In 1918, shortly after his nineteenth birthday, Ellington married a childhood friend and neighbour, Edna Thompson, and, less than a year later, they had a son whom they named Mercer. Another child came soon but died in infancy. The marriage to Edna was not happy. He remained with her several years before they permanently separated, and he continued to support her generously after the break-up. Ellington remained married to Edna until she died in 1966. Enormously respected throughout his life, he died of cancer in New York City at the age of 75.

Duke – who was 6 feet 1 inch, and whose weight fluctuated wildly, for he loved to eat – was extremely urbane and gracious in his manner. He was a ladies' man, a charmer and a flatterer. Even while still living with Edna, he had numerous affairs and, according to his son Mercer, during an argument over one of them

Edna slashed his face with a knife, leaving a permanent scar. Duke always loved the attention women paid him, and his son believed that at least part of the reason he went into show business was because it was 'a good way to get a girl to sit beside you and admire you as you played the piano'. Ralph Gleason, writer and jazz critic, recalls standing with Ellington in the wings of a theatre while his band was playing. A trumpet solo was in progress and, as Duke watched, two of his musicians – who had a reputation for using drugs – sat in their chairs, heads drooping, nodding off. Duke shook his head and said, 'I don't understand it at all. I'm a cunt man myself.' But Ellington, according to Mercer, 'never seemed to be interested in the perfect woman. If she had a scar, or was slightly misproportioned – big-busted, big-hipped or a little off-balance – then he was more interested.' At the notorious House of All Nations in Paris, after the spectacle was over and the girls had lined up, he was asked by a friend to take his pick. Ellington replied, 'I'll take the three on this end.' He had so many women that he had to develop tricks to deal with all of them. He got into the habit of giving everybody four kisses, thus making it impossible for anyone to know with whom he was actually involved. When someone would ask about the usual number of kisses, Duke's standard reply was 'once for each cheek'. In 1972, during a week-long festival, so many of his women showed up – and stayed in the same hotel as he – that he would get a friend to take two of them out to dinner while he took yet another woman up to his room.

His marriage to Edna ended after Duke had a passionate affair with an attractive actress. Although Mercer calls it 'one of the most serious relationships of his life', the anonymous woman left Duke because he refused actually to divorce Edna and marry her. Mildred Dixon, who caught Ellington's eye from the chorus line at the Cotton Club, moved in with Duke in 1930 and stayed for almost a decade. Personable and intelligent, Mildred was Duke's 'Sweet Babe', but her charms paled next to Beatrice Ellis, a striking half-black, half-Spanish showgirl who also worked at the Cotton Club. She spent the next thirty-seven years answering to the name of Evie Ellington and patiently waiting for Duke's infrequent trips to their lavish New York City apartment. Even when the globetrotting Ellington breezed in to relieve Evie's loneliness, they were rarely seen together in public. His sister Ruth was the 'official' hostess, and her possessiveness and Evie's greed were the major reasons why Duke never married Evie.

Until Edna died in 1966, he maintained that a divorce would be very expensive and Evie wanted to keep her deluxe standard of living. After Edna's death, when Evie was certain Duke would marry her, he flatly refused – even when she pulled a gun on him. Evie resigned herself to a solitary life without a marriage certificate and Duke rang her daily, wrote her touching notes and showered her with flowers, candy and fruit.

In 1959, Duke met nightclub singer Fernanda de Castro Monte, who later became Madame Zajj in 'A Drum Is a Woman'. Tall, blonde and fortyish, Fernanda accompanied Ellington on many of his world tours and was introduced as the 'Countess'. Mercer remembers the farewell she gave Duke after they met in Las Vegas: '. . . She was very smartly dressed in a mink coat. Just as the train was about to pull out, she opened the coat. She had nothing at all on under it, and she wrapped it around him to give him his goodbye kiss. With that, she left him to cool off.' Fernanda had expensive tastes and introduced Duke to vodka and caviare (which he touted as an aphrodisiac). When she started making demands, Ellington told her that he was legally married to Evie, who was so jealous of Fernanda that she threatened Duke with her gun a second time.

Fernanda de Castro Monte was the fifth and final woman of influence in Ellington's life. He had affairs with many other women (some of whom divorced their husbands for him), but none of them made much of an impact on Duke's life. To the end he insisted, 'Music is my mistress, and she plays second fiddle to no one.'

C.H.S. and Eds. (Lists 20, 22, 42, 52)

♣ Havelock Ellis
2 February 1859 to 8 July 1939

Called the 'Darwin of sex', Havelock Ellis was principally known as a sex educator and the author of a seven-volume work issued between 1897 and 1928 entitled *Studies in the Psychology of Sex*.

Son of a sea captain and a doting mother, Ellis was born in Croydon, Surrey. He attended private schools in London. At 16, in poor health, he was sent to Australia on his father's ship. There he worked as a teacher for four years, too shy to be effective. Returning to London, he entered St Thomas's Hospital at 22 to study medicine. After qualifying, he practised briefly in the

London slums. He gave up medicine for writing. At 30 Ellis published his first book, *The New Spirit*. Shortly afterwards he became interested in sex, then a taboo subject. Through interviews and research, Ellis gathered material on human sexuality and wrote about it. The first volume of his *Studies in the Psychology of Sex* series, entitled *Sexual Inversion*, dealt with homosexuality. The book was banned in England for 'obscene libel'. Nevertheless, Ellis continued to pour out books on aspects of human sexuality. Although widely known, he lived close to poverty most of his life. He was 64 when he had his first commercial success with *The Dance of Life*.

During his lifetime, Ellis defended homosexuals and woman's rights, and pioneered open discussions on sex. He gave free advice on sex to anyone who wanted it, and could not understand why Freud charged patients for the same help. Ellis was a sweet and humane man, part scientist, part mystic. Birth-control crusader Margaret Sanger found him a 'tall angel', blue-eyed, handsome, with a distinctive flowing white beard. He died in Ipswich of a throat ailment at the age of 80.

Not until he was 25 did Havelock Ellis have any sexual experience with a woman. He had read a novel, *The Story of an African Farm* by Ralph Iron, and wrote a fan letter to the author. The author proved to be an attractive woman named Olive Schreiner, a 29-year-old feminist and novelist. They corresponded, then met. Olive, who wanted to be dominated, expected a strong man and found in Ellis an awkward and withdrawn intellectual. They became friends, and he gave her his daily journal to read. Going through it, she realized that he was sexually inexperienced. Olive, who had had several affairs with men, decided she could rectify that and eventually marry Ellis. She lured him to Derbyshire for a weekend and during their first walk together, she put her hand on his crotch to feel his penis. Intent on consummation, she lay nude with him on a sofa. He caressed her and kissed her vagina. He could not get an erection, and finally suffered premature ejaculation. This happened again and again. 'She possessed a powerfully and physically passionate temperament', Ellis admitted, and he could not match it. They settled for a close and enduring friendship. She remained uninhibited with him. Once, in Paris together, observing some bronze vessels in the Louvre, Olive spoke seriously of the handicaps women suffered. 'A woman,' she said, 'is a ship with two holes in her bottom.' Eventually, Olive returned to South Africa and married, without great success, a farmer-politician.

Havelock Ellis was 31 when he became involved in his greatest
love affair. Edith Lees, a 28-year-old former social worker, was
tiny, curly-haired, pretty and outspoken. Edith, who ran a girls'
school, was drawn to Ellis upon reading his first book. He liked
her brightness and intelligence. When she proposed marriage, he
worried about his privacy and meagre finances, but Edith promised him 'space' and agreed to share their expences. They shared
the cost of a wedding ring, and married in December 1891. Edith
did not know Ellis was impotent until their honeymoon in Paris.
He did not even attempt to have intercourse with her. While she
had told Ellis she had had affairs with several men, she had not
told him she liked women more. Edith mourned the baby she
could never have with Ellis, and settled for his fondling in bed,
still thinking him 'beautiful' and her spiritual lover. She agreed to
a marriage of companionship, but not for long. Three months
after their wedding, she informed him that she was having a
torrid affair with a woman named Claire. Unhappy but tolerant,
Ellis interviewed Edith on lesbianism for a book he was writing
on homosexuality. After breaking with Claire, Edith had another
affair with a fragile painter named Lily. After Lily died, Edith
turned her attentions back to her husband. Their twenty-five-
year marriage was stormy. Edith was a manic depressive. When
manic, she redecorated and rented cottages, gave lectures as Mrs
Havelock Ellis (her favourite was on Oscar Wilde), wrote books
and plays, founded a film company. When depressed, she sat at
her female lovers' graves, had several nervous breakdowns, and
three times tried to commit suicide. When she resumed her
lesbian affairs, Ellis continued to love her and resumed his own
sexless affairs. He outraged his wife when he fell in love with the
24-year-old daughter of a chemist friend, a woman he referred to
as Amy – her real name was Mneme Smith – and whom he
continued to be close to until she married. He was 57 when he
met and became enchanted by Margaret Sanger. This relationship
brought Edith back from a lecture tour in the USA and gave her
one more nervous breakdown. Ellis was constantly attentive to
Edith . . . her doctor told him she was on the verge of insanity. In
September 1916, she died in a diabetic coma.

Shortly afterwards, a charming young Frenchwoman, Françoise Cyon, entered Ellis's life. Françoise wanted to collect her fee
for having one of Edith's books translated into French. Drawn to
Ellis's kind understanding, she came to him again for marital

advice. She had had a child by a lover, and a second by her husband, Serge Cyon, an insensitive Russian journalist she had recently left. During her treatment by Ellis, Françoise fell in love with him. On 3 April 1918, she wrote to him, 'I am going to write a very difficult letter. Yet it must be written if I want to find peace of mind. The truth is, Havelock Ellis, that I love you.' He tried to warn Françoise of his impotence. He wrote to her of his many dear women friends. 'But there is not one to whom I am a real lover . . . I feel sure that I am good for you; I am sure that you suit me. But as a lover or husband you would find me very disappointing.' Puzzled, she replied, 'I will have nothing but what you offer; it is the very flower of love.'

In bed with him she learned of his problem, but was undeterred. They masturbated each other. She lavished love on him unconditionally, treating him as virile, a potentially good lover. And, miracle of miracles, he responded. Aged 60, he had his first erection with a woman. More followed and he enjoyed sexual intercourse at last. Their relationship was idyllic, marred by only one incident. Ellis asked her to be friendly with one of his admirers, an urbane minor novelist and advocate of free love named Hugh de Selincourt. While Ellis was out of town, Françoise allowed De Selincourt to seduce her. He was a mighty lover. He hated to wear a contraceptive device and had trained himself to copulate at great length, bringing his women to orgasm without ejaculation himself. Françoise lost herself in his pleasure. When Ellis learned about the affair he was wounded, feeling she had found a younger and better lover. Françoise tried to gloss over the physical aspect of her affair. Ellis answered, 'Do you imagine that coitus is unimportant? Olive said to me once that when a man puts his penis into a woman's vagina it is as if (assuming of course that she responds) he put his finger into her brain, stirred it round and round. Her whole nature is affected.' Françoise pleaded with Ellis, writing to him, 'You have been the beloved, the lover, the friend most divine. You are still this, will always be . . .' She gave up De Selincourt, and returned to Ellis. She worked as a teacher, and lived separately with her sons. She wanted to move in with Ellis, but he could not support her. Then, from America, Margaret Sanger offered her a salary as Ellis's secretary. Françoise, at last able to pay her share of their expenses, joined him for what was left of his life. They had twenty-two warm years together. Françoise, keeper of the flame, died in 1974.

Ellis, the sexual reformer, had had two celebrated quirks. At

156

the age of 12, while accompanying his mother to the London Zoo, Ellis saw her pause and urinate on an isolated gravel path. Hearing of this, his favourite sister told him, 'She was flirting with you.' Decades later, after lying down fully clothed to caress Françoise for the first time, he followed her into the bathroom to watch her urinate. He enjoyed having Françoise urinate when they went walking in the rain. She termed his interest in urolagnia a 'harmless anomaly'. Ellis asked many of his new women friends for photographs of themselves in the nude.

I.W. (Lists 1, 6, 7, 10, 26, 30, 44, 49, 51)

♣ Farouk I
11 February 1920 to 18 March 1965

The last monarch to rule Egypt, Farouk was known for his gluttony, promiscuity, capriciousness and kleptomania. While he began his reign at 18 with high ideals, these quickly deteriorated under the impact of his monumental physical and emotional problems. He could weep over the death of a rabbit one moment, then pick a cat up by the tail and dash it against a wall the next. One of his first acts as king was to have his cars (more than one hundred of them) painted fire-engine red, and make it illegal for any other cars to be that colour, so he could speed through the countryside without police interference. In a short time, he had alienated his allies and his own army to such a degree that revolutionaries were able to take over in an effortless coup. Farouk went into exile at the age of 32. The deposed king's possessions, including a vast amount of pornography and the world's largest stamp collection, were auctioned off, bringing over a million dollars into the coffers of the new Egyptian republic. Farouk's erotica – the 'nudie' playing cards, the pulp porn, the X-rated films, and even the manacles which he supposedly used to chain women to his bed – were a small part of his vast hoard. During his reign, he filched enough to fill several storehouses – he had bottle caps and toothpaste tubes, clocks and coins, a ceremonial sword and assorted medals stolen from the dead body of Reza Shah Pahlavi of Iran as it passed in state through Cairo, and even Winston Churchill's heirloom gold pocket watch.

At 18, Farouk fell in love with and married pretty, 17-year-old Safinez Zulficar, whose name he legally changed to Farida ('the

Only One'). Within a few years, he openly began having other women. By creating for himself an image as an insatiable lover, Farouk successfully hid from his subjects the embarrassing fact that he had underdeveloped genitals and a low sex drive. He began each day with a banquet of not only eggs but countless dishes of meat and fish, and he swilled fizzy drinks by the gallon – obesity was the predictable result. It was even considered admirable for the 6 foot ruler to weigh in at 21 stone 6 pounds. Lack of virility, however, was another matter. Though he began having bouts of impotence at 23, he attempted sexual intercourse with an estimated 5000 women in his lifetime. He consulted hormone specialists and hunted for aphrodisiacs, trying amphetamines, hashish mixed with honey and caffeine pills, stopping only at powdered rhinoceros horn. While pelting other guests at nightclubs and gambling casinos with spitballs, he flirted with desirable women. Those who resisted his invitations were captured and deposited in 'harems' at any one of his five palaces. He often coveted married women and tried to blackmail them into divorcing their husbands. He flaunted women in front of his wife – girls would, according to biographer Hugh McLeave, 'scamper up the backstairs and make merry with the king until sunrise'. None stayed long. After nearly eleven years of marriage and three daughters – but no son – Farouk divorced the estranged Farida. According to rumour, Farida asked Farouk to go ahead with the divorce after a French opera singer was seen leaving his bedchamber. In a futile attempt to regain the affection of the Egyptian people, he later married a commoner, Narriman Sadek, a 16-year-old who reminded him of another woman he had once desired. Narriman went with him into exile in Italy in 1952, but she returned to Egypt and obtained a Moslem divorce in 1954. Farouk established himself in Rome where, on a dwindling fortune, he enjoyed his role as European playboy. Here he met 18-year-old aspiring actress Irma Minutolo when she appeared in a beauty contest – she lost the contest, but won Farouk. He paid for her singing lessons and moved her into his apartment building. Irma remained his friend until his death, but his infatuation did not prevent his prowling the cabarets of Rome in a constant search for additional female companionship. Farouk died at 45, after a night of gluttony at his favourite restaurant, accompanied by his latest girlfriend.

J.H. (Lists 5, 8, 11, 34, 38, 52)

♣ William Faulkner
25 September 1897 to 6 July 1962

Nobel Prize-winner for Literature in 1949, William Faulkner (he added the 'u' himself) was born in New Albany, Missouri, not far from Oxford, which was to become the model for his town of 'Jefferson', in the fictional county of Yoknapawtawpha – the setting for most of his novels and stories. His ancestors were wealthy and powerful Southerners, ruined by the civil war. His father, who owned a livery stable and hardware store – both of which failed – was business manager of the state university. Faulkner – shy, slow-moving, and soft-spoken – was the eldest of four brothers. He dropped out of high school after two years and worked in a bank. When the First World War broke out, he tried to enlist in the army, but was rejected because he was only 5 feet 5 inches tall and underweight. He joined the Royal Air Force in Canada and, though the war ended before he could see action, his experiences left him with a lifelong love of aeroplanes. He returned home and took several odd jobs to earn enough for 'paper, tobacco, food, and a little whiskey', while he read voraciously and began to write. In 1925, he met Sherwood Anderson, who recommended Faulkner's first novel, *Soldier's Pay*, to his own publisher.

The hard-drinking, nattily attired, pipe-smoking Faulkner made little money from his fiction and was forced to go to Hollywood, where sporadically, for more than a decade, he wrote for the screen, while he continued writing novels and short stories. 'I write when the spirit moves me,' he said, 'and the spirit moves me every day.' By 1946, his books were out of print but, upon publication of *The Portable Faulkner*, his star rose rapidly. Although he despised ceremonies, he interrupted a drinking spree and came out of his alcoholic stupor long enough to accept the Nobel Prize in 1949. He won the Pulitzer Prize for *A Fable* in 1954, and travelled abroad extensively for the State Department. In May 1962, he returned to Oxford, the town he had made famous in his novels. He died there a few months later of a coronary thrombosis, his wife and family by his side.

As a teenager, Faulkner's first love was the daughter of a neighbour, Estelle Oldham, but she married another and moved to China, leaving Faulkner shattered. He was usually attracted to small, childlike women, like his next love, Helen Baird, to whom he dedicated his novel, *Mosquitoes*. Eventually she spurned him

159

and married someone else. Eleven years after Estelle's departure for China, she returned, divorced; after courting again, she and Faulkner married in 1929. Their first child, Alabama, died soon after birth. They had a second daughter and named her Jill. Although their marriage was rocky and both drank heavily, neither moved towards divorce.

While in Hollywood, Faulkner met Meta Carpenter, ten years his junior and secretary to director Howard Hawks, for whom Faulkner was also working. Meta was very attractive and petite, and a fellow Southerner. Faulkner pursued her ardently and they became lovers. He was, according to her, a very passionate lover. 'In the art of love, Bill, the restrained, remote man by day, was seized with a consuming sexual urgency. . . . Sexual gratification made voluble and outgoing. He told bawdy stories and kissed the blushes that inflamed my skin.' Faulkner reportedly told Meta, 'I've always been afraid of going out of control, I get so carried away. . . .' He was a romantic (he once covered their bed with gardenia and jasmine petals), and he often presented her with erotic drawings and erotic poems like:

Meta
Bill
Meta
who soft keeps for him his love's long girl's body sweet to fuck.
Bill.

In a letter he wrote, 'For Meta, my heart, my jasmine garden, my April and May cunt; my white one, my blonde morning, winged, my sweetly dividing, my honey-cloyed, my sweet-assed gal. Bill.' In 1937, she married someone else, but kept in touch for the next sixteen years. In 1950, Faulkner met Joan Williams, a 21-year-old writer. They became lovers, but the difference in their ages proved too great and the couple broke up in 1953.

In a 1925 letter to his mother he had written, 'After having observed Americans in Europe I believe more than ever that sex with us has become a national disease. The way we get it into our politics and religion, where it does not belong anymore than digestion belongs there. All our paintings, our novels, our music, is concerned with it, sort of leering and winking and rubbing hands on it. But Latin people keep it where it belongs, in a secondary place. Their painting and music and literature has nothing to do with sex. Far more healthy than our way.'

C.H.S. (Lists 10, 25, 35)

♣ W. C. Fields
29 January 1880 to 25 December 1946

William Claude Dukenfield was the product of English working-class parents who lived in Philadelphia, a city he always spoke of with disgust. He left home at the age of 11 to pursue a career as a vaudeville juggler, adopting the stage name W. C. Fields. In 1915, he settled in New York and worked in various Broadway reviews, notably the *Ziegfeld Follies*. He moved to Hollywood to break into the movies, and people soon flocked to the local theatre to see the man with the bulbous nose, cigar and top hat be tormented by children and dogs in films like *Tillie and Gus* (1933), *The Bank Dick* (1940) and *Never Give a Sucker an Even Break* (1941). Much of Fields's boyhood was spent in poverty, and as an adult he was constantly fearful of being broke. As a result, his girlfriends found him tight-fisted.

In 1900, Fields married Hattie Hughes, his vaudeville assistant, who bore him a son named Claude. Although he faithfully supported his wife and child for forty years, he called them 'vultures' who were always after his money, and he very rarely saw them. A typical Fields letter to Hattie in 1933 began, 'I am in receipt of your complaint No. 68427. . . .' Fields and Hattie never obtained a legal divorce.

For seven years during the 1920s, Fields shared an apartment with Ziegfeld showgirl Bessie Poole, who also bore him a son. Although Fields never publicly acknowledged the child, he sent Bessie a cheque every month. Friends said of Fields that he changed mistresses every seven years, but the truth is few of his loves lasted that long. His stinginess, drinking and unwarranted suspicion were more than most women could take. In Hollywood, Fields began to hire detectives to follow his girlfriends. One of them, a New York showgirl, fell in love with her detective and married him.

In 1932, when Fields was 54 years old, he was introduced to 24-year-old Carlotta Monti – a dark-haired, olive-skinned beauty of Italian–Mexican–Spanish descent. He doffed his stovepipe hat, bowed low and said, 'It is a pleasure, my dusky beauty.' On their first date, Monti asked him if he had ever been married. 'I was married once,' Fields replied. 'In San Francisco. I haven't seen her for many years. The great earthquake and fire of 1906 destroyed the marriage certificate. There's no legal proof. Which proves that earthquakes aren't all bad.' In her book, *W. C. Fields and Me*, Carlotta describes their love life: 'Beginning with the first intimate night together when we consummated our love ... it was ecstasy.... Woody [her pet name for Fields] seemed starved for real love and affection, and I gave it to him in large quantities.... He was as much a perfectionist in his lovemaking as he was in his juggling. He never dropped a cigar box accidentally and, by the same token, he never fumbled during a golden moment.' However, alcohol eventually disrupted his sex drive completely. Carlotta put up with Fields's eccentricities for the last 13 years of his life. He would sometimes leave piles of money around the house to test her. Wise to him, she would add $5 to the pile to confuse him. When it came her turn to be followed by a detective, she responded by leading him on long meandering drives around the California countryside, knowing that Fields would be charged by the mile. As soon as he got his first bill from the detective agency, Fields ended the surveillance. When Fields died in 1945, his final words were, 'Goddamn the whole friggin' world and everyone in it but you, Carlotta.'

'Women', he once remarked, 'are like elephants to me: I like to look at them, but I wouldn't want to own one.'

M.J.T. and D.W. (Lists 8, 25, 30, 42)

♣ Kitty Fisher
1738 to 10 March 1767

Prostitutes, unlike courtesans, rarely gain renown; they sell their bodies for money, are unselective in their mates and emotionally indifferent to their partners. Catherine Maria (Kitty) Fisher was an exception. She was one of the most famous prostitutes in history, known to students of harlotry and nursery rhymes. Born in Soho and raised a Lutheran by poor German parents, Kitty somehow received a good education. On maturity, she was apprenticed to a milliner. In those years, milliners' shops were showcases for attractive young women seeking lover, patron or husband. Kitty was extremely attractive: small and dainty, with grey-blue eyes, a tilted nose, a generous mouth and a provocative manner, she was also intelligent, high-spirited and a witty conversationalist. Before long she was a kept woman, then a high-class prostitute. Kitty was never a streetwalker, nor did she work at a brothel. Instead, she occupied her own elegant flat in London. She had the outer dignity and poise of a lady, was a theatre-goer and horsewoman, had an expensive wardrobe, and enjoyed the high life.

While toiling behind the milliner's counter, Kitty was wooed by the son of an English merchant, an army ensign (later to become a lieutenant general) named Anthony Martin. He was handsome enough to be nicknamed the 'Military Cupid'. Despite his parsimony, Martin overwhelmed Kitty with gifts. She soon moved into his house in Leicester Square. Low on funds, Martin was relieved when the army transferred him abroad.

Kitty was not alone for long. Eminent men rushed to her door. Kitty decided to sell her favours for a life of luxury. Charging 100 guineas for a night in her bed, Kitty accepted all-comers. Among her lovers were Thomas Medlycott, heir to a vast estate, who introduced her to the opera, Captain Keppel, a naval officer, who introduced her to London society; First Lord of the Admiralty George Anson, who brought Kitty into the British royal circle; General John Ligonier, the most popular soldier in England, and the tenth Earl of Pembroke, aide-de-camp to King George II, who was so enchanted by Kitty that he settled £1000 a year on her. To these, Kitty added six lovers from the House of Lords. She thought she had reached her peak when Edward Augustus, Duke of York, and younger brother of King George III, called. After he had spent the night with her, Kitty decided to charge him no more than her usual 100 guineas. Instead, the duke handed her a £50 note. Kitty contemptuously placed the £50 on her bread and butter and ate it for breakfast. Then she barred the duke from her bed.

In one year, Kitty spent £12,000. The publicity she received was enormous. When she ordered out-of-season strawberries at 20 guineas a box, all of London was wide-eyed; when one of her clients paid Joshua Reynolds £50 to paint her, no one was surprised. Later, Reynolds painted her again, as Cleopatra, and reproductions were hawked throughout the city. While she was entertaining the dwarfish Lord Montfort and received word that Lord Sandwich, a rival for her affections, was about to visit her, she quickly shoved her pigmy peer under her hoopskirt and walked him safely out of sight. Parliament roared with delight at the story. Kitty's greatest scandal occurred in St James's Park. Wearing a smart riding habit, she was taking her daily gallop. The sudden appearance of a column of soldiers frightened the mount. The animal reared, and Kitty tumbled off. The incident resulted in this memorable verse in *Universal Magazine*:

Dear Kitty, had thy only fall
Been that thou met'st with in the Mall,
Thou had'st deserved our pity;
But long before that luckless day,
With equal justice might we say,
Alas! poor fallen Kitty!

In her heyday, she met notables ranging from King George II to Casanova (she missed only Dr Samuel Johnson, who was not at home when a friend brought her to meet him). Casanova wrote, 'the celebrated Kitty Fisher came to wait for the Duke of XX, who was to take her to a ball. She had on over a hundred thousand crowns' worth of diamonds. Goudar told me I could seize the opportunity to have her for 10 guineas, but I did not want to do so. She was charming, but she spoke only English. Accustomed to loving only with all my senses, I could not indulge in love without including my sense of hearing.'

After six years on her back, Kitty retired. In 1765, she met John Norris Jr, an ex-member of Parliament and heir to a fortune. Although a notorious womanizer, and a feckless spendthrift, Norris loved Kitty. They were married in Scotland, against his family's wishes. Several months passed before her father-in-law, after considerable soul-searching, received her in his house in Kent. A chronicler observed, 'She made an excellent wife, as she at once set about reforming her husband and retrieving his fortunes.' That winter she was happy but ill (with tuberculosis). Five months after her wedding, en route to a water cure, she died in a tavern in Bath. She was buried in the Norris family vault, in her best ball gown. She was only 29.

I.W. (List 19)

♣ F. Scott Fitzgerald

24 September 1896 to 21 December 1940

As the young author who christened the 1920s 'the Jazz Age', Fitzgerald enjoyed early success as spokesman for a rebellious generation. However, his popularity had waned by the end of the decade, and when he died at 44, not one of his books was in print. Ironically, his novels *The Great Gatsby* and *Tender Is the Night* are regarded as classics of American literature.

While still a boy in St Paul, Minnesota, Francis Scott Key Fitzgerald was more comfortable in the company of girls than with his own sex. He made a sincere effort to play football in school, but preferred Mr Van Arnum's dancing class, where a gentleman danced with a handkerchief in his right hand so he would not soil the back of the girls' dresses. Scott's father, who was by no means coarse, once said he would give $5 to hear his son swear. In contrast to his contemporary, Ernest Hemingway, Scott was offended by blood, sweat, grime and the seamy side of life. His stories and novels dealt mainly with the very rich, whose intrigues and decadence captivated his middle-class, Irish Catholic imagination. Scott's first novel, *This Side of Paradise*, was about flaming youth at Princeton University, a hotbed of alcohol and indiscriminate kissing. The book was quite scandalous for 1920, and as a result it sold well. At the age of 23, Fitzgerald was a best-selling author with all the attendant money, fame and opportunities. He married Zelda Sayre, the daughter of an Alabama judge, and with her began a relationship that lasted ten years and spanned two continents. Scott never again duplicated his initial literary success. Although his subsequent novels were well received by critics, the books did not sell. *Gatsby* earned him about $1200, a third of what the *Saturday Evening Post* paid him for quickly written short stories. So Scott stayed busy writing commissioned stories, at first to support his and Zelda's extravagant life-style, and, later on, to pay for Zelda's care after her nervous breakdowns. In 1937, deeply in debt to hospitals and friends, Scott went to Hollywood to write screenplays for MGM. The pay was good, but Fitzgerald often found himself at odds with the Hollywood establishment and eventually lost his contract with the studio. He was at work on a novel about the film industry, *The Last Tycoon*, when he died of a heart attack. Eight years later, Zelda was burned to death in an asylum fire.

A few of Fitzgerald's biographers have speculated that the author was a closet homosexual. Their evidence is circumstantial, however, for he had no documented homosexual experiences. He was often described as having delicate, 'feminine' features, and a picture of Fitzgerald in drag for a college review prompted a burlesque house to offer him a job as a female impersonator. He once donned a gown and attended a University of Minnesota dance with a friend, Gus Schurmeier, but it was done as a prank. According to Scott's friends and acquaintances, he would launch into drunken tirades against 'fairies', and the frequency of these outbursts led some to think he protested too much. Scott once told his friend Edmund Wilson that he longed to go with a handsome young man for an amorous weekend to the seaside. But he never actually went, and so the debate continues.

Fitzgerald did have a fetish for which there exists more solid evidence. He was greatly excited by women's feet. His view of feet as sex objects, a self-described 'Freudean [sic] complex', compelled Scott to keep his own bare feet modestly hidden. On the beach, he would bury them in the sand rather than expose them to public view. Scott was likewise ashamed of another part of his body – his penis. Zelda once told him that he could never satisfy her or any other woman, saying his problem was 'a matter of measurements'. His ego shattered, he consulted Hemingway, who suggested that they compare organs and afterwards declared that Scott's was normal sized. Fitzgerald was unconvinced, so Hemingway took him to look at statues at the Louvre. But even this failed to restore Fitzgerald's self-esteem. Years later, he asked an experienced prostitute named Lottie how his penis compared to others, and she assured him that it was technique that mattered to women and not size. This opinion was later echoed by Sheilah Graham, Scott's mistress, who wrote a rather backhanded defence of Scott's dimensions: 'Personally,' she said, 'given the choice between a donkey and chipmunk, I might choose the latter.'

Sex was one of Scott's warm-up preparations for writing, and he often made love as though he had a deadline to meet. After spending a night with him, Lottie commented to a mutual friend, 'He was nervous and I thought maybe that was why he was so quick about it. I asked him if that was his usual way and he said yes, so I didn't take it personally, like he wanted to get it over with.' Lottie then gave Scott a few pointers, for which he was grateful.

As an army lieutenant stationed in the South, Scott met Zelda at the Montgomery Country Club dance. The strikingly beautiful, blonde 17-year-old was surrounded by a pack of hopeful young men, but Scott would not be outdone: 'I was immediately smitten and cut in on her. She was the most beautiful girl I had ever seen in my life. And from the first moment I simply had to have her.' Scott later said Zelda had been 'sexually reckless' during their courtship. He had wanted to postpone sex until their wedding night, but Zelda delighted in flouting conventions, and they became lovers a year before their marriage. Scott's Catholic upbringing made him reluctant to use any form of birth control, yet

166

he never appeared to share Zelda's guilt about the three abortions she had during their marriage. Their union produced only one child – a girl called Scottie. Both Scott and Zelda were extremely jealous and one rarely went anywhere without the other. Once, Isadora Duncan flirted openly with Scott, and Zelda flung herself down a flight of stairs in protest. When Zelda found herself attracted to a handsome French aviator named Édouard Jozan, Scott went so far as to lock her in their villa for a month to keep her away from Jozan. The affair was probably quite innocent, and it is doubtful that Zelda and the flier ever slept together. Still, Scott was tormented for years by the episode.

Scott contended that he was unfaithful to Zelda only after she had been committed. In the summer of 1935, while Zelda was hospitalized, Scott lived at a resort hotel in Asheville, North Carolina. There, he blatantly carried on with a married woman named Rosemary, who was holidaying with her sister. It was also in Asheville that he met the prostitute Lottie, who recalled an evening when Scott made the mistake of spouting white supremacist rhetoric in her presence: 'I asked if he'd ever gone to bed with a coloured girl. He gave me the damnedest look, like I accused him of sleeping with his sister. Before he could answer, I told him that he had. Yes, not once or twice, but a dozen times. . . . When he got over that shock, he walked away like I had leprosy and told me to put on my clothes.'

Scott's companion for the last three years of his life was Sheilah Graham, a young, attractive, English-born columnist living in Hollywood. She shocked Scott at the outset of their affair by admitting she had had eight lovers before him. As Graham described it in her book, *The Real F. Scott Fitzgerald*, it was probably Scott's first healthy, uncomplicated relationship: 'In all our time together, I don't remember seeing him naked. But I was just as shy about my own body. However, this modesty did not prevent us from having a good time sexually. We satisfied each other and could lie in each other's arms for a long time afterwards, delighting in our proximity. It was not exhausting, frenzied lovemaking but gentle and tender, an absolutely happy state.' The rumour persists that Fitzgerald suffered his fatal heart attack while in bed with Sheilah Graham. However, according to her, he felt a pain while sitting in an easy chair reading the *Princeton Alumni Weekly*, tried to rise and collapsed to the floor, dead.

M.J.T. (Lists 5, 8, 20, 47)

167

♣ Errol Flynn
20 June 1909 to 14 October 1959

One of the greatest swashbucklers in cinema history, Errol Flynn was among Hollywood's top stars in the late 1930s and early 1940s, appearing in such films as *Captain Blood, The Charge of the Light Brigade* and *The Adventures of Robin Hood*.

Flynn stood 6 feet 2 inches, and his handsome looks rivalled those of any film idol. Born in Tasmania, of Irish-American parentage, Flynn was a chronic runaway as a youth. He left home for good after secondary school, and spent the next few years travelling the South Seas. In the early 1930s he was leading an expedition to New Guinea when he met film producer Charles A. Chauvel, who later cast him as Fletcher Christian in the semi-documentary *In the Wake of the Bounty*. Flynn landed a contract with Warner Brothers and spent the next fifteen years playing action-adventure heroes in sea tales, costume epics and war pictures.

In the 1950s, Flynn moved first to Europe and then to Jamaica, meanwhile making a series of unsuccessful films. He aged quickly – no doubt owing to high living, alcohol and narcotics – and died of a heart attack at 50.

Flynn boasted that he had spent between 12,000 and 14,000 nights making love. Although he had three wives – actresses Lili Damita and Patrice Wymore, and Nora Eddington – Flynn preferred to live apart from his wives and four children, claiming, 'The only real wives I have ever had have been my sailing ships.'

Biographers have surmised that his emotional indifference to women was due to his relationship with his mother, Marelle Young Flynn, who instilled in her son the idea that both sex and his genitals were dirty. Flynn was also obsessed with a fear of castration, having once been attacked by a knife-wielding Indian rickshaw driver. The blade, which barely missed Flynn's organs, left a deep scar in his groin. Despite his constant sexual urges, Flynn rarely bragged about his endurance as a lover, but did claim to practise oriental sexual techniques learned in Hong Kong. He was concerned about being able to perform whenever called upon, and was known to apply a pinch of cocaine to the tip of his penis as an aphrodisiac. His enjoyment of sex was heightened by watching other couples make love, and he also got a tremendous kick out of exhibiting himself – with a full erection – to his 'straight' male friends. Flynn even installed a one-way mirror at home so that he could observe his guests making love.

He often indulged his taste for kinky sex in Mexico, where one could see men and women copulate on stage or have intercourse with animals. Unrepentant Flynn even urged his son Sean to follow in his footsteps, once sending $25 for 'condoms and/or flowers'. Errol Flynn had a penchant for teenage girls. Nora Eddington was barely 18 and pregnant when they married, and at the time of his death he was planning to marry Beverly Aadland, 17. Flynn would often drive with David Niven to Hollywood High School, where he would linger, lamenting that the beautiful young girls he saw were 'jailbait' or 'San Quentin Quail'.

In fact, Flynn's reputation stemmed partly from his being charged with statutory rape. In 1942, he was accused of having had sex with Betty Hansen, 17, and with Peggy LaRue Satterlee, 16. According to Hansen, a waitress with aspirations to become a studio employee, she had flirted with Flynn at a tennis party at the house of one of his friends. Feeling ill, she had gone upstairs to lie down. Flynn followed her and, meeting with no resistance on her part, took off her clothes except for her shoes and socks. Then, she explained, he 'put his private parts in my private parts'. Satterlee, who claimed Flynn had forced her to have intercourse twice on his schooner, *Sirocco*, said that the actor had not made any effort to uncover her feet either. After a much-celebrated trial, Flynn was acquitted amid suspicions that the charges were not based on fact but reflected the desire of certain corrupt city officials to extort large bribes from the studio bosses. Also, the defence was able to establish that pending charges against the two girls – Hansen for oral intercourse and Satterlee for an illegal abortion – had been dropped after they agreed to testify against Flynn. Neither of these activities had involved Flynn, who emerged from the trial characterized as a 'charming rogue', and with his popularity enhanced. During the latter part of the Second World War servicemen began to use the expression 'in like Flynn' to denote a successful night with a woman. Flynn reportedly grew to despise both this expression – which implied he was a fun-loving rapist – and the snickers that greeted him when he walked into a room, but he still had not learned his lesson. Years later, he was charged with raping an attractive young French girl. Again he was acquitted, but the publicity intensified his self-destruction, which by this time included a dependence on vodka and an addiction to morphine.

A.L.G. and Eds.
(Lists 3, 8, 11, 17, 20, 22, 31, 34, 42, 50, 51, 52)

❦ Henry Ford
30 July 1863 to 7 April 1947

Ford epitomized a traditional American hero – the self-made man. Born on a farm near Dearborn, Michigan, he left school at 16 and died a billionaire at 83. His life abounds in contradictions. An enlightened employer who doubled the minimum wage and shortened the work day, he devised the five-day week to speed up production, hired informers to spy on workers, and fought unions with terror tactics. Inherently magnanimous, he often treated people with contempt and alienated his friends. A philanthropist, he published virulent anti-Semitic articles, and in 1938 was awarded a medal by Adolf Hitler.

Contradiction extended to Ford's love life. He was a straitlaced guardian of sexual morals, yet evidence suggests that he fathered a son adulterously. Ford's marriage seemed ideal. It had been love at first sight when he met pretty Clara Jane Bryant, a farmer's daughter, at a village ball. They wed when he was 24 and she 22. One child, Edsel, was born after four years. Smart, even-tempered, unselfish, Clara would go along with her husband's enthusiasms even if it meant letting him run a petrol engine in her sink or serving meals composed mainly of soyabean products. In one rare instance, she 'interfered' in his business affairs, begging him to end his resistance to unions and avert bloodshed; he followed her advice. Spending millions in charitable undertakings, Clara detested waste. She mended her petticoats and underwear and continued to darn Ford's socks after he became a millionaire. Clara died in 1950, three years after Ford.

A different picture emerges from John Dahlinger's *The Secret Life of Henry Ford* (1978). Dahlinger asserts that he is Ford's son, born in 1923. According to Dahlinger, his mother, beautiful Evangeline Côté (a cousin of Tyrone Power), caught Ford's eye when, still in her teens, she began working in an office at his plant. Clara's opposite, Evangeline charmed Ford, thirty years her senior, with her headstrong and vivacious ways. Ford arranged her marriage to one of his executives, Ray Dahlinger. He built the Dahlingers a magnificent home adjoining his, with a secret stairway leading to Evangeline's bedroom. Ford shocked nurses by visiting her new baby at the hospital. Little Dahlinger was showered with gifts and attentions by Ford and encouraged to play with Ford's grandchildren. Once, when an artist needed a model for the tycoon as a boy, Ford asked young Dahlinger, not one of his own grandsons, to pose for the portrait. Both Evangeline and her husband held important positions with the Ford company until Mrs Ford's death. Dahlinger says that the new regime, headed by grandson Henry Ford II, aware of gossip concerning the Dahlingers, tried to suppress all traces of Ford's association with them.

M.B.T. (Lists 25, 33)

♣ Benjamin Franklin
17 January 1706 to 17 April 1790

Franklin was the tenth of seventeen children born to the wife of a Boston soapmaker and candlemaker. At 12, he was apprenticed to his brother James, a printer. The ambitious boy learned quickly, and by his twenties he was public printer for Pennsylvania, New Jersey, Delaware and Maryland. He began his political life as clerk of the Pennsylvania Legislature (1736–51) and postmaster of Philadelphia (1737–53). During this period, he undertook his famous experiment with electrical phenomena. Franklin's wealth and reputation grew rapidly; in 1757, he was sent to London to protect the interests of Pennsylvania. In 1775, he returned to America, and the day after his arrival he was named as delegate to the Second Continental Congress. There he helped draft the Declaration of Independence. Then he was sent as emissary to France to solicit funds and military aid for the American Revolution. He stayed on in France as a celebrity after his replacement by Jefferson, but finally returned home in 1785. Two years later, the 81-year-old statesman attended the Constitutional Convention, and after his motion for adoption the constitution was unanimously approved. When Franklin died eulogies poured in from around the world, and Philadelphia staged the most impressive funeral in its history.

Franklin had a strong sex drive well into his seventies. He learned to control this drive as an adult but, while a young man on his own in Philadelphia, he wrote, 'That hard-to-be-governed Passion of Youth had hurried me frequently into intrigues with low Women that fell in my way, which were attended with some Expense and great Inconvenience, besides a continual Risque to my Health by a Distemper which of all Things I dreaded, tho' by great good Luck I escaped it.' One of the inconveniences alluded to was an illegitimate child. The baby, called William, was raised

171

by Franklin and his common-law wife Deborah Read. Franklin spent much of his married life away from Deborah; from 1757 until her death in 1774, they enjoyed less than two years together because of her fear of sea travel – which Franklin did everything in his power to feed. He was, however, genuinely fond of her, although she was plain and unintellectual. They had two children, a daughter Sarah and a son who died at the age of 4.

Franklin was a man whom women loved – not for his looks, but because he treated them as friends and equals and individuals. He had many affairs but, despite numerous references to kissing and embracing, most were platonic. Later affairs fell into the category of amorous friendships; full-blown passion was avoided. One such was with Catherine Ray, a young woman Franklin met in Boston in 1754. They journeyed by carriage to Newport together, but what happened between them remains speculation. He kept in close touch with Catherine throughout his life. He tried to repeat his flirtation with Catherine's cousin Betty under similar circumstances; she later angrily told her father, 'Don't you ever ask me to ride with that old fool again!' Franklin had a knack for ingratiating himself with his landladies and their children. His wife Deborah was the daughter of a family he had boarded with and, when in London, he became very close to Mrs Margaret Stevenson, his landlady, a widow with a daughter named Polly. In his memoirs, Franklin was very discreet about his relationship with Mrs Stevenson, although it lasted five years – and later ten years – at a stretch. They were considered a couple, and Deborah once received a letter from Franklin's old friend William Strahan, warning her 'to look after [her] interest', because Franklin was undergoing 'repeated and strong temptation'. Polly may also have been Franklin's lover, but Franklin was probably more of a parent, friend and confidant to the girl. She was at his side when he died.

Franklin's reputation as a ladies' man was established in France. He was 70 when he first arrived in Paris, but his zest for women hadn't diminished. Again becoming intimate with his landlord's family – he called the Chaumonts' tiny eldest daughter 'my pocket wife' – Franklin had two of his 'affairs' in the Chaumonts' house, both of them passionate in their way. The first began in the spring of 1777, when he met Madame Brillon de Jouy, beautiful and in her early thirties, an accomplished musician and composer. She was extremely romantic and Franklin saw much of her. On one famous occasion Franklin played chess with

172

a mutual friend beside Madame Brillon, while she had a bath (the bathtub was covered with a plank). Though he would have enjoyed being more intimately involved, she never consented.

But the love of Franklin's later life, perhaps his entire life, was Madame Helvétius, widow of the philosopher. The centre of attention at her estate in Auteuil, she was aristocratic, though rather bohemian. They had great affection for each other and Franklin wrote her many letters. In 1779, he proposed and was turned down, but their deep *amitié amoureuse* continued through 1785, the year Franklin returned to America, and was then maintained in a tireless correspondence.

Well into old age, Franklin was an advocate and practitioner of nude air baths. Polly Stevenson commented, 'He is fond of being in his *Birthday Suit*, and has not the least apprehension of *catching cold* in it.' Franklin was very unselfconscious about his own nudity. Once he was taking one of his air baths when he saw a friend's maid approaching with a letter he was anxious to receive. He absentmindedly went out to meet her and she ran away screaming, later telling her master that the Indians had killed Franklin and the chief himself had chased her.

In 1745, 39-year-old Franklin wrote a letter of sexual advice that was to become one of the best-known letters in American history. The original, in the files of the US Department of State, was considered too racy to release to the public until 1926. While Franklin addressed the letter to a 'friend', it is not known whether he wrote it for the amusement and edification of his peers or whether he sent it to an actual acquaintance. If the latter, his friend had apparently asked for advice on handling his sexual urges. Benjamin Franklin suggested that he find a wife:

25 June 1745

My dear friend:

I know of no Medicine fit to diminish the violent natural inclination you mention; and if I did, I think I should not communicate it to you. Marriage is the proper Remedy....

But if you will take this Counsel, and persist in thinking a Commerce with the Sex is inevitable, then I repeat my former Advice that in your Amours you should *prefer old Women to young ones*. This you call a Paradox, and demand my reasons. They are these:

1. Because they have more knowledge of the world, and their Minds are better stored with Observations; their Conversation is

more improving, and more lastingly agreeable.

2. Because when Women cease to be handsome, they study to be good. To maintain their Influence over Man, they supply the Diminution of Beauty by an Augmentation of Utility. They learn to do a thousand Services, small and great, and are the most tender and useful of all Friends when you are sick. Thus they continue amiable. And hence there is hardly such a thing to be found as an old Woman who is not a good woman.

3. Because there is no hazard of children, which irregularly produced may be attended with much inconvenience.

4. Because through more Experience they are more prudent and discreet in conducting an Intrigue to prevent suspicion. The Commerce with them is therefore safer with regard to your reputation; and regard to theirs, if the Affair should happen to be known, considerate People might be inclined to excuse an old Woman, who would kindly take care of a young Man, form his manners by her good Councils, and prevent his ruining his Health and Fortune among mercenary Prostitutes.

5. Because in every Animal that walks upright, the Deficiency of the Fluids that fill the Muscles appears first in the highest Part. The Face first grows lank and wrinkled; then the Neck; then the Breast and Arms; the lower parts continuing to the last as plump as ever; so that covering all above with a Basket, and regarding only what is below the Girdle, it is impossible of two Women to know an old from a young one. And as in the Dark all Cats are grey, the Pleasure of Corporal Enjoyment with an old Woman is at least equal and frequently superior; every Knack being by Practice capable of improvement.

6. Because the sin is less. The Debauching of a Virgin may be her Ruin, and make her for Life unhappy.

7. Because the Compunction is less. The having made a young Girl *miserable* may give you frequent bitter Reflections; none of which can attend making an old Woman *happy*.

8th and lastly. They are so grateful!!! . . .

Your Affectionate Friend,
Benj. Franklin
J.N. (List 26)

174

♣ Frederick II of Prussia
24 January 1712 to 17 August 1786

Frederick the Great's childhood was unhappy. His father, the tyrannical King Frederick William I, decreed that his heir be raised as a soldier, excluding poetry, the arts and philosophy from his schooling. But the boy had a strong taste for these and later became an accomplished composer and flautist. His father was determined to eradicate these 'effeminate' interests, and years of squabbling ensued. Frederick I's discipline included public beatings of his son, and young Frederick was sometimes forced to kiss his father's boots. There was scant mourning when, in 1740, the king died and Frederick II succeeded him. The first year of Frederick's rule typified the opposite poles of his personality. He speedily invited numerous artists to Berlin, instituted freedom of the press, and even wrote a treatise on monarchy. But, that same year, he invaded neighbouring Silesia and embarked upon the first of the many wars of his reign. After forty-six years of prosperous rule, Frederick the Great died in bed from a chill he caught while reviewing his troops.

As a boy of 9, Frederick wrote, 'One must not love too strongly.' What triggered his pained outburst is unknown, but Frederick's later life provided ample justification for his caveat. At 18, for instance, Frederick, by then an army officer, conspired with friends to abandon Prussia for England's more intellectual society. His father discovered the plan and had his son and a confederate arrested. They were charged with desertion and tried, and the friend – thought by the king to be his son's lover – was beheaded before Frederick's eyes. The king also ordered that 16-year-old Dorothea Ritter – a rector's daughter whom Frederick briefly courted – be flogged and sentenced to a lifetime of hard labour in the hemp spinneries at Spandau.

His father's wish was for Frederick to marry Elisabeth Christine, daughter of a minor Prussian noble. In 1733 they married, although Frederick did so without enthusiasm; he knew he would never love her. None the less, again at his father's urging, Frederick tried hard to provide an heir, promising that his efforts in the bed Frederick William gave the honeymooners would shortly produce offspring. His efforts failed, however, and, shortly after his father's death, Frederick and his wife (who faithfully loved him) took separate apartments. He rarely saw her, and upon his return from the Seven Years' War greeted her coldly, saying,

'Madame is fatter.' While they never divorced, their marriage, for all practical purposes, was finished.

Visitors to Frederick's palaces in subsequent years often commented upon the predominantly male character of his court, and rumours of the Prussian king's homosexuality abounded. Certainly Frederick did have intimate ties with many males, and he wrote to a curious nephew advising avoidance of 'Greek pleasures' (sodomy, especially anal intercourse) because, from his 'personal experience', he could vouch that it was 'not pleasant'. Voltaire, a frequent visitor to Frederick's court, also propagated the rumour by writing of Frederick's homosexuality. Frederick often spoke disparagingly of women; in one instance, speaking of the biblical Solomon, Frederick remarked that, where King Solomon found his harem of 1000 women not enough, 'I have only one [Elisabeth Christine] and that is too much for me.' Women were important to him, however, and he was probably bisexual. Frederick's adolescence, despite his father's meddling, featured many infatuations with girls. In 1728, Frederick and his father visited the elector of Saxony, who hoped to titillate the king by showing him one of his two beautiful mistresses – naked. Although the king was shocked, the 16-year-old prince apparently took the hint. According to his sister Wilhelmina, who was a confidante, Frederick made the woman his first mistress. Before marriage, three years later, Frederick fell in love with 23-year-old Luise de Wreech, a colonel's wife. It was rumoured that she bore him a daughter, who died within a few months. And in 1744, when the dancer Barberina enchanted Frederick's court, stories of their affair circulated throughout Prussia.

Some biographers allege that Frederick contracted a venereal disease as an adolescent, and that lack of proper treatment necessitated an operation later which removed part of his penis and rendered him impotent. While this would help explain Frederick's evident lack of interest in sex, there is no proof of such an operation.

R.M. (List 14)

176

♣ Sigmund Freud
6 May 1865 to 23 September 1939

Freud was the father of psychoanalysis. Terms relating to his theories concerning the development of personality and the sexual origins of neuroses have been absorbed into our everyday speech – for example, Oedipus complex, libido, repression, penis envy and death wish.

Sigmund Freud was his mother's first-born and the favourite of eight children; his father had four sons by a previous marriage. Always an excellent student, Freud attended the University of Vienna. It took him eight years to graduate; he could not settle on one course of scientific study. Ambitious as well as intellectually curious, Freud finally chose medicine because, as a Jew in Vienna, his opportunities in his first career choice – politics – were limited. He was not religious, but retained strong ties to his heritage. His research into the nervous system led to study of related diseases and their possible cure. He experimented with hypnosis, became enthusiastic about cocaine as a therapeutic substance, and in 1886 established a private practice specializing in nervous disorders. That year, aged 30, he married Martha Bernays.

In the late 1890s, Freud suffered a serious psychoneurosis, precipitated by the agonizing death of his father and his own fading interest in sex after the birth of his last child. In the process of analysing the disturbing dreams he was having at the time, he began making use of the 'talking cure' – psychoanalysis – which had been developed by his teacher, Dr Josef Breuer. For the next forty years, Freud lived a life of domestic stability and formidable achievement, gathering around him a circle of disciples, notably Carl Jung, Alfred Adler, Sandor Ferenczi and Ernest Jones. When the Nazis came to power in 1933, they burned Freud's works as 'Jewish pornography', but not until 1938 did he escape to London. Princess Marie Bonaparte of Greece, a friend and former patient, paid £20,000 ransom for his safe passage. Freud spent his last year in London, with cancer of the jaw and palate, and died there in 1939.

Freud made a career of sifting through the sexual secrets of others, yet took pains to conceal his own private life. He destroyed many letters; some that survived are in the Library of Congress, unavailable to scholars until the year 2000. At 16 his first love, Gisela Flüss, rejected him; he responded by becoming infatuated with her mother. Until he was 26, Freud showed no renewed interest in women. In 1882, Freud met Martha Bernays, a slim, pretty 21-year-old girl from a traditional Jewish family. They were engaged for four years, exchanging hundreds of letters and seldom meeting, although he was a resident at a nearby hospital. Freud was a passionate and jealous suitor in his correspondence. In 1884, he wrote, 'Woe to you, my princess, when I come. I will kiss you quite red and feed you till you are plump. And if you are forward you shall see who is the stronger, a gentle little girl who doesn't eat enough or a big wild man who has cocaine in his body.' They finally had enough money to marry in 1886, and eventually settled into a Vienna apartment they would occupy until 1938. Within nine years Martha had six children. In 1895, her sister Minna Bernays came to stay for two years. Evidently Freud was faithful, but became a distant husband. He was devoted to his work, and Martha was absorbed by domestic duties deemed proper to a wife and mother. She arranged the entire household for her husband's convenience, keeping children and servants out of his way, tending to his meals and wardrobe – she even put the toothpaste on his toothbrush. Looking back, Freud admitted that Martha never seemed at ease with him.

During Freud's self-analysis, he developed dramatic emotional ties to Dr Wilhelm Fliess, a Berlin ear, nose and throat specialist. There was a strong attraction between the two men; they wrote constantly and met occasionally for 'congresses', as they termed their discreet rendezvous. Freud wrote, 'I am looking forward to our congress as to a slaking of hunger and thirst ... I live gloomily ... until you come and then I pour out all my grumbles to you, kindle my flickering light at your steady flame and feel well again.' Fliess was receptive and caring. He tried to persuade his friend to give up smoking twenty cigars a day. (Freud never analysed his habit, although he had observed that smoking, drugs and gambling were substitutes for the 'primal addiction' – masturbation.) At one of their congresses, Freud fainted, and later remarked about the incident, 'There is some piece of unruly homosexual feeling at the root of the matter.' The friendship ended in 1903, largely due to Freud's complicated reaction to Fliess's theory of a universal bisexual impulse. At first, Freud rejected the idea, then claimed it as his own, and planned to write a major book on it, giving Fliess only nominal credit. Freud came to believe in a strong bisexual aspect to every personality, and said, 'Every sexual act is one between four individuals.'

It has been speculated that Freud and his sister-in-law Minna were lovers. Indeed, Minna's bedroom was accessible only through that of Sigmund and Martha. Larger and heavier than her sister, Minna was, according to one neighbour, also prettier than Martha. Of the two, she was considerably more intellectual, and Freud found her a good conversationalist and a sympathetic ear for his thoughts on psychoanalysis. Freud once described Minna as being like himself – they were both 'wild, passionate people, not so good', whereas Martha was 'completely good'. Freud loved to travel and, when he took his extended summer vacations, Minna often accompanied him. Martha stayed at home. The main source for the story that Freud actually had a love affair with Minna was Freud's disciple Carl Jung. Reportedly, Jung had remarked that Minna and Martha had separately approached him about the problem of Freud's passion for Minna. Jung told an American professor that, on one occasion in 1907, when Jung had been Freud's guest in Vienna, Minna approached him and poured out her secret. Jung said, 'From her I learned that Freud was in love with her and that their relationship was indeed very intimate.' Upset, Jung confronted Freud about the matter and suggested he be analysed by an outside therapist. Jung offered himself as the analyst. Freud coldly rejected the suggestion.

Freud had a voracious appetite for sex – as an intellectual pursuit. When he was only 41 he wrote to Fliess, 'Sexual exitation is of no more use to a person like me.' He lived by a strict moral code. Even though his theories stressed the power of unconscious sexual impulses, Freud edited such wishes out of his own behaviour. He was, after all, a married man, and he had said that no marriage was secure until the wife had succeeded in making herself a mother. After six children in rapid succession, his desires may have been quenched by anxieties about contraception. In 1908, he said, 'Marriage ceases to furnish the satisfaction of sexual needs that it promised, since all the contraceptives available hitherto impair sexual enjoyment, hurt the fine susceptibilities of both partners and even actually cause illness.' In 1909, he came to the USA with Jung and other colleagues to deliver a series of lectures. One morning, upon awakening, Freud confided to Jung he was having erotic dreams about American women. 'I haven't been able to sleep since I came to America,' confessed Freud. 'I continue to dream of prostitutes.' 'Well, why don't you do something about it?' said Jung. Freud recoiled in horror. 'But

I am a married man!' he exclaimed.

Freud's theories described the forces shaping human behaviour as sexual. But culture siphoned off the instinctive energy of sex and sublimated it into social functioning. Freud's own life epitomized the viewpoint he thought tragic, but true: 'The sexual life of a civilized man is seriously disabled.'

K.P. (Lists 14, 21, 25)

♣ Clark Gable
1 February 1901 to 16 November 1960

Clark Gable reigned as King of Hollywood for more than thirty years, starring in sixty-one films between 1930 and 1960. Often cast as the ultimate macho male, Gable became one of the screen's greatest sex symbols. His portrayal of a newspaper man in *It Happened One Night* won him an Academy Award, but he gained his most lasting fame as Rhett Butler in *Gone With the Wind*.

Gable was raised by a strong-minded but indulgent stepmother without much interference from his itinerant oil-driller father. Never much of a scholar, Gable dropped out of high school in his junior year and, after putting in some time at a tyre factory in his home state of Ohio and in the Oklahoma oil fields, he decided to become an actor. Ignoring his father, who said that 'acting was for sissies', Gable worked his way across the country as a roustabout in a travelling tent show. Ending up in Portland, Oregon, he joined a small theatre group, where he received his first real dramatic training. More interested in the theatre than films, Gable nevertheless went to Hollywood and began working as an extra on film sets. Although studio executives were slow to realize Gable's potential, women quickly recognized his sexual magnetism. When MGM caught on, the studio fixed his decaying, crooked teeth and began grooming him as an 'outdoorsy, he-man' type. Gable remained modest even after his rise to stardom, and would make a point of striding through screaming hordes of fans to sign autographs, saying that, if it wasn't for them, he wouldn't have a job. An impeccable dresser who carried his 6 foot 1 inch frame with grace, Gable was obsessed with cleanliness and would take several showers a day, and shaved not only his armpits but his chest as well. Somewhat of a loner, he preferred the company of extras and studio technicians – men with whom he could drink and fish and hunt – to that of his film-star peers. He refused to let his fame go to his head and mumbled after winning the Oscar, 'I'm still going to wear the same size hat.'

That women loved Gable and that he loved them is made evident by the dozens – perhaps hundreds – of affairs he carried on throughout his career. Some said he had a fixation for older women and pointed to his first two marriages as proof. But those marriages seem to have been more a matter of convenience than passion. Gable's first wife, Josephine Dillon – his acting coach and seventeen years older than he – later claimed that she and Gable had no physical relationship – that it was a marriage 'in name only'. Gable next married a wealthy 46-year-old Houston divorcée, Ria Langham, who encouraged and mothered him considerably at the beginning of his career. Gable himself admitted to a preference for older women and once remarked, 'The older woman has seen more, heard more, and knows more than the demure young girl. . . . I'll take the older woman every time.'

Still, Gable wasn't firmly trapped in an older-woman syndrome. During one of his first leading roles he jumped into a red-hot affair with his co-star Joan Crawford, who was 25 at the time. Crawford was to credit Gable later with 'more sheer animal magic than anyone in the world', which she attributed to the fact that 'he had balls'. She added that she didn't believe that any woman who worked with Gable 'did not feel twinges of sexual urge beyond belief'. Although Crawford and Gable were to remain friends for many years, they stoically cooled their romance on studio orders, since they were both married to other people at the time.

Then he met Carole Lombard, the Hollywood actress who was to become the greatest love of Gable's life. The quiet and reserved Gable was instantly attracted to the petite, blonde actress's zaniness and ribald humour. The two adopted the incongruous nicknames of 'Ma' and 'Pa' for each other and became inseparable. Lombard loved to pull pranks on Gable such as leaving a gift-wrapped knitted 'cock-warmer' in his dressing room with a note: 'Don't let it get cold. Bring it home hot for me.' Irreverent about his sexy image, she would tease him by pretending she'd arranged to make his 'cockprint' as well as his footprints and handprints in front of Grauman's Chinese Theatre. Lombard was once heard to remark, 'I adore Clark, but he's a lousy lay.' Lombard gamely trekked alongside Gable on his fishing and hunting expeditions, sleeping in the open and once even making love in a duck blind. When Gable's divorce from Ria became final, the two eloped to

Kingman, Arizona. After their marriage, Lombard tamed considerably to fit in with Gable's more sedate ways, causing a friend to comment that she was a changed person from the one who had once flippantly remarked during a press conference that Gable wasn't circumcized. The only thing that marred the happiness of 'Hollywood's favourite couple' was their failure to have children. 'They were forever checking sperm', a friend said, and 'tried every position known to humans', according to another. 'They would have done it hanging out a window if somebody said you got pregnant that way.' But, no matter how much Gable loved Lombard, he would never be a one-woman man and Lombard would periodically explode when rumours grew too hot about Gable's escapades with his current leading lady.

Gable was devastated by Lombard's death in a plane crash just three years after they were married. 'Ma's gone', he said brokenly to a group of friends when her body was finally recovered. He was to spend the rest of his life searching for another Lombard. After going through an endless parade of women ranging from a Palm Beach socialite to the daughter of a fishing resort owner, he recklessly plunged into a marriage with Lady Sylvia Ashley. The match ended quickly and Gable was to say later that he was drunk when he married her. At the age of 54, Gable married (a fifth and final time) a former actress ten years his junior who was as close a facsimile to Lombard as he was likely to find. Fair-haired, tiny, lovely Kay Spreckles was willing to fit herself into the mould set by Lombard, and she and Gable led a quiet life on their ranch until he died of a heart attack after making *The Misfits*. They had one son, John, who was born five months after Gable's death.

Gable was promiscuous and often was indiscriminate about his bedmates. Screenwriter Anita Loos noted that Clark had 'that old early American male idea that you must take on any girl that comes your way'. Although the King could snap his fingers and get almost any woman he wanted, at times he preferred to go to bed with high-priced call girls. Asked why, when he could have it for free, Gable replied, 'Because I can pay her to go away. The others stay around, want a big romance, movie lovemaking. I do not want to be the world's greatest lover.' He also did not confine himself to attractive women. When an army buddy with whom he was stationed in Europe during the Second World War asked Gable why he was going out with such 'a dog', Gable said, 'Well, she's there.' Gable had one long-term love affair – it lasted more than a decade – with a diminutive, homely Hollywood writer that was a secret to all but a few of his intimates. He slept with this woman regularly, and she once remarked to her closest friend, 'Whenever Clark got on top of me and entered me, and started going, it never amounted to much and was never very good. But then I would open my eyes, and realize this was *the* Clark Gable – Gable himself – and only then would I truly feel excited.'

Gable also took advantage of the ready supply of leading ladies, making love to them both on and off the screen. Once, when looking at an MGM publicity photo which displayed the studio's female stars, Gable exclaimed admiringly, 'What a wonderful display of beautiful women and I've had every one of them!' Gable's name was linked romantically with nearly all his co-stars, from Grace Kelly to Ava Gardner to Jean Harlow, whether there was substance to the rumours or not. The King not only played the role of the quintessential male; he was one. More than one actress was to remark, 'I think every woman he ever met was in love with him.' Marilyn Monroe said she 'got goosebumps all over' when he accidentally touched her breast. Or, as Joan Blondell put it, 'He affected all females, unless they were dead.'

L.K.S. (Lists 7, 11, 20, 27, 28, 42, 43, 45)

♣ Mahatma Gandhi
2 October 1869 to 30 January 1948

Gandhi was the youngest, smallest and favourite child of the middle-aged prime minister of the minor principality of Porbandar in western India and the minister's fourth wife. Solitary, shy and plain (with a big nose and jug ears), he enjoyed a close relationship with both parents, particularly with his deeply religious mother. The turning points of his childhood were marriage at the age of 13, in the Hindu tradition, and the death of his father three years later, at the very moment Gandhi was sexually importuning his pregnant child bride. This left him with a lifelong sense of sexual guilt – eventually sublimated in political activism. At 18, taking a vow not to touch wine, women or meat, he went alone to study law in England for three years, a formative period for him. He had great difficulty satisfying his prodigious appetite with British vegetarian cuisine. But, despite temptation, particularly at the hands of middle-aged landladies eager to assuage his needs, he succumbed to nothing more than a temporary dandyism.

183

Gandhi came into his own during twenty-one years spent in South Africa, arriving in 1893 as a lawyer for a Muslim firm and becoming a leader of the Indian community there. He began to experiment with 'nature cures' and communal living. And at the age of 37 he took the Hindu vow of *brahmacharya* (celibacy), to free himself for a lifetime of political and religious leadership. Gandhi's political philosophy was a combination of truth and force, a form of passive resistance or militant non-violence. By means of civil-disobedience campaigns and symbolic protest demonstrations – later by dramatic public fasts – he would counter might with right and return good for evil, compelling the strong to acknowledge the force of the weak.

In 1915, Gandhi returned to India to tackle colonialism. Rejecting all western influences, he established a simple, austere lifestyle in his ashrams (communal retreats). He adopted the spinning wheel as a symbol of traditional self-sufficiency, spinning cloth to replace imported fabric. He devised a series of symbolic confrontations with the British, culminating in 1947 in Indian independence. Soon afterwards, working to bring peace between Hindus and Muslims, he was assassinated by a Hindu fanatic.

With his small, frail body, naked except for a loincloth and metal-rimmed spectacles, Gandhi confronted the key issues of his time: tradition and modernization, colonialism and nationalism, identity and faith. The one question he was never able to resolve, and which continued to plague him into old age, was sex. Marriage at the age of 13, Gandhi recalled, meant at first only the acquisition of a 'strange girl to play with'. It also meant that, assuming the traditional authority of the Hindu husband, he might dictate to his bride. But Kasturbai Makanji, also 13, was stubborn and strong-willed, and spent nearly half of her first two years of marriage at home with her parents. She was submissive only when it came to sex. For Gandhi, who had been coached by his brother's wife, marriage launched a period of sexual self-indulgence. Constantly preoccupied with erotic urges, his schoolwork suffered. Kasturbai remained illiterate ('lustful love left no time for learning') and Gandhi henceforth sought intellectual companionship elsewhere. He shared the Hindu concern with digestion and excretion, and the worship of semen as the vital life force, its loss debilitating to body and mind. Celibacy, in fact, is not uncommon among older Hindu males. But, for Gandhi, highly sexed and in his mid-thirties, it involved a great struggle. A combination of factors motivated Gandhi's final resolve to forswear sex. He believed that abstinence was the only morally acceptable form of birth control; after five sons, he wanted no more children. He wished to conserve all his energy for a life of service.

For Gandhi, there was a parallel between sexual and political exploitation. His philosophy of passive resistance, he wrote, was inspired by the indomitable Kasturbai: 'Her determined resistance to my will ... made me ashamed of myself and cured me of my stupidity in thinking I was born to rule over her.' Celibacy was simply a form of non-violence between the sexes. But, until her death in 1944, while she and Gandhi were serving time in prison for civil disobedience, Kasturbai reserved a peasant distrust of the women who surrounded her husband. For, although the traditional Hindu vow required a celibate to avoid the opposite sex altogether, Gandhi spent the rest of his life tempting fate. He was a great flirt who adored women – and they were useful to his movement. Beginning in South Africa with 17-year-old Sonja Schlesin, he had a long line of secretary–nurses who served him with great devotion and slavish obedience. Over the years, in addition to taking dic a on, these women assumed the duties of massaging, bathing, ? d even sleeping with him. Such was Gandhi's appeal that women came from far and wide. Not all Gandhi's relations with the opposite sex, however, were entirely platonic. The struggle to remain sexually pure, he wrote, was 'like walking on the sword's edge.' He continued to be tormented by nocturnal em ssions, to which he confessed publicly as a form of atonement, ir to his late sixties. Then there was the scandal of the naked young girls he slept with, to keep him warm and 'test his resolve'.

He had been experiencing 'shivering fits' in the night, so he asked young women in his inner circle – all virgins or young brides – to warm him with their bodies. For some of them it was an ambivalent experience. Abha Gandhi, the wife of a grand-nephew, began sleeping with the Mahatma when she was 16, and was eventually asked to remove all her garments. Her husband was so upset that he offered to keep the old man warm himself! Gandhi refused his offer.

Some of Gandhi's girls were motivated by jealousy of one another and their fear of losing favour. Manu Gandhi was a distant cousin, who slept with the Mahatma from the age of 19. He would lean on her and Abha, his 'walking sticks', when he went out; and during his fasts Manu would monitor his vital functions and administer enemas. 'The more they tried to restrain themselves and repress their sexual impulses', one of Gandhi's disciples said about the women in his entourage, 'the more over-sexed and conscious they became.' Ironically, Gandhi scolded her (also a celibate and a healer) for sleeping naked with one of her patients. In fact, in matters of sex as well as politics, the Mahatma simply wrote his own rules.

C.D. (Lists 2, 7, 21, 32, 44)

❦ David Garrick
18 February 1717 to 20 January 1779

No English actor before him had been paid so much or had received such adulation from an adoring public. Superb in tragedy, a genius at comedy, he revolutionized acting by intro-ducing a naturalistic style. As actor–manager of Drury Lane Theatre for three decades, he made important innovations in all aspects of theatrical production.

Garrick had only a limited amount of English blood in his veins. One grandfather was a French Huguenot refugee named de la Garrique, and the other was Irish. This son of a poor army captain set out with fellow immortal Samuel Johnson from their homes in Lichfield in 1737 – with fourpence between them – to seek their fortunes in London. Abandoning a plan to study law, Garrick eventually joined his brother in opening a wine business. However, enamoured of the theatre, he quietly took up acting and, on 19 October 1741, burst upon the public as Shakespeare's Richard III. An astonished Alexander Pope said, 'That young man never had his equal, and never will have a rival.' In 1747, Garrick became part owner of Drury Lane Theatre, which he managed until his retirement in 1776. During these years he displayed an amazing versatility in a wide range of roles, keeping Shakespeare before the public (in 1448 performances), and thus handing down a great dramatic tradition to posterity. Garrick died at 61, suffering from gout, kidney trouble and herpes, and was buried in Westminster Abbey. He left a fortune of £100,000.

Garrick was attractive and magnetic in appearance, though only 5 feet 4 inches tall. His large features were dominated by brilliant black eyes, set in an incredibly mobile face. Skilful and graceful in dancing and fencing, he was pursued by glamorous actresses, but he had no desire for casual sex. While seeking a

186

'soulmate' to share his life, he fell deeply in love with actress Peg Woffington, an impudent and enchanting Irish beauty. Honest, warm, generous, intelligent, and a brilliant performer, she had only one fault: she couldn't say no to the admirers who pursued her. Garrick addressed verses to her, hoping to reform and marry her. He even bought her a wedding ring to try on. She returned his love and was faithful to him 'in her fashion'. They agreed to live together – a daring experiment at that time – but Garrick could not adjust to Peg's carefree ways. After six months they separated, although they continued to see each other. Peg gradually began to reconsider the advantages of married life. As a member of a profession thought to be socially disreputable, she wanted to be made an 'honest woman'. But Garrick hesitated. For him, fidelity was a necessity. Insulted by his doubts, she cried, 'From this moment I separate myself from you. . . .' The next day, she returned his present with a letter dismissing him. He did the same, but kept a pair of diamond shoe buckles she had given him. She wrote for them, but he begged to be allowed to keep them as a memento. Deeply hurt and angry, Garrick wrote verses decrying her infidelity. She in turn spread stories that he had treated her shabbily. After many lovers and a brilliant career, she died at 46 due to a paralytic stroke.

The break with Woffington was good for Garrick, clearing the way for the great romance of his life. He found his ideal woman in Eva Maria Veigel, a Viennese dancer called 'La Violette'. This exquisite star of the opera ballet was reputedly a protégée of the Empress of Austria, and when in England she lived with the family of Lord Burlington (some believed her to be his natural daughter). She first appeared in London in 1746 and was talked of everywhere. Garrick met her and fell in love; she had seen him in one of his stage roles and was already in love with him. Lady Burlington opposed Eva's match with a mere player, and every obstacle was thrown in the lovers' path. It is said that a clever doctor finally got Lady Burlington's consent by telling her that the only remedy he could prescribe for the lovesick Eva was marriage to Garrick. Garrick and Eva were united on 22 June 1749. The wealthy actor settled £10,000 on his wife, plus £70 per year pin money. After a perfect honeymoon, they moved into a house five minutes' walk from the theatre. She retired from the stage forever to devote herself completely to her husband. Not a shred of correspondence exists between them (though Garrick saved everything for his future biographers), because in thirty years of marriage they were never parted for a single day. Nothing was complete for him without her; she even accompanied him to his rehearsals, and he relied on her judgement completely. Though childless, their marriage never lost its bloom; his gallantry toward her was legendary. Dr Johnson used to tease Garrick about Eva's despotism: '*He* durst not do such a thing. His wife would not *let* him!' Her friendliness and hospitality were famous. The two of them were 'friend-making, everywhere friend-finding souls', strangers to a day's solitude. When Garrick died, he left Eva two houses and a large fortune; she was to have forty-three years of widowhood. She cherished his memory and, although courted by a Scottish judge, never remarried. When she died in 1822, aged 98, her maid draped her coffin with her wedding sheets.

Garrick's numerous love poems stressed that what was physical or sensual in a woman was less important to him than wit, charm, soul and mind – attributes that are impervious to the passage of time.

M.B.T. (List 42)

♣ Paul Gauguin
7 June 1848 to 8 May 1903

Born in Paris – three-quarters French, a quarter Peruvian Creole – young Paul Gauguin was taken to live in Lima, Peru, in 1851, when Napoleon III staged a coup d'état in France. Nudity was commonplace in South America, and these early experiences affected him strongly. All his life he felt most comfortable among naked women. Paul returned to France with his mother in 1855, and at 17 he decided to explore the world as a sailor. Six years later, he quit the sea for the more respectable but no less uncertain life of a stockbroker. The French Bourse enriched him for a time but, when the Paris exchange crashed in 1883, he decided to concentrate on painting. The decision ruined his marriage, doomed him to a lifetime of penury, and gave the world some of its most treasured art.

Gauguin befriended other painters of the period, among them Pissarro, Cézanne and Van Gogh, and joined in the Impressionist exhibitions of the 1880s. For ten weeks, towards the end of 1888, he lived and worked with Van Gogh in 'the Yellow House' in Arles, France. Their incompatibility drove Gauguin to Paris. Increasingly alienated from his wife as well as from Western civilization, Gauguin managed to sell thirty paintings in 1891, and he set sail for Tahiti. Except for a brief return to Europe in 1893, he spent the rest of his life in the South Seas, painting and sculpting. He died embittered and poor, in the Marquesas Islands.

From his early days as a teenage seaman, to his last months as a dying syphilitic on the Marquesas Islands, Gauguin had an extremely active sex life. With his marriage to Mette Sophie Gad – a tall, blonde Danish governess – in 1873, he settled into what promised to be a life of respectability and comfort. In 1883 Gauguin's decision to leave the Bourse stunned and outraged Mette, who hoped that this was just some phase Gauguin was going through. His in-laws in Copenhagen, where the couple lived for a time, ridiculed him. The resultant strain and lack of money caused the Gauguins to separate. Yet, even after leaving for Tahiti, he clung to the hope that his wife and five children would one day join him there. They never did.

In Tahiti in 1891, Gauguin found artistic inspiration and all the breasts he could fondle. At first he revelled in the local custom of welcoming a different native woman into his hut each night, but soon learned that such promiscuity hindered his work. He longed for his own *vahine* (woman). He set out to find one, and at a neighbouring village he was offered the hand of Tehura, a nubile native barely into her teens. Gauguin was instantly attracted. Assured that she was entering the union willingly and that she was free from disease, he took her to his hut. After a week's trial marriage, she agreed to stay. With Tehura by his side, frequently as his model, the artist produced much work. Inspired one night by her fear of the *tupapau*, or evil spirit, he created *The Spirit of the Dead is Watching*.

In 1893, he sailed for France, leaving a pregnant Tehura behind. In Paris, he renewed his relationship with a former mistress – a simple, withdrawn seamstress named Juliette Huet. He also began a disastrous affair with a 13-year-old waif known as Anna the Javanese, who was half Indian, half Malay. She kept him from his work and, when they went to Brittany, her unpopularity among the townspeople was immediately evident. One afternoon, Anna – whose superior attitude and outlandish clothes offended the villagers – stuck out her tongue and thumbed her nose at a group of children who were making fun of her. The incident touched off a melée that ended with Gauguin being kicked unconscious by a gang of fifteen fishermen. Gauguin had barely recuperated when Anna deserted him after carefully stripping his studio of all valuables except his paintings.

When Gauguin returned to Tahiti in 1895, he expected to cohabit with Tehura. But she had meanwhile married an islander. Although she did visit the painter for about a week as a sort of hut-warming present, she was frightened by his syphilitic sores and went back to her husband. Gauguin had lost his mate, but found many others. 'My bed has been invaded every night by young hussies running wild', he complained at one point. 'Yesterday I had three.' Looking for a 'serious woman for the house', he briefly settled down with a pretty 14-year-old named Pahura, but she was not as stimulating as Tehura. Still, he did a nude of her, *Arii Vahine* (The Noblewoman), which he considered 'the best I have ever painted'.

In 1901 he moved to a 1¼ acre lot on one of the Marquesas Islands, where he built a hut that he decorated with pornographic photos. In a bed into whose wooden frame Gauguin had carved an erotic scene, he slept with virtually any native woman willing to overlook the open sores festering on his legs. Whenever a new girl entered his hut, he would explore her body underneath her dress and say to her, 'I must paint you.' His syphilis grew progressively worse, but a heart attack eventually killed him in 1903.

Gauguin had reflected, 'In Europe intercourse between men and women is a result of love. In Oceania love is a result of intercourse. Which is right? The man or woman who gives his body is said to commit a small sin. That is debatable. . . . The real sin is committed by the man or woman who sells his body.

'Women want to be free. That's their right. And it is certainly not men who stand in their way. The day a woman's honour is no longer located below the navel, she will be free. And perhaps healthier, too.'

Gauguin's son by Tehura, named Emile, boasted of his illustrious parentage and always hoped to become a painter himself. Emile died in poverty at the age of 80 in January 1980.

W.A.D. (Lists 3, 8, 9, 11, 18, 20, 21, 22, 25, 35, 39)

♣ George Gershwin
26 September 1898 to 11 July 1937

Born Jacob Gershvin in a tough Jewish section of Brooklyn, Gershwin gave no hint of his extraordinary talent as a boy. But, at the age of 10, Gershwin heard the sounds of a violin drifting through an open window and this 'flashing revelation of beauty' led him to take up the piano. In 1913, he became a staff pianist with a Tin Pan Alley publishing firm – and began his prolific stream of compositions. His 1919 hit, 'Swanee', sung by Al Jolson, established his fame and allowed him to pursue more ambitious undertakings, including scoring Broadway shows and Hollywood films, often with his older brother, Ira, as lyricist. Despite his successes, Gershwin was plagued by nervous and digestive disorders. He rigidly limited his diet to easily digested foods like cereals. To combat constipation and chronic depression, he was psychoanalysed by Dr Gregory Zilboorg. He saw Zilboorg five times a week for a year, and the pair got along so well that they went on vacation to Mexico together. Gershwin was not all gloom and constipation, however. He liked parties, and enthusiastically plunged into a variety of projects – from juggling to painting. His vitality remained undiminished until his sudden death, at 38, from an inoperable brain tumour.

Women by the score were attracted to his dark, athletically trim good looks. Gershwin slept with many of them but, unsated by the flood of women who pursued him, he indulged in frequent trips to brothels where he gladly bought more sex. He even asked a friend how one went about 'keeping' a woman. When informed of the cost involved, he dropped the subject. A scorecard of Gershwin's lovers would list hundreds, even thousands, of partners, and he often bragged of his conquests and prowess – he occasionally enjoyed sex with two women at the same time. Aware of his sexual reputation, he once offered to bestow upon a young woman the privilege of sleeping with him before her marriage. She declined. But one trip to a bordello undid his boasting. While having his pleasure in a Parisian brothel, a pair of his friends – unbeknown to Gershwin – bribed the madame for a look through a peephole which gave a clear view of Gershwin's performance. What they saw, they reported later, was mechanical sex hastily consummated. Gershwin's interest in lovemaking, despite a multitude of lovers, was perfunctory. Although he believed that sex stimulated his creativity, Gershwin's chief interest – always – was music. Once, while at a party, for example, Gershwin sat with a pretty girl on his lap. Invited to play a few tunes on the piano, Gershwin bolted from his chair so rapidly that the young lady tumbled to the floor. He had simply forgotten her presence when music was mentioned. In another instance, after learning a woman he had loved had married another, Gershwin commented, 'If I wasn't so busy, I'd be upset.' Ironically, Gershwin, despite his vigorous pursuit of sexual pleasures, retained some prudishness. His sister Frances discovered this when, upon saying 'darn' in public, Gershwin slapped her for uttering an expletive. And he frequently rebuked her if her skirts rode above her knees.

Because of Gershwin's many lovers, his biographers inevitably seek to identify *the* woman of his life – the one he loved best. Dozens of candidates included composer Kay Swift, to whom he dedicated his *Song-Book* compositions; actress Paulette Goddard, whom he urged to leave her spouse, Charlie Chaplin; French starlet Simone Simon, who presented Gershwin with a gold key to her Los Angeles home; and dancer Margaret Manners, whose son took the name Alan Gershwin and, in 1959, wrote an article for *Confidential* magazine entitled, 'I Am George Gershwin's Illegitimate Son'. Was he? The evidence on both sides is unconvincing. Only one fact is certain: Gershwin never loved one woman enough to marry her. With some insight, Oscar Levant – a close friend – quipped, 'Tell me, George, if you had to do it all over again, would you fall in love with yourself again?'

R.M. (Lists 9, 20, 22, 28, 42)

♣ André Gide
22 November 1869 to 19 February 1951

This Nobel Prize-winning writer is best known for his semi-autobiographical novels (among them *The Immoralist* and *The Counterfeiters*), which deal with homosexuals and the duty of each individual to shape his own moral code. A champion of homosexuality, Gide gave literary respectability to this hitherto taboo subject.

Paris-born to both wealth and position, Gide lost his father, a law professor, when he was 11. His overprotective, puritanical mother dominated her only child. A sickly dunce in school, he was once expelled for masturbating in class. Weeping, his mother took him to a doctor, who threatened to castrate him to make him desist. Neurotic and anxiety-ridden, at 13 Gide fell in love with his 15-year-old cousin, Madeleine Rondeaux, whom he called his 'mystic lodestone' and worshipped all his life. At 20 he received his baccalauréat and thenceforth devoted his time to music, writing, travel and social causes. At 25 he declared he was a pederast: a man whose object of desire is a male child or adolescent. None the less, after the death of his mother, he married his cousin Madeleine. (The marriage was never consummated.) For the rest of his life he was torn apart by the polarization of the sensual and spiritual aspects of his nature. His writing was an attempt to reconcile the conflict. Gide's frankness, expressed in his works, shocked the public and deeply hurt his wife. Although he was a major literary influence of his time, the Catholic Church banned his works. Honours were withheld until 1947, when – at 78 – he received both a doctorate from Oxford University and the Nobel Prize for Literature.

Gide suffered from 'angelism', an aberration which precluded intercourse with a beloved or idealized object; in his case, the angel was his wife. Cultured, intelligent, almost saintly, she never complained about their platonic relationship, content with his spiritual half as long as she could believe it was all hers. But at 47 Gide fell in love with Marc Allégret, the 16-year-old son of the best man at the Gides' wedding. Their liaison developed into a lasting friendship. Gide records that he experienced the torments of jealousy for the first time when Marc returned home late one night after visiting artist–writer Jean Cocteau. In retaliation for Gide's 'spiritual infidelity', Madeleine burned all his letters to her. Throughout his life, Gide maintained that he had loved her alone. She died, still devoted to him, in 1938.

His family's brutal attempt to repress his sexuality tended to link sensuality with guilt in his mind. Because of his mother's attitudes, he thought 'good' women had no sexual feelings and feared prostitutes as much as 'vitriol throwers'. Homosexual copulation he once described as being like 'a huge vampire feeding upon a corpse'. Because most forms of homosexual activity were repellent to him, when he discovered he was a pederast, the solitary masturbation of his childhood was replaced by reciprocal masturbation with young partners. After his mother died, Gide agonized over his sexual identity and suitability for marriage. Sexual attempts with women continued to fail, whereas encounters with young boys had been consistently satisfying. He consulted a doctor about his tastes, and confessed to what he thought was a hopeless perversion. The doctor examined him, listened to Gide's account of feeling sexually 'normal' only in the arms of boys, and then gave him some optimistic advice: 'Get married. Get married without fear. And you'll quickly realize that all the rest exists only in your imagination.'

Gide's first sexual experience, at 23, was with a 14-year-old Arab who loafed around his hotel in Tunisia. Ali offered himself in the sand dunes and, after a feigned hesitation, Gide submitted joyfully. Later he tried to 'normalize' himself by having intercourse with Meriem, a 16-year-old female prostitute who resembled a child. While he was with her, he wrote, he pretended she was her little brother, a young lad 'black and slim as a demon'. Meriem's 'treatments' were terminated when Gide's mother came to Africa to nurse him through tuberculosis.

The following year, in Algiers, Gide met Oscar Wilde, and Wilde's lover, Lord Alfred Douglas. One night, Wilde procured a young musician, Mohammed, for Gide, who regarded the episode ever afterwards as the high point of his sexual experience. 'After Mohammed had left me, I spent a long time in a state of quivering jubilation and, although I had already achieved pleasure five times with him, I revived my ecstasy over and over again and, back in my hotel room, prolonged the echoes of it until morning.'

In Algeria, Gide formed strong attachments to his beautiful 15-year-old servant boy, Athman, whom he called a 'black pearl'. When he wrote to his mother about bringing Athman back to Paris, to 'help in the house', Madame Gide wouldn't hear of it. For a month they fought, exchanging increasingly exasperated letters. At his mother's ultimatum that *her* servant would leave if a 'Negro' were brought into the house, Gide relented. He was miserable at having to leave the boy, but four years later he returned to Algeria, found Athman, and took him back to Paris.

At 46, Gide began a heterosexual affair with Elizabeth van Rysselberghe, the daughter of an old friend. He passed her a note saying he would like to give her a child – a wish fulfilled in 1923 when their daughter Catherine was born. He acknowledged this child and lived to be a grandfather.

As a boy, Gide found that his sexual excitement was stimulated 'by a profusion of colours or unusually shrill sweet sounds', and also by the 'idea of destruction'. He was aroused when he spoiled a favourite toy or heard a story about crockery being smashed to

194

pieces. Later he was attracted to crippled, deformed or monstrous children, in whom he recognized some aspect of himself.

M.B.T. (Lists 6, 7, 12, 14, 17, 20, 25, 39)

♣ William Gladstone
29 December 1809 to 19 May 1898

The son of a Liverpool merchant who made his fortune in the West Indian slave trade, Gladstone was an introspective young man, always very self-critical. As a boy, he was deeply religious and wanted to become a clergyman. However, his father considered the ministry a useless profession, ordering his son to study law at Oxford and use that as an entry into politics. Dutifully, Gladstone followed his father's directions. His early evangelical bent never left him and later, as prime minister, he consistently made political decisions based on religious moral grounds. During sixty-two years in politics, Gladstone championed a variety of causes, including international disarmament, political and electoral reforms and Irish home rule. After serving a fourth term as prime minister, he left office in 1894, and died four years later aged 88.

Most of his life, Gladstone was emotionally and mentally torn between puritanical sexual attitudes and a strong sex drive. This conflict resulted in frequent, intense sexual frustration and rather odd attempts at sublimation. Throughout his life he kept a diary which revealed that, soon after puberty, he had an overwhelming desire to masturbate, saying that the urge came upon him 'again and again like a flood'. This perfectly normal desire produced tremendous guilt – Gladstone describing these feelings as 'most dangerous and degrading temptations'. Gladstone rarely, if ever, gave in to the urges and he was a virgin until the age of 29.

From 1835, Gladstone desperately proposed to a series of women, but it was not until 1839 that Catherine Glynne agreed to marry him. Affectionate, young, intelligent and pretty, she came from an upper-class family, and finally relieved Gladstone of his virginity on their wedding night. Through their nearly fifty-nine years of marriage, the Gladstones loved each other sincerely. However, after only several weeks of providing sexual satisfaction for Gladstone, Catherine became pregnant – as she was to do repeatedly over the next fifteen years. She produced four sons and four daughters. So again Gladstone found himself deprived of an adequate sex life, since proper Victorians felt that sex was taboo during pregnancy. He also had frequent, prolonged separations from his wife due to political responsibilities.

Guiltily, Gladstone began reading pornography. He may have been introduced to this delight by his friend Richard Monckton-Milnes while they were at Oxford. Milnes, a one-time Conservative MP and a wealthy literary patron, had perhaps the most extensive and celebrated pornographic library in Victorian England. After several years of marriage, Gladstone resumed his work – begun at Oxford and temporarily abandoned – of 'rescuing' London's prostitutes. This charitable endeavour was long considered to be a rather eccentric, yet innocent, vocation. Gladstone walked the streets of Soho or another red-light district until accosted by a prostitute, whom he then tried to 'reform', persuading her to enter a home for former prostitutes that he had founded.

In more than forty years of this work, Gladstone achieved a degree of success, but his intimate conversations with these women may have been a form of voyeurism. The question of whether or not Gladstone had sexual relations with them has never been answered. He swore to his son that he had never 'been guilty of the act which is known as that of infidelity to the marriage bed'. However, scholars have noted that, in Victorian terms, this ruled out coitus but not other sex acts such as fellatio.

In 1851, Gladstone visited a beautiful young prostitute named Elizabeth Collins and later made a cryptic entry in his diary: 'Received (unexpectedly) remained 2 hours: a strange humbling scene. . . .' In the next weeks, he had two more long visits with Miss Collins. One biographer, Matthew, notes that on this and on other occasions with prostitutes, Gladstone's diary 'certainly suggests . . . that he was guilty of other [sex] acts.' Gladstone also disclosed in his diary that he was a self-flagellant, asking, 'Has it been sufficiently considered how far pain may become a ground of enjoyment?' He seems to have whipped himself as a form of punishment and as a means of lessening his sexual longings. These masochistic episodes were indicated by a mark representing a whip placed next to the dates when they occurred. It is interesting to note that Gladstone found it necessary to scourge himself after each visit with Miss Collins.

R.J.F. (Lists 20, 21, 32, 34, 35, 36)

🍂 Johann Wolfgang von Goethe
28 August 1749 to 22 March 1832

The first-born child and only son of a highly cultured Frankfurt family, Goethe was accomplished in music, art and six languages when he left home for law school in 1765. An attractive young man with a beaky nose and large, dark eyes, he affected a bohemian appearance and manner in his student days at the University of Leipzig. His short novel *The Sorrows of Young Werther* made suicide for love fashionable among the young in Europe and also established him as a popular novelist. Frankfurt society took him to its bosom, and the Duke of Weimar invited him to join his court in 1775. After a few months of debauching with the 18-year-old duke (throwing plates from palace windows and perhaps engaging in orgies), Goethe settled down to serious work as chief minister of state (inspecting mines and issuing military uniforms), and an austere way of life (he gave up coffee and stopped wearing a wig). For the rest of his life, except for two journeys to Italy, Goethe lived at Weimar, where he wrote his masterpieces, managed the theatre, and studied science (he founded morphology and his work on plants foreshadowed Darwin's). Goethe wrote volumes about the state of his romantic feelings. The tension that helped him create also existed in his love affairs – he was often involved in bizarre triangles with two different women (one innocent, one experienced, for example), and the course of his romances rarely ran smooth.

One biographer postulates that Goethe may have had problems with premature ejaculation as a young man and did not have actual intercourse until he was 39. This has been neither proved nor disproved. Goethe did indeed have a free-flowing, intense personality and was deeply affected by the merest physical contact. A kiss could throw him into ecstasies. The women Goethe loved were often unattainable – several were engaged or married to his friends. Charlotte Buff, who inspired *The Sorrows of Young Werther*, was engaged to Goethe's friend Johann Christian Kestner. Though he had relationships with aristocratic intellectuals, he had a predeliction for pretty, earthy women of inferior social station. Round-faced Käthchen Schönkopf, an innkeeper's daughter and perhaps his first real love, is typical. One moment he was indifferent to her, the next writing to a friend: 'But I love her. I believe I would take poison from her hand. . . . We are our own devils, we drive ourselves out of our own Edens.' His passion for Friederike Brion, a parson's daughter, was a 'magic garden', yet he wrote, 'One isn't an atom happier when one gets what one wanted.' Some biographers claim he left her not only broken-hearted, but with child.

During his period in Frankfurt society, he became engaged to Lilli Schönemann, a banker's daughter. After several dramatic partings and reconciliations, the engagement ended when Goethe left for Weimar in 1775. Did they have intercourse? Lilli's later claim that she owed him her 'moral existence' would indicate not, yet there is a puzzling entry in his autobiographical notes which reads: 'Episode with Lili. Prelude. Seduction. Offenbach.'

At Weimar, Goethe had a ten-year, probably platonic, relationship with Charlotte von Stein, married and the mother of eight, an intellectual, seven years older than he. He sent her more than 1500 letters, writing little else during this period.

After his journey to Italy in 1786–8 to discover the classical world, he met Christiane von Vulpius, a worker in an artificial-flower factory. Stocky and black-eyed, she loved the theatre, dancing, clothes, wine – and Goethe. He called her his 'force of nature'. She moved in with him and stayed until the end of her life. When he was away on occasion, they wrote to each other – alluding to an unborn child as *das Pfuiteufelchen* ('the-little-it's-a-damned-shame') and she referred to Goethe's penis as Herr Schönfuss ('Mr Nicefoot'). When they had been together more than fifteen years, he wrote asking for a pair of 'danced-out shoes' to 'press against his heart'. He married Christiane in 1806, after the French invasion of Germany, during which she had saved him from being shot by two soldiers. His marriage seemed to arouse in him yearnings for other women – among them Minna Herzlieb, who inspired 'sonnet fever', and Marianne von Willemer, married to a friend. Christiane died in 1816. When Goethe was 74, he proposed to his 'daughterling', Ulrike von Levetzow, then in her late teens. She turned him down.

A.E. (Lists 1, 3, 11, 25, 26)

❧ Maxim Gorki
28 March 1868 to 18 June 1936

Aleksei Maksimovich Peshkov chose the word '*gorki*' – 'the bitter one' – as his pseudonym. It reflected the brutal poverty of the peasants in czarist Russia. Called the greatest proletarian in Soviet literature, Gorki was exiled in 1906 for his revolutionary activities. For years he lived in Italy, but returned to the USSR for good in 1928 as a hero. His complete works, published posthumously, fill thirty volumes.

Gorki was torn by conflicting sexual values. His romantic ideals forever clashed with harsh realities. Raised by his impoverished grandparents, Gorki yearned to find some sweetness in life. At 13, he fell in love with an elegantly beautiful young widow. She gave him books of poetry, encouraged his passion for reading, and inspired in him an idea of womanhood and sex which profoundly affected him. He thought of her as 'Queen Margot', visited her on Sunday instead of going to mass, and confided his secrets as she lay in bed listening. Once he watched her dress. 'She put on her stockings in my presence; and I felt unembarrassed; there was something clean in her nakedness.' He arrived one day and was surprised to find her in bed with a man. 'Actually, I did not believe my queen gave her love like other women,' he later wrote, and from that time on he had trouble accepting the co-existence of passion and purity in women. Gorki learned early about sex. It was easy enough to observe in the squalid lower depths of peasant life, but it was like a hastily gulped meal, affording no real enjoyment. Later, his stories described raw sexual scenes, coarse to the point of brutality, but without sensuality, and inevitably they were coloured by his moralizing.

In 1887, Gorki was a confused 19-year-old in desperate need of love and affection. He despaired of ever saving himself from poverty and loneliness, and finally attempted suicide. He shot himself but, instead of hitting his heart, the bullet lodged in a lung. Recovering but still miserable, he visited a hunchbacked psychiatrist, whose advice was: 'Find yourself a girl who knows how to play; she'll be good for you.' Gorki found a married woman ten years older than himself. Olga Kaminskaya was witty and charming and had lived in Paris, but Gorki's ardour turned to agony when she refused to leave her husband. He moved away but, two years later, in 1892, they met again. When Gorki heard she was living alone, he fainted with delight. They married and moved into a bath-house located in the backyard of a priest with a drinking problem. For two years, they were intensely in love; he was enthralled with her slim, girlish figure and her affectionate ways. When she began having affairs in almost compulsive fashion, he left her.

In 1896, Gorki was working on a newspaper. He fell in love

with proof-reader Catherine Pavlovna Volzhina, a dedicated revolutionary ten years his junior. They married and soon had two children, but the marriage was not happy. She was bright and tough – he once called her 'an enraged canary' – and they remained friends after the marriage disintegrated. They did not formally divorce, which later proved to be a disastrous mistake.

After an interlude of living with a young prostitute, whom he claimed he was reforming, he took up with actress Maria Feodorovna Andreyevna, a married woman, in 1901. She accompanied him on a trip to America in 1906, where he was welcomed by President Theodore Roosevelt, Mark Twain and William Dean Howells. Gorki introduced Maria Feodorovna as his wife. Since he was touring to gain support for the revolutionary cause, the czarist government was eager to discredit him. The Russian embassy broke the news that Gorki was travelling with his mistress. The American press, calling him an anarchist and a bigamist, fanned the public's outrage, the roster of big names withdrew its support, and his tour collapsed. Hotel after hotel refused Gorki and Feodorovna rooms, while one indignant manager ran them out with the words, 'This is not Europe. . . .' The New York *Independent* mused about 'respectable ladies' who 'used to press their money upon the Russian committees with the stipulation that it be used for dynamite. They were anxious to aid and abet murder, but they could not countenance matrimonial quirks.'

As a teenager, Gorki had attended sex orgies, but not as a participant. Instead, he would stand against a wall and sing folk songs to the revellers, hoping thereby to redeem their debauched souls.

M.B.T. (Lists 17, 34)

♣ Francisco de Goya
30 March 1746 to 16 April 1828

Raised mostly in Saragossa, Goya set out early to become an artist. His career was one of steady progress – designer of royal tapestries, member of the prestigious Academy of San Fernando in Madrid, court painter to both Charles III and Charles IV – until a near-fatal illness struck in 1792, when he was 46. He lay for a time paralysed and nearly blind, and complained of dizzy spells and strange noises in his head. Syphilis was diagnosed. He recovered in a year but was thereafter stone deaf. In 1795, he was chosen to succeed his brother-in-law Francisco Bayeu as painting director at the Academy of San Fernando, but his deafness was a handicap so he accepted the title of honorary director. Despite the political upheaval during and after the French occupation of Spain (1808–14), Goya managed to survive as court painter. Even his sensual 'Maja' paintings somehow escaped the wrath of the Inquisition, though formal charges of obscenity were lodged against him. But a crackdown on liberals in 1824 so threatened his security that he took refuge in Bordeaux, France, where he lived and worked in self-imposed exile.

While young, Goya sowed acres of wild oats, and once while studying art in Rome he raided a convent to kidnap an upper-class Italian girl boarding there. This led to a duel, which Goya won, and to a love affair with the Italian girl. In 1773, settled in Madrid, Goya called on a friend he had met during his travels, Francisco Bayeu, who was the official court painter for King Charles IV and Queen Maria Luisa. Francisco introduced Goya to his sister Josefa, an attractive russet blonde, disarmingly simple and honest. Entranced by Josefa, Goya seduced her. She was four months pregnant when Goya was forced to marry her in 1775. Five months later, their first child, a son named Eusebio, was born. The boy did not survive his childhood. In all, Josefa gave birth to five – possibly six – children, but only one, a son named Xavier, lived to maturity. The marriage proved profitable to Goya in another way. His brother-in-law had court connections, and thus Goya procured a steady job in the royal tapestry factory. Once Goya had an entrée to meeting aristocratic ladies, his wife Josefa faded into the background of his life. Goya painted only one portrait of her.

The most desirable aristocrat was the headstrong, spirited, promiscuous, 20-year-old Duchess of Alba, already married seven years to the moody Marquis of Villafranca. Goya lusted for her from the first day he saw her. He had reason to. Her beauty was breathtaking. A contemporary said of her, 'The Duchess of Alba does not have a single hair on her head which would not kindle the flame of desire. There is not a more beautiful thing in the world. . . . When she walks in the street everybody watches her from the windows and even the children stop playing in order to look at her.' Goya met the duchess casually at a social gathering. Then, one day in the summer of 1795, she called on him at his studio. After that, he began to see the duchess more often. He wanted to possess her, and she wanted him. At last, she granted him her 'final favours'. Ecstatically, Goya confided in a letter to his friend Zapater, '*I finally know what life means.*'

When the duchess's ailing husband died in 1796, she withdrew to her estate in Andalusia to mourn the occasion properly. She took Goya along. They stayed together for several months. He devoted himself to painting and making love with her regularly. She posed for him both clothed and naked. Goya painted her respectfully dressed in black, but wearing rings on the index and middle fingers of her right hand; one ring was inscribed 'Goya', the other 'Alba'. Moreover, she was shown pointing down to a phrase scratched in the sand that read 'Solo Goya' ('Only Goya'). Other representations of the duchess in Sanlucar were more revealing. There were hundreds of sketches. many showing her quite nude. 'One of them', wrote a contemporary, 'shows the lady's beautiful nakedness from the back, with her buttocks, waist, and hips exposed.' The duchess allowed Goya to save the drawings. On one of these he wrote, 'It is madness to keep this, but each according to his own taste.' Returning to Madrid, the duchess temporarily abandoned Goya for an older man, Lieutenant General Don Antonio Cornel. Embittered, Goya painted three pictures of the duchess depicting her flightiness – one showing her with a double face. But, by 1799, she was back with Goya, posing for the two paintings that became the artist's most popular works – *The Naked Maja* and *The Clothed Maja*. The clothed version was hung in front of the naked one for propriety. Goya's nude of her was the first such oil to be depicted, in the words of André Malraux, as 'erotic without being voluptuous'. These two paintings the duchess kept for herself. They were later inherited by Manuel de Godoy, the Queen of Spain's lover. The Duchess of Alba died suddenly in July 1802. She remembered her love for Goya in her will by bequeathing the sum of 3500 reales annually to Goya's son Xavier Goya. Ten years later, Goya's wife Josefa died. The painter's son had married a wealthy trader's daughter and had his own residence. Goya was left quite alone.

He moved out of Madrid to a place by the side of the Manzanares river. There he met Leocadia Zorrilla de Weis, a lively and liberal-minded young woman still married to a businessman, Isidro Weis. Soon her husband petitioned for a separation from his wife on the grounds of her 'misbehaviour and infidelity'. Undoubtedly Goya, at 68, was making love to Leocadia. In 1814, she gave birth to a girl whom she named Rosarito. Goya doted on the little girl and trained her to paint, hoping in vain that Rosarito was talented. In 1824, fearful of the excesses of a new government in Spain, Goya, accompanied by Leocadia and little Rosarito, fled to France and settled down in a small house with a garden in Bordeaux. Hot-tempered Leocadia often argued with Goya, but generally she amused and looked after him. Goya spent his time walking, painting a little, napping a lot. He died at the age of 82.

W.A.D. and I.W. (Lists 18, 20, 21, 25)

♣ Jean Harlow
3 March 1911 to 7 June 1937

The reigning sex queen of the thirties, Jean Harlow played humorous film roles in which she was the platinum blonde floozy with a heart of gold – the 'combination good kid and slut'. Among her best-known films are *Hell's Angels*, *Public Enemy*, *Bombshell* and *Red Dust*.

Jean was born Harlean Carpenter in Kansas City. Her mother divorced her dentist husband and two years later married Marino Bello, an Italian–American of uncertain profession with gangster connections. Marino and 'Mama Jean', as she was called, managed Jean's career and leeched large sums of money from her. The family moved to Hollywood when Jean was a teenager, and her first important part was in *Hell's Angels*, a fabulously expensive Howard Hughes production. Hughes coined the term 'platinum blonde' for Harlow (her almost white hair was to become her greatest trademark) and got his costumier to design the lowest-cut evening gown ever photographed for the screen. Jean, wearing very little to begin with, caused a sensation when she uttered the immortal line, 'Do you mind if I slip into something more comfortable?' The next step was to super-stardom, although Mama Jean, Marino and Jean's friends still called her by her childhood nickname: 'the Baby'.

Stories about her amorous life range from one extreme to another – that Harlow was sex-crazed and promiscuous; that Harlow hated sex; that Harlow was a normal, healthy girl who just had bad luck with men. Probably a little of each is true. One thing her biographers do agree on is that she had her first sexual experience at 16. Partly in order to escape from a girls' boarding school in Illinois, she eloped with 21-year-old Charles McGrew, the son of a wealthy investment broker, but the newlyweds' families separated them almost immediately. They probably never saw each other again, and a divorce was obtained in 1929. Jean remembered her first act of love as 'messy' and not very satisfying.

She had no other lovers until she married her second husband, Paul Bern, in 1932. This was a highly unusual and much gossiped about courtship. Bern was a small, moustached, weaselly looking man twice her age – an odd choice for a woman who had her pick of the great Hollywood leading men. Most likely, she was seeking a father figure – and enjoyed Bern's apparent interest in her mind rather than her body. It is true that Bern was suave, intellectual and gentlemanly – he was Irving Thalberg's assistant at MGM, and was called Hollywood's 'little father confessor' because he loved listening to other people's problems. Before he married Jean, he had an unusual arrangement with another girl: he set her up in a Hollywood flat and visited her every afternoon. The girl would disrobe and lie naked on the bed, while he read poetry to her. Then they would have tea and he would leave. But the mystery of the Harlow–Bern liaison has still not been solved. The most famous story of the fateful wedding night and following weeks is as follows. After a happy wedding, the couple went to their home to consummate the union. Several hours later Jean's agent, Arthur Landau, received a tearful phone call from his distraught client. He picked her up outside the house, and she revealed that a drunken Bern had beaten her with a cane – leaving long, ugly welts all over her snowy body. He had also bitten her thighs so savagely that they bled. Jean spent the remainder of her wedding night with the Landaus. Entering the house the next morning, Landau found the nude Bern weeping, and exclaiming, 'Every man I know gets an erection just by talking about her. Arthur, didn't I have the right to think Jean could help me at least that much?' Apparently Bern had the penis and testicles of an infant boy, and was completely impotent. (A variation on the story was told by Jean's maid who quoted Bern as saying, 'The Baby's still a virgin.') Whatever happened was not good – but they kept up appearances for the sake of Jean's career. Finally, one night two months after the wedding, Bern entered Jean's usually locked bedroom. He strode in wearing an enormous dildo – with huge testicles and a bulb which shot water out of the end of the artificial penis. Jean burst into hysterical laughter, and Bern pranced around the room sporting the giant phallus until the two of them removed it and flushed it down the toilet. The next evening, probably while Jean was out (the sequence of events is uncertain), the butler discovered Bern's naked body sprawled before a full-length mirror. It was drenched in his wife's favourite perfume, Mitsouko. Bern had shot himself in the head with a .38 pistol. The note he left gave the press a field day. It read: 'Dearest Dear, Unfortunately this is the only way to make good the frightful wrong I have done you, and to wipe out my abject humiliation. I love you. Paul. You understand that last night was only a comedy.' Three days later the body of a blonde was found in the Sacramento river. The suicide was Dorothy Milette, who had claimed to be Bern's common-law wife before Jean had married him.

A distraught Jean turned to promiscuity – as self-punishment, to find out what sex was all about, and because she suddenly wanted to have a baby. She cut her hair very short (studio heads were furious when they found out), wore a black wig and sunglasses, and began to pick up men, starting with a salesman with whom she spent two nights in a sleazy hotel in San Bernardino. She met one of her pick-ups in front of a San Francisco cinema showing *Red Dust*, her latest film with Clark Gable. The man told her she resembled Jean Harlow and ought to go to Hollywood to try out for the job of stand-in or double. But Harlow could be choosy – when Louis B. Mayer himself propositioned her, dangling a fur coat as bait, she turned him down. In any case, her attempts to get pregnant failed; she was sterile.

The last of Jean's 'three marriages of inconvenience', as she called them, was to Hal Rosson, a talented and successful cameraman. Rosson resembled Paul Bern, and was sixteen years older than Jean. The couple happily eloped in 1933, but the marriage lasted only eight months. No one knows exactly why, though it is speculated that Mama Jean's and Marino's interference led to the break-up. The complaints Jean filed for the divorce proceedings were ridiculous; for example, she charged that he was ruining her career by reading in bed until late at night, thus making her sleepy on the set.

Jean's final affair was with actor William Powell, probably her one true love. Like Bern, he was intelligent and suave; he even resembled him physically. Powell was 43 to her 24, and on the third anniversary of their first date he brought Jean a cake with a card saying, 'To my three-year-old from her Daddy'. They were probably engaged at the time of Jean's sudden collapse at the age of 26. She quickly died of uremic poisoning because Mama Jean was a Christian Scientist and would not allow her to have medical help until it was too late. It is believed that, at her funeral, Powell was the one who placed in her hand a single gardenia, her favourite flower, along with a note that read, 'Good night, my dearest darling,' and that the empty plot next to Jean and her mother's graves is reserved for him.

Harlow was the first actress in Hollywood to appear regularly in films without a bra; in fact, she rarely wore any underwear. When a high school teacher reprimanded her for this, the 15-year-old replied, 'I can't breathe when I'm wearing a brassière.' She also rubbed her nipples with ice to make them stand out for the camera, and dyed her pubic hair platinum to match the hair on her head.

A.W. (Lists 2, 6, 17, 24, 42)

♣ Franz Josef Haydn
31 March 1732 to 31 May 1809

Haydn was of humble origin. The son of a wheelwright, he spent his first few years in a tiny village in lower Austria and, at the age of 5, was sent to nearby Hainburg, where he lived with a cousin, a choirmaster, who trained him. Three years later, he became a choirboy at St Stephen's Cathedral, Vienna. Deeply impressed by his days in Hainburg when 'floggings were more common than food', Haydn sacrificed freedom for financial security and later signed on as a music director to the aristocratic Esterházy family, with whom he remained for thirty years. The strict contract went so far as to stipulate that he 'abstain from vulgarity in eating, drinking and conversation'. But he was a kindly, down-to-earth man, who clung to old-fashioned habits and refused to give up his powdered white wig even when it went out of style. He was loved by his musicians, and old and young alike began calling him 'Papa Haydn' when he was only 35. As he became increasingly feeble with age, and physically unable to compose, he exclaimed to a friend, 'I really am a living keyboard.'

Haydn was a late developer. Although he lived in risqué bohemian circles in Vienna until his late twenties, there is no evidence that he ever touched a woman during that time. The young composer's innocence clearly showed itself while accompanying a young countess on the pianoforte. The lady leaned forward to see the music better and her fichu fell open, exposing her breasts. 'It was the first time I had ever witnessed such a sight!' the 27-year-old musician exclaimed to a friend. 'I was embarrassed, my playing stopped, and my fingers lay idly on the keys.' Shy, and uncertain of his unproven abilities with women, Haydn found that his looks didn't bolster his self-confidence. Shorter than average and with stubby legs, the composer also had a swarthy face deeply pitted by smallpox; his large aquiline nose was disfigured by an abnormal tissue growth. Haydn considered himself ugly and often remarked that attractive women drawn to him 'were at any rate not tempted by my beauty'.

When Haydn finally fell in love, he chose the daughter of a wigmaker, but she had already set her heart on becoming a nun. Her father cajoled the disappointed musician into marrying the girl's sister. This marriage proved a disaster. The shrewish and jealous Anna Maria Keller flaunted her disdain for her husband's profession by using his manuscripts as liners for pastry tins or curlpapers for her hair. The couple's childlessness did not help. Haydn once justified his roving eye by saying that his wife was 'unable to bear children and therefore I was less indifferent to the pleasures of another woman's bed'. Although Haydn was for all purposes a 'married bachelor', he remained faithful – at least in spirit – for nearly twenty years of marriage. Then he suddenly succumbed to the charms of an Italian opera singer – also unhappily married. Nineteen-year-old Luigia Polzelli's dark eyes and delicate figure were undoubtedly more entrancing than her mediocre voice, but Haydn loved her dearly for several years, at one point promising to marry her if and when they both became free. He somewhat morbidly referred to that vow after her husband died, saying, 'Perhaps the time will come for which we have so often wished, when four eyes shall be closed.' But, by the time Anna Maria died, the flame uniting Haydn and Luigia had waned, probably hastened by her increasing demands for money as well as Haydn's first trip to England where he met ladies more cultured than his Italian mistress. However, the conscientious Haydn continued to send her money throughout his life. It is said that Luigia's second son was Haydn's, although the composer never acknowledged him, treating both her boys with equal affection.

Haydn also entered into an intense friendship with an English widow while his wife was still alive; it seems unlikely that the relationship was physical. Madame Rebecca Schroeter was 'still a beautiful and attractive widow, though over 60,' Haydn declared, 'and had I been free, I should certainly have married her.' It is not known why the two suddenly stopped writing to each other.

Haydn carried on many flirtations throughout his career, but seemed to prefer to keep women on a pedestal. Affairs of the heart played a small part in Haydn's life, and perhaps he turned to writing operas as consolation for the lack of passionate, lasting love in his life.

L.K.S. (List 1)

♣ Ernest Hemingway
21 July 1899 to 2 July 1961

Hemingway's major novels, *The Sun Also Rises, A Farewell to Arms, For Whom the Bell Tolls* and *The Old Man and the Sea*, often mirrored his adventurous life, recreating his physical sensations while hunting big game, bullfighting and soldiering. At the same time, his aesthetic sensibility drew wide critical acclaim and brought him both a Pulitzer Prize and the Nobel Prize for Literature.

Hemingway's life has been called a 'never ended rebellion' against his middle-class past. The son of a doctor, Hemingway was raised in a Chicago suburb, in a family dominated by its women, including his four sisters, a nurse, and a cook. His mother made him wear girl's clothing for several years, and held his elder sister Marcelline back a year so the two could enter school together, as twins. At 15, he ran away from home, but returned in order to finish high school. After the First World War, during which he saw front-line action as an ambulance driver in Italy, he went to Paris as a journalist. There Hemingway developed his crisp style and achieved initial fame and success as a novelist. He craved yet resented being in the limelight, carefully creating a virile public image of the man seeking out adventure as boxer, hunter, wartime correspondent and soldier all over the world. In later years he lived contentedly in Cuba. After Fidel Castro seized power in 1960, Hemingway moved to a house in Ketchum, Idaho, but the loss of his Cuban farm hurt; he became anxiety-ridden and depressed, and was unable to write. Hemingway twice underwent electric-shock therapy at the Mayo Clinic. Two days after returning to Ketchum from one of these sessions, he took his life with a shotgun.

In keeping with his masculine image, Hemingway portrayed

himself as a great lover. He told Thornton Wilder that, as a young man in Paris, his sex drive was so strong he had to make love three times a day; also, he ostentatiously consumed sex-sedating drugs to quiet his raging libido. His family, however, reported that he didn't even begin dating until he was a junior in high school. ('About time,' they said.) He was never comfortable with casual sex, although he later boasted he was 'an amateur pimp'. He compared intercourse to bicycle racing – the more you do it, the better you get at it. Hemingway liked to dominate his women, believing that the man 'must govern' sexual relationships. Three of his four wives appear to have accepted that rule. The exception was his third wife, Martha Gellhorn, who said afterwards that 'Papa' Hemingway had no redeeming qualities apart from his writing. (Hemingway called their marriage his 'biggest mistake'.)

In his letters, Hemingway told of having many unusual bed partners, including a black harem he maintained while on an African safari. His strident womanizing led contemporaries to question his manhood. Some observers, including former mentor Gertrude Stein, implied that he was a latent homosexual. In fact, on one occasion in Spain – while walking to the bull ring with his friend Sidney Franklin, the Brooklyn-born matador – Hemingway spotted a very obvious homosexual across the street 'just minding his business'. Hemingway snorted, 'Watch this.' He strode across the street, and without warning he smashed his fist into the homosexual, knocking him down and hurting him. Satisfied, Hemingway rejoined Franklin. However, there is certainly no evidence to suggest that Hemingway ever had a homosexual relationship; Hemingway himself commented that he had been approached by a man only once in his life.

''Course, Hemingway's big problem all his life, I've always thought,' Sidney Franklin once told author Barnaby Conrad, 'was he was always worried about his Picha [penis]. The size of it, that is.' 'Small?' Conrad wondered. '[Franklin] solemnly held up the little finger of his left hand with his thumbnail at the base,' Conrad reported. 'He appraised it with a critical eye; then he raised his thumbnail up a fraction of an inch in re-evaluation.' ''Bout the size of a thirty-thirty shell,' he said. Papa Hemingway was a straight man in bed, and he preferred women who 'would rather take chances than use prophylactics'. He abhorred any sexual arrangement that violated his sense of propriety. He wasn't always the best performer and sometimes experienced stress-induced impotence.

Hemingway boasted of his sexual prowess, claiming he had made love to a wide variety of women including Mata Hari, Italian countesses, a Greek princess and obese prostitutes in Michigan where he spent many youthful summers. He also claimed he had made love to some of Havana's most outrageous prostitutes – who bore such nicknames as Xenophobia, Leopoldian and the International Whore. In truth, his relationships were considerably more chaste than this and his attitudes towards sex almost prudish. His 'loveliest dreams' were inhabited by Greta Garbo and his friend Marlene Dietrich, and in real life he preferred submissive, shapely blondes or redheads. Friends and acquaintances thought him 'a puritan', and Hemingway himself blushed when accosted by a prostitute, feeling that only those 'in love' could make love. Married four times (and producing three sons), he always regarded his divorce from first wife Hadley Richardson as a 'sin' he could never expiate. Although their first few years together were nearly ideal, their marriage was doomed when Hemingway met and fell in love with Pauline ('Pfife') Pfeiffer, a beautiful sycophant who became his second wife. Hadley agreed to a divorce only after she had forced Pauline and Ernest to stay apart for one hundred days. Hemingway's second marriage lasted twelve years on paper, but far less in reality. The relationship ended for sexual reasons: after Pauline twice gave birth by Caesarian section, they had been forced to practise coitus interruptus because her Catholicism precluded the use of prophylactics.

Hemingway met Martha Gellhorn while reporting on the Spanish Civil War from Madrid. They were quickly drawn to each other, but their passions cooled after marriage, and they were divorced five years later, in 1945. It was Ernest's shortest marriage and a cosmic mismatch. Ernest did not like Martha's independence (she was an accomplished writer in her own right) or her sharp tongue. He wanted blind adoration and submission, which Martha could not give.

Hemingway's fourth wife, Mary Welsh, was in many ways made to order. She was patient, reverent and beautiful (and nine years younger than Hemingway). He called her his 'pocket Rubens'. The marriage lasted for the remainder of Hemingway's life largely because Mary overlooked his often difficult behaviour. Hemingway continued to enjoy a number of dalliances, and made no effort to keep them secret.

As a young man he had preferred older women (Hadley was

eight years his senior). From middle age on, he enjoyed the company of much younger women. A number of these women were clearly models for Hemingway's fictional characters; one may have inspired Brett Ashley in *The Sun Also Rises* and another Renata in *Across the River and Into the Trees*, but none won his heart completely. He never let them get too close, lest they try to run his life. 'I know wimmins,' he told one friend, 'and wimmins is difficult.'

Hemingway had several unusual theories about sex. He believed that each man was allotted a certain number of orgasms in his life, and that these had to be carefully spaced out. Another theory was that, if you had sex often enough, you could eat all the strawberries you wanted without contracting hives, even if you were allergic to the fruit.

J.A.M. (Lists 5, 20, 27, 28, 39, 48)

♣ Jimi Hendrix
27 November 1942 to 18 September 1970

Life magazine called Jimi Hendrix 'a rock demigod', the *New York Times* called him the 'black Elvis', and John Lennon called him the 'Pied Piper of rock'. As a guitar player, Jimi was unique, outstandingly daring, and innovative. As a performer, he wore outlandish, crazy clothes, writhed, snaked, and moaned on stage. He played his guitar at earsplitting volume with teeth, tongue, or elbow – but mostly, it seemed, with his crotch. One of the most sexual performers in history, Hendrix thrust his groin madly against the guitar, and rubbed it between his thighs, often ending these orgasmic episodes by smashing the guitar to bits in an explosion of love and fury. At the Monterey Pop Festival, in 1967, after a particularly explosive performance, he caused a sensation by dousing his guitar with lighter fluid and setting it on fire. He eventually grew tired of all these histrionics, wanting to be appreciated for his musical ability.

On stage, Jimi was a wild man. Offstage, he could be anything – polite and gentlemanly, someone you could bring home to your mother (except for his clothes and general appearance) – or angry and destructive. Sometimes he was painfully withdrawn, shy and inarticulate. And then again he could be voluble and gregarious. Possibly Jimi was as confused about himself as everyone else. He

211

frequently had fits of violence and tears, beating up girlfriends and smashing furniture, for which he apologized abjectly afterwards.

Jimi Hendrix's father was an easygoing black gardener in Seattle, his mother a hard-drinking American Indian, his stepmother Japanese. For most of his life, Jimi was not especially conscious of his 'blackness', and chose friends and lovers from all races and nationalities. He learned to play the guitar at an early age, left home to join the army, became a parachutist and was discharged when injured. Then he began his travels, playing back-up guitar for acts like the Isley Brothers, B.B. King, Sam Cooke, Wilson Pickett, Ike and Tina Turner, King Curtis, James Brown and Little Richard. In 1966, he was discovered in New York by Chas Chandler, formerly of the Animals. Chandler took him to England, put him together with two English musicians, and managed the Jimi Hendrix Experience. They took England by storm, but scandalized mothers and teenyboppers in America when opening the show for the clean-cut Monkees. The Experience was thrown off the tour amid great publicity. Jimi handled success relatively well at first, but eventually business and legal difficulties, the pressures of the road, and the break-up of the band exhausted and depressed him. Jimi was a heavy drug user who would try everything – LSD, uppers, booze – and he also snorted a little heroin. But he was *not* a drug addict. The manner of his shocking, sudden death at 27 added to the reputation. He took too many sleeping pills, and died of suffocation, having inhaled his own vomit. Some called it suicide, but it was undoubtedly at least as much an accident as Janis Joplin's tragic drug death three weeks later.

The consummate superstud, Hendrix is something of a sexual legend today. His appetite was voracious, and he often indulged it with three or more girls simultaneously. He was exotically good-looking, famous, and women flocked to him. One girl said his member was 'damn near big as his guitar'. He was one of the major black sex symbols for white women in the 1960s. Jimi started early. Never shy about finding women, although self-conscious about his skinny chest and long arms and legs, he had his first sex at 12. At 15, he was expelled from high school for holding hands with a white girl during class. When his teacher confronted him with this crime, he replied, 'What's the matter? Are you jealous?' Jimi's immense popularity and his cooperation with groupies (he called them 'Band-Aids') led to an unusual experience. In Chicago, two chubby, teenage groupies devised a scheme to make themselves something special on the competitive market. They called themselves the Plaster Casters, dedicated to making moulds, and ultimately true-to-life reproductions of rock stars' penises. Although one of the girls had the job of performing fellatio, it was often difficult for the stars to sustain their erections in the wet plaster. But not Jimi. One of the Plaster Casters wrote, 'He has got just about the biggest rig I've ever seen! We got a *Beautiful Mould*. He kept his hard for the entire minute. He got stuck, however, for about fifteen minutes (by his hair) but he was an excellent sport – didn't panic . . . actually enjoyed it and balled the impression after it was set. In fact, I believe the reason we couldn't get his rig out was that it wouldn't *get soft*!'

Despite his rampant promiscuity, Jimi had a number of intimate relationships, but these would still be second to his guitar, which he called his 'Electric Lady'. His greatest love was probably Kathy Etchingham, an attractive red-headed English girl with whom he was seen on and off in London for over three years. She said that Jimi 'used girls like some people smoke cigarettes', and he had children in Sweden, America and Germany. Kathy usually didn't mind his groupie infidelities. There were occasions, though, when one or the other was jealous, and there were fights. During one of these, Jimi fractured Kathy's nose with his foot. She took her revenge by hitting him over the head with a frying pan while he was asleep. Once, she was attacked and viciously beaten by four jealous groupies. Later, when Kathy married, her husband agreed that she could stay friends with Jimi. There were a number of other girls with whom Jimi had involved relationships, but never monogamously.

One long-lasting, unconventional relationship was with groupie Devon Wilson. Devon was black, tall, voluptuous, regal (she looked like Jimi), bright and wily. She was hungry for sex and heroin – the latter Jimi did not approve of. She had been a teenage prostitute, was rescued by composer Quincy Jones, and eventually became Queen of the Groupies. She served for years as Jimi's lover, pimp, secretary, drug procurer and Girl Friday. In return, he gave her companionship, a salary, sex, love of a sort and a distinguished position among her peers – writing a song about her called 'Dolly Dagger' (a wordplay on her on-off affair with Mick Jagger, of whom Jimi was a little jealous).

One (rare) unconsummated passion was with singer Marianne Faithfull, then Mick Jagger's girlfriend. One night, after playing

213

in a London club, Jimi seated himself between Mick and Marianne at their table, turned his back to Mick and whispered in Marianne's ear that he 'wanted to fuck her and that she should leave Mick who was a cunt and come with him, right now'. Marianne refused.

When Jimi met Monika Danneman, a tall German ice-skating instructor, he played a whole concert to her in the midst of a crowd of thousands. Flattered, she played it cool for a while. Monika did fall madly in love with Jimi, who was her first lover. She claimed they were going to be married, which friends doubted. True love or not, it was Monika who was with him the night he died.

A.W. (Lists 2, 4, 11, 22, 31, 39, 42)

♣ Henry VIII
28 June 1491 to 28 January 1547

The second son of Henry VII, Henry Tudor was blessed with magnificent looks. He was 6 feet tall, fair and powerfully built – and he had a formidable mind. In his teens he became the embodiment of the Renaissance man, excelling not only at tennis and jousting, but in music, art, philosophy and other scholarly pursuits. Foreign ambassadors vied with native eulogists in praising his auburn hair, his golden beard, his 'extremely excellent calf'. He loved dancing and feasting, pageantry and fine dress. Sir Thomas More said of him that he 'has more learning than any English monarch ever possessed before him,' and asked 'What may we not expect from a king who has been nourished by philosophy and the nine muses?' Henry, however, was also self-righteous, wilful and temperamental. During the first twenty years of his reign he drained the royal coffers to finance court entertainment and warfare. (He more than replenished them when he broke off religious contact with Rome, and confiscated the wealth of the monasteries.) Toward the end of his life he developed syphilitic leg ulcers, which prevented him from taking any physical exercise. The man who could tire four or more horses in a day and was considered the leading athlete in the nation became obese and piglike, walking with a limp and had to have his legs, of which he had been so proud, constantly bandaged. This affliction, plus repeated disappointments in love, turned Henry into an irascible and unpredictable monarch. Weakened by a number of illnesses – including malaria and alcoholism – he died at 55. Despite his failings, he left England a stronger, more unified, kingdom than it had ever been.

At 12, Henry was betrothed to Catherine of Aragon, the 18-year-old widow of his brother Arthur. (Arthur and she had been married six months when Arthur died.) But Henry did not wed Catherine until his succession to the throne two months before his 18th birthday. His first sexual experiences were with peasant girls when he was 16. Six weeks after his coronation, Henry married Catherine, who wore white to show the world that, though she and Arthur had been briefly married, she was still a virgin, and fit, therefore, to be Henry's wife. The daughter of King Ferdinand of Spain, she was dainty and graceful, loved to dance, and dressed in bold, bright colours. She was also Henry's intellectual equal. She taught him Spanish and decided to learn English herself. Henry adored her with the ardour of first love. But soon Catherine's troubles began. Her first child, a girl, was stillborn; then a son died shortly after birth. Henry grieved, especially over the son, but soon turned his attention toward consoling his wife. A second son was stillborn; a third was born prematurely and died. Finally Catherine gave birth to a healthy baby, her daughter Mary, who would one day become queen. Despite his disappointment at the child's gender, Henry was delighted to be a father at last, saying, 'If it is a daughter this time, by the grace of God the sons will follow.' But, during the next three years, Catherine had two more miscarriages and another stillbirth; then, at 35, she stopped conceiving. So much childbearing took its toll on Catherine's appearance; her figure had thickened and her face had coarsened. Henry, at 25, was in the prime of life, and had begun an affair with 17-year-old Elizabeth Blount, one of Catherine's ladies-in-waiting. Henry was ecstatic to have a young lover, and England was never so tranquil as when he carried on with his 'Bessie'. Six months after Catherine's last baby, Elizabeth gave birth to a male child who was christened Henry Fitzroy and taken away to be raised in semi-royal privacy as the Duke of Richmond. He died in 1536.

Henry stopped seeing Elizabeth, and began an affair with Mary Boleyn, daughter of Sir Thomas Boleyn and Lady Elizabeth Howard. Mary, at 18, had just returned from the French court. Two years later, her sister Anne, aged 15, also returned from that court, and became one of Catherine's ladies-in-waiting. During the next four years, while Henry slept with Mary, Anne fell in love with a young courtier named Sir Henry Percy, who was banished from court soon after the king became infatuated with Anne. As Anne reached her 19th year, Henry realized that he was in love with her.

Anne Boleyn was more bewitching than beautiful. She was small, with long dark hair and fiery eyes, and she was said to have three breasts. Anne had become sophisticated at the French court, and had been hardened by her heartbreak over Sir Henry Percy. Moreover, she had learned by her sister's example. Anne refused to become Henry's mistress, and thereby changed the course of history. Henry decided he must have a divorce. Henry's self-righteousness would not allow him to admit that he wanted to exchange his old, worn-out wife for a new one. Instead, he quoted the bible and informed Catherine that for the last twenty years they had been living in sin. Catherine, who loved Henry, insisted that she was a virgin when she had married him, and would not agree to a divorce. Henry waited unsuccessfully for the pope to approve his divorce, which would ensure the legitimacy of his future issue in the eyes of the English people. 'The king's great matter,' as it came to be called, dragged on for six years, while Anne held Henry at bay. Finally, Henry divorced the English Church from Roman Catholicism, making himself head of both church and state. He married Anne, who had at last become his mistress and was pregnant. The English people would not accept her as queen – their loyalty remained with Catherine – and a reign of terror began, in which anyone who opposed Henry's marriage or his being the sovereign ruler of both church and state was tortured and burned, drawn and quartered, or boiled to death. As Henry's wife, Anne began to show the sharper edges of her nature. Henry was soon advising her to 'wear the bridle of reason'. When Anne's first child was a daughter, Henry was bitterly disappointed. If his first wife had not been a good 'broodmare', Anne apparently was no better. Three miscarriages and one stillborn son later, Henry was through with her. Five men – including her own brother – were accused of having had sex with the queen (they were all, in fact, innocent), and all five were sent to the block along with Anne. Anne would not be blindfolded, and the executioner found her eyes so disarming that he got someone to distract her while he took off his shoes and stole up beside her to cut off her head.

For some time, Henry had had his eye on Jane Seymour, one of

216

Anne's ladies-in-waiting. Jane was as plain as Anne had been sparkling. She was simple, sweet and good-natured, and her submissive ways appealed to Henry. They married, and Jane gave birth to a boy, later to become Edward VI, but she herself died soon afterwards. Henry was devastated. Of the four wives he outlived, Jane was the only one for whom he wore black.

Within a few years, Henry wanted to make Germany an ally, and began to look for a German bride. Anne of Cleves was one prospect. Holbein painted a flattering portrait of her, and Cromwell, Henry's chief administrator, recommended her heartily. Henry was lusty for love, and travelled, laden with presents, to meet her boat. When he saw this Anne he was immediately repelled by her appearance. She was tall, spoke a guttural German, and her face was pitted by smallpox. Though they went through with the marriage, it was never consummated. When Henry asked Anne to resign her title, she was so relieved not to be beheaded that she instantly agreed.

Meanwhile, Henry had become taken with yet another lady-in-waiting. Catherine Howard was the most beautiful of Henry's wives. At 18, she was fair, slender and merry, and her laughter was often heard echoing down the castle halls. When her uncle informed her that she was to marry Henry Catherine protested that she was in love with Thomas Culpeper, who happened to be the king's favourite courtier. Her uncle convinced her, however, that her personal wishes did not matter. Henry felt that he was in love for the first time. At 50, he was having an Indian summer, and his lust for Catherine was insatiable. He caressed her in public much more than he had his other wives – in fact, he could not keep his hands off her. Catherine tried to please Henry. She avoided Culpeper as best she could, while poor Tom, as the king's favourite, was called to his bedside when he was not with Catherine, where Henry would recall the joys he had shared with his fresh young wife in excruciating detail. But soon rumours began circulating; Henry's archbishop discovered that in the past Catherine had been wild – sexually involved with one of the boys who would pay nightly visits to her boarding school. Henry laughed it off at first. But when the court began to pour forth its evidence he cried in public for the first time. Wanting desperately to find a way to overlook Catherine's premarital indiscretions, he prolonged her life. But, when it was discovered that she was currently in love with Thomas Culpeper, he flew into a rage. Catherine, her former lover, and Culpeper were executed. Before the block Catherine announced, 'I die a queen. But I would rather die the wife of Thomas Culpeper.'

It had left Henry a very old and broken man. He had given Catherine his all, only to discover that she had never really let him into her heart – she was the first woman to whom he had not come first. But a year and a half later fortune smiled on him again in the form of Katherine Parr, who had a long nose, short neck, respectable body and well-shaped, ardent mouth. By the age of 31, she had been widowed twice. She was cultured and tactful. When, in 1543, Henry proposed marriage she let out a shriek, saying that it would be better to be his mistress. But she soon took pity on the ageing monarch, and pity developed into warm affection. She was a patient nurse for him in his old age; Henry had grown fat and needed constant care. They were married four years before Henry succumbed to his many illnesses. Though he had loved his last Katherine well, he asked to be buried next to Jane Seymour, 'the woman who died in order to give me a son'.

J.H. (Lists 8, 18, 24, 25, 32, 38)

♣ Adolf Hitler
20 April 1889 to 30 April 1945

Dr Leonard L. Heston, professor of psychiatry at the University of Minnesota, investigated Hitler and came to one conclusion: 'Sexual deviations of several kinds have been suggested, but the fact remains that very little is known about Hitler's sex life. Ignorance has fostered blatant speculation. The evidence is: he was regarded as sexually normal by his physicians and those who knew him through the war. Eva Braun, his mistress, was thought by all to be normal. Hitler was an emotional person who certainly grieved deeply and appropriately following the death by suicide of an earlier mistress, Geli Raubal. Eva Braun voluntarily came to Berlin during the last days, elected to marry Hitler, and then to die with him. Hitler was certainly capable of sustaining for a lengthy period a relationship involving profound affectional ties. Saying more would be sheer speculation.'

Gossip that Hitler might be homosexual was scoffed at by his colleague Albert Speer: 'Such accusations have no truth. Hitler's worries and long hours often made his sex drive taper off and he would request drugs . . . to help, but as to being a homosexual –

no!' According to Glenn B. Infield, in his study of Hitler's secret life, the Führer was normal: 'The testimony of the women whom he slept with, and many are still alive, proves that he appreciated female flesh. They laugh at the accusation that he was a homosexual, and their evidence is convincing.'

The preponderance of evidence suggests that Hitler's longest and most publicized love affair – with Eva Braun, who was to become his wife – involved little more than sexual intercourse. Twenty-three years younger than Hitler, Eva became his mistress-in-residence in 1932. Intellectually limited, the Bavarian beauty compensated for her lack of brains with a shapely, athletic body that had but one flaw: a vagina too small for normal sex. Eva underwent painful corrective surgery, doggedly enduring secret and lengthy post-operative treatments. (Her gynaecologist promptly died in a car accident shortly after announcing a full recovery had been achieved.) As Hitler's mistress, Eva kept a confident but low profile, seldom appearing with her lover in public. In her diary, she was less sure, writing, 'he needs me only for certain purposes ... this is idiotic'. Otto Skorzeny, Hitler's chief of commandos, once reported a conversation in which Eva had confided, 'He doesn't even take his boots off, and sometimes we don't get into the bed. We stretch out on the floor. On the floor he is very erotic.' Indoors, Hitler encouraged Eva to cavort in the buff by hinting that she seemed 'too hot in her clothes'. He preferred to strip her himself, removing her garments with fumbling fingers that nearly drove her crazy with frustration. Outdoors, he insisted she swim or sunbathe nude, while he took photographs to add to his huge pornographic collection. Usually, the shots were close-ups of her buttocks. He declared this peculiar angle was necessary to prevent her from being recognized should the prints fall into 'the wrong hands'. Trapped in his Berlin bunker, while the Russians were about to overrun the city, Hitler married Eva in the early morning hours of 29 April 1945. The following day, in a suicide pact, Eva took cyanide and Hitler ended his life with a bullet.

Underground rumours swept Germany during the 1930s suggesting that the real reason for the Nazi party leader's fanatical devotion to duty was that he was impotent. Jokingly, the wags pointed to his typical pose at public functions during which he clasped his hands protectively in front of his genitals and wisecracked that he was 'hiding the last unemployed member of the Third Reich'. The small group of women who became intimate with Hitler, and survived the experience, assured interrogators that he was not impotent. Subsequent to their affairs with the Führer, many of his mistresses either committed suicide or were murdered by the Gestapo to protect Hitler's reputation. What seems not to be absolutely certain, and based mostly on shreds of gossip and guesswork, is that Hitler's chosen females learned that their revered leader specialized in coprophilic sadomasochism.

Hitler's one true love appeared to be Angela ('Geli') Raubal, the 21-year-old daughter of his half-sister. In September 1929, the attractive brunette came to join her mother, the housekeeper at Hitler's sumptuously furnished Prinzregentenplatz apartments in Munich. Forty-year-old 'Onkel Adolf' promptly appointed himself guardian–protector, gave her an adjacent bedroom, and jealously assigned guards to keep the Viennese girl a virtual prisoner. Flattered by the attention, she revelled in the uncle–niece relationship at public occasions and privately they became lovers, but possibly with bizarre, unexpected twists. According to rumours, along with coprophilic demands Hitler claimed artistic privilege to draw precisely detailed, pornographic sketches of Geli, posing her in every obscene position he could devise. 'My uncle is a monster,' she reputedly sobbed to friends, 'you would never believe the things he makes me do.' Terrified, yet unable to escape, Geli endured the sadomasochistic perversions for two years. The chambermaids responsible for tidying up the bedroom could only gossip among themselves over the 'very strange and unspeakable' abnormal sexual relations that had taken place. As compensation and to even the score, Geli not only seduced Hitler's long-time companion and chauffeur Emil Maurice and copulated with the willing security guards assigned to her, but had sex with every young man with whom she could secretly establish a liaison. In 1931, unable to accept the gilded captivity any longer, she shot herself through the heart, using Hitler's personal 6.35 mm Walther pistol. Ironically for the millions of people who later died because of Hitler's rule, a despondent Führer had to be closely watched to ensure that he, too, did not commit suicide.

In the mid-1930s, Hitler met Renate Müller, then 29 and an established star in German films. The petite, blue-eyed blonde – a typically Aryan beauty – accepted a command invitation for sex in the private quarters of Germany's master. In October 1937, the meetings ended abruptly. Renate Müller either jumped forty feet from her Berlin apartment window, or was thrown out on Gestapo orders, after being charged with secretly having a Jewish lover.

Other female intimates met equally tragic fates. In 1939, Englishwoman Unity Mitford shot herself while in Munich. With a bullet lodged in her brain, she lingered on as a human vegetable for nine years. Earlier, Suzi Liptauer hanged herself after an overnight rendezvous. Maria 'Mimi' Reiter also attempted suicide but survived. The reasons behind these strange suicide attempts and deaths? Hitler's unnatural bedroom behaviour? Possibly. But the truth remains unproved.

Soviet doctors, after performing an official autopsy on Hitler's burned corpse, reported a curious fact: 'In the scrotum, which is singed but preserved, only the right testicle was found. The left testicle could not be found in the inguinal canal.' Seemingly, Hitler was born with but one.

Of the seven children conceived by his mother Klara, four died prematurely, one was moronic, and another was hidden from public view as an idiot. Her marriage was so close to being labelled incestuous that the pope had to give the couple a special dispensation. This in-breeding led Hitler to fear that his own blood was 'tainted'. He used leeches to 'purify' it, and had numerous samples drawn so he could visually reassure himself. His pathological, festering hatred of the Jews was perhaps due to a suspicion that his paternal grandmother, Anna Maria Schickl-gruber, had been seduced by her Jewish employer's student son. While an unmarried servant girl, she produced Hitler's father, Alois.

Eds. (Lists 7, 25, 37, 49, 50)

♣ Billie Holiday
17 April 1915? to 17 July 1959

Billie wrote, 'Mom and Pop were just a couple of kids when they got married. He was 18, she was 16, and I was 3.' Pop was an itinerant guitarist and, though poor, Mom would feed any musician who drifted through Baltimore. A childhood trauma left Billie with a permanent fear of corpses – her great-grandmother died in her sleep, and her stiffened arm had to be broken in order to release the just-awakened Billie from its grasp. Eleanora Fagan Holiday was a tomboy and her father called her Bill. She called herself Billie after her favourite film actress, Billie Dove. She attended school only to the fifth grade. After a lifetime of heroin addiction, police harassment and jail, she died at 44 of heart and liver failure.

Ten-year-old Billie was sentenced by a judge to a Catholic reform school. Her crime – being raped by a middle-aged neighbour, Mr Dick. The event was 'bloody and violent', as was her first voluntary sexual encounter two years later with an older musician on her grandmother's parlour floor. Around that time she started running errands for a whorehouse, where she heard her first jazz records. As a teenage prostitute in New York City, she preferred white customers because blacks took too long. A black man she refused to service tipped off the cops and she was jailed for prostitution. Later she admitted to having had lesbian relationships while in prison, but claimed she had taken a passive role.

In her first singing job, she refused to pick up customers' tips from the table in the customary manner – using her vaginal lips – and consequently the other girls started calling her 'Lady'. She wore no underwear on-stage; one night she expressed her sentiments to an unappreciative audience by raising her skirts as she stalked off. 'Lady Day' could sing with real passion, and the men she chose to sleep with gave her violent inspiration. She liked them big and pretty. Of one drummer she remarked, 'They don't call him "Big Sid" because he's six foot three you know.' In her twenties, she had many musician-lovers, and often sang with her pretty face marred by black eyes and her body covered with bruises. If her friends warned her away from a bad character, she went after him with more determination than ever. Men used her and spent her money; before long, she had a reputation as an easy mark.

The dates of various events in Billie's life, like that of her engagement to a young pianist named Sonny White, are uncertain. Her relationship with Sonny was no rougher than most of Billie's casual affairs, but both supported their mothers, and the problems involved ended the romance. Tenor-sax player Lester Young was the best friend Billie ever had. His obbligati matched Billie's moods so perfectly that the records they made together are her finest. Lester shortened her last name and called her 'Lady Day'; she affectionately called him 'Pres', short for 'President'. It is interesting that, through all their years together – recording, on the road, nightclubbing – their friendship was never physical.

The music they made together shows that Lester touched Billie as no other man could and years later, when they had parted, he told a writer 'She's still my "Lady Day".'

In 1941, Billie met her husband-to-be, the handsome businessman Jimmy Monroe. Jimmy 'smoked something strange'. When their marriage began to founder, she thought joining Jimmy in his opium habit would restore the lost magic, but before she was 30 she was separated from him and living with trumpeter Joe Guy, then 25 years old. That relationship was a triangle – Billie, Joe and her heroin. Drug busts and tours eventually separated them and Billie's next choice of a lover, John Levy, proved a disaster. Levy managed a nightclub and gave her a singing job when nobody else would. He bought her nice clothes, gave her jewellery, and gradually took over her finances. Although she was making $3500 a week, she had to beg for pocket money. Levy eventually left Billie and her band stranded and broke during a tour in the South.

The year 1956 brought a second marriage for Billie. She was devoted to Louis McKay, a club owner and her manager, but they filed for divorce in California in late 1958. 'Lady Day' died before the divorce decree was finalized.

J.M. (Lists 14, 16, 19, 39, 42)

♣ J. Edgar Hoover
1 January 1895 to 2 May 1972

As director of the US Federal Bureau of Investigation from 1924 until his death forty-eight years later, John Edgar Hoover organized the FBI into a scientific law-enforcement agency which mercilessly prosecuted small-time gangsters and political dissidents and maintained files on thousands of Americans from all walks of life. Hoover dominated federal law enforcement for so long that, in 1971, Martha Mitchell was able to remark, 'If you've seen one FBI director, you've seen them all.'

'I was in love once when I was young,' Hoover remarked, 'But then I became attached to the Bureau.' In fact, there is no evidence that Hoover ever made love. He did date in high school, but never 'went steady'. He became captain of the school cadets and his friends teased him that he was 'going steady with Company A'. He was a champion debater, particularly when arguing against women's suffrage. His father died when he was 26 years old and Hoover, a devoted son, chose to live alone with his mother for the remainder of her life – 17 years. He never married, expressing the belief that women are a hindrance to the development of a man's career.

Hoover's only intimate friend for the last forty-four years of his life was Clyde Tolson, a tall native of Missouri, who served as confidential secretary to three US secretaries of war before joining the FBI in 1928. Periodically, rumours spread that J. Edgar Hoover and Clyde Tolson were homosexual lovers. Hoover took these charges very seriously, claiming that they were made by 'public rats', 'gutter-snipes', and 'degenerate pseudo (which he pronounced 'swaydo') intellectuals'. When Hoover died, Tolson received most of Hoover's $551,500 estate, as well as the flag that had draped his coffin. Although Hoover and Tolson were definitely a tight couple, it is true that two men can remain close friends for decades without engaging in sex together. And Hoover was not without certain traditional attitudes of male sexuality. For example, he displayed a gallery of famous nudes in his home, including Marilyn Monroe's celebrated calendar photo. He enjoyed cracking jokes about sex, and it was rumoured that he kept pornographic magazines in his desk. He had his own private collection of mild erotica. The 'OC' files (official and confidential) were kept in Hoover's office under lock and key. These files contained potentially embarrassing information, sexual and otherwise, about government officials and various public figures.

Sometimes, when his agents turned up a particularly juicy item, Hoover would pass it on to the current president and to members of the cabinet. However, the OC files were also said to contain stories about the extramarital affairs of Franklin D. Roosevelt and his wife Eleanor, as well as incidents from the lives of Richard Nixon and John F. Kennedy.

Once, FBI agents raided the apartment of black radical Angela Davis and found some photographs taken while she and her boyfriend were making love. When Hoover learned of these photos, he was outraged that they hadn't been brought to him immediately, and the agent who had held them back was denied his next promotion. The FBI began tapping the phone of the Rev. Martin Luther King Jr in 1957. Eventually, in 1964, Hoover obtained tapes that proved King had engaged in extramarital sexual activities, and Hoover made copies available to members of the press, to Congress and to President Lyndon Johnson. Prior to King's audience with the pope in August 1964,

224

Hoover had sent the pontiff derogatory information about King, but the Pope ignored Hoover and went ahead with the meeting as scheduled. While King was preparing to go to Stockholm to receive the Nobel Peace Prize, Hoover's attacks on his character reached a peak. During one session with reporters, Hoover called King 'the most notorious liar in the country'. Three days later, Hoover and Tolson had excerpts of the hotel tapes sent to King's wife, Coretta. Also enclosed was an unsigned note addressed to Dr King which threatened release of the tapes and said, 'Your end is approaching ... you are finished.... You are done. There is but one way out for you. You better take it before your filthy, abnormal fraudulent self is bared to the nation.'

Hoover once commented, 'I regret to say that we of the FBI are powerless to act in cases of oral-genital intimacy, unless it has in some way obstructed interstate commerce.'

D.W. (Lists 15, 29, 35, 42)

♣ Howard Hughes
24 December 1905 to 5 April 1976

The son of a millionaire who manufactured oil-drilling equipment, Howard Hughes was born in Houston, Texas. An only child, he was spoiled by both parents but especially by his mother Allene, who worried over young Hughes constantly. Allene instilled in her son her own phobias, including a profound fear of germs, which years later would dominate Hughes's life. During his childhood, Hughes had only one close friend and rarely took part in any group activities at school; what he liked most was to ride his horse around the countryside.

Hughes was an indifferent student who appeared to have little ambition or direction. But, after his mother died (when he was 16), and his father's death two years later, Hughes revealed a strong personality. He got a court to declare him legally an adult, bought out his relatives' shares of the Hughes Tool Company, and thus took over total control of the family business. A millionaire at 19, he moved to Hollywood, where he directed and produced films, including the First World War aerial epic, *Hell's Angels*. By the early 1930s, Hughes had a new passion – aviation. He founded the Hughes Aircraft Company, bought control of Trans-World Airlines (TWA), and personally designed new, experimental aircraft. Serving as his own test pilot, he set a new airspeed record in 1935, and soon broke the transcontinental and transworld records. He also crashed three times, suffering serious injuries.

As early as 1944, Hughes had his first nervous breakdown. While his economic empire grew over the next two decades, Hughes's mental condition deteriorated dramatically. Surrounded by aides who never suggested he seek psychiatric help, Hughes withdrew into bedrooms in mansions and penthouses where he used box after box of Kleenex – spreading the tissues over everything he came in contact with – in his obsessive war against germs. For at least the last decade of his life, he was chronically paranoid and addicted to codeine and Valium. Weighing less than 7 stone and with long shaggy hair, Hughes died at the age of 70 en route from Acapulco, Mexico, to a hospital in Houston. He left an estate valued at $2.3 billion.

A very shy teenager, Hughes had few if any dates and little experience with women. After his father's death, he decided to marry Ella Rice, a young Houston socialite. A vivacious extrovert, Ella turned down his proposal. However, Hughes made his aunt, who had married into the Rice family, intervene. Finally, Ella's mother agreed Hughes would be an asset to the family and arranged the marriage. Hughes and his bride moved to Los Angeles, where the marriage proved disastrous. Intoxicated with the excitement of Hollywood, Hughes paid little attention to his wife, while spending an increasing amount of time in the company of film people. After three years, Ella left and sued for divorce. Hughes's reaction to this set a pattern for the future – feeling betrayed, he never saw or spoke to Ella again. After her departure, Hughes began a pursuit of Hollywood film stars which continued for thirty years. Actress Billie Dove was his first conquest, but Hughes did not want their affair publicized. When he learned that Dell Publications had printed a one-shot 'magazine' featuring himself and Billie on the cover, Hughes bought the entire printing before it could be distributed. Billie Dove was genuinely in love with the 6 foot 4 inch tall, dark-skinned young Texan. This was unfortunate, since he dropped her for no apparent reason after a short affair and never spoke to her again. Katharine Hepburn was another love. Hughes would follow her across the country in his private plane. Finally, Hepburn terminated the romance, explaining to a friend that Hughes bored her.

Ginger Rogers was also linked with Hughes. But their relationship ended when she found Hughes in bed with another actress.

One actress widely assumed to have been romantically involved with Hughes was Jane Russell. Although they were close for years, they were never lovers. Hughes was particularly concerned, however, with Jane Russell's breasts and how they appeared on screen. After viewing rushes of the film *Macao* starring Russell, Hughes wrote a three-page memo describing in detail the kind of brassière she should wear to enhance her assets. Other film actresses associated with Hughes included Marian Marsh, Hedy Lamarr, Jean Harlow, Ida Lupino, Ava Gardner, Lana Turner, Terry Moore, Yvonne Schubert and Carole Lombard.

Probably no other person in history invested as much money in his sex life as did Howard Hughes, who obsessively searched for the woman with the most perfect face, body, and especially breasts. Besides his heavily publicized affairs with well-known actresses, Hughes established another outlet for his sexual urges. Over the years, he developed a system for procuring young women for what became a veritable harem. Hughes operatives across the country were told of their boss's need for new faces and bodies. These agents found likely candidates, promised them screen tests and film careers, and then shipped them off to Los Angeles. At one time, Hughes owned or leased five houses in different areas of Los Angeles. Each one was occupied by a hopeful starlet or showgirl – kept on salary. Thus, whichever neighbourhood Hughes found himself in, he would have privacy and a girl. Hughes himself was constantly looking for talent in magazines, on television and on the streets. He set up his own detective agency to research and contact these prospects. One friend, studio executive Bill Fadiman, was sent to investigate the star of the Ballet de Paris, Zizi Jeanmaire, after Hughes saw a picture of her. When Fadiman heartily approved of what he saw, Hughes bought the entire ballet company and installed it on the second floor of the RKO Writers Building. He hired a writer to do a screenplay for the company and set about seducing Jeanmaire. After two years of failure, Hughes abruptly dropped both ballet and film project.

Another victim of Hughes's obsessional desire was Italian actress Gina Lollobrigida. When approached by a Hughes agent and asked to come to Hollywood, she was thrilled. On arrival, she was whisked off to the Town House Hotel and kept a virtual prisoner – she had a twenty-four-hour guard and was permitted to see no one. Happily married to a dentist in Italy, she wanted no part of Hughes's advances, so Lollobrigida finally escaped and returned to Italy.

Beauty contests were always a good field for Hughes's reconnaissance missions. In 1960, after viewing the Miss Universe pageant on television, Hughes ordered his detectives to contact seven of the finalists, successfully installing them in a Los Angeles hotel. The operation failed when all seven became suspicious of the promises of stardom and bolted for home. At one point during the 1950s, a Hughes aide claimed there were 108 active files on various candidates for Hughes's bedroom. After reading the files and checking the photographs of these women, Hughes decided which should be contacted – his favourites were teenage brunettes with large breasts. At least one such seduction operation backfired. A 15-year-old blonde with a 40 inch bust was brought to Hollywood from North Carolina. Her mother, who had also gone west, suggested a trip to Palm Springs for her daughter, herself and Hughes. He readily agreed and once there took the girl to bed. In the middle of their lovemaking, the mother burst into the room, claiming her daughter had been ruined. To avoid statutory rape charges, Hughes was forced to settle out of court for $250,000.

In 1957, aged 51, Hughes married 31-year-old film star Jean Peters, whom he had dated off and on for eleven years. He would not allow her to shave her body hair (he liked hair on women). When Peters posed in bathing suits for fan magazines, her legs and thighs had to be retouched. Why the couple married remains a mystery. Hughes was already mentally unbalanced, and Peters gave up her career to live in seclusion with him. Some time during the early 1960s, Hughes's sex life ended when his overwhelming fear of germs precluded physical contact with another person. Sex was replaced by drugs and round-the-clock viewing of films and television. Finally, in 1970, Jean filed for divorce, not having seen Hughes for over three years.

In the early 1940s, Hughes had a big chow named Chang. Chang got into a fight with another dog. When Hughes tried to separate them, the other dog bit him on the penis. It took six stitches to sew up the wound. Although it temporarily disabled him, the injury didn't seem to have lasting effects. However, Hughes never owned another pet.

R.J.F. (Lists 3, 7, 17, 22, 25, 45, 46)

'Victor Hugo was a madman who believed himself to be Victor Hugo', said the poet Jean Cocteau, summing up the extravagances and contradictions of a man who was larger than life both in literature and in love. This supremely self-centred genius championed the rights of the poor and the downtrodden at the same time that he emblazoned his walls with the motto '*Ego Hugo*'. He amassed a fortune, and yet insisted on being buried in a pauper's coffin.

An immense man of gargantuan energy and robust health, he slept less than four hours a night, wrote standing up, and boasted that he never had a thought or a sensation that was not grist for his writer's mill. His disillusionment with the regime of Louis Napoleon drove him into exile in 1851, and for nearly twenty years he lived and worked on Guernsey, creating a bizarre and ornate personal environment of architectural whimsy, made up of secret staircases, hidden rooms and eccentric decorations. Here he wrote feverishly and explored the occult. When he finally returned to France, he was again active in politics and literature, vigorous almost to the end. His dying words echo the contradictions of his life: 'I see a black light.'

When Hugo married at the age of 20, he was a virgin, but on his wedding night he coupled with his unsuspecting young wife, Adèle Foucher, nine times. She became exhausted by his sexual athleticism and, after five difficult pregnancies in eight years, she called a halt to their sex life. The marriage was shaken further when Adèle fell in love with Hugo's friend, the literary critic Sainte-Beuve. Although the affair was probably not consummated, it nearly led to a duel between the two men. The rupture with Adèle only temporarily disrupted Hugo's sex life. In fact, his appetite had merely been whetted by his wife. He had been married eleven years and was world famous for his novel, *The Hunchback of Notre Dame*, when in 1833 he began an affair with the raven-haired, dark-eyed beauty Juliette Drouet. An actress and mistress of a series of famous and wealthy men, she taught him the varieties of sensual pleasure. He was soon able to make the boast 'Women find me irresistible.' And obviously they did. He began one of the most amazingly active sex lives ever recorded. It was not unusual for him to make love to a young prostitute in the morning, a willing actress before lunch, a compliant courtesan as an aperitif, and join the also indefatigable Juliette for a night of sex. He maintained a certain level of activity almost to his death bed – diary entries at the age of 83 record eight bouts of love over the four months before his death.

He craved affairs with women who were passionate, witty and challenging – but he often settled for sheer numbers. His powerful personality and fame were strong aphrodisiacs and he enjoyed a dazzling parade of willing partners. They were almost exclusively young and, as he grew older, often young enough to be his granddaughters. He was perfectly willing to have liaisons with married women, but not if they were living with their husbands. Any other woman, or girl, who was young, amenable and attractive was fair game.

Juliette, who was the great love of his life, tolerated his prodigious activity. But, by the time she was in her thirties, her beauty had begun to fade – no doubt due in part to the cloistered existence Hugo forced upon her. By 1844, she had been temporarily displaced by Léonie d'Aunet, a young noblewoman who had run away with a painter. The affair turned into a shocking scandal when Léonie's jealous husband arranged to have the couple tailed by the police, who caught them in flagrante delicto. Although Hugo escaped punishment by claiming his proviileges as a member of the peerage, Léonie was thrown into jail for adultery. Upon Léonie's release from prison Hugo divided his time equally between Léonie and Juliette. Eventually, Léonie was deposed, but Juliette's reinstatement as his primary love did not in any way limit the scope of Hugo's conquests. She herself estimated that he had sex with at least 200 women between 1848 and 1850. Even at age 70 he managed to seduce the 22-year-old daughter of writer Théophile Gautier, and it is possible that he was carrying on an affair with Sarah Bernhardt simultaneously. Despite the myriad of women who claimed his attentions, Hugo always returned to Juliette as his 'true wife'. Their love affair lasted fifty years. During most of that time, they had to live separately. When possible, Hugo visited her ever day. As for Juliette, her devotion was unswerving. She wrote him 17,000 love letters. At 77, she died in his arms and, although his sex drive continued during the remaining two years of his life, her death seemed to break his spirit at last.

Rumours abounded during his lifetime, as they have since, that he carried on an incestuous relationship with his daughter Léopoldine, but no conclusive proof of this exists. He was apparently a voyeur, and something of a foot fetishist, and he was excited by intrigue and mystery. He often admitted his mistresses through secret staircases and entertained them in hidden rooms even when this was not really necessary.

To his young grandson who walked in on the 80-year-old Hugo in the embrace of a young laundress, he exclaimed, 'Look, little Georges, that's what they call genius!'

R.W.S. (Lists 1, 7, 8, 10, 11, 20, 21, 22, 25, 26, 31, 34, 43, 47)

♣ Henrik Ibsen
20 March 1828 to 23 May 1906

Ibsen was the second child of a tyrannical merchant in Skien, a small town in Norway. Rumoured to be illegitimate, he experienced a lonely childhood which left him fearful of intimacy. At 16, he left home, was apprenticed to an apothecary, and spent his free time reading, painting and writing poetry. Unsociable and withdrawn, he nevertheless moved to Christiania (now Oslo) to study medicine.

Ibsen's career as a playwright began by chance when he was offered the job of 'dramatic author' with the Norwegian Theatre in Bergen. For six years, he lived with bitter poverty and failure, but he did learn his craft. He described this time as 'a daily abortion'. In 1856, however, the theatre produced his play, *The Feast of Solhaug*. In that year, he met his future wife, Suzannah Thoresen. She was devoted to him and, after they married in 1858, followed him into a twenty-seven-year self-imposed exile – mainly in Rome, Dresden and Munich. Ibsen was obsessed with fame, but it did not come easily. He was regarded as a dramatist whose heretical ideas on marriage, religion and human behaviour were outrageous and immoral. When he finally returned to Norway at the age of 63, he had become internationally famous. After suffering two strokes which robbed him of physical vigour, he died at 78.

Ibsen, the great exponent of realism, was so timid about sex that he was reluctant to show his genitals to a doctor. He loved risqué stories but could not bring himself to use them in his works. As a young man, he was notoriously shy with women, but this did not prevent him from becoming involved with Else Jensdatter, a servant ten years his senior, while he worked as an

231

apothecary's assistant. Ibsen was 18 when Else bore him a son.

As a young man in Bergen, Ibsen met Rikke Holst, a 15-year-old to whom he proposed. He had been so shy that she had to initiate their affair by chasing him up his hotel stairs and flirtatiously hitting him in the face with her bouquet. Rikke's father disapproved of Henrik, however, and, when he once caught the young student making love to his daughter, he turned 'green with anger'; Ibsen, not very heroically, fled the scene.

As success widened his circle of friends, Ibsen met the woman he would marry. Suzannah Thoresen was a clergyman's daughter. She had ankle-length chestnut hair, great vitality and radical views. Ibsen wrote to her that, if she would join her destiny to his, he could become someone important in the literary world. They were married in 1858. Ibsen called Suzannah 'my cat', and depended on her entirely. She believed that the highest thing a woman could do was to accompany her loved one into battle and 'set his vision aflame'. Their son, Sigurd, was born in 1859.

Ibsen had an enduring obsession with young women. According to Suzannah, he looked at their pretty maids, but only 'aesthetically, as one looks at a statue or painting'. As a renowned author, he cultivated various young women, having discovered fame to be a powerful aphrodisiac. But he was unwilling or unable to translate his desires into action. Young women became enamoured of him, and he responded by modelling his heroines on them. If they fired his passion, he only expressed it in his imagination. Ibsen fantasized that if he were rich he would buy the finest ship in the world, engage a gypsy orchestra, and sail off to some tropical island with a few good friends and 'the most beautiful young women in the world'. His longing for young girls was apparently never consummated, but their companionship offset his feelings of sexual inadequacy. In foreign countries, he would receive several girls in his hotel room, give them signed photographs of himself and kiss them, but he was fearful of performing the sex act itself.

Ibsen never created a scandal or embarrassed his wife, but in 1889 an infatuation for Emilie Bardach, an 18-year-old Viennese girl, led him to consider divorce and remarriage, and to tour the world with his new love, whom he called his 'May sun in a September life'. Emilie returned to Vienna and, although they kept up an affectionate correspondence, she was replaced in his heart by another young admirer, Helene Raff. This relationship, too, was one of sublimated passion.

232

In 1891, when he was 63, Ibsen had an emotional involvement with 27-year-old Hildur Andersen, a concert pianist whom he had met when she was 10. Now, knowing her as a woman, he wanted to be with her constantly. Whenever his wife was off on a trip, Ibsen would spend all his time with Hildur. Once, away on an extended trip, Suzannah received a letter from her stepmother warning her that rumour had it Ibsen was in love with Hildur and planning to get a divorce and marry her. Suzannah immediately wrote to her husband repeating what she had heard. Shaken, Ibsen replied to his wife that none of what she'd heard was true, that her stepmother was 'mentally confused' and a 'damned old sinner' for trying to stir up trouble. That was the end of Hildur. Even when he was seriously ill, and Hildur asked to visit him, Suzannah would not permit it. Many of these young women inspired characters in Ibsen's plays. Emilie Bardach became the prototype for *Hedda Gabler*. Another woman Ibsen knew inspired the character of Nora in *A Doll's House*. Ibsen was appalled by the case of a young wife, Laura Kieler, who had been unjustly committed to a lunatic asylum – simply for borrowing money and forging a cheque – by her indignant husband. By writing these plays, Ibsen inadvertently became the champion of the 'new woman', who was defined by one Danish literary critic as 'self-possessed and sceptical'.

'Most people die without ever having lived', Ibsen maintained 'Luckily for them, they don't realize it.'   A.S.M.

❧ Christopher Isherwood
b. 26 August 1904

British-born author Christopher Isherwood is probably best known for his quasi-autobiographical 'Berlin novels', one of which, *Goodbye to Berlin*, introduced the character Sally Bowles and was the basis for the hit musical *Cabaret*. The slender, 5 foot 7 inch Isherwood spent time in pre-Hitler Germany and chronicled much of the decadence of that society in his fiction. With his good friend W. H. Auden, with whom he collaborated on several plays, Isherwood left Europe in 1939 and emigrated to the USA, settling in California and working on films, including *The Loved One*. An American citizen since 1946, Isherwood is a student of Vedanta, and has written extensively on the various aspects of Hindu philosophy. He is also an active supporter of gay liberation, having openly admitted his homosexuality in his book, *Kathleen and Frank*.

Asked when he first came to the realization of his own homosexuality, Isherwood replied, 'Quite early – by the time I was 10 or so, in the sense of being physically attracted to boys at school. I managed to have orgasms with them while we were wrestling and I guess some of them had orgasms, too, but we never admitted to it. I fell in love a lot during my teens, but never did anything about it. I was very late in getting into an actual physical affair. That happened while I was in college. . . .' It was his partner's idea. When Isherwood protested, the other young man locked the door and sat on Isherwood's lap. 'Other experiences followed, all of them enjoyable but none entirely satisfying,' according to Isherwood. This was because he was suffering from an inhibition common to upper-class homosexuals of the time – he couldn't relax with his British peers. He needed 'a working-class foreigner'. Isherwood found his answer in Berlin when he visited Auden in 1929. The fact that the Germans were 'simple and natural about homosexuality' was a welcome change. In one of Berlin's homosexual bars he found the type of blue-eyed blond boy who represented for Isherwood 'the whole mystery-magic of foreignness'.

After returning to England, he was hired as a tutor for a young boy in a remote village on the coast. Isherwood's autobiography, written in the third person, recounts the scene: 'While Christopher was there, he had his first – and last – complete sexual experience with a woman. . . . They were both drunk. . . . She liked sex but wasn't the least desperate to get it. He started kissing her without bothering about what it might lead to. When she responded, he was surprised and amused to find how easily he could relate his usual holds and movements to this unusual partner. . . . He also felt a lust which was largely narcissistic; she had told him how attractive he was and now he was excited by himself making love to her. . . . Next day, she said, "I could tell that you've had a lot of women through your hands. . . ." He asked himself: "Do I now want to go to bed with more women and girls? Of course not, as long as I can have boys. Why do I prefer boys? Because of their shape and their voices and their smell and the way they move. And boys can be romantic. I can put them into my myth and fall in love with them. From my point of view, girls can be absolutely beautiful but never romantic. In fact, their utter lack of romance is what I find most likeable about them. They're too sensible." '

Back in Germany in 1930, Isherwood met the boy on whom he modelled 'Otto Nowak' in *Goodbye to Berlin*. Otto was a bisexual with a dramatic nature and 'a face like a very ripe peach'. By 1932, the affair had cooled and Otto was replaced by 17-year-old Heinz. After Hitler came into power, Heinz and Isherwood wandered around Europe, from country to country, living like a 'happily married heterosexual couple' until 1937, when Heinz risked a visit to Nazi Germany, where he was arrested and imprisoned for homosexuality and evading conscription. Heartbroken, Isherwood returned to London and allowed himself to be comforted by a variety of young men.

He also had the companionship of Auden. About his relationship with Auden, Isherwood has written: 'Their friendship was rooted in schoolboy memories and the mood of its sexuality was adolescent. They had been going to bed together, unromantically but with much pleasure, for the past ten years, whenever the opportunity offered itself. . . . They couldn't think of themselves as lovers, yet sex had given friendship an extra dimension.'

When Isherwood came to Hollywood in 1939, he met Aldous Huxley and Swami Prabhavananda. For a while, he stayed at the swami's monastery where he, like the other devotees, practised celibacy. But he did not completely neglect his love life. His boyfriends during the 1940s included William Caskey, a young photographer from Kentucky with whom he lived for several years.

In 1953, Isherwood met 18-year-old Don Bachardy, with whom he was to establish a lasting relationship. He currently lives in Santa Monica, California, with Bachardy, who has gained recognition as an artist and has collaborated with Isherwood on a play and some film scripts.

Isherwood has always maintained that he is very happy with his sexual preference. Although Auden once baited him by calling him a 'repressed heterosexual', Isherwood offers his own definition of what it means to be a homosexual: 'It seems to me that the real clue to your sex orientation lies in your romantic feelings rather than in your sexual feelings. If you are really gay, you are able to fall in love with a man, not just enjoy having sex with him.'

C.H.S. (Lists 12, 20, 25)

♣ Edward Jenner
17 May 1749 to 26 January 1823

British surgeon Edward Jenner discovered the process of vaccination, and with single-minded devotion fought and virtually conquered smallpox. He was also a naturalist who made important studies of the cuckoo.

At 29, Jenner was heartbroken when a girl he desired rejected him. Five years later he met the lovely Catherine Kingscote. At the time, Jenner was conducting his first experiment with a hot-air balloon, in imitation of the Montgolfier brothers. The experiment came to the attention of Catherine's father, who happened to witness the balloon's descent. Kingscote requested a repeat performance and Catherine released the second balloon. Her dark curls and white skin captivated Jenner, and they were married in 1788, after a long courtship and engagement. At first marriage distracted Jenner from his quest for a smallpox cure, and Catherine was doubtful that the disease could be eradicated. Eventually she came to share her husband's dream, supporting his work for the twenty-seven years of their marriage. The Jenners had two boys and a girl. The first child, Edward, was mentally retarded, and died of tuberculosis at 21. Not long afterwards, Catherine began to show signs of TB. Wishing to devote all his time to his wife, and not wanting to expose her to the dirty London air, Jenner turned down an offer of a very high-paying practice in that city. They remained in the country, happy at least to be spending more time together than ever before. When Catherine died after a five-year illness, Jenner retired from public life, dying eight years later at 74.

A.W. and J.M. (List 33)

♣ Jack Johnson
31 March 1878 to 10 June 1946

He was the first black world heavyweight boxing champion. In forty-eight years he engaged in one hundred and thirteen bouts and lost only seven. Ring historian Nat Fleischer called him 'the greatest heavyweight of all time'.

Raised in a poor family of nine in Galveston, Johnson ran away from home at 12, and in five years on the road he learned to be a boxer. He was soon beating the best fighters around and was in line for a shot at the heavyweight title held by a tough Canadian, 5 foot 7 inch Tommy Burns. But Burns flung insults at Johnson and ignored him, until baited by a $35,000 promoter's offer. The match was held outside Sydney, Australia, with Burns seven to four favourite. In the fourteenth round, a venomous right from Johnson knocked Burns flat. Champion Jack Johnson returned to a segregated, racist America, refusing to play Uncle Tom, flaunting his power and arrogance. The seething press and boxing crowd sought a White Hope. Johnson crushed them all. Novelist Jack London begged in print, 'Jeff, it's up to you!' – and the undefeated, invincible white Jim Jeffries came out of five years' retirement to take care of the black. The fight of the century was staged on the blazing afternoon of 4 July 1910, in Reno, Nevada. The 6 foot 2½ inch Jim Jeffries squared off against the 6 foot 2¼ inch Jack Johnson. 'The great Jeffries was like a log,' reported the Associated Press. 'The reviled Johnson was like a black panther.' In the fifteenth round, Johnson knocked out Jeffries.

Race riots exploded throughout the USA. Johnson ignored them. In his beret and silk suits, sipping wine through a gold straw, enjoying his own Chicago cabaret, driving a Stutz Bearcat, starring in *Othello*, sleeping with innumerable white women, he was on top of the world. The whites had to get rid of him. Found guilty on a trumped up morals charge, Johnson escaped to Europe for five years. Eager to return home, he defended his crown against lumbering 6 foot 6 inch Jess Willard in Havana on 5 April 1915. Johnson was knocked out by Willard in the 25th round. Johnson claimed he had thrown the fight to get back to America and obtain a pardon. Experts claimed Johnson lost because he was out of shape. He got no pardon but spent a year in Leavenworth Prison, working as athletics director. He died at 68 in a motor accident.

When Johnson boasted, as allegedly he once did, 'I can get any white woman in Chicago I want' – or when the press reported his affairs and marriages with young white ladies – the white population of America became enraged. Once, one hundred Texans prepared to converge on Chicago to lynch Johnson. In Congress, Republican Seaborn A. Roddenberry of Georgia introduced a constitutional amendment banning inter-marriage between blacks and whites, shouting, 'No brutality, no infamy, no degradation in all the years of southern slavery, possessed such villainous character and such atrocious qualities as ... states which allow the marriage of the negro, Jack Johnson, to a woman of Caucasian strain.' Race riots set off by Johnson knocking out white men and bedding white women caused the death of nineteen people in seven years. Johnson's explanation for his behaviour was simple: 'I didn't court white women because I thought I was too good for the others. It was just that they always treated me better. I never had a coloured girl that didn't two-time me.' Most white men felt threatened by Johnson's sexual prowess. They imagined he had a gigantic penis that their women loved. When Johnson heard this, he laughed and decided to threaten his white tormentors further. Dressing to spar in public, he would wrap gauze bandages around his penis to enlarge it and go out before the spectators in the skintight trunks of the time, displaying the mammoth bulge at his crotch. There was talk of forcing Johnson to wear loose boxing trunks instead of skintight ones. But former bareknuckle heavyweight champion John L. Sullivan announced, 'The size of a nigger's penis is not to be discussed in public.'

At 20, Johnson married a childhood sweetheart, a lightly coloured girl named Mary Austin. When he refused to quit prize-fighting, she divorced him in 1901. Then he began living with Clara Kerr, an attractive black girl. They travelled everywhere together until Clara ran off with a white man in Johnson's entourage, taking with her Johnson's clothes and all the cash she could find. Years later, Johnson heard Clara was in a New Jersey jail for murdering her husband. Learning she had killed in self-defence, Johnson helped her win acquittal, and bought her a small hotel.

Disenchanted by black women, Johnson turned to whites. He became involved with an Irish girl from New York, Hattie McLay, daughter of a respectable jeweller. He took her to Europe, and to Australia where he won the championship. When he got back to Chicago with Hattie, he broke with her because she was an alcoholic and had been sleeping with his manager. Then Johnson fell for Belle Schreiber, brought up in Milwaukee and called 'the prettiest white whore' in Chicago. Belle worked in the classiest bordello in America, the Everleigh Club, run by two young Kentucky sisters, Aida and Minna Everleigh, which featured thirty exotic boudoirs furnished with marble-inlaid brass beds covered with white cashmere blankets, perfume sprays over the beds and mirrored ceilings. The baths were gold. Among the club's regulars were James J. Corbett, Ring Lardner and John Barrymore. Belle Schreiber was one of the higher paid prostitutes, receiving $50 a time. Meeting Johnson, she offered to live with him, and he accepted. Belle accompanied Johnson to San

Francisco. There, at his hotel, he found Hattie had just arrived for a reconciliation. The women bumped into each other and fought, but Johnson parted them and promised to keep both happy. He would make love to Hattie, then to Belle, and to avoid the press he would use a rope outside Belle's window to get down and back to his quarters. One night, as he descended the rope, the hotel owner's daughter pounced on him, grasping for his crotch. 'She wanted the sight and feel of my privates', Johnson said. 'Like she thought I was built of leather down there. I've never seen a girl get so frantic.' To stop her screams, Johnson had intercourse with her, but the next night, he refused her, insisting he could not satisfy three women. Furious, the girl told her father the champion had raped her. Her father confronted Johnson, accusing him of 'ruining his poor little baby, with his gigantic, oversized thing'. Johnson paid off the hotel owner to suppress any bad publicity.

Shortly afterwards, at a race track, Johnson met a 28-year-old white woman, Etta Terry Duryea, a tall, slender blonde who had recently divorced an Eastern horse-racing tycoon. Johnson began living with her, truly loved her, and married her in Pittsburgh in 1909. The press was in an uproar from coast to coast. Etta became deeply depressed. Johnson wanted children, but she refused, and began to sleep in a separate bedroom. Johnson then became the first black regular at the Everleigh Club. At heart he was devoted to his wife but, on 11 September 1912, Etta put a gun to her head and committed suicide. (When Johnson died, he was buried beside her in Chicago's Graceland Cemetery.)

Three months after Etta's death, Johnson hired a pretty 19-year-old white girl from Minneapolis, Lucille Cameron, as his secretary. They lived discreetly apart, but slept together. Lucille's mother heard about it and stormed into town. She insisted Johnson be charged with abducting her under-age daughter. Headlines condemned Johnson, lynch crowds gathered, but defiantly Johnson married Lucille. The reformers decided to get Johnson once and for all, and employed the Mann Act – the federal white slavery law of 1912 that made it a crime to transport a woman across state lines for immoral purposes. The government needed a witness and found one in Belle Schreiber, who was determined to have her revenge on Johnson. She told authorities that Johnson had taken her over one state line after another for debauchery, prostitution, unlawful sexual intercourse and crimes against nature. On 13 May 1913, a jury found Johnson guilty. He was sentenced to one year and one day in jail. Out on bail, Johnson, at the urging of his mother, posed as a Canadian baseball player and left the country.

He spent five years in exile with Lucille. In France, he had affairs with Mistinguett, the leggy star of the Folies Bergère, and with actress Gaby Deslys. In Germany, he had a fling with Mata Hari. Later, in Hollywood, he had an intense relationship with actress Lupe Velez. After twelve years of marriage Lucille quietly divorced him. In August 1925, Johnson married the last of his white wives, Irene Marie Pineau, another blonde who divorced her white husband for Jack. His love for her, Johnson said, knew no equal. By this time, there was no public fuss. Despite his public arrogance, Jack Johnson was an easy-going, affable fellow. He just had the misfortune of being born at the wrong time.

I.W. (Lists 9, 39)

♣ Janis Joplin
19 January 1943 to 4 October 1970

Born into a middle-class family in a conservative Texas backwater, Janis was made to suffer for her non-conformity at an early age. She had an artistic bent and liked to read and paint, but neither activity was respected by her high-school peers. Her 'beatnik' life-style, coupled with the fact that she was overweight and had severe acne, earned her the cruel nickname of 'Pig Face'. In college she was nominated for 'Ugliest Man on Campus', so she adopted a self-defensive pose for the rest of her life – that of a hard-drinking, good-time mama. Ever trying to become one of the boys, she often crossed into nearby Louisiana for the honky-tonk life. There she discovered the blues. She began imitating the style of Bessie Smith and performed for free, or the price of a drink, in cafés and roadhouses near Port Arthur.

She left home to join Big Brother and the Holding Company, a San Francisco-based rock band, as their lead singer. Janis's virtuoso performance at the first Monterey Pop Festival (captured in the film *Monterey Pop*), coupled with the success of Big Brother's second album, 'Cheap Thrills', pushed Janis into the national spotlight and made a cult figure of her. She openly used drugs and alcohol daily, and pressured the manufacturers of Southern Comfort into giving her a fur coat for all the free publicity she'd given them. Adored by her fans, she was feared by her promoters.

240

Yet, at the height of her fame, she often wistfully confided to friends that what she really wanted was a home life. When friends pleaded with her to stop using hard drugs, she told them, 'Let's face it, I'll never see 30.' While recording her third album in 1970, she returned to her room at the Landmark Hotel in Hollywood and injected a large shot of unusually pure heroin. A member of her entourage found her the next morning, dead of an overdose at 27.

When Janis was 18, she made an ill-fated first trip to San Francisco, seeking the bohemian life she had dreamed of as a high-school student. She moved in with a man who tired of her, and kicked her out. Throwing her arms around his knees as he walked up a San Francisco hill, she begged him not to leave her. He kept walking, dragging Janis behind him. It was a cathartic moment for her. She picked herself up, said, 'OK, Daddy, what the fuck,' and resolved never again to beg for love. Strung out on methedrine, broke and alone, she tried to sell her body for $5 a trick and was devastated when prospective clients either laughed at her or ignored her completely. She eventually returned to Port Arthur to lick her wounds. She said of herself in this period, 'I'd 've fucked anything, taken anything. . . . I did. I'd take it, suck it, lick it, smoke it, shoot it, drop it, fall in love with it. . . .'

In 1966, she made her second trip to San Francisco with an emissary from Big Brother, who made love to her in order to secure her services as a singer. Later, she delighted in telling people how she had been 'fucked into being in Big Brother'. Her constant graphic remarks about her love life became a Joplin trademark. Although her primary interest was heterosexual, Janis often enjoyed sex with women, and sometimes liked to indulge in threesomes with her girlfriends and men she picked up at random. She had a come-on style all her own and frequently frightened potential sex partners with the directness of her approach: 'I thought we'd go back to the dressing room and get it on.' For these casual encounters she favoured 'pretty young boys' of 16 or 17. The school-yard taunts she had suffered stayed with her to the extent that she was unable to handle her sexy, onstage image, although her performances had the same effect on men that Jimi Hendrix's and Mick Jagger's did on women. She frequently commented that she was too ugly to attract men, and was heard to lament, 'I'm a big star and I can't even get laid.' Actually, she got laid quite a lot, but seldom more than a few times by the same person. Once, after a long train trip, she complained that there were over 365 men on board and she'd had sex with only sixty-five of them. Terrified of rejection, she histrionically faked orgasm at times, feeling that if she didn't have one it was *her* fault. On other occasions, she wore partners down with demands for non-stop sex. She never let pick-ups become too close, because she feared being financially exploited.

Janis made a distinction between sex for the hell of it and serious relationships, and even considered marriage with one of her lovers. Her most serious relationship with a 'star' involved Kris Kristofferson, with whom she fell in love. Unfortunately, a romantic triangle occurred when one of Janis's female lovers fell for him too. She also had a four-month affair with singer Country Joe McDonald, who described her as 'pretty' and 'a very feminine woman'. 'My music isn't supposed to make you wanna riot!' she declared. 'My music is supposed to make you wanna fuck!'

M.J.T. (Lists 9, 11, 14, 22, 26, 42)

🍀 James Joyce
2 February 1882 to 13 January 1941

When the elder Joyce – a Dublin tax collector – sank into alcoholism and eventually lost his job, young James was withdrawn from an exclusive Jesuit-run boarding school, and for two years the brilliant boy educated himself. At 17, he entered another Jesuit institution, University College in Dublin, and briefly considered becoming a priest, but rejected the idea because it required a vow of celibacy. Joyce fell in love with a semi-educated Dublin chambermaid, Nora Barnacle, on 16 June 1904, a date to which he assigned all the happenings in his novel *Ulysses*. Refusing to be married by 'a clerk with a pen behind his ear or a priest in a nightshirt', Joyce took Nora as his common-law wife and they left for the continent in October 1904. They eventually married in 1931, urged on by their daughter Lucia.

In Europe, Joyce earned a precarious living by teaching conversational English and writing reviews in Trieste, Zurich and Paris. Until 1912, there were rare visits to Dublin, which Joyce considered stifling to artists like himself. After years of drudgery – and a series of twenty-five painful operations for iritis, glaucoma and cataracts, which left him at times nearly blind – he finally began to enjoy a comfortable income from his writing. Lanky, bespectacled and shy, Joyce never permitted himself an off-colour remark in the presence of a woman. Yet he became famous for his unbuttoned prose, and in December 1920 *Ulysses* was banned for its obscenity in the USA and England.

In his student days, Joyce had haunted Dublin's seedy 'Nighttown' red-light district, where he lost his virginity at 14. In his early twenties he gave up prostitutes, saying he longed to 'copulate with a soul'. The soulmate he chose, Nora Barnacle, remained his lifelong companion. He saw himself as a weak child in need of Nora's motherly discipline and once wrote to her: 'I would be delighted to feel my flesh tingling under your hand. . . . I wish you would smack me or flog me even. Not in play, dear, in earnest and on my naked flesh. I wish you were strong, *strong*, dear, and had a big full proud bosom and big fat thighs. I would love to be whipped by you, Nora love!'

The small-breasted, boyishly built Nora adapted well to the role of dominatrix, addressing Joyce as 'simple-minded Jim' and describing him to others as 'a weakling'. While Joyce's work earned him worldwide praise, Nora made no secret of her disdain for it. Despite the fact that *Ulysses* became famous for its psychological penetration of the female mind, Nora asserted that Joyce knew 'nothing at all about women'. Still, Nora was faithful to him throughout their long relationship, even though she confided to friends that Joyce wanted her to go to bed with other men 'so he'll have something to write about'. Joyce was never at a loss for words in his letters to Nora. In 1909, when he was away from Ireland on business, he wrote her lusty letters packed with scatological endearments and praises for her soiled underwear: 'The smallest things give me a great cockstand – a whorish movement of your mouth, a little brown stain on the seat of your white drawers . . . to feel your hot lecherous lips sucking away at me, to fuck between your two rosy-tipped bubbies. . . .' When he didn't hear from her, he wrote again with words of apology: 'Are you offended, dear, at what I said about your drawers? That is all nonsense, darling. I know they are as spotless as your heart.' Nora's drawers, and what was in them, kept Joyce's pen quite busy. He was a true underwear fetishist and even carried a pair of doll's panties in his pocket. Fortified by alcohol, he would sometimes slip the tiny underpants over his fingers and cakewalk them across a café table, to the bewilderment of onlookers. The author spent much of his time in cafés and bars, chatting with other writers and artists. Joyce was less interested in exchanging ideas with his intellectual peers than in avoiding intercourse with Nora:

drinking himself flaccid provided an effective means of birth control.

While teaching English in Paris, Joyce fell passionately in love with one of his students, Amalia Popper, the daugher of a wealthy Jewish businessman. An unrequited love, it was thwarted by Amalia's father, who gently warned the writer not to take advantage of his position of authority. The experience kindled in Joyce a nagging desire for a dark Semitic woman.

In early 1919, Joyce found his ideal in a Zurich woman named Marthe Fleischmann. He described to a friend the circumstances under which he first saw Marthe: 'She was in a small but well-lit room in the act of pulling a chain.' Through this unabashed first encounter, Marthe had unwittingly endeared herself to the coprophile Joyce, who later that night explored 'the coldest and hottest parts of a woman's body'.

During Joyce's early forays into Nighttown he contracted syphilis, which he treated himself by cauterizing the chancre. The treatment eliminated the symptom, but not the disease, and it is believed that the author's chronic eye trouble stemmed from this disease. However, he died in Zurich after an operation for a duodenal ulcer.

M.J.T. (Lists 7, 20, 35, 37, 49)

♣ Carl Gustav Jung
26 July 1875 to 6 June 1961

A German–Swiss contemporary of Sigmund Freud, Jung was the creator and father of analytical psychology, which incorporated many of his theories, including those of the collective unconscious, the attitude types (extrovert and introvert) and the four function types (thought, intuition, feeling and sensation).

A strange and imaginative child (son of a minister and, according to a family legend, the great-grandson of Johann Wolfgang von Goethe, through an illicit liaison), Carl had visions, one of God defecating on a cathedral. He developed a lifelong interest in folklore from listening to peasants' tales, and claimed he had two personalities. Though he wanted to be an archaeologist, he chose medicine as a profession for practical reasons. In 1903, married and practising psychiatry at a Zurich clinic, he began a study of word-association, which led him to correspond with Sigmund Freud. The two met in 1907 – Jung thought Freud 'the first man of importance I had encountered'; Freud thought Jung 'magnificent'. They had their differences – for example, Freud wasn't keen on Jung's interest in parapsychology, nor was Jung a total believer in Freud's sexual theories. When their collaboration came to a bitter end in 1913, Sandor Ferenczi, an associate of Freud, quipped, 'The Jung no longer believe in Freud.' Jung went on to develop his own 'school', run his institute, write his books, and travel to New Mexico and Africa to study primitive cultures. From these studies, he formulated his theory of mythological archetypes common to all cultures. At his retreat in Bollingen, on Lake Zurich, he himself built a tower-shaped house and annexe, to which he could withdraw. When there, he led a simple life cutting his own wood, carving stone and meditating.

Jung was a bull of a man, 6 feet 1 inches tall with rough-hewn features and visionary eyes. His sense of humour was robust (Freud once defended its coarseness) and witty ('Show me a sane person and I'll cure him for you.'). He had a ferocious temper and a tendency to be callous – he once called a patient with a syphilis phobia a 'filthy swine'. His leaning toward the grandiose may have inspired his initial admiration of Hitler ('a spiritual vessel') and the Nazis ('the twilight of the Gods'), which earned him just reproach from Jews; his reply was that they were paranoid. By 1939, he had changed his mind about Hitler and deemed him 'more than half crazy'. His son Franz called him 'maddening and marvellous'. He cheated at games and was a poor loser, walked around the garden dressed only in ragged shorts, and was a gourmet cook. He loved detective novels and dogs. 'The Sage of Zurich' died aged 85.

It was 22 years after its occurrence that, in a letter to Freud, Jung finally confessed to one of the significant events in his sex life: '. . . my veneration for you has something of the nature of a "religious crush" because of its undeniable erotic undertone. This abominable feeling comes from the fact that as a boy I was the victim of a sexual assault by a man I once worshipped.' The man has never been identified. The incident, he felt, made the transference of his male patients repugnant to him. His relationship with Freud was marked by intense quarrels and emotional reconciliations, during one of which Freud fainted and was carried to a couch by Jung. Both admitted the homosexual overtones in their natures, never given physical expression; both were basically heterosexual.

Jung's early loves included a village girl he met only briefly but with whom he was enraptured; a friend's good-looking but slightly cross-eyed mother; and a French-Swiss girl he nearly became engaged to as a student.

Emma Rauschenbach, whom he married in 1903, was the love of his life. When he was a young medical student, visiting family friends, he caught sight of her – a 15-year-old in braids, standing on a staircase – and remarked to a friend, who did not take him seriously, that she would be his wife. Six years later, she was. Emma was intelligent and pretty but had been burdened at 12 by her father's dependence upon her when he went blind. Jung, eloquent and intellectual, represented an exciting escape. Jung later wrote of their honeymoon at Lake Como: 'My wife was apprehensive – but all went well. We got into an argument about the rights and wrongs of distributing money between husbands and wives. Trust a Swiss bank account to break into a honeymoon in Italy.' They had five children – four girls and a boy. It is not known whether they practised contraception, though Jung wrote Freud that he tried 'every conceivable trick to stem the tide of these little blessings'. At first their marriage was idyllic. By 1906, however, Jung was having dreams – one of which, about two horses, was interpreted by Freud as 'the failure of a rich marriage'. Jung replied, '. . . I am happy with my wife in every way . . . there has been no sexual failure, more likely a social one.' The dream held, he believed, 'an illegitimate sexual wish that had better not see the light of day'.

In 1907, he became briefly infatuated with a woman he met while travelling with Emma in Abbazia. In 1909, one of his patients wanted him to impregnate her; he confessed that his professional relationship with her had 'polygamous components'. However, these two experiences only set the stage for the other important woman in his life – Toni Wolff, thirteen years his junior and elegant, with a delicately modelled face, who came to him as a patient in 1910. Later, during his 'confrontation with his unconscious', a near-breakdown which began in 1913 and lasted several years, she helped him search out his *anima*, the female element of his nature. In Jung's typecasting of the women in his life, she was the *femme inspiratrice*, while Emma was wife and mother. Emma was jealous, but Jung had his heart set on a triangle, which he later justified in theories about marriage in which the 'many-faceted gem' (Carl), needing more than the 'simple cube' (Emma), looks outside the marital relationship for satisfaction. So powerful was his personality that he came close to

246

convincing both women that the triangle was ideal. It lasted for almost forty years. Emma and Toni both became practising analysts. Emma gave lectures on the Holy Grail and exchanged advice with Freud; Toni developed original theories about female function types. However, Toni, restive in her role as mistress in straitlaced Zurich, began to demand divorce. Jung said no, and began to criticize her – for example, when he saw her new apartment he said, 'Only Toni would have gone to live in a place with marble pillars and a study like Mussolini's.' Toni, heartbroken, drinking and smoking too much, died at 64 of a heart attack. Emma died two years later in 1955 – she and Jung had been married fifty-two years. 'She was a queen! She was a queen!' cried Jung after her death.

Many of his followers were young women intellectuals, known jocularly as the *'Jung-Frauen'*, who tended to adore him for his bear-like appeal, his sensibility, his empathy with women. An old woman patient of Jung's, whom Freud called a 'phenomenally ugly female', was to Jung a pleasant woman who 'had such lovely delusions and said such interesting things'.

Among his women friends was flamboyant Olga Fröbe-Kapteyn, supposedly an ex-circus rider, who created Eranos, a discussion group for intellectuals which met at her home. The meetings at least once degenerated into debauchery; an anonymous participant said it was the 'nearest I ever came to wicked abandonment in my life'. Jung was there, 'bubbling over with wit, mockery, and drunken spirit'. Some of these women claimed to have been his lovers. One gave him poor marks in lovemaking while another, Jolanda Jacobi, claimed he was undersexed. A cynical Jungian countered, 'Presumably *she* hadn't been his mistress anyway.'

Ruth Bailey, an Englishwoman he met in Africa who was his friend for more than thirty-five years, became his housekeeper and companion after Emma died. He was then over 80 and cantankerous. After a quarrel about two tomatoes, he advised her, 'All you have to remember is not to do anything to make me angry.'

'The prerequisite for a good marriage . . .' he remarked, 'is the licence to be unfaithful.'

A.E. (Lists 10, 16, 21, 49)

247

♣ Edmund Kean

4 November 1787 to 15 May 1833

Kean ranks with David Garrick and Sir Henry Irving as one of the three greatest tragedians in the English-speaking theatre. Watching this actor of the Romantic School portray Hamlet, Othello, Richard III or Shylock was, as Coleridge put it, 'like reading Shakespeare by flashes of lightning'.

Although he would later claim to be the illegitimate son of that infamous rake the Duke of Norfolk, Kean was actually the child of itinerant street-hawker, strolling player, and occasional prostitute Ann Carey and apprentice surveyor Edmund Kean. He was indeed born out of wedlock but his only connection with Norfolk was through Charlotte Tidswell – a woman who later became his mentor and surrogate mother. Charlotte had once had an affair with the profligate duke. Early in life, Kean showed talent and Ann Carey, to her profit, promoted him as a child actor. Kean, however, rebelled at this exploitation and at 15 ran away from home to spend the next twelve years in provincial theatres and county fairs in an assortment of plays and bawdy entertainments, competing with dwarfs, mermaids and educated pigs.

In 1808, Kean married Mary Chambers, an Irish actress of little talent, who was several years older than he. The couple had two sons, Howard and Charles. The little family struggled on in the provinces, eking out a living, until Kean made his London debut at Drury Lane as Shylock, in 1814. Unfortunately, he was so well schooled in dealing with failure that he was unable to handle success. He drank and whored to such extremes that, by the age of 40, although renowned as a great tragedian, he was unable to learn any new roles. Towards the end of his career, people came to see him as though visiting a favourite picturesque ruin. He died at the age of 45 – gout ridden, syphilitic and mentally unstable – after collapsing on the Covent Garden stage while playing the role of Othello.

Whatever sexual attraction Kean and his wife Mary had had for each other soon wore off. If the rigours of hand-to-mouth theatrical touring dampened her ardour, it only stimulated his. From early in their marriage, what little money they earned went to buy not only food and lodging but drink and prostitutes for Edmund. During these lean years, his lack of money limited his carousing, but when he became one of the best-paid actors in London he was able to abandon all restraint. He was a small man, with dark curly hair and flashing eyes and, although not unattractive to women, he seems to have been titillated by paying for sex. He entertained several prostitutes and an occasional small-time actress each evening in his dressing room during intermissions. As a result, the Drury Lane house manager could never predict how long an intermission would be needed.

Kean enjoyed the company of the types of people he knew well – pugilists, drunkards and actors. He took wild midnight horse-back rides, kept a pet lion, and formed the scandalous Wolves Club in 1815. Supposedly a group of fellow actors dedicated to philanthropy, the club soon degenerated into orgies and non-stop drinking bouts at its meetings.

One night as he played Othello in Somerset in 1816, a society matron, Charlotte Cox, was overcome by his performance. She rose, screamed and fainted. Annoyed at first, Kean was flattered when he realized what had caused the commotion. He stopped the performance, had the lady lowered from her box to the stage, and took her to his dressing room to be revived. She was not a particularly attractive woman, but Kean fell in love with her and, during the following years, he enjoyed this opportunity to carry on an affair with an aristocrat – a lady who was, moreover, a lady only in the drawing room. In the bedroom, she was insatiable. Charlotte proved a bit too insatiable, however, when she pressed to be publicly acknowledged as Kean's mistress. While Kean's wife tolerated wenches in his dressing room, she would not accept a serious mistress. Kean was terrified that someone who knew about his liaison with Charlotte would tell Mary. In one breath he was the hot-blooded romantic hero: 'You are my fate,' he wrote to Charlotte, 'my heaven or my hell!' But in his next letter he would warn: 'Caution be our password!' The matter came to a climax when Charlotte's husband, a middle-aged and respected alderman, sued Kean for 'criminal conversation' with his wife. Their letters, introduced as evidence, were declared too scandalous to be read aloud in court. Kean, who was ordered to pay £800, toured America until the scandal blew over. Before the trial, Charlotte had already turned to an affair with her husband's clerk, Whatmore. Mary also deserted Kean. Without either mistress or wife, he drank more heavily and became even more promiscuous, continuing his sexual activity almost to the end of his life. He abstained only when syphilis prevented him from coupling with that evening's wenches.

R.W.S. (Lists 11, 17, 18, 20)

♣ John F. Kennedy
29 May 1917 to 22 November 1963

After Kennedy was gunned down by an assassin in Dallas near the end of his first term, his time in office came to be characterized as the '1000 days of Camelot'.

Born into the wealthy and tight-knit Irish Kennedy clan, the man who would become president forty-two years later was instilled from birth with a fiercely competitive spirit, fuelled by a demanding father who wouldn't accept 'second best' from any of his four sons. Jack Kennedy graduated cum laude from Harvard. He was plagued with a weak back all his life and also suffered from Addison's disease. Despite the fact that 'at least one half of the days that he spent ... were days of intense physical pain', Kennedy refused to act the invalid and carried on an active life enjoying sailing, swimming and other sports. A casual dresser, Kennedy nevertheless carried his 6 foot 1 inch, 12 stone 7 pound frame with a certain elegance, and when president he took care to look good. After serving as US senator from Massachusetts, Kennedy narrowly defeated Richard Nixon in the 1960 presidential race. He was a serious politician, who readily admitted his mistakes and took full responsibility for the Bay of Pigs fiasco. However, he was also capable of being lighthearted, prompting one of his aides to remark, 'This administration is going to do for sex what the last one [Eisenhower's] did for golf.'

Kennedy prided himself on being a sexual athlete and was known for his popularity with women. He viewed sex as a natural need and once offhandedly remarked to Harold MacMillan that, if he went too long without a woman, he suffered severe headaches. One of his closest friends, George Smathers, described his colleague as having 'the most active libido of any man I've ever known'.

Kennedy's initiation into the sexual world took place in a whorehouse in Harlem with a school friend at the age of 17. Although his reputation as a playboy was still developing during his college days, he managed to get in trouble at least once for having girls in his room. From there, he progressed to a more dangerous female entanglement that nearly jeopardized his naval career. While stationed in Washington, Kennedy became involved with Danish journalist Inga Arvad – whom he affectionately called Inga-Binga – and who was also suspected in intelligence circles of being a Nazi spy. When government officials

250

intervened, Kennedy rapidly moved on to other conquests.

During his congressional years, Kennedy was rarely without female companionship, although the word among some Georgetown women was that the senator was a disappointment in bed and had a talent for making love with one eye on the clock. Indeed, former Senator Smathers commented, 'in terms of the time he spent with a woman, he was a lousy lover. He went in more for quantity than quality.' Others also indicated that Kennedy enjoyed the pursuit and conquest almost more than the act. Kennedy himself once told reporters, 'I'm never through with a girl until I've had her three ways.' According to Smathers, 'No one was off-limits to Jack – not your wife, your mother, your sister.' During their Senate days, Kennedy and Smathers shared a pied-à-terre where they could carry on discreet affairs. Once, when Smathers was called away to the Senate, leaving Kennedy with their dates, he returned to find the ambitious senator chasing both girls around the apartment. Having two girls at once was one of Kennedy's 'favourite pastimes', Smathers said.

When Kennedy finally decided in his mid-thirties that he needed a wife, he eschewed the voluptuous starlets and models he was usually attracted to, and chose Jacqueline Bouvier. A nervous thoroughbred of impeccable family, elegantly attractive Jackie was the ideal wife for a presidential candidate. However, marriage did not mean monogamy to Jack Kennedy, and the opportunity for sexual liaisons was wide open on the campaign trail. Kennedy maintained a cool nonchalance: when aides once became frantic over a picture showing Kennedy lying next to a nude and very buxom brunette on a Florida beach, the candidate merely smiled and remarked, 'Yes, I remember her. She was great!' Another time, when a landlady took pictures of Senator Kennedy leaving the apartment of his 21-year-old secretary with whom he was having an affair, he simply brushed the incident aside.

Fond of swimming nude in the White House pool, Kennedy was even fonder of being accompanied by well-endowed beauties similarly unclothed. A number of women were secreted in and out of the White House when Jackie was absent, and two secretaries, referred to by Secret Service agents as 'Fiddle and Faddle', were reputedly kept on the staff for Kennedy's personal convenience. That Jackie knew of her husband's infidelities seems fairly certain; it was reported that Kennedy's father offered her a million dollars not to divorce his son on the brink of the presidential campaign. Friends said Jackie would turn a blind eye to Kennedy's affairs, although once, discovering a pair of panties stuffed in a pillowcase, she icily asked, 'Would you please shop around and see who these belong to? They're not my size.' However, despite Kennedy's wanderings, the two shared a certain intimacy, and the White House staff had strict orders not to disturb them when they retired to their quarters in the early afternoon while their children were napping.

While alive, John F. Kennedy's sex life was considered taboo by the world press, but, twelve years after his death, with the USA in a post-Watergate mood, women began appearing from every direction to tell their stories of indulging in fleshly pleasures with the martyred president. Kennedy's taste in women ran the gamut from starlets to society women to obscure secretaries and airline stewardesses. Stripper Blaze Starr claims to have spent twenty minutes making love to Kennedy in a closet in a New Orleans hotel suite in 1960, while her fiancé, Gov. Earl Long, held a party in the next room. In the closet, Kennedy found time to tell Blaze the story of President Harding making love to Nan Britton in a White House closet. Divorced painter Mary Pinchot Meyer said that she had an affair with Kennedy in 1962. They smoked marijuana together in the White House and he wrote her love letters. She kept a diary of the affair: this disappeared after she was murdered in October 1964.

Kennedy's most notorious affair involved a dark-haired beauty later investigated for having close connections with the Mafia. Judith Campbell Exner met Kennedy before he became president, but their affair continued during his early days in the White House. Kennedy was generous and once insisted on buying her a fur coat, Exner said; his generosity did not continue in the bedroom. His favourite way of making love was supine, which was partially due to his back problem but also made it seem as if the woman was there 'just to satisfy the man'. Kennedy tried to talk her into a ménage à trois one night while a tall, thin woman waited for them in the bedroom. Judith refused, even though he told her, 'I know you; I know you'll enjoy it.'

Part of Kennedy's attraction was his humour, according to a former mistress who says she enjoyed Kennedy 'not because he was so great in bed, although he wasn't bad, but because he had such a great sense of fun'. This stood Kennedy in good stead when he encountered an infrequent rejection. After he had attempted unsuccessfully to seduce Pulitzer-Prize-winning historian Dr Margaret Louise Coit, she asked him, 'Do you do this to all the women you meet?' 'My God, no,' he replied, 'I don't have the strength.'

The young president's name was linked with many Hollywood actresses, including Gene Tierney and Jayne Mansfield. But his most famous liaison was with Marilyn Monroe. Monroe, who sang a sexy happy birthday in her breathy whisper at Kennedy's 45th birthday party in Madison Square Garden, was reportedly smuggled aboard Kennedy's plane after their affair began in 1961. Despite his promiscuity, Kennedy maintained a certain detachment and rarely became emotionally involved with his women. As he himself readily admitted, he never lost himself in passionate affairs, explaining, 'I'm not the tragic lover type.'

L.K.S. (Lists 9, 11, 20, 22, 26, 43, 44)

♣ Aly Khan
13 June 1911 to 12 May 1960

Aly Khan was once heir apparent to Aga Khan III of India, but his international pursuit of fast cars, horses and beautiful women cost him the post of spiritual leader to over twenty million Muslims of the Ismaili sect which had been held by his father.

Born in Italy and reared in Europe, Prince Aly Suleiman Khan inherited a fortune and learned early how to enjoy it. In 1929, after the death of his mother, Aly threw himself into London society (where he had been sent to study law). The short dark teenager had distinctive, exotic looks, boundless energy and skill at racing cars and horses which won him fame and the adoration of that year's debutantes. He went on to compete in European motor races and hunt on African safaris, while managing his horse-breeding farms and villas in Ireland, France, Switzerland and Venezuela. The Allies found his daring and fluency in English, French and Arabic invaluable during the Second World War, awarding him the Croix de Guerre and the US Bronze Star for his work in intelligence. Though some consider his greatest conquest Rita Hayworth, whom he married in 1949, he earned deep respect as Pakistan's delegate to the UN, where he served from 1958 until his death in a car accident two years later.

Two aspects of motor racing and army service re-appeared in his career as a lover: speed and logistics. With houses all over the world, he had only to capture a woman's attention and he could woo here wherever he wished. His blitzkrieg involved the 'eyes-across-the-crowded-room' approach: staring intently at the chosen prey until he had her attention. Then he fixed an introduction, following it up with dozens of roses, constant phone calls, and attention to his victim's every whim and desire. The international hostess Elsa Maxwell wrote that Aly danced with a woman 'slowly and rapturously, as though it is the last time he will ever hold her in his arms. . . . When he tells a woman he loves her, he sincerely means it at the moment. The trouble is that a moment passes so quickly.' Even a married woman could carry on an affair discreetly with the prince, who always travelled with a crowd of people and kept everyone guessing who, among the current crew, was the chosen one. A bewildered member of Parliament, Mr Loel Guinness, told a divorce court in 1936 that he had left a happily married woman, his beautiful blonde wife Joan, with such a retinue, and returned from a business trip to find she wanted a divorce to marry Aly Khan. Joan was Aly's first wife and she gave him two sons, Karim (who became the fourth Imam when Aly's father died in 1957) and Amyn.

Though Aly continued to stalk other women, he didn't bother to ask Joan for a divorce until he met sultry Rita Hayworth on the Riviera in 1948. As competition, Aly had Hollywood's leading men as well as the Shah of Iran, also holidaying there and planning seductions of his own. Aly won, gallantly helping Rita forget her inattentive husband Orson Welles by whisking her off to Paris, London and Madrid. For Rita, seeking privacy and respite from a gruelling Hollywood schedule, marriage to Aly was a bitter disappointment. He felt alone with anything less than a mob, she said. She took their daughter Yasmin back to America, becoming the first woman to walk out on Aly Khan. They divorced in 1953 and Aly renewed old interests, shuttling between countries on visits, and often not leaving his hotel suites. His father once became incensed when a delegation of Ismailis, in London on a visit from India, were kept waiting in the lobby for over an hour while Aly entertained a young woman upstairs. Aly's reputation had grown to such an extent that one friend claimed, 'You were déclassé, démodé, nothing, you hardly counted, if you'd not been to bed with Aly.'

Though Aly changed women as often as cars and horses, his romances were so intense that few women complained. Juliette Greco admired his perfect timing; and Kim Novak found that other people seemed only 'half alive' compared to Aly. Even actress Gene Tierney – at first so unimpressed she thought to

254

herself on meeting him, 'that's all I need, some Oriental super-stud' – became smitten and hoped at one time to marry him. But none of his romances had quite the historical import of his dalliance with Thelma, Lady Furness – the Prince of Wales's companion until she fell for Aly. Angered, Edward VIII turned to the American divorcée Wallis Simpson, for whom he eventually gave up the throne of England.

Aly's claim that 'I think only of a woman's pleasure when I'm in love' came out of a unique education given him by an Arab doctor in Cairo, where his father sent him as a boy for instruction in the sex technique called *Imsák*. A woman described it this way: 'No matter how many women Aly went with, he seldom reached climax himself. He could make love by the hour, but he went the whole way himself not oftener than twice a week. He liked the effect it had on women. He liked to get them out of control while he stayed in control – the master of the situation.'

'They called me a bloody nigger,' he once declared, 'and I paid them out by winning all their women.'

B.B. (Lists 22, 31, 51)

♣ Peter Kropotkin
9 December 1842 to 8 February 1921

Russian revolutionary, geographer and author, Kropotkin was the foremost leader and thinker of the anarchist movement. He believed in decentralized, cooperative societies where human creativity could bloom unfettered by rulers, priests and government. Kropotkin was greatly admired not only by fellow revolutionaries, but even by many who frowned upon anarchism. Oscar Wilde called him one of the two really happy men he had known. Perhaps this happiness was due in part to his marriage in the winter of 1878–9 to Sofia Grigor'evna Anan'eva, a Polish Jew fourteen years his junior. They married 'rationally', without a religious ceremony, and made a private agreement to renew their relationship every three years. Though Kropotkin rarely discussed his wife, and barely mentioned her in his autobiography, their system must have worked – for she adopted the anarchist cause and remained her husband's devoted companion throughout their lives.

A.W. and J.M.

♣ Lillie Langtry, née Emilie Charlotte Le Breton
13 October 1853 to 12 February 1929

The most celebrated 'professional beauty' of Queen Victoria's London, Lillie was an artist's model, an actress, and the mistress of princes and millionaires. Her beauty and wit were praised by Wilde, Twain and Shaw, among others. Gilbert and Sullivan said of her, 'Oh, never, never, never since we joined the human race/Saw we so exquisitely fair a face.'

Lillie was born on Jersey, the daughter of a clergyman. As a child she was a tomboy, but by the time she was 16 her father had been obliged to repulse several suitors. To console the girl, he allowed her a trip to London. Dazzled by city life, she vowed to live there one day. Escape from Jersey came in the form of Edward Langtry, a moderately well-to-do yachtsman whom she married when 21. Edward provided her with a passport to London society.

Lillie was 5 feet 8 inches tall and had masses of red-gold hair. She had a flawless complexion and at the height of her fame appeared in advertisements for Pears soap. One of the first celebrities to endorse a commercial product, Lillie was paid £132, a sum matching her weight in pounds. Lillie posed for the most famous artists of her day, among them Whistler, Millais and Burne-Jones. Her image – reproduced on postcards – was displayed on the walls of army barracks, student dormitories and ship's cabins, thus originating the pin-up fashion. When she was 24, all manner of men desired her. The famous 78-year-old French author, Victor Hugo, once toasted her, 'Madam, I can celebrate your beauty in only one way – by wishing I was three years younger.'

She made her theatrical debut in 1881 and, although her acting talents were uneven, she nevertheless became the toast of both England and America, playing opposite such leading men as Lionel Atwill and the young Alfred Lunt. In Texas, the infamous Judge Roy Bean renamed his saloon the Jersey Lily and moved it to the town of Langtry, Texas. After the judge's death, Lillie was bequeathed his revolver, which had reputedly been used several times to defend her honour.

In 1897, while Lillie was enjoying international acclaim, her hapless husband Edward died broke in an insane asylum. Two years later, she married a baronet, Hugo de Bathe, and became Lady de Bathe. Using £55,000 of her own money, she remodelled

256

a derelict London playhouse, the Imperial Theatre, and spent the next two decades amusing herself with acting, baccarat and occasional visits to her friend Queen Alexandra. When she was 64 and a grandmother, most of her admirers had fallen away. On a visit to New York, she was seen visiting public dance halls where she paid gigolos 50c to dance with her. Yet, vestiges of her beauty remained. Oscar Wilde had predicted she would 'be a beauty still at 85' – and she was a beauty still upon her death at 74. Hugo de Bathe was useful to her as an official escort after her retirement to Monaco in 1918, but mostly occupied himself with chorus girls and debutantes in Nice. Lillie died, wealthy and alone, in Monaco in 1929.

Lillie enjoyed sex, but not nearly so much as she enjoyed her own glamour and notoriety. Sex was the serious business of her life, her ladder to the top. She believed that scandal was the best form of publicity and provided ample fodder for Victorian gossips. In Lillie's heyday, London's most ambitious hostesses entered her name as a matter of course on any guest list that included her obese lover Albert Edward, Prince of Wales (later King Edward VII). She was also romantically linked with both American millionaire Freddie Gebhard and George Alexander Baird, one of the wealthiest men in England. The mercenary Lillie used these relationships to amass a fortune in diamonds, townhouses, a racing stable and plenty of ready cash. For the most part, Lillie's men tended to be rich, ineffectual and easily dominated. 'Men are born to be slaves,' she once remarked. Edward Langtry was a sexual dud and a drunkard, and when his fortune dwindled he was of no use to her at all. Freddie Gebhard catered to her every whim, tolerating her peccadilloes with doglike loyalty. George Baird delighted in beating Lillie, but every time he did so she made him pay her £5000. She could be haughty with her lovers. Crown Prince Rudolf of Austria–Hungary gave her an emerald ring. Angered by an argument with him, she yanked off the ring and threw it into the fireplace. The crown prince fell to his knees, desperate to retrieve the emerald from the burning coals. Disgusted, Lillie told her friends, 'I couldn't love him after that.'

It was Lillie's dominant nature that Prince Albert found attractive. Lillie's open disregard for Victorian morality not only enthralled Albert but he was even faithful to her for a time. They would meet regularly at the homes of friends, ostensibly for tea, and were given adjoining accommodation during weekend retreats. The intimate details of their affair were kept discreetly hidden, although the fact that they were lovers was no great secret. When Prince Albert once complained, 'I've spent enough on you to buy a battleship,' Lillie snapped back, 'And you've spent enough in me to float one!' Edward Langtry, meanwhile, was bribed into silence. Lillie remained Albert's mistress until she playfully dropped a piece of ice down his back at a party. The prince was not amused and abruptly ended the affair.

On the rebound, Lillie consoled herself with yet another prince, Louis Alexander of Battenberg, Albert's nephew. Louis, an officer in the Royal Navy, was perhaps the only man Lillie ever really loved and the father of her only child, a daughter named Jeanne-Marie. To Lillie's credit, she was never a hypocrite about her many affairs and could even be amused by bawdy items such as this one from a scandal sheet of the time: 'We heard that Mrs Langtry has lost her parrot. . . . That the lady possessed such a bird we were unaware, but we knew she had a cockatoo.'

M.S. (Lists 8, 10, 11, 17, 22, 41, 42, 46)

♣ Charles Laughton
1 July 1899 to 15 December 1962

Laughton was one of the most powerful and versatile character actors in both British and American films theatre. He won the Motion Picture Academy Award as Best Actor in 1933 for his performance in *The Private Life of Henry VIII*.

'I have got a face like an elephant's behind,' said Laughton once, and this, with his large girth, made his desire to go on the stage seem strange to his hotel-keeping British parents. After serving in the First World War, during which he was a frontline soldier and was gassed, he returned home to take up his apprenticeship in the respectable family business. Finally, at 26, he convinced his parents to subsidize his training at the Royal Academy of Dramatic Art in London. Before long he was a well-known and sought-after character actor. His film roles as King Henry VIII, as Captain Bligh in *Mutiny on the Bounty* (1935), and as Sir Wilfred Robarts in *Witness for the Prosecution* (1957) won him Oscar nominations. Laughton died in Los Angeles in 1962 of bone cancer.

Laughton made love with one woman in his entire lifetime – actress Elsa Lanchester, his wife for thirty-three years – and with countless and mostly nameless young men. He met Lanchester at a rehearsal in 1927. Her initial response to him was not romantic: 'He was plump, well, fat really, and pale.' But they hit it off; they could talk, they amused each other, and they shared an interest in art and flowers. They fell in love, a love sorely tested over the years, and married in 1929. The first two years of their marriage were happy and prosaic and, apparently, nothing happened to give the young bride a hint that her husband was homosexual. Then, as a result of a very ugly row with a boy prostitute who insisted that he hadn't been paid, Laughton was forced to admit to his wife that he had long been a practising homosexual, mostly with young hired companions. Upon hearing Laughton's confession, Elsa was dazed. She could only say, 'It's perfectly all right. It doesn't matter. I understand.' But it did matter. For the next week Elsa was stricken with deafness. As she told Charles Higham, 'I suppose I shut my ears off. I have since realized, or was told, that it was probably a sort of reaction to some news I really didn't want to hear.' Finally, she was able to discuss the incident with Laughton. 'Later on, I asked Charles what had happened. And he told me he was with this fellow on our sofa. The only thing I could say was, 'Fine. OK. But let's get rid of the sofa.' After that, she would not consider having children. Although Elsa claimed she was not fond of children, Laughton believed that she could not stand the idea of bearing a child whose father was a homosexual. Yet their marriage continued, even though their sex life dwindled rapidly to nothing. They remained in love, and continued to live together as close companions. Sexually, they both satisfied themselves with outside partners. Elsa had occasional affairs with other men over the years, and Laughton resumed his search for young males – the younger and, in most cases, the more anonymous, the better.

Laughton went through a short period of therapy to try to alter his sexual tastes, but soon gave it up. Although he would be sporadically troubled by guilt and fears of scandal (homosexuality was then against the law), the pattern was set. His wife kept her distance from most of his handsome young men but, in a few cases, got to know them quite well. 'When he was with one in particular,' she once said, 'I used to go to the market every day and get two peach pies for them. I didn't mind. I don't mind a bit of peach pie myself.'

Over the years apparently only two men held Laughton's interest. One was a lean, handsome young actor whom Laughton met in 1941. He was involved with the young man off and on for over twenty years. When Laughton died, the young actor was a pallbearer. The other male love of his life was a tall, good-looking member of the showbusiness community he met in 1959. The two travelled widely together until Laughton's death.

R.W.S. (Lists 10, 12, 20, 42, 46)

♣ D. H. Lawrence
11 September 1885 to 2 March 1930

David Herbert Lawrence wrote the most outspoken novels of his day, books banned for their explicit descriptions of sexual activity. *Women in Love* (1920) had to be privately printed while *Lady Chatterley's Lover* (1928) was expurgated until a landmark 1960 court decision allowed publication of passages featuring illicit intercourse.

Lawrence was the dearly loved son of a proud, possessive mother who scorned her coarse husband, a Nottinghamshire coal miner. The frail and sickly 'Bert' grew up surrounded by doting women, suffering agonies of frustrated 'animal' feelings in the repressive late Victorian atmosphere. At the age of 16 he suffered a severe sexual trauma, followed by pneumonia, after being cornered and threatened with exposure of his private parts by a rowdy group of factory girls. 'I loved my mother like a lover,' Lawrence admitted after her death in 1910. A schoolteacher by day, he spent his nights working out his mother fixation in his early masterpiece, *Sons and Lovers* (1913), a classic variation on the Oedipus theme. Trying to exorcise his mother's influence, he elaborated a philosophy of sex as the motive force of life, as almost a religious state of grace. Always thin and consumptive, never particularly virile, with tousled hair, a 'flaming' red beard, and eyes 'intense as blue stars', Lawrence attracted by the force of his personality a succession of wealthy, titled patronesses. 'Income on two legs', he called these women, who subscribed to the Lawrentian sexual mystique and subsidized his nomadic lifestyle. (The writer repaid their devotion by satirizing female 'culture vultures' in his novels.) So acutely sensitive that he could not tolerate the nerve-jangling excitement of city life, Lawrence roamed all over rural England and southern Europe. He also travelled to Ceylon, Australia, the American Southwest

260

and Mexico, described in travel essays. From 1928 until tuberculosis killed him at 44, Lawrence was constantly on the move.

Lawrence's young manhood was dominated by the struggle (recounted in *Sons and Lovers*) between his first sweetheart, Jessie Chambers, and his mother, both possessive women who wanted to 'wheedle the soul' out of him. He was first initiated into the 'mystery of sex' at 23 by the local pharmacist's wife, Alice Dax, who has described how, finding him stuck over a poem, she 'gave Bert sex' to prompt his creative imagination. Jessie may have surrendered to him physically, but the two were never able to overcome their sexual timorousness together. Lawrence abandoned Jessie for another friend, the more sexually alluring Louie Burrows, whom he had known since he was 15. 'Strong and rosy as the gates of Eden', she too proved to be too 'churchy' for the writer's taste. Although all three women had good reason to feel ill-used by Lawrence, so powerful was his influence on them that Jessie Chambers lived her whole life in the shadow of Lawrence's rejection, Alice Dax remained celibate in his memory, and Louie Burrows married only after his death.

In 1912, Lawrence fell in love and ran away with Frieda Weekley, a member of the aristocratic German Von Richthofen family, who was at the time of their meeting married to one of Lawrence's professors. '[Lawrence] touched a new tenderness in me,' explained the buxom blonde Frieda, who abandoned her husband and three children to follow and later marry the impoverished writer six years her junior. 'There was nothing for me to do but submit.' Actually, Frieda was a handsome Aryan 'giantess' of a woman, who had been initiated into Freudian sexuality by an earlier lover. Anything but submissive, Frieda enjoyed a brawling love–hate relationship with Lawrence, a lifelong contest of wills punctuated by public quarrels and broken crockery. This was because Lawrence, the messiah of sexual liberation, also espoused male chauvinism. ('I do think a woman must yield some sort of precedence to a man,' he once said to the author Katherine Mansfield. 'Men must go ahead . . . women must follow, as it were, unquestioningly.') He even counselled beating recalcitrant wives. But Frieda, who was more than her husband's equal physically, refused to submit to such treatment. Sexually, also, there was evidence of incompatibility. They were never able to achieve simultaneous orgasm, admitted Lawrence, who accused his wife, and *all* women, of having 'sex on the brain' – a curious complaint for a man himself obsessed by the subject. But the Lawrences seem to have met one another's deep-seated emotional needs. Frieda, who wore the long full skirts, aprons and closely fitted bodices of his beloved mother, functioned as the writer's earth mother. 'And I hope to spend eternity,' Lawrence wrote in a poem, 'with my face down-buried beneath her breasts.' Frieda indulged in harmless dalliances with Italian peasants and Prussian officers, while Lawrence, the working-class guru of sex, was occupied with his rich benefactresses. These included the eccentric Lady Ottoline Morrell, who was supposed to reign over Lawrence's utopian colony of Rananim (founded on 'the complete fulfilment in the flesh of all strong desire') but instead ended up as the sinister Hermione in *Women in Love*; Cynthia Asquith, an unattainable patrician beauty whom Lawrence is said to have made love to through his writings and paintings; and Mabel Dodge Luhan, an American heiress and writer who gave Lawrence a one hundred and sixty-six acre ranch in New Mexico but failed in her attempt to 'seduce his spirit'. Mrs Luhan was not physically attracted to Lawrence but sought physical union with him because the 'surest way to the soul is through the flesh'.

Lawrence was something of a prude. He was offended by lewd tales, and considered sexual intercourse indecent any time except in the dark of night. He probably also suffered from impotence, aggravated by his exhausting bursts of creative energy and by his worsening tubercular condition. Dorothy Brett, one of his most devoted followers, has described how Lawrence climbed into her bed one night but was unable to consummate the relationship. Lawrence's 'sexual potentialities', according to another friend, were 'exclusively cerebral'. 'Even if we can't act sexually to our complete satisfaction,' Lawrence wrote à propos of *Lady Chatterley's Lover*, 'let us at least think sexually, complete and clear.... This is the real point of this work. I want men and women to be able to think sex, fully, completely, honestly and cleanly.'

Lawrence professed to be 'shocked' by the effete homosexuality of the British intelligentsia, but would say 'I believe the nearest I have come to perfect love was with a young coal-miner when I was about 16.' Occasionally frustrated in his relations with women, he exalted a sort of mystical communion of men, a 'blood brotherhood'. He was also fascinated by the male physique, which he celebrated in the nude wrestling scene in *Women in Love*. In fact, Lawrence seems to have had more of his mother in him than his father; women may have worshipped him, but men considered him effeminate and joked about his domestic virtues. The messiah of sex was happiest when peeling potatoes or scrubbing floors, as Norman Douglas once pointed out, not without malice. Lawrence's friend and biographer Richard Aldington said, 'I should say DHL was about eighty-five per cent hetero and fifteen per cent homo.'

C.D. (Lists 1, 14, 17, 35, 37, 46)

❦ T. E. Lawrence
15 August 1888 to 19 May 1935

Lawrence of Arabia was short (5 feet 5½ inches) and born out of wedlock. His Anglo-Irish father, Sir Thomas Chapman, had run off to Wales with Sarah Maden, the governess hired to care for his daughters. Known as 'Mr and Mrs Lawrence', the couple had five sons, the second of which was T.E. There has been speculation that Lawrence's heroic drive was in part an attempt to redeem his mother's name. He so impressed the Bedouins with his zest for austere desert life – driving his camel hard, walking the hot sands in his bare feet, and facing violent desert storms – that they followed him on numerous guerrilla raids against the Turkish-controlled railway and during the seizure of Aqaba in the First World War. After the war, he served as a technical adviser to the British delegation at the Paris Peace Conference of 1919, and lobbied strongly for Arab independence. Between 1919 and 1920, he wrote his war memoirs, *The Seven Pillars of Wisdom*, twice, having burned the notes and lost the final draft of the first copy. His exploits and writings brought him to the attention of such men as Winston Churchill and George Bernard Shaw, who lionized him and indirectly drove him back into the ranks of the military in a search for anonymity. He joined the Royal Air Force as private J. H. Ross in 1922, but was exposed by the press and had to leave. He then joined the Royal Tank Corps as T. E. Shaw (a name he assumed legally in 1927), and had worked his way back into the RAF by 1925, where he remained as an aircraftsman until his death. He died in a motorcycle accident near Bovington Military Camp in Dorset, aged 46. The controversy surrounding his death was appropriate to his life. One story had him being run off the road by a mysterious car driven by British agents because the government feared his political views and ambitions. Another story had his death being faked by the British so that they could smuggle him into the Middle East for espionage.

Fellow Oxford student Vyvyan Warren Richards first declared his love for Lawrence in 1905. But later Richards told biographers Philip Knightly and Colin Simpson that Lawrence 'had neither flesh nor carnality of any kind. . . . He received my affection . . . my total subservience, as though it was his due. He never gave the slightest sign that he understood my motives or fathomed my desire. . . . I realize now that he was sexless – at least that he was unaware of sex.' Lawrence did, however, try to form a serious relationship with a woman while an undergraduate. Janet Hallsmith, his childhood friend, was surprised when he abruptly proposed. She laughed at him since they had not even kissed or discussed their feelings and she had hoped to marry his brother. Lawrence was hurt, but they remained friends. How much more aware of sex Lawrence was six years later during an archaeological dig in Asia Minor is uncertain. But he did enjoy the company of a teenage boy named Dahoum, whom he took camping and hiking and brought home to England in the summer of 1913. He adorned his house in Carchemish with a statue he had carved of Dahoum in the nude. He probably dedicated *The Seven Pillars of Wisdom* as well as his efforts in the Arabian campaign to the boy, who died of typhus in 1918. From the dedication:

> *I loved you, so I drew these tides of men into*
> *my hands and wrote my will across the sky in stars*
> *To gain you Freedom, the seven-pillared worthy house,*
> *that your eyes might be shining for me.*

The crucial sexual encounter of Lawrence's life may or may not be as he described it in *The Seven Pillars of Wisdom*. He told many versions of the story, and he was an 'infernal liar' according to Charlotte Shaw, wife of George Bernard and a mother figure to Lawrence. The crux of the story as it appears in the book is that Lawrence was captured by the Turks while on a reconnaissance mission in Deraa in 1917, and was sexually molested by the Turkish bey and beaten by the bey's guards. In a confessional letter to Charlotte Shaw, however, Lawrence admitted to having given away his 'bodily integrity' in order to 'earn five minutes' respite from the pain'. He told Colonel R. Meinertzhagen that he allowed himself to be sodomized not only by the bey but by his servants too. The factual account seems almost secondary to the vivid, almost loving, detail with which Lawrence described the incident in his book. Speaking of a Turkish corporal who has just kicked him 'yellow' with a spiked boot, Lawrence wrote, 'I remember smiling idly at him, for a delicious warmth, probably sexual, was swelling through me.'

Lawrence liked to be spanked with a birch rod on his bare buttocks to the point of seminal emission, according to one friend. Whether it was to 'purify' himself after his degradation at Deraa or to atone for his parents' scandalous relationship, he went to great, imaginative lengths to keep himself 'birched'. He went to 'beating parties' in Chelsea organized by an underworld figure named Bluebeard, and his arrangement with John Bruce, a young Scots bunkmate, is well documented. Lawrence told Bruce that a relative, whom he called the Old Man, was keeping him on a financial string and threatening to expose his bastardy if he didn't do as he was told. In 1968, Bruce detailed the beatings: . . . before Lawrence left for India there had to be another beating . . . on the old man's orders [it] was a ferocious one . . . twelve strokes. When Lawrence returned from India in 1929 it was another twelve. . . . In September the same year he had a flogging at my house in Aberdeen . . . he came all the way from Cattewater, Plymouth, had breakfast and a flogging and caught the next train back. The worst beating of all was in 1930. . . . There was another beating in 1931 . . . and another in 1934. . . . On this last occasion the Old Man made him travel . . . on his motor bike.' Bruce was also told to describe the birchings – and Lawrence's reactions to them – in letters Lawrence said he himself would deliver to the Old Man. As it turned out, the Old Man was a figment of Lawrence's imagination, and the letters' only purpose was to excite him further. As he himself wrote in his latter days, 'The period of enjoyment, in sex, seems to be a very doubtful one. I've asked the fellows in this hut . . . they all say it's all over in ten minutes: and the preliminaries – which I discounted – take up most of the ten minutes. For myself, I haven't tried it, and hope not to.'

D.R. (Lists 12, 15, 25, 35, 36, 37, 39)

265

♣ Robert E. Lee
19 January 1807 to 12 October 1870

General Robert E. Lee is remembered as a symbol of the Confederate Army in the American Civil War, although he personally
opposed slavery, secession and war. The seceding states were only
loosely bound in the Confederacy, but Lee's surrender of the
Virginia Army at Appomattox is generally considered to have
ended the war. His ancestors on both sides had been instrumental
in the American Revolution and in shaping Virginia's colonial
history, but no family fortune remained at his birth. He graduated well from West Point, though his second lieutenant's pay did
not make him a great 'catch' – except to Mary Custis, heiress to
several plantations. One afternoon, after reading from Scott's
latest novel to Mary and her mother, Lee quietly proposed to
Mary over a piece of fruitcake. Mr Custis reluctantly agreed to the
marriage. The wedding was held in grand Southern style in June
1831, and contrasted with the life-style the couple adopted afterwards. Mary insisted they live only on Lee's salary. Her health
was poor, eventually leaving her an invalid, but she bore seven
children in fourteen years.

Lee was a respected figure in Virginia society – often seen in
the company of pretty girls at social functions, but always faithful
to his wife. On the occasion of the birth of his first son the proud
father told a friend, 'I would not be unmarried for all you could
offer me.'

A.W. and J.H. (List 21)

♣ Ninon de Lenclos
May 1620 to 17 October 1705

Ninon was the most celebrated French courtesan of her day. She
lived by the philosophy of Epicurus – placing most importance on
the quality of life's pleasures than quantity. Still, in twenty years,
she managed to fill her carnal dance card with the names of 4959
men.

Ninon's father was a musician and a pimp, who educated his
daughter in worldly things. At 12, she could dance, play the
harpsichord and appreciate literature. In addition to social graces,
Ninon studied human relationships, both sexual and platonic,
and resolved early on to resist the traditional female role: 'I soon

saw that women were put off with the most frivolous and unreal privileges, while every solid advantage was retained by the stronger sex. From that moment I determined on abandoning my sex and assuming that of the men.' Her parents died before she was 20; but she was more than prepared to face the world alone. Ninon, financed by admirers, established a salon in Paris, where she entertained the most prominent literary and political figures of seventeenth-century France. She also founded a School of Gallantry for aristocratic boys, who were taught basic Epicureanism and the art of pleasing a woman. 'Men lose more hearts by awkwardness than virtue preserves,' she told her pupils.

She was striking – a perfect oval face topped by reddish-blonde ringlets; dark eyebrows and eyes, and a body that inspired poets and painters. According to legend, she was visited on her 18th birthday by a mysterious old man who offered her a choice of three gifts – the highest rank, immeasurable riches or eternal beauty. Supposedly, Ninon chose the last and lived her eighty-five years as an unfading rose. She aged gracefully, but aged none the less, and her long career as a progressive thinker ended with one last gesture – she willed money for books to young Voltaire. Ninon loved eroticism, but shunned outright debauchery. Her salon was not a hotbed of free love; on the contrary, it was quite respectable to be a member of Ninon's inner circle, where art and philosophy were the principal topics of discussion. She did not sleep with all her admirers. The playwright Molière and philosopher Saint-Evremond maintained only a platonic relationship with her. The rest of her male friends fell into three groups – payeurs, martyrs and favourites. The payeurs supported her in exchange for visiting rights, but their visits were rare. When she eventually achieved financial independence, she dismissed them. The martyrs haunted her salon, while the favourites shared her bed for as long as she willed. Ninon often broke off her affairs at their peak. This way, both she and her lover retained nothing but pleasant memories of the relationship. Her disregard for religion prompted King Louis XIV's mother, Anne of Austria, to have her confined in a monastery. Ninon's friends quickly obtained her release, but there is no evidence that she was anxious to leave. Of her nearly 5000 recorded lovers, 439 were monks. It was rumoured that Ninon maintained an active love life until death. Actually, she retired as a courtesan at 50, thereafter amusing herself with occasional adventures.

When Ninon was 15 years old, she succumbed to the persuasive powers of Saint-Etienne, a notorious seducer of virgins. However, once Ninon lost her virginity, Saint-Etienne was no longer interested. She next became infatuated with the charming and handsome Chevalier de Raré. Ninon ended the affair when her mother's health failed and there was little time for romance.

After her mother's death, Ninon began to accept money from her first payeur, Coulon, a disagreeable drunkard. About now, she met her first real love, Gaspard de Coligny. To her great disappointment, she found Coligny completely inadequate, lacking both stamina and technique. She later learned that Coligny was more enthusiastic in bed with men. He left her to return to his 'pretty boys'. Determined to find a virile lover, Ninon simultaneously carried on affairs with the Abbé Dessiat and the Maréchal d'Estrées. However, when she became pregnant, the question of paternity had to be settled by the dice. Thus, the Maréchal d'Estrées was named as father of Ninon's first child. She was said to have also given birth to a child by the Chevalier de Méré, over 70 years old when he courted her. Advanced age was seldom a barrier to Ninon, who reportedly had the power to resurrect even a long-dead libido.

As a rule, Ninon retained a 'favourite' for a few months at the most. The Marquis de Villarceaux was an exception; she lived at his country estate for three years and once spent eight days in bed with him, allegedly to speed his recovery from an illness. After she had ended the affair, she recommended Villarceaux to a friend, Madame Scarron (later Madame de Maintenon, wife/mistress to Louis XIV), who was greatly in need of sex. The woman's marriage to writer Paul Scarron, another friend of Ninon, was clouded by Madame Scarron's inhibitions and her husband's paralysis. Ninon came to the woman's rescue with the right man. It was not the first time she had set up a female friend with an ex-lover. She advised Madame de la Suze on the sexual expertise of various men, and Ninon's evaluations were always accurate.

Two men who ranked low on Ninon's list of competent lovers were soldiers, the Comte de Navailles and the Duc d'Enghien. Navailles fell asleep while she was preparing for bed, so she donned his uniform and crawled under the covers with him. Navailles awakened, and what followed is not known. It is certain, however, that Ninon never again took a blond as a lover. Enghien stayed awake but, in spite of his reputation as a formidable warrior, failed her on the bedroom battlefield. Afterwards, she quoted to him the maxim 'A hairy man is either passionate or strong.' Then she added, 'You must be very strong.'

The Comte de Sévigné also rated poorly in Ninon's estimation. She seduced him to annoy his lover, an actress of whom Ninon was jealous. But the attraction was purely political, for she found him to be 'a man impossible to define . . . a soul of boiled beef, a body of damp paper, with a heart like a pumpkin fricasseed in snow'. Her victory won, she quickly abandoned the comte.

A tragic incident supposedly occurred when Ninon was in her sixties, after she had retired. She still received a few young men, the sons of close friends, and educated them in gentlemanly virtues. One of them, the son of Monsieur de Gersay, fell in love with Ninon. She had reasons for discouraging his attentions – he was, in fact, her son. The boy was unaware of this because Ninon had insisted that Monsieur de Gersay keep it secret. She tried to thwart the young man's attentions by pleading age. She called his passion for her 'ridiculous' and sent him away. But she called him back, having decided to reveal their true relationship. Before she could speak, however, he began again to profess his love. Ninon angrily protested, 'This dreadful love cannot go on. Do you realize who you are and who I am?' Taken aback, he repeated the word 'mother', went out into Ninon's garden and fell on his sword, killing himself.

M.J.T. (Lists 2, 19, 22, 24, 26, 43, 46)

♣ Nikolai Lenin
22 April 1870 to 21 January 1924

Part German Lutheran, part Kalmuck Buddhist, part Great Russian, and perhaps part German Jew, Vladimir Ilyich Ulyanov was the third of six children born to a public-school inspector in Simbirsk (now Ulyanovsk) beside the Volga river. In May 1887, his elder brother was hanged for plotting to assassinate Czar Alexander III. Seven months later, young Vladimir was arrested for participating in a student demonstration.

Well before 1901, the year he adopted his famous *nom de guerre*, the short, stocky, Mongol-eyed Marxist theoretician had committed himself to revolution. He was first imprisoned in 1895, and for the next twenty-two years directed the Bolsheviks from exile in Siberia, Switzerland, Germany, France, England and Poland. When the peasants rose spontaneously against the Romanovs in March 1917, Lenin seized his opportunity. Multiple revolutionary factions struggled for the Russian leadership, but in November Lenin demanded – and took – full control. Lenin's six-year command was ruthless and bloody, and as he lay dying he feared that he had betrayed the principles and workers he had sought to represent. He also feared his legacy would be even worse: in his last dictated memorandum he urged Stalin's removal as general secretary of the party; a year later Lenin was dead – poisoned, Trotsky and others speculated, at Stalin's command.

The revolution was Lenin's whole life, and it is small surprise that three of the women he loved were intimately involved with it, and a fourth left him because of it. Little is known about his brief affair with Apollinaria Yakubova in 1895. She organized and leafleted for Lenin's illegal activities; evidently he proposed to her and was rejected. In 1894, Lenin met Nadezhda Konstantinova Krupskaya. A year older than Lenin, attractive but severe with her dark hair drawn back tight, Krupskaya was already an active Marxist. Lenin was exiled to Siberia in 1897, and the following year, when Krupskaya was also sentenced to three years' exile, she requested permission to spend it with her fiancé – Lenin. The government agreed on condition that the couple marry immediately, which they did, in July 1898.

Some scholars speculate that their marriage was basically a political expedient, but Krupskaya and Lenin were wonderfully suited to each other: she was happy serving the revolution he personified, and he acquired a willingly subordinate comrade who was also secretary, aide, cook and party official. Their marriage lasted until his death. Krupskaya continued to live thereafter in the four-room apartment they had shared in the Kremlin until her own death at the age of 70 on 27 February 1939.

In 1905, living in St Petersburg (now Leningrad) under the name of William Frey, Lenin met Elizabeth de K. She was pretty, intelligent, adventurous, independently wealthy and recently divorced. At their third meeting, 'Frey' told her he wanted to hold clandestine meetings in her flat. She agreed. Some evenings the secret meeting had only two members. Although their affair lasted nine years, on and off, their different worlds were impossible to reconcile. Elizabeth's was literary, artistic, gracious and bourgeois – while Lenin's was uncompromisingly radical. 'It's quite obvious,' he told her once, 'that you will never make a Social Democrat.' 'And you,' she replied, 'will never be anything *but* a Social Democrat.' Elisabeth d'Herbenville Armand – known as Inessa – spoke French, German, English and

Russian. According to various accounts, when 31-year-old Elisabeth met Lenin in Paris in the spring of 1910 she had already left her wealthy young husband (taking her five children) and lived with her brother-in-law; left the brother-in-law to study with feminist Ellen Key; left Key for radical activity after reading Lenin's *What Is To Be Done?*; been arrested, imprisoned and exiled; and escaped exile. She was soon as devoted to Lenin as to his cause. Despite Lenin's relationship with Inessa, Krupskaya also enjoyed the younger woman's bright company, and they hiked, travelled, and sometimes even lived, together as a threesome. Indeed, Inessa was with the Lenins, or on assignment or in prison on behalf of the movement, from the time she met Lenin until her death from typhus in 1920. At her funeral Lenin was so shocked that friends could not approach him, and at least one observer felt that the decline of his health and power dated from that October burial.

W.A.H. (Lists 9, 29)

♣ Franz Liszt
22 October 1811 to 31 July 1886

Son of a Hungarian nobleman's servant, Liszt was a child prodigy. The European aristocracy, for whom he would spend his life playing, was impressed by the boy's talents and financed his musical education. Acknowledged as the greatest pianist of the day, he travelled from Portugal to Turkey to Russia, and achieved widespread fame in the process. In 1848 he accepted the directorship of the Weimar court theatre. During the next thirteen years he instilled new life into European music, not only with his concerts and operatic productions, but through encouraging new composers such as Richard Wagner. After leaving Weimar, Liszt spent eight years in Rome, where he became an abbé of the Roman Catholic Church. After his Roman period, Liszt spent seventeen years playing, teaching and directing in Rome, Weimar and Budapest. Liszt's genius brought him such wealth that in mid-career he ceased to work for money, devoting his efforts to fund-raising for worthy causes. In his waning years, the rigours of travelling for these charitable enterprises weakened him, and in 1886 he died of pneumonia in Bayreuth, Germany.

Throughout his career, Liszt demanded respect from his aristocratic audiences, and constantly sought to elevate the status of

271

artist above that of servant. On one occasion, he refused to play for Isabella II after he was denied a personal introduction to her because of Spanish court etiquette. Another time, he halted a performance and, with head bowed and fingers poised above the keyboard, waited until Czar Nicholas I of Russia ceased speaking. Despite these flashes of hauteur his passionate style ensured his popularity. Liszt's fame brought him feminine adulation. His appearances caused a sensation as his female admirers sought souvenirs, one lady even stripping the cover from a chair that had supported the revered posterior. Lovers were his for the taking, and he had dozens, especially among the noblewomen who made up his audiences and pupils.

Crushed at 17 when he was forced to break off a romance with Caroline di Saint-Crieg, one of his aristocratic pupils, Liszt withdrew into a period of fierce practice, refining the extraordinary skills that would bring him society's adoration. His earliest substantial liaison was with Countess Adèle de la Prunarede, but he broke off the affair upon learning that the countess had a second lover. Liszt's first long-term relationship began in 1835, when the Countess Marie d'Agoult left her husband and children in Paris to join Liszt in Switzerland, where she bore him three children. (Their daughter Cosima later became Richard Wagner's wife.) In 1839, however, the couple separated, their relationship strained by Liszt's loss of interest and his friendship with Frédéric Chopin's mistress George Sand (q.v.), cigar-smoking writer of risqué novels who loved to sit under the piano while Liszt played. When the countess challenged Sand to a duel at one point – the chosen weapon was fingernails – Liszt locked himself in a closet until the ladies calmed down.

Liszt's name was soon linked with Lola Montez, a hot-blooded and beautiful Spanish dancer who had achieved notoriety by baring her breasts when introduced to King Louis I of Bavaria. When Liszt tired of their stormy affair, he deserted Montez while she was napping in a hotel room and left money to pay for the furniture he knew she would destroy in her rage. Liszt's sexual affairs were the talk of European musical society. His mistresses included the eccentric Italian-born Princess Christine Belgiojoso, who had the body of a deceased lover mummified and kept in a cupboard; Russian Baroness Olga von Meyendorff, known as the 'Black Cat' because of her tight-fitting black clothing; the young Polish Countess Olga Janina, who threatened to shoot and poison Liszt when he broke off their relationship; and the famous courtesan Marie Duplessis, who inspired *La Dame aux Camélias*.

The longest affair of Liszt's life was with Princess Carolyne von Sayn-Wittgenstein. This intellectual Polish noblewoman left her Russian husband and her feudal estates to join Liszt in Weimar, where she spent hours lying on a bearskin rug wearing a turban and smoking a hookah while Liszt played the piano. Liszt hoped to marry the princess; this led him to Rome where he sought papal approval for the princess's divorce – a suit which was thwarted by her Russian husband's influential connections. By this time, Liszt's feelings toward Carolyne had begun to cool, and he was relieved that the divorce was denied.

Liszt's sexual exploits continued into his autumn years, and he was frequently involved with a pupil young enough to be his granddaughter. He claimed, however, that, because of his reverence for virginity, he never 'seduced a maiden'. Even though he feared impotence – and used a variety of stimulants to prevent its onset – he had a longer list of lovers than almost all of his contemporaries. Liszt's only comment was, 'I didn't take a big enough bite of the apple.'

J.Z. (Lists 22, 25, 26, 52)

♣ Jack London
12 January 1876 to 22 November 1916

London remains one of the most widely translated American authors – especially in the Soviet Union, where his socialist philosophy has had a wide appeal.

Survival was taking shape as the theme of his life while he was still in the womb. 'A Discarded Wife: Why Mrs Chaney Twice Attempted Suicide' was the *San Francisco Chronicle* headline seven months before Jack's birth. 'Driven from house for Refusing to Destroy her Unborn Infant – A chapter of Heartlessness and Domestic Misery,' it continued. The unborn baby was Jack. The abandoned mother-to-be was Flora Wellman and she was *not* Mr Chaney's wife. Flora and W.H. Chaney, two San Franciscan occultists, had been cohabitating, but Chaney claimed he was impotent at the time and furthermore did not want this child. Despite the publicity and the turmoil, Flora had a successful delivery and Jack was raised on the tough waterfront by his stepfather John London. An independent youth, he set out at 14 – using his stepfather's surname – to see the world. He lived as a tramp (and once spent a month in jail because of it), explored the Klondike for gold, and hunted seal in Siberia. Though he made California his home, the lure of travel and adventure never dimmed. He visited the slums of London, sailed the south Pacific, and was a war correspondent during the Russo-Japanese War. Refusing doctor's orders to change his drinking habits and his life-style, he died from an overdose of morphine and atropine at the age of 40.

'Prince of the Oyster Pirates' they called him when he sailed in San Francisco Bay. It was with the 'Queen of the Oyster Pirates', a girl named Mamie who came with the boat he bought when he was 15, that he enjoyed his first sexual encounter.

'Latently homosexual' was how Joan London described her father's relationship with his best friend George Sterling. But there was nothing latent about his heterosexual relations. His friends called him the 'Stallion', and one biographer characterized him as 'a sexual anarchist'. The essence of man–woman sex for London was embodied in a story he told of meeting a woman on a train and romping in bed with her for three days while the train chugged East, and a maid baby-sat for the woman's child. When the train stopped, London bade the woman a final farewell, having got all he wanted.

London desired two things from a wife: a son, and tolerance for his infidelities. The first great love of his life, the pale and delicate Mabel Applegarth, would also have given him a dictatorial mother-in-law. Mabel was one of the first 'nice' girls London met in Oakland in the 1890s, and he worked hard to raise himself to her social status. He never raised himself high enough for her mother though and, after London had courted Mabel unsuccessfully for several years, his ardour cooled. The woman he married in 1900 gave him two daughters and a divorce. Bess Maddern, who was a good friend of Mabel's, could not tolerate his straying. (He believed that resisting the temptations of the flesh was a waste of willpower.) Bess named Anna Strunsky – Jack's longtime friend in the socialist movement and his co-writer on *The Kempton Wace Letters* – as the other woman, and the couple separated in 1903. Bess never suspected that the other woman was in fact Charmian Kittredge, Bess's confidante during the separation.

Jack married Charmian in Chicago in 1905, as soon as he had been granted a divorce in California. Illinois, which did not recognize divorce until a year after such decrees were granted, declared the marriage to Charmian invalid. In the uproar that ensued, the lecture tour Jack was on at the time was cancelled, his books were banned in various parts of the country, and an organization called the Averill Women's Club passed a resolution condemning both college football and Jack London. To London, Charmian was worth the tempest. She could box and fence like a man, enjoyed travel, and earned one of the highest appellations Jack could pin on a female – 'Mate-Woman'. But they did not live happily ever after. In 1911, after Charmian gave birth to a sickly daughter who lived only three days, a bitterly disappointed London became 'one wild maelstrom', embarking on nightly debauches to assuage his grief at not being able to father a son. Charmian was aware of a world filled with 'slim-ankled potential rivals', and began playing a game friends called 'breaking it up', wherein she would not allow him to be alone with another woman for more than two minutes. But women continued to fling themselves at 'God's own mad lover', as the blue-eyed, curly-haired, muscular writer referred to himself. The Londons' marriage deteriorated to a state of bitter coexistence. It was during his last few years, when his kidneys began to fail, that they journeyed to Hawaii where Jack, depressed and ill though he was, met the last love of his life. He fell deeply in love, but never revealed a single detail about the woman. (George Sterling later told Joan London of the existence of that affair – but nothing else.) London couldn't bring himself to demand a separation from Charmian, having more or less given up on life. The Londons spent their final years sleeping in separate wings of their home in Glen Ellen, California, with Jack vowing that he would take to bed any woman who might give him the son that he had always wanted. When he died, Charmian, who had suffered chronic insomnia due to her fear of losing her husband to another woman, slept for a day and a half.

D.R. (Lists 8, 17, 20, 22, 26, 43)

♣ Louis XIV
5 September 1638 to 1 September 1715

Whether or not Louis himself believed that he was a 'visible divinity', he insisted that his subjects so regard him. He taxed the French people mercilessly to support the ostentatious life of his royal court and nearly bankrupted France to build the incomparable pleasure palace at Versailles. The monarchy Louis inherited from his father was plagued by rebellious nobles, who in forty years had fought eleven civil wars against the throne. Louis XIV brought the French nobles under royal control by offering them positions at his court, where he seduced them with wine, women and fortunes, all to be had by courting Louis's favour. His elaborate system of patronage extended beyond politics to the ladies at court, where it was estimated there were never less than three hundred women scheming for the king's attentions. He was not reluctant to bestow wealth and prestige upon those who participated in his dalliances.

Although scarred by childhood smallpox, Louis XIV was an athletic and witty charmer and an indefatigable lover. Married twice, he had innumerable affairs with noblewomen and palace servants alike, and was generous to them all. His women were confidantes as well as lovers, and he decreed legitimate his many chidren born out of wedlock. However, torn between his licentious nature and the constant urgings of his religious counsellors to atone for his many sins, Louis was often as harsh in his treatment of others' sins as he was lax in controlling his own. In 1674, he ordered the noses and ears of all prostitutes found servicing the soldiers stationed within five miles of Versailles to be cut off.

Although sexually initiated at 16 by a court seamstress who threw herself naked into his arms, Louis's first real love was Marie Mancini, a niece of his closest political adviser, Cardinal Jules Mazarin. Their affair lasted two years, until Mazarin and Louis's mother convinced him to send her away from court. To bring about peace between France and Spain, Louis married Marie Thérèsa of Austria, daughter of the Spanish king. Queen Marie Thérèsa was a plain if not ugly woman, religious but determined to do her 'duty' – at least twice a month – by her husband, even if it meant sharing their living quarters with his mistresses. She bore six of Louis's children, although only one, the Dauphin, survived infancy. The solitary scandal occurred when a rival for Louis's affections, Madame de Montespan, claimed that Marie Thérèsa had borne a black child after being given a black dwarf by an African prince. The queen said that during her pregnancy the dwarf once frightened her – an incident that caused the child to be born black. Marie Thérèsa died in the convent in which she spent most of her later years.

Louis, of whom Voltaire said, 'He liked the ladies, and it was reciprocal,' conducted his court as a never-ending party. Surrounded by fawning attendants from morning to night (when he used Versailles's labyrinth of secret passages to visit his current lovers), Louis directed every detail of the continuous round of hunts, dances and royal dinners that established his court as the centre of European culture. And the women were encouraged in their prestige-seeking flirtations with the king by 'their families, fathers, mothers, even husbands'.

While pursuing his homosexual brother's wife, Louis fell in love with one of her attendants, Madame Louise de la Vallière, who became his secret, then official, mistress. La Vallière's place in the king's heart and court was usurped by one of her closest friends, Madame de Montespan, wife of the Prince of Monaco. A woman of intelligence and voluptuous beauty, the Marquise de Montespan used her influence as Louis's mistress to rule the social life of the palace for many years. Since she had gained the king's affection and ascended to his bedchamber by treachery, de Montespan was well aware that there would be romantic plottings against her by the other women of the court. Her attempt to keep Louis faithful led to the most famous scandal of their day, the Affair of the Poisons. In her anxiety, Madame de Montespan first resorted to love potions and charms. Then, despairing of their effectiveness, she submitted to black masses conducted by a mad priest. During these secret ceremonies, she would lie naked on an altar (with her face and breasts covered in deference to her rank) while the priests chanted and fondled her body. It was alleged that she even participated in the sacrifice of infants, whose hearts and entrails were burned, powdered, and added to love potions which were slipped into the king's food. Madame de Montespan was accused of attempting to poison her rivals and of planning to poison the king himself, reasoning that, if she couldn't have him, no one else would. Louis never gave public recognition to these accusations, but he dismissed her from bed and court after providing her with an ample estate. After numerous short-lived romances, Louis became enthralled with Madame de Maintenon, the widow of satirist Paul Scarron, and the former governess of the king's children. A deeply religious woman who had been disgusted by the sexual demands of her crippled husband (in his partially paralysed state, he was forced to consummate their marriage orally), Madame de Maintenon at first rejected Louis's attentions and his request that she become his mistress. Because she burned their love letters following Louis's death, it is only speculation that they slept together before they were secretly married when she was 48, he 45. (It has even been suggested that she was technically a virgin when they married.) Their morganatic marriage ceremony, during which the king gave her his left hand instead of his right, entitled this woman of common birth to be the king's wife without the rights or inheritance claims of a queen. Considered frigid by nature and morally repelled by Louis's extramarital affairs, she struggled to reform the king and save his soul, while still satisfying his lusts. Still, the 'peasant queen' did her best, and she shared the king's bed until he died of gangrene five days before his 78th birthday. A true voluptuary, Louis XIV remained lusty and vigorous until the end, the Sun King both in and out of bed.

R.S.F. (Lists 2, 17, 21, 22, 26, 31)

♣ Louis XV
10 February 1710 to 10 May 1774

Because Louis inherited the throne as a child, the first years of his reign saw a regent and ministers in control of France. As a youth, Louis dedicated himself to hunting and regular church attendance – pursuits he followed throughout his life. Official occasions required, however, that the boy king appear before his subjects. Those appearances scarred him, leaving Louis forever fearful of crowds, extremely shy, and consistently aloof in his dealings with strangers. In 1723, Louis reached his majority under prevailing French law. Two years later, he married Maria Leszczyńska, daughter of Stanislas II, the deposed king of Poland. In 1743, upon the death of André Hercule de Fleury – who had replaced the Duke of Bourbon as chief minister – Louis insisted he would take complete control. None the less, Louis still preferred the pursuit of love. His mistresses often meddled in the affairs of state. The Marquise de Vintimille is blamed for France's involvement in the War of the Austrian Succession (1740–48).

Strikingly handsome, Louis had a sensuous face and a well-developed body. At 15, his sexual maturity was apparent. Since he loathed his 5-year-old fiancée, the Spanish Infanta, his chief minister instead affianced him to the 23-year-old Maria. During preparations for the wedding, Louis's tutors worried about how he could be taught the art of lovemaking. They decided to hang pictures of sex acts on the walls of his study. For first-hand instruction, Louis turned to Madame de Falari and lost his virginity in her bed. Although Louis's intellect is occasionally

278

belittled, he learned the subject of sex thoroughly; on their wedding night, Louis made love to his wife seven times. Maria dutifully gave Louis ten children, but her enthusiasm for sex paled beside his hearty appetite. As she pointed out, she was always 'in bed, or pregnant, or brought to bed'.

Although she grew to bore the king, Maria remained married to Louis until her death in 1768; however, their marriage was in name only from 1738. Maria, having suffered a miscarriage, was told by her doctor to refrain from sex. As a result, she locked Louis out of her bedroom. Shortly afterwards he made public his affair with Madame de Mailly, one of the five de Nesle sisters. Within months, Louis's fickle affections turned to Mailly's sister, the Marquise de Vintimille. That affair ended when she died giving birth to his child. Louis turned next to a third de Nesle sister, the dazzling Madame de Châteauroux. She, too, soon died after emerging from a sick bed to heed Louis's call. The youngest sister amused Louis briefly and found herself rewarded by being married to a duke. Only one sister escaped Louis's attentions. Her husband objected to sharing her with the king.

In 1745, Louis took his mistress Jeanne Poisson, who became the Marquise de Pompadour – perhaps the central figure in his life. Pompadour, an accomplished and charming woman (even Maria liked her and said, 'If there must be a mistress, better this one than any other,'), had long dreamed of becoming part of the royal family. As a child of 9, a fortune-teller thrilled her by predicting she would one day be the king's mistress. After drawing Louis's attention to herself at a ball, she became his 'official mistress'. Her husband grudgingly accepted a legal separation. Pompadour was privy to the secrets of state and the resources of the nation's treasury. Her love of luxury and interference in politics caused the people to resent her as well as the king. Described by Louis as 'the most delicious woman in France', Pompadour valiantly tried to keep pace with his unflagging sex drive. She took aphrodisiacs and lived on a diet designed to heighten her passion – vanilla, truffles and celery. But, she herself confessed, she was ' very cold by nature'. In 1751, her health weakened by a chest infection, she ended her sexual relations with Louis. It was not the king's body she wanted – 'It's his heart,' she said. Pompadour remained Louis's closest confidante and lived in apartments connected to his by a staircase until her death in 1764.

After the break in physical relations with Pompadour, the virile king turned to a succession of lovers – often young prostitutes. At the Parc aux Cerfs, a four-room hideaway in Versailles, a parade of mistresses satisfied him. Very few knew that their lover was the king. They were told that he was a rich Pole. Girls were nearly always in residence there; few stayed long, as new lovers moved in to replace old ones whose charms had waned. Only Louise O'Morphi – a former model for the painter Boucher – stayed long. In his memoirs, the libertine Casanova claimed he had procured her for the king, but she may have been brought to Louis by his regular pimp, his valet Lebel. She arrived when 15½ years old, and instantly captured the king's affection. But that, too, cooled after several years and one or two children, when O'Morphi indiscreetly asked the king about Pompadour. 'On what terms are you, then, with your precious old girl?' she inquired. He sent O'Morphi packing for her boldness but arranged a marriage for her with a minor noble.

In 1768, Louis took his last important mistress, the voluptuous Comtesse du Barry. The daughter of a monk and – Parisian gossips claimed – a former prostitute, du Barry's affair with Louis outraged the French. Louis was not to be shaken, however. When Cardinal Richelieu asked why he kept her, Louis replied, 'She makes me forget that soon I will be 60.' Du Barry remained with Louis until his death from smallpox.

R.M. (Lists 20, 21, 22, 31)

♣ Martin Luther
10 November 1483 to 18 February 1546

Dominated by autocratic parents, Luther was often beaten by his father, a copper miner. As a result, Luther suffered throughout a sickly and sad childhood. His impoverished family slept together naked – thus providing the impressionable youngster with an opportunity to witness sexual acts. Although he found school boring, Luther entered law school, but quickly abandoned his legal education and entered an Augustinian monastery. Ordained in 1507, his order sent him to the University of Wittenberg, where in 1512 he received a theology doctorate.

Luther's antipathy toward the Church grew. On 31 October 1517, he posted on the door of the Castle Church in Wittenberg his scandalous ninety-five Theses. In the Theses, Luther denounced the Church practice of selling indulgences. (An

280

indulgence was sold to a sinner by the Church to lessen the punishment for a sin.) Labelled a 'drunken German' by Pope Leo X, Luther appeared before an ecclesiastical court and shocked the assembled clergymen by accusing the pope of being 'no better than any other stinking sinner'. Excommunicated, he faced execution, but escaped and was harboured by German knights who supported his cause. He resurfaced as a folk hero a year later, and became the acknowledged leader of the Reformation.

Throughout his life, Luther suffered from indigestion, constipation, kidney stones and haemorrhoids, but his painful ailments did not hamper his crusade to reform the Catholic Church. He was supported by a vociferous following and his influence continued long after his death.

As spiritual head of a new Church that celebrated but two sacraments – baptism and communion – Luther advocated the elimination of clerical celibacy. He believed sex was not sinful and insisted intercourse was as necessary as eating and drinking. Luther supported marriage for the clergy and he practised what he preached. Shortly after breaking from the Catholic Chuch, he made arrangements to help nuns escape their cloisters. One of them, Katharina von Bora, became his wife after one of the other nuns he had aided rejected his proposal. Luther married the reddish-haired runaway nun to spite the pope, avenge his hatred for the devil, and please his father – who was concerned that the family name should not die out. The excommunicated monk insisted nothing could cure his lust, not even marriage, but he learned to live with this lust, and apparently remained faithful to Katharina.

Prior to marrying Katharina, Luther spoke of his 'temptations of the flesh' and said that he and many fellow monks at the Augustinian monastery in Erfurt, Germany, had experienced 'nocturnal pollutions'. Luther frequently waited more than a year to change his bed sheets, permitting them to become saturated with the smell of sweat, and after his marriage he often touched 'specified parts' of his wife's body while being tempted by the devil. The devil lost his greatest battles 'right in bed, next to Katie'. Luther had a lifelong personal battle with Satan, who manifested himself in a variety of disguises. Luther was known to cry out to the devil, 'I have shit in the pants, and you can hang them around your neck and wipe your mouth with it,' and boasted he could drive away the evil spirit 'with a single fart'. He had an intimate relationship with his bowel movements and regularly wrote home giving a score of his defecations.

Although he believed women were emotionally weaker than men, and craved sex more intensely, Luther confessed in a 1519 sermon that his own sexual desires were overpowering. He considered sex a natural function ordained by God, and therefore supported the ideal that an impotent man should supply a sexual partner for his wife. Luther and his wife had six children of their own, and raised eleven orphans as well. Their marriage lasted twenty-one years, from 1525 until Luther's death from a stroke in 1546. Despite his religious radicalism, Luther wasn't ready for a domestic reformation. He believed the man should rule his wife and she should give him not only love but also honour and obedience. In Luther's eyes, women were meant to stay at home: 'The way they were created indicates this, for they have broad hips and a wide fundament to sit upon.' He preferred bigamy to divorce and thought that, if a married man needed another female companion to satisfy his sexual needs, he should feel free to take a second woman as a mistress.

A.K. (Lists 7, 21, 32, 34, 44, 45, 49)

☘ General Douglas MacArthur
26 January 1880 to 6 April 1964

MacArthur was an imposing figure. Nearly 6 feet tall with a spare build, his battered cap, sunglasses, and corncob pipe became his trademarks. Enemies considered him imperious, cold, calculating; friends regarded him as warm, understanding, brilliant. Everyone knew he was vain. When asked to explain his numerous successes, MacArthur said, 'I believe it was destiny.'

He was born in the armoury building at Fort Dodge in Little Rock, Arkansas. His father had been a civil war general. His dominating mother supported MacArthur's military ambitions from childhood. Inevitably, MacArthur went to West Point, where he graduated first in his class. Eventually, he commanded the 42nd Division in France in the First World War. After this, MacArthur served successively as President Herbert Hoover's army chief of staff for four years, and as President Franklin D. Roosevelt's for one. Retiring from the American military in 1937, MacArthur accepted Philippine President Manuel Quezon's appointment as Field Marshal of the Philippines, thereby becoming the highest paid military officer in modern history. In 1942, with America's entry into the Second World War, General MacArthur was made commander of all Allied forces in the Pacific arena. He accepted the Japanese surrender in 1945, and became virtual dictator of Japan during the postwar reconstruction period. In 1950, he led UN troops in defence of South Korea against North Korea and China. Eager to expand the war, MacArthur directly disagreed with President Harry Truman, who wanted to limit the conflict. In April 1951, President Truman fired MacArthur and recalled him to the USA. Returning to a hero's welcome, MacArthur briefly considered running for the presidency.

General MacArthur was the most decorated man in American military history, but in love he lost two major battles before achieving victory. As a West Point cadet, with his mother living nearby, MacArthur took out girls from colleges in the area. Credited with engagements to eight different young women, MacArthur often denied it: 'I do not remember being so heavily engaged by the enemy.'

His first love was Louise Cromwell Brooks, a divorcée, socialite, heiress to millions, who liked parties, jazz and bathtub gin during prohibition. MacArthur met Louise at a party. He immediately proposed marriage, and she accepted. They had a large wedding on St Valentine's Day in 1922. MacArthur's mother refused to attend. The couple settled down in Manila, where MacArthur liked to spend his leisure with President Quezon and his Filipino circle. The high-society whites with whom Louise associated found MacArthur's friends unacceptable. This led to a marital rift, and during the next few years Louise constantly tried to persuade MacArthur to leave the military. When he refused, she left him. In June 1929, she sought a divorce. MacArthur agreed, on 'any grounds that will not compromise my honour'. The heiress went to court in Reno and cited MacArthur's 'failure to provide'. Granted the divorce, Louise returned to her social set and eventually had two more marriages and two more divorces. In his memoirs, MacArthur summarized their union briefly and did not mention his wife's name.

The general's next skirmish with the opposite sex was also unsuccessful. In Manila, five months before being transferred to Washington DC, MacArthur had an exquisite young Eurasian mistress. Her name was Isabel Rosario Cooper, the daughter of a Chinese woman and a Scottish businessman. She had danced in a Shanghai chorus line, and called herself an actress when

MacArthur met her. A lobbyist who met her recalled, 'She looked as if she were carved from the most delicate opaline. She had her hair in braids down her back.' MacArthur brought her to Washington, and installed her in a suite at the Hotel Chastelton. He supplied her with kimonos, black lace underwear and a fur coat, but almost no street clothes. He did not want her to go out. He gave her a poodle to keep her company, wrote her love letters, and while on official visits to Paris and Vienna he sent her postcards. Isabel complained, and at last MacArthur gave her a car, chauffeur and money. When MacArthur was abroad, Isabel visited local nightclubs and seduced several men. She also went to Havana and blew all her money. MacArthur continued to keep her presence his secret.

He made one mistake. He provoked the enmity of the country's leading political gossip columnist, Drew Pearson, who had called him 'dictatorial' and 'disloyal', and had been sued by MacArthur for $1,750,000. By then tired of Isabel's infidelity and extravagance, MacArthur had broken with her. However, Pearson, investigating MacArthur, uncovered the affair. Pearson located Isabel, who was broke. He 'rented' six letters the general had written; several of them were passionate love letters, dating back to late 1930. One was in response to Isabel's request that the general secure a job for her brother, and it contained an enclosure from MacArthur of 'Help Wanted' advertisements from a newspaper. The last letter from MacArthur, postmarked 11 September 1934, carried a chilling dismissal and a plane ticket to take Isabel back to the Philippines. Isabel made it clear she had no intention of returning. Beside paying her for the letters, Drew Pearson bought Isabel some new street clothes and found her a hiding place in Baltimore. After spending $16,000 in legal fees (a tidy sum in depression years), General MacArthur suddenly dropped the lawsuit against Drew Pearson. No further explanation was given. Obviously, a compromise had been reached. On Christmas Eve 1934, MacArthur's representative gave $15,000 in $100 bills to Drew Pearson's agent, who acted on Isabel's behalf. In return, MacArthur received his original letters back, although Pearson kept copies. With the $15,000, Isabel left Washington and opened a beauty salon in the Midwest. Then she moved to Los Angeles where, in 1960, she committed suicide. Shortly after his tangle with Pearson, MacArthur was relieved of his post as chief of staff and transferred to the Philippines.

General MacArthur's mother died in 1935, but this period of

grief was alleviated by an encounter that brought the general happiness. On a ship bound for Shanghai, he met vivacious, cultured Southern belle Jean Marie Faircloth. By the time the ship docked, MacArthur and Jean were in love. After a year and a half's courtship, they married in New York, in April 1937. Their honeymoon was cut short because the groom had to hurry back to Manila to oversee the graduation of his newest Filipino recruits. Jean understood: she loved the military life. Jean had a son, Arthur, in 1938 and was the best wife MacArthur could hope for, and he knew it.

J.M. (Lists 17, 26, 39, 46)

♣ María Luisa
9 December 1751 to 2 January 1819

María Luisa, who was Queen of Spain during the turbulent era of the French Revolution, scandalized the courts of Europe by using her royal bodyguards as a recruiting ground for sexual playmates. She elevated her most enduring paramour, Manuel Godoy, from guardsman to prime minister. When the Spanish monarch was overthrown in 1808, the queen went into exile accompanied by not only her husband but her lover as well.

María Luisa was a Bourbon by birth and marriage. Her father was the brother of Charles III, King of Spain; her mother was the eldest daughter of Louis XV of France; and María Luisa was married at the age of 14 to her cousin Charles, heir to the Spanish throne. Educated by the philosopher Condillac, the aggressive and articulate María Luisa was considered twice the man her amiable but slow-witted husband was. She was also said to be a frivolous, imperious woman with insatiable sexual appetites. As a dark-eyed young woman, she was shapely and graceful, but she had aged by her mid-thirties due to her many pregnancies (she gave birth to twelve children, losing five in infancy and miscarrying several others), dental disease (she was toothless by 37) and, it was widely believed, sexual excesses. According to the Russian ambassador in Madrid, 'Her complexion is now greenish, and the loss of almost all her teeth – which have been replaced by artificial ones – have given the coup de grâce to her appearance.' While all Europe seethed with revolutionary discontent, the Queen of Spain sought solace for lost beauty through a long succession of lovers.

285

María Luisa's infidelities were the scandal of Spain, a strictly moral country. Soon after her marriage, she created her own court in the Casita del Principe – the Little Prince House – and began deceiving her husband with grandees such as the Count of Teba, the Duke of Abrantes and Don Juan Pignatelli, exiling the last-named to France because of his partiality to a fairer face. Other lovers were banished by María Luisa's reproving father-in-law, Charles III. Only her husband, who became Charles IV on the death of his father in 1788, remained happily oblivious to his wife's promiscuity. 'If queens felt tempted to sin,' he once naively remarked, 'where would they find the kings or emperors to sin with them?'

Hitherto sovereign in her sexual caprices, María Luisa became enthralled at 37 by handsome 21-year-old guardsman Manuel de Godoy, an impoverished provincial nobleman whose brother had preceded him into the royal bed (and thence into exile). Godoy, amusing, indolent and sensual, aroused in her a grand passion compounded of lust, maternal instinct, hero worship and jealousy. The balance of sexual power shifted to Godoy, who in 1792 at the age of 25 became prime minister. 'It is difficult to imagine,' French ambassador Bourgoing wrote to Paris, 'that a young man without any previous political experience could have been appointed to one of the most important ministries; a man whom the queen's love demands leave little time to dedicate to government affairs.' Three years later, after a catastrophic war against France, he was elevated to 'Prince of Peace', second in stature only to the King of Spain. Most of Godoy's diplomacy was devoted to handling the queen. The Prussian ambassador described their typical day: 'At eight o'clock in the morning Godoy goes to his country house riding school where the queen joins him every day at nine o'clock, while Charles IV is away hunting. The riding takes place until eleven. At one o'clock in the afternoon Godoy returns to the Palace to be present during the queen's lunch, which is one of his "duties". Afterwards, he goes to his rooms, which are located under the queen's. María Luisa soon joins him, using a secret staircase.' Aristocratic ladies vied for Godoy's favours, emerging rumpled and flushed from the prime minister's chancery, while their husbands contributed to his growing personal fortune. There was also Josefa (Pepita) Tudo, a beautiful, plump, dark-haired commoner who bore Godoy two bastard children. To break up this affair, María Luisa arranged for her lover's marriage to the king's cousin, the

Countess of Chinchon, in 1797. The latter, however, could not abide her husband, who continued to sleep with Pepita.

Jealousy drove the queen, absurd in her girlish frocks, into further sexual excesses. 'To appease the queen's unnatural sensuality,' the French ambassador reported, 'the assiduity of the king, the fleeting attentions of the Prince of Peace, and the frequent assistance of the choicest of the bodyguards, are all required.' During periods of estrangement from Godoy, María Luisa consoled herself with others: an Italian named Malaspina, whom she goaded to intrigue against Godoy; Don Luis de Urquijo, promoted by the queen to first secretary of state; and Don Manuel Malló, another handsome guardsman rewarded for his services with a carriage and horses so splendid that even the phlegmatic Charles took notice.Godoy is said even to have provided the queen with lovers. Whatever the case, the bond between María Luisa and her favourite was so compelling it lasted the rest of her life. Godoy fathered two of the queen's children, a son named Francisco and a daughter named Maria Isabella. Far from being suspicious, Charles was genuinely fond of Godoy, to whom he abdicated all power and responsibility. This aroused the undying enmity of the heir apparent, Ferdinand, who conspired to overthrow the regime, but then Napoleon installed one of his brothers as King of Spain, and María Luisa and Charles were exiled. With them, as fulcrum of the royal sexual triangle, went Godoy and his assorted children, legitimate and otherwise – joined shortly by Pepita. This complicated ménage survived until the death of María Luisa in Rome, followed by her husband's three weeks later. Free at last, Godoy moved to Paris, marrying Pepita in 1828. Bored and weary of their poverty, Pepita returned to Spain alone in 1833.

C.D. (Lists 21, 22)

♣ Karl Marx
5 May 1818 to 14 March 1883

Descended from a long line of rabbis, Karl was baptized at the age of 6 in the Evangelical Church in his home town of Trier, Prussia, at the request of his father, who had repudiated the family faith. Later, Karl himself rejected all religion ('Religion is the opium of the masses') and has been accused, probably justly, of anti-Semitism.

At 16, he fell in love with aristocrat Jenny von Westphalen, whom he married eight years later, after completing his education. (He received his doctorate from the University of Jena.) The inflammatory articles he wrote for literary–cultural magazines in several European cities were partly responsible for his expulsion from three of those cities – Paris, Cologne and Brussels. He was also active in the underground socialist movement. In Paris, he met Friedrich Engels, son of a wealthy textile manufacturer, who became his lifelong collaborator. Among their joint works is the *Communist Manifesto* (1848) written for the Communist League.

In 1849, he moved to London, 'where the next dance [revolution] begins,' he said hopefully. Engels came too, to work at his father's textile firm in Manchester. Their hopes for revolution ended in disappointment when the British refused to comply. Money was Marx's bête noire. He refused to be a 'money-making machine', so he and his family lived on what he earned writi g and on handouts from Engels and relatives. The Marx children were trained to say to bill collectors, 'Mr Marx ain't upstairs.' (Later family fortunes improved.) Only three of their seven children grew to maturity and, of those three, two committed suicide. Marx spent his days in the reading room of the British Museum where he did research for *Das Kapital* and the articles and editorials he and Engels wrote for the *New York Daily Tribune*. His physical condition was poor – run-down and nervous. He rarely bathed and for the last twenty years of his life he was afflicted with boils all over his body. In addition, he suffered from liver and eye problems. A Victorian autocrat, Marx was prone to sarcasm and intolerant of others' opinions. Nicknamed the 'Moor' for his swarthiness, he grew a flowing beard to emphasize his resemblance to a statue of Zeus he kept in his study.

The only serious romantic love of Marx's life was green-eyed, auburn-haired Jenny, four years older than he and daughter of a baron. Gentle and scholarly, she also had style and a streak of vanity. Named 'Queen of the Ball' one year in Trier, she was pursued by suitors but chose Karl, whom she called pet names, like '*Schwärtzwildchen*' ('little black wild one'). Both families were against the marriage. In her extravagant and well-written love letters, she talked of 'All the bliss that was and will be', though their passion for each other was not consummated until after their marriage.

In 1843, Karl and Jenny were married in a Protestant church. The couple honeymooned in Switzerland, financed by Jenny's mother. They carried their money in a two-handled strongbox, which they purposely left open in hotel rooms so that anyone could take from it. Their first child was born in Paris. Jenny took the baby girl home to show her off and wrote to Karl that she was afraid to return to Paris for fear they would make another baby which, of course, they did. Fear of pregnancy – and another mouth to feed – haunted their marriage. Marx was a family man. Though he referred to Jenny as 'mercurial' and complained in letters of her 'floods of tears', he also said, to Engels, 'When I see the sufferings of my wife and my own powerlessness, I could rush into the devil's jaws.' They faced evictions for non-payment of rent and even had to borrow the money to pay for a coffin when 1-year-old Francizka died. In happier moments, on Sundays, the whole family went for picnics in London parks. In a graphic account of the Marx ménage, a Prussian police spy once told of an oilcloth-covered table littered with sewing, manuscripts, toys and chipped cups – and of how he was offered a chair from which 'the children's cooking' (play) was not removed.

The only scandal that touched the family was Karl's affair with the family servant, Helene Demuth ('Lenchen'), a delicately beautiful peasant girl who had joined the von Westphalen family as a maid at 11 or 12 and was 'given' to Jenny in 1845 by her mother. Lenchen ruled the family with an iron hand and could beat Marx at chess. In 1851, she gave birth to a child, Henry Frederick, fathered by Marx who did not acknowledge him. The child was raised by a foster family. Marx met the boy only once, in 1882. Lenchen worked for the Marx family until Karl's death, in 1883, two years after Jenny died. Then she went to work for Engels.

Marx had a least two minor flirtations – one with 33-year-old Frau Tenge, a cultured Italian married to a wealthy landowner, and another with his cousin, Antoinette Philips, nineteen years younger than he, who in 1863 nursed him through a painful attack of boils. During his recovery, Marx wrote of Antoinette's 'dark eyes shining dangerously as she pampers me'.

He was paternal – the practice of wife-beating so enraged Marx that he claimed he would have flogged a wife-beater 'to the point of death'. Politically, he was against bourgeois marriage (though he had such a marriage himself) because it kept women in a state of slavery. Ironically, he deeply disapproved of Engels's mistress because she was of the lower classes. The reverse side of Marx shows a corresponding vulgarity. He was fond of erotic French poetry of the sixteenth century, used language like 'cock' and 'toss-off'', and liked to tell dirty jokes, though never in mixed company.

A.E. (Lists 21, 35)

♣ Mata Hari
7 August 1876 to 15 October 1917

An exotic dancer famous for her sensational nude performances, Mata Hari was the toast of Europe in the early years of this century. In 1917, she was executed by a French firing squad for acting as a German spy. It has never been proved, however, that she was a double agent.

Eighteen-year-old Gertrude Margareta Zelle, her convent schooling over, answered an Amsterdam newspaper advertisement supposedly placed by an army officer seeking a wife. This was a joke, but the officer – balding 39-year-old Rudolph MacLeod – did wed Margareta. For the next two years they lived in Holland, where she bore their son Norman. When MacLeod was reassigned to the Dutch East Indies, he took his family with him. There Margareta had another child, Jeanne; flirted with young officers and planters (arousing MacLeod's jealousy); and watched Javanese temple dancers, who inspired her future career. MacLeod drank, was unfaithful, and beat her. At least once, he threatened her with a loaded gun. One story, probably apocryphal, states that their son was poisoned by a native soldier incensed over MacLeod's seduction of his girlfriend, the boy's nurse. Margareta later claimed that she strangled the poisoner – with her bare hands, of course. The MacLeods returned to Holland, separated, and, by 1904, Margareta was in Paris, without husband or child. 'I thought that all women who ran away from their husbands went to Paris,' she said.

At her debut as an oriental dancer, she met Emile-Etienne Guimet, the owner of an oriental art museum, where she gave an electrifying performance of oriental dances, dressed in jewelled bra and diaphanous draperies in a setting of palms, bronze statues and garlanded columns. Theatre critic Edouard Lepage described her appearance in the hyperbole typical of the times: 'Her flexible body at times becomes one with the undulating flames, to stiffen suddenly in the middle of contortions ... with a brutal gesture, Mata Hari rips off her jewels ... throws away the ornaments

that cover her breasts. And, naked, her body seems to lengthen way up into the shadows! ... she beats the air with her shattered arms, whips the imperturable night with her long heavy hair....'
Some sources say that she never danced completely nude, but always concealed her breasts, which had been bitten and thus permanently disfigured by MacLeod. By then, she had become Mata Hari (Malay for 'eye of the day', the sun), complete with story – she was the child of a 14-year-old Indian temple dancer who had died giving birth; was raised by temple priests who taught her dances sacred to the Hindu god Siva; danced nude for the first time at the age of 13 before the altar of a Hindu temple. She looked the part – tall, dark, strong-featured and velvety-eyed. Her career rocketed – she was a sensation in most of the major capitals of Europe. And she was a scandal – the directress of one of her performances went so far as to force her to wear a piece of red flannel, nappy-like, at her crotch.

The spy plot, true or not, began on the day the First World War was declared, and she rode through the streets of Berlin with a police official. It was high drama: the bottles of invisible ink given her by the Germans (she threw them into a canal, she said); her German code number, H 21; her seduction of high German officials (for money, love, or secrets?); her agreement to spy for the French for the million francs she needed to impress the father of the love of her life, Vadime de Massloff, a Russian captain; her grandiose plans for manipulating noblemen through jealousy, greed and lust; the French spies tailing her in Madrid.... She was arrested by the French in February 1917. Some say she greeted the arresting officers while sitting naked on a couch in her hotel room. This is no more true than the rumour that she took milk baths while Parisian children starved or that she danced nude in her cell at St. Lazare Prison. The file on her was six inches thick, but the evidence was inconclusive. A tube of 'secret ink' in her possession turned out to be oxycyanide of mercury, which she injected into herself after making love as a birth-control method. Her aged lover, Maître Clunet, defended her at her trial; another lover – Jules Cambon, of the Ministry of Foreign Affairs – testified on her behalf. A third lover, old and amiable General Messimy, sent a letter written by his wife which asked that the general be excused from testifying since he didn't know the defendant. At that, Mata Hari laughed, 'Ah! He never knew me! Oh, well. He has a nerve!' The jury laughed at her, but humour did not save her from the firing squad.

The nun who came to fetch her on the day of her execution chastised her for showing too much leg while putting on her stockings in front of the prison doctor. She was dressed to the nines. On the way out of prison, she was asked whether she was pregnant – according to French law, a pregnant woman could not be executed. This question arose, some say, from a last-ditch attempt by Clunet to save her – he had even claimed to be the father of the unborn child. She was shot at the polygon of Vincennes, at her own request without blindfold. It is not true that she pulled open her coat to reveal her naked body, so astounding the firing squad that not one man could squeeze a trigger. Nor did a playboy aviator boyfriend strafe the field. Nor did another lover – inspired by the plot of the opera *Tosca* – bribe the firing squad to use blanks, put her in a ventilated coffin, and bury her in a shallow grave so that he could spirit her away. The truth? No one claimed her body, so it went to a medical school for dissection. Was she guilty? The question remains unanswered.

Though she accepted money for sex, she was so infatuated by 'the Uniform' that she often slept with soldiers for nothing. Judging by her letters signed 'your loving little wife', she was intimate with MacLeod before their marriage. Her long string of later lovers included innumerable military men of several nationalities; the Crown Prince of Germany; the head of a balloon company; the president of the Dutch council; two boys, 17 and 18 respectively, when she was close to 40. Her price, when sex was a business deal, was $7500 a night – or so she claimed. Upon occasion, Mata Hari turned a candidate down – an American munitions salesman with bad table manners, for example.

Her first important lover was Lieutenant Alfred Kiepert, a rich, married landowner in the German Hussars, who set her up in an apartment in 1906. About a year later, they parted and she returned to Paris with the story that she had been on a hunting trip in Egypt and India. But in 1914, they were together again.

In 1910, she had lived in Touraine as mistress of Xavier Rousseau, a stockbroker. He came down for weekends at their hideaway, the Château de la Dorée, where once she rode a horse up and down the outer staircase. After they split up, he became a champagne salesman. His wife claimed that Mata Hari had ruined him.

After Rousseau came Edouard Willen van der Capellen – rich, married and a colonel in the Dutch Hussars. But her passion reached full flower with her Russian captain, Vadime de

Massloff, whom she visited in 1916 in Vittel, a French resort in the military zone. He was recuperating from a wound; she may have been spying. When she was arrested, several photographs of de Massloff were found in her hotel room. Written on the back of one was : 'Vittel, 1916. In memory of some of the most beautiful days of my life, spent with my Vadime, whom I love above everything.' When jailed, she wrote a pathetic letter to an interrogator begging for news of de Massloff. Yet de Massloff claimed their relationship had been a minor affair.

To what extent Mata was capable of real passion cannot be determined. Her love life was so entangled with her profession and with her espionage activities that her emotions remain unfathomable. For instance, she was capable of cruelty. She killed her pony by plunging a gold stiletto into its heart, simply because she didn't want anyone else to ride it. And she had a fierce temper: she once pushed a wardrobe down a staircase. Cornered by an interrogator, she flung a glass of water on his trousers. 'I never could dance well,' she maintained. 'People came to see me because I was the first who dared to show myself naked to the public.'

A.E. (Lists 17, 19, 24, 25, 41, 42, 44)

♣ W. Somerset Maugham
24 January 1874 to 16 December 1965

Because his father was the English solicitor to the British embassy in Paris, Maugham was born in France and French was his first language. When he was 8, his mother Edith died of tuberculosis, and two years later his father died of stomach cancer. The loss of his mother scarred him for ever. The orphaned boy was sent to England, placed in the care of his father's brother, a Whitstable clergyman. The atmosphere seemed alien and loveless, and Maugham suffered. At the strict King's School in Canterbury, he developed a stammer. Because of ill-health, he was sent to Germany, where he enrolled at Heidelberg University. There he secretly began to write. At 18, on his return to England, his uncle pressured him to take up medicine. Maugham reluctantly entered the medical school of St Thomas's Hospital in London. After five years, he was a doctor and on his own. But instead, he wrote full time and published short stories. At 23 he had already published his first novel, *Liza of Lambeth*. In the decades that followed, he turned to playwriting, and when he was 34 had four hit plays running in London at once. At 41 he returned to the novel and brought out his autobiographical classic *Of Human Bondage*.

He travelled constantly: to the South Sea Islands, China, India, Italy, North Africa, Mexico. During the First World War he served as a British agent in Switzerland and Russia. In 1928, he bought a Moorish residence on the French Riviera, the Villa Mauresque at St Jean Cap Ferrat, his home for the rest of his life. Here he entertained the likes of Winston Churchill, H. G. Wells and Noel Coward. Maugham's appearance in his heyday was that of a natty gentleman, 5 feet 7 inches, dark hair and moustache, his manner diffident and remote; yet (despite his stammer) he was a witty storyteller. In his last years he was not afraid of death. 'Death, like constipation, is one of the commonplaces of human existence,' he told a friend. 'Why shy away from it?' In his 92nd year, partially demented, often angry, sometimes euphoric, he died of lung congestion.

Maugham was bisexual. While most gossip made him out to be largely homosexual, one of his oldest friends, author Beverly Nichols, said he 'was not predominately homosexual. He certainly had affairs with women.... He had no feminine gestures nor mannerisms.'

At 16, while studying in Heidelberg, Maugham had his first sexual encounter. His mate was 26-year-old Ellingham Brooks, an attractive moneyed Cambridge graduate, who devoted himself to travel and reading. Returning to London, Maugham was afraid to consort with male homosexuals there because copulating with them was a criminal offence. Only five years before, Oscar Wilde had been sent to jail for two years for practising homosexuality. So, while still a medical student, he turned to women. 'One Saturday night,' he confessed, 'I went down Piccadilly and picked up a girl who for a pound was prepared to pass the night with me. The result was an attack of gonorrhoea.... Undeterred by this mishap, however, I continued whenever I could afford it.' Shortly afterwards, Maugham shared a flat with a friend, Walter Payne, an accountant who was good at obtaining girls, 'small-part actresses, shopgirls, or clerks in an office'. When Payne was tired with a girl, he passed her on to Maugham, who would take her to dinner and then to bed. 'There was no romance in it, no love, only appetite.' In the two decades to follow, Maugham had a number of sexual affairs with well-known women. One was Violet Hunt, a feminist who edited the *Freewoman*. Violet was 41 and Maugham

294

29 when she confided in her diary that she had seduced him. Another was Sasha Kropotkin, daughter of Peter Kropotkin, the Russian anarchist who lived in exile in London.

There were two important mistresses in Maugham's life. One he loved, and the other he married. The first was Ethelwyn Jones, known as Sue Jones, whom he always referred to as Rosie, since he had used that name for her in his novel *Cakes and Ale*. The daughter of a successful playwright, she was a sparkling 23, a divorcée and a rising actress when Maugham met her. After a few meetings, Maugham took her to his room and made love to her. He guessed she wanted to marry him. 'I didn't want to do that,' he wrote long after, 'because I knew that all my friends had been to bed with her. That sounds as though she were something of a wanton. She wasn't. There was no vice in her. It just happened that she enjoyed copulation and took it for granted that when she dined with a man sexual congress would follow.' Later, when Sue was in a play in Chicago, Maugham had second thoughts. He pursued her and proposed. When she turned him down, he was stunned. But Sue was already pregnant by another man and soon married the son of the sixth Earl of Antrim.

The other mistress, the one Maugham married, was Syrie Barnardo Wellcome. Her father, a German Jew, had founded the orphanages known as Dr Barnardo's. At 22, Syrie, shapely and lively, met and married 48-year-old Henry Wellcome, an American-born pharmaceutical giant. The marriage was a disaster. Syrie had an affair with Gordon Selfridge, also American-born and a London department-store tycoon. Annoyed, Wellcome got her to sign a deed of separation. Maugham met Syrie in 1911, and found her gay, smart, charming. By 1913, they were sleeping together. She wanted a baby by Maugham, and eventually he gave her one, a daughter named Elizabeth. Wellcome, who had hired detectives to record his wife's adultery, now sued for divorce, naming Maugham as co-respondent. Syrie tried to kill herself, but survived. Once she was divorced, Maugham did what he felt to be the right thing. He married her, on 26 May 1917. It was a poor, one-sided marriage. She loved him and constantly wanted sex, but Maugham would not cooperate. In a letter to Syrie, Maugham cruelly outlined his complaints: 'I married you because I thought it the best thing for your happiness and for Elizabeth's welfare, but I did not marry you because I loved you, and you were only too well aware of that.' They went their own way. She became a renowned interior decorator, doing houses for

Tallulah Bankhead and Wallis Simpson. Syrie had cause to complain: she had lost her husband to a man and to homosexuality. She asked for a divorce, and in 1929 got it.

Meanwhile, Maugham had found his greatest love in France during the First World War. Gerald Haxton was born in San Francisco but had been raised in England. He was slightly taller than Maugham, brown-haired, blue-eyed, pock-marked, somewhat dissipated in appearance. Many women thought him handsome. Some men thought him evil. Haxton was 22 and Maugham 40 the night they met. Maugham asked him what he wanted out of life. Haxton said, 'Fun and games. But I've not got a cent. So I want someone to look after me.' They went up to Haxton's quarters, undressed and got into bed. After they'd made love, Maugham whispered, 'You needn't worry about the future, Gerald, because I'll look after you.' For almost thirty years, until Haxton's death of edema of the lungs, Maugham looked after him. Haxton served as Maugham's secretary–companion on the Riviera and during his travels. Throughout the years Haxton – a drunkard, gambler and liar – dominated Maugham in a strange way, but he was cherished as caretaker and lover. And in their travels, because he was a good mixer, Haxton provided Maugham with raw material for some of his best characters and stories. Also, to give his employer sexual variety, Haxton turned procurer. In 1924, Haxton found Maugham teenage boys in Mexico. In Indo-China, Maugham had the happiest love encounter he had ever known, with a young boy in a sampan. In New York, in 1943, the 69-year-old Maugham had an affair with 17-year-old schoolboy poet and admirer David Posner. In his thorough biography, *Maugham*, author Ted Morgan quoted a letter from Posner on Maugham's lovemaking: 'He wasn't particularly virile, but he was full of lust. He was rather businesslike about sex, but it's equally true that there were occasions when he spent a long time just fondling. . . . He profoundly disliked women sexually . . . he was very disturbed once when he saw me with a girl.'

After Haxton's funeral, Maugham took on a new secretary–companion. This was Alan Searle, a kind young man who had been a hospital social worker and had once had an affair with Lytton Strachey. Searle devotedly adored Maugham, and considered him the best lover he had ever known. In 1962, Maugham, upon hearing that his daughter Elizabeth might have him confined for incompetence, followed the advice of a French lawyer and adopted Alan Searle as his son, disowning

296

Elizabeth as his legal daughter. Elizabeth hauled her father into court in Nice, proved her legitimacy, and had Searle's adoption nullified. On his deathbed, Maugham's last words were spoken to Searle: 'I want to shake your hand and thank you for all that you've done for me.'

I.W. (Lists 8, 12, 14, 17, 18, 20, 25, 26, 46)

♣ Guy de Maupassant
5 August 1850 to 6 July 1893

Two occurrences in Maupassant's youth, spent near Dieppe, France, scarred him for life. One was the separation of his parents when he was 11 years old. Raised by his strong, neurotic mother, Maupassant adored her, hated his father, despised all husbands, and remained a bachelor. The other was the discovery that he had syphilis, which he had either inherited or contracted. He claimed he was cured of it, but he wasn't, and in his later years it destroyed him. Living in Paris and studying law, he began to write, with his mother's friend Gustave Flaubert as his stern mentor. Quitting law, Maupassant worked for ten years as a government clerk, mostly for the naval ministry. When he was 30, his first published short story, 'Boule de Suif', caused a sensation, and three years later he published his first novel, *Une Vie*, called by Leo Tolstoi 'the best French novel since *Les Misérables*'. After that, writing steadily, Maupassant became rich and famous, ultimately possessing four dwellings and two yachts. He was a powerful man, able to row a boat fifty miles in a single day. But syphilis killed him in the end. He became ill, began to hallucinate, and tried to cut his throat. Committed to a Paris lunatic asylum, he died there at the age of 42.

Guy de Maupassant was one of the most prodigious lovers in modern French history. In a quarter of a century of steady lovemaking, he reportedly had sexual intercourse with thousands of young women. He was prouder of his sex exploits than of his books. He possessed three qualities that made him a much sought-after lover: the ability to go on and on in his couplings without coming; the ability to have multiple orgasms; the ability to bring most women to a climax. He credited his carnal successes, above all, to his intelligence. He said, 'Most people are inclined to think that the lower classes . . . are better lovers than those who live sedentary lives. I don't believe that. . . . It needs

297

brains to give another the greatest possible amount of pleasure.'

From the age of 12 to 15 he masturbated 'occasionally'. Then he had his first love affair. 'When I was about 16 I had a girl, and the delight she gave me cured me of self-abuse.' He never forgot the feel of her loins or the way she gasped, 'Enough, enough!' Later, he enjoyed consorting with prostitutes, and at the peak of his fame preferred wealthy young society women, favouring those who were married and Jewish. Maupassant was very matter-of-fact about his endurance, and insisted that successive sex bouts did not exhaust him. 'I'm as tired after two or three times as I am after twenty,' he once said. 'I've counted twenty and more. Surely you know that in two or three times you exhaust your stock of semen so that you can go on afterwards without further loss.' When Flaubert doubted his endurance, Maupassant had a book-keeper accompany him to a Paris brothel as a witness, and there he 'had six girls in an hour'. Another time, to impress and 'stagger' Bobukin, a visiting Russian writer, Maupassant picked up a dancer at the Folies Bergère, took her to a nearby brothel, and in front of his visitor had sexual intercourse with her six times in a row. When he finished with her, he went across the hall and had sex three more times with a young prostitute.

Whenever Maupassant saw an attractive woman, he wanted her. In 1889, on his only visit to London, he was taken to lunch at an Earls Court restaurant by Henry James. Noting a beautiful woman at the next table, Maupassant asked James to 'get her' for him. James was never more horrified. Most of these women Maupassant wanted only once. A handful he saw frequently. All of them were married. One affair – with Marie Kann, a wealthy young brunette – lasted eight years. Maupassant wrote her 2200 love letters. Another of his long-lived affairs was with Blanche Roosevelt Macchetta, born in the USA, who married a Milan nobleman and became a marchesa. She was a shapely redhead, who made a brief singing debut at Covent Garden, then became a published novelist. She bedded down with Maupassant regularly at his country retreat in Etretat and admitted enjoying 'the maximum of sensual pleasure' with him. For variety, Maupassant sometimes liked his women on the kinky side. After Gisèle d'Estoc – who affected close-cropped hair and men's clothes – had had an affair with Emma Bouer, a trapeze artist with the Cirque Médrano, and had stabbed her in a fight, Maupassant took up with Gisèle. Often Gisèle shared her broad-hipped lesbian ladies, as well as hashish or ether, with him.

298

One day, journalist Frank Harris went for a walk in the country with Maupassant. Harris recalls a conversation as follows:

'"I suppose I am a little out of the common sexually," he [Maupassant] resumed, "for I can make my instrument stand whenever I please."

'"Really?" I exclaimed, too astonished to think.

'"Look at my trousers," he remarked, laughing, and there on the road he showed me that he was telling the truth.'

I.W. (Lists 4, 9, 11, 18, 20, 26, 31, 52)

⚜ Aimee Semple McPherson
9 October 1890 to 27 September 1944

Founder of the International Church of the Four-Square Gospel, Sister Aimee was the spiritual leader of thousands and one of the foremost big-money evangelists of the early twentieth century.

Aimee Elizabeth Kennedy spent her childhood in rural Ontario, Canada, in an atmosphere of religious fervour. Her father was a Methodist farmer, her mother a Salvation Army zealot who consecrated Aimee's life to the Lord's service a few weeks after she was born. As a teenager, Aimee shocked her pious parents with her desire to become an actress. She eventually managed to satisfy all concerned by combining religion and show business in a successful, money-making formula still widely emulated.

Aimee first started on the revival circuit with fiery Pentecostal preacher Robert Semple, whom she married at 17. Semple died of typhoid fever in Hong Kong, where the young couple had set up a mission. The 19-year-old widow returned home with her infant daughter and soon married Harold McPherson, a grocery clerk. After the birth of a son, Aimee coaxed her husband into accompanying her and the children on the hallelujah trail. McPherson quickly became disgusted with life under Aimee's revival tent and ordered his wife to settle down, so she left him and continued her wanderings. He divorced her in 1921 for desertion.

In 1918, Aimee set up her headquarters in Los Angeles, then as now a hotbed of religious cults. She began to receive newspaper publicity for her faith-healing services and quickly accumulated a large following. An attractive, dynamic woman, she was widely criticized for her Paris gowns, make-up and tinted blonde hair. Her massive concrete church, called the Angelus Temple, was famous for its theatrical religious spectacles. On one occasion, Sister Aimee donned a policeman's uniform and rode a motorcycle down the centre aisle to introduce a sermon on the consequences of breaking God's law. During the 1930s, her Four-Square Church was the centre of a series of internecine intrigues and law suits. In a celebrated fight with her mother, Aimee broke the old woman's nose. After a third unhappy marriage, Aimee began to shy away from publicity. Her death from an overdose of barbiturates in an Oakland, California, hotel room was ruled an accident.

Aimee used to declare that her ideal man would be 6 feet tall, have wavy hair and play the trombone. In fact, her men adhered to no such specifications. Kenneth Ormiston, a radio engineer for her church station, was tall and slender, but he had a receding hairline and bat ears. If he did play the trombone, he kept it to himself. Ormiston was already married. In addition, he was an agnostic who refused to treat Sister Aimee with the respect she was accustomed to, and she found this attractive.

On 18 May 1926, the superstar evangelist was reported missing while swimming in the ocean off Venice, California. For days, her followers searched for her body, and two of the faithful died during the search. Five weeks later, Aimee turned up in Agua Prieta, a town near the Mexico–Arizona border, with a fantastic tale of having been kidnapped and held captive in Mexico. Her clean clothes and fresh appearance gave little credence to her story, and a county grand jury decided to investigate. It was revealed that, during the time Aimee claimed she had been held by gangsters in a shack in the Sonora desert, she was actually enjoying an idyllic month with Ormiston in a rented cottage in Carmel, California. Aimee was forced to sever her relationship with Ormiston to preserve her career. By her own admission, she was often lonely, and the tenets of her church forbade a divorced person to remarry while an ex-spouse was still living. Nevertheless, Aimee eloped in 1931 with 30-year-old David Hutton Jr, a baritone who weighed 17 stone 12 pounds. They met when he sang the role of Pharoah in one of Aimee's biblical productions. The couple had been married two days when Hutton was named as defendant in a $200,000 breach-of-promise suit, initiated by a woman who worked in a massage parlour. The plaintiff was awarded damages of $5000, and when Aimee heard the news she pitched forward in a faint, fracturing her skull. After her recovery, she left on a European tour without Hutton. He divorced her during her absence, and for a time eked out a living as a nightclub singer described as 'Aimee's man'.

She indulged herself in discreet affairs in a special flat in Los Angeles. One of these was with a Hearst Newspapers reporter she had hired to ghost-write her autobiography. Another was with rising young comic Milton Berle, who remembers her as a worldly and passionate woman who charmed him into her apartment and made love with him in front of a homemade altar – candles, crucifix, Calvary scene and all.

In 1936, the *Los Angeles Times* reported that unknown persons were demanding money in return for refraining from releasing nude photographs of the evangelist, but the pictures never surfaced. Still, she was often a target for innuendo and obscene phone calls. Like it or not, Aimee had become a sex symbol – 'the evangelist with pulchritude', as one reporter called her.

M.J.T. (Lists 17, 32)

♣ Adah Isaacs Menken
15 June 1835 to 10 August 1868

Famous worldwide as the 'Naked Lady' because of her semi-nude stage appearances, Adah had beauty, wit and intelligence, and became mistress, friend and confidante of many literary celebrities of the nineteenth century. She was years ahead of her time. She smoked cigarettes in public, bobbed her hair and took numerous lovers, openly defying the strict morals of the mid-1800s. The stage vehicle that propelled her to stardom was a play called *Mazeppa*. The highlight of the play occurred when Adah, wearing a skin-coloured body stocking, was tied to the back of a horse and carried off the stage. Tame by present-day standards, the scene was nevertheless erotic enough to make *Mazeppa* the most risqué play of its time. When Adah appeared on stage in the silver-mining boom town of Virginia City, the miners showered her with silver nuggets, named a mine after her, and gave her fifty shares in it. After viewing a performance of *Mazeppa* in the Nevada outback, Mark Twain was so fascinated with its star that he visited Adah at her hotel. He found her sipping champagne while feeding her lapdog sugar cubes dipped in brandy. Twain showed her some of his work, inviting her criticism, and even wrote a riddle about her beautiful hands.

Adah was 5 feet 7 inches tall, weighed 9 stone, and had high breasts and long, supple legs that prompted one theatre critic to remark, 'Such calves! They were never reared on milk.' She composed poetry praised by Swinburne, Whitman and George Sand. Yet this poetess was not beyond fighting a duel with pistols, as she did when a woman in Paris accused her of stealing her man. Adah, an expert shot, drilled a hole in her opponent's hat, which prompted a quick apology. Adah died in Paris of an internal abscess, probably resulting from syphilis. She was only 33 years old.

At 18, Adah was invited on an expenses-paid holiday in Cuba by Austrian Baron Friedrich von Eberstadt, who met her in New Orleans. Adah's impoverished family urged her to go – the baron had promised to subsidize the clan while he and Adah were away. So she was seduced – and just as easily abandoned, and left in Cuba without a peso to her name. At first, she sold her body for the cost of a meal, then the price escalated to $3, and eventually topped out at around $200 for a night in her bed. As she 'performed' in order to get the price of her return passage to New Orleans, Adah stared at the ceiling and dreamed of revenge.

In 1856 she married Alexander Isaac Menken, the bland son of a Cincinnati dry-goods merchant. But she had seen too much of the world to be content with him, and in 1859 left to go to New York City. Believing she had been divorced by Menken, she married John C. Heenan, the American bare-knuckle boxing champion. When news of their marriage was made public, Alexander Menken came forward to say that he had never, in fact, divorced his wife but would now do so. The ensuing scandal further established Adah in the public eye as a wild and debauched woman, and people flocked to see her perform at the Bowery. Her husband, the 6 foot 2 inch Heenan, was also in the limelight. In 1860, he travelled to England to challenge the British heavyweight champion, Tom Sayers, for the world title. In the forty-second round, when Heenan seemed to be winning, spectators broke into the ring and stopped the fight. It was called a draw. But Heenan lost his next fight – one with his wife – when Adah divorced him in 1861. Adah went on with her romances. A subsequent marriage to newspaperman Robert Newell also ended in divorce. Riverboat gambler James Barkley was her final husband. Adah was seven months pregnant on the day of the wedding. Three days later, she left for Europe and never saw Barkley again, but she bore him a son named Louis.

Adah Menken spent the last years of her short life in Europe, where she was both a social and stage success. Perhaps the sweetest triumph of her life came when she encountered in Vienna the baron who had stranded her in Cuba years before. Professing his love for her, the baron tried once again to seduce her. But Adah held out, demanding in exchange no less than an introduction to Emperor Franz Josef. The baron arranged it, and at a palace reception she was presented to the austere emperor. Upon meeting him, Adah stripped off her sequined cloak and stood before him in a tight-fitting flesh-coloured gown – at a distance of ten feet, she looked nude. Unaccustomed to being flashed at in court, the emperor stormed out of the room. The baron was thus ruined in Viennese society.

In later years, none of Adah's contemporaries knew she had spent time in Havana as a prostitute, yet her experience no doubt showed. She wrote in her diary: '[Bret Harte] had the gall to tell me last night that I'd feel at home in one of the bawdy houses we passed while driving to supper. . . . I did deny, of course, but was none too convincing.' She complained that Harte would slap her hard on the backside if she failed to laugh enough at his jokes. On the other hand, the poet Swinburne was probably more anxious to proffer his own behind to Adah's blistering palm. Swinburne was rumoured to be impotent with women, but enjoyed being flogged and, when Adah accepted a £10 offer from Dante Gabriel Rossetti to bed the masochistic poet, she probably did not realize what the task ahead involved. Whether their relationship was sexual or not is debatable, but very few women offered Swinburne the intellectual stimulation that she provided.

Alexandre Dumas *père* was not so sexually inhibited when he took up with Adah towards the end of his life. She and the author of *The Three Musketeers* would regularly spend weekends at Dumas's estate outside Paris, where they would engage in the type of 'swordsmanship' the old man was famous for.

M.S. (Lists 8, 17, 18, 19, 42, 46)

❧ Edna St Vincent Millay
22 February 1892 to 19 October 1950

At the age of 20, Millay became an overnight literary sensation with the publication of her poem 'Renascence'. Writing from a uniquely feminine point of view, she enjoyed popular as well as critical acclaim. In 1923, she received a Pulitzer Prize, the first ever awarded to a woman.

The eldest daughter of a divorcée, Millay grew up in a remote town on the Maine coast as 'Vincent', the surrogate man of the family. Her mother was a free-spirited woman who worked as a nurse to raise her three daughters as a tight little band of creative women. Thanks to a benefactress the young poetess was able to enter Vassar College – belatedly – when she was 21. Rebelling against this 'pink and grey college' from which men were excluded, she smoked secretly, disregarded campus rules, and escaped after graduation to the uninhibited freedom of New York's Greenwich Village. There she worked intermittently as an actress, while writing poetry and pseudonymous magazine articles which paid the rent. 'My candle burns at both ends,' Millay wrote, and it became the epigraph of the dawning twenties. The petite red-haired poetess, half Irish and half American, was enchantingly beautiful but also intense, highly-strung, and prone to mental and physical breakdown. In 1923, she married Eugen Boissevain, an importer of Dutch–Irish ancestry, who waited on her hand and foot during the twenty-five years of their marriage.

Millay had an intoxicating effect on both men and women. Her sexual ambivalence revealed itself early in attachments to older women. On one occasion, a young doctor suggested that her recurrent headaches might stem from 'an occasional erotic impulse towards a person of [her] own sex'. Millay replied, 'Oh, you mean I'm homosexual! Of course I am, and heterosexual too, but what's that got to do with my headache?'

Her first serious lover, the playwright and radical Floyd Dell, described her as a 'Snow Princess, whose kiss left splinters of ice in the hearts of the mortal men who loved her'. Equally fearful of desertion and of the confines of traditional femininity, incapable of emotional surrender, she rejected Dell and a succession of other lovers. At one point, Dell unsuccessfully tried to persuade her to enter therapy to deal with what he called her 'sapphic tendencies', which to him meant her compulsive plunging into one love affair after another.

An exception to her usual pattern was poet Arthur Davison Ficke, who was already married and hence safely unattainable. They consummated their passion in a whirlwind thirty-six hours during the First World War, and remained lifelong admirers of each other. However, to Millay, it seemed only proper that Ficke would always be unattainable. When he proceeded to fall in love with another woman after divorcing his first wife, she accepted it complacently and even became friendly with his new sweetheart.

304

Another lover was author Edmund Wilson, who became infatuated with the poetess at first encounter. 'Edna ignited for me both my intellectual passion and my unsatisfied desire, which went up together in a blaze of ecstasy that remains for me one of the high points of my life,' Wilson wrote in his memoirs. He was able to joke about her many lovers (the 'alumni association', he called them), and on one occasion Wilson and his friend John Bishop playfully divided her in half for the evening, Wilson embracing the lower part of her body and Bishop the upper half. But Millay's extreme promiscuity wounded Wilson deeply. 'What my lips have kissed, and where, and why,' she wrote in one poem, 'I have forgotten. . . .'

Eugen Boissevain, whom she finally married, represented a safe harbour, the supremely indulgent parent figure. He nursed Millay back to health, bought her a farm and an island off the Maine coast, and managed every domestic detail down to washing his wife's hair. Theirs was an 'open marriage', Boissevain insisted, but Millay was so fiercely protective of her privacy that the identity of the extramarital lover described in the sonnets in *Fatal Interview* (1931) remains unknown. In a sense, the identity of her lovers was subordinate to the feelings they engendered within her.

C.D. (Lists 9, 10, 14, 22)

❧ Yukio Mishima
14 January 1925 to 25 November 1970

The most colourful and prolific author to emerge in postwar Japan, Mishima wrote numerous plays, stories, novels and journalistic pieces which earned him a worldwide reputation.

Mishima's father was a minor bureaucrat who deeply admired Hitler and Nazism. His mother was a second-class citizen in a household dominated by her mother-in-law. Mishima was literally a prisoner in the possessive old woman's darkened sick room until he was 12 years old; he grew into a brilliant, languid, morbid youth obsessed with fantasies of blood and pain. He began to write during adolescence, and at 16 was already a central figure in the new romantic school of Japanese literature, having shunned his given name, Kimitake Hiraoka, and adopted his pen name to conceal his writing from his anti-literary father. Later in life, the author would write out 'Yukio Mishima' in Japanese so that the characters also read 'mysterious devil bewitched with death'. As he told friends, 'It's eerie, but that's the way to write my name.' Exempted from military service because of poor health, he worked in an aircraft factory during the Second World War. Later, he accepted a prestigious civil service job but quit in order to devote himself exclusively to writing. In 1949, *Confessions of a Mask*, a masterful autobiographical novel dealing with homosexuality, appeared, and Mishima became an international celebrity. He delighted in shocking the Japanese public and affected a Westernized demeanour. He was overjoyed when people mistook him for a gangster, and played the lead in a Japanese film called *Tough Guy*.

Despite his homosexuality, Mishima took a wife and had two children. Fascinated with the physical activity he had missed as a boy, he became an avid bodybuilder, attaining both the fifth-rank black belt grade in Japanese swordsmanship and the second-rank black belt in karate. He became a fanatical nationalist and the leader of a private army of some 100 young, right-wing zealots. In 1970, he led four members of his toy army, the 'Shield Society', into a suicide raid upon the office of a general of the army self-defence forces in Tokyo and took the general hostage. From a balcony, he exhorted a regiment of soldiers to revert to the prewar militarism and emperor worship he so admired. When the troops laughed at him, he disembowelled himself in the ancient ritual of seppuku – or hara-kiri – and was also beheaded with his seventeenth-century samurai sword by a follower, who then committed suicide.

As a boy, he drew pictures of beautiful knights dying of their wounds, and was appalled to learn that a favourite picture represented Joan of Arc and not a young man as he had thought. Thereafter, he hated the sight of women in men's clothes, and once angrily reprimanded his wife for appearing in trousers. At 12, he had his first orgasm looking at a picture of St Sebastian bound and pierced by arrows. At the same time, he fell in love with a male classmate, and as a consequence developed three lifelong fetishes – masculine armpit hair, sweat and white gloves. He became a frantic masturbator, finding release in Marquis de Sade-like fantasies of death and cannibalism. In his youth, he attempted to interest himself in women, and while studying law was briefly involved with a woman he called Sonoko. On the day she married someone else, Mishima got drunk for perhaps the only time in his life. With the fame earned from *Confessions*, he grew bolder, often entertaining friends at gay cafés in Tokyo. He favoured young roughnecks, and on a trip to New York in 1952 he cruised gay bars looking for his ideal white male. From New York, he went to Rio, where he haunted city parks in the afternoons and often brought young boys back to his hotel. When a friend asked how he managed to communicate with the youths, Mishima answered that in the homosexual world 'you don't need a common language'. He added that he was interested in the process of courting females but entirely uninterested in performing 'the final act' with a woman. As if to demonstrate the truth of this, Mishima later phoned his friend for help because a Japanese woman was trying to seduce him in his hotel room.

The author flew to Paris, becoming good friends with composer Toshiro Mayuzumi. Mishima asked Mayuzumi to take him to a 'bar for pederasts' and later railed at the composer because Mayuzumi – who could speak French – monopolized all the boys.

Women tended to shy away from Mishima because of his odd physique. He was 5 feet 2 inches, with a weightlifter's torso set on top of skinny, underdeveloped legs. A crewcut revealed that his head was shaped like a lightbulb. In a magazine poll, 50 per cent of female readers questioned stated they would rather kill themselves than marry the famous novelist. The girl who did become his wife in 1958, Yoko Sugiyama, was faced with the enmity of Mishima's mother, Shizue, who jealously treated him more like a lover than a son. Even in company, Mishima would address Shizue in intimate terms, causing speculation about the mother/son relationship. Mishima regarded his pretty, round-faced wife as a near-equal and often invited her to mix with his friends, thus breaking Japanese tradition.

After he became a celebrity, Mishima found himself pursued by what he called the 'literature virgins'. He liked to tell the story of how he had almost been smothered to death in the breasts of a tall American woman who insisted on dancing with him at an embassy function. However, Mishima's true erotic interest was in a painful, gory death, and sooner or later everyone who knew him heard him say that seppuku was 'the ultimate form of masturbation'. The author's companion in suicide was a 25-year-old 'soldier' named Masakatsu Morita, who was once referred to by friends as Mishima's 'fiancée'. Morita – who was also fascinated by death – had pledged his life to Mishima.

'I am desperate to kill a man,' Mishima had said. 'I want to see red blood.'

M.S. (Lists 7, 12, 14, 15, 20, 25, 36, 37, 39)

♣ Amedeo Modigliani

12 July 1884 to 24 January 1920

The youngest child of a Jewish merchant family, Modigliani was born in Livorno, Italy, just as a business crash forced his father into bankruptcy. A peculiarity of Italian law helped the family: a bankrupt could keep a bed in which a woman had recently given, or was about to give, birth. At the moment of Modigliani's birth, officials were seizing the household goods, but the family took full advantage of the law – the maternal bed was heaped with personal possessions and valuables. That incident – good fortune salvaged from a dire predicament – is perhaps symbolic of Modigliani's life.

But in 1895 and 1898 Modigliani contracted typhus. Forced to leave school, he turned to painting which, except for a four-year period sculpting, was his life. Moving to Paris in 1906, Modigliani was swept up in the bohemian milieu of that city's artists (including Picasso). A prodigious drinker, Modigliani often stumbled through the streets drunk – and sometimes naked. His fights with other men over women were legion. He consumed enormous amounts of cocaine and hashish. In 1917, his one-man show – the only exhibition of his work during his lifetime and consisting almost entirely of female nudes – was closed by police, who judged his paintings indecent. Modigliani continued to paint until tubercular meningitis killed him. His fame while alive was restricted to the Parisian art community, but by 1922 he had become internationally acclaimed.

Modigliani loved women – hundreds, maybe even thousands, were possessed by this elegantly handsome painter. While still a schoolboy, he was aware of his good looks. Legend places his loss of virginity at 15 or 16 years of age, when he made love to a maid employed by his family. Although he occasionally visited brothels, his favourite sex partners were his models. During his career, he had hundreds of models. Most sat for him in the nude, and – before the painting sessions closed – they made love with him. His preferred subjects (and lovers) were working-class women – such as the peasant girls who took in laundry for a living. Flattered by the attractive artist's attentions, these docile women eagerly gave themselves to him.

Despite his many partners, Modigliani loved only two women. The first was Beatrice Hastings, an aristocratic British poetess five years his senior. They met in 1914, made love that first night, and became inseparable. They drank, danced and fought. Modigliani beat her frequently. When enraged – usually because she had paid attention to another man – he would drag her down the street by her hair. She inspired him, however, and in the bloom of their love he entered his most prolific period of painting, with Beatrice often sitting as his model. None the less, this affair did not last. Beatrice fled from him in 1916. They never saw each other again.

Modigliani mourned this loss, but not for long. In 1917, he met Jeanne Hébuterne, a 19-year-old art student from a French Catholic family. Jeanne – a tiny, pale girl – and Modigliani set up house on the Côte d'Azur within months of their first meeting – despite her parents' opposition to the Italian Jew. She not only modelled for Modigliani, but saw him through his final, failing years, as his fragile health worsened due to his debauchery. In November 1918, they produced a baby girl and, in July 1919, Modigliani vowed to marry Jeanne 'as soon as the papers arrive'. Why they never married remains a mystery. They were devoted, had another child, and remained together until Modigliani's death, six months after his promise. As the painter lay dying in Paris, he supposedly suggested that Jeanne join him in death 'so that I can have my favourite model in Paradise and with her enjoy eternal happiness'. Jeanne was in despair on the day of Modigliani's funeral. Pregnant with a second child, she jumped out of a fifth-floor window to her death.

R.M. (Lists 2, 11, 20, 22, 36, 37, 44)

♣ Mongkut
18 October 1804 to 1 October 1868

This King of Siam is known to the Western world as the inspiration for the Broadway musical, *The King and I*.

Few people in history have had such a sudden and radical change in their sex lives as did Mongkut at the age of 46. He began normally enough, marrying early and fathering two children. When he turned 20, he followed tradition by leaving his family to become a monk, intending to return in a few months. However, while he was away, his father died and Mongkut's elder half-brother became king. To avoid any hint of political intrigue, Prince Mongkut remained a monk and spent the next twenty-six years celibate.

In 1851, his half-brother died, and Mongkut became king. He moved from his monastic quarters to the luxurious Inner Palace in Bangkok, which he shared with 3000 women. No other men were allowed in the Inner Palace except priests and an occasional doctor; these visitors had to be escorted by members of the all-female palace guard. Assuming the throne in early April as Phra Chom Klao, Mongkut wasted little time returning to action. By mid-August he had taken thirty wives, and early in 1852 royal children began appearing. By the end of his seventeen-year reign, he had fathered 82 children, sixty-six of whom were alive when he died.

The rigid laws of custom stipulated that he spend the period between 11.00 a.m. and 1.00 p.m. each day being 'attended by the ladies of the palace'. Unlike his predecessors, Mongkut felt that he had more than enough wives and concubines. In the most dramatic reform of his career, he announced that his wives and concubines, if they wished, could leave the palace to return to their parents or to marry other men. Only the mothers of his children could not remarry. Very few women took advantage of the king's offer.

D.W. (Lists 8, 21, 22)

♣ Marilyn Monroe
1 June 1926 to 5 April 1962

Marilyn Monroe began life as Norma Jean Mortensen, the daughter of Gladys Monroe Baker Mortensen, a hard-working but emotionally unstable Hollywood film cutter, and Gladys's second husband, Edward Mortensen, of Norwegian extraction and uncertain employment, who disappeared shortly before she was born. Norma Jean had a deprived childhood during the Depression. She boarded with one family until she was 7, joined her mother until Gladys was institutionalized for paranoid schizophrenia, and spent the next three years in an orphanage and foster homes. Grace Goddard, her mother's best friend, took care of her from the age of 11 until her marriage at 16. Escaping into a world filled with Saturday matinee images, Norma Jean fantasized about a father who looked like Clark Gable, about glamorous seduction scenes involving tropical islands, yachts, palaces. She also had a recurring dream in which she took her clothes off in church and the shocked congregation silently admired her naked splendour. Marriage to Jim Dougherty, a blue-collar saviour, protective and possessive, soon proved disappointing. Contradicting the lurid tales she would later tell of having been raped and sexually abused, even impregnated, as a foster child, Dougherty reported that his Norma Jean was a virgin. In any case, she became bored with playing house and was relieved when her husband went overseas in 1944. While working in a war plant, she was discovered by a photographer. Norma Jean loved to pose, and the camera (her only true lover, some would say) revealed a beautiful young woman, eager to please and be noticed, voluptuous yet vulnerable, a combination of allure and innocence. Ambitious for stardom, she divorced her husband, became a popular model (photographer André de Dienes fell in love with her and proposed), and in 1946 presented herself at the studios of Twentieth Century Fox. She demonstrated remarkable 'flesh impact' in a silent screen test, on the basis of which the studio signed her, lightened her dull blonde hair, and changed her name to Marilyn Monroe.

Marilyn emanated a strong sexual aura, by all accounts. She thought about sex constantly, considering it with every man she met, but would describe herself as selectively promiscuous, submitting only to men she liked, the main requirement being that they be 'nice'. Her preference was usually for older men: kindly, warm father figures.

Hollywood in the late 1940s was an 'overcrowded brothel', in Marilyn's words, and she needed all the help she could get to move up from third-string blonde at Fox. Her first patron was veteran producer Joe Schenck, then nearly 70. Schenck wined and dined the starlet, invited her regularly to his home and office, where he would fondle her breasts and talk about the old days, while she performed fellatio. Schenck introduced Marilyn to Harry Cohn, the tyrant of Columbia Pictures, but she was fired after her first film – allegedly for rejecting Cohn's sexual demands. Comedian Milton Berle, who succeeded where Cohn failed, claimed, 'She wasn't out to please me because I might be able to help her ... [but] because she liked me.' At the time, she was also in love with Fred Karger, her vocal coach, who enjoyed her sexual favours but did not reciprocate her feelings. An intimate glimpse of Marilyn's sexuality in this period is afforded by Anton LaVey, then an 18-year-old accompanist at a strip joint where the 22-year-old actress worked briefly after being fired from Columbia. LaVey, who had a two-week affair with Marilyn

311

in motels (or, when they were broke, in her car), describes her as sexually passive, a tease who enjoyed the ogling admiration of men but not much else. Marilyn's biographers are inclined to agree. Fred Guiles wrote that she was 'too self-absorbed to respond to men most of the time', while Norman Mailer concluded that she was 'pleasant in bed, but receptive rather than innovative'. And Marilyn was still pathetically insecure. 'I don't know if I do it right,' she murmured after making it with actor Marlon Brando. Or she would jump into bed, nude, pleading, 'Don't do anything but just hold me.' (One loving friend who did a lot of holding was Bob Slatzer, a writer who claims to have been married to Marilyn in Mexico, briefly, until she changed her mind.) But with most men sex was simple and reassuring: 'They were also so full of confidence and I had none at all, and they made me feel better.'

Johnny Hyde, a top Hollywood agent, succeeded Schenck as Marilyn's patron. Hyde was short, dapper and at 53 had a serious heart ailment. He was infatuated with Marilyn and wanted to marry her, but she refused. He gave her a sense of security, a new wardrobe, and paid for plastic surgery on her nose and chin. Most important, Hyde used his influence to line up Marilyn's best early roles, both as kept women, in *Asphalt Jungle* (1950) and *All About Eve* (1950). Marilyn didn't enjoy sex with Hyde, but would fake ecstasy so he wouldn't be offended.

When Marilyn signed her first big contract, she is said to have exclaimed, 'That's the last cock I'll have to suck.' In fact, she was setting her sights higher. Fooling around with one-time roommate Shelley Winters, she made a list of the men she'd like to sleep with. The names included an eminent man Marilyn would marry, another she would seduce, and Albert Einstein. Shelley Winters later came across a photo of the scientist inscribed to Marilyn 'With respect and love and thanks.'

Joe DiMaggio was Marilyn's first real hero-lover, a great baseball star. Just retired at 37, he was still in prime shape, a fitting complement to the blonde bombshell who would become a superstar with the release of *Gentlemen Prefer Blondes* and *How to Marry a Millionaire* in 1953. (Even the revelation of the nude calendar, for which she had posed when she was broke, seemed to augment her career.) Unfortunately, however, DiMaggio didn't want his wife to be a superstar after their 1954 marriage. The strong, silent type, proud, possessive, and old-fashioned, he detested Hollywood and was outraged by the public display of his wife's sexual charms. He disliked Marilyn's drama coach and mentor Natasha Lytess, who retaliated by suggesting that Marilyn got along better with women.

Trying to break away from her studio-imposed stereotype of the sexy blonde, Marilyn left Hollywood for the East Coast, where she thought she had finally found a man interested in more than her body. Playwright Arthur Miller, whom she had first met in 1950 ('He sat and held my toe and we just looked into each other's eyes'), was as respected in radical intellectual circles as DiMaggio was in baseball circles. They were married in 1956. Lena Pepitone, her maid, described Marilyn's daily life in New York between acting classes and sessions with a psychiatrist. While Miller worked in his study, the actress would lie alone in her bedroom, sipping champagne and talking for long hours on the telephone, or listening to 'Frankie' records and admiring her naked image in the mirrors. (She also preened before a full-length picture of DiMaggio in the closet.) Totally uninhibited, Marilyn belched and farted constantly, she rarely bathed, although she did take the trouble to bleach her pubic hair, which gave her infections ('I want to feel blonde all over'), and owned no underwear. She ate in bed, wiping her hands on the sheets, which had to be changed frequently, particularly when she had her period. At first the Millers embarrassed friends with their physical possessiveness. After one night of lovemaking, Marilyn would not let her maid change the sheets, saying, 'I want to lie on these all day.' Then Marilyn suffered two miscarriages, despite corrective surgery, followed by increasing depression. Her later films were completed with great personal difficulty (and mounting cost to the producers, for Marilyn, taking revenge, was chronically late or absent altogether). Unable to sleep, she became a heavy barbiturate user, drugging herself into oblivion. More than once, Miller rescued her from accidental overdosing. After collaborating on *The Misfits* (1960), the Millers were divorced – prophetically, on the day that John F. Kennedy became president.

Now approaching 35, alone and desperately worried about ageing, Marilyn was hungry for reassurance. She had engaged in a highly publicized affair with Yves Montand, her co-star in *Let's Make Love* (1960), who stunned her by ending the affair, not wanting to leave his wife, Simone Signoret. Marilyn had hoped for more than a fling. And there were meetings in seedy hotels with Danish journalist Hans Jørgen Lembourn, whose hands made her sleep, she said. She went bar-hopping, according to her maid, entertained her handsome chauffeur, and became intimate friends with her masseur, Ralph Roberts. DiMaggio occasionally stayed overnight, but they still disagreed about Marilyn's career. Another old friend and sometime lover was Frank Sinatra, whose sexual demands and protective dominance so excited and pleased her that she indulged in fantasies of marriage. Then Sinatra introduced her to the Kennedys. 'Can you imagine me as first lady?' Marilyn mused to her friend Bob Slatzer in 1962. She was enjoying secret assignations with the president at his brother-in-law Peter Lawford's Santa Monica beach house, at the Beverly Hills Hotel and on the presidential jet. She bought a house and moved back to L.A., she told friends, because 'it sure beats hanging around [hotel rooms] for God Himself [Jack Kennedy] to show up'. Kennedy's performance was 'very democratic' and 'very penetrating,' she giggled. 'I think I make his back' feel better,' she joked to her masseur. John Kennedy liked to pat and squeeze her, Marilyn said, but was embarrassed on putting his hand up her dress under the table at a dinner party to discover she wore no underwear. He began to be annoyed by her lateness and constant telephone calls – and was fearful of publicity. Marilyn was becoming too hot to handle by the time JFK's 45th-birthday fund-raiser was held at Madison Square Garden that May – Marilyn stole the show singing 'Happy Birthday'. By June, cushioning the blow of rejection, the president had handed her over to his brother Bobby. Bobby and Marilyn consummated their relationship in a car outside Lawford's house, it was rumoured, and Marilyn began fantasizing about marriage again. When her trust proved to be devastatingly misplaced, and RFK changed his phone number to escape her calls, she talked idly about calling a press conference to blow the whistle on him.

Suicide – or murder? Marilyn's moods during that last summer of 1962 swung from gaiety to despair, the latter dampened by pills and daily psychiatric sessions. She had been fired from her last picture for absenteeism, and was despondent over her inability to hold a man – 'to fulfil anyone's total needs,' she wrote in a letter, never mailed, to DiMaggio. Her life had been so disordered, with so many rehearsals for death, that it came as a shock but not a total surprise when she was found dead of an overdose early one Sunday morning. There was later speculation that Marilyn Monroe had been the victim of murder. But the physician who pronounced Marilyn dead, Dr Hyman Engelberg, told us that there was no question the actress had taken her own life. The love goddess was dead, ironically, for lack of love.

C.D. (Lists 2, 6, 22, 24, 42, 44, 45)

♣ Lola Montez
? 1818 to 17 January 1861

Irish-born Marie Dolores Eliza Rosanna Gilbert achieved world-wide notoriety as Lola Montez. A dancer and actress, her true calling was performing as a courtesan. Franz Liszt, Alexandre Dumas *père* and King Louis I of Bavaria were among her conquests. Lola's outrageous behaviour made her name synonymous with liberated female sexuality in the mid-nineteenth century. Screaming she 'never would thus be thrown alive into the jaws of death', 18-year-old Eliza Gilbert – the headstrong daughter of a Spanish mother and a British father – rejected the marriage her mother had arranged to a 60-year-old judge in India while Eliza was away at an English boarding school. Ironically, one of her mother's lovers, 30-year-old Lieutenant Thomas James, rescued the beautiful Eliza by seducing her and then marrying her in 1837. Four years later, the philandering lieutenant deserted Eliza and eloped with the wife of a fellow officer. Claiming Eliza had committed adultery with a Lieutenant Lennox of the Madras Cavalry after he left her, Lieutenant James obtained a well-publicized judical separation in 1842 (requiring a special Act of Parliament).

Unable to remarry during her husband's lifetime and seeking a way to support herself, Eliza studied Spanish dancing in Seville and Madrid for four months. As Donna Lola Montez, she opened in London with the sensual dance 'El Olano' at Her Majesty's Theatre in 1843. Her initial performance was disastrous – she was booed offstage by a group of men headed by Lord Ranelagh, whose bed she had spurned. News of this debacle provoked Lola's sanctimonious mother to wear mourning clothes and to announce her daughter's death. Undaunted, Lola learned to step to the footlights and successfully win over her audiences even when hostile claques threatened her performances. Her beauty and personality, not her limited talent, kept her on stages for the next fourteen years. Her 'Spider Dance' was popular enough to make male audiences clamour for encores. It featured Lola in brightly coloured layers of petticoats over flesh-coloured tights. During the course of the dance, each petticoat was lifted and inspected for imaginary spiders, which were shaken off and stamped to death. The spicy fandango concluded with a naughty flash of Lola's legs. When she could no longer attract theatre audiences, Lola held receptions, charging a dollar for a ten-minute chat and an additional 50 cents for a handshake. In her last years, she became a devout Episcopalian and concentrated her efforts on saving prostitutes. In 1861, at the age of 42, Lola Montez succumbed to syphilis contracted almost two decades earlier. She died on an old mattress on the floor of a cheap room in Hell's Kitchen, a New York City slum. Aldous Huxley wrote, 'When you met Lola Montez, her reputation made you automatically think of bedrooms.' She used sex to obtain wealth and prestige rather than as an expression of love, and had no difficulty finding lovers willing to play and pay on her terms. No wonder, considering one reporter's description of her: 'There was about her mouth something provoking and voluptuous which drew you. Her skin was white, her wavy hair like the tendrils of woodbine, her eyes tameless and wild, her mouth like a budding pomegranate. Add to that a dashing figure, charming feet, and perfect grace.'

Franz Liszt had a brief affair with Lola in 1843, but found her so demanding that he didn't have time for his music. One day, Liszt left Lola sleeping in their Paris hotel room, paid the manager 'for the furniture she will break when she discovers my absence', and fled to the Riviera.

At the height of his fame, Lola had a brief fling with Alexandre Dumas *père*. She abandoned herself to his bed 'strewn with rose petals and surrounded by ice buckets of wine', which he called his 'theatre designed for the art of love'. Dumas introduced her to the cultural-political circle which included singer/actress Madame Stoltz, Frédéric Chopin and George Sand. Like Stoltz and Sand, Lola affected men's clothing and cigar smoking until she realized both detracted from the femininity which was her primary asset.

At Sand's salon, Lola met the one true love of her life, handsome literary critic and newspaper publisher Alexandre Henri Dujarier. Lola rediscovered in Dujarier's arms the tender feelings she had so long suppressed. But, during the course of the relationship, the quiet and sober Dujarier was unaccountably transformed into a drunk who was often abusive to Lola in public. In 1845, he provoked a duel with one of his newspaper's contributors and was killed. Before she met Dujarier, Lola had said, 'The moment I get a nice, round, lump sum of money, I am going to try to hook a prince.' In 1846, she became mistress of Henry, Prince of Ruess. When renounced by Henry, she travelled to Bavaria, where she charmed 60-year-old King Louis I.

Braving the outrage of his court and the Church, Louis gave her land and riches, wrote poetry for her, and titled her the Countess von Landsfeld. Lola 'rather liked a row' and her fiery temper kept her busy boxing ears or horsewhipping anybody who dared to cross her. Her unpopularity with the Bavarian people, combined with vehement attacks by the Church, eventually brought both Lola and Louis into disfavour. In 1848, Louis was forced to banish her and abdicate the throne in favour of his son, Maximilian II. Louis and Lola corresponded for years, and some biographers believe they were secretly married. He died of syphilis in 1868.

In 1849, in London, Lola married George Trafford Heald, a wealthy officer, ten years her junior. Less than a month later, Lola was arrested for bigamy after Heald's maiden aunt discovered she had never divorced Lieutenant James, her first husband. After the first day in court, Lola persuaded Heald to flee the country with her. Their life together was tempestuous – once she stabbed him in the chest. Another time, she publicly humiliated him when he ran out of money while she was playing roulette. 'Learn that he who has the honour to accompany Lola must always have money at his command,' she shouted as she slapped him. Heald became an alchoholic and finally left her.

Lola's syphilis began to take its toll. A three-month-long illness left her weak and bald. Bewigged and impoverished, Lola took dancing lessons to regain her muscle control, and then she booked a tour through Belgium and Germany. She made her American debut in New York in December 1851. In 1853, she met Patrick Purdy Hull, the editor of the *San Francisco Whig*, in New Orleans. He persuaded her to return to California with him, and there she made (and quickly spent) a fortune performing her Spider Dance. Far removed from the jurisdiction of the English courts, Lola married Hull on 1 July 1853. Disgusted by her flirtations and extravagances, he filed for divorce a few weeks later, upon learning of his wife's affair with Dr Adler, a German physician in America. Adler subsequently died in what appeared to be a hunting accident.

Lola's last affair was with Noel Follin, a married actor who had come to California during the Gold Rush. Follin was selling tickets in a box office when Lola picked him up and made him her agent and lover. Two years later, when her popularity in California waned, he arranged a tour of Australia for her. Again the Spider Dance attracted audiences. The next year, on the night of his 29th birthday, Follin and Lola were returning to San Francisco by ship when they quarrelled over the division of the profits from the tour. Follin apparently seized Lola's bag of gold and jumped overboard. His body was never recovered.

In 1845 her former patron, Alexandre Dumas, said of Lola: 'She has the evil eye, and is sure to bring bad luck to anyone who closely links his destiny with hers. If ever she is heard of again, it will be in connection with some terrible calamity that has befallen a lover of hers.' Dumas's prediction proved chillingly accurate.

H.B. and L.S. (Lists 8, 17, 18, 41)

♣ Wolfgang Amadeus Mozart
27 January 1756 to 5 December 1791

This most prodigious of all child prodigies, born in Salzburg, Austria, began music lessons at 4 with his violinist father, Leopold, a stern but loving disciplinarian. Composing from the age of 5, at 6 Mozart astonished European royalty as he and his gifted sister made the first of many arduous concert tours. A virtuoso on violin, organ and harpsichord, he was called a *'Wunderkind'* and showered with attention. Yet he remained completely natural and affectionate.

His adult life was a sharp contrast to his younger years. Short, pale, insignificant in appearance, he could not command the interest of aristocratic and ecclesiastical patrons as a serious and mature composer. He never found an official post that paid enough to enable him to devote himself fully to the major works he longed to write. Precious time was wasted giving perfunctory lessons and grinding out potboilers. His life was a long losing struggle against rivals, illness and poverty. He and his wife Constanze did not live within their financial means. Pleasure-loving, they were unable to keep money from vanishing, not least because of their generosity to all-comers. Mozart died at 35 of kidney disease brought on by overwork and malnutrition. He was in debt to his tailor and upholsterer, as well as his friends. A heavy rainstorm prevented his wife and friends from accompanying the coffin to the graveyard. Not until seventeen years later did Constanze realize that Mozart's remains had been dumped into an unmarked pauper's grave.

Pampered by women as a child, he was precociously aware of

their looks. Mozart enjoyed flirting, saying that, if he had had to marry every girl with whom he flirted, he would have been a husband one hundred times over. At 21 he carried on a playfully indecent correspondence – full of double meanings – with his favourite cousin Maria Anna Thekla Mozart.

While on tour Mozart lost his heart the first time. The object of his affections was Aloysia Weber, 16, a lovely girl studying to be an opera singer. Encouraged by her designing mother, she flirted with Mozart, who was enchanted. They played and sang together by the hour. Wolfgang's father heard about it and ordered him back from his tour since he thought the 'loose-living' Weber clan socially beneath the Mozarts. Some months later Wolfgang returned to Mannheim to find that Aloysia, now a member of the Munich opera, had forgotten him. Their meeting was so awkward that Mozart sat down at the piano and played a ribald song to cover his hurt feelings. Long after Mozart's death, Aloysia was asked why the relationship had cooled and she replied, 'I did not know, you see. I only thought he was such a *little* man.'

At 25, Wolfgang transferred his affection to Aloysia's younger sister – uneducated, unmusical Constanze. When writing to his father, Mozart described her as plain, but said she had a good heart and wonderful housekeeping skills. This time Mother Weber used strong tactics to keep Mozart in the family. She spread the story that he was being too familiar with Constanze, then told him people were talking and she feared for her daughter's reputation. The conniving mother engineered an ultimatum: he must stop seeing Constanze or sign a marriage contract which stipulated that if he defaulted he would have to pay three hundred gulden ($150) a year. Wolfgang certainly had no intention of giving up Constanze, and she proved her good heart by tearing up the contract as soon as he had signed. Their wedding took place when he was 26, she 19. The nine-year marriage was genuinely happy. The Mozarts were companionable and physically compatible. Constanze was tolerant, uncomplaining, and usually pregnant and ailing – only two of her six children survived. A visitor once found the couple dancing around their living room in each other's arms to keep warm. They had no money to buy wood. When Mozart died, Constanze was hysterical with grief. Later her second husband, Nissen, helped her write the first biography of Mozart, whom she survived by fifty years.

Legend attributes many extramarital affairs to Mozart, but he was no Don Juan like the hero of his opera; when he and librettist

319

da Ponte required a living model for that character, they called in Casanova for advice. Mozart's strenuous work habits were not conducive to dalliance. Until the end of his life, he wrote to his wife almost daily whenever they were separated. His letters brim with warmth and affection. In them Mozart seems the ideal of marital fidelity. Also, by his own admission, he avoided promiscuity because of the perils of venereal disease.

In his youth, Mozart wrote a number of letters to his mother and his favourite cousin, Maria, which indicated that he was something of a coprophiliac. In one letter he wrote to Maria: 'Oh my arse is burning like fire!... Perhaps some muck wants to come out!... what is that? – Is is possible .... Ye gods! – can I believe those ears of mine? Yes indeed, it is so – what a long, melancholy note!... I shit on your nose and it will run down your chin.... Do you still love me?' The moment Mozart became interested in the Weber sisters, his anal references ceased.

Eds. (Lists 21, 49)

♣ Benito Mussolini
29 July 1883 to 28 April 1945

Mussolini was born in the northern Italian town of Dovia in the district of Romagna, the son of a blacksmith and a schoolteacher. An unruly child, he was expelled from two elementary schools after attacking fellow students with his penknife. Still, he was an intelligent boy and managed to get both an education and teaching credentials. At 18, he worked as a schoolteacher in a small village near his home town, until his reputation as a satyr cost him his teaching contract. Mussolini gained a modicum of fame as a socialist orator, journalist and general rowdy. By the time he was 26 he had been jailed six times for inciting violence against authority. He was expelled from the socialist party for advocating war with Austria. When the First World War began, Mussolini enlisted in the army and was wounded by shrapnel. On his return, he founded the *Fascisti* to fight socialism and Bolshevism, accumulating over three hundred thousand followers. By 1922, the Fascists were powerful enough to intimidate King Victor Emmanuel III into appointing Mussolini, then 39, the youngest prime minister in Italian history. Under Mussolini's dictatorship, Italy's economy was stabilized, public works were started, and the country prospered. But Mussolini's desire for expansion, coupled with his alliance with Hitler, proved fatal, and in 1943 he was ousted from power. Two years later, no longer protected by the Germans, Mussolini and his faithful mistress Clara Petacci were shot by Italian partisans.

A superstitious man, the *Duce* might well have attributed his downfall to plain bad luck. He had a mortal fear of hunchbacks, cripples and open umbrellas. He painted shamrocks on the hood of his red Alfa-Romeo, and never ventured anywhere without a small statue of St Anthony, the patron saint of healing, in his pocket. He fainted at the smell of incense or ether and, though he was involved in several duels and battles, corpses made him squeamish. Blessed with a speaking voice that could charm the multitudes, Mussolini was less charismatic close up. He seldom bathed or changed his shirt, and once offended Queen Elena of Spain by attending a reception with a two days' growth of beard.

Initiated into the world of the flesh by a prostitute at 16, Mussolini never tired of the pleasure women afforded him. During his teens, he admitted to 'undressing every girl I see with my eyes'. When he did undress a woman, it was seldom all the way, since most of his early encounters took place on staircases, against trees, or on the banks of the river Rabbi. The undisputed master of the 'quickie', Mussolini as prime minister would receive female petitioners in his office and seduce them on a window seat or on the floor, rarely taking the trouble to remove his trousers and shoes. He was loath to let women spend the night beside him, afraid they would laugh at his nightshirt. Actually, it would have been unwise for any woman to laugh at him. When he was 18, he stabbed a woman with the pocket knife he always carried, and, once, when Clara Petacci angered him, he struck her soundly enough to send her flying against a wall. He viewed women as mere 'objects to plunder', and plunder them he did, sometimes seven in rapid succession. He only asked that they be plump and wear no perfume – criteria met by Italian peasant girls.

In his teens, Mussolini frequented prostitutes. He soon discovered that he had a way with women and could charm them into bed for free. He seduced his cousin and several of her friends, as well as any country girl who caught his fancy. His first steady partner was Angelica Balabanoff, a Russian socialist agitator fourteen years his senior. She lost interest in the egotistical 19-year-old because she doubted his sincerity as a socialist. While teaching in Tolmezzo, in the Alps, Mussolini carried on an affair with his landlady, a married woman named Luigia. She was extremely jealous and would rip out and burn pages in his notebooks on which he scribbled the names of women he had read about in history books.

In 1909, he fell in love with Rachele Guidi, one of his former students, who was working as a barmaid in his father's inn. As a socialist, he was ideologically forbidden to marry, and when he proposed that they live together out of wedlock, Rachele's mother would not hear of it. So Mussolini produced a pistol and said, 'You see this revolver, Signora Guidi? It holds six bullets. If Rachele turns me down, there will be a bullet for her and five for me. It's for you to choose.' At that, the signora gave them her blessing. They finally did marry several years later, during the First World War, for practical reasons. One of Mussolini's mistresses, Ida Dalser, bore him a son and began calling herself Signora Mussolini, and she began running up bills using that name. So the *Duce* wed Rachele and clarified the situation. Ida died in a mental institution in 1937; her son, Benito Albino, was killed during the Second World War. Though a devoted family man, Mussolini was still a Fascist. He bossed and occasionally beat Rachele, and even threw things at his beloved daughter Edda. However, Rachele was equally capable of violence. When the *Duce* returned home drunk one night and ran amok in their flat, smashing what few furnishings they had, she warned him the next day, 'If you ever come home again in that state, I'll kill you.' Knowing she meant it, he gave up alcohol for good. On the other hand, Mussolini was never so intimidated by his mistresses. Magda Fontanges, a French journalist with whom he had an affair, wrote in *Liberty* magazine that one of Mussolini's first acts of courtship was to choke her jokingly with a scarf.

Of all the *Duce*'s mistresses, the dark beauty Clara Petacci was by far his favourite. Their relationship lasted over ten years and, although he loved her dearly, he was permanently bound to Rachele and his family and refused to leave them. Clara understood this and managed to console herself with the luxurious apartments Mussolini provided her. It was in one of these love nests that Rachele finally confronted Clara. Livid throughout the brief meeting, Rachele sarcastically noted the luxury in which her husband kept his 'whore', and prophetically told Clara that one day 'they'll take you to Piazzale Loreto' – a meeting place for down-and-out prostitutes. The Piazzale Loreto was where Clara's and the *Duce*'s bodies were hung by their heels after their execution. For a while, Clara's skirt dangled around her face, until it was tied in place for the sake of modesty. She and Mussolini had spent their last night together in a farmhouse and, although the partisans would have let her live, she insisted on dying with her lover. Loyal to the end, she flung herself in front of Mussolini at the instant the first shots were fired.

Mussolini contracted syphilis while living in Tolmezzo, perhaps from his landlady Luigia. He was so distressed about having the disease that he almost shot himself. A friend intervened and convinced him it would be wiser to see a doctor. He was never cured, and it has been speculated that his bungled war efforts resulted from brain damage caused by the disease. Syphilis, unless properly treated, is known to result in megalomania and exaggeration of emotions – traits which were plainly visible in the *Duce*'s character.

M.J.T. (Lists 8, 18, 20, 26, 36, 37, 40, 43, 45)

♣ Carry Nation
25 November 1846 to 9 June 1911

Among the most famous of all temperance reformers, Carry Nation was a crusader whose enthusiasm in the war against vice has scarcely been rivalled. She raged against alcohol, tobacco, sex, politics, government, Freemasonry, lawyers, foreign foods and Theodore Roosevelt – to name only a few. She was and is best known for her 'hatchetations' – destroying bars and other dens of iniquity single-handed with a hatchet.

She was born Carry Moore in Kentucky; her father was a prosperous slave-owning stockdealer, and her mother suffered from the delusion that she was Queen Victoria, complete with royal carriage and sceptre. There were a great number of eccentrics in her family, notably one aunt who, at full moon, made repeated attempts to climb on to the roof and transform herself into a weathervane. Carry's odd relatives and her own early religious visions probably served to influence her development towards fanaticism. Although erratically educated, Carry was a qualified teacher. She became interested in temperance in 1890. At that time, she was a resident of Kansas, which was a dry state. When a new US Supreme Court ruling permitted wet states to export alcoholic drink in 'original packages' to dry states, Carry

323

felt the law of Kansas was being undermined and began her crusade. With a handful of female followers, she marched on saloons. While they sang hymns outside, Carry stormed into the saloons and wielded her hatchet. She was in and out of jails more than thirty times, paying her fines by lecturing and selling souvenir hatchets. In her heyday, she was a forbidding figure: nearly 6 feet tall and weighing 12 stone 8 pounds, she wore stark black and white clothing, with a hatchet brooch pinned to her bosom. She died at 64 in Leavenworth, Kansas. Her legacy was the 1919 Prohibition Amendment to the US Constitution.

Carry's mother and numerous aunts trained her to look upon every man as a potential seducer. Thus, when she received gentlemen callers, there was no hand-holding or hayriding. Instead, they discussed literature or the bible. She said of herself, 'Oh, I was a great lover,' and in her autobiography, she wrote, 'There are pages in my life that have had much to do with bringing me in sympathy with the fallen tempted natures. These I cannot write, but let no erring, sinful man or woman think that Carry Nation would not understand, for Carry Nation is a sinner saved by grace.' However, her concept of sin was so exaggerated that she was probably referring to her fantasies.

In 1865 Charles Gloyd, a handsome young doctor from Ohio, became a boarder in the Moore household. Although Mrs Moore forbade the two young people to be alone together, Gloyd managed to woo Carry. One day he caught her in his arms and kissed her on the mouth. She covered her face with her hands and cried, 'I'm ruined! I'm ruined!' Their courtship lasted two years. Things took a turn for the worse on their wedding day, when Gloyd showed up drunk for the ceremony. Carry wrote of the days that followed, 'I did not find Dr Gloyd the lover I expected. He was kind but seemed to want to be away from me; used to sit and read, when I was hungry for his caresses and love.' After a few months, she left him at her parents' urging; she was pregnant and on the verge on a nervous breakdown. Six months later, her husband died from drink.

Several years later, living with her daughter and mother-in-law, Carry was in financial difficulty. Within six months, she was married to David Nation, an extremely ugly widower nineteen years her senior, a minister and a lawyer. Their marriage was rocky, and Carry was bitter that she had not found true love. Her new husband resented her over-zealous Christianity and religious visions and, although she wept at his lack of affection, she found sex repugnant. After twenty-four miserable years together, Nation divorced Carry on grounds of desertion. In her final analysis, men were 'nicotine-soaked, beer-besmeared, whiskey-greased, red-eyed devils', and 'two-legged animated whiskey flasks'. In addition to fighting her whisky war, Carry was a feminist; she preached against corsets and advocated a mat-riarchal society.

The product of a deeply repressed sexuality, Carry's hatred of all things sexual and her aggressive tactics in fighting them became increasingly warped. She began her career of interference by attacking necking couples and lecturing them on the evils of buggy-riding and 'spooning', brandishing a ferocious-looking umbrella with a sharpened tip. (She had not yet picked up the hatchet.) She also stopped women on the street to alert them against seduction, describing it in graphic anatomical detail. She established a 'Home for the Wives of Drunkards', and a news-paper call the *Hatchet*. Her column, 'Private Talks to Boys and Girls', warned of the evils of self-abuse, and its language was so explicit that one reader called it 'a blueprint for masturbation'. Claiming that God had told her to use a hatchet, she began to wreak havoc. To protect themselves, some bar owners hired bodyguards, equipped their bars with trapdoors, or kept cages of rats to let loose on unwelcome visitors. One saloon keeper even designed a portable bar with the strength of a tank, which he planned to take on tour through the dry states in open defiance of Carry and her hatcheteers. One of her most celebrated smashings occurred in Wichita, at the Hotel Carey. Famed for its lovely interior decoration, the bar proudly sported a life-size painting of a nude Cleopatra bathing, along with scantily clad attendants. When Carry saw it, she proceeded to destroy the bar single-handed, causing thousands of dollars worth of damage. She told the bartender, 'It's disgraceful! You're insulting your mother by having her form stripped naked and hung up in a place where it is not decent for a woman to be when she has her clothes on!' Not wishing to risk similar treatment, a hotel owner in New York City abjectly draped with cheesecloth the naked statue of Diana decorating his lobby.

A.W. (List 32)

♣ Horatio, Lord Nelson
29 September 1758 to 21 October 1805

Nelson began his naval career at 9, when his mother died and an uncle took the frail and sensitive boy to sea. After tasting high adventure in the Arctic and the West Indies, he contracted malaria in the Indian Ocean and was sent home. But he studied for and won a commission, and at the age of 20 commanded his first ship. The hazards of the profession were to take their toll. In 1780, he contracted yellow fever during an otherwise successful mission against the Spanish at San Juan, Nicaragua. In 1794, at Bastia, Corsica, a French shell fragment blinded him in one eye. Shipboard diet eventually claimed most of his teeth. After a victory off Cape St Vincent in south-west Portugal had won him a knighthood and catapulted him into national prominence, he went ashore to oversee a ground assault on Tenerife, in the Canary Islands, and his right elbow was shattered by grapeshot; the arm was amputated. Then came a forehead wound at the Battle of the Nile, and later a shot pierced his shoulder and chest. After this last blow, he died on board ship in 1805, just as the outcome of his greatest victory – Trafalgar – was assured. Contemporaries described Nelson as a bag of bones who cut a poor figure in uniform. While he relished his fame and felt he deserved even more recognition, he was awkward, even boorish, at social gatherings. Yet he never failed to live up to his reputation in battle. He was a brilliant tactician and strategist, a fearless leader, and a sensitive paternal figure to his men.

Until he reached the age of 27, Nelson's love life amounted to a series of unreciprocated passions far outpaced by his naval career. Then, in the West Indies, he met Fanny Nisbet, an intelligent and poised widow several months his senior. He wrote home, 'I think I have found a woman who will make me happy'. But his official responsibilities caused the courtship to drag on for two years. In 1787, they married and returned to England for six years of domestic tranquillity.

Unfortunately, Nelson was eventually sent to Naples to gather reinforcements against the French. There, in 1793, he met the love of his life – Lady Emma Hamilton, 28-year-old wife of the 63-year-old Sir William Hamilton, the scholarly British ambassador to Naples and the owner of the Portland Vase. The shy Captain Nelson – while respecting Hamilton – was taken aback by the beauty of his young wife. Emma Hamilton, with her grey eyes, long auburn hair, and shapely body (hardly concealed since she shunned underwear) was one of the most beautiful women of the age. Born a blacksmith's daughter in Cheshire, she had travelled a hard road to her present position. When a favourite cousin had been forced into service on a British warship, Emma had pleaded with the ship's captain, and bartered her body for the boy's release. At 17, she bore the captain a daughter, who was farmed out to relatives. Abandoned by the captain, Emma none the less realized the value of her charms. She obtained a job with a quack, Dr James Graham, whose Temple of Health featured a canopied Celestial Bed, rented to the impotent who wished to restore their virility; Emma performed erotic dances in the nude. Displaying her wares, she was seen and hired as a model by painters Gainsborough, Thomas Lawrence and Joshua Reynolds. Romney painted her as Venus, Circe, Mary Magdalene, Joan of Arc and herself. One of her longest affairs was with the Hon. Charles Francis Greville, a dilettante who made her his mistress. Greville, conscious of a rich uncle's will, turned her over to his ageing relative, Sir William Hamilton. Emma had her revenge. She married Hamilton and took Greville's inheritance as her own.

In 1793, she met Nelson and the attraction was mutual. But his stay was too brief for love to flourish. He returned to sea and to war. Satisfying his sexual needs with his mistress Signora Adelaide Correglia, whom he called 'Dolly', (and probably with several others), his mind was on Emma Hamilton. Not until five years later did Nelson return to Naples. He was famous now, an admiral and a living legend. He was also prematurely middle-aged, a semi-cripple missing some teeth and racked by coughing spells. 'Oh God! Emma cried when she saw him. 'Is it possible?' She fainted into his one arm. Under her husband's roof, she nursed Nelson with asses' milk and entertained him with her dancing. On his 40th birthday, she arranged a party with 1800 guests. Emma's hero-worship was as complete as it was indiscreet. In their nine weeks together, their great love began. Although both were married, Nelson felt himself above convention, and Emma was guided by impulse. She was soon pregnant by Nelson. Still, Nelson and Hamilton displayed nothing but admiration and respect for each other, and throughout the years of absence Nelson continued to write loving letters to his wife Fanny.

But, when Nelson returned to England in the Hamiltons' company, this strange trio found that scandal had preceded them.

Although the masses thronged about their Hero of the Nile, Nelson was publicly snubbed by King George III and soon abandoned any serious attempts at concealing the affair. When Nelson embarked on his next mission, he left the pregnant Emma behind. Nelson worried about Emma's pregnancy, believing this to be her first. He wrote long letters to her swearing he would be faithful and 'could be trusted with fifty virgins naked in a dark room'. He asked her to prepare 'the dear thatched cottage' (a veiled reference to her anatomy) for his return, saying that he 'would not give it up for a queen and a palace'. There is little doubt that Sir William knew the parentage of 'his' daughter – particularly after Emma named her Horatia. As the old diplomat explained to his nephew, 'I am determined that my quiet shall not be disturbed; let the nonsensical world go on as it will.' Fanny somehow kept her hopes alive for a while, until her last touching letter was returned marked, 'Opened by mistake by Lord Nelson, but not read.' Divorce was impossible, for Fanny had committed no transgression. Meanwhile, Nelson sent money to Emma with instructions to buy them a country home, Merton Place.

When Nelson returned to England, Sir William's health was rapidly failing. Nelson and Emma took turns keeping vigil by the sickbed; the elder statesman finally died in 1803 with his wife and her lover by his side. For a time, Emma took mourning seriously; the old man had been a benevolent and forgiving husband. But now she no longer had to divide her attention between two men. At Merton Place, Emma, Horatia and Nelson spent several blissful months together.

Then duty called once more – Nelson seemed to know it would be his last mission. Before engaging the French fleet at Trafalgar, he wrote a will bequeathing Emma and Horatia to the nation. After Nelson's death, Britons chose to distinguish between Nelson's professional and personal legacies: while heaping posthumous honours on their hero, they totally ignored his mistress and daughter. Emma spent all her money drinking, gambling and giving wild parties. She sold her home – and Nelson's relics – to survive, but still spent nine months in a debtors' prison. Later, she moved to a farmhouse outside Calais, France, and sent her daughter to an English school. Drunk, fat and shapeless, Emma died in 1813, aged 50.

E.Z. and I.W. (Lists 8, 17)

❧ Sir Isaac Newton
25 December 1642 to 20 March 1727

Newton was born three months after the death of his father, a poor farmer. Until he was three years old, he had no rivals for the love and attention of his mother Hannah. Then she married Barnabas Smith, a minister, and the couple moved away to a nearby village. Newton was left in his grandmother's care for the next eight years. He remained devoted to his mother, even in the face of apparent abandonment, but hated his stepfather. Later, he remembered 'threatening my father and mother Smith to burne them and the house over them'. Hannah had three children by Smith. When Smith died, she and 11-year-old Isaac were reunited. Perhaps his fixation on her developed new dimensions at that point. Anyway, she remained the central figure in his life.

Newton became a recluse, an absentminded, ascetic and devoted scientist, often simply forgetting to sleep or eat.

He apparently felt some sort of tender feelings for Anne Storey, the stepdaughter of a family he boarded with while he was at school. They may have been formally engaged for a short time, but almost certainly did not have a sexual relationship. They parted in 1661, when Newton went to Cambridge, but remained good, if distant, friends over the years.

Students of Newton are divided about his sex life. Some insist he died a virgin. Others, referring to rumours circulating during and after his life, believe that he had at least one great love affair. It seems that Newton did indeed love Fatio de Duillier, a handsome young Swiss mathematician. The two men were inseparable companions for several years, starting in 1687, when Fatio was 23. They shared a burning interest in science and mathematics – whether they also shared a bed is speculation. For reasons known only to themselves, Newton and Fatio broke off their relationship in 1693. They exchanged occasional letters for the rest of their lives, but the friendship remained distant. For the next eighteen months, Newton suffered a complete mental breakdown. He was depressed and hostile, and had delusions that his friends had abandoned him. He retaliated by writing poisonous letters, accusing them of betrayal and deceit. To John Locke he wrote, 'Sir, being of opinion that you endeavoured to embroil me with women and by other means, I was so much affected by it . . . 'twere better if you were dead.' When Locke calmly and kindly replied, Newton apologized, explaining he had been delirious from lack of sleep and didn't know what he was writing.

A rather mysterious 'love triangle' developed between the young, witty and beautiful Catherine Barton, Newton's niece who lived in his London home for over twenty years, Charles Montague and Newton. Contemporary observers believed that Newton may have connived at an affair between Catherine and the increasingly influential Montague (later Lord Halifax) in order to gain a highly paid position as Master of the Mint. Later historians, putting the theories of Freud to work, have suggested that Newton enjoyed the affair between Montague and Catherine because he identified with Montague and saw Catherine as an embodiment of his own mother. He could thereby enjoy a vicarious sexual relationship with his mother, who, though she had deserted him early in life, he loved deeply. Some have even suggested that he himself actually had an affair with Catherine. The most reasonable consensus, however, seems to be that Newton had no sexual interest in women.

R.W.S. (Lists 15, 29)

♣ Friedrich Nietzsche
15 October 1844 to 25 August 1900

Nietzsche was one of the most important philosophers of modern times, best known for his great work *Thus Spake Zarathustra*. His controversial theories included the idea of the 'superman' – the healthy, virile, noble man who achieves his highest potential through individualism, shunning all dogma and tradition. Nietzsche's reputation was distorted when his work became wrongly associated with Nazi thought, although he himself despised anti-Semitism in any form. Nietzsche was born into a moral, upright, prudent German family. When his father died four years later, the boy was left in a household of women: mother, sister, aunts. Shy, studious and precocious, he showed early signs of genius. He also began to show the ill-health that was to torture him all his life. At only 26, he became a professor of philology. But after several years his migraines and failing eyesight became so painful that he gave up his post and, with a pension from the University of Basel, devoted himself to writing. Increasingly stricken by his headaches, he spent much of his life travelling Europe, visiting one health resort after another and writing in solitude. One highlight of his youth was his friendship with the composer Richard Wagner and his wife Cosima. Nietzsche was so often at odds with his own mother and sister that the Wagners were, in a way, the first family he had ever known. However, half from a need for independence, and half from revulsion at Wagner's bigotry and anti-Semitism, he completely broke with him. In 1889, when Nietzsche was 45, he collapsed in tears on a street in Turin, after flinging his arms round the neck of a cab horse that was being mistreated by its owner. For the next eleven years, he lived in a lunatic asylum, and under the care of his mother and sister.

There are two versions of Nietzsche's sex life, one constructed by scholars and biographers, the other a torrid outpouring from Nietzsche himself, written in the asylum while he was suffering from a creeping paralysis probably caused by syphilis. These steaming notes were smuggled out of the asylum by a patient, and not published until 1951, fifty years after Nietzsche wrote them, under the title *My Sister And I*. Because he was mad when they were written, it is impossible to say where reality finishes and fantasy begins. True or not, they shed a startling light on the great man's psyche. The accepted version of Nietzsche's *amours* is as follows.

As a young man, the timid, intellectual Nietzsche had no romances – he was in love with ideas. But he did visit prostitutes once or twice, and thus contracted syphilis. In *My Sister And I* he wrote, 'I did a great deal of maturing in Leipzig, a vast amount of masturbating, and not nearly as much whoring as I should have.' Wagner thought Nietzsche's nervous state of mind was due to too much masturbation, and advised cold showers.

Nietzsche's first 'love' was Cosima Wagner, although he gave no indication of his feelings during their friendship. After his collapse in Turin, he sent her a note which read, 'Ariadne, I love you.' (He likened himself to Dionysus.) When brought to the asylum he told the doctors, 'My wife, Cosima Wagner, has brought me here.'

In 1876, when Nietzsche was 32, he spent some time in Geneva where he met a Dutch girl named Mathilde Trampedach. After knowing her for only a few days, he proposed to her by letter the last night of his stay. It was a formal, not very passionate, letter, and she refused him. He wrote in *My Sister And I*, 'I was terrified at the thought that she might accept my rash proposal. . . . But the stars favoured me that day, and the pretty Dutch girl turned me down.'

331

When Nietzsche was 38, he met the great love of his life, Lou Andreas-Salomé. His friend and fellow philosopher Paul Rée introduced the 20-year-old Russian girl, who years later became Rilke's mistress and Freud's confidante. She was rather plain, but very bright and independent. She was impressed with Nietzsche's elegant and gracious manners, and appreciated his genius. The three of them developed a friendship and they excitedly made plans for a study group based on Nietzsche's ideas. They called themselves the 'Trinity' and decided to live together. The group was to be entirely intellectual – the baseness of passion would not enter into it. But Rée and Nietzsche both fell in love with Lou. Neither one admitted it, and they began to live together in assorted, changing alliances which added to their problems. Neither Rée nor Nietzsche ever made love with Lou – in fact, she probably remained a virgin for several years after her marriage to a theologian.

Deeper trouble started when Nietzsche tried to create a friendship between Lou and Nietzsche's sister Elizabeth, who was bossy and possessive about her brother and no intellectual competition for Lou. Elizabeth had never had any grasp of Nietzsche's philosophical ideas and later slanted them to suit her own anti-Semitism. She even forged letters and documents in her brother's hand. A complicated quarrel ensued between Elizabeth and Lou: Elizabeth denounced their ménage à trois – and Lou said it had been her brother's wish all along to drag sex into it. (Rée encouraged Lou to think this.) Tortured letters and recriminations ensued, which nearly drove Nietzsche mad with anguish and rage. Though he had once called Lou 'the most intelligent of women', he now referred to her in a letter to a friend as 'that scraggy dirty she-monkey with her false breasts'. The break with Lou and Rée was final – yet Nietzsche still loved them, and missed Lou desperately. Though he was now aligned with his sister, it didn't last long. She had married an ardent anti-Semite, Dr Bernhard Foerster, and gone off with him to South America to start a German colony based on the proto-Nazi principles of Aryan supremacy. That was too much for Nietzsche and, though there was a later reconciliation, it was only superficial.

There ended Nietzsche's love life. Not until he reached the lunatic asylum and wrote *My Sister And I* did the sexually repressed philosopher pour forth his regrets and lust like a burst dam. His most shocking confession was his story of incest with his sister. He said it began when she crawled into his bed on the night their baby brother died. She made a habit of playing with

332

his genitals 'as if they were special toys of hers', 'She haunted the world of my senses with those marvellous fingers of hers, driving me to a premature and hopeless awakening. So that for a whole spasm of my life I was unable to think of beauty or pleasure except in terms of her eyes and her damnably wonderful fingers. So refurbishing my life that in place of the strange goddess who visits the imagination of every normal adolescent I could only look forward to headaches and a sister.' He said this love-play lasted into their adolescence. The crowning point of his shame came when his Aunt Rosalie called him to her deathbed, and told him she knew everything.

Next he wrote, 'There have been, in all, four women in my life. The only two who brought me an approximate amount of happiness were prostitutes. Elizabeth was beautiful enough, but she was my sister. Lou was intelligent enough (a little too intelligent sometimes), but she refused to marry me.'

He then told the story of his first love affair – not with a prostitute, but with a married woman – a blonde, nymphomaniacal countess. The 30-year-old countess, trying 'to quench the flame of her uterine passion', seduced the 15-year-old boy. Sexually hungry, yet castrating and cruel, the countess goaded Nietzsche until he grabbed a riding whip and flogged her. She was aroused by the taste of the whip. This led Nietzsche to conclude that 'cruelty does not quiet down the lust of a woman, but on the contrary intensifies it to a fever pitch'. One night, he wrote, she sneaked into his school dormitory disguised as a man, and beat him with a blunt instrument. As he was about to pass out, she became excited, and made love to him. She further humiliated him by being on top during the sex act. His next encounter, he wrote, was with a prostitute – a sultry, brunette 'semi-Indian girl'. It was passionate, erotic and satisfying – but, alas, she gave him syphilis.

There are also pages of grief over Lou Andreas-Salomé – references to having made love to her (untrue, of course), fantasies about her body, and promises that if he ever recovered from his illness he would *act out* his philosophy, and thrill her with his manliness. He called Lou his good angel warring with his bad angel, Elizabeth. And finally he wrote, 'Having been separated from the love of my life (Lou), the love that made me human, I made my desperate plunge into the fires of madness. . . .' Most of all, the mad philosopher wrote that he wanted a woman – any woman. But it was too late.

A.W. (Lists 9, 18, 20, 24, 39, 40)

333

✤ Waslaw Nijinsky
12 March 1890 to 8 April 1950

During his brief but glorious career as premier danseur of the Imperial Russian Ballet at St Petersburg's Maryinsky Theatre and of Diaghilev's Ballets Russes, Nijinsky performed the leading male roles in such works as *Le Spectre de la Rose*, *Petrouchka* and his masterpiece, *Le Sacre du Printemps*. Rejecting the conventional forms of classical ballet, he perfected leaps in which he appeared to hang in mid-air. His daringly original choreography and dramatic acting spurred the art of ballet to great heights, and earned him a reputation as a genius.

The son of dancers, Nijinsky was born in Kiev, in the Ukraine. 'A delicate child, awkward, temperamentally backward and slow thinking', he began dancing early, and by the age of three was touring with his parents' troupe. As a student he demonstrated unparalleled ability, and once performed ten entrechats – crossing and uncrossing the legs – in a single jump. When Nijinsky was 9, his father deserted the family in favour of a pregnant mistress. His mother urged him all the harder to excel in dance, since a ballet career would ensure money and prestige. He graduated from St Petersburg's Imperial School of Dancing in the spring of 1907, and joined the Imperial Russian Ballet as a soloist. In 1909, he met dance impresario Sergei Diaghilev. When he danced in Paris with the Ballets Russes, he created a sensation. In 1911, Nijinsky was dismissed from the Imperial Ballet for appearing on stage without his full costume. He was promptly offered a place in the Ballets Russes. There, Nijinsky choreographed and danced his most legendary roles. *L'Après-midi d'un Faune* created a minor scandal in 1912; in the final scene Nijinsky simulated masturbation. The police warned him to rewrite the scene or risk having the show closed. He refused to change the passage, but no performances were actually raided.

In 1913, he married Countess Romola de Pulszky. The marriage offended Diaghilev so much that he dismissed his star. Nijinsky then formed his own dance troupe, which toured for about a year, appearing in London and America. But Nijinsky was no businessman, and the company failed. During the First World War, he was imprisoned in Austria-Hungary on charges of spying for Russia. Forbidden to perform, he did not resume his career until 1916. He again toured, but in 1919, at 29, Nijinsky had a nervous breakdown. He stopped dancing, was plagued by insomnia, headaches, persecution mania, schizophrenia and depression. Until his death from kidney disease in 1950, he lived most of his last 30 years in a Swiss mental institution.

Nijinsky's tumultuous love life contributed significantly to his insanity. He was passive in love, perhaps because he reserved his full vitality for the stage. A naive and beautiful young man, Nijinsky began an intimate relationship with 30-year-old Prince Pavel Dmitrievich Lvov in 1908. Tall, blue-eyed and handsome, Lvov was instantly attracted to the muscular Nijinsky. The prince initiated his friend into the intoxicating delights of nightclub life, and also gave him his first homosexual experience. However, Lvov was disappointed with the dancer's small penis; as one biographer described him, 'Nijinsky was small in a part where size is usually admired.' The prince was not possessive, and even arranged Nijinsky's first sexual experience with a woman – a prostitute. He was frightened and repelled by the encounter.

Lvov was generous and won the heart of his lover. But after a few months the prince withdrew, having tired of the dancer he considered just 'another of his toys'. Before they parted, however, Lvov introduced Nijinsky to Sergei Diaghilev. Twenty years older than Nijinsky, Diaghilev was an unabashed homosexual whose only experience with a woman (his 18-year-old cousin) had resulted in venereal disease. The two men became lovers. Nijinsky had grown accustomed to being passed around, but his initial lovemaking with Diaghilev disturbed him. 'I trembled like a leaf,' wrote Nijinsky. 'I hated him, but pretended. . . .' 'Chinchilla', as Diaghilev was called because of the white streak in his dyed black hair, stripped his lover of independence. He scrutinized Nijinsky's personal and professional life, and warned him against sleeping with women – such acts would impair his dancing. So persuasive was Diaghilev that Nijinsky once turned down an offer from Isadora Duncan, whom he met in Venice in 1909. She had suggested to Nijinsky that he father her next baby. Diaghilev repeatedly encouraged his lover to consent to a ménage à trois with a young boy, but Nijinsky was already finding the sex act extremely difficult with even one person. By 23, he felt he was growing too old to be Diaghilev's 'boy'. In September 1913, while the Ballets Russes was en route to South America aboard the SS *Avon*, Nijinsky became engaged to coquettish Romola de Pulszky. She was 23, the daughter of Hungarian actress Emilia Markus. Romola had been pursuing Nijinsky for months, and

335

even took up ballet in order to be near him. According to Hungarian tradition, an engagement authorized freedom to indulge in premarital sex. But, whether because of Nijinsky's shyness, the language barrier or Nijinsky's emphatic desire for a proper Catholic wedding, they did not make love until after their wedding in 1913. Diaghilev was surprised and insulted, and retaliated by dismissing Nijinsky. He refused to answer his former lover's letters. Soon after the marriage, Nijinsky gained another admirer, the Duchess of Durcal, a beautiful redhead, who fell so hard for him that she offered herself as his mistress. Romola agreed, and Nijinsky had sex with the duchess. He regretted it later, saying, 'I am sorry for what I did. It was unfair to her, as I am not in love. . . .'

As Nijinsky's mental health deteriorated, he and Romola slept apart. Sometimes he would slip out at night and walk the streets, searching for prostitutes – just to talk. He would return home, sexually aroused by these women, and masturbate in his bedroom '. . . in order to protect myself from catching a venereal disease'. Romola had the first of their two daughters in 1914 – the second was born in 1920 – and a few years after that Diaghilev re-entered Nijinsky's life. Romola objected to this, and even brought a 500,000 franc lawsuit against him, as compensation for her husband's past performances in the Ballets Russes. She won the suit, but Diaghilev never paid. Instead, he made an overt move to win back Nijinsky. She pulled one way, Diaghilev pulled the other, and Nijinsky, no longer dancing and with no outlet for his frustrations, lapsed into catatonia.

A.K. and K.P. (Lists 5, 12, 14, 20, 24)

♣ Aristotle Onassis
20 January 1906 to 15 March 1975

Onassis was the son of a prosperous Greek tobacco merchant in Smyrna, Turkey. A likeable but rebellious youth, he was suspended from several schools, once for pinching the backside of a woman teacher. In 1922, the Turks launched brutal attacks on the resident Greek population, and 16-year-old Onassis and family fled to Athens. Although he hoped to emigrate to the USA, he was discouraged by the thought of having to wait for several years; instead, he set sail for Argentina. He arrived in Buenos

Aires with only a few hundred dollars in his pockets. By means of personal daring and business acumen, he first established himself in the tobacco business and then branched out to his real love, shipping. He became a millionaire at 25, and through investments in shipping – especially oil tankers – he amassed one of the great personal fortunes of the postwar era.

As a youngster, Onassis was sexually precocious. He had to be restrained from seducing the family laundress at the age of 11. A few years later, he received his initiation from his 25-year-old French teacher whose scanty dress, owing to the scorching weather, fired his lust. 'Mademoiselle, you are arousing me against my will . . . nothing can stop me from violating you!' The women of Argentina found Onassis, with his intense dark eyes, equally irresistible. Later, as a young man about town, he savoured New York City night life during the 1940s in the company of his tall blonde mistress, Ingeborg Dedichen. Ingeborg was an aristocrat who helped advance Onassis's career as well as teach him the social graces. Of this period Ingeborg has written: '. . . he would lick between the toes. . . . He would embrace every part of my body and cover me with kisses. . . .' Yet, passionate though Onassis was, this affair descended into a series of beatings administered by the jealous Onassis and an attempted suicide by Ingeborg.

Following a brief Hollywood fling with a number of screen stars, Onassis finally married for the first time at 40. Tina Livanos, the petite 17-year-old daughter of a rival shipowner, was to bear his two children, Alexandra and Christina. But this idyllic existence was shattered by the appearance of the greatest love of his life, opera singer Maria Callas (q.v.). When Greek meets Greek, the result is a tug of war, but, in the case of Callas and Onassis, it was love at first sight. Their affair was conducted openly, and they understood each other emotionally, intellectually and sexually. Although opera bored him, Onassis enjoyed the worldwide success and fame of his fiery lover. They never married, but they remained close to each other until the day of Onassis's death.

In 1968, Aristotle Onassis (who had been divorced from Tina for some years) stunned the world by wedding the beautiful widow of a beloved, slain president of the USA. Onassis had known Jackie Kennedy casually for some time, but it was thought he was 'too short, too old, too dark, and too coarse' to be a suitable successor to John F. Kennedy. The eyes of the world

337

focused on Skorpios, the site of the wedding, and from that moment on, this May–December couple (Jackie was a generation younger than Ari) found themselves bathed in an unending glare of publicity. The text of the pre-nuptial contract allegedly contained over one hundred clauses, covering everything from money to sleeping arrangements. A steward formerly employed by Onassis claimed that the contract provided for separate bedrooms for the couple at all times and released Jackie from any obligation to bear Onassis's children. Onassis offered affection and the protection of wealth to a woman who had been shattered by the violent death not only of her husband but of her brother-in-law as well. In return, Jackie offered Ari warmth and the companionship of one of the most glamorous of women. But their carefully constructed relationship was soon shattered by the death of Onassis's only son. Thrown into a deep depression, Onassis could no longer indulge Jackie's extravagant and capricious ways. He turned to Callas for comfort and contemplated a divorce. However, death in the form of myasthenia gravis put an end to his plans.

Onassis could be described as a 'roaring' heterosexual. His boudoir humour tended towards the explicit. Once he asked Ingeborg Dedichen to examine him for piles. As she investigated, Onassis wafted a not so gentle breeze in her startled face. On another occasion, when harassed by a photographer, Onassis took him into the gents', where he said he would show him the secret of success. Unzipping his fly, he revealed an asset that may best be described as physical rather than fiscal.

J.M.M. (Lists 2, 4, 22, 25, 39)

♣ La Belle Otero
4 November 1868 to 10 April 1965

Often called the last of the great courtesans, La Belle Otero (or Caroline Otero) was the professional name of Augustina Otero Iglesias, from Valga in Galician Spain. Officially she was a dancer, singer and actress in the world's music halls, but really she was mistress of some of the most famous men in the world. During her lifetime, she made and lost approximately $25 million.

The illiterate daughter of the town prostitute, Otero grew up fatherless and in poverty. At 11, she was brutally raped by the village shoemaker, who had become excited by her dancing. This left her with a broken pelvis, unable to bear children. She left Valga the next year and wandered to Barcelona, realizing, like so many young girls before her, that prostitution was the only way to survive.

When 14, she met a Catalan named Paco Colli, who had been a dancer all his life. He taught Otero the ways of the stage – dancing, singing, acting – and became her pimp, since she had to continue sleeping with men to support Paco and herself. Paco also took her to the French Riviera where, in 1889, he decided to marry Otero. She declined and instead became a music hall star and courtesan until she retired more than twenty-five years later. In her heyday, Otero was as famous as any Hollywood star. Of her American debut on 1 October 1890, the New York *Tribune* headline declared, 'Otero Conquers New York'. A reviewer for *The New York Times* marvelled, 'She appears to dance all over. Every muscle, from her dainty toes to the crown of her head, is brought into play, and the consequent contortions are wonderful and, at times, startling.' A compulsive gambler, she occasionally mixed business with pleasure. An employee at the casino in Monte Carlo maintained that Otero, broke, went to bed at a nearby hotel with eleven men. He added that she never spent more than half an hour away from the gaming tables during this marathon. In her lifetime, she lost an estimated $20 million at the casino. Asked what she would have otherwise done with that money, Otero replied, 'I might have endowed a university for prostitutes. Think of the variety of courses we could have offered.'

It was said that she was a nymphomaniac, and sought to punish men in retaliation for her childhood rape. In any case, Otero was a strikingly beautiful woman, 5 feet 10 inches tall, with measurements of 38–21–36. Her face was oval, her hair black and silky, her teeth white. Her friend, French writer Colette, said that Otero's breasts 'were of curious shape, reminding one of elongated lemons, firm and upturned at the tips'. An anonymous source added that Otero's breasts 'preceded her by a quarter of an hour'. The coarse edge to her speech titillated her patrons, and she believed in always making a man feel like a king in the bedroom, whether he was royalty or not. In her prime, Otero charged $10,000, or the equivalent in jewellery, for a night of her services.

According to Otero's autobiography, in 1898 a group of men

with whom she had been having affairs for several years gathered to give her a birthday party. The guest list included King Leopold II of Belgium, Prince Nicholas I of Montenegro, Prince Albert of Monaco, the Grand Duke Nikolai of Russia and Albert, Prince of Wales, who would become King Edward VII.

Otero made love with Baron Lepic in a hot-air balloon floating two hundred feet over the river Aude in France. On 15 June 1902 the New York *World* reported that 'the gondola remained high above the earth for more than an hour'. Sixty years later, Otero purred, 'It was an experience every woman should enjoy.'

Otero did not limit herself to royalty. William K. Vanderbilt, of the eminent American family, offered Otero a yacht and showered her with $250,000 worth of jewels, including the pearl necklace Napoleon III had given the Empress Eugénie.

Her five-year affair with the Shah of Persia brought many jewels. 'He was a dirty, smelly old man, and very strange in his desires,' she recalled. 'He visited me every afternoon at two o'clock and left at five. Ten minutes later one of his servants would be at the door to hand my maid a gold, inlaid cassette, lined with velvet. It contained a single jewel but a very magnificent stone – diamond, ruby, pearl, jade or emerald, some worth as much as 25,000 francs. I would remove the jewel and return the box.'

Otero later wrote that she did not always enjoy sex, but was unfailingly hospitable. In the 1890s, Prince Albert of Monaco earned low marks because he had trouble getting an erection. Eventually he did, and Otero told him he was 'formidable' – whereupon he 'strutted around the room'. The grateful Albert set her up in a choice apartment and gave her jewellery worth more than $300,000. 'He was not a very virile man and I don't think he got his money's worth,' Otero concluded. 'But, as long as he didn't care, neither did I, and he seemed to enjoy taking me where we could be seen together publicly.'

In 1894, Prince Nicholas of Montenegro (who would become his country's first and last king) moved into the flat Albert had given Otero. The lissom prince was in his early fifties, and their relationship lasted several years. After presenting Otero with 'a simply gorgeous diamond bracelet and at least five . . . beautiful watches', he persuaded her to visit his palace. Otero later complained, 'I saw practically nothing the whole trip . . . all the Prince wanted to do was to make love to me so I obliged.' Sixty-year-old King Leopold II of Belgium 'was not very generous at the start but I taught him how to give. He was an apt student.' They met in 1894, and were part-time lovers for three or four years. Leopold, said Otero, gave her several lush residences.

One of the richest men in the world, Nicholas II, Czar of Russia, had a bad complexion and rarely bathed – 'he really stank'. He was still shaken from an assassination attempt six years earlier: 'There were always half-a-dozen huge, black-bearded armed guards at our bedroom door, some more at every window, and, if there was a rear exit, he'd have half a regiment posted there. It almost felt like I was undressing in an army barracks or a bull-fighting arena. If I moved a chair suddenly or dropped a perfume bottle, Nick would jump out of bed screaming with fright.' But Otero 'grew quite fond of him' even though 'he had the strangest views about sex'.

When Otero returned to Paris in September 1897, Prince Bertie was waiting. 'He was surprisingly virile and generous', but he had to disappoint her one night in London when his official mistress, Lillie Langtry, arrived.

The Khedive of Cairo saw her perform and, after three torrid days in his palace, gave her a ten-carat diamond ring with a setting of twelve pearls worth half a million francs at the time.

In Monte Carlo in 1905, Otero 'deflowered' 19-year-old King Alfonso XIII of Spain. 'He was rather aloof at first,' she remembered, 'but I taught him how to relax.' In 1913, at the age of 27, he set the 44-year-old Otero up in Madrid in the last apartment she would ever occupy courtesy of a royal client.

Otero's 40th birthday found her with a new lover – Aristide Briand, later France's greatest statesman and winner of the 1926 Nobel Peace Prize. Otero, sensing his future greatness (because his appearance did not foretell such a future) said, 'He was ... hideously ugly. He was fat. He dressed like a slob – often there'd be remains of an omelette on his vest – his nails were black, but there was a fascination to him I never found in any other man.' He could only afford 'an occasional cheap jewel and flowers,' Otero recalled. 'Once ... he made love to me eight times before morning. And he was 50 years old at the time.' Their affair lasted ten years.

When La Belle Otero retired in 1914, she had a fortune and, for a while, the money kept coming, occasionally from secret benefactors. In 1935, at 66, she was still attractive, but age eventually crept up on her and her money disappeared in the casinos. She was alone when she died of a heart attack aged 97 in

Nice. Otero never had any regrets about her life. 'I have been a slave to my passions,' she admitted, 'but never to a man.'

A.L.G. and L.S. (Lists 2, 16, 19, 22, 24, 39, 41, 42, 43, 46)

❧ Nicolò Paganini
27 October 1782 to 27 May 1840

The most renowned violinist of the nineteenth century, Paganini was encouraged by his father, an amateur musician, and quickly outstripped all the available teachers in Genoa. Having studied and practised assiduously in his youth, Paganini never picked up the violin as an adult except for a rehearsal or a concert, or to tune it. 'I have laboured enough to acquire my talent,' he said. 'It is time I should rest myself.'

A gambler and womanizer, Paganini was nevertheless adored not only in Italy but all over Europe. In Vienna, shop windows were filled with a variety of goods all adorned with his portrait. The local royal family usually attended his concerts wherever he appeared, and his musical skills attracted numerous female admirers. His reputation for licentiousness and his physical appearance – pale, waxen face and long, dark, stringy hair – encouraged detractors, as did his habit of wearing an enormous cloak to ward off a chill, even in summer. Paganini suffered from poor health all his life, and finally died of a degenerative disease of the larynx. Legends had circulated that Paganini was not only in league with the devil but had been imprisoned for murder, and consequently his burial in consecrated ground was delayed for five years.

Paganini was 40 before he looked for anything in a woman other than large breasts, a small waist and slender ankles. Although he often said that he wanted to marry, a peaceful domestic liaison eluded him all his life. The musician's existence took on a peculiar pattern revolving around his concert tours, sexual adventures and flagging health. After playing a number of concerts, he would retreat, usually with a woman, to restore his energy and spirits. The first of these was a Tuscan lady of rank who fell in love with him around the turn of the century and whisked him off to her chalet.

When Elise Bonaparte Baciocchi – Napoleon's sister and the Princess of Lucca – appointed him director of music at Piombino

342

in 1805, many suspected he was fiddling with more than his violin. He also spent much of his time with an unidentified woman said to be a lady-in-waiting and far more beautiful than the difficult, plain princess. While Elise took siestas after lunch, Paganini slipped through a side door of the palace to rendezvous with this mysterious lover. He left the court in 1813 to devote his time to concerts.

While Paganini's violin playing was admirable, his treatment of women was not. The sole exception was his first love, Eleanor de Lucca, the one person outside his family remembered in his will. The harshest treatment befell 17-year-old Angelina Cavanna, whom Paganini met in Genoa in 1808. A tailor's daughter, the lovely Angelina insisted on marriage before sleeping with him. Paganini allegedly agreed to her terms, but enticed her to travel with him to a small Italian city, ostensibly to be married. There was no marriage and, when Angelina became pregnant, Paganini abandoned her. (The baby was stillborn.) Later he was sued by Angelina's father and thrown into prison. In his defence, Paganini claimed that the girl had lived in 'great liberty' before she knew him and became his companion voluntarily. Paganini's longest liaison was with dancer Antonia Bianchi. The tempestuous relationship began in 1815 and ended thirteen years later when her jealousy provoked violence. He paid her 2000 scudi to renounce her rights to their son, Achille, and leave him in peace.

Simply seeing a beautiful woman could drive the violinist to distraction and he would go to incredible lengths to woo her, always with sex in mind. Even when he was older, Paganini could inspire passion in women both personally and through his concert performances. One German baroness left her husband for Paganini. He ultimately rejected her and she retreated to a convent and died alone and forgotten decades later. The musician himself was not fated to be lonely, but the only true harmony he ever found was in his music.

M.O. and E.K. (List 42)

♣ Louis Pasteur
27 December 1822 to 28 September 1895

Pasteur, French chemist and microbiologist, was the first to use vaccines for rabies, anthrax and chicken cholera. He saved the beer, wine and silk industries of France and other countries with his work on fermentation, and invented pasteurization.

Pasteur virtually lived his life in university laboratories. Working as a professor of chemistry at the University of Strasbourg, Pasteur married the university rector's daughter, Marie Laurent, in May 1849, and the Pasteurs were very happy. Marie agreed that the laboratory should come before everything else. Only the early deaths of three of their five children marred their marriage. Pasteur's last twenty-four hours were spent on his deathbed with one hand holding a crucifix and the other hand resting in his wife's hand.

A.W. and J.M. (List 33)

♣ Adelina Patti
19 February 1843 to 27 September 1919

A coloratura soprano, Patti reigned for fifty-six years as undisputed queen of world opera, the most popular and richest prima donna of the late nineteenth century.

She came from a musical family. Her father was Sicilian, her mother Roman, and Adela Juana Maria Patti was born in Madrid while her parents were on tour. She was only a few years old when her father moved the family from Italy to America, where he helped manage New York's Astor Place Opera House. Patti made her US singing debut at the age of 8. She sang at Covent Garden in *La Sonnambula* at 18, and was an overnight sensation. Soon she took Europe by storm. She could sing a role to herself twice and know it, and at the height of her career had a repertoire of forty-two operas. Chiefs of state showered her with diamonds. In 1881, using her own luxurious private railway carriage, she began to give concerts (at $5000 a performance) around the USA featuring popular songs like 'Comin' Thro' the Rye'. Summoned to Windsor Castle, Patti sang 'Home, Sweet Home' for Queen Victoria, who wept at its conclusion. On another occasion, Jenny Lind was also moved to tears upon hearing Patti. Verdi proclaimed Patti the greatest singer he had ever heard. In her prime, Patti was described by an admiring critic as a young woman with a 'delicately chiselled head, fine mobile features, and the guileless eyes of a doe – white marble turned into flesh, surrounded by a dark frame of hair'. Poorly educated, Patti was not intellectual. A friend said he 'never perceived in Adelina the least interest in the higher problems of mankind'.

The major interest in her life, next to singing, was men. In 1868, when she was 25, she married Henri, Marquis de Caux, equerry to Napoleon III. The emperor had seen Patti perform in Paris, and had sent the marquis backstage to convey his congratulations. Middle-aged, dapper, refined – but with an income of only ten thousand francs a year – Henri became infatuated. She liked him, and the idea of a title, but she never loved him. At their Catholic wedding Patti wore a virginal white satin gown, though she was already sexually experienced. A guest at the wedding breakfast was Giovanni Mario, the handsome 58-year-old Italian tenor who had played opposite Patti in many operas. During the breakfast, Mario leaned over to British music critic Sutherland Edwards and whispered, 'The marquis, much as he might be attached to his fascinating bride, has never made love to her as much as I, her constant lover, have done.'

The marriage produced no passion and no children. After seven years Patti fell in love with her new leading man, the Italian tenor Ernest Nicolini, to the distress of his wife and five children. The Marquis de Caux was furious. He forbade his wife to appear on a stage with Nicolini again. Patti ignored her husband and the two starred in *La Traviata* in St Petersburg. Enraged, the marquis cornered Patti in her dressing room and shouted that her adultery had besmirched the title he had brought her. 'You can take your title back!' Patti cried, scooping up a handful of jewellery and throwing it in his face. The marquis hit her. She screamed. Stagehands had to break down her door to evict her husband. The pair separated in 1877. It took Patti eight years to get a French divorce, and then only after she agreed to give the marquis half her fortune. His share came to one and half million francs. Even before the divorce, Patti and Nicolini had been living together in Craig-y-Nos Castle on their magnificent rural estate in south Wales. His billiard room was illuminated by the first electric lights to be installed in a country house in Britain, and she had her private theatre. He was 52, she 43, when they finally married in a Protestant ceremony in June 1886. The happy union lasted a dozen years, until Nicolini's death in 1898. Less than a year later, Patti, almost 56, married her third husband, Baron Rolf Cederström of Stockholm, thirty years her junior. They remained together until her death nineteen years later. The baron lived until 1947.

Adelina Patti was not as sexually straight as she seemed. Occasionally, she desired something different in a heterosexual partner. One day in 1882, when 39, she was riding in her carriage in New York, gazing out at the shop-fronts, when she saw Bunnell's Curiosity Dime Museum. Something in the window caught her attention. She stopped her carriage, stepped down and walked across. She stared at a photograph advertising the appearance of an attractive male midget named General Mite. The midget's actual name was Dudley Foster, and he came from Nova Scotia. He was 20 years old, less than two feet tall – actually, his height was twenty-two inches – and he weighed ten pounds. Something about him excited Patti. She went into the museum, and told Foster she would like to take him home for a while. The midget was delighted. Patti made arrangements with the proprietor and carted the tiny Foster off to her boudoir. Their subsequent bizarre affair was the talk of show business for years.

I.W. (Lists 6, 25, 42)

♣ Cora Pearl
1835 to 8 July 1886

Despite her poor manners, incomprehensible French and penchant for cruel practical jokes, Pearl enjoyed a long reign as the most popular courtesan in the Paris of Napoleon III.

Cora was born Emma Elizabeth Crouch to a family of sixteen children in Devon. Her father was a musical director and the composer of 'Kathleen Mavoureen', a popular ballad which he sold for £20. Cora, however, did not sell herself so cheaply, and the time came when a single night with her cost ten thousand francs. The age at which Cora began her career is uncertain; she was apparently young enough to be lured into a low-class pub by promises of sweets. There, a merchant gave the naive girl her first taste of gin. When she woke up in his bed the next day, he gave her £5. Thus, she began her career. That same day, she left home and soon began an apprenticeship in a London brothel, whence she moved to Paris, where she worked independently. Among her customers were the wealthiest and most powerful men of her day, whom she collectively called her 'Golden Chain' of lovers. Later in life, Cora wrote her memoirs and sent excerpts to former clients, offering to delete certain parts for money. The extortion was apparently a success, for the published version made dull reading. Cora liked practical jokes. She once lured a prominent Parisian into a compromising position in her bedroom, only to throw open the closet doors and reveal a contingent of his friends. Another time Cora gave a dinner party at which she was brought naked on a silver platter to win a bet. She had wagered she could serve 'a meat nobody could cut'. She was plain, but she had beautiful skin and hair and her body was one of the most perfect in France, so she earned a vast fortune. Ironically, when Cora died of cancer at the age of 51, she was penniless and alone.

Cora arrived in Paris in 1858 with the proprietor of the Argyle Rooms, a seedy London brothel where she had perfected her skills. The trip was for pleasure rather than business, but duty eventually called and Cora's patron returned to England without her. She took up with a sailor, but when he shipped out she was fortunate enough to meet a mysterious man known as 'Roubisse', who procured for her the first in her 'Golden Chain'.

For six years she was mistress to Victor Massena, third Duc de Rivoli. The staid aristocrat indulged her every whim, yet Cora later described him as 'the man who received the least in return'. Throughout their relationship, which ended in 1869, she had many other lovers. One of these was 17-year-old Prince Achille Murat, a greatnephew of Napoleon I. While the young man was not rich, Cora helped him spend what money he did have. He fought (and won) a duel over Cora's bills once, and got so badly into debt that Emperor Napoleon III sent him to Africa.

Once Cora herself fought a duel with Marthe de Vère, over a good-looking Serbian prince. Riding whips were the weapons. Both Cora and Marthe remained in seclusion for a week to let their face wounds heal. The prince, in the meantime, disappeared. After Murat the next link in Cora's Golden Chain was William, Prince of Orange, heir to the Dutch throne. The Prince of Orange had little besides money, and Cora found him tiresome. However, a woman who would bathe nude in a champagne-filled, silver tub in front of her dinner guests might find most men tiresome. Cora was ice-skating when she was picked up by the Duc de Morny, the second most powerful man in France – the emperor's half brother. 'Cora on the ice?' he said to her. 'What an antithesis!' She replied, 'Well, since the ice is broken, take me for a drink.' De Morny was a stepping stone to Prince Napoleon, known to his friends as Plon-Plon, who fell in love with Cora. The prince installed her in a grand house and gave her twelve thousand francs monthly. But her crude manners and coarse-accented French annoyed the prince at times, as did her habit of entertaining hordes of men. During one party, when Cora was the

347

only woman at a table full of male admirers, she coyly remarked, 'There is only one of you with whom I am still a virgin.'

Although there is no conclusive evidence that Plon-Plon's cousin, Napoleon III, was among Cora's lovers, it is reasonable to assume that he was. It was a rare man indeed who did not sample Cora's perfect body, and it is unlikely that the emperor overlooked her.

For a time, all Paris was buzzing with the tragic story of one of Cora's lovers, Alexandre Duval, who had ten million francs. Duval showered Cora with gifts of carriages, horses, jewellery, furnishings. He once gave her a book, which she contemptuously tossed aside, not realizing that its one hundred pages consisted of one thousand franc banknotes. Despite the lavish presents, Cora treated Duval with disdain. And, when he eventually shot himself in her house, Cora coldly remarked, 'The dirty pig. He fucked up my beautiful rug!' Duval eventually recovered from both the bullet wound and his devotion to Cora.

Cora's spurned lovers might have been gratified to see her later – hungry, homeless and whoring desperately in the slums. An English journalist, Julian B. Arnold, stumbled upon Cora in Monte Carlo, where she sat weeping on a kerb. Taking pity on her, Arnold brought her home to his villa until he could arrange transport to Paris for her. That night, as Arnold sat reading in his study, Cora entered in a dressing gown. She let the gown fall to the floor and stood naked before him. 'A woman's vanity,' she said, 'should be my sufficient excuse. I found it difficult to rest until I had shown you that, if Cora Pearl has lost all else, she still retains that which made her famous – a form of loveliness.'

M.S. (Lists 2, 19, 22, 41, 44, 46)

♣ Samuel Pepys
23 February 1663 to 26 May 1703

As England's first secretary of the Admiralty, Pepys doubled the size of the English Navy and greatly increased its efficiency, establishing a tradition of order and discipline that allowed Britannia to rule the waves in the centuries that followed. However, the 1,250,000 word diary he kept from 1660 to 1669 was what immortalized him.

Despite humble origins, Pepys's intelligence and dilligence allowed him to climb in society until, under King James II, he was one of the most powerful men in England. At his marriage to Elizabeth Marchant de Saint-Michel, a poor but beautiful 15-year-old, Pepys was a factotum, or general servant, for his cousin Admiral Edward Montagu (later the Earl of Sandwich). After serving as a clerk and secretary, Pepys began his rise in the naval bureaucracy, later becoming a trusted confidant of King Charles II and King James II. By 1678, Pepys's attacks on corruption had made him many enemies – some powerful enough to have him put in the Tower of London, charged with treason and popery. However, he survived and, during the reign of King James II, controlled a larger budget that any other department of state. He had a peacful retirement, enjoying friendships with Dryden, Wren and Newton.

Pepys's diary, kept between the ages of 26 and 36, is extraordinary not only for descriptions of great historical events, but for its honest revelations. The reader can identify with Pepys's bouts of constipation and jealousy, his pride at acquiring a new pocket watch or periwig, and his struggles with his barely controllable sex drive. He kept the diary hidden and protected himself further by writing in shorthand. Certain passages, particularly those dealing with his affairs, were further disguised by the scattered use of words from Spanish, French, Dutch, Greek, Italian and Latin. For example, on 3 June 1666, Pepys noted '... and so to Mrs Martin and there did what *je voudrais avec* her, both *devante* and backward, which is also *muy bon plazer*.' On 28 November the same year: '... and Pegg with me in my closet a good while, and did suffer me *a la besar mucho et tocar ses cosas* upon her breast – wherein I had great pleasure....' The diary was first published in 1825, but even the ten-volume Wheatley edition of 1893–9 left out ninety passages that dealt too explicitly with sex and defecation. Not until the 1970s were these sections finally made public.

Samuel Pepys had been married four years when he began his diary. Young Mrs Pepys, petty and annoying as she might sometimes appear, endured some pettiness herself. On 19 December 1661, Pepys called her a 'whore' because her ribbons didn't match. On 9 January 1663, he tore up all the letters he had written to her. On 5 April 1664, he was so angry with her that he pulled her nose; and, on 19 December 1665, he punched her in the eye. On 12 July 1667, he pulled her nose again. None the less, he always felt guilty afterwards. On 23 October 1662, after sporting together in bed, Pepys described himself and Elizabeth as 'a very happy couple'. However, 1663 was to change their relationship. Elizabeth persistently complained because her husband made her stay at home and deprived her of the pleasures of London. Finally Pepys surrendered, allowing her to take dancing lessons from a married man named Pembleton. It wasn't long before Pepys was outrageously jealous. On 15 May, he checked to make sure his wife was wearing drawers. On 24 May, he noticed Pembleton leering at her during church services. Two days later, he hurried home during the afternoon. Finding his wife and Pembleton alone, he sneaked upstairs to see if any of the beds had been used. (They hadn't.) Meanwhile, Elizabeth was becoming jealous of Samuel's growing closeness with her maid, Ashwell. Pepys solved the problem in mid-June by sending his wife and Ashwell to the country for two months.

Previously, Pepys had engaged in minor extramarital flirtations, but nothing serious. For example, on 6 February 1660, he had 'a very high bout' with Mistress Ann. 'I rattled her up.' And, on 12 August of that year, he wrote of shopgirl Betty Lane, 'I was exceeding free in dallying with her and she not unfree to take it.' But in 1663, with his wife out of town, he met Betty Lane again and their affair shifted gear. July 18: 'I had my full liberty of towzing her and doing what I would. Of which I am heartily ashamed, but I do resolve never to do so more.' However, on 24 September, with his wife back in London, he returned to Betty Lane and 'did what I would with her, but only the main thing'. Again he resolved 'never to do the like again'. On 16 January 1664, he 'did what I would' with Betty Lane once again and wrote, 'I hope it will be the last occasion of my life.' It wasn't. While his wife was in the country again, Pepys learned that Betty Lane had married and was now Mrs Martin. His reaction? 'I must have a bout with her very shortly to see how she finds marriage.' Three days later, being in 'an idle and wanton humour', he had his bout and scored twice in an hour.

By this time, Pepys was ready to branch out. Attracted to 'Bagwell's wife', he seduced her in small steps for a year until, on 15 November 1664, he was able to boast to his diary, '. . . after many protestings by degrees I did arrive at what I would, with great pleasure'. And a month later (the day after he punched his wife in the eye): 'I tried to do what I would and against her will I did enough for my contentment.' Eventually he broke down Mrs Bagwell's resistance completely, but not before injuring his left forefinger in a struggle with her on 20 February 1665.

For the next three years, Pepys kissed and played with the

breasts of many women, mostly of the lower classes. However, he only 'did what he would' with a handful, one of whom was Doll Lane, Betty's sister, with whom he first became involved in 1666 while Betty was pregnant. On 21 October, he 'might have done anything else'.

All this time Elizabeth Pepys was unaware of her husband's infidelities, although jealous of his friendships with women and angry at rumours that had circulated in her absence. But, in October 1668, Pepys's extramarital bubble burst, because of his involvement with a girl he never even had sex with. Deborah Willet came to work for the Pepyses on 30 September 1667. She was a pretty young virgin whose breasts were just beginning to develop. By 22 December, Pepys had kissed her for the first time, and by the following August was touching her 'with great pleasure'. Then came 25 October 1668: '. . . and after supper, to have my head combed by Deb, which occasioned the greatest sorrow to me that ever I knew in this world; for my wife, coming up suddenly, did find me imbracing the girl *con* my hand *sub su* coats; and endeed, I was with my *main* in her cunny. I was at a wonderful loss upon it, and the girl also. . . .' Not knowing how much his wife had seen, Pepys admitted nothing, but that night Elizabeth became so upset that she admitted for the first time that she was a Roman Catholic. The Pepys household was extremely tense for two weeks, with Elizabeth watching her husband's every move and making sure that he didn't so much as smile at Deborah Willet. On 9 November, he managed to fling a note to Deborah, telling her that he had denied ever having kissed her and advising her to do the same. However, the next day, when he returned home from the office for lunch, Pepys found his wife 'mightily troubled again, more than ever, and she tells me that it is from her examining the girl and getting a confession now from her of all, even to the very *tocando su* thing with my hand. . . .'

Understandably outraged by her husband's infidelity and lying, Elizabeth forced Pepys to dismiss Deborah Willet. But the night before she left, he confessed to his diary, '. . . the truth is, I have a great mind for to have the maidenhead of this girl, which I should no doubt to have if *yo* could get time *para* be *con* her – but she will be gone and I know not whither.' However, he also noted the next day that he had made love to his wife 'more times since this falling-out than in I believe twelve months before – and with more pleasure to her then I think in all the time of our marriage before'. Within the week, Pepys had tracked down Deborah

Willet, kissed her, and given her fatherly advice. But Elizabeth found out and demanded that Pepys write a letter to Deborah in which he called her a 'whore' and said he hated her. This he did, but only after Will Hewer, Pepys's lifelong friend, agreed to deliver the letter and, with a wink, assured Pepys that Deborah would never see the offensive portions.

Eventually Samuel and Elizabeth were reconciled. However, on 9 April 1669, Pepys was back with Mrs Martin, doing what he would, and also with her sister, now Mrs Powell. On 15 April, he even met with Deborah in an alehouse and kissed her and touched her breasts. Six weeks later, the threat of losing his eyesight forced Pepys to give up his dairy. On 10 November, Elizabeth, after a high fever, died at 29. Shortly afterwards Pepys became passionate with witty young Mary Skinner. Twenty years later, she moved in with him, without scandal, and she nursed and consoled him in his old age. Not surprisingly, Pepys never re-married – preferring, no doubt, to do what he would for the rest of his life.

D.W. (Lists 3, 35, 49)

♣ Eva Perón
7 May 1919 to 26 July 1952

María Eva Duarte was born in Los Toldos, a poverty-stricken village on the pampas, about 150 miles from Buenos Aires. Eva was the fourth child born to Juana Ibarguren as the result of her unmarried liaison with Juan Duarte, a married small landowner. Faced with a bleak future, Eva left for Buenos Aires at 14 in the hopes of a theatrical career. At first, her provincial accent and manner worked against her, but eventually she became one of the leading actresses on radio. She was tall for an Argentine woman – 5 feet 5 inches – with dyed honey-blonde hair, large, dark-brown eyes, an attractive face and a tendency towards plumpness, which she determinedly controlled. She was barely literate.

Her ambitions led her to cultivate the company of widowed colonel Juan Perón, whom she met in 1934. She moved in with him, and married him in 1945. With Eva at his side, Juan Perón became president–dictator of Argentina. Not content to be a conventional first lady, Evita unleashed her venom on the rich and her personal enemies alike, but won the hearts of the poor of Argentina – whom she called *los descamisados* (the shirtless ones).

They revered this peasant who stood before them in regal attire, and backed her as she promoted women's suffrage, organized workers, and, under the guise of the Eva Perón Welfare Foundation, pumped millions of dollars of government money into welfare programmes (and her Swiss bank accounts). When she died of cancer of the uterus at 33, Evita was mourned as a saint.

Eva Perón had a complex personality. As vindictive as she was charismatic, she used sex as a means to wealth and power – no doubt her true loves. Although 27 per cent of the children born in Argentina were illegitimate, as she was, there was tolerance – but no honour and no chance of advancement from the lower classes. A woman in Argentina society had only one option – sex – and Eva knew how to use it. When she married Juan Perón, she sought to conceal all evidence of her past; much of what remains is rumour and gossip.

It is sometimes assumed that she began her career in Buenos Aires as a prostitute; although she later tried to legalize the red-light district, it is unlikely that she ever worked the streets. Instead, she became the mistress of one more influential man after another. She posed for pornographic photographs (later collected and destroyed), and she was supposed to be 'good on her knees' - in other words, she offered her men fellatio. Nevertheless, she was unable to shake off the 'little whore' tag. There is a story – possibly apocryphal, but illuminating – about an incident on an official trip to Milan. While travelling in an automobile with a retired admiral, she was jeered by an angry mob. She turned to her companion and cried, 'Do you hear that? They're calling me a whore.' To which the admiral allegedly replied, 'I understand perfectly. I haven't been to sea in fifteen years, and they still call me admiral.'

Information on the men in her life is often less obscure, but there are still discrepancies. At 14, she offered her sexual services to a second-rate tango singer, José Armani, if he would take her to Buenos Aires. He agreed, and she was on her way. (The story was later changed – with popular singer Agustin Magalis being credited as her first lover.)

Eva soon realized that a tango singer was not much help in the big city, and by the time she was 15 she had latched on to Emilio Karstulovic, magazine publisher and man-about-town. Soon she gravitated toward more useful men – photographers and producers. Those who knew her say Eva was basically a shrewd, cold, asexual woman whose interest was power, not love. Yet she did have charm, and she used it on Rafael Firtuso, the owner of the Liceo theatre, who cast her in one of his productions, and on a soap manufacturer, who provided her with the best cosmetics.

Then came Perón, a handsome ladies' man with a penchant for teenage girls. Eva was 24 and he 48 when they met. They made love their first night together, and before long she had convinced her new lover – a man who supported Hitler and Fascism – that he should rise to be head of government. She became both his inspiration and champion, and his adviser.

After Eva's death, Perón founded the infamous Union of Secondary School Students, which quickly became the means by which young girls were procured for his pleasure and that of his officers. The union was highly organized, with branches in every secondary school in the country. Officers scouted comely prospects and sent the most alluring to regional 'recreation centres'. These centres included luxurious quarters and a permanent staff of doctors to handle pregnancies and venereal diseases. Perón had his own private recreation centre and often spent his afternoons with some teenage girl who was far from home and unable to resist the powerful president of the country. In 1955, Perón was ousted from Argentina by a coup and settled in Madrid. He returned to power for a brief period in 1973 but, without his wife in her furs and diamonds, could regain little popularity.

Although Eva was probably faithful to her husband during their marriage, there is one instance where a man's power and wealth were irresistible. She first met Aristotle Onassis during the Second World War, through sending food parcels to Nazi-occupied Greece. When Eva was in Europe in 1947, Onassis made a special effort to meet her. After a formal lunch, he asked one of her escorts to arrange a more private meeting. He was promptly invited to her holiday villa on the Italian Riviera. No sooner had he arrived than they got into bed and made love. Afterwards, she cooked Onassis an omelette and he gave her a cheque for $10,000 to donate to one of her favourite charities. He later described the omelette she had cooked that afternoon as 'the most expensive I have ever had'.

The legend of Evita continues: in the late 1970s, a Broadway musical based on her career, written by Andrew Lloyd Weber and Tim Rice, won international acclaim.

A.L.G. and Eds. (Lists 2, 19, 24, 26)

🍀 Philippe I, Duc d'Orléans
21 September 1640 to 9 June 1701

Philippe I, Duc d'Orléans, was the younger brother of King Louis XIV. He distinguished himself militarily but, apparently jealous of Philippe's success in battle, Louis refused him any further commands and encouraged his dissipation. Philippe spent the remainder of his life as one of Louis's courtiers, and became the French court's most notorious homosexual. He was also known for his tendency to dress as a woman in public.

Historians equivocate over the reasons for Philippe's early homosexual tendencies. Some argue that his feminine leanings were evident from birth; others say they were the result of a childhood seduction by the homosexual Duc de Nevers. Most agree, however, that it was politically inspired – his mother, Anne of Austria, fearing that Philippe might some day challenge the rule of her first-born, Louis XIV, deliberately raised him in the company and habits of women. Left largely uneducated, he spent his days gossiping, playing, and dressing up like a girl. This continued into adult life, according to Charlotte Elisabeth, his second wife.

Surprisingly, he proved a courageous fighter despite his lack of formal military training, and won several major battles for his increasingly envious brother Louis. Perhaps he shocked the enemy into submission – he would ride into battle wearing make-up, powder, ribbons, and jewellery, but without a hat in order to show off his elaborate hairdo. Jealous, vain, and petty, he strutted on heels as tall as stilts and once burst into tears when his lover, the Chevalier de Lorraine, refused to give him a new face-cream recipe.

In 1661, he married Henrietta Anne, the sister of his cousin Charles II. They had two daughters. Although he cared little for Henrietta, he was wildly jealous about her suspected relationship with his brother Louis, and was equally furious with her for her role in persuading Louis to banish the Chevalier de Lorraine. When Henrietta died unexpectedly in 1670, people immediately suspected the Chevalier of poisoning her. The following year, he married the German princess, Charlotte Elisabeth, who bore him a son and a daughter.

Since Louis refused to share his power with his brother, Philippe spent his time indulging himself. According to his German wife: 'Monsieur thinks of nothing but his male favourites.

He spends whole nights in orgies with them, and gives them enormous sums of money.' It was also rumoured that he associated with members of the Sacred Fraternity of Glorious Pederasts, who were sworn to ignore women, using them only to produce heirs – all members wore a medallion depicting a man stepping on a woman. A favourite pastime at meetings was to perform fellatio. During the last months of his life, Philippe became more subdued. When he finally succumbed to death after a fit of apoplexy in 1701, Louis was genuinely grieved.

M.W. (Lists 11, 12, 14, 16, 48)

❧ Pablo Picasso
25 October 1881 to 8 April 1973

Born in Málaga, Spain, son of José Ruiz Blasco, an art teacher and sometime painter, Picasso had little formal education or artistic training, being clearly superior to his teachers. When Picasso's father realized the scope of his son's genius, he purportedly gave him his own brushes and colours, and did not paint again. In his late teens, Picasso discovered the bohemian life in Barcelona and continued to follow it in Paris, where he was immediately inspired by the streets of Montmartre and the works of Toulouse-Lautrec, Van Gogh and Cézanne. He was from the beginning extraordinarily prolific. From the age of 20, in accordance with Spanish custom, he signed his works with his mother's maiden name – Picasso. In 1904, he moved to Paris. There, he and Georges Braque, working together, founded the Cubist movement. The outbreak of the Spanish Civil War in 1936 ended Picasso's political apathy; he became a passionate Loyalist, and the destruction of a small Basque town by Hitler's bombers inspired what many consider his masterpiece, the huge *Guernica*. Throughout both world wars he remained in France.

Picasso's energy was relentless – habitually a late riser, he saw his friends in the afternoons and then worked far into the night. Although he was only 5 feet 3 inches tall the intensity of his black eyes and his often explosive presence gave the impression of a much larger man. He enjoyed his wealth and fame, earning millions each year from his enormous output – estimated as 14,000 canvases, 100,000 prints and engravings, and 34,000 book illustrations. When Picasso died at 91 in his French hillside villa, he left an estate valued at $1.1 billion.

Beauty and relative youth were the only consistent qualities he desired in women. Usually before and always after a sexual relationship began, his wives and mistresses became his models.

Fernande Olivier was the partner of Picasso's early life in Paris. She was a green-eyed, auburn-haired, voluptuous young woman whom he met one day at the common water tap of the run-down Montmartre tenement where they both lived. She was four months his senior, which prompted him, then all of 23, to speak of her to his friends as 'very beautiful – but old'. She later described him as having 'a sort of magnetism which I could not resist', but resisting was not Fernande's style. She liked posing, preferably in a reclining position, and did not object when lack of money to buy shoes prevented her from leaving the flat for two months. Picasso provided, if at times meagrely, for their most urgent needs, and for entertainment there was always lovemaking. Picasso adored Fernande and was obsessively jealous – 'Picasso forced me to live like a recluse,' she said later.

Periodically, Picasso's restless nature required both a change in models and in sources of inspiration. Marcelle Humbert, whom he called Eva, perhaps as an assurance to her that she was now his first woman, was as small and delicate as Fernande had been robust. Because their romance occurred during Picasso's Cubist period, no portraits of her exist, but she is immortalized in the words *'ma jolie'*, which appear variously inscribed in several of his paintings (two works bear the words, *J'aime Eva*). She died in 1915 of tuberculosis.

In 1917, Picasso was persuaded to go to Rome with Jean Cocteau and the Ballets Russes. There he designed the curtain for Diaghilev's new ballet *Parade*. Walking at night with the dancers along moonlit Roman streets, he singled out Olga Koklova, the diminutive daughter of a colonel. Her upper-class background and tastes appealed to him as solid and lasting values. His bohemian life had died with Eva; he was becoming rich and famous. Something essentially Spanish and bourgeois in his nature told him it was now time to settle down and start a family. He took Olga to Spain, introduced her to his friends and relatives, painted her in a Spanish mantilla, and married her not only in the obligatory civil ceremony, but in the Russian Orthodox service as well. Then he installed her in a luxuriously decorated Parisian flat with – as if with a premonition of failure – twin beds.

Picasso's first son, Paulo, was the product of that already disintegrating marriage. His first daughter, Maïa, was born in

1935 to his mistress and model, the large and lovely, blonde, blue-eyed Marie-Thérèse Walter. Picasso was delighted. Olga had grown increasingly demanding and neurotic, and Picasso had taken his revenge by painting a series of female monsters with shrivelled breasts and exaggerated sexual organs. His conjugal unhappiness and sexual deprivation produced deformed female figures in his art, but, once the warmhearted Marie-Thérèse appeared, the sunken breasts became round and firm, the mouths smiled, and the figures, although still distorted, exuded sensual joy. After Maïa was born, his affair with her mother became complicated by parental responsibility. Picasso was then attracted by the dark eyes and serious expression of Dora Maar, whom he first saw seated at a nearby table at the Deux Magots café. A photographer and a painter herself, Dora Maar could not only converse intelligently on the creative process, but do so in Spanish. Picasso was charmed. Soon Dora Maar was making regular visits to the Paris studio, and paintings of a woman with flowing hair began to appear. Dora Maar offered Picasso intellectual as well as sexual companionship; unfortunately, she matched his ferocious temperament and depressions with her own. The series of paintings of women weeping are all of Dora Maar.

In his 60s but with no apparent diminution of sexual energy – 'his sexual gluttony was becoming obsessive,' wrote a friend – Picasso acquired a new young painter, Françoise Gilot, as his mistress. Although she was, at the time, the sole occupant of Picasso's bed, Françoise soon discovered that Olga, Marie-Thérèse and Dora Maar all still played their roles in his life. Summers in the south of France were enlivened by the presence of Olga, who dogged their footsteps on the street and at the beach, raining verbal abuse on the couple. In Paris, Thursdays and Sundays were set aside for visits to Marie-Thérèse and Maïa, and during holidays daily letters arrived outlining in detail for Papa Picasso the events and concerns, particularly financial, of their lives. Picasso insisted that Françoise accompany him when he called on or had a lunch engagement with the now scornful and bitter Dora Maar. Forcing the women of his life to relate to each other, however violently, was for Picasso one of the more amusing aspects of longevity.

Some 40 years younger than Picasso, Françoise Gilot had a relationship with him that was more complicated than those of her predecessors. Whenever Françoise became dissatisfied with her role, Picasso prescribed maternity as a cure; their son Claude

358

and daughter Paloma were the result. Living with Picasso was too hard, as it turned out; after seven years, Françoise took the children and left. Picasso was furious. 'There's nothing so similar to one poodle dog as another poodle dog, and that goes for women, too,' he said. Françoise later married Dr Jonas Salk.

Picasso's last relationship of any duration was with a young divorcée, Jacqueline Roque, who moved in after Françoise left. She organized his affairs and devoted herself to his well-being. When Olga died in 1955, Picasso was at last free to remarry; and he and Jacqueline were wed in 1961. Jacqueline was less voluptuous than Fernande, less delicate than Eva, less graceful than Olga, less sweet than Marie-Thérèse, less intelligent than Dora Maar, less talented than Françoise. But her own expectations may have been less, too. She was loyal, capable, willing – and beautiful, like all of his women. At different times – and with varying degrees of passion – Picasso had loved them all. But there had always been something of anger and hatred. Picasso authority Pierre Cabanne pointed out, 'Sex stimulation was the basic motive force of his lyrical flights; desire, with him, was violence, dismemberment, tumult, indignation, excess.' A reference in the *Diaries of Anaïs Nin*, Cabanne felt, gave a clue to Picasso's attitude toward women. Alice Paalen, the wife of the Surrealist painter Wolfgang Paalen, who was one of Picasso's mistresses, is quoted as saying that one of his joys was to deny women their climaxes. As Paul Éluard wrote in transcribing a graphological analysis of him in 1942: 'Loves intensely and kills the thing he loves.'

'For me', Picasso had declared, 'there are only two kinds of women – goddesses and doormats.'

N.C.S. (Lists 8, 10, 22, 25, 26, 31)

♣ Édith Piaf
19 December 1915 to 11 October 1963

Édith Giovanna Gassion was born on a pavement in a poor district of Paris. She was promptly deserted by her mother, and later by her acrobat father too. Consequently, Édith and her half-sister Momone were raised in their grandmother's house of prostitution. Momone, who was younger, became Édith's confidante and alter ego; they remained close in later life. Édith was discovered and renamed by her first impresario, who took her off the street to sing in his cabaret. To him, she looked like a sparrow, so he used the French slang term for that bird – *piaf* – for her stage name. She had a rich, throbbing voice which often reduced audiences to tears. Maurice Chevalier came to hear her sing, and exclaimed, '*Cette môme; elle en a dans le ventre.*' ('That kid, she's got it inside.')

Thin, only 4 feet 10 inches tall, Piaf looked plain and frail. But her passion for life and love shone in her large, luminous eyes. 'I've got sagging breasts,' she said, 'a low-slung ass, and little drooping buttocks ... but I can still get men!' She drank enthusiastically and excessively for years, and alcohol – combined with drug problems, several car accidents and a turbulent emotional life – killed her at 48. Thousands paid homage at her Paris funeral, and many years later her fans were still placing flowers on her grave in Père Lachaise cemetery.

Piaf's sexual activity was prodigious. She had already slept with many men before she was 15, and couldn't remember the first one. Like a romantic schoolgirl, she fell desperately in love with each of them. Although she made millions of francs and thousands of dollars singing in Europe and the USA, she gave most of it away; she bought wardrobes of clothes for her lovers, and provided generous financial assistance to friends – like Charles Aznavour – and lovers alike. When Piaf died, she left nothing. She was attracted to all kinds of men, and even jokingly subdivided her affairs into 'the streets', 'the sailors', 'the pimps', 'the flings', 'the professors' and 'the factory' group; the latter consisted of new singing talent discovered by Piaf, notably Yves Montand. 'You never know a guy till you've tried him in bed,' she said. 'You know more about a guy in one night in bed than you do in months of conversation. In the sack, they can't cheat!'

Regardless of the circumstances, Édith Piaf enjoyed innumerable lovers. During her early days of singing in the street, all she could afford was a hotel room with one bed. One young lover, Louis Dupont, didn't object to sharing the bed with Édith and Momone. 'There was a deep purity in Édith,' said Momone, 'which nothing ever spoiled. Three in a bed may not be right, of course, but at 17 and as poor as we were, love is so marvellous, it's made silently. It lulled me and I dropped off to sleep like a little kid.'

Despite the many men, there was only one true love – a shy, muscular and graceful Arab–French prizefighter. Marcel Cerdan already had a wife and three sons. Called the 'Moroccan Bomber', he took the middleweight crown from Tony Zale at

Madison Square Garden on 21 September 1948. Even when Cerdan was in training for the Zale return fight, Piaf needed to be with him constantly. She took a room in the Waldorf-Astoria for appearances' sake, but it was Momone who used it.

A year later, Piaf was in New York while Cerdan held boxing exhibitions in Europe. She missed him terribly and persuaded him to visit her, insisting that he travel by plane rather than ship. He was killed when his plane crashed in the Azores. Momone had to have her sister sedated to prevent her suicide.

Among Piaf's other lovers were actors Eddie Constantine, Yves Montand (one of the few men she was faithful to) and John Garfield, whom she spotted when he was in a play in Paris. She sat through the performance every night for weeks, entranced by this 'handsome beast'. Finally she spent the night with him. He didn't try to see her again until months later, and by then she had lost interest. Piaf claimed not to believe in marriage, but she was married twice – first in 1952, to singer Jacques Pills. They divorced five years later. In the last year of her life, she married Theo Sarapo. The 26-year-old Greek hairdresser and singer was deeply devoted to her and, after she died, he cradled her body in his arms for hours.

For Piaf, men with blue eyes were especially irresistible, but she was not indifferent to the charms of any man. Each time she fell in love, it was love at first sight. Her need for love produced such tension that she slept with her hands clenched into fists. She was so obsessed by love that, as Momone said, 'She went wild. She ate her heart out, she was jealous and possessive ... she howled, she locked her guys up. She was demanding, she was unbearable; they slapped her around and she cheated on them.'

She once said to her sister, 'Can't have a house without a man, Momone. It's worse than a day without sunshine. You can get along without the sun – there's electricity. But a house without some guy's shirt lying around, where you don't run across a pair of socks, or a tie ... it's like a widow's house – it gets you down!'

B.J. and K.P. (Lists 2, 22, 25, 42)

🍀 Ezra Pound
30 October 1885 to 1 November 1972

An eccentric figure with a billowing cape, a 'fox's muzzle' beard, and one long, dangling earring, Pound affected a personal style as distinctive as his verse. After abandoning doctoral studies at Pennsylvania University, he worked briefly as a professor of Romance languages at Wabash College in Crawfordsville, Indiana, then left for Europe in 1908. While teaching in London he developed a non-academic interest in one of his pupils, Dorothy Shakespear. They married in 1914. After the First World War, they moved to France, and later to Italy. Meanwhile, Pound was working on the *Cantos* and lending invaluable support to Hemingway, T.S. Eliot, Joyce and other struggling writers. By the time the first rumblings of the Second World War were heard, he was praising Mussolini and Hitler. Pound's vehement denouncements of the American war efforts over Rome Radio resulted in his being indicted by the USA on nineteen counts of treason. Arrested outside his home at Sant' Ambrogio, Italy, in 1945, he spent six months in an American army stockade before being shipped back to the USA. At his trial in Washington DC, in February 1946, he was judged 'of unsound mind' and confined to St Elizabeth's Hospital for the criminally insane. Finally released in 1958, he returned to Italy, worked sporadically for a few years, then lapsed into silence for the last decade of his life. At the end he lamented, 'Everything that I touch, I spoil. I have blundered always.'

Getting engaged was one of Pound's favourite pastimes as a young man. When he was 19, he established a liaison with 34-year-old concert pianist Katherine Ruth Heyman, who gave him an heirloom diamond ring. At about the same time, he became engaged to poet Hilda Doolittle (H.D.), who recorded in her journal that Pound's 'fiery kisses' were 'electric, magnetic'. Another young poet to fall under Pound's sway was Hilda's friend Frances Gregg. After his relationships with Frances and Hilda had cooled, he became engaged to Mary Moore and gave her the diamond ring entrusted to him by Miss Heyman. Complications with women continued to dog his steps. His landlady found a woman in his bed one morning after he had left for work at Wabash College and, as a result of the incident, Pound lost his teaching job. Although he claimed that the girl was merely a destitute actress on whom he had taken pity, members of the community were outraged.

Pound sailed for Europe, where he served as Katherine Heyman's concert manager before meeting Dorothy Shakespear, whose mother was a close friend of W. B. Yeats. Dorothy had all the necessary prerequisites for a wife. She was 'beautiful and well-off' and had 'the most charming manners'. But Pound was not destined to settle into a conventional marriage for long. In 1922, eight years later, he was introduced to fellow American expatriate Olga Rudge, a pretty, dark-haired concert violinist in her mid-twenties. She thought him 'the handsomest man she had ever seen' and he considered her 'a great goddess'. When the goddess became his mistress, Pound began leading a double life, spending winters with Dorothy and summers with Olga. In 1925, Olga gave birth to his daughter, Mary; and the following year Dorothy bore his son, Omar. In 1944, when the Germans forced Pound and his wife out of their home in the Italian port of Rapallo, they moved in with Olga for the rest of the war. Although no angry words were ever spoken in the household, Pound's daughter recounts that the air was always heavy with tension because Dorothy and Olga despised each other. During the final stages of Pound's life, as his health declined and he became increasingly reclusive, Dorothy proved physically unable to care for him. Consequently, his last years were spent with Olga, who would accompany him to the Montin trattoria in Venice. According to one restaurant employee, 'he never said a word and always sat with his chin on his chest, sometimes muttering'. After Pound's death at 87, Olga Rudge stayed on in Italy, and today, according to one Venetian, 'listens all day, at the loudest volume, to tapes of Ezra Pound reading his poetry — perhaps not having heard his voice much when he was alive, she wants to do so now'.

Pound wrote, ' . . . it is more than likely that the brain itself is, in origin and development, only a sort of great clot of genital fluid held in suspense or reserve. . . . There are traces of it in the symbolism of phallic religions, man really the phallus or spermatozoid charging, head-on, the female chaos. . . . Even oneself has felt it, driving any new idea into the great passive vulva of London, a sensation analogous to the male feeling in copulation.'

Eds. (Lists 8, 10)

♣ Elvis Presley
8 January 1935 to 16 August 1977

Presley was born into an extremely poor Mississippi family, and received a guitar when he was 11 because his parents couldn't afford to give him the bicycle he wanted; the guitar was also intended to keep him out of trouble. Wanting to be different, young Elvis began to personify both the rebel and the good boy. On one hand, he wore sideburns and wild pink and black clothes and worshipped James Dean. On the other, he was deeply religious (and would remain so), going to church regularly with his parents. After high school, he got a job as a lorry driver. Making his first record cost him $4 – it was a birthday present for his mother. Sam Phillips of Sun Records heard Elvis, and Phillips had often said 'If I could find a white man with the Negro sound and the Negro feel, I could make a billion dollars.' So it all began with Sun, and Elvis's sexy, powerhouse performances. The curling lip, sultry hooded eyes and animal sexuality of the gyrating hips have often been described. Presley's performances elicited from women of all ages a form of erotomania – mass sexual frenzy. In 1955, 'Colonel' Tom Parker became Elvis's adroit manager; that same year, Presley signed with RCA records and bought his first Cadillac – pink – for his mother.

Elvis's scandalous behaviour outraged the world: Hedda Hopper called him 'a menace to young girls'. (She later reversed her position and did the twist with him at a Hollywood party.) He was given such nicknames as 'Elvis the Pelvis' and 'Sir Swivel Hips'; and worst of all for Elvis, he was denounced from countless pulpits. Billy Graham said he wouldn't want his daughter to meet Elvis. Elvis just didn't understand; gospel singing and revival meetings were his musical roots. Deeply hurt, he defended himself in conversation with his mother. 'I don't feel sexy when I'm singin'. If that was true I'd be in some kind of institution as some kind of sex maniac.' In 1955, the Florida police forced him to perform without moving. By 1956, he had made his first million; by 1957, he had moved his parents and grandmother into a twenty-three-room Memphis mansion called Graceland and, by the age of 30, was the highest paid performer in the history of the music business. During his lifetime, he grossed more than a billion dollars. When he appeared on the *Ed Sullivan Show*, from the waist up, he was seen by 54 million Americans, and his television ratings were higher than President Eisenhower's.

Between 1961 and 1967, he gave no public performances. After leaving a two-year stint in the army in 1960, Elvis concentrated on making a stream of stunningly corny movies in Hollywood. In 1968, he reappeared on the musical scene with a Christmas television special before a live audience, and began to perform again. But there was another side to this embodiment of the American Dream: flying a thousand miles with his entire entourage for a peanut butter and jelly sandwich; living by night (Elvis could never go out – he'd have been mobbed); shooting television sets during his violent outbursts. He surrounded himself with up to fifteen southern buddies – dubbed the 'Memphis Mafia' – employed as bodyguards, valets and royal jesters to the King. Any slight displeasure could result in a terrifying fit of Presley's temper. Graceland became a weird prison and Elvis's life was increasingly bizarre.

Elvis's drug use – some of his employees called him 'a walking drugstore' – began in the army with Dexedrine. He later took uppers, downers and painkillers in pill form or injected, and in his last years lived in a total narcotic haze. He developed a number of obsessions: with guns, motorcycles, badges, uniforms and police paraphernalia. In addition, he had a severe health problem and grew unquestionably fat. Knowledge of these difficulties drove his fans crazy – God was not allowed to decay – but at the age of 42, he was found dead from a heart attack in his Graceland bathroom. It is belived that he did not die from an overdose, although ten different kinds of drugs were found in his bloodstream. President Carter eulogized him, saying ' . . . he was a symbol to people the world over of the vitality, rebelliousness and good humour of his country'. Mass hysteria followed Elvis's death. Girls claimed to be making love to his ghost. The Graceland lawn was covered with fainting women, who did not want to live in a world without Elvis.

Numerous biographers have insisted that Elvis's greatest love was his mother, Gladys. She lived for her son, and had always told him that, even though he came from poor country people, he was as good as anybody. When she died in 1958, Elvis was crushed.

Apart from his mother, there was one great love in Elvis Presley's life: Priscilla Beaulieu. While stationed in Germany as a soldier, Presley met a pretty little 14-year-old, the daughter of a US army officer. 'Cilla', as he called her, was feminine, unspoiled and remarkably mature for her age – exactly suited for the

365

pedestal upon which Elvis liked to place the women he loved best. He talked her father into allowing her to be shipped to Graceland, where Elvis installed her, sending her to Catholic school and then to finishing school. Before her arrival, Elvis had shown a snapshot of her to his stepmother, and said, 'I've been to bed with no less than one thousand women in my life. This is the one, right here.' According to Elvis's secretary, he started sleeping with the 15-year-old girl right away. Years later, Priscilla made a discreet mention of their premarital relationship in a *Ladies Home Journal* interview. But Elvis had his cake and ate it too. He usually did not allow Priscilla to accompany him to Hollywood, where he had constant affairs. The list of stars with whom Elvis had been linked is virtually endless, and includes Ann-Margret, Juliet Prowse and Tuesday Weld. Elvis's amours were not always with the famous. One woman, Virginia Sullivan – a cashier in a movie theatre – claimed to have been his lover for fourteen years, from 1953 to 1967. They had what she described as 'comfortable sex'. Elvis married Priscilla in 1967, when she was 21. Exactly nine months later, their daughter Lisa Marie was born. While the marriage was good in the beginning, it was subject to increasing strains. Priscilla was tired of waking up to face the Memphis Mafia at her breakfast table; tired of living at Graceland and going weeks without seeing her husband. And Elvis was still sleeping around, while the Memphis Mafia was expected to cover it up. Worst of all, when Elvis was at home, he and Priscilla had no privacy – he even took his entourage on their holidays.

After five years of marriage, Priscilla announced to Elvis that she had fallen in love with another man and was leaving. The rival was Mike Stone, her karate teacher. Elvis was shattered: he had lost his most valuable possession. The couple separated in 1972, and divorced in 1973. Priscilla's final settlement was $2 million. Although the divorce was relatively amicable, Elvis was deeply wounded. He found release in drugs, women, work and food. The most important woman after Priscilla was the tall, willowy Miss Tennessee of 1972, Linda Thompson. She was a Southern model – beautiful and utterly devoted to the King; she was a virgin when she met him. She moved into Graceland, and the relationship lasted several years. When Elvis started dating other women – and invited Linda along as a third – the affair petered out.

In the last year of his life, Elvis had an affair with 19-year-old Ginger Alden, Miss Memphis Traffic Safety of 1976. He gave her the customary Cadillac and an $85,000 ring. She was with him the night of his death.

Elvis wasn't lying when he told his stepmother that he had slept with more than one thousand girls. And that was *before* he married Priscilla. At the beginning of his career, he was shy, and more interested in succeeding for the sake of his mother than in busying himself with sex. But Elvis had access to countless women, all over the world, who were dying to make love to him. Between 20 and 30, when he was young and in good health, he frequently had two or three women a day. Towards the end of his life, drugs dampened his desire for sex ('Bed,' he would say, 'is for sleeping on') and sometimes angry, unravished dates complained to the Memphis Mafia. However, it was strictly understood that the boys were not to fool around with a girl Elvis might still want, although their dates were fair game for Elvis.

According to three ex-bodyguards who wrote *Elvis: What Happened?* a biography of him, the King had distinct sexual preferences: did not like a large bosom, preferring shapely legs and buttocks. He liked his woman petite and feminine ('girl-type girls'), and his biggest turn-off was big feet. He also detested male homosexuals. Another sexual bromide was the knowledge that a woman had been married, or had children. He once dropped a girlfriend flat when he discovered she was a mother. He was also a confirmed voyeur – he had a two-way mirror in his bedroom, so he could secretly watch other couples; he had mirrored ceilings, and liked to videotape his sex. He would also give his girl of the moment a sleeping pill, and put her in his bedroom before going to a nearby room, where he would watch two especially pretty prostitutes have sex. When this show had sufficiently excited him, he would 'make a dead run to his bedroom and make it with his girl'. His overall preference in women ran to the young and inexperienced – because they were less likely to make comparisons or reject him. The King, for all his glory, was extremely insecure.

A.W. (Lists 3, 9, 11, 20, 22, 25, 34, 42, 49, 50)

♣ Grigori Yefimovich Rasputin
?1871 to 30 December 1916

Rasputin, born in a Siberian village, was the third and last child of Efim Akovlevich, a prosperous farmer, and Anna Egorovna, who may have been a Mongol from Tobolsk. As a young man, Grigori gave every indication of following in his father's footsteps

– with a farmer's appetite for work, hard drinking, and loose women. At 20, he married a local girl, Praskovia Feodorovna Dubrovina, and fathered four children. Around 1900, he joined a heretical religious sect known as the Khlist. These flagellants believed that man must sin first in order to be redeemed later, and they practised a variety of bizarre sexual customs and rites. Expelled from his native village by the more respectable priests, Rasputin wandered through rural Russia, performing cures and initiating hordes of women into the rituals of the flagellants. By 1905, he had settled in the capital, St Petersburg, where tales of his 'miraculous' healing powers brought about an audience with Czar Nicholas and Czarina Alexandra. The imperial couple had a son, Alexis, a haemophiliac, and Rasputin's apparently genuine ability to ease the boy's suffering won him immense favour, especially with Alexandra. Rasputin used her protection to build his own influence, and at the same time scandalized St Petersburg with his wild sexual antics. In 1916, a gang of conservative noblemen assassinated him. After drinking poisoned wine, and being shot and beaten, Rasputin was tied up and thrown into the icy Neva river, where he finally died from drowning.

Rasputin was undoubtedly one of the most profligate sexual adventurers in history. He seems to have been born with an overabundance of natural lust which, according to his daughter Maria, seemed to 'radiate' from his 13 inch penis. Even as a young boy, his magnificent phallus was the delight of all the village girls, who observed him swimming in the nude – as they were – in a local pond. But his real initiation into the world of sex came at the hands of Irina Danilova Kubasova, the young and beautiful wife of a Russian general. She enlisted the help of six of her maids in a mass seduction of the 16-year-old Rasputin, and lured him into a bedroom. When he stripped and followed her to the bed, the maids suddenly leaped out of hiding, dousing him with cold water and grabbing his penis. Following this episode, he sported with prostitutes in his native village, even after his marriage to Praskovia Feodorovna. According to his daughter, a sexual frolic with three Siberian peasant girls whom he chanced on while swimming in a lake led Rasputin to a religious revelation of sorts, and he soon joined the Khlist, who not only allowed but actively encouraged the indulgence of the flesh. Thus converted, Rasputin embarked on a journey through Russia, during which he found numerous women with whom to celebrate his peculiar rites, which included Bacchanalian orgies, complete with partner-swapping 'in any convenient place, the woods, a barn, or the cottage of one of his converts'. His doctrine of redemption through sexual release allowed a multitude of guilt-ridden women to enjoy themselves sexually for the first time, despite the grubby, slovenly appearance of the 'holy satyr'. As biographer Robert Massie noted, 'making love to the unwashed peasant with his dirty beard and filthy hands was a new and thrilling sensation'. Even the sophisticated women of St Petersburg fell under Rasputin's sexual sway. He set up shop in a flat and the ladies gathered to wait for an invitation to his bedroom, which he called the 'holy of holies'. So fashionable did his attentions become that the husbands of his conquests sometimes bragged to one another that their wives had 'belonged' to the incredible Rasputin; one of his steady customers, an opera singer, often telephoned her mentor for no other reason than to sing him his favourite songs. Typically, he could be found in his dining room, surrounded by lovely 'disciples', sometimes sitting with one of them on his lap, stroking her hair and whispering softly of the 'mysterious resurrection'. He would begin to sing and the women joined in. Soon the singing would erupt into wild dancing, which itself often led to passionate swoonings and trips to the 'holy of holies'. At one of his sessions in St Petersburg, Rasputin abruptly launched into a graphic description of the sex life of horses. He then roughly seized one of his distinguished guests and said, 'Come, my lovely mare.'

Even Rasputin's death had sexual overtones. His murder was plotted by men jealous of his power. His assassins invited him to a midnight repast, and fed him poisoned cakes and wine. One of the murderers, Felix Yussupov, was a prince, who was reputed to have homosexual tendencies, and who had been rebuffed several times for his advances to the mystic. When Rasputin grew dazed from the poison, Yussupov sexually abused him, and then shot him four times. Rasputin fell, still alive, and another attacker pulled out a knife and 'castrated Grigori Rasputin, flinging the severed penis across the room'. A servant recovered the penis and turned it over to a maid who, at the last account, was living in Paris in 1968. Inside a polished wooden box she preserved the organ which looked '. . . like a blackened, overripe banana, about a foot long. . .'

Rasputin's willing sex partners – often anonymous – are legion. He had probably been enjoying himself with the village girls long before Irina Danilova seduced him.

Dunia Bekyeshova, who at 14 was one of the girls who helped Irina take Rasputin, later became a servant of the priest's family and his lifelong mistress. Another of the many conquests noted by Rasputin's daughter was Olga Vladimirovna Lokhtina, wife of a minor nobleman. The list goes on and on, including actresses, military wives and – when no one else was available to quell his mighty lust – chambermaids and prostitutes. Certainly the most patient of all his women was his wife Praskovia, who suffered his lifelong infidelities without complaint, shrugging them off by saying tolerantly, 'He has enough for all.'

W.L. (Lists 4, 9, 10, 11, 20, 22, 31, 32, 43, 44)

❧ Rembrandt van Rijn
15 July 1606 to 4 October 1669

Rembrandt had a prodigious output which included over 600 paintings, 300 etchings and almost 2,000 drawings.

The gifted son of a Dutch miller and a baker's daughter, he studied art first in Leiden, his native city, and later in Amsterdam. In 1631, when almost 25, he moved to Amsterdam permanently, establishing himself as the city's leading portrait painter. Three years later, he married the wealthy heiress Saskia van Uijlenburgh. Commissions poured in, and 'numerous' paying pupils came to study with him. Knowing or caring little about money management, he developed extravagant tastes and spendthrift habits, ostentatiously collecting art, jewellery, and antiques. As a result, from 1639, he never seemed to be out of financial trouble. In 1642, Saskia died, leaving an infant son, Titus, the only one of their four children to reach adulthood. Throughout the 1640s, Rembrandt developed a more innovative and introspective style, considered daring by many of his stolid Dutch clients. In 1665, internationally famous, but out of fashion at home, he was declared bankrupt; his house and possessions were sold at auction. After the early death of both his son and his mistress, Hendrickje Stoffels – who had helped to stave off his creditors – Rembrandt became increasingly isolated. Even though his eyesight was failing, he continued to develop artistically; some of his greatest works were done a year or so before his death. Although Rembrandt has been described as ugly, with ears like jug handles, a bulbous nose and a coarse, sensual mouth, at least three women loved him devotedly. He returned their affection as far as he was able, using them more as conveniences than love objects, because he was 'married to his art'.

His marriage to Saskia brought him wealth and contact with a higher social class. She was not beautiful, but she represented the world to which he aspired to belong; he idealized her and used her as the model for a series of portraits and sketches. Saskia died aged 30, worn out with childbearing and endless daily chores. A clause in her will stipulated that Rembrandt would lose the income from her estate if he remarried. He respected her wishes in the legal sense, but did not deprive himself of female companionship. Twenty years after her death, needing ready cash, he sold the tomb over her grave.

The next woman in Rembrandt's life was Geertghe Dircz, nurse to 10-month-old Titus. The painter made shrewish Geertghe his mistress and approved when she made a will in Titus's favour. When he subsequently fell in love with Hendrickje Stoffels, a young servant girl, Geertghe abruptly left. Jealous and hurt, she sued Rembrandt for breach of promise. The court ordered him to pay her 200 guilders a year. She later had a nervous breakdown, and he had to pay the cost of maintaining her in a mental hospital. Rembrandt's sincerest affection probably went to Hendrickje, who attended to his needs, modelled for his paintings, and bore him a daughter. Plump, red-haired, and prettier than Saskia, she was completely unselfish. But he did not legalize their relationship, because of the terms of Saskia's will. In 1654, when Hendrickje was six months pregnant, she was called before a panel of ecclesiastical judges, reprimanded for her illicit relationship with the artist, and excommunicated. She faced this ordeal of public humiliation alone, because Rembrandt was indifferent to formal religion and did not accompany her. Yet she remained staunchly loyal to him until her death in 1663.

Despite his shabby treatment of the real women in his life, Rembrandt often depicted them as goddesses in his paintings. His nudes combined sensuality with tenderness; and he individualized women's bodies as much as their faces. He was convinced that everything human, even physical love, was an appropriate subject for art, and he was not above shocking the puritannical with 'lewd' etchings.

M.B.T. (Lists 17, 21, 35)

♣ Rainer Maria Rilke
4 December 1875 to 29 December 1926

Rilke, the great Austrian poet, was born in Prague, and raised by his unbalanced mother as a girl for his first six years. Later, his father sent him to a military school in Linz, but he dropped out because of poor health. He also left a commercial school in Linz, Austria, and the University of Prague. Rilke published his first volume of poems at 19, then went to Munich to write. All his life, Rilke travelled in Europe, producing a steady stream of poetry. He also visited North Africa and Egypt, and called Russia – where he met Tolstoi – his spiritual home. But he preferred Paris. For a time Rilke was Auguste Rodin's secretary. Then the European aristocracy 'adopted' him, installing him in a series of villas and castles. Princess Marie von Thurn und Taxis-Hohenlohe became his patroness in 1909. Rilke found in her the mother figure he had longed for, and to her he opened his heart. During the First World War he served briefly as a clerk in the Austrian army. Intellectual and artistic women were always drawn to the graceful Rilke, although he was no Adonis. With his long head, large nose, receding cleft chin and droopy moustache, he seemed 'ugly, small, puny' even to Princess Marie. Rilke preferred the company of women, yet would bolt as soon as he felt his solitude and work threatened. He practised nudism, flirted with the occult, and believed in nature cures. 'The Santa Claus of loneliness', as poet W. H. Auden called him, died near Montreux, Switzerland.

'I am no good at love, because I did not love my mother,' Rilke once confessed. At other times he complained about the suffering and despair that his erotic relationships had brought. Because he found very little pleasure in sex, with many women he preferred the role of a good friend. But there were certainly exceptions.

At 16, while at the commercial school in Linz, he had a love affair with an instructor several years his senior and they eventually ran away together. Next year he fell in love with and became engaged to Valerie von David-Rhonfeld, an aspiring artist a year older than him. Three years and 130 love letters later, Rilke broke off the engagement.

In 1897, Rilke met Lou Andreas-Salomé, a well-known author and the daughter of a Russian general. Although she was married and 13 years his senior, they quickly became lovers. Rilke's diary suggests that she may even have borne his child. Rilke, Lou and her husband made a trip to Russia, returning a short time later –

this time passing themselves off as cousins. This was Rilke's most enduring relationship with a woman, not counting Princess Marie's platonic friendship. Even after Rilke and Lou parted, they continued to see each other and corresponded for the rest of Rilke's life. Lou, an amateur psychoanalyst, wrote years later that, of Rilke's 'many fears', his biggest was the girlish fear of his penis. She alluded to Rilke's sexual infantilism and revealed that a physical difficulty with his genitals made erections painful for him. She also interpreted his fears as a 'displaced, converted guilt over masturbation'.

Rilke married German sculptor Clara Westhoff in 1901. Their daughter Ruth was born the same year. But the Rilkes soon went their separate ways without bothering to get divorced. As with Lou, Rilke had met and corresponded with Clara for years.

In 1914, pianist Magda von Hattingberg considered living with Rilke forever, but then decided that she did not love him as a woman should love a man. 'For me he is the voice of God, the immortal soul,' she said. The following year, the flamboyant painter Loulou Albert-Lazard became his mistress in Munich. In the winter of 1918, Rilke wrote impassioned letters to poet Clair Studer, with whom he had a 'short ecstatic flowering of physical love'. Then there was 17-year-old Marthe Hennebert, a pathetic Parisian waif with whom Rilke carried on a lover–father affair from 1911 to 1919. And, in Switzerland in 1921, he had an erotic liaison with the Russian painter Baladine Klossowska.

Rilke also was linked romantically, but not necessarily sexually, with many other women, including poet Regina Ullmann and Countess Francesca von Reventlow. His last love was a young Egyptian beauty, Mrs Nimet Eloui Bey, whom Rilke met shortly before his death. It is said that, while picking roses for her, Rilke pricked his finger. An infection developed, and the doctors who treated it discovered that Rilke had leukemia. He was dead within weeks.

Among his unpublished manuscripts, there were seven poems glorifying the human phallus; in these the sexual act is extolled in religious metaphors. The essence of earthly splendour is our 'lovely' sex, which Christianity has always sought to suppress. 'Why did they make our sex homeless for us?' Rilke lamented. He even thought that deification of sex was possible, yet Rilke confided to Princess Marie, 'All love is an effort for me, a difficult task....'

R.J.R. (Lists 2, 5, 35, 44, 48)

373

♣ Erwin Rommel
15 November 1891 to 14 October 1944

German general Erwin Rommel was acclaimed even by his enemies for his spectacular military successes. Fighting in North Africa during the Second World War, Rommel was nicknamed the 'Desert Fox' because of his daring surprise attacks. In 1944, Rommel was arrested by two of Hitler's generals and accused of having conspired to murder the Führer. Although critical of Hitler, and a friend of the conspirators, Rommel was not involved in the assassination plot. Given the choice between a trial and poison, Rommel took poison.

In 1916 Rommel had married Lucie, an attractive, dark-haired 22-year-old. She completely dominated Erwin. He made no secret of his adoration for his wife and had a deep emotional dependence on her, hating to be away from her. So devoted were the couple that they wrote to each other daily when separated – thousands of their letters still exist. The Second World War kept Lucie and Erwin apart a great deal. Rommel, who by 1944 was a hero, was often approached by attractive women. On one such occasion, he commented to General Wilhelm Meise, 'You know, Meise, some of those girls are so attractive I could almost be a rat!' But it was only talk – Rommel's fidelity was unshakable. Lucie and Erwin had one son, Manfred. On 14 October 1944, Rommel was visited by Hitler's generals. Solemnly, he bade farewell to Lucie and Manfred, telling his beloved wife, 'In fifteen minutes I will be dead.'

A.W. and J.M.

♣ Franklin Delano Roosevelt
30 January 1882 to 12 April 1945

Charismatic and handsome, though partially paralysed by polio in 1921, Franklin Roosevelt was a strangely elusive extrovert. Behind the jauntiness exemplified by his up-tilted cigarette holder and sweeping cape was a man who did not often indulge in confidences.

An only child, Franklin was the product of an aristocratic family. He was adored by his mother Sara, who later interfered constantly in his marriage. At Harvard, some of those in his social circles considered him a lightweight and called him 'the feather duster'.

374

In 1905, he married a distant cousin, Eleanor Roosevelt, by whom he had five children who lived to maturity. He went on to law school and a political career interrupted by his bout of polio at 39. He fought his way back from the life of an invalid by exercising – particularly in mineral waters. Never again able to stand without braces or support and afraid of dying in a fire, he practised crawling as an escape measure. He campaigned to become governor of New York in 1928 from a specially equipped car. His promise was to help 'the forgotten man at the bottom of the economic pyramid'. He won the election, and four years later was elected President of the USA. His New Deal included the Works Progress Administration (WPA) and he also introduced social security. He led the USA through the Second World War.

Roosevelt had patrician looks – a firm jaw, finely chiselled nose (with pince-nez accentuating it), level brow – and a flirtatious magnetism which appealed to many women. He preferred tall and straightlaced, even prudish women. Eleanor Roosevelt had been raised with Victorian strictness and was perhaps even more the product of old-fashioned virtues than her contemporaries. Lucy Mercer, with whom Roosevelt had an affair, and Marguerite (Missy) LeHand, with whom he may have had an affair, were products of Catholic childhoods and noted for their reticence.

In 1916, he began an affair with Lucy, originally hired as Eleanor's secretary. Lucy came from a well-to-do family which had suffered financial reverses. Stately, with a velvety voice, she was mysterious and elegant. She accompanied Franklin (without Eleanor) on a weekend yachting cruise up the Potomac, and they registered for one night as man and wife at a Virginia Beach motel.

Franklin returned from a trip to Europe as assistant secretary of the navy in 1918, and was ill with pneumonia. Eleanor sorted his incoming mail for him and found Lucy's love letters. In a family conference, with Sara Roosevelt present, Eleanor offered him his freedom, but they decided to stay together, perhaps for political reasons, provided Franklin never saw Lucy again. In 1920, Lucy married, but much later, just before Franklin's death, they met (without Eleanor's knowledge), though probably not for sexual intimacy. Lucy, along with several other people, was with Franklin at Warm Springs when he died. Eleanor was absent. According to most sources, Franklin and Eleanor, who had never kissed before their marriage, stopped having sexual relations some time between 1916 and 1918. Their relationship was cool, though not without affection.

In 1923, Missy LeHand, 23 years old and good-looking, became his secretary, and was probably in love with him. On more than one occasion, while cruising on the *Larooco*, the Roosevelt houseboat, she was seen sitting on his lap. While Eleanor was away, Missy acted as hostess for Franklin; she was his companion, listener, conscience. One Roosevelt son, Elliott, believes she was Franklin's mistress; his son James does not. At 41, Missy had a stroke, which left her without speech. In despair, she swallowed chicken bones in an abortive suicide attempt. For a while, she lived at the White House and Franklin often wheeled himself into her room to see her. In his will, he left her half the income from his estate to pay her medical bills. Though she died before he did, he did not change his will.

Other women named as FDR's possible lovers were Dorothy Schiff, once owner and publisher of the *New York Post*, and Princess Martha of Norway, who lived in the United States during the Second World War.

Roosevelt was a modest man. He could make light jokes with his children about sex, but he didn't often talk about it. He was shocked when a male guest on the *Larooco* paraded about naked. He was certainly capable of sexual activity in spite of his paralysis. In 1923, three doctors testified to that by writing, 'No symptoms of *impotentia coeundi* [inability to copulate].'

A.E. (List 21)

♣ Jean Jacques Rousseau
28 June 1712 to 2 July 1778

The Swiss-born French philosopher, novelist and political theorist was the author of such works as *The Social Contract* and the autobiographical *Confessions*. His writings on romance, education, government and morality greatly influenced the leaders of the French Revolution and the Romantic movement. His philosophy is epitomized in the concept that man is naturally good and all contact with society is corrupting. So controversial and influential was Rousseau that George Sand called him 'St Rousseau', Voltaire and David Hume called him 'a monster' and Tolstoi said that Rousseau and the Gospel were the two greatest influences in his life.

After a dispute forced Rousseau's widowed watchmaker father

to flee Geneva, Jean Jacques and his brother François were left with an uncle. François was soon apprenticed, and Jean Jacques was sent to live with a minister who taught him the classics. At the age of 16, he left Geneva for a lifetime of travel. In love with nature, he tramped about the countryside and, after working for a notary, an engraver and a lackey, he eventually became a music teacher. At 37, he won an essay contest and turned to writing, and by 46 he was famous. He became immensely popular in high society, although he railed against the oppression of the masses. In 1762, when his book *Emile* was condemned by both Church and State, he escaped Paris, was expelled from Berne, and found refuge in London where he stayed for a year. Near the end of his life, Rousseau's tendency towards paranoia and reclusiveness grew worse. He was sure that his friends were plotting to discredit him. In part, his fears were well based, since he had repeatedly outraged his best friends with insults or wildly extravagant philosophies. A lonely and melancholic man, troubled for most of his life with physical and emotional pain, he sank into intermittent periods of mental illness before his death outside Paris.

Good-looking and romantic, Rousseau was attractive to women. But his love life was chaotic. His first profound sexual experience was as a child. Having committed some minor offence, he received a spanking from his teacher, Mademoiselle Lambertier. He later wrote, 'Who would believe that this childhood punishment, suffered at the age of 8 at the hands of a spinster of 30 [he was in fact 11 and she 40], was to determine my tastes, my desires, my passions, my very self for the rest of my life?' He was left desperately craving more. However, the astute teacher, realizing what she had started, never spanked him again. Poor Jean Jacques – it was too late. He suffered 'erotic frenzies' which led him to intense fantasies of being spanked. But worse than these troubling frenzies were the long-term effects of the spanking: 'I have passed my life in silent yearning among those I loved most. Never daring to mention my peculiar taste, I achieved at least some satisfaction from relationships which retained a suggestion of it. . . . To lie at the feet of an imperious mistress, to obey her orders, to be forced to beg her forgiveness – this was for me a sweet enjoyment.'

There was only one person with whom Rousseau truly lived out his masochistic dreams. In his brief youthful liaison with the 11-year-old Mademoiselle Goton, he was satisfied. She 'played the schoolmistress' with him and spanked him, though 'this was a favour which had to be begged for on bended knees'. To his delight, she 'allowed herself to take the greatest liberties with me without permitting me to take a single one with her. She treated me exactly like a child. . . .' After a short time, the two precocious youngsters were separated.

During his youth, he was given to extravagant, uncon-summated infatuations with older women. And in due time he learned the facts of life, from the buxom Madame de Warens. He received an introduction to her house at Chambéry, Savoy, and lived with her and her lover–caretaker Claude Anet. Rousseau grew devoted to her, calling her *'maman'* while she called him 'little cat'. Five years later, *'maman'* offered Rousseau her favours – to be shared, of course, with Anet. The 'little cat' was 21 and she was 34 – it was time for him to become a man. She gave him a week to consider the proposition. He consented but, instead of being excited, he was repelled at the thought of having sex with her. For, after five years, Rousseau felt more like her son than her lover, saying, 'I loved her too much to desire her.' It turned out that Madame de Warens was cold in bed, and Rousseau didn't enjoy himself – 'Twice or thrice, as I pressed her passionately to me, I flooded her breast with my tears. It was as if I were committing incest.' He turned to fantasizing about other women while he was making love to her. The ménage à trois continued until Anet died in 1734. Rousseau stayed with Madame de Warens for three more years, finally leaving to seek his fortune when she brought in another young lover to live with them.

Rousseau's next romantic adventure began in 1745. At a hotel in Paris, he became infatuated with the chambermaid, 24-year-old Thérèse le Vasseur. Their affair lasted for the rest of his life. He told her from the start, 'I shall never leave you, but I shall never marry you.' After twenty-three years, he did marry her, in a spur-of-the-moment ceremony which he conducted himself. In a letter to a friend, he recommended a quarter of a century as a sensible length of time for a trial marriage. Thérèse was pretty, kind and a good cook, but completely unsuited intellectually to Rousseau. She could barely tell the time, never learned to spell correctly, was unable to remember the months of the year or count money. She was remarkably devoted to Rousseau consider-ing his difficult nature and cruelty towards their five bastard children. Despite her protests, Rousseau insisted each one be given at birth to the Foundling Hospital. His reasons were absurd – for example, he claimed that, since they weren't married, it was the only way to 'save her honour'. In later years, he was racked with grief over his actions, but never asked her for a spanking, and reported that she too was cold in bed. Interestingly, this was not the report of James Boswell (an ardent admirer of Rousseau), who constituted, as far as is known, Thérèse's only infidelity. Boswell wrote that he and Thérèse 'mated' thirteen different times. Thérèse told Boswell that, while he was 'vigorous' in bed, Rousseau's lovemaking lacked 'art'.

Rousseau encountered his wildest passion when 44. Countess Sophie d'Houdetot was a plain married woman. The problem was not Sophie's husband, but that she was devoted to her lover – an officer friend of Rousseau's who was often away. As usual, Rousseau 'loved her too much to possess her'. But that didn't stop him from trying: 'The continuance over three months of ceaseless stimulation and privation threw me into an exhaustion from which I did not recover for several years and brought on a rupture [a hernia] that I shall carry with me to the grave ... such was the sole amorous gratification.' All in all, he decided that it was the first and only time he had truly fallen in love; and Sophie served as inspiration for the terrifyingly moral Julie in his novel *The New Héloïse*.

Rousseau had numerous sexual eccentricities. He had the odd habit of going into raptures over inanimate objects. When living with Madame de Warens, he would wander through her house, kissing her armchair, the bedcurtains, even the floor. Another female friend sent him 'an under-petticoat which she had worn and out of which she wanted me to make myself a waistcoat. . . . It was as if she had stripped herself to clothe me. . . . In my emotion I kissed the note and the petticoat twenty times in tears.' (Thérèse thought he was mad.)

As a young man, Rousseau went through a period of exhibitionism. He would hide in dark alleys and, when a woman passed by, he would expose his buttocks, hoping that some day some bold female would spank his behind in passing. One time, he flashed before some girls fetching water at a well, admitting in *Confessions* that the sight was 'more laughable than seductive'. When one of the girls gave a cry of alarm, Rousseau was confronted by an intimidating posse consisting of an angry man and several old women with broom handles, but managed to worm his way out of trouble.

One of Rousseau's most incredible sexual escapades occurred early, while he was living in Venice. Although he claimed to

379

loathe prostitutes, he occasionally visited them. One such local beauty was Zulietta, a woman he elevated to goddess-like proportions in his mind. But, on his first visit to her, as he was about to 'pluck the fruit', he became deeply upset and began to cry. How, he wondered, could it be that this divine being was a mere prostitute? He decided there must be something wrong with her, 'a secret flaw that makes her repulsive'. She managed to cheer him up and, when he was about to enter her, he suddenly discovered the secret defect: 'I perceived that she had a malformed nipple, I beat my brow, looked harder and made certain this nipple did not match the other.' Casanova had enjoyed Zulietta three years earlier and mentioned no such flaw. But Rousseau 'started wondering about the reason for this malformation ... I was struck by the thought that it resulted from some remarkable imperfection of Nature.... I saw clear as daylight that I held in my arms some kind of monster rejected by Nature, man and love.' When he pointed this out to her, she scornfully told him to 'leave the ladies alone and go and study mathematics'.

Much of Rousseau's unhappiness was directly traceable to an extremely painful bladder ailment which troubled him all his life. He suffered a congestion of the trigones, or posterior part of the urethra, and inflammation of the bladder which caused frequent, incomplete and painful urination and fever. He needed a chamber pot constantly when his bladder tormented him and Thérèse had to insert a catheter into his penis, but this often did not work. Sex became so painful for him that he gave it up entirely for the last twenty-three years of his life, returning to masturbation.

A.W. (Lists 2, 6, 9, 20, 21, 36, 37, 44, 46, 49)

♣ Peter Paul Rubens
28 June 1577 to 30 May 1640

Many of Rubens's more than 3000 works featured women who seemed 'made of milk and blood'. Better than any other painter, he knew how to express the colour gradations of a full female body. His plump figures were not only the ideals of his time, but certainly more rewarding to paint, with their fleshy hollows, mounds and dimples. Early in his life, Rubens was a royal favourite in most European courts, becoming immensely rich as a result.

Though he painted bacchanalia and fat billowing buttocks, Rubens had the deportment of a Flemish banker and the manners of a diplomat. His parents had fled the troops of the Spanish Duke of Alba which were murdering, raping and pillaging Calvinists, intellectuals and merchants in the Netherlands. The refugee family settled near Cologne. His father, Jan Rubens, secured an appointment as financial and legal adviser to 26-year-old Princess Anne of Saxony, a beautiful, blue-eyed blonde whose husband, William of Orange, had left her in a castle for several years while he sought to recapture the Netherlands from Spain. Anne and Jan had a long, embarrassingly public affair which culminated – after Anne's pregnancy – in her banishment and Jan's imprisonment. Eventually the princess bore a girl; soon afterwards, Anne returned to her family in Saxony, where she died five years later. Eventually released from prison, Jan Rubens found that he and his immediate family, shunned by fellow refugees, were not allowed to return to Cologne. Peter Paul Rubens was born at this time. While Peter was still a youth, his father died, and later the family returned to their native Flanders. As a teenager, Rubens had to give up his schooling so that his mother could pay off the dowry for his sister's marriage, and he was made page in the court of the Countess de Lalaing. Perhaps he learned his courtly ways there, but he suffered from the countess's cruel games, which included dressing up the young pages as girls to entertain her female guests. Eventually, Rubens persuaded his mother to take him away from court and began his studies in painting. He rapidly surpassed his various teachers and went on to become Europe's most illustrious painter. He married twice, siring eight children whom he attended with much more interest than most fathers of his time. Friend of Pope Paul V, emissary of Marie de Médicis, and knighted by Charles I, Rubens built up an estate so large that it took five years to take an inventory of it. Crippled by gout in his final years, he died in his sixties.

During his years of study and work in Italy (1600–1608), Rubens had many casual affairs, usually with Italian actresses and prostitutes. His first serious love affair was with an unidentified Roman aristocrat. Although she apparently returned his feelings, her parents ended the relationship between their daughter and the unknown foreign artist. At 32, Rubens married his first wife, 18-year-old Isabella Brandt from Antwerp, a year after returning from his travels. Isabella was lovely, tall and dark-haired. Though most of his artist colleagues were philanderers, Rubens was not. The couple had three children of their own and adopted his brother's two after he died. Isabella was probably his model for many of the Madonnas of his early work. She died at 35 and Rubens lamented losing her.

After Isabella's death, Rubens had a year-long affair with Suzanne Fourment, the lush model in his famous painting *Chapeau de Paille*. The discreet relationship ended when Suzanne married another man. Two years later, at 53, Rubens married Suzanne's dazzling, buxom 16-year-old sister, Helena, who became his favourite model, and he gloried in painting her naked. Assisted by troops of apprentices and helpers, Rubens painted his fair, pink-and-white Helena, who had radiant health and a generous body. Helena is featured in many of Rubens's works, and is the prototype of the 'Rubens woman'. He painted her being hauled by the horses of captors, rescued, raped – or lost in divine thought and sensuous play. Kenneth Clark wrote, 'Rubens's women are both responsive and detached . . . happy but not at all self-conscious.' This marriage was happy, too. Helena gave Rubens five children, the last born almost nine months after his death.

R.G.P. (Lists 2, 6, 9, 20, 21, 36, 37, 44, 46, 49)

❧ John Ruskin
8 February 1819 to 20 January 1900

Appointed Slade Professor of Fine Art at Oxford in 1870, Ruskin was Britain's first art professor as well as an eminently successful author, critic and lecturer. He spent his declining years at Brantwood, his estate overlooking Coniston Water, supported by the income from his published writings. His inherited fortune had long since been expended in philanthropy, support of a huge retinue and bad investments.

At 16, armed only with such sexual knowledge as his puritanical mother had chosen to reveal, Ruskin had set sail on the sea of love, and promptly foundered. His first affair – with 14-year-old Adèle Domecq, the daughter of his father's French partner – wavered for four years, fed by copious love letters expressing romanticized desire. Ruskin's hopes were abruptly ended in 1840, when his mother declared that a Roman Catholic marriage was '. . . too monstrous to be possible'. Eight years later, Ruskin tried again. He dutifully courted – with his mother's approval – a beautiful Scottish cousin named Euphemia Gray, and married her in 1848. The stunned bride learned that her spouse was neither able nor willing to have sexual intercourse. His excuses ranged from hating children to protecting her pristine beauty from the ravages of pregnancy. Shocked but patient, Effie agreed to a compromise in which Ruskin would 'marry' her when she reached 25, a full five years away. But, in 1854, Ruskin unilaterally extended the deadline. During a stormy fight, Effie learned the real cause of his impotence. An angry Ruskin confessed that he'd been disgusted by sex on their wedding night because women, unlike marble statues, have pubic hair. Effie won an annulment the same year, after an embarrassing medical examination had verified her virginity.

In 1858, Ruskin – regressing emotionally – began a tragic relationship with Rose La Touche, a 9-year-old Irish schoolgirl brought to him for art lessons. His nympholeptic affection gradually turned to idealized love over the next eight years, nurtured by his contact with other young girls whom he taught at Winnington Hall. When his 'Rosie' was 18, and he 47, Ruskin proposed marriage. Rose asked him to wait three years. He counted the days. She was in turn affectionate and evasive. When she was 21, she rejected Ruskin. There were two reasons. For one thing, she was unable to reconcile the conflict between his scepticism and her own fervent Catholicism. For another, Rose had heard of his 'physical infirmities' when he had been married to Effie Gray, now Lady Millais. A family friend asked Ruskin, 'Was it true that you were incapable?' Ruskin denied it. He said he had not loved Effie when he had married her, but knew he could have completed their sexual relationship once he came to love her. But in a letter Effie warned Rose against marrying Ruskin. His mind, she wrote, was 'inhuman'. In 1875, Rose died, a bedridden hysteric beset by both mental and physical ills. The grief-stricken Ruskin unexpectedly found a long-lost love letter from Rose after a séance at which her spirit allegedly appeared. He considered the discovery to be an omen and carried the letter in his breast pocket – preserved between gold leaves – until his death.

Ruskin's paternal grandfather was insane, and he himself was a manic depressive. At 21, he had an eighteen-month-long collapse, precipitated by frustration in love. His writings, tuned to his mental state, were cyclic. Ruskin's many obsessions led to nightmares so garish that he feared to sleep and believed he was going insane. In his lectures, he often claimed that he had been given an exceptional knowledge of God. Ruskin had a mental breakdown in February 1878 and recurrent attacks of varying severity throughout the rest of his life. In old age, his powers of concentration were sharply curtailed by fits of depression, delusions of persecution and a sense of gloom that sometimes ended in violence. Nevertheless, in his saner moments, between 1885 and 1889, he produced the twenty-eight-part autobiography *Praeterita*. With this, the final curtain descended on what Ruskin wryly labelled '... the not, I hope, unentertaining history of the Don Quixote of Denmark Hill'.

W.K. (Lists 3, 17, 29, 30)

♣ Bertrand Russell
18 May 1872 to 2 February 1970

Bertrand Russell, British philosopher, mathematician and pacifist, achieved scholarly renown with *Principia Mathematica* (1910–13), which he wrote with A. N. Whitehead. Russell also wrote numerous more popular works, including *History of Western Philosophy* (1945), *Marriage and Morals* (1929) and his *Autobiography* (1967–9).

Russell, like Voltaire, was the 'laughing philosopher' of his generation. An elfin animated face surmounted his slight, aristocratic body. His irreverent wit and personal magnetism were part of a huge appetite for life. Yet, also like Voltaire, he was a deeply passionate man whose rage at public policy often gave him, in newspaper photographs, the aspect of an avenging angel. Throughout his life, he attacked conventional wisdom on everything from sex, education and religion to women's rights, politics and nuclear arms. Born into one of England's oldest families and raised by his austere Presbyterian grandmother, Russell was a shy, oversensitive child much concerned with his 'sins'. His rejection of religion at 18 led him to mathematics in search of 'whether anything could be known' – a lifelong pursuit. An outspoken pacifist, he was jailed as a security risk in 1918, but supported the allies in the Second World War. Russell had almost achieved an affectionate popular following by the time he won the Nobel Prize for literature in 1950. But his controversial stands on the Vietnam War, Kennedy's assassination and nuclear testing sullied his reputation in the eyes of 'authority'. In his late eighties, he led protest marches and sit-down demonstrations and was again jailed. 'I do so hate to leave this world,' he said, shortly before he died peacefully at 97.

'At 15,' Russell wrote, he was 'continually distracted by erections, and I fell into the practice of masturbating'. He suddenly dropped the practice at 20 'because I was in love'. Alys Pearsall Smith – from a prominent Philadelphia Quaker socialist family – was five years older than Russell. He determined to marry her and first kissed her four months after he proposed. His grandmother vigorously fought the match, calling Alys a 'baby-snatcher' and 'designing female' and whispering dire stories of insanity in both families. The couple speculated about the frequency of their future sexual intercourse, but both remained virgins until their marriage in 1894. Their sexual difficulties during their honeymoon 'appeared to us merely comic,' Russell reported, 'and were soon overcome.' Alys, educated to think of sex as God's grudge against women, supposed that her carnal desires would be properly infrequent, but Russell 'did not find it necessary' to argue the matter. Though both believed in free love, neither practised it; their first five years together were happy and highly moral.

About 1901, however, Russell fell in love with Evelyn Whitehead, gifted wife of his collaborator A.N. Whitehead. This relationship, never physical, came as an 'awakening' to Russell, who underwent an almost mystical 'change of heart' in many of his feelings and views. Suddenly realizing – during a solitary bicycle ride – that he no longer loved Alys, he quite promptly told her so. 'I had no wish to be unkind,' he wrote, 'but I believed in those days (what experience has taught me to think possibly open to doubt) that in intimate relations one should speak the truth.' For nine more years, Russell and Alys maintained the façade, but occupied separate bedrooms and were thoroughly miserable. 'About twice a year,' Russell wrote, 'I would attempt sex relations with her, in the hope of alleviating her misery, but she no longer attracted me, and the attempt was futile.'

One of his first tentative flings involved a young secretary with a matchless Victorian name – Miss Ivy Pretious. In 1910, he met Lady Ottoline Morrell, wife of Liberal MP Philip Morrell. Russell described Lady Ottoline as 'very tall, with a long thin face something like a horse, and very beautiful hair'. Their sexual relationship was furtive; Ottoline had no desire to leave or embarrass her husband. Philip appreciated their discretion. Russell left Alys that spring and did not see her again until 1950, when they met as 'friendly acquaintances'. Lady Ottoline 'made me much less of a Puritan,' he wrote and, though they had stormy quarrels, they remained lovers until 1916 and close friends until her death in 1938.

Russell had stopped being a puritan. After 1910 – though married three more times – he was never again monogamous until extreme old age. His private life was a chaos of serious affairs, secret trysts and emotional tightrope acts that constantly threatened, if never quite exploded into, ruinous scandal. In his letters to Ottoline and other lovers, his conscience drove him to confess, even though he 'made little of' his escapades with other women. Surprisingly most of his lovers tolerated his wanderings and each other well.

During his first American lecture tour in 1914, Russell became intimate with Helen Dudley, daughter of a Chicago surgeon, and invited her to England. 'My darling,' he wrote to Ottoline, 'please do not think that this means *any* lessening of my love for you.' When Helen actually arrived, however, Russell felt 'an absolute blank indifference to her'. By this time, he had taken up with Irene Cooper Willis, a talented, beautiful researcher. But Irene feared scandal and Russell hated caution. 'I wish to goodness I had not made love to her,' he told Ottoline.

In 1916, Russell met Lady Constance Malleson, a 21-year-old, auburn-haired actress (stage name Colette O'Neil). Her marriage to actor Miles Malleson was 'open' by mutual agreement, and Russell remained her lover until 1920, often spending holidays with the couple. They renewed their affair three times over the next thirty years and Colette always sent roses on his birthday. But his affections for Colette 'could never make a *shadow* of a difference to what I feel for you,' he wrote to Ottoline.

Russell desperately wanted children. In 1919, he met Dora Black, a suffragette also interested in children without the fetters of marriage and monogamy. Still in love with Colette, and regularly confiding in Ottoline, Russell went to China to take a post at Peking University – Dora went with him. She was eight months pregnant when they returned to England in August 1921. 'From the first we used no precautions,' said Russell. Having agreed on a 'marriage compatible with minor affairs', and with their baby due in one month, they married. After a second child, the Russells established the experimental Beacon Hill School. Its liberal policies included advocacy of free love for those on the staff, and Russell enjoyed several affairs with young female teachers. While he was philandering at school and during lecture tours in the USA Dora had an affair with American journalist Griffin Barry, and bore him two children. Russell clearly resented this application of his theories: he had said in their marriage contract, 'If she should have a child that was not mine there would be a divorce.' Strained beyond endurance, the marriage ended in 1935.

Russell felt he didn't know any woman until he had slept with her. In *Marriage and Morals*, he advocated both trial and open marriage, exceedingly radical ideas for 1929. He did not think he could 'remain physically fond of any woman for more than seven or eight years'. Dora wanted another child by him, but he 'found it impossible'. His affair with 21-year-old Joan Folwell was typical. 'My only fear,' he told her, 'is lest you may find me inadequate sexually, as I am no longer young . . . . but I think there are ways in which I can make up for it.' She reported years later, 'I had dinner with him and the third time I slept [with him] . . . this lasted over three years. But the sleeping wasn't a success so I gave him up.' For all his galloping satyriasis, Russell apparently suffered frequently from impotence.

In 1930, he began a long affair with Patricia 'Peter' Spence, his children's young governess. They married in 1936, and a son was born the next year. The family spent the war years in the USA where 'Peter' Spence became increasingly unhappy. Russell's daughter recalled their unpleasant domestic life: 'She had found marriage to the great man something of a disappointment. His passion . . . was replaced by kindly courtesy and a show of affection thinly unsatisfying to a romantic young woman.' By 1946, now in his seventies, Russell took up with the young wife of a Cambridge lecturer; their relationship lasted three years. Colette, whom he saw for the last time in 1949, wrote to him bitterly, 'I see everything quite clear now, and it seems a dreary end to all our years. . . . Three times I've been drawn into [your life] and three times thrown aside.'

Peter Spence divorced Russell in 1952. Later that year he married his old friend Edith Finch, an American teacher and author. Russell, cooled at last from his self-declared inability to damp his 'abnormally strong sexual urges', finally enjoyed a successful marriage. And Colette sent him red roses on his last birthday.

J.E. (Lists 1, 8, 9, 10, 22, 25, 42)

♣ Lillian Russell

4 December 1861 to 6 June 1922

In the era just before radio and motion pictures, when the great medium of entertainment was the stage, Lilian Russell was *the* American star. Celebrated for her great beauty, her clear soprano voice, and her flamboyant life-style, she specialized in light operatic and musical comedy roles, reigning as the toast of Broadway for some thirty years. Russell exuded a sexual magnetism comparable to that of Marilyn Monroe. She was surrounded by wealthy and titled suitors who showered her with flowers, furs, jewels ($100,000 worth from one anonymous admirer alone) – even cold cash. But, like the latter-day sex goddess, Russell also had a streak of vulnerability which involved her in a succession of disastrous marriages.

At 18, Russell married Harry Braham, the musical conductor of her first show. She bore him a child which died while in the care of a nursemaid. (The parents were busy at the theatre at the time.) The Brahams' marriage never recovered from this loss. Seduced again by music, she eloped a few years later with Edward Solomon, a composer and conductor who neglected to tell his bride he was already married, and also failed to provide for Russell and their daughter. Husband number three was Giovanni Perugini (real name: Jack Chatterton), a caricature of the handsome tenor, vain, fatuous and, as it happened, gay. Theirs was derisively called 'a marriage of convenience – his', for Perugini was so absorbed in the advancement of his career that he left Russell a 'kissless bride'. ('I love you too much to defile you,' he claimed.) Russell, who passed her wedding night playing poker, was not amused, particularly when her husband began verbally abusing her in public. She left Perugini after two months of marriage when he tried to throw her out of a seventh-storey window. Perugini told a newspaper reporter: 'Do you realize the enormity of this woman's offence – her crime? Do you know what she did to me ? Why, sir, she took all the pillows; she used my rouge; she misplaced my manicure set; she used my special handkerchief perfume for her bath ... Once she threatened to spank me, and she did, with a hairbrush, too. You can't expect a fellow to take a spanking with equanimity, can you?'

Russell was painted in the press of the Gay Nineties as a modern Jezebel. It was rumoured that she smoked cigarettes (which ladies simply did not do), conducted orgies on the tiger skin rugs in her New York townhouse, and had been seen with a circus strong man. Actually, she was involved in a longstanding affair with Jesse Lewisohn, heir to a copper fortune and a fellow poker player. Together they made up a frequent foursome with Diamond Jim Brady, the larger-than-life salesman of steel railway carriages, and Edna McCauley, a woman whom Brady passed off as his niece for twelve years. Unhappily for Russell, however, this was to be another star-crossed love affair: Lewisohn eloped with McCauley, leaving Russell to console herself with Brady. In fact, theirs was a unique friendship. It centred around their huge appetites. One appetite they shared was a taste for high living. Brady over-indulged himself in everything except alcohol. It was his habit to give away everything he owned once a year, and then to replace it all in a flurry of buying. He customarily wore up to $250,000 of precious gems. Their second shared appetite was a mutual passion for eating. Russell was by now a well-upholstered 11 stone 11 pounds, and Brady was a king-size 17 stone 12 pounds. Russell was the only woman he had ever met who could keep up with him at the table – the two of them often got together just to gorge themselves on several trays of well-buttered sweet-corn. (Brady often single-handedly demolished the entire pantry at Charles Rector's restaurant on Broadway. After his death, his stomach was found to be six times normal size.) Brady proposed marriage to Russell several times, once by spilling a million dollars into her lap. She declined with thanks, fearing it would wreck a beautiful friendship – but she often took him along on her dates with other men.

In her fifties, Russell retreated from the stage to a second career, as a syndicated columnist offering advice on health, beauty and love. She also used her fame in the cause of women's suffrage; when, as the greatest sex symbol of her day, with a profile that was practically a national institution, she marched the length of New York's Fifth Avenue in the great suffrage parade of 1915, it was one of her proudest performances.

C.D. and M.S. (Lists 17, 38)

♣ George Herman 'Babe' Ruth
6 February 1895 to 16 August 1948

The best-known baseball player in the history of American sport, he was the first to gain world renown. In the Second World War, when Japanese troops charged a US Marine emplacement, they shouted, 'To hell with Babe Ruth!' Babe Ruth *was* America. Born into a poor Baltimore family, he was saved from becoming a juvenile delinquent when his exasperated parents sent him to St Mary's Industrial School. Excelling at baseball, he played for the Baltimore Orioles, was signed by the famous Boston Red Sox, and finally sold to the New York Yankees. Lovable and sentimental, he was also undisciplined, crude, bawdy and vulgar. Although a selfish hedonist, Babe Ruth never forgot the advice Mayor Jimmy Walker of New York gave him: to remember that he was the idol of millions of 'dirty-faced kids' out there, and should behave accordingly. After retiring from the Yankees in 1934, Ruth's ambition was to become a team manager. But no one would hire him as a manager because of his irresponsibility. His last years were embittered, before he died of throat cancer at 53. Over one hundred thousand fans paraded past his bier in Yankee Stadium, 'the house that Ruth built'.

His appetites were gargantuan. His excesses included eating (a stack of mutton chops for breakfast, endless hot dogs throughout the day), gambling, drinking, carousing and copulating. Hardly a day passed during his career when he did not have sex with at least one woman. He liked women as much as baseball. He had no favourites, bedding women who were tall, short, fat, thin, beautiful, ugly: there were socialites, film starlets, secretaries, other men's wives, and whores in every big city in the USA. Whenever the team arrived in a new town and moved into a hotel, Babe Ruth left his suitcase with team-mate Ping Bodie and hastened out to find some young woman. He was usually gone all night. When a reporter asked Bodie what Ruth was really like, Bodie said he did not know. 'But you room with him,' the reporter persisted. Bodie shook his head. 'I don't room with him. I room with his suitcase.' At other times, Babe Ruth entertained women in his hotel. In Detroit, he once rented four adjoining rooms, purchased a piano, and invited team-mates and stray women to a party. After a while, Babe stood on a chair, waved his beer glass and bellowed, 'All right ladies, any girl who doesn't want to fuck can leave right now!'

He was insatiable and possessed great stamina. In St Louis he took over a whorehouse for an entire night, stating he was going to have sex with every woman in the house. After that, he took them on one by one, mounted each successfully, and in the morning celebrated by consuming an omelette made with eighteen eggs.

Robert W. Creamer researched and described Babe Ruth in action – sexually – in his excellent biography, *Babe*: 'One teammate, asked if Ruth had an exceptionally big penis, frowned a little as he searched his memory and shook his head. "No, he said. It was normal size ... Babe's wasn't noticeably big. What was extraordinary was his ability to keep doing it all the time. He was continually with women, morning and night. I don't know how he kept going." He was very noisy in bed, visceral grunts and gasps and whoops accompanying his erotic exertions. "He was the noisiest fucker in North America," a friend recalled.'

All this activity sometimes got Ruth into trouble. Biographer Ken Sobol noted, 'The circumstances of one unsavoury rape in which he had been involved were already known to several sportswriters.' Late in 1922, Babe Ruth was slapped with a paternity or breach-of-promise suit for $50,000 filed on behalf of Dolores Dixon, a teenage employee in a Manhattan department store. She claimed that she had become pregnant by Ruth, who had promised to marry her, and had committed statutory rape. Ruth called it blackmail, his lawyer called it extortion. The matter went to trial in 1923, but was settled out of court.

During his busiest years in bed with other women, Ruth had a wife whom he sorely neglected. Helen Woodford, an attractive auburn-haired Texas girl, had been a waitress in a Boston café when Ruth fell in love with her. They were married in 1914 in a Catholic Church near Baltimore. He was 19 and she 17. Throughout their fourteen years of marriage, Helen's life with Ruth was hell. He gave her furs, an eighty acre farm, an adopted daughter named Dorothy, but neither time nor fidelity. His affairs caused her to have a nervous breakdown. She left Ruth in 1928, and the following year died in a fire. Ruth mourned her briefly. Three months later, he married Mrs Claire Merritt Hodgson, who was classy and still a beauty when she moved to New York to become a model and part-time actress. Ruth was introduced to her at a ball game and had been having an affair with her when Helen died. He married Claire in April 1929. Claire tamed him, changing his entire life-style. She put him on a strict diet,

391

curbed his drinking and saved his money. She forced a ten o'clock curfew on him when he went to parties, and she knew about all the other women. 'The Babe brought out the beast in a lot of ladies the world over,' she wrote in her autobiography, 'and I enjoyed very much setting them straight on their problem.' To the end, their marriage was a happy one.

I.W. (Lists 11, 17, 22, 31)

✤ Donatien Alphonse François de Sade
2 June 1740 to 2 December 1814

Because de Sade was imprisoned by royal decree for staging orgies during which he whipped and sodomized young women, his name has become synonymous with unlimited sexual licence, especially the licence to derive pleasure from inflicting pain – sadism. Briefly, the facts of his remarkable life are these.

After two brief incarcerations for 'outrageous debauchery', the young and handsome Marquis de Sade, lieutenant governor of four royal provinces, was forced to transfer his quest for strange pleasures from Paris to his ancestral chateau in the south of France. When five Marseilles prostitutes accused him of attempting to sodomize and poison them, his mother-in-law obtained a *lettre de cachet* (a royal order for indefinite detention without trial) and eventually put him away in 1777 for twelve and a half years. In prison, he became a prolific writer, churning our conventional work as well as frenzied erotica. At last, the French Revolution freed him, when the Constituent Assembly abolished *lettres de cachet*. He was now Citizen Sade, a pamphleteer, orator, and a living legend for having incited, from his tower cell, the historic storming of the Bastille. Promoted to revolutionary judge during the Reign of Terror, he found himself incapable of demanding his mother-in-law's execution when her case came before him. He was denounced as a moderate, escaped the guillotine only by luck, and turned to a theatrical career. In 1801, he was prosecuted by the Napoleonic regime's censors, ostensibly for his erotic novel *Justine*, but actually for a pamphlet lampooning Napoleon and his wife, Josephine. He was found criminally insane and lived out his life at Charenton asylum, where the director allowed him to stage dramas in which he often acted the villain's part. De Sade's career had begun by 18 October 1763. Jeanne Testard, 20, a fan-maker and part-time prostitute, had entered a house of assignation with an elegant, auburn-haired young nobleman. He led her to a small inner room draped in black; its walls, on which religious art mingled strangely with pornography, featured a large collection of whips.

Later, he explained, she would flog him with one of them, and she could choose one with which to be flogged. Meanwhile, perhaps an enema or a little sodomy...? She declined both, but was forced at gunpoint to smash a crucifix.

Unfortunately for de Sade's future victims, his in-laws, the Montreuils, were influential at court. After fifteen days in jail, Sade professed repentance and was released. The Paris police warned brothel keepers not to supply him with any more prostitutes for his private orgies. As a result, he began to pick up amateurs. On Easter Sunday 1768, he accosted Rose Keller, a thirtyish widow lately reduced to public begging, politely conducted her to a house in the suburbs, and made her strip and lie face down on a couch. He then began to beat her with a whip of knotted cords, pausing several times to rub a white ointment into the lacerations. Her screams for pity seemed only to energize him, until he stopped with an appalling, orgasmic cry. Keller was able to escape and find help. Although she was bribed into silence by de Sade's family, the authorities had already taken a statement from her. De Sade was jailed as an example to the many other sexually depraved aristocrats. He earned a quick release by getting his wife, the uncomplaining Renée-Pélagie, pregnant again when she visited him at the jail. Paroled, he was ordered to live quietly on his estate in the south. He and his family went there – and for company invited his wife's lively younger sister, Anne-Prospère, who was soon his wife in all but name. That winter, a private world of pleasure was created in the old chateau of La Coste; erotic spectacles were staged and the entire household, including not only de Sade's sister-in-law but his wife, took part willingly in elegant indecencies. Too elegant, it seems, for when de Sade visited nearby Marseilles to collect a debt he instructed his valet Latour to procure several young women for the most violent orgy yet. Four waterfront prostitutes, aged 18 to 23, were subjected by de Sade to a complicated ritual in which each was in turn beaten and ordered to beat him; in between beatings they were offered various combinations of anal and vaginal intercourse with de Sade and, alternatively or simultaneously, Latour. All the women were repeatedly offered handfuls of anise-flavoured *bonbons*. That same evening de Sade attempted a similar orgy with another prostitute. Hours later, she and one of the girls used earlier were vomiting uncontrollably; they had overdosed on Spanish Fly, a common aphrodisiac of the time. De Sade and Latour fled the city but were condemned to death in absentia and executed 'in effigy'. Caught and jailed in Sardinia, de Sade escaped and lived the next few years as a fugitive.

In May, 1774, the *lettre de cachet* obtained by Madame de Montreuil seemed about to lapse with the accession of a new king. Sade lost no time in realizing his latest fantasy: he would lure young girls to the chateau and personally undertake their sex education. Anne-Prospère had now left him, but his wife Renée-Pélagie was his ally in everything. With her support, he engaged an experienced procuress who recruited five 15-year-old girls and a small boy, supposedly for domestic service. There were orgies that Renée-Pélagie may have directed. The outcome was more tragedy: two girls escaped, one needing medical treatment; the parents of three began legal action; the procuress had a baby by de Sade, departed, and was jailed by *lettre de cachet* (Madame de Montreuil's work) to stop her from talking, and the baby died of neglect. Undaunted, de Sade found older replacements through a corrupt local monk who assured anxious parents that the 'discipline' at the chateau was well up to convent standards.

Early in 1777, news arrived from Paris that de Sade's mother was dying. Although he had never cared for her, he set off at once. Since friends had warned him of Madame de Montreuil's intentions, it seems likely that he wanted to be caught, and he was. In prison de Sade discovered two enduring sources of sexual satisfaction: masturbation and literature. His imaginary orgies were so successful that he never attempted real ones again. Renée-Pélagie, loyal throughout his imprisonment, divorced him on his release. He soon formed a lasting relationship with the young actress Marie-Constance Renelle; he lived with her for a while in a hayloft at Versailles, baby-sitting for her little son and earning a few sous as a stagehand. She followed him to Charenton asylum, and seems not to have minded when this fat, rheumaticky, partially blind old man enlivened his last two years there with a pretty young woman from the asylum's laundry.

By the end of young de Sade's military service as a cavalry officer, he was hiring one woman a day. His down-at-heel father was delighted when the bourgeois but wealthy family of Renée-Pélagie de Montreuil suggested her as a suitable bride; marriage would steady the boy, he thought. Meanwhile de Sade had

394

actually fallen in love with a count's daughter, Laure de Lauris. She left him with a beautiful memory and a venereal infection.

Renée-Pélagie was pious and frigid, but de Sade impressed her charming young mother and her blonde and sexy younger sister (the story is told that he asked to marry the sister instead). His first arrest threw the entire family into shock. Almost with relief, Madame de Montreuil noted that, after his release, he followed the approved fashion and began keeping mistresses. There was Mademoiselle Colet, a popular actress at the Comédie Italienne; another actress, the buxom Mademoiselle Beauvoisin, whom he took south and allowed to pass as his wife; then a *poule de luxe*, Mademoiselle Dorville; then several ballet dancers, one of them an expert flagellator. Renée-Pélagie knew nothing of these affairs, but Madame de Montreuil did. What she did not know was that de Sade had an isolated suburban house outside Paris where he regularly staged bisexual orgies; one of them, at which he had flogged four women and then served them dinner, was the talk of the sexual underworld. It was to this house that he took Rose Keller – for a job, according to her testimony: for a debauch, according to his.

We know little of the Marseilles victims except their names and ages: Mariette Borelly (23), Marianette Laugier (20), Rose Coste (20) and Marianne Laverne (18), of the morning orgy; and Marguérite Costa (25), of the one attempted in the evening. Marguérite brought the first complaint, followed by the other four together. Latour, de Sade's partner in the affair, was said to be a nobleman's son; de Sade would switch roles with him socially as well as sexually, addressing him as 'Monsieur le marquis'. Latour and Anne-Prospère, who had stayed on at La Coste, accompanied de Sade when he fled over the border to Italy. Renée-Pélagie, a woman of such saintly character that de Sade must have worked hard indeed to corrupt her, was in the uncomfortable position of being her sister's rival. When de Sade was finally jailed, she became in good conscience what she had always tried to be – the perfect wife. The affair of the 15-year-old girls was so effectively hushed up that we cannot even be certain of their names. One of their successors was Catherine Trillet, known as Justine; promoted from the kitchen to de Sade's orgies, she would not leave him even when her father turned up brandishing a pistol. Her predecessor as household favourite was Gothon, Renée-Pélagie's personal maid, who remained fond of him and sent him fruit and jam in prison.

During his early prison years de Sade enjoyed, by letter, a platonic relationship with Marie-Dorothée de Rousse, his former housekeeper; he had always tended to separate sex from friendship. For a few months after his release he lived with a widow of 40, la Présidente de Fleurieu, but left her for the more sympathetic Marie-Constance Renelle, of whom he wrote, 'This woman is an angel sent to me by heaven.' In the asylum, with the director's connivance, she passed as de Sade's illegitimate daughter. We know that his last mistress, Madeleine Leclerc, was only 12 when de Sade's eyes first lighted on her and 15 when she became his mistress (he was 72); that her mother hoped the marquis would launch her as an actress; and that she shaved her pubic hair.

The original medical analyses of de Sade's case were oversimplified and now are out of date. New material – letters, diaries, etc. – which has come to light recently suggests that de Sade can no longer be regarded as a good example of sadism. Rather, he appears to have been a man with multiple personalities and a powerful intellect, who ended up disavowing the novels for which he is infamous, and whose cruelties were more theatrical than real. It was his irresponsibility as a member of the ruling class, not his complexes, that made these excesses criminal. De Sade claimed that the extreme thickness of his sperm made ejaculation painful. The diagnosis is unlikely, but the symptom may explain his algolagnia (pleasure in both receiving and inflicting pain). His anal obsession is more puzzling, since he despised homosexuals: he may have enjoyed sodomy just because the law forbade it. Perhaps, because of his experiences as a former cavalry officer, he liked to 'ride' (and whip) anything resembling horseflesh. More likely, he was so terrified by the wild emotions that women aroused in him that he tried to subdue them in order to subdue himself.

J.M.B.E. (Lists 3, 9, 11, 14, 17, 18, 20, 22, 24, 25, 26, 34, 35, 36, 37, 40, 52)

♣ George Sand

1 July 1804 to 8 June 1876

Armandine Aurore Lucie Dupin was raised by her grandmother on the family's country estate at Nohant, 150 miles south of Paris. Her two years formal education at a convent ended when, after a stint as leader of the *diables* (bad girls), she turned pious and talked of becoming a nun, whereupon her deist grandmother yanked her out of school. At the age of 17, Aurore inherited Nohant. After an unsuccessful marriage, which produced two children, she ran off to Paris and began her writing career, taking George Sand as her pen name. When her first novel, *Indiana*, was published in the spring of 1832, it was a resounding success, the first of many.

A champion of women's rights, she billed herself as 'the Spartacus of women's slavery'. However, her heroines, often caught in marital traps, nearly always won their freedom through fortuitous turns of fate (for example, a husband's accidental death). According to one critic, 'In George Sand, when a lady wants to change her lover, God is there to facilitate the transfer.' Unfortunately, in real life, Sand usually had to make the transfer herself.

Interpreters of George Sand have called her fickle and heartless; have labelled her bisexual or lesbian; have hinted at incest (in view of her enormous love for her son Maurice) and at a covert maternal instinct that encouraged her to take younger lovers. The cigar-smoking woman whose sexuality has aroused such interest was once described by Charles Dickens as resembling 'the queen's monthly nurse'. She was short and swarthy, with heavy features and dark eyes. Her manner was brusque. In her intellect and passion for living lay her sensual appeal.

Her first sexual encounter was probably with neighbour Stéphane de Grandsagne when she was 16 or 17. Grandsagne may have fathered her daughter Solange, born in 1828. At 18 she married 27-year-old Casimir Dudevant, who proved to be a drunken boor and beat her from time to time. Although she left him – and their children – in 1831, they were not legally separated until 1836.

It was in Paris that her love life really began. Her first Parisian lover, Jules Sandeau, with whom she briefly collaborated on a book, was typical of the men who attracted her – younger than she by seven years, frail, blond and artistic. Long after their affair had ended, Sandeau, still bitter, described her as a 'graveyard'. Bad endings were to become typical of her love affairs.

Sand needed to be in love to enjoy sex. A short experiment in loveless copulation with writer Prosper Mérimée was a disaster. Though some of her lovers accused her of frigidity, it seems that in truth she was like many women – passionate when aroused by romance, indifferent when not. She spoke of biting, beating and kissing Sandeau; and of Michel de Bourges, a married lover

397

whom she adored in spite of his bald ugliness, she confessed he caused her to 'tremble with desire'. When rejected, she suffered – even grovelled. As her stormy relationship with Alfred de Musset drew to a close, she cut off her hair and sent it to him.

With Frédéric Chopin – tubercular, aristocratic, an opium smoker, and six years younger than she – Sand ran the gamut. In 1838, at the beginning of their relationship, she compared his attitude toward sex to that of an old woman and wailed, 'Can there ever be love without a single kiss, and kisses without *volupté?*' Long before the end of their nine years together, he complained that she wouldn't sleep with *him*.

Among her other lovers were engraver Alexandre Damien Manceau, who lived with her in calm serenity from the time he was 32 (she was 45) until he died fifteen years later, and a painter called Charles Marchal, 39 to her 60, whom she called her 'fat baby'.

Gossip linked her with others. Gustave Planche, a literary critic who was careless about personal hygiene, fought a duel to defend her literary honour against another critic who had attacked her novel *Lélia* (the shots misfired; the sales of *Lélia* shot up). It is not clear whether she ever had sex with him. Nor is it clear whether she had sex with women, notably with actress Marie Dorval, to whom she wrote letters that would today be considered erotic but were common-place among women friends at the time. Example: '. . . in the theatre or in your bed, I simply must come and kiss you, my lady, or I shall do something crazy!'

A.E. (Lists 14, 17, 25)

❦ Jean-Paul Sartre
21 June 1905 to 15 April 1980

As novelist, playwright and philosopher of existentialism – a philosophy which holds that people are responsible for their actions, even in a random, absurd universe – Sartre had an international influence on the post-Second World War generations.

Son of a French naval officer who died a year after his birth, Sartre was raised by his mother, Anne-Marie Schweitzer (her first cousin was Albert Schweitzer) in his grandparents' Parisian home. A timid, ugly child, Sartre had virtually no childhood friends and retreated into fantasy, especially after he discovered books at the age of 4. Even though he was over-protected by his mother and dominated by his grandfather, Sartre developed an assertive personality. After he entered the Ecole Normale Supérieure, Sartre rejected his mother's and her parents' influence and bourgeois life. After graduating, he became a leftist teacher and writer. While serving with the French army as a weatherman in 1940, he was captured and jailed by the Germans. Six months later, he was released and joined the Resistance as a propagandist. After the war, Sartre's genius flowered and his reputation – based on plays like *No Exit* and novels such as *Nausea* – became worldwide.

Politically, Sartre was associated with communism and advocated proletarian revolution. He wrote political pamphlets and participated in demonstrations. After the Hungarian Revolution of 1956, he broke with the Stalinists and later drifted towards Maoism. In 1964, he was awarded the Nobel Prize for Literature, but refused it because he felt it was being offered by the forces of conservatism. A man who had renounced materialism for the world of ideas, Sartre, who chain-smoked and constantly took amphetamines, died of pulmonary congestion after a heart attack in 1980.

At 19, Sartre met a woman named Camille at a funeral. The 22-year-old Camille had been seduced by a family friend as a child and had worked in brothels since the age of 18. For four days and nights the young lovers stayed in bed until relatives finally forced them apart. Their relationship lasted – on and off – for over five years, until Camille tired of Sartre's poverty and found a wealthy older lover.

In 1929, while at university, Sartre met Simone de Beauvoir, an intelligent and attractive fellow student who became a famous feminist writer. Sartre was infatuated, and Simone was impressed by the tremendous intellect of this 5 feet 4 inches tall, wall-eyed man. They quickly became lovers, and their relationship lasted over fifty years. However, Sartre hated what he called 'bourgeois marriage' and renounced the institution along with parenthood. During their early years together, Sartre and Simone discussed extensively their ideas about love, commitment, marriage and sex. They agreed their relationship should be open: they would support each other in times of need, but also allow each other 'contingent loves'.

In 1934, while studying in Berlin, Sartre exercised his rights for the first time and had an affair with Marie, the wife of another student. Back in Paris for Christmas, Sartre informed Simone

399

of the affair. By February, Simone told the supervisor where she was teaching that she was having a nervous breakdown and needed a leave of absence. Heading directly for Berlin, she met Marie, and her fears were removed when Marie and Sartre explained that theirs was only a temporary relationship which did not threaten Sartre's commitment to Simone.

Back in Paris, Simone took one of her students under her wing, tutoring her and allowing her to live in her apartment. When Sartre returned to Paris, he also took a liking to this Russian emigrant teenager, Olga Kosakiewicz. At this time, Sartre experimented with mescaline and for months afterwards had temporary hallucinations. Olga would accompany Sartre on walks, during which he would vividly describe giant lobsters that were following them. This nurse–patient relationship developed into a sexual relationship and a subsequent living arrangement that included Simone. In her autobiographical novel, *She Came To Stay*, Simone tells how the younger woman usurped her lover and states, 'There is something absolutely valid and true in jealousy.' Finally, after four years, Olga found another lover and left. However, Simone and Sartre continued to support Olga – emotionally and financially – for the next thirty years.

During the last half of the 1940s, Simone had an affair with American writer Nelson Algren. At the same time Sartre, who never seems to have been afflicted with any jealousy, had an affair with a New York woman identified only as Dolores.

Although they had their 'contingent loves', Sartre and Simone always nurtured their own relationship. But, during the 1950s, the couple moved further apart than they had ever been before. Simone developed a relationship with Claude Lanzmann, a journalist seventeen years younger than she. While she and Sartre still travelled together, Simone lived with Lanzmann. Sartre, who constantly sought female companions, explained his behaviour by stating, 'But the main reason I surround myself with women is simply that I prefer their company to that of men. As a rule I find men boring'. Therefore, while Simone was cohabiting with Lanzmann, Sartre chose as his companion a 17-year-old Jewish Algerian girl named Arlette Elkaim. When Sartre almost married Arlette to prevent her deportation and because he thought her pregnant, the relationship between Sartre and Simone was nearly destroyed. However, Sartre adopted the girl instead. After Lanzmann left Simone in 1958, Sartre and she again became constant companions, more deeply in love than ever. During the last two decade of Sartre's life, they travelled together and took care of each other until their fifty-one year affair ended when Sartre died, with Simone at his bedside.

R.J.F. (Lists 10, 20, 25)

♣ Arthur Schopenhauer
22 February 1788 to 21 September 1860

Called 'the philosopher of pessimism', Arthur Schopenhauer is famous for *The World As Will and Idea*, in which he challenged the dominant idealism of his time with the concept of the will to live as the prime mover of human life and the basic cause of human suffering.

Schopenhauer looked the part of a philosopher – small and slight with a large head and piercing blue eyes. Always well-dressed, he had intense moods, extreme pride, and little patience for anyone who dared disagree with him. Both his parents were headstrong, intelligent and short-tempered. His mother Johanna was jealous of his talents, and they fought constantly. Once she threw him downstairs. His father was a stern, successful Danzig businessman who committed suicide in 1805. Schopenhauer admired his father and tried to continue the family business. He hated it, and when his mother encouraged him to study philosophy, he eagerly concurred. The widowed Johanna moved to Weimar, 'the city of poets', where she became a popular novelist and salon hostess. Although disapproving of her frivolity, young Schopenhauer followed her in 1813. He was shocked to find a young man, Müller von Gerstenberg living with her. Despite Johanna's insistence that it was platonic Schopenhauer thought she had committed an indiscretion. He told her, 'Choose between von Gerstenberg and me!' She chose von Gerstenberg, and Schopenhauer never saw his mother again.

While he was battling with his mother in Weimar, Schopenhauer had a quiet affair with Karoline Jägermann, leading actress at the Court Theatre and recognized mistress of Duke Karl August. Few details are known of their relationship, except that Schopenhauer thought of her more romantically than of any other woman in his life. When *The World As Will and Idea* was published, Schopenhauer moved to Italy. There he indulged his strong sensuality. Believing sexual passion was 'the most distinct

401

expression of the will', he gave it free rein, admitting, 'I am not a saint.' In Italy – where 'the only sin is not to sin' – he met a rich, distinguished and beautiful woman, known only as Teresa. He considered marriage, weighing her faults and virtues, but backed out when she embarrassed him publicly by swooning over Lord Byron. Schopenhauer wrote, 'I was afraid of the horns of cuckoldry.'

He returned to the University of Berlin, but his lectures drew tiny audiences. In Berlin, he was sued for personal injury by a middle-aged seamstress, Caroline Marquet, whom he had physically thrown out of his apartment, because she had repeatedly irritated him by sewing there. She won the case, and he had to pay damages for the rest of her life. After this, he left again for Italy. His misogyny was becoming more apparent as he made love to many women, regarding all with contempt. For him the sexual impulse was 'a demon that strives to pervert, confine, and overthrow everything,' and he blamed women for the resulting havoc. His philosophy explained love as a deceit played by nature to suit her only purpose: procreation. 'It is only the man whose intellect is clouded by his sexual impulse that could give the name of the fair sex to the undersized, narrow-shouldered, broad-hipped, and short-legged race.' Despising women, he thought they possessed only one virtue: the sexual allure of youth, which would fade after marriage. He could be charming, though, to young and pretty ladies, with his mastery of languages, literature, and occasional magic tricks.

After one happy year, he retreated to Munich, desperately ill with syphilis. Bedridden for months, Schopenhauer feared the disease would destroy his mind. Recovered, he wrote an article which presented his theory of tetragamy. This advocated that two men share a woman as a wife until she was past childbearing age, whereupon they should marry a second young woman, whilst continuing to care for their first wife. Later, his essay 'On Women' (published as *Parerga* in 1851) established his permanent reputation for misogyny.

Yet he never banished women from his life. In a journal he wrote of a 'Fräulein Medon', a charming actress. He courted and won her and again thought of marriage. In his analysis, she was 'quite satisfactory' both as a lover or as a wife. Once again his caution and cynicism emerged. He was in love, but he was also a philosopher; his pessimism won and marriage was dropped. For Schopenhauer, confidence in the immortality of his work was more meaningful than any children he could have. He died alone, at 72, of a lung haemorrhage.

Schopenhauer had resented his desires, but never denied them: 'The more I see of men the less I like them; if I could but say so of women too, all would be well.'

C.L.W. and L.S. (List 18, 23)

❧ Bessie Smith
1894 to 26 September 1937

The greatest blues singer of them all, Bessie Smith, was born into total poverty in Chattanooga, Tennessee. She was a tall, heavy, very dark black woman who wore strange hats and colourful costumes on stage. She had a quick temper and would not hesitate to attack a man or woman with her bare fists. Bessie especially hated to see black people behave with servility toward whites. Occasional bouts of alcoholism were a problem in her personal life, although they rarely affected her performances. She never learned the value of money, and would hand out cash to strangers. At the same time, she was tight-fisted about paying her own performers and crew. Despite her lusty, violent, pleasure-seeking ways, Smith was religious and would attend church whenever possible. The rumour that Smith died because a white hospital refused to treat her after a car accident is false, but this has persistently been used as an example of Southern racism. Bessie – who hated racism as much as anyone – died at the Afro-American Hospital in Clarksdale, Mississippi, where she had been taken after receiving first aid from a white doctor who happened on the scene of the accident.

Smith was married young to Earl Love, who came from a prominent black Mississippi family. The wedding took place after the First World War (the exact date is unknown), and Love died soon after.

In 1922, Bessie met Jack Gee, a watchman who falsely claimed to be a policeman, and moved in with him. Gee was illiterate, but managed Smith's career for a while. Because of his carelessness, Bessie received only $125 per recording, and no royalties during her entire career.

In fairness to Gee, although he took advantage of Bessie later on, their affair began before Bessie was discovered. In 1923, they married in a simple ceremony. The marriage was good at the beginning, but deteriorated into wild jealousy in less than three years. Once, on tour, Bessie heard Gee was 'messing around' with a chorus girl in her show. Without bothering to verify the story, Bessie beat up the girl and threw her out of their railway carriage on to the tracks. Gee appeared on the scene and stopped to comfort the bleeding girl. An outraged Bessie emerged from the car and emptied Gee's own pistol at him as he fled down the tracks. The train left without Gee.

Bessie was not innocent of indiscretions herself. She had her own lover on tour, a young male dancer named Agie Pitts. Bessie's affair with Pitts ended when she was jailed for beating another chorus girl. Pitts, entrusted with $1000 bail money to free Bessie, left town instead and was soon jailed himself. Despite violence, infidelities and Gee's opportunism, the couple seemed unable to break up. Whenever Gee was around, the fun-loving, carousing Bessie would be on her best behaviour. They never divorced, but a final separation did occur. In 1929, Gee financed a show with Bessie's money, making his girlfriend, Gertrude Saunders, the star. This hurt Bessie more deeply than anything else Gee had done. Reading about the show in a newspaper, she took a cab to the hotel where Gee and Saunders were staying. Saunders was out when Bessie arrived, but the ensuing fight with Gee left furniture in the hotel room in a shambles, and Bessie emerged bleeding. Though Gee was reunited briefly with Bessie, he returned to Gertrude and Bessie's married days were over. Bessie took it very hard, and began drinking heavily. A brief affair with blues singer Lonnie Johnson did not relieve her loneliness. The Great Depression finally began to affect Bessie, a year and a half after most other performers had been forced to give up. But she still toured and, when her troupe stopped in Chicago, an old platonic friendship with bootlegger Richard Morgan grew into the love she had never had. Morgan genuinely admired Bessie both as an artist and a person, and she was happier than she had ever been. Morgan was tall, handsome and a sharp dresser, and he liked a good time as much as Bessie did. His profitable bootlegging and management of Bessie's business affairs helped end her financial decline. He also filled the void left by Gee and Bessie's adopted son Jack Jr (whom Gee had kidnapped and placed in foster homes). Bessie and Morgan lived together happily until Bessie's death in 1937.

It is not known when Bessie began to enjoy sex with women, but the first proven affair was in late 1926. Lillian Simpson was a young chorus girl in Bessie's show who regularly slept in Bessie's room in the railway carriage. One night, Bessie kissed Lillian publicly in the car: the girl objected. Bessie threatened to throw her out of the show, saying, 'The hell with you, bitch. I got twelve women on this show and I can have one every night if I want it.' The girl attempted suicide four nights later. Bessie saved her life, and the episode seemed to release Lillian's inhibitions, for she never complained again. But the troupe feared Gee might visit the tour at any time, as he usually did when he ran out of money, and discover the lesbian affair. Gee finally caught Bessie in a compromising situation with another girl named Marie. He chased them through the hotel corridors, and Bessie hid in a girlfriend's room, terrified. When Gee ran down the street thinking Bessie had escaped from the hotel, Bessie quickly told the entire troupe to grab what they could carry and run for the train depot. Still in pyjamas, the entourage quietly slipped out of Detroit in a darkened railway carriage.

Another of Bessie's fears was that Gee would discover her visits to 'buffet flats'. Buffet flats were small, private establishments run by women, which featured gambling, sex shows and kinky or straight sex for the customers. Bessie went only to watch, afraid word would get back to her husband if she participated.

The lyrics of Bessie's songs were masterpieces of sexual double entendre. A classic example is 'Kitchen Man', in which 'Madame Bucks' who is 'quite deluxe' receives notice from her cook:

> *His frankfurters are oh so sweet*
> *How I like his sausage meat*
> *I can't do without my kitchen man*
>
> *Oh how that boy can open clams*
> *No one else can touch my hams*
> *I can't do without my kitchen man*
>
> *When I eat his donuts, all I leave is the hole*
> *Anytime he wants to, why he can use my sugarbowl.*

J.M. (Lists 14, 20, 34, 42)

♣ Ruth St Denis
20 January 1878 to 21 July 1968

Born Ruth Dennis and raised on a farm, America's 'First Lady of Dance' had been in love with the theatre since, aged 9, she saw a circus with a finale of 100 dancing girls in angel costumes made of ribbons, and then went home and cut up a pair of old curtains to make her first dance costume. She was world famous from her first tour in 1906, which included her well-known dance 'Radha', until one of her last appearances, at 87, with Ted Shawn to celebrate their fiftieth wedding anniversary (although they had been separated for over thirty years). Together they had founded Denishawn ('every brick a one-night stand'), where pupils like Martha Graham learned techniques that became the basis for modern dance.

After dancing 'The Resurrection' in her sixties, St Denis said a few words about religion and art, and the need to recognize all kinds of love. Then she paused and blurted out, 'And boy! Do I know about all kinds!' Since she was a virgin when she married at 36, her knowledge grew from a concentrated series of affairs, some with 'impossibly' young men whom her husband called 'pimply faced'. She engaged in these affairs although both she and Shawn called their sex life together 'highly satisfactory'. That her many early romances were unconsummated was alternately credited to devotion to career, travelling with mother and brother, or developing a 'strange aversion to what I thought sex to be', because of all the older men who had tried to seduce her. These men included her first producer David Belasco (who gave her her stage name), wealthy adventurer Stanford White, and a string of devoted suitors in cities around the world. In performance, the mere sight of her body brought 'gasps of appreciation', but it was dance characterized as pure rather than voluptuous – the French 'disillusioned' her by calling it 'sexless'. (She was not disillusioned but incensed when the sculptor Rodin asked to sketch her, then dropped his pad and began kissing *'ces beaux jambes, ces jambes extraordinaires'*, proving, she said, that he was 'only an ordinary French sensualist!').

In 1914, Ruth St Denis met, married and went into theatrical partnership with Ted Shawn. She was 36, and the 22-year-old ex-divinity student from Kansas City did not have an easy time of it. He proposed, she declined; Shawn then went to work, convincing Ruth's protective mother that the match was a good one

406

for reasons of love and art. When she gave in, Ruth's resolve crumbled. The morning of 13 August 1914, she said to Ted, 'Come on, let's go down to City Hall and get this thing over with.' She insisted on deleting the word 'obey' from the vows, and refused to wear a wedding ring – to her a symbol of subjugation. They did not consummate the marriage until October. Ruth St Denis was not ready to adjust to the role of bride. Fourteen years older than Shawn, she was a star and was used to having her own way. Like St Denis, Shawn was probably a virgin when they married, and he was willing to let her set the tone of their sexual life together.

Once she discovered sex, however, St Denis turned into a middle-aged sensualist, giving herself 'wholeheartedly' to sexual experience, careful to use 'every birth control method from medieval times to the present' to protect her lithe body from the potential ravages of childbearing. (Shawn had desperately wanted children.) There were many lovers, and St Denis kept her husband up to date on each one. Walter Terry, in his biography *Ted Shawn, Father of American Dance*, explored the more painful aspects of the marriage. He reported Shawn saying, 'Ruth was searching for romance in all directions except me.' Of one lover, still a teenager, Shawn exclaimed, 'If he were any younger he'd be a foetus!' Some of the men were 'as much poetical as physical' affairs; one such man became the mayor of a town Shawn revisited years later. The mayor confessed, 'I went up into the hills with her and, frankly, I had screwing in mind but all she wanted to do was to read poetry to me by moonlight.'

St Denis was never in doubt about who came first in the relationship. Ted was given second billing both on stage and at home – a situation she considered only right, given her confidence in her genius and her importance. One of St Denis's closest friends said about her, 'It is impossible to like Miss Ruth. She really isn't likeable at all. . . . But it is possible to love her. That's all you can do with someone like that.' What was 'pure, unadulterated, ghastly suffering' for Ted ended during one tour when they both fell in love with the same handsome young man, to whom Ted felt 'a strong, overwhelming sexual attraction'. Shawn speculated that his homosexual tendencies had always been there and blamed their manifestation on Ruth. If she had been a reasonably faithful wife, he claimed, he would never have fallen in love with a man. One day, Ted looked at his wife and saw her as nothing more than an old coat tossed over a chair. In that moment, the spell evaporated. St Denis said, 'But he never loved the old coat.... He married a goddess [who] didn't exist, except on stage. The deception was of his own making, not mine.' Shawn won the young man, and St Denis left for California, threatening to sue for divorce and name her husband's new lover as co-respondent – though she never did.

Then began their 'spiritual separation' – never a divorce – while St Denis continued to pursue the sex she 'adored' but still wrote romantically of their relationship as 'probably one of the great love stories'. In her late eighties, she told an interviewer that finally her art served only God, that physical love was a thing of the past. 'But,' she exclaimed, 'don't believe for a moment I don't still think about it!'

D.M.L. and K.P. (Lists 1, 10, 22, 25)

♣ Gertrude Stein
3 February 1874 to 27 July 1946

Gertrude Stein's avant-garde writing style and odd, masculine appearance helped establish her as an eccentric in the minds of the American public. Her home in Paris, shared with her lover, Alice B. Toklas, served as the gathering place for expatriate writers and artists during the years between the First and Second World Wars.

Born in the USA of fairly well-to-do and restless parents, Stein spent her early years with her family in Vienna and Paris before returning to settle in Oakland, California. Her weak-spirited mother died of cancer when Stein was 14, leaving her tyrannical father to browbeat his daughter into studying medicine. He died three years later, but was an early influence on her feelings toward men. Later she would write, 'Fathers are depressing.' At Radcliffe College, she studied psychology under William James, then entered Johns Hopkins Medical School for graduate study, only to drop out four years later, distracted by her first lesbian love affair, and her subsequent inner struggle to accept her own sexuality – so at odds with the standard mores of the time. She moved to Paris, living off money left to her by her parents. There, she shared a home with her brother Leo, an art critic. The two began collecting Cubist paintings, which were new and daring at that time. Painters like Picasso, Matisse and Braque became close friends, and began visiting regularly. During this period she wrote three books – *Q.E.D.* written in 1903 but not published until 1950, a cathartic account of her struggle with lesbianism; *Three Lives*, published in 1909 and well received by the public; and *The Making of Americans*, not published until 1925. After fighting with his sister, Leo moved out and Alice B. Toklas moved in, becoming Stein's adviser, protector and lover for the next thirty-eight years. As Stein's literary reputation grew, so did the number of writers and artists who came to visit – people like Fitzgerald, Sherwood Anderson and Hemingway. With her short-cropped hair, thick girth and loud laugh, Stein seemed unlikely material for the powerful artistic figure she became – one who could make or break reputations. Her most popular book was her autobiography, *The Autobiography of Alice B. Toklas*, published in 1933. Stein died in 1946, leaving her estate to Toklas, who kept possession of her art collection until 1961, when it was appropriated by the Stein family and sold at auction for $6 million.

Gertrude Stein had problems accepting her lesbian tendencies in her first affair with fellow student May Bookstaver. May's passionate nature led her to other affairs, leaving Stein to agonize over her own sexuality, because it was so opposed to her middle-class upbringing. Not until later, when she met and 'married' Alice B. Toklas, could she accept her feelings for women: 'Slowly it has come to me that any way of being a loving one is interesting and not unpleasant to me.'

Stein was living in Paris, presiding over a salon populated by Picasso and other painters of future renown, when she met Alice B. Toklas in autumn 1907. Toklas, raised in San Francisco, was well educated; on a visit to Europe, she was invited to see Stein's collection of art. She was shy and lean; Stein was heavy-set (soon to exceed 14 stone 10 pounds). Mabel Dodge Luhan remembered them both, saying of the 30-year-old Toklas, 'She was slight and dark, with beautiful grey eyes hung with black lashes – and she had a drooping, Jewish nose, and her eyelids drooped, and the corners of her red mouth and the lobes of her ears drooped under the black folded Hebraic hair, weighed down as they were, with long heavy Oriental earrings.' And of the 33-year-old Stein she wrote, 'Gertrude Stein was prodigious. Pounds and pounds and pounds piled up on her skeleton – not the billowing kind, but massive, heavy fat. She wore some covering of corduroy or velvet and her crinkly hair was brushed back and twisted up high behind her jolly, intelligent face.' It was love at first sight for both. Alice Toklas visited again, and finally Stein invited her to move in. Toklas proof-read one of Stein's books, then typed 1000 manuscript pages of another. Eventually, said Mabel Dodge Luhan, Toklas became Stein's 'hand-maiden'. But their love was mutual. Stein proposed to Toklas. 'Care for me,' she urged. 'I care for you in every possible way.... When all is said one is wedded to the bed.' Alice Toklas accepted, and so began an almost husband–wife relationship, with Stein the provider, and Toklas minding the house and bills, and in general keeping Stein's life running smoothly.

Stein maintained close relationships with men as well, although they were non-sexual in nature. She was close friends with Hemingway, although she disliked his outlook. She once chastised him for his prejudice against lesbians: 'You know nothing about any of this really, Hemingway. You've met known criminals and sick people and vicious people. The main thing is that the act male homosexuals commit is ugly and repugnant and afterwards they are disgusted with themselves. They drink and take drugs, to palliate this, but they are disgusted with the act and they are always changing partners and cannot be really happy. In women, it is the opposite. They do nothing that they are disgusted by and nothing that is repulsive and afterwards they are happy and they can lead happy lives together.' Hemingway, for his part, said of Stein, 'I always wanted to fuck her and she knew it.'

As she grew older, Stein made her disgust with heterosexuality more evident, but her life with Toklas was a contented one, and apart from their lesbianism almost conventional. Both were faithful and loving, calling each other by private pet names – Toklas was 'Pussy', Stein 'Lovely'. But the relationship was not without passion, as related by Stein in a 1917 piece, 'Lifting Belly', a long rhapsody of lesbian love. In the following quote, 'Caesars' and 'Cow' are symbols of sexual pleasure.

Kiss my lips. She did.
Kiss my lips again she did.
Kiss my lips over and over and over again she did....
I'll let you kiss me sticky ...
I say lifting belly and then I say lifting belly and Caesars.
I say lifting belly gently and Caesars gently. I say
Lifting belly again and Caesars again.... I say lifting
belly Caesars and cow come out. I say lifting belly
and Caesars and cow come out.
Can you read my print?

She writes to Alice. Alice answers 'yes'.

In 1946, Stein insisted upon surgery for cancer. About to be wheeled into the operating room, she turned her head to Toklas and said, 'What is the answer?' Toklas did not reply. Stein nodded and said, 'In that case, what is the question?' These were her last words to her beloved. Gertrude Stein died that night under anaesthesia, convinced she was a genius, one of three geniuses she had known – the other two being Pablo Picasso and A. N. Whitehead. Alice Toklas lived for another twenty-one years, heartbroken and lonely. At 89, she said simply to a friend, 'I miss her; I still miss her very much.'

M.W. and Eds. (List 13)

🍀 Stendhal
23 January 1783 to 23 March 1842

'Literary fame is a lottery. I am taking out a ticket whose winning number is 1935,' wrote Stendhal in his autobiographical work *The Life of Henri Brulard*. His 'ticket' won. This French writer of the nineteenth century wrote, he said, for the 'happy few', and has been appreciated far more in the twentieth century than in his own. Someone once asked Stendhal what his profession was, and he answered, 'Observer of the human heart.' The heart he observed was often his own – he described it with candour and accuracy in his voluminous journals. He was self-conscious, partly because of his appearance. Though he had a radiant smile and well-shaped hands, Stendhal had lost most of his hair early and chose to cover his pate with a purplish wig; his nose was thick, his cheeks fat, his legs short. In later life, he developed a paunch. Once he expressed the desire to be a tall, blond German. To compensate for his unprepossessing appearance, he developed a brilliant wit. 'I'd rather be a chameleon than an ox,' was his motto, and a chameleon Henri Marie Beyle was, with more than two hundred pseudonyms, Stendhal among them. In contrast, his writing was simple and direct, and he worshipped the truth. When 16 he left his home town of Grenoble and his materialistic father to study at the École Polytechnique in Paris. However, instead of enrolling, he lived in a garret and roved the streets expecting to find damsels to rescue. He himself was the one who was rescued – by a distant relative, Noël Daru, who found Henri ill, gave him a room in the Darus' Paris home, and got him a secretarial job with the ministry of war. In 1800, Stendhal travelled to join Napoleon's army in Italy, a country he adored for the rest of his life. Until 1814, he served on and off in the army – in 1812, he was with Napoleon during the retreat from Moscow. Battle disgusted him. On returning to Paris, suffering from unrequited love for an Italian woman, Stendhal contemplated suicide – but immersed himself in his writing instead. In 1828, the Austrian police expelled him from Milan as a subversive, but a magnanimous Stendhal nevertheless published his enthusiastic tribute to Italy, *Roman Journal,* the following year. In 1831, he accepted a consulship in Civitavecchia, in the Papal States. Here he felt intellectually isolated and bored. Although his official duties were light during the next seven years, he started three books which he never completed. He died of a stroke aged 59, his *chasse de bonheur* (pursuit of happiness) over. As he requested, his tombstone was engraved with the words '*Arrigo Beyle, Milanese, Visse, Scrisse, Amò*' (Henri Beyle, Milanese, He lived, He wrote, He loved). A fitting epitaph for the creator of *Beylisme*, a method of deliberately cultivating the senses and the mind, which was expressed in the equation: Happiness = love + work.

Many of the women Stendhal loved were unattainable, including the first. He wrote, 'I wanted to cover my mother with kisses, and that there not be any clothing. . . . I always wanted to give them to her on the breast.' She died when he was 7. Stendhal was also erotically aroused by paintings ('To bathe like that with lovely women!' he mused, standing before a landscape showing nudes in a stream), music, nature – and the glimpse of his Aunt Camille's thigh as she descended from a wagon.

As an adult, his love objects were often married women who refused to sleep with him. This did not lessen his relentless, though awkwardly shy, pursuit of them. And, while he couldn't always have what he wanted, he still enjoyed an active sex life. His first encounter, in Milan in 1800, was probably with a prostitute. He said of it, ' . . . the violence of my timidity and of the experience have absolutely killed my recollection'. However, he never forgot the result – a venereal disease, possibly syphilis, plagued him intermittently for the rest of his life. In spring 1806, he recorded another casual sexual encounter, this one with a serving maid in a doorway. Afterwards, he accompanied her to her room for more sex, then left in the morning 'thoroughly disgusted and ashamed' – but he also contemplated returning to her room to try anal intercourse. His sexuality was affected by his state of mind. Of one sexual failure (followed in the morning by victory), he said that anxiety 'agitated my mind too much for my body to be brilliant'. In a depressed mood in summer 1821, he attended a party where the guests were young men and prostitutes. During the orgy, he was impotent with the prostitute Alexandrine – a 'complete fiasco', he said. She rejected his offer to bring her to orgasm manually, and then reported his impotence to the rest of the company, thus generating a story that circulated around Paris. His novel *Armance* was about an impotent man. Yet he wrote of having intercourse with a woman seven times in a row and of additional many-times-in-one-night bouts with other women. At 50, he confessed his interest was waning so that he could 'quite easily pass a fortnight or three weeks without a woman'. Although he was overwhelmingly heterosexual, he was once attracted to a Russian officer sitting next to him in a theatre. 'If I had been a woman, this lovable officer would have inspired me with the most violent passion.' He died a bachelor.

In 1835, by the shores of Lake Albano near Rome, Stendhal wrote in the sand the initials of his major loves:

$$a \quad d \quad\quad i \quad l \quad ine \quad pg \quad de \quad\quad r$$
$$V.\ A\ .\ A\ .\ M\ .\ M\ .\ A\ .\ A\quad .\ A\quad .\ M\quad .\ C.\ G.\ A\ .$$

He mused on the 'amazing follies and sillinesses' they made him commit and noted that he had not even possessed all of them. He loved one enough to list her twice. In Stendhal's order, the initials probably referred to the following women.

V. – Virginie Kubly, a tall, married actress whom he worshipped from afar while a teenager in Grenoble. Seeing her approach in a park, he fled from the 'burn' of her closeness. He never spoke to her.

Aa. and Apg. – Angela Pietragrua ('Gina'), a married Milanese, with flashing eyes, whom he met in Milan in 1800. He was too shy to tell her of his love. In 1811, again in Italy, he pursued and finally made love to her. To mark the occasion, he had his suspenders embroidered 'Ap 22 September 1811', and wrote, 'It seems to me that perfectly pure pleasure can come only with intimacy; the first time, it's a victory; in the three following, you acquire intimacy.' Their affair was studded with quarrels, signals (half-open windows) and barriers (two nuns sleeping in an adjoining bedroom). Gina's performance in bed with another man, which he watched – unbeknownst to her – through a keyhole, made him think of 'puppets ... dancing before my eyes'. Initially it made him laugh, then depressed him. They broke up in an art gallery with Gina 'clinging to my garments and dragging herself on her knees. . . . assuredly she never loved me more than on that very day'.

Ad. – Adèle Rebuffel, whom he met while having an affair with her mother. She was then a child of 12. In his four-year pursuit of Adèle, the furthest he got was to put a hand on her breast.

M. – Mélanie Guilbert (called Louason), an actress with whom he lived in Marseille from summer 1805 to spring 1806. On an outing in the countryside, he saw her bathe nude in a river, a vision like the painted nudes that aroused him when he was a boy. After she went back to Paris, he wrote, in disillusionment, 'I desired passionately to be loved by a melancholy and slender woman who was an actress. I was, and I didn't find sustained happiness.'

Mi. – 'Minette', or Wilhemine von Griesheim, blonde daughter of a Prussian general, rebuffed his advances.

Al. – Angéline Béreyter, an opera singer with whom he had a three-year affair, during which she taught him songs from various operas. Sometimes she had as many as nine orgasms a night, but he complained that their physical happiness robbed him 'of much of my imagination'. In a list of his lovers, he said he never loved her.

Aine. – Alexandrine Daru, wife of his cousin Pierre, double chinned and decent, who never gave in to his blandishments – like caressing her gloves as though they were her hands, and tracing an 'A' in the sand.

Mde. – Mathilde Viscontini Dembowski ('Métilde'), a sympathizer with the revolutionary movement in Milan, whom he loved, unrequitedly, from 1818 to 1821. For her, he turned down other women – though not all, as a case of venereal disease contracted in 1819 attests. Once he undertook to follow her to another town, where he contrived to pass by her in a disguise consisting of green spectacles and a large overcoat. She inspired his book *On Love*, a 'scientific' study of love, in which he explained his concept of 'crystallization' – love so powerful it transforms one's beloved into a perfect being. The book sold seventeen copies in its first ten years of publication. By the end of 1820, his pursuit of Métilde reached *'le dead-blank'*.

C. – Countess Clémentine Curial ('Menti'), married, was 36 to his 41 when their affair began. Once, for three days, he stayed cooped up in a cellar, while she brought food and emptied his chamber pot and provided sex. In love with someone else, she

414

ended the relationship in 1826, causing him great pain. When she was 47, he tried to revive their affair, but she said, 'How can you love me at my age?' and refused to consider it.

G. – In 1830, Giulia Rinieri, a 19-year-old aristocratic virgin, attempted to seduce Stendhal saying, 'I am perfectly aware, and have been for some time, that you are old and ugly,' and then she kissed him. After hesitating for several months, he slept with her, then later that year asked for her hand in marriage but was rejected.

Ar. – Alberthe de Rubempré, married, witty, a little crazy, was in love with the occult. Their affair lasted six months, but he was in love with her a 'month at most'. After he died, she tried, in a séance, to summon up the shade of 'poor Henri'.

His diary of 1 August 1801 reads: 'Like many others, I'm embarrassed when it comes to —— a respectable woman for the first time. Here's a very simple method. While she's lying down, you start kissing her lightly, you titillate her, etc., she begins to like it. Still, through force of habit, she keeps defending herself. Then, without her realizing what you're up to, you should put your left forearm on her throat, beneath her chin, as if you are going to strangle her. Her first movement will be to raise her hand in defence. Meanwhile, you take your —— between the index and middle finger of your right hand, holding them both taut, and quietly place it in the ——. . . . It's important to cover up, the decisive movement of the left forearm by whimpering. . . .

A.E. (Lists 11, 15, 18, 20, 34)

♣ Leopold Stokowski
18 April 1882 to 13 September 1977

Born in London, Stokowski was the son of an immigrant Polish cabinet maker and his Irish wife. Leopold had learned to play the violin, piano and organ before he was 13. While working as a church organist, Stokowski was discovered by a wealthy member of the congregation who sponsored him at the Royal College of Music, after which he entered Queen's College, Oxford. Stokowski then studied in France and Germany and, in 1909, the ambitious young musician became conductor of the Cincinnati Symphony Orchestra, although he was without experience as a conductor. From Cincinnati, he went to Philadelphia where, in the next three decades, he created a symphony orchestra that gained world renown. A great experimenter, Stokowski was one of the first conductors to record classical music and the first to introduce electrical instruments in the orchestra. Working in Hollywood during the late 1930s, he was musical supervisor for Disney's *Fantasia* and performed in two other films. After an amazingly productive and creative career, Stokowski died in his sleep in Nether Wallop, Hampshire, aged 95.

Tall, handsome, slender and blond, Stokowski devoted almost as much time and energy to the seduction of women as he did to music. Of his early affairs we have only rumours until 1906, when he met concert pianist Olga Samaroff – born Lucie Hickenlooper. After five years as lovers, they married. Stokowski demanded that his new wife give up her career to help further his. For a decade, she used her time and influence to secure his advancement. However, upon moving to Philadelphia, Stokowski began his bedroom wanderings, and in 1923 Olga – tired of her husband's domineering personality and sexual escapades – sued for divorce.

After this, Stokowski conducted sexual affairs openly – with Philadelphia society women, actresses and chambermaids. Also, he became well known for his association with female students of Philadelphia's prestigious music school, the Curtis Institute. His liaisons with these students became so notorious that the local citizens referred to Curtis Institute as Coitus Institute. Stokowski showed little prejudice in his selection, sleeping with single and married women alike. He referred to his sex companions as 'nurses' because, in his words, 'They are angels of mercy who rejuvenate us.' (Stokowski's sexual partners praised his general performance but complained of his sporadic impotence.)

In 1926, at the age of 44, Stokowski suddenly dropped his 19-year-old debutante girlfriend to marry Evangeline Johnson, an heiress to the Johnson and Johnson fortune, whom he had known for three weeks. A liberated woman active in social causes, Evangeline accepted her new husband's claim that he needed his sexual wanderings to stimulate his musical creativity.

During the 1920s and 1930s, Stokowski's musical fame and reports of his bedroom conquests raised him to the rank of a national sex symbol. This was reinforced in 1937 when Stokowski seduced Greta Garbo – she reported, 'I felt the electricity going through me from head to toe'. During this tumultuous affair, the couple resided in Italian villas where Stokowski introduced Greta to yoga. However, after ten months, the flame suddenly died and so did Stokowski's second marriage. Complaining of her husband's dominating personality, long absences and headline affairs with movie stars, Evangeline sued for divorce.

Stokowski continued his libertine ways until 1945, when he stopped off in Reno, Nevada, on his way from New York to Los Angeles. There he married Gloria Vanderbilt, who had just divorced her first husband. Like his two previous wives, Gloria was beautiful, young (23), and rich – two years earlier she had inherited $5 million. At the age of 63, Stokowski had changed little. His demands on Gloria led her to a psychiatrist who helped her become more assertive which, in turn, ended the marriage. In 1962, she sued Stokowski for divorce.

After this last divorce, Stokowski's sexual adventures decreased in frequency, probably because he was then over 80. However, until his death fifteen years later, Stokowski continued to have occasional affairs.

R.J.F. (Lists 8, 22, 25, 26)

♣ Marie Stopes
15 October 1880 to 2 October 1958

A contemporary of American birth-control crusader Margaret Sanger, Stopes established the first birth-control clinic in Great Britain, where, through her numerous writings, she advocated healthy, pleasurable sex lives for women.

She and her younger sister were the product of an essentially sexless marriage. Her mother, who was 40 when Marie was born, confused sexual ignorance with virtue and, because of her influence, Marie remained a virgin for the first thirty-six years of her life, including a five-year marriage. At this unhappy juncture in her life, Marie turned from botany and coal research, in which fields she was a recognized authority, to write a manual called *Married Love*. In 1918, this book, and its companion work entitled *Wise Parenthood*, created an international sensation, mostly because it treated the subject of birth control openly. (Both books were banned by the US postal authorities as 'obscene'.) The publication of her books, and the largely positive public response to them, inspired Stopes to found the Society for Constructive Birth Control and Racial Progress. She also engaged the religious establishment, especially the Catholic Church, in a battle for the minds of the masses. That battle reached its climax in a prolonged

417

libel suit brought by Marie against the Catholic doctor Halliday Sutherland. In a book of his own on birth control, he had questioned Marie's qualifications for dealing with the subject and accused her of 'exposing the poor to experiment' in offering them the means to control birth. On a third appeal before the House of Lords, the suit was settled in favour of Sutherland. Marie was made to pay a modest fine and court costs, but the publicity surrounding her trial generated enormous sales of her book, which compensated for her losses.

Q: With regards to your husband's parts, did they ever get rigid at all?
A: On hundreds of occasions on which we had what I thought to be relations, I only remember three occasions on which it was partially rigid, and then it was never effectively rigid. . . .
Q: And he never succeeded in penetrating into your private parts?
A: No.

Marie was a certified virgin when she gave testimony in a London divorce court in 1916. A sympathetic court annulled her marriage to Dr Reginald Gates who, in five years, had failed to consummate their marriage.

Actually most of Marie's sex life deserved sympathy. She didn't get her first kiss until she was 24 – from a married Japanese who was culturally opposed to kissing and had to be shown how. She'd met Kenjiro Fujii in 1904, while they were both researchers at the University of Munich. She played down her interest in him by ridiculing his shortness in letters written home to her mother, but in private she would wrap herself tightly in a girdle to simulate the feeling of his arms around her. After five 'physically pure' years, the relationship ended when Fujii, who was by then divorced, developed a psychosomatic illness at the thought of marriage to Marie. Although against lesbianism throughout her career, Marie none the less attracted the attention of two older women. Clothilde van Wyss, one of Marie's teachers at North London Collegiate, and Dr Helen McMurchy, a Canadian she met in 1908, both took a passionate interest in Marie; however, biographer Ruth Hall doubts that either relationship ever became overtly sexual since Marie was so naive she didn't know what masturbation was until she was 29. Marie finally learned about sex from books and Aylmer Maude, a translator of Tolstoi, twenty-two years her senior. He had come to live with Marie and Reginald Gates a year after their 1911 marriage, and it was he who first pointed out the abnormality of her relationship with Gates. Maude became Marie's confidant and platonic lover, and Reginald Gates threw him out of his house. Marie finally lost her virginity in 1918 to H. V. (Humphrey Verdon) Roe, her second husband and partner in her birth-control campaign. The Roes viewed birth control as a means of purifying their race, with Marie at one point suggesting that Britain pass a bill to 'ensure the sterility of the hopelessly rotten and racially diseased. . . .' In the latter group, she put her daughter-in-law, who married Harry, Marie's only child. Mary suffered from nearsightedness and Marie railed against the marriage as a eugenic disaster.

In reality, it was Marie's second marriage that was the disaster. In 1938, after years of frustration, she demanded and received from Roe a letter in which he confessed his own sexual inadequacy and granted her the right to carry on extramarital affairs. Despite the existence of such a letter and the attraction that existed between Marie and younger men, it seems probable that she lived vicariously, and that the high point of her sexual life may well have been 1918. Even as a septuagenarian, Marie maintained that her real age was 26. On her 70th birthday, her son wrote to her: 'Darling mummy, Very many happy returns on your 26th birthday. Isn't it funny that never again will we be the same age, and that from next March on I will be older than you.'

D.R. (Lists 1, 10, 17)

♣ August Strindberg
22 January 1849 to 14 May 1912

Sweden's greatest playwright was the fourth child born to his parents – who had wed just a few months before his birth. Strindberg had a tormented youth. His father was declared bankrupt, and the family's poverty forced Strindberg to wear ill-fitting hand-me-downs and consequently suffer the taunts of his schoolmates. Strindberg adored his mother, but she clearly favoured her eldest son. In 1862, when Strindberg was 13, his mother died. Within a year, his father remarried – and Strindberg found himself in continuing conflict with an aloof father and a stepmother whom he jealously hated. Strindberg grew bored with his lectures and studies at the University of Uppsala. He failed to gain a degree and turned to writing. Supplementing his meagre literary earnings by working as a librarian, Strindberg laboured long on his first play, and was crushed when the Swedish Royal Theatre rejected it. He persisted at his writing but, for consolation, turned to alcohol – he was a prodigious drinker – and to mystical pursuits including alchemy (he claimed he had discovered how to transform baser metals into gold). Those around him suspected he was sinking into madness. He proclaimed that the spirit of Edgar Allan Poe, who had died in the year Strindberg was born, had entered his body. But his powerful, often viciously satirical, writing continued – and won him, by the time of his death, the general respect of his fellow Swedes, who regarded him as their most brilliant writer.

Brought up in a family that adhered to Pietism – a gloomy, hell-fire Lutheran movement – Strindberg found that his early thoughts of sex were coloured by his religious devotion. It horrified him when, at 14, he stumbled upon a slim volume entitled *Warning of a Friend of Youth Against the Most Dangerous Enemy of Youth*. Because he had masturbated, he feared he was 'condemned to death or lunacy at the age of 25'. To regain salvation, he immersed himself in a theology class. During this time he had his first adolescent infatuation, with the 30-year-old daughter of his landlord. Ephemeral as that was, it paved the path for dozens more – and also for Strindberg's escape from the religious doctrines he found unsatisfying.

His independence growing, the blond-haired blue-eyed teenager took to passing his evenings by dancing and flirting with a parade of young girls, especially fragile brunettes – perhaps because they reminded him of his beloved mother. Strindberg himself was aware of the possible link: 'Are my feelings perverted because I want to possess my mother? Is that an unconscious incest of the heart?' Incestuous or not, Strindberg's burning desire was to have a tranquil, married home life with a wife more devoted to him than his mother had been. He would have been happy, he once mused, if at 16 he had married a pleasant woman and taken a simple job.

While Strindberg married three times, the peaceful home life he yearned for was never his. Despite his avowed preference for old-fashioned women – he stridently denounced Henrik Ibsen's *A Doll's House* – his enduring lovers were complex, ambitious and independent. When he met Siri Von Essen, his first wife, it was – as always for Strindberg – love at first sight. She was married to an army officer and coincidentally lived in Strindberg's boyhood home. Whereas Siri's rakish husband thought her frigid, Strindberg thought her chastely pure. Their two-year affair ended in marriage. Unhappily for Strindberg, Siri wished to pursue her theatrical ambitions and when she won success as an actress she lost Strindberg. He accused her of having affairs with both men and women and implored his friends to spy on her. Strindberg and Siri fought, frequently and loudly. After 14 years and four children, their marriage ended in divorce, with Siri – to Strindberg's sorrow – retaining custody of the children.

A year later, he was pursuing Frida Uhl, an Austrian journalist. Days before the marriage ceremony, the wedding was nearly halted because Strindberg (mistakenly) thought Frida had been the model for a scandalous painting of a bare-backed odalisque, or harem girl. With this rift mended, the marriage went forward – only to dissolve within two years, in part because of Strindberg's obsession with what he perceived to be Frida's promiscuity. They had one child, a daughter, who remained with Frida.

Strindberg saw his last wife, Harriet Bosse, acting the part of Puck in *A Midsummer Night's Dream*. A few social meetings fired his desire for her, even though Harriet was thirty years younger than the 52-year-old playwright. 'Would you like to have a baby by me?' he asked. She agreed, they wed, and she soon produced Strindberg's sixth child. But Harriet, like Siri, wanted to act, and Strindberg – as ever – wanted a domesticated wife. Again, he imagined infidelities. When, after the birth of their child, Harriet bought a new cloak to show off her restored figure, Strindberg snappishly inquired if she had bought the garment 'to walk the streets'. She cried. They made up. That cycle, and the battles, continued for three years until this marriage, too, ended in divorce – with Harriet keeping the baby, a daughter to whom Strindberg remained devoted until his death from stomach cancer eight years later.

R.M. (Lists 15, 21, 25)

✹ Algernon Swinburne
5 April 1837 to 10 April 1909

Born of noble ancestry in London, the eldest child of a naval captain, Swinburne cut an odd-looking figure. He had a puny physique, an oversized head covered with carrot-coloured hair atop severely sloping shoulders and a springy gait. His high-pitched voice turned into a falsetto during times of excitement, and a nervous constitution produced an effeminate manner, trembling hands, and cataleptic fits. Yet his ambition was to be a soldier until his father prudently scotched the idea. In 1861, Richard Monckton Milnes introduced Swinburne to the writings of the Marquis de Sade, whom he emulated thereafter. His first success, *Atalanta*, was followed by volumes of poetry generally criticized for their obscene content. Heavy drinking and carousing so undermined the poet's fragile constitution that, in 1879, he lay near death. At this time he was 'adopted' by Walter Theodore Watts (later Watts-Dunton). Watts-Dunton was also a writer, who nursed Swinburne back to health at The Pines – Watts-Dunton's estate – where he lived until his death thirty years later. During this time, he produced many volumes of poetry and criticism. Although Watts-Dunton clearly saved the dissolute poet from an early grave, some critics charge that he also smothered Swinburne's genius.

Swinburne acquired a taste for flagellation at Eton's infamous flogging block. He once rinsed his face with cologne before a whipping in order to heighten his senses. He later was a regular customer at a flagellation brothel in St John's Wood. Euphemistically referred to as the 'Grove of the Evangelist', the house featured rouged blonde girls who whipped while an elderly lady collected clients' fees. Swinburne observed, 'One of the great charms of birching lies in the sentiment that the floggee is the powerless victim of the furious rage of a beautiful woman.'

Swinburn was obsessed with flogging. It dominated his whole life, his every fantasy, and a great deal of his writing. His poems were shocking enough to earn him insults, full as they were of heterosexual S & M fantasy, and oozing with references to death, delirium, and hot kisses. *Punch* called him 'Swine Born'; a critic accused him of 'grovelling down among the shameless abominations which inspire him with frenzied delight'; and Carlyle described him as 'standing up to his neck in a cesspool, and adding to its contents'. But his unpublished works would have prostrated the critics, had they read them, for they had titles like *The Flogging-Block*, *Charlie Collingwood's Flogging* and *The Whippingham Papers*. Some of these writings appeared anonymously in *The Pearl*, an underground journal of Victorian erotica. Swinburne, nostalgic for the glorious Eton beatings, wrote a letter to his homosexual poet friend George Powell, who was at the

422

school: 'I should like to see two things there again, the river – and the block.' He asked for news of Eton whippings – 'the topic is always most tenderly interesting – with an interest, I may say, based upon a common bottom of sympathy'. Powell sent him a special present: a used birch rod. Swinburne was delighted – he only wished he could be present at an Eton birching. 'To assist unseen at the holy ceremony . . . I would give *any* of my poems.' Powell next sent him a photograph of the flogging block. Swinburne was happy, but wished for an action picture. 'I would give anything for a good photograph taken at the right minute – say the tenth cut or so –' An 1863 letter to his friend Milnes finds Swinburne irritated that Milnes would stoop to flogging a boy of the lower classes. Birching, he argued, was an aristocratic sport.

Besides his friendship with Powell, he was close to the homosexual painter Simeon Solomon, who sent Swinburne drawings depicting flagellation. Swinburne once chased Solomon around the poet Rossetti's home while both were naked. And his letters imply homosexuality. At an Arts Club dinner, Swinburne got drunk and professed a horror of sodomy, but wouldn't stop talking about it. He appears to have been impotent with women. In an attempt to cure him of his bad habits, Rossetti once paid Adah Isaacs Menken – a popular entertainer and lover of the period – £10 to sleep with Swinburne. After several attempts, she returned the fee explaining that she had been 'unable to get him up to scratch', and couldn't 'make him understand that biting's no use!' Perhaps to refute rumours of his homosexuality, Swinburne boasted to friends of the 'riotous concubinage' he had enjoyed with Adah. The nature of the relationship between Swinburne and his mentor Watts-Dunton remains unclear. In Swinburne's last will he was named as the poet's sole heir.

Flagellation was not Swinburne's only quirk. He also was inordinately fond of babies, especially plump, cherubic ones. He loved to cuddle and caress them. He collected baby pictures and kept on his desk a figurine depicting a baby hatching from an egg. His close relationship with Bertie Mason, the 5-year-old nephew of Watts-Dunton, so alarmed Mrs Mason that she temporarily removed her son from The Pines. The lad's absence inspired Swinburne's book of poems, *A Dark Month*.

An extraordinary account of Swinburne's experiences with George Powell in a French cottage is given by Guy de Maupassant, who visited them when he was 18. After lunch 'gigantic portfolios of obscene photographs' were produced, all of men.

Maupassant recalled one of an English soldier masturbating. At a second luncheon, Maupassant tried to decide if the two men really were homosexuals. His conclusion was that they had sex with their pet monkey, and with clean-cut 14-year-old servant boys. The monkey, he further reported, had been hanged by one of the jealous servant boys.

Another young man claimed to have visited Swinburne when he was living in a tent on the Isle of Wight, again with a monkey which he dressed in women's clothes. Swinburne made advances toward the boy, after expounding on 'unisexual love'. At this, the jealous monkey attacked the visitor. Swinburne persuaded his young man to return for a second lunch. This time the main course was grilled monkey. Oscar Wilde said that Swinburne was 'a braggart in matters of vice, who had done everything he could to convince his fellow citizens of his homosexuality and bestiality, without being in the slightest degree a homosexual or a bestializer'.

Russian novelist Ivan Turgenev once asked Swinburne what was the most original and unrealizable thing he would like to do. 'To ravish Saint Geneviève,' the poet replied, 'During her most ardent ecstasy of prayer – but in addition, with her secret consent!'

W.A.D. and A.W. (Lists 6, 7, 14, 20, 35, 36, 37)

♣ Pëtr Ilich Tchaikovsky
7 May 1840 to 6 November 1893

Though strong, handsome and abundantly talented, Tchaikovsky suffered from neurasthenia throughout his life. This precarious emotional condition was touched off when his governess, Fanny Durbach, left the family in 1848. This was the first in a series of painful separations from mother figures which he was to experience. The next came when his mother died when he was 14, leaving him so inconsolable that twenty-five years later he wept uncontrollably for days after coming across a packet of her letters. He taught at the Moscow Conservatory of Music and threw himself into Moscow night life, but even his successes had a pathetic side. The first time he conducted a piece of his own in public, he hallucinated that his head was going to come off unless he held it absolutely rigid. He didn't conduct in public again for ten years. In 1866, he suffered a nervous breakdown one night while composing, and was so frightened by the experience that he gave up nocturnal composing forever.

He called the murky undercurrent of his sexual life 'Z', using the letter in his diaries to refer to his homosexuality (alternately called 'This' when writing to his homosexual brother, Modest). 'Z tortures me unusually today,' reads one diary entry. Another reads, 'Was very tortured not by the sensation of Z itself, but by the fact that it is in me.' Who his homosexual lovers were is uncertain, since he so feared exposure that he kept his activities extremely circumspect. One likely candidate, however, is Vladimir Shilovsky, his favourite student at the conservatory and his frequent, often secret, travelling companion to whom he dedicated two of his early piano pieces. Another is Vladimir (Bob) Davidov, his nephew, whose attraction for him is made clear in a number of diary entries. 'Oh, how perfect is Bob,' he wrote in one, and 'Am terribly reluctant to go away from here. I think it's all on account of Bob,' he wrote in another. Havelock Ellis called the *Sixth Symphony*, which Tchaikovsky dedicated to Davidov, 'the homosexual tragedy'.

His agonizing homosexuality, and the earlier heartbreak at losing Fanny and then his mother, made it almost impossible for him to have a normal relationship with a woman. The closest he came to such a thing was with Désirée Artôt, a French opera singer he met in 1868 while she was touring Russia. He fell madly in love with her and they became engaged, but his friends' concern that he would fall into Désirée's shadow awakened his own fears and caused him to postpone the wedding. Artôt resumed her tour and almost immediately married a Spanish baritone. Tchaikovsky was crushed.

In 1877, he married Antonina Ivanova Milyukova, his student at the conservatory. Antonina had professed undying love in her letters, and determined to marry him despite his admission of homosexuality. By all accounts, she was deluded and stupid, constantly imagining that men were trying to seduce her and unable to name a single piece of her husband's music. Tchaikovsky married her out of pity but, three months after the marriage, the composer fled and spent the rest of his life trying to extricate himself from the commitment. He attempted suicide, standing up to his armpits in the Moscow River one October night in the hope of catching pneumonia. He tried confessing to adulteries he hadn't committed in order to secure a divorce, but she wouldn't hear of it. He even contemplated murdering Antonina.

Finally he learned of her own adultery in 1881, but hesitated to seek a divorce for fear she might expose him. In the ensuing years, she became increasingly deranged and carried on an endless string of affairs which resulted in several children. None the less, Tchaikovsky faithfully supported her until his death in 1893. Three years later, she was committed to an asylum, where she died in 1917.

As odd as his marriage was, it was no more bizarre than his relationship with Nadezhda von Meck, a wealthy widow nine years Tchaikovsky's senior, with such an addiction to music that she included pianists (among them Debussy) as members of her household staff. She fell in love with Tchaikovsky's music and was his patron for fourteen years. They communicated solely by letter, filling three volumes of often intimate correspondence. Even when he occupied an apartment of hers in Italy and she lived half a mile away in a villa, the two never spoke. In 1890, for some unknown reason, she broke off all communication with Tchaikovsky and, when he lay dying in St Petersburg three years later, he repeated her name over and over again in what Modest described as a 'reproachful tone'.

D.R. (Lists 12, 15)

♣ Alfred, Lord Tennyson
6 August 1809 to 6 October 1892

Tennyson's early life was often troubled. There were family problems, and his work was not well received. Worst of all, his dearest friend, Arthur Hallam, died suddenly in 1833, sinking the poet into almost suicidal depression. The tide of Tennyson's luck turned at last when he married Emily Sellwood in 1850.

In 1836, Tennyson's brother married Emily's sister, and at that wedding Tennyson met Emily again, after a previous acquaintanceship. Alfred and Emily corresponded constantly for several years, despite her father's disapproval. Mr Sellwood thought Tennyson's religious views too liberal, his taste for port and tobacco unsavoury, and his lack of regular income unsuitable. In 1840, he forbade Alfred and Emily to write to one another. Alfred despaired. He refused his mother's offer of money (which she supposed might mollify Mr Sellwood); he also refused to undertake commercial writing, saying, 'I only write what I feel, and will never write anything else.' Not until 1850, ten years later, were

426

the two reunited. They had seen each other only once, by accident, in the interim. Alfred sent Emily *In Memoriam*. The poem
and its financial success seemed to impress the stern Mr Sellwood
at last. Tennyson said the wedding, in 1850, was 'the nicest
wedding' he had ever attended, even though the dresses and the
cake arrived too late for the ceremony. It was a blissful marriage,
despite the tragedy of the first child being stillborn. After Tennyson saw his dead baby boy, he wrote, 'Dead as he was I felt proud
of him. . . . I am glad I have seen him.' And, 'He lay like a little
warrior, having fought the fight and failed. . . .' Two healthy
children, Hallam and Lionel, followed. Tennyson delighted in his
sons. One of his favourite sayings was, 'Make the lives of children
as beautiful and happy as possible.'

Emily was an intelligent, plucky woman, who impressed
Alfred's friends, including Thomas Carlyle. But his friends'
praise paled beside her husband's adoration. Emily was his most
important literary adviser, and he always requested her final
criticism before a poem's publication. Tennyson wrote: 'I am
proud of her intellect.' In her diary, Emily confided, 'If it were
not faithless, I should be afraid of so much happiness as I have.'

A.W. and J.M.

♣ William Tilden Jr
10 February 1893 to 5 June 1953

In 1950, a poll conducted by the Associated Press proclaimed that
Big Bill Tilden was the greatest tennis player of the first half of
the twentieth century, and some of America's leading sports
writers called him the greatest US athlete in any sport at any time.
Perhaps these writers hoped to bring solace to a one-time giant – a
closet homosexual – who was living out his last years in disgrace
and near-oblivion.

He was Mr Tennis to the world and to himself, a dazzling star
dedicated to the game he dominated. Yet he was always marked
for personal tragedy. Seven years before his birth, Selina and
William Tilden had watched in horror as all three of their babies –
two girls and a boy – died one by one during a diptheria epidemic.
The following year Selina Tilden bore their fourth child, Herbert.
Still stunned by her loss, longing for a daughter, she yielded
Herbert's upbringing to his father. Seven years later, with the
appearance of another son, Selina's maternal instincts resurfaced.

She named her new baby William Tilden Jr, but from the beginning she called him June (short for Junior) and he became an obsession. To keep him close, she convinced herself he was a sickly child. When June reached school age Selina refused to relinquish him, hired tutors for his lessons, and deprived him of playmates. June adored his mother. When she spoke to him of sex, it was to warn him of the frightful venereal diseases that could result from genital contact. Not until he was 18, and illness confined Selina to a wheelchair, was June released – to become Bill, at last. Young Tilden moved in with two maiden relatives and was sent to school for the first time. He went to the University of Pennsylvania. During his freshman year in college, news of his mother's death affected him so severely that he withdrew and returned to an earlier school as a tennis coach. There his two lifetime passions merged: the need to excel at tennis, and the desire to cultivate the affection and playing skills of young boys. His own game remained unspectacular until he was 27. For the next six years he never lost a championship match. At 29, an operation that removed the upper joint of a middle finger seemed only to improve his game. In 1920, he became the first American to win the men's singles at Wimbledon. Between 1920 and 1930, he led the US Davis Cup team to victory in seven consecutive years.

Success transformed him into an egocentric prima donna. Dubbed 'Big Bill' although he was no more than 6 feet 1½ inches tall, he became arrogant, opinionated and belligerent. He was also messy, unwashed and frequently smelly. After matches he would return to the locker room but refuse to disrobe and shower in the presence of his team-mates. Not one of them ever saw his naked body. He chain-smoked, drank strong black coffee, and ate almost nothing but steak and ice cream. With growing fame, he had affected a British accent as he consorted with the world's notables, including four US presidents. In Hollywood he was partnered with Errol Flynn, Spencer Tracy and Montgomery Clift on Charlie Chaplin's tennis court. At Clifton Webb's he coached Greta Garbo, Katharine Hepburn, and Tallulah Bankhead. After his first arrest on 23 November 1964 and subsequent detention in a California honour farm for 'contributing to the delinquency of a minor', most of his acquaintances fell away. Despite his considerable professional earnings and two inheritances, this tormented man died alone in a Hollywood side-street apartment, almost destitute. His money had long since been dissipated on a

428

pasha-like life-style, ungrateful boys and disastrous investments, most notably a brief stage career wherein he financed and played the lead in Bram Stoker's *Dracula*.

In his autobiography *My Story* Tilden spoke of boyhood crushes on pretty girls. He claimed that, upon reaching manhood, he considered marriage, and later suffered from unrequited love at the hands of some of Hollywood's most famous women – all a pathetic fabrication. Actually, he recognized early on that he was 'different'. At 10, somehow escaping Selina, he embarked on a five-year fondling affair with another boy. Traumatized by his mother's preachings, living at a time when words like pregnancy and menstruation hid behind euphemisms – and homosexuality was absolute taboo – he fought to sublimate his sexual urges in tennis. He never enjoyed a fulfilling homosexual love affair, and it is unlikely he ever had complete physical contact with another human body, male or female. Mostly he fondled his boys and masturbated privately, increasing this activity as his career faded. Although he minced on to the tennis court before launching into his powerful game, very few knew his secret. In *Lolita*, Vladimir Nabokov's nymphet takes tennis lessons fron Ned Litam – 'Ma Tilden' spelled backwards – but no one openly exposed him.

Describing the incident that led to his downfall, Tilden wrote, 'I met one lad on the court who showed unusual promise ... Somehow we drifted into a foolishly schoolboyish relationship ... Coming home from a movie ... we indulged in horesplay ... We were stopped by the police in Beverly Hills.' As a consequence, Tilden spent almost eight months at a California honour farm, polishing kitchen pots, setting the table and serving other inmates. Arrested a second time after he violated a five-year parole by consorting with a minor, Tilden protested, but to no avail. The youth he had pursued identified Tilden unhesitatingly, even mentioning that missing joint on Tilden's middle finger. He also testified that Tilden 'was playing with my privates'. This time Tilden was sent to a road camp. In his sensitive, definitive biography *Big Bill Tilden*, Frank Deford wrote of Tilden's Philadelphia funeral, 'He was placed ... at the feet of his mother, so that at last he could be her child again, for good, at peace.'

S.W. (Lists 12, 15, 17, 29, 45, 48)

429

♣ Leo Tolstoi

9 September 1828 to 20 November 1910

Born into an aristocratic Russian family, Tolstoi was orphaned as a child and raised by relatives. He left Kazan University to manage the family estate but preferred the social whirl of Moscow and St Petersburg, where he lived a profligate life. Disgusted with his aimlessness, Tolstoi went to the Caucasus in 1851 and joined the army. There he worked on his first novel, the semi-autobiographical *Childhood*. When it was published a year later, Tolstoi became a literary celebrity. In 1862, at the age of 34, Tolstoi married 18-year-old Sofya (Sonya) Andreevna Behrs, who bore his thirteen children and encouraged him to write. Although his novels and short stories made him rich and famous, and his family life was relatively happy, Tolstoi became dissatisfied with himself. During the last stages of work on *Anna Karenina*, he experienced a moral and spiritual crisis. He questioned the purpose of life and even contemplated suicide. His anguish ended after he became a Christian and discovered that faith in God could give meaning to one's existence and unite people into a brotherhood of universal love and justice. He adopted the Sermon on the Mount as his personal credo. In order to live according to his new convictions, Tolstoi adopted peasant dress, worked as a farm labourer, and tried to dispose of his property. He eventually transferred his estate to his wife and children and gave Sonya the right to publish his earlier books. Turning away from his previous literary style, Tolstoi concentrated on writing moralistic fiction and social and religious essays. His teachings attracted many followers. To Tolstoi's great resentment, Sonya was unwilling to join him in his ascetic life-style, which strained the marriage. The household was in constant turmoil, and in 1910, at the age of 82, Tolstoi finally left Sonya for good. Ill-prepared both spiritually and physically for such a journey, he collapsed at the small railway station of Astapovo. As he lay dying in the stationmaster's house, Sonya was not allowed to come to his bedside until he was unconscious and could no longer recognize her. Seven days later he was dead.

Tolstoi lost his virginity at the age of 16 in a way that was considered commonplace for a man in the 1800s – to a prostitute. As he recounted it later, 'The first time my brothers dragged me to a brothel and I performed the act, I sat down afterwards at the foot of the woman's bed and cried.' Throughout his life, Tolstoi's remorse and his sexual desires fed upon each other. 'Regard the company of women,' he wrote in his diary, 'as a necessary social evil and avoid them as much as possible.' He did not heed his own advice. As he later admitted to Anton Chekhov, he was 'insatiable'. While living on his estate in 1849, he seduced one of the servants, a dark-eyed virgin named Gasha. He asked himself with distaste, 'Is what has happened to me wonderful or horrible? Bah! It's the way of the world; everybody does it!' A short time later he became involved with another servant. At 69 he remembered 'Dunyasha's beauty and youth ... her strong womanly body. Where is it ? Long since, nothing but bones.' He also had an incestuous desire for a distant aunt, Alexandra Tolstoi. He called her 'delicious' and 'unique' and even dreamed of marrying her.

Prosperous and successful as a writer, Tolstoi began to look for a wife, even though he was not very confident about his appearance. (He had a broad nose, toothless mouth, thick lips and half-closed eyes.) After discarding Axinya, his peasant mistress of three years who had given him a son, he decided to marry Sonya who was proud to be the wife of a famous author. But the marriage was doomed when, shortly before the wedding, he forced Sonya to read his diary where every one of his sexual exploits was described in explicit detail. He wanted her to know everything about him, but she interpreted his action as meaning he had only a physical love for her. Their first night together was a confrontation between a satyr and a virgin bride. Two weeks after their wedding night, Sonya wrote that 'physical manifestations are so repugnant', and throughout her married life she was never able to enjoy sex fully. His wife's innocence and apprehension only inflamed Tolstoi's lust. The seducer of coarse farm girls was to come to enjoy family life immensely, glorifying familial harmony and stability in the first of his masterpieces, *War and Peace*. Although he wrote in defence of individual freedom, he was a tyrant under his own roof and believed that a woman should devote herself to her husband's happiness. Sonya did her best to please him. She took care of the household and assisted him while he wrote. She copied *War and Peace* seven times before he was satisfied with the draft.

In 1889, Tolstoi stunned Sonya with *The Kreutzer Sonata*, a work in which he urged people to renounce sex and adopt celibacy. Marriage, he explained, must be avoided, since a Christian should abstain from all sex. After publication, Sonya was mor-

431

tified to find herself pregnant. 'That is the real postscript to *The Kreutzer Sonata*,' she wrote angrily. Try as he could to follow his new beliefs about sex, Tolstoi failed – again and again. His sexual drive remained undiminished, as indicated by Sonya's references to his passion in her diary. Not until he was 82 could he admit to a friend that he was no longer seized by sexual desire. Tolstoi blamed Sonya for making him want her and for letting him fall into sin. For her part, Sonya loathed his moral hypocrisy and disliked his constant advances. The fact that he smelled like a goat and had feet covered with sores and dirt did not help. He later described to Maxim Gorki the remorse he felt about sex: 'Man can endure earthquake, epidemic, dreadful disease, every form of sprititual torment; but the most dreadful tragedy that can befall him is and will remain the tragedy of the bedroom.'

Seven years after the first publication of *The Kreutzer Sonata*, Tolstoi and Sonya suffered another marital crisis when Sonya fell in love with a longtime family friend, pianist and composer Sergey Tanayev. The girlish attentions she paid to Tanayev infuriated Tolstoi. He called the relationship her 'senile flirtation', and referred to her as a 'concert hag'. Hurt and humiliated, he was greatly relieved when her innocent passion began to wane a year later. Tolstoi gradually confided less and less in Sonya, and she began to feel that he had rejected her as a wife, except for the sexual aspects of their relationship. Their frequent quarrels occasionally ended with threats by Sonya to run away and kill herself. Despite Tolstoi's guilt feelings, the mornings after nights of sex were about the only harmonious times they enjoyed. When she suspected that Tolstoi and his favourite disciple, Chertkov, were drafting a will bequeathing Tolstoi's works to the public, she became hysterical and accused her 81-year-old husband of having homosexual relations with Chertkov.

Tolstoi's advice regarding lust was summed up in his diary: 'The best thing one can do with sexual desire is (1) to destroy it utterly in oneself; next best (2) is to live with one woman, who has a chaste nature and shares your faith, and bring up children with her and help her as she helps you; next worse (3) is to go to a brothel when you are tormented by desire; (4) to have brief relations with different women, remaining with none; (5) to have intercourse with a young girl and abandon her; (6) worse yet, to have intercourse with another man's wife; (7) worst of all, to live with a faithless and immoral woman.'

A.S.M. and L.L. (Lists 11, 16, 20, 21, 26)

Henri de Toulouse-Lautrec

25 November 1864 to 9 September 1901

The only surviving child of an eccentric count and his shy and patient wife, Lautrec suffered two falls as an adolescent which broke both his thighbones. He was left crippled for life; his growth was frozen at 5 feet 1 inch. This greatly disappointed his father, who had been counting on a strong and healthy son to join him when he went hunting and debauching. Ugly, deformed and shorter than his peers, Lautrec had a personal charisma and quick wit which made him popular in the louche artistic circles of Paris in the late 1880s and throughout the 1890s. He became well known on the streets of Montmartre, dressed in baggy trousers, an overlong overcoat, and a bowler hat, and sporting a beard, bamboo cane and pince-nez. Despite his blue-blooded origins, Lautrec felt most at home with society's outcasts, and devoted extended periods of his life to living in brothels and frequenting lesbian bars. Alcoholism, syphilis and general abuse of his health led to his death in his mother's arms two and a half months before his 37th birthday.

Although he wasn't very tall, Lautrec had unusually well-developed sexual organs, even for a man of normal size. His genitals were so out of proportion to the rest of his body that he compared himself to a 'coffeepot with a big spout'. Coming from an aristocratic family, Lautrec was introduced to brothels early. Because he was misshapen and somewhat grotesque, marriage with a woman of his own class was considered unthinkable. He moved to Montmartre when 19 and divided his time between painting and observing Paris night life. He began having sexual affairs with some of his models, in particular Marie Charlet, a teenage adventuress who gossiped about the painter's sexual prowess.

In 1885, Lautrec became involved with model Suzanne Valadon, the mother of artist Maurice Utrillo and an artist herself. For three years, they carried on a stormy affair which ended abruptly when he learned that Valadon's threats of suicide were in fact play-acting. After the break-up with Valadon, Lautrec painted six studies of Rosa La Rouge, a red-haired prostitute from whom he contracted syphilis.

In 1891, Lautrec prepared his first poster for the Moulin Rouge and his fame began. Following a break-up with another lover, Berthe La Sourde, he began regularly frequenting brothels, and by 1894 had taken up residence in a high-class house of prostitution in the Rue des Moulins. He lived in this brothel and others virtually for the rest of his life. This unusual living arrangement provided Lautrec with the opportunity to indulge completely his sexual appetite, while simultaneously allowing him to observe and paint unposed nude and semi-nude women. 'The professional model is always like a stuffed owl,' he said. 'These girls are alive.'

He lived with prostitutes day in and day out. He played cards with them, laughed with them and surprised them in their beds. He shared their meals and brought in pâtés and fine wines to brighten up the menu. He kept track of each woman's birthday and brought them all presents. On their days off, Lautrec would invite these women of the night to his studio and take them to a restaurant or to the circus or a theatre. But, when he began to tire of brothels, Lautrec moved on to lesbian bars, particularly La Souris and Le Hanneton, near the Place Pigalle. Here, also surrounded by women, he again became a popular figure who could be consulted for advice.

In 1897, Lautrec fell in love with a young relative named Aline, who had just left a convent. For a while he foreswore cocktails (which he had helped popularize), talking of entering an alcoholism clinic, and drinking only port. But, when Aline's father forbade Lautrec to see his daughter, the artist plunged deeper than ever into the Paris underworld, eventually being sent to a mental asylum with delirium tremens. Within months of his release, he was drinking heavily again. He was finally stricken with paralysis in 1901.

An extreme sensualist, Lautrec periodically concentrated on different parts of the female body. It was said that he could caress a woman's hand for an hour. Red hair drove him to ecstasy. His friend, Thadée Natanson, described how Lautrec would 'purr with delight as he plunged his face into a woman's bosom, wrapping her two enormous breasts around him like a comforter made of human flesh'. Lautrec would 'clutch a pair of women's stockings that had fallen to the ground, roll them into a ball and inhale their scent with his eyes closed'.

At one point, Lautrec became obsessed with the actress and dancer, Marcelle Lender. For more than twenty nights he reserved the same seat in the orchestra stalls, so that he could watch her dance the bolero. When asked why he kept returning, Lautrec replied, 'I simply come to see Lender's back. Take a

good look at it you've never seen anything so magnificent.'
Apparently he was impressed with her nose as well. According to
Natanson, Lautrec loved the sight of finely chiselled nostrils
since, due to his size, it was the first thing he saw as he looked up
at a woman's face.

D.W. (Lists 4, 7, 18, 20, 22, 50)

♣ Mao Tse-Tung
26 December 1893 to 9 September 1976

The principal architect of modern China, Mao was born in the
village of Shaoshan in Hunan Province, the oldest son of wealthy
peasants. Graduating from Hunan Normal School in 1918, he
went to Peking, where he studied Marxism. Three years later, he
became one of the founders of the Chinese Communist Party.
Mao rallied the peasants and organized them into an army skilled
in the tactics of guerilla warfare. By 1934, Chiang Kai-shek's rival
Kuomintang forces had surrounded the peasant Red Army. To
escape, Mao led his 100,000 followers on a 6000 mile retreat
marked by starvation, battle, disease and death to a safer area in
north-west China. When the Long March was over a year later,
only 5000 of those who started had survived the journey. Mao
eventually emerged as the most powerful man in the party: in
1949, he defeated Chiang and established the People's Republic
of China.

A good part of Mao's success as the foremost leader in China's
long revolutionary struggle can be attributed to his unwavering
identification with the masses. Though personally deploring the
harsh life into which he was born, he retained many peasant
habits, and articulated the discontent and longings of his people.
He was also a serious student of the Chinese classics, an avid
reader, and an accomplished speaker and writer. But he cared
nothing for his personal appearance (during his youth he didn't
care about his body odour), and was indifferent to what he ate,
smoked until his teeth blackened, talked openly about his bowel
movements, and once even dropped his trousers in the company
of Europeans in order to cool off on a hot day. Yet he turned these
drawbacks into strengths. He inured himself to physical hard-
ships and deprivations, was largely impervious to personal criticism, and retained a strong sense of humour. He was probably

one of history's least egotistical leaders.

By his own admission, he was a somewhat introverted youth. Several times he endured periods of sexual abstinence while concentrating on political problems, but appears to have been wholly heterosexual and appreciated beauty and intelligence in his women. His first adult relationship with a female was an odd one which contributed greatly to the shaping of his political thought. By 14, he had alienated his task-master father with his dreamy devotion to romantic literature. To jar the boy out of his indolence, Mao's father arranged a marriage for him with an older girl. Though appalled by the situation, Mao went through the traditional wedding ceremonies (perhaps the only time he did so in his four marriages), then refused to live with his bride. Later he claimed he had never touched her. This act of rebellion inaugurated his lifelong fight against Chinese traditions.

A decade of spasmodic education and odd jobs followed, after which Mao settled down to serious journalism and incipient revolutionary work in Peking. He seems to have had few romantic involvements, and he probably remained a virgin until he met Yang Kai-hui, a beautiful fellow revolutionary. According to Edgar Snow, an American journalist who interviewed Mao extensively during the late 1930s, Mao and Yang joined in a 'trial marriage' before formalizing their bonds around 1921. By freely choosing each other, they flouted tradition. Their radical peers thought them the ideal revolutionary couple. During the fighting with Chiang Kai-shek's Kuomintang forces in 1927, Mao left Yang and his children in Changsha for safety. Three years later, the Kuomintang captured Yang there, and publicly executed her for refusing to renounce Mao, who was by then a major communist leader. Many other members of Mao's family were killed over the next twenty years, and he lost track of most of his children (whose number is not known) in the upheaval of the times.

Although Yang had never disavowed Mao, by her death he was already living with another beautiful co-revolutionary – Ho Tzu-chen, a girl about half his age. They married soon after Yang's death. Ho was to become the millstone in Mao's private life. When the Long March started in 1934, she had two children and was pregnant with a third. She was severely wounded and the rigours of the march destroyed her mental balance. Mao and Ho became violently antipathetic and were divorced in 1937. Mao's abandonment of a disabled veteran of the Long March alienated many of his followers. Ho was sent to Moscow for psychiatric treatment, but her condition only worsened. Eventually she was placed in a Shanghai mental hospital.

Before breaking completely from Ho, Mao flirted with several presumably promiscuous women. Lily Wu, a graceful actress and interpreter, captivated him and was charged by Ho with alienating Mao's affections. In 1938, he shocked the Chinese Communist Party leadership by taking up with a movie actress whose reputation was even less savoury and whose commitment to the revolution was suspect. This was Lan Ping (Blue Apple), who soon changed her name to Chiang Ch'ing (Azure River). She was poor but ambitious, and resorted to Shanghai's casting couches to get better parts. Rumours spread that she had been the mistress of Chang Keng, a director and Communist Party official, and the wife of Tang Na, an actor and film critic. When she jilted Tang Na, leaving their two children with him, he threatened to kill himself. The press sensationalized the story, putting the blame on Chiang Ch'ing and making her the target of malicious gossip. After marrying Mao in 1939, she became an obscure housewife – a role said to have been ordained by the party leaders. Chiang later revealed something of her relationship with Mao in a famous epigram: 'Sex is engaging in the first round, but what sustains interest in the long run is power.' Chiang Ch'ing's quest for power began during the 1960s when she resurfaced as the driving force behind the Cultural Revolution. Mao's feelings about her in this period are a major enigma in his life. By the 1970s, Mao was clearly estranged from her (she had to apply in writing to see him), and after Mao's death Chiang Ch'ing's fall came swiftly when her early promiscuity and other sins were widely publicized.

Paradoxically, Mao – who one way or another abandoned four wives – was always a crusader against the oppression of women. The essence of Mao's ideas about woman's liberation was that the 'double standard' had to be eliminated in order to give women the same freedom as men.

R.K.R. (Lists 1, 20)

♣ Mark Twain
30 November 1835 to 21 April 1910

Samuel Langhorne Clemens was born in Florida. His pen name –
'Mark Twain' – was derived from a call used on riverboats when
sounding water depths. He began his writing career as a journalist, and eventually turned to fiction. Though a brilliant writer,
there was a tragic side to his life. Yielding to convention, Twain
funnelled his writing into a socially acceptable mode, and did not
complete or attempt to publish many of his beloved creations. His
work was profitable, as were his many lecture tours, but he
repeatedly lost fortunes by sinking money in bad business
schemes.

Twain's amorous life was dominated by a single figure – that of
his wife, Livy. Although he had had sweethearts before he met
her, he was probably a 34-year-old virgin when they married in
1870. Shown Livy's picture by her brother, he instantly fell in
love with her. Her family was highly respectable and, even
though Twain was making good money lecturing, it wasn't easy
to convince her parents, but marry her he did. Besides giving him
three daughters, Livy set about reforming him. Looking upon
him as a wayward child, her pet name for him was 'Youth'. Twain
told a friend, 'After my marriage she edited everything I wrote.
And what is more – she not only edited my works – she edited
me!' He added, 'I would quit wearing socks if she thought them
immoral.'

Believing her to be the essence of female perfection, he never
criticized her. And, though he delighted in teasing her and playing practical jokes, he generally obeyed her. Livy was a partial
invalid all her life because of a fall on the ice in her youth, so
Twain happily doted on his wife and nursed her. He remained
madly in love with Livy until her death in 1904. The loss for
Twain was enormous – he never recovered his happiness, and
barely wanted to live without her.

Twain may well have been mostly impotent by the age of 50.
This is strongly indicated in a number of his lesser-known
humorous writings. But he never said it directly, stating in his
memoirs that he would tell the truth about himself, but not the
sexual truth, since Rousseau had taken care of that in his *Confessions*. He probably never made love to anyone but his wife,
although his longtime personal secretary, Isabel Lyon, set her
sights on him after Livy died. He found the woman repulsive,

and wrote to a friend, 'I could not go to bed with Miss Lyon. I would rather have a waxwork.' He explained that she was 'an old, old virgin, and juiceless, whereas my passion was for the other kind'.

A curious fact about Twain is that he delighted in writing obscene poems, ballads and essays. He had them printed privately in very small quantities, if printed at all. He complained, 'Delicacy – a sad, sad false delicacy – robs literature of the two best things among its belongings: family-circle narratives and obscene stories.'

The most famous of his sexual/scatological works is *1601: A Tudor Fireside Conversation*. This hilarious essay was written in Elizabethan language – with Queen Elizabeth, Raleigh, etc., exchanging lewd tales and insults. Twain sent a copy of it to his friend the Rev. Joseph Twitchell, and the two of them would take it to a favourite spot in the wood and roar with laughter over it.

One of Twain's poems begins 'Constipation, O constipation,' and an address given to a men's club (the Stomach Club) is entitled *Some Remarks on the Science of Onanism*. *The Mammoth Cod* is a song and speech written for another men's club, the Mammoth Cods, who were devoted to cod-fishing, drinking and revelry. ('Cod' is an old-fashioned euphemism for 'penis'.) The song includes the lines: 'Of beasts, man is the only one/Created by our God/Who purposely, and for mere fun/Plays with his Mammoth Cod!' He called the song a hymn for children and imagined it 'sung by hundreds of sweet, guileless children' in Sunday schools. 'I fail to see any special merit in penises of more than the usual size,' he wrote in the cod essay. 'What more can they achieve than the smaller ones? ... In this, as in everything else, quality is more to be considered than quantity. It is the searching, not the splitting weapon that is of use. I really don't know whether I have such a thing as a "Cod" about me. I know there is a conduit about my person which is useful in conveying the waste moisture of the system, but that is the only use I have ever put it to, except the natural one of procreation. I may be excused for this, for it would be a shame to have the kind of man I am die out with myself. As for what men of the world call pleasure ... I know nothing about it and care less. My recollection of it is that, while it was, perhaps, pleasant, it was so brief and transitory that it was not worth my while to repeat.'

Equally revealing is this excerpt from *Letters from the Earth*: 'During twenty-three days in every month (in the absence of pregnancy) from the time a woman is 7 years old till she dies of old age, she is ready for action, and *competent*. As competent as the candlestick is to receive the candle. Competent every day, competent every night. Also, she *wants* that candle – yearns for it, longs for it, hankers after it, as commanded by the law of God in her heart.

'But man is only briefly competent; and only then in the moderate measure applicable to the word in *his* sex's case. He is competent from the age of 16 or 17 thenceforward for thirty-five years. After 50 his performance is of poor quality, the intervals between are wide, and its satisfactions of no great value to either party; whereas his great-grandmother is as good as new. There is nothing the matter with her plant. Her candlestick is as firm as ever, whereas his candle is increasingly softened and weakened by the weather of age, as the years go by, until at last it can no longer stand, and is mournfully laid to rest in the hope of a blessed resurrection which is never to come.'

Twain goes on to calculate that while a man is good for 100 acts of love a year for fifty years, a woman is good for 3000 a year as long as she lives, an average of ten a day. It put man's lifetime total (according to Twain's arithmetic) at 5000 'refreshments' and woman's at 150,000. He therefore recommended that men receive a one-fiftieth interest in one woman, while women receive a male harem.

Perhaps the most telling work of all is a poem entitled 'A Weaver's Beam': 'Behold – the Penis mightier than the Sword/That leapt from Sheath at any heating Word/So long ago – now peaceful lies, and calm/And dreams unmoved of ancient Conquests scored.'

Twain in later years became obsessed with little girls. His interest clearly bordered on the sexual. He formed his favourites into a club: they were called 'Angel Fish' separately (each was given an angel-fish pin) and the 'Aquarium' en masse. The average age for an Angel Fish was 13, and girls over 16 were rarely eligible. When one Angel Fish abandoned Twain for the company of young men Twain was extremely jealous. His secretary wrote, 'his first interest when he goes to a new place is to find little girls', and 'off he goes with a flash when he sees a new pair of slim little legs appear, and if the little girl wears butterfly bows of ribbon on the back of her head then his delirium is complete'.

A.W. (Lists 1, 3, 35, 49)

♣ Rudolph Valentino
6 May 1895 to 23 August 1926

Rodolfo Guglielmi di Valentina D'Antonguolla, from the small town of Castellaneta, Italy, was a wayward boy and a daydreamer. He worked just hard enough to get through agricultural school, after which he took a holiday in France and squandered his family's hard-earned money at night spots and restaurants. He had to borrow to get home. His mother was horrified by the change in him – he now associated with showgirls and 'loose' women. Rather than run the risk of disgrace, his parents shipped him off to the USA. He arrived in New York City as Rodolfo Guglielmi, 18, friendless and unable to speak the language.

Rodolfo first sought work as a gardener and was employed on a millionaire's estate until he wrecked his boss's motorcycle. He went hungry for a time and was locked out of his hotel room for non-payment of rent. But he learned English quickly and, with his suave European charms, he procured jobs as a dancing partner for unescorted ladies at cabarets and hotels. Women clamoured to dance with the flirtatious young man who was soon offered professional dance spots. He tangoed with socialite Joan Sawyer until he appeared as a witness against her in a divorce trial in which Joan was named as a co-respondent. After that, he once again had difficulty finding work. In 1916, he was arrested, along with a Mrs Georgia Thym, in a vice and white slavery investigation. 'Many persons of means, principally "social climbers,"' said *The New York Times*, 'had been blackmailed after discreet visits to [Mrs Thym's] house.' Why Rodolfo was there was never clarified, but he was jailed for a few days as a 'material witness'. The charges against him were apparently dropped, but rather than face the possibility of deportation he left New York. After joining a musical comedy show that folded, he went to San Francisco where he sold bonds for a while. After that, he took a job as a dancer with an Al Jolson act that was moving to Los Angeles. There he tried desperately to break into films. From 1917 to 1921, he played bit parts as a 'foreign type' or a 'villain' until scriptwriter June Mathis spotted him and helped him land the role of Julio in *The Four Horsemen of the Apocalypse*. Between 1921 and his death from peritonitis at 31, the man known as Rudolph Valentino acted in fourteen completed films. He was perhaps best loved for his role in *The Sheik*, in which he played passion personified.

Valentino had a sexual-fantasy film image which no mortal could sustain in real life. But women found the tall, lean young man polite and impeccably, though sometimes gaudily, dressed. When he arrived in Hollywood, Valentino fell for Jean Acker, an aspiring young actress. They were kindred spirits, both looking for that big break. Their marriage in 1919 was impetuous and, as soon as the ceremony was over, Jean knew she had made a 'big mistake'. Before Valentino could scoop up his bride for the traditional ride across the threshold, she dashed inside ahead of him and bolted the door. Valentino spent his wedding night alone and the marriage was never consummated. Friends suspected that Jean had been in love with someone else, and she admitted that she had married the struggling actor out of pity. Rather than set up house with her husband, she moved in with a female friend. Ironically, Jean sued Valentino for divorce on grounds of desertion. The actor counter-sued and, after it was admitted in court that they had never had sex, he won an interlocutory decree of divorce which became final at the end of a year – in March 1923.

But, late in 1920, while at work on *Uncharted Seas*, Valentino met Natacha Rambova (real name Winifred Shaughnessy), stepdaughter of cosmetic tycoon Richard Hudnut, the woman who became the moving force in his life. As a strong-willed, ambitious teenager, she ran away from home to join Kosloff's Russian ballet company. When Valentino met her, she was working on another set with Russian actress – and purported lesbian – Alla Nazimova, as a costume and set designer. In Natacha, Rudy found his greatest love – she made him 'touch ecstasy', he once said. They were married before his divorce became final. The groom was promptly arrested on charges of bigamy and was jailed for several hours while bail was raised. Valentino was once again forced to admit in court that his marriage hadn't been consummated, and the charges were dropped. Though he and Natacha lived apart until they could legally remarry, she became a part of his life and career. He trusted her judgement and bowed to her decisions. After his great success in *The Sheik*, she envisaged him as another Douglas Fairbanks appearing in epic films rather than in the 'small, trifling, cheap, commercial pictures' Paramount gave him. For almost two years – late 1922 to early 1924 – he made no movies because of contract disputes in which, at her instigation, he protested against the parts he was getting and the studio's treatment of Natacha.

Rudy and Natacha married legally in 1923, and the newlyweds

earned a living by dancing for the Mineralava Company, promoting beauty clay. To supplement their income, the Valentinos wrote a book of poetry called *Day Dreams*. The contract problems ended when an independent film-maker agreed to shoot Valentino's films and let Natacha act as consultant. She became involved in every facet of his pictures, provoking the press to say that she wore the pants in the Valentino family. They jeered at the platinum slave bracelet she gave him. Her mistake, she said later, was to incorporate 'beauty' into his films. It was beauty that hurt his career – in the films in which Natacha 'meddled', Valentino seemed effeminate. In *Monsieur Beaucaire*, he wore powdered wigs and a heart-shaped beauty spot on his face. The publicity became vicious: *Photoplay* ran an article stating that 'All men hate Valentino', and the Chicago *Tribune* ran an editorial called 'Pink Powder Puffs', which blamed Valentino for the fact that a powder-vending machine had been installed in the men's room of a Chicago ballroom. Finally, the independent film-maker refused to work with the Valentinos and scrapped a film they had already begun. United Artists approached Valentino with a lucrative contract, but it banned Natacha from their sets. Valentino tried to assuage her feelings by backing her in her own endeavour, a movie called *What Price Beauty?* It failed miserably and critics detected lesbian-fantasy scenes in it. Once she no longer shared his career, Natacha wanted no part of Rudy's bed. Valentino insisted that what he really wanted was a homemaker, not a business partner. He told the press, 'Mrs Valentino cannot have a career and be my wife at the same time.' They were divorced in 1925.

The 'Great Lover' was a bachelor again. Detectives herded him home if he got too friendly with strange women – the studio didn't want more bad publicity if Valentino should turn in a less-than-successful amorous performance. But no one could keep him away from Pola Negri. He met the actress through Marion Davies, mistress of William Randolph Hearst. As Pola wrote in her autobiography, 'Valentino's true sexuality reached out and captured me.' She was fascinated, she said, by 'the way in which he used his body', and he took her in 'a perfect act of love'. Valentino preferred sex first and intimate conversation afterwards. She found him a very accomplished lover, able to size up a woman and judge exactly the right approach which would manoeuvre her into bed. Once, he decided that strewing rose petals on Pola's bed would do the trick – and it did. Pola hoped to marry him, though as a form of New Year's resolution in 1926 he betted that he would still be a bachelor by 1930. No one knows whether he would have won – after a brief illness, he died in 1926. Thousands of men and women trampled over one another to view the body; some women who never knew him committed suicide, and for years a 'Lady in Black' visited his grave on the anniversary of his death.

W.A.D. and V.S. (Lists 8, 42, 46)

♣ Vincent Van Gogh
30 March 1853 to 29 July 1890

Born in Zundert, the Netherlands, Van Gogh was a clergyman's son. At 16, he was apprenticed to art dealers Goupil and Co., working first in their office in The Hague and later at their branches in London and Paris. After wandering from job to job, he eventually turned to religion. In 1879, Van Gogh ministered to the poor in Le Borinage, a Belgian coal-mining region, until a conflict with church authorities led to his dismissal. In despair he found solace in painting, but regrettably he lived to see only one painting – *The Red Vine* – sold. He lived on an allowance from his devoted brother Theo. Van Gogh's ideas were too unorthodox for his time. For example, he once had a fight with his art instructor at the Antwerp Academy of Art over the proper way to draw a woman. Asked to draw the Venus de Milo, Vincent gave her large hips, enraging his teacher, who slashed at the drawing. 'God damn you!' yelled Vincent. 'A woman must have hips and buttocks and a pelvis in which she can hold a child!'

In 1886, he moved to Paris, where he fell in with Toulouse-Lautrec and Gauguin. Towards the end of 1888, he and Gauguin lived and worked together in Arles. Although they were prolific, they were temperamentally incompatible, and their love/hate relationship provoked many feuds. During one quarrel, Gauguin refused to eat at the same table with Van Gogh, citing hygienic reasons and their differing outlooks on life. After another heated argument, Van Gogh – jealous of Gauguin's success with the Arles prostitutes – cut off part of his own left ear. The incident had definite sexual overtones – Van Gogh put the ear in an envelope and took it to a prostitute who preferred him to Gauguin. When the lady opened the envelope containing the bloody ear, she fainted. Van Gogh suffered recurrent fits of

444

madness, voluntarily spent a year in an asylum, and ultimately committed suicide by shooting himself in the stomach while hiding behind a manure heap in a farmyard. He was 37. The failure to find lasting female companionship throughout his life perhaps contributed to his breakdown and suicide.

One of Van Gogh's early bouts of depression followed his rejection in 1874 by Ursula Loyer, his landlady's daughter. After concealing his feelings for months while working for the Goupil Gallery in London, he suddenly blurted out his love to the shocked and repelled girl. This happened again with his recently widowed cousin Kee Stricker Vos, who was visiting the Van Gogh's home in Etten. Again, he hid his feelings until they erupted in an urgent proposal of marriage. 'No! Never, never!', Kee replied and promptly returned to her parents in Amsterdam. This time Van Gogh did not give up so easily. Using borrowed money, he gave chase to Amsterdam, where he interrupted the Strickers during dinner. When he was announced, Kee ran out before he could talk to her. The Strickers tried to be polite, but Van Gogh would not leave until he saw his love. On his third visit, he plunged his hand into the flame of an oil lamp, vowing to keep it there until Kee appeared. Now more determined than ever to keep this apparent madman away from their daughter, the Strickers bluntly told Van Gogh that his suit was pointless.

By this time, Van Gogh was sexually frustrated. 'I must have a woman or I shall freeze and turn to stone,' he once complained. Taking to the streets, he discovered that he liked prostitutes, because they were 'sisters and friends' to him, outcasts like himself, and would not reject him. Van Gogh preferred faded, slightly older, prostitutes whom he could nurture. He soon found the ideal candidate in a pregant prostitute named Clasina Maria Hoornik, whom he called 'Sien' – 'His Own'. She and her 5-year-old daughter moved in with him, and she soon bore Van Gogh a son, Willem, whom he adored. Much to the shame of his family, Vincent lived with Sien for more than a year and considered marrying her. In return, Sien posed for him (she is the crouched nude figure in the 'Sorrow' lithographs) and gave the artist a case of gonorrhoea that put him in hospital for more than three weeks. He did not resent this, however, feeling that the rigours of her childbearing were a far greater burden. But the idyll passed, as he saw Sien's true colours: she was slovenly, bitchy and usually drunk. From then on, he no longer referred to her by name, but called her 'the woman with whom I live', or just

445

'the woman'. When she eventually returned to the streets, Van Gogh lost his 'family' and left The Hague.

Finally, in 1884, a woman actually chased Van Gogh. She was Margot Begemann, his next-door neighbour in Nuenen, a dowdy, sexually repressed 41-year-old spinster who thought the artist was her last opportunity for marriage. Van Gogh compared her to a Cremona violin mangled by inept craftsmen. Yet, whether from pity or genuine affection or both, Van Gogh agreed to marry her. When her parents forbade the union, Margot responded by swallowing strychnine, which Vincent forced her to vomit. The marriage never took place.

In 1887, Van Gogh confided to his sister that he was going through a string of meaningless affairs 'from which I emerge as a rule damaged and shamed and little else'. He frequented Parisian brothels with friends like Toulouse-Lautrec, had an affair with a female café owner, and reportedly with a 19-year-old boy. He contracted venereal disease from time to time and complained of increasing impotence. When asked why he didn't sketch in brothels for money, he replied that he wasn't 'good enough meat' to entice the women to pose for free.

In a letter to a friend, Van Gogh expounded on the sexual/artistic merits of his fellow craftsmen. Degas, he said, 'does not like women, for he knows that if he loved them and fucked them he ... would become insipid as a painter. He looks on while the human animals, stronger than himself, get excited and fuck.... Rubens! Ah, that one! he was a handsome man and a good fucker.... [Delacroix] did not fuck much, and only had easy love affairs, so as not to curtail the time devoted to his work.' And so on about Courbet, Cézanne, and even Balzac.

Van Gogh summed up his comments pithily when he wrote, 'Painting and fucking are not compatible; it weakens the brain.... If we want to be really potent males in our work, we must sometimes resign ourselves not to fuck much.'

He said, 'The world seems more cheerful if, when we wake up in the morning, we find we are no longer alone and that there is another human being beside us in the half-dark. That's more cheerful than shelves of edifying books and the white-washed walls of a church....'

W.A.D., E.K. and A.W. (Lists 14, 18, 20)

♣ Giuseppe Verdi

10 October 1813 to 27 January 1901

Verdi was born to poor, illiterate parents in the tiny town of Le Roncole, in the Duchy of Parma. As a child he displayed a genius for music that was noted and encouraged by a local merchant, Antonio Barezzi, who became Verdi's sponsor and lifelong friend.

Verdi's first opera had its premiere at La Scala, in Milan, in 1839, and was a modest success. He completed his second opera, a comedy, in a state of depression following the death from unknown diseases of his young wife and their two children. The work was a failure. In his grief and frustration, Verdi vowed to write no more for the stage. But he was persuaded by La Scala's powerful impresario Merelli to undertake the composition of *Nabucco*, and this opera's overwhelming success in 1842 established Verdi's reputation. In spring 1851, Verdi moved his permanent address to a farm at Sant' Agata, outside Busseto, where he composed his most famous works. He died in Milan half a century later after a stroke, wealthy, famous, and – according to Arrigo Boito, librettist for Verdi's last two operas, *Otello* and *Falstaff* – fighting death until his last breath.

Despite mid-nineteenth-century gossip, which had Verdi sleeping with every attractive woman he met, the evidence suggests that there were only two important romances in his life, plus three affectionate friendships – almost certainly platonic. Verdi's first love was Margherita Barezzi, the eldest daughter of his sponsor in Busseto. Their marriage lasted from May 1836 until Margherita's death in June 1840. Verdi returned to Milan, and after the success of *Nabucco* the young widower became much sought-after in Milanese salons.

Between 1842 and 1847, Verdi's name was linked with three women in particular, but two of these relationships were clearly social in nature. Verdi's liaison with the diva Giuseppina Strepponi (1851–97) *was* romantic, however, and, when they started living together openly in 1848, it caused a flurry in artistic circles from Paris to Milan. Strikingly different from Verdi's shy and gentle first wife, Giuseppina was highly independent. She had supported her family since she was 19 and had been a very successful prima donna before her voice failed. Although unmarried, she already had two children by the time she met the handsome, black-bearded young composer. Although Verdi always valued the professional advice of this remarkably

447

intelligent woman, he expected his mistress to perform the traditional functions of housekeeper and wife. She gladly complied, remarking, 'Not everybody can write *Aïda*, but somebody has to pack and unpack the trunks.' When Verdi brought Giuseppina to Sant' Agata in 1851, the local populace was scandalized. Women turned their backs on her in the market, and people refused to sit beside her at church. Furious, Verdi closed the doors of his home to all but his closest friends and maintained his distance from the town even after he and Giuseppina married in a small village in Savoy in August 1859. Why they waited so long to do so has never been adequately explained, but Verdi defended their right to privacy.

During the 1870s, Giuseppina suspected Verdi of having an affair with the diva Teresa Stolz, who became a frequent guest. The situation apparently turned to confrontation during which Giuseppina laid down the ultimatum, 'Either this woman leaves the house or I leave it.' The hotblooded Verdi reportedly replied, 'This woman stays or I blow my brains out!' The domestic crisis was weathered, however, and La Stolz continued to deny rumours linking her with the maestro. As for Verdi – so intent on safeguarding his privacy through his long life – not a single love letter written by him survives. Thus, the nature of his relationship with Teresa Stolz will probably always remain a mystery.

W.A.H.

♣ Paul Verlaine
30 March 1844 to 8 January 1896

The great French writer Verlaine was well known for his bohemian life-style and bisexual love affairs, including one with the poet Rimbaud.

His father was a comfortably off army officer, his mother a simple woman who kept the foetuses of her three stillborn infants in glass jars and jealously indulged her only surviving child. Throughout his life, Verlaine would remain his mother's beloved son – weak and irresponsible, demanding yet sexually ambivalent.

Verlaine remembered that he was 'overcome by sensuality' at the age of 12 or 13, but his personal slovenliness and ugliness aroused antipathy rather than attraction. His face was broad and flat with narrow slanting eyes set under thick brows. Children

448

taunted him, while a teacher said he looked like a degenerate criminal. At school, Verlaine was attracted to younger boys with whom he formed 'ardent' friendships. At about 17, Verlaine became a regular patron of female prostitutes, exploring with great relish the borders of illicit pleasure and pain. He also demonstrated a congenital weakness for alcohol, with a preference for the deadly green absinthe. After an extended period of debauchery, he met and in 1870 married a young girl who seemed the epitome of unsullied virginity. Verlaine settled down briefly to a civil service job before the Franco-Prussian War erupted, and the arrival in Paris of Arthur Rimbaud in 1871 ended for ever any semblance of bourgeois respectability in Verlaine's life. Their affair lasted for two years, followed by eighteen months in prison for having assaulted Rimbaud. While in jail, Verlaine consoled himself with religion.

Henceforth, Verlaine lived as a sexual vagabond, wandering from one disastrous affair to another, alternating between violence and penitence, sobriety and debauchery, quarrels and reconciliation – all the while distilling the essence of his experience into verse. Even during affairs he lived with his mother in a tempestuous, frequently violent, love-hate relationship. After his mother's death in 1886, Verlaine returned to heterosexuality for the first time since his marriage. His health was declining (his many complaints included cirrhosis of the liver, a heart condition and a 'bad leg', possibly caused by tertiary syphilis), and he spent nearly half of his last years happily ensconced in public hospitals, where he was cared for like a baby and regaled as a celebrity. Before his death of pneumonia, he was elected 'prince of poets', the greatest living French poet.

For Verlaine, it was love at first sight when he met a proper 16-year-old who admired his poetry. Having already seen the poet in literary circles, Mathilde Mauté was not put off by his looks. Indeed, the infatuated Verlaine was so happy, she later wrote, that 'he ceased to be ugly, and I thought of "Beauty and the Beast", where love transforms the Beast into Prince Charming.' During their ten-month engagement, Verlaine remained adoringly devoted and chaste, writing trite poetry which idealized love. Marriage, however, revealed 'Beauty' to be a vain and snobbish bourgeoise, while 'Prince Charming' reverted to the 'Beast'. He began to drink again and alternated between gentleness and brutality. He once tried to set his wife's hair on fire, and in a burst of rage hurled his infant son against a wall. Finally, he

449

ran away with the 17-year-old poet Rimbaud. After an unsuccessful attempt to seduce her husband into returning home, Mathilde obtained a formal separation and eventually divorced him. It had been a mere three years from her first encounter with Verlaine to his final desertion.

Rimbaud was the boy-genius of French poetry, a beautiful, precocious teenager who wrote startlingly original verse, and was also, by all accounts, an insufferable hooligan, ruthlessly perverse, and gratuitously sadistic. His philosophy of exploring every form of love, suffering and madness, in order to achieve poetic 'truth', made him sexual fair game for Verlaine. Preceded by some of his poems and a letter of introduction sent to Verlaine, Rimbaud arrived in Paris dirty and penniless. Verlaine put him up at his in-laws', where he was living at the time, then housed him with a succession of friends. (One of them, a homosexual musician, introduced the boy to hashish.) Day and night the two poets caroused, drinking and engaging in deliberately provocative displays of public affection. Privately, Verlaine introduced Rimbaud to 'nights of Hercules', the exhilarating 'love of tigers'. Of the two, Rimbaud was clearly the dominant partner. Verlaine, who considered himself 'a feminine' seeking love and protection, fell under the spell of the 'infant Casanova' with his irresistible combination of beauty, genius and violence. Rimbaud, testing his powers, slashed Verlaine with a knife just to amuse himself, and taunted him about his marital respectability. In July 1872, the two poets ran away together, apparently with the financial assistance of Verlaine's mother, who was jealous of Mathilde. The escapade lasted for the better part of a year, which Verlaine would forever remember as a time of 'living intensely, to the very top of my being'. They explored the Belgian countryside, then crossed the Channel to London, living in cheap hotels and lodgings. They made a perfunctory effort to support themselves by giving French lessons, but were glad to fall back on Verlaine's indulgent mother, who estimated bitterly that Rimbaud cost her 30,000 francs.

It was a period of great creativity for Verlaine, but also a time of constant bickering and vituperation, as Rimbaud vented his self-disgust and his hatred of being dependent on the older poet. Unable to bear it any longer, Verlaine left abruptly in July 1873 for Brussels. Dispatching suicide notes to all concerned – including his wife – he waited to be rescued. Verlaine's mother arrived first, followed by a truculent Rimbaud. In the drunken emotional disorder of the occasion, Verlaine turned his suicide weapon on Rimbaud, shooting him in the wrist. Threatened again and fearful of another attack, Rimbaud called the police, who arrested Verlaine and proceeded to explore his sexual proclivities. Medical examination revealed signs of homosexual intercourse. Verlaine was subsequently sentenced to two years in prison for attempted manslaughter. Released in January 1875 – six months off for good behaviour – Verlaine sought out Rimbaud. The latter repelled these advances by knocking him out and leaving him by the roadside. Rimbaud soon abandoned poetry and lived the rest of his short life as a mercenary adventurer, dying of cancer in 1891. Verlaine, never one to harbour a grievance, would remember their time together as the apex of his life – intellectually, emotionally and physically – a time of pleasure so intense it bordered on pain.

Verlaine spent the rest of his life divided between demon lovers and mother figures, the opposite poles of sexual attraction for him. While teaching in a provincial school in 1879, he met a young student whose impudence and opportunism reminded him of Rimbaud. Lucien Létinois at 19 was a handsome and straightforward peasant. Lucien accepted the effusive affection and financial support of the 35-year-old poet, only to complain privately that he wished they had never met.

Verlaine maintained the sentimental fiction that Lucien was his adopted son. He took Lucien to England and paid his expenses in London while he taught in Hampshire. The poet gave up his teaching post and rushed to London to rescue Lucien upon learning that he had fallen in love with a young British girl. Then Verlaine bought a farm in France and installed Lucien's family to help run it. The venture was a romance of rural life that ended in bankruptcy. When Lucien went into the army, Verlaine became a camp follower, composing fatuous verse about 'the handsome erect soldier'. Yet Verlaine, fortified by his religious conversion in prison, seems to have stopped short of sexually seducing his 'son'. When Lucien died of typhoid in 1883, the poet had him buried in a coffin draped in virginal white cloth. He then launched into a period of drunken homosexual vagabondage.

There was a young Parisian artist and writer named F. A. Cazals who became for a time the poet's platonic friend, heir and obsession. But Verlaine, liberated by the death of his mother, spent his last years – when not in hospital – alternating his time between two ageing prostitutes. Philomène Boudin and Eugénie

Krantz were both slatterns who satisfied his adolescent craving for tainted sex and stimulated his masochism with their physical and verbal abuse. They were also greedy, urging him to write poetry which they exchanged for cash at his publisher's office. Composed under the influence of absinthe and the broomstick, these poems reveal preoccupation with thighs, breasts and buttocks.

Verlaine's mistress Philomène had come equipped with a pimp who extended his protection to the poet, while Eugénie, who was semi-retired, gave him greater stability. Eugénie was with Verlaine when he died and presided over his funeral in widow's weeds. She soon drank herself to death with the proceeds from a lively trade in bogus literary souvenirs.

C.D. (Lists 12, 14, 15, 17, 18, 20, 35, 37)

♣ Victoria
24 May 1819 to 22 January 1901

Victoria's father, fourth son of King George III, died when she was an infant. She grew up simply at Kensington Palace, sharing a room with her mother and companionship with her German governess, Baroness Lehzen. Despite a solitary childhood, she was a merry, mischievous and wilful child; her imperious tendencies were reinforced on becoming heir apparent at 11 and queen at 18.

The young Victoria was a romantic figure. Although less than 5 feet tall and with a hearty appetite that would lead to stoutness, she was fair and charming. During the first visit of her cousins Ernest and Albert, 16-year-old Victoria danced and romped to her heart's content. 'All this dissipation does me a great deal of good,' she remarked.

The most prized match in the world of her day, Victoria was courted by a succession of royal suitors, many of them her cousins. She described them all in her diary with enthusiastic approval, particularly the tall, dashing Grand Duke Alexander – heir to the Russian throne – with whom she fell a little in love. But the dominant male figure during her first years on the throne was Lord Melbourne, Prime Minister of England, a gallant, sophisticated, erudite man who educated the young queen in her public role and took private pleasure in gossiping with her on the sofa at Windsor Castle. The widowed Melbourne, forty years older than his pupil, has been described as 'more than a father,

452

less than a lover' to Victoria. They spent hours each day together, obviously delighted with one another's company, and corresponded when they were separated even briefly.

Although susceptible all her life to strong men with roguish charm, Victoria chose to marry her cousin Albert, a young German princeling with operatic good looks, because she found him pure, gentle and winning. As queen she was the one to propose marriage, and she maintained her ascendancy during an engagement otherwise noted for fervent embraces and ecstatic letters. 'I am the Sovereign,' Victoria reminded her betrothed, denying his request for a quiet honeymoon. Shortly after the 20-year-olds were wed, Albert complained to a friend that he was only 'the husband, not the master of the house'. But his influence grew every day, and with every night, and with every royal pregnancy (of which there were nine). By the second child, Albert had succeeded in supplanting the governess, Baroness Lehzen; by the third, the royal 'I' had been changed to 'we'.

The wedding night injuction to 'Close your eyes and think of England' has been attributed to her; but she also wrote with such frankness of the delights of the marriage bed that her journal was destroyed after her death. She hated pregnancy ('a complete violence to all one's feelings of propriety') and complained of the 'shadow side of marriage', the sexual slavery of woman to man – yet she liked to call Albert her angel, worshipped him effusively, and presented him with gifts of nude works of classical art. When advised to have no more children, she is said to have replied to her doctor, 'Oh, Sir James, can I have no more fun in bed?' However, Victoria was naive about some aspects of sexuality. In 1885, when presented with the anti-homosexual Criminal Law Amendment, she crossed out all references to females. Lesbianism simply did not exist, insisted the queen. Victoria's and Albert's was by any account an intimate companionship. What the straitlaced and abstemious consort lacked in passion he made up for in devotion, calling Victoria 'little wifey' in German, choosing her bonnets, and even putting her stockings on for her. He knelt at her feet and held her hand while enduring the queen's emotional outbursts. Both were jealous and possessive – Albert of influence over his wife, Victoria of attractive women, even her oldest daughter. For the queen was the child in the royal family, enjoying in her patient and protective husband the father she never knew. Albert's public role was to foster the national climate of piety and prudery. Lacking the queen's natural vigour, he damaged his health irreparably in a fit of hysterical indignation over the Prince of Wales's illicit escapades. After Albert's sudden death at 42, Victoria was consumed with grief and longing, and never forgave Bertie. But she consoled herself with Albert's nightshirt clutched in her plump arms, a portrait of him on his pillow, and a cast of his hand nearby.

The usual image of the widowed Victoria is a plump, plain figure, with bulbous eyes and a little kerchief on her head, mourning for her sainted Albert. Remarriage was unthinkable, but there were diversions. Chief among these was John Brown, a burly, brusque Scots manservant who became the queen's closest companion after Albert's death. Victoria's son and successor, Edward, was appalled at her attachment to Brown. He ordered a wooden pavilion, which had been a favourite resting place of his mother's when she went on outings with Brown, to be dismantled. Victoria promptly commanded that it be rebuilt, and retaliated by giving Edward the silent treatment for several weeks. The pavilion most likely harboured drinking companions and not lovers, since Victoria and Brown shared a fondness for whisky. Victoria for her part publicly acknowledged Brown as her 'friend and most confidential attendant', refusing to give him up despite scandalous rumours that they were secretly married. (It has even been argued that Victoria bore Brown a son, who died a recluse in Paris at the age of 90.) Brown himself died in 1883.

One of Victoria's last conquests was Benjamin Disraeli, who as prime minister became the queen's close friend and confidant. Also a bereaved spouse, Disraeli was a romantic who consoled and flattered Victoria, restoring her taste for power by making her Empress of India. Although Victoria once paid 'Dizzy' the honour of visiting him at his country house, he declined another royal visit when on his deathbed, saying, 'No, it is better not. She will only ask me to take a message to Albert.'

C.D. (List 21)

♣ Voltaire
21 November 1694 to 30 May 1778

François-Marie Arouet, the author of *Candide*, was the son of a minor government functionary in Paris. Having little use for his family, in his youth he often claimed to have been born out of wedlock and he suspected that his real father was the Abbé de

Châteauneuf, since it was the abbé who enabled him to acquire an excellent liberal education at a Jesuit school. At an early age, he showed a remarkable talent for writing, adopting his pen name in his early twenties. From the onset, Voltaire was enormously successful in chic Parisian society. He was brilliant, witty and satirical in a culture that valued smart conversation and an agile mind. His acerbic epigrams were widely quoted, his plays enjoyed long runs, and his books sold briskly. He was an indulgent man who forgave most debts and personal affronts. Yet he rarely forgave intellectual insults, and was unable to contain his irreverence. Advocating such radical causes as inoculation against disease, religious tolerance, trial by jury, and the right of a people to choose its rulers, Voltaire flaunted the royal censors, his sometime patron King Frederick the Great of Prussia and his good friend King Louis XV. Voltaire spent much of his life in danger of arrest or in exile. An avid Anglophile, he often took refuge in England, where he made friends with Pope and Congreve. Finally elected to the French Academy in 1746, he promptly attacked his colleagues in a series of satirical essays. 'If there is an author in this country with whom I have not quarrelled,' he once wrote, 'his work is not worth reading.'

'It seems to me that I am in no degree made for passion. I find something a bit ridiculous in love . . . I have made up my mind to renounce it for ever,' Voltaire wrote at 25. At 46, he said he was too old to make love. And at various times he claimed to be impotent, either because of his age, illness, predilection or boredom. Yet, by the time he was 30 Voltaire had already had lengthy affairs with perhaps a dozen women, including the Duchess de Villars, wife of the Marshal of France, and the famous actress Adrienne Lecouvreur, and probably a few homosexual liaisons as well. At 79, he tried so hard to seduce an attractive young woman that he fainted three times, although he himself attributed his fainting to the awe in which he held the girl.

Voltaire never married, but he had three particularly important lovers. When he was 19 and living in The Hague, he fell desperately in love with Catherine Olympe Du Noyer, the teenage daughter of a gossip journalist. Pimpette, as she was called, was pretty and kind, and their affair very nearly led to elopement and marriage. However, Pimpette's mother and Voltaire's guardian had other plans for the children. They ended the affair forcibly, and Voltaire returned to Paris alone.

In 1733, Voltaire met the woman who would be his lover,

friend and intellectual companion for the next sixteen years. Gabrielle-Emilie Le Tonnelier de Breteuil, the Marquise du Châtelet, was *le philosophe*'s ideal mate. She read Latin and Italian, translated Newton's *Principia* into French, and developed Leibnitz's system of philosophy in her highly regarded book, *Institutions de Physique*. Although he called her 'the divine mistress', he was not above looking at her with a critical eye: ' . . . I frequently wish she were less learned and her mind less sharp, that her appetites for the making of love were less voracious and, more than all else, that she would acquire both the ability and desire to hold her tongue on occasion.'

At first, their affair was so publicly passionate it caused comment even among their friends, but as time went on it became less an engagement of bodies than an intense romance between two brilliant and well-matched minds. Although one of Emilie's female contemporaries described her as 'a great desiccated creature without any curves, covered with diamonds, and wearing cheap underclothes', her portraits suggest she was rather handsome. In any case, Voltaire loved her deeply, and wrote about her virtually every day of their lives together. The gradual cessation of their sex life put a severe strain on the relationship. Forced to look elsewhere for physical satisfaction, Emilie began an affair with the Marquis de Saint-Lambert, ten years her junior. An undistinguished poet and dramatist, the handsome Saint-Lambert's chief occupation was seducing other men's mistresses. To make matters worse, at 43 Emilie found herself pregnant. She died in 1749, six days after bearing Saint-Lambert's child. Voltaire wrote, 'I have not merely lost a mistress, I have lost the half of myself – a soul for which mine was made. . . .'

Not *all* was lost, however. Since about 1745, Voltaire had been having an affair with Marie Louise Mignot Denis, his bright and witty niece (such relationships were not considered incestuous in Voltaire's time). In fact, while Emilie had been writing passionate letters to Saint-Lambert, Voltaire had been busy corresponding with Mme Denis. 'I shall never be happy until I can live with you,' he wrote. 'I cover your adorable body with kisses.' The young widow had found comfort in her uncle's arms when her husband died, and upon Emilie's death she returned the favour. If, as some scholars suggest, she was attracted by Voltaire's considerable wealth, she none the less loved him, fulfilled his desires, and maintained his household until his death.

W.A.H. (List 12)

♣ Richard Wagner
22 May 1813 to 13 February 1883

Wagner was an arresting figure, with piercing blue eyes set in a large head, severe features, and an initially reserved manner. He had little formal musical education but was adept from childhood at reading music. He became his own librettist, and his operas are recognized as much for the prose as for the musical scores. Unfortunately, his amazing talent doomed Wagner to continual disappointment when his works were produced because no musician or performer could conduct, act or sing them as well as he.

Richard was well aware of his capabilities and was noted for his conceit. He regularly regaled friends with dramatic readings of his writings, and these – plus his incessant, passionate conversation – ensured he was always the centre of attention. One evening when his guests were peacefully chatting, Wagner was so annoyed that he screamed until all eyes once again were riveted on him. Richard sincerely believed that because of his genius it was the duty of others to support his extravagant life-style, which required money (provided by friends, patrons and his salary from conducting jobs). Wagner's creativity demanded sensuous surroundings. No angular objects, such as books, no noise or commonplace odour was allowed to remind him of the real world. Rooms were draped with satins and silks, violet and red predominating. Thick carpets covered the floors, perfumes scented his chambers, and natural light was muted. He dressed in luxury, favouring lace shirts, satin trousers, fur-lined slippers, and satin or silk dressing gowns. The combination of opulent tastes and financial irresponsibility caused Wagner to spend one night in a debtors' prison and he had to leave two cities hastily to avoid arrest. (One of these escapes required that he, his wife, and their dog cross the Russian border; if caught, they would have been shot.) In later years, Wagner adopted a vehement anti-Semitism that sometimes embarrassed his family and his benefactors. He was more talk than action, though, and the three men who were responsible for his last production – *Parsifal* in 1882 – were Jews. At 13 he had boarded with another family and enjoyed 'pretending to be too sleepy to move so that I might be carried to bed by the girls'. Wagner detested being alone and constantly sought out feminine company. He felt that women, much more than men, had the capacity to understand and sympathize with him and with his art. His fondness for them carried him through many affairs, both before and after his marriage. He wanted a woman unquestioningly devoted to him and willing to be devoured in return. His lovers ranged from intellectuals to maids and covered all age groups. They included one amiable young woman who also served as his housekeeper and cooked and cleaned in pink pantaloons to please him.

However, his most notorious attachment was not to a woman but to 18-year-old Louis II, King of Bavaria. The blatantly homosexual king idolized Wagner's music and provided the composer with housing and money. Infatuated with the older man, Louis addressed Wagner in letters as 'My loved one' and 'Darling of my soul'. Wagner reported spending hours with the king engaged in earnest conversations about art and music or simply sitting in enraptured silence. The king evidently wasn't enough, however, since Wagner was simultaneously living with Cosima von Bülow (later his wife). The royal liaison was ended after a year and a half by the king's advisers, who objected to Wagner's 'unwholesome influence' on the monarch.

In 1836, Richard married Christiane Wilhelmine 'Minna' Planer when she was 27 and he was 23. The pretty, sedate leading lady of a regional theatre troupe had been ardently pursued by its young conductor for two years, rejecting his proposals several times. Their marriage was largely composed of twenty-five years of fights, jealousy, intellectual and emotional differences, and separations. Minna steadfastly stood by Wagner during his poverty-stricken early years, but his inability to remain debt-free and his flights of imagination alienated her sensibilities. Moreover, Wagner expected her to be content keeping house while he pursued his extramarital loves and his work. In 1847, Wagner tried to convince 37-year-old Minna that she was too old and frail for sex. Minna finally agreed with him eleven years later, when her heart trouble was aggravated by the discovery of her husband's affair with Mathilde Wesendonk.

In April 1848, Wagner met Jessie Laussot, a beautiful, 21-year-old English woman whose husband subsidized Wagner. Jessie's intellectual capacities endeared her to Wagner and they plotted to flee to Greece together. But her husband discovered the plan, threatened to shoot Wagner, took his wife to the country and, when Richard followed, got the police to run him out of France. At the end, Wagner felt that Jessie had failed him: she had not rushed to his side against all odds.

Several years later Wagner, in his early 40s, became involved with another patron's wife, Mathilde Wesendonk – his inspiration for *Tristan und Isolde*. Richard revered her as his muse and insisted that their relationship was totally virtuous. Scrupulously honest, Mathilde made her husband her confidant and convinced him to support Wagner financially, provide him with a house next to their own, desist from sexual relations with her, and maintain warm, friendly relations with the composer. Minna Wagner did not agree that their love was pure after she had intercepted a hotly worded letter. In a rage, she went first to her husband and then to Mathilde. Mathilde, aghast that Wagner had neither been honest with his wife nor mollified her anger, became estranged from the composer and returned to her husband's bed. Minna moved out and, except for brief periods, the Wagners did not live together again.

At 50 Wagner became the lover of 25-year-old Cosima von Bülow, whom he had known for ten years. She was the daughter of his friend Franz Liszt and the countess Marie d'Agoult, and the wife of his favourite pupil and dear friend Hans von Bülow. Five years earlier, Wagner had been involved with her older sister Blandine, who was prettier, but Cosima was to become his true love. On their honeymoon, the von Bülows went to Zurich, where they visited Wagner at the Asyl – Mathilde's country home. Minna was also there. When Mathilde visited the Asyl, Wagner's trio – Minna, Mathilde and Cosima – was assembled under one roof. In the beginning, Cosima was openly shared by Wagner and von Bülow, but eventually she left her husband, taking their two children, and went to live with Wagner and the two children she had borne him. After Minna died and von Bülow sued for divorce on grounds of infidelity, Cosima and Richard were married in 1870. Cosima ran the household and Richard's life efficiently, and seemed the woman best suited to live with the genius on a daily basis. Wagner died in Cosima's arms after a heart attack. She clung to his body for twenty-four hours, then cut off her long hair and placed it in the coffin on his heart.

P.A.R. (Lists 25, 41)

❦ The Duke of Wellington
1 May 1769 to 14 September 1852

Born Arthur Wesley (the family reverted to the original Wellesley in 1798) in Dublin, the future general impressed no one as a youth, least of all his mother, who pronounced him 'food for powder and nothing more', and packed him off to military school. The turning point came in 1793, when he abruptly renounced gambling and burned his treasured violin – to concentrate on his military career. It paid off. He served with distinction in India from 1797 to 1805, led British forces to victory in the Peninsular War during 1808–14 and outfoxed Napoleon at Waterloo in 1815. He was made a duke in 1814.

With wavy brown hair, bright blue eyes, and a slim 5 feet 9 inch physique, the handsome Wellington had a stiff, aristocratic bearing and spoke rapidly in clipped phrases. He was admired not only for his military genius and personal attractiveness, but also for his unimpeachable integrity. Hailed as saviour of Europe, Wellington was magnanimous in victory, refusing to divide France among the victors and indeed withdrawing from that country as soon as conditions permitted. He served as commander-in-chief of the British Army and in 1828 became prime minister. He personally pushed through parliament the critical Catholic Emancipation Bill, but his rigid opposition to parlimentary reforms forced his resignation in 1830. The iron shutters he subsequently used to protect his house from hostile crowds – coupled with the 'iron hand' he had always wielded in military affairs – inspired *Punch* to dub him the 'Iron Duke'. Wellington's fall from grace was only temporary, and in later years he was appointed to many important governmental posts. His death inspired national mourning. After an imposing state funeral, he was buried in St Paul's.

Wellington married only once and had two sons. He first proposed to Catherine 'Kitty' Pakenham, daughter of Lord Longford, in 1793, when she was 21, pretty and shapely. But her family objected to the union because Captain Wesley, as he was then known, was unable to support her in appropriate style. As he rose in rank and word reached him that the Pakenhams were now eager for the match, he felt honour-bound to keep his word, even though, upon seeing Kitty again, he exclaimed 'She has grown ugly, by Jove!' They were married in 1806. Kitty idolized her husband, privately and publicly. But his career caused prolonged separations and rumours of his philandering hurt Kitty deeply. While living with his army in France after the Battle of Waterloo, he met the young actress Mademoiselle George. She later boasted that she had been the mistress of both Wellington and Napoleon. Wellington, she claimed, was the 'stronger' lover. In

1825, the 39-year-old former courtesan Harriette Wilson published her memoirs, revealing her sexual relationship with Wellington.

Among the more respectable women fluttering about Wellington was Lady Frances Shelley, who first met him after his return from the Peninsular campaign. Once asked why she had spurned the advances of an Austrian baron, she replied, 'Know, sir, that I have resisted the Duke of Wellington.' In defence, Wellington responded wryly, 'I must say that I was never aware of this resistance.' Such stories quickly found their was back to Kitty and only hastened the disintegration of the marriage. The duke and duchess quarrelled often. To the duke's distress, Kitty never fulfilled the role of Duchess of Wellington. She was criticized for reading during carriage rides, instead of acknowledging passers-by, but she did so for fear that, being extremely shortsighted, she would not recognize old acquaintances. It took Kitty's approaching death in 1831 to bring the couple together. 'It is a strange thing,' Wellington lamented, 'that two people can live together for half a lifetime and only understand one another at the very end.'

Outside his marriage, the woman closest to Wellington was Harriet, wife of Charles Arbuthnot, who served as treasury secretary from 1809 to 1823. Among all his female admirers, only she remained tactful in public. They shared political conversation, jokes and confidences. Many believed they were having an affair. Remarkably, their close relationship was accepted, even encouraged, by her husband. Mrs Arbuthnot's death in 1834 moved Wellington to tears. However, he quickly pulled himself together to look after the grieving widower, who thereafter leaned heavily on Wellington for support.

Shortly before Harriet's death, Wellington received a bible from Anna Maria Jenkins, a 20-year-old evangelist who had recently converted a condemned murderer and who now claimed divine inspiration for a fresh mission – to bring the Duke of Wellington 'a new birth of righteousness'. At her invitation, the duke visited her and wasted little time on amenities. 'Oh, how I love you!' he reportedly cried at their first meeting. On his next visit, he made a proposal of sorts, though rather vague about whether his intention was marriage or simply an affair. Jenkins pressed hard for marriage, but never managed to trap him. Over the next seventeen years, they exchanged nearly four hundred letters, and even after he stopped writing in 1851 she continued

461

to press her case by mail until his death.

Throughout his long life, many other women vied for Wellington's attention. His marriage meant nothing to Mrs John Freese, whom he met in India. As godfather to her son, he raised the child in his own household. The beautiful Lady Frances Wedderburn-Webster attracted Wellington in Brussels. He took time to dash off notes to her on the morning of and the day after the Battle of Waterloo. In 1816, Marianne Caton Patterson of Baltimore enchanted him. Although he hesitated to relive his anguish by seeing Waterloo again, he consented to guide her on a personal tour of the battlefield. Lady Charlotte Greville (daughter of the Duke of Portland) was reported to have had a passionate affair with Wellington in 1820, but pressure from her husband and son forced her to end it.

Even old age provided no respite for Wellington. Mary Ann Jervis, a singer and the daughter of Lord St Vincent, sought to snare the duke after his wife died. For seven years, she spread false rumours of their intimacy, even pretending to be pregnant, only to earn from him the nickname the 'Syren'. In 1847, Wellington, who was already nearly deaf, politely refused a marriage proposal from 32-year-old Angela Burdett-Coutts, a banking heiress. And, at 80, Wellington again set tongues wagging by appearing at parties with Margaret Jones, wife of a member of parliament and then in her early twenties.

When asked by a lady if he had really received as much female adulation as was rumoured, Wellington replied with his distinctive shortness, 'Oh yes! Plenty of that ! Plenty of that!'

W.A.D. (Lists 20, 22, 25, 26)

❦ H. G. Wells
21 September 1866 to 13 August 1946

Herbert George Wells was the fourth and last child of Joseph and Sarah Wells. His father – easygoing and self-indulgent – ran a china shop and earned extra money by playing cricket. His mother was a rigid, deeply religious woman who constantly reminded her husband that his entire life was a failure. Wells said that his parents had a foolproof method of birth control – they slept in separate rooms.

To escape the drudgery of the lower middle-classes young Wells turned to books and daydreaming. His fantasies often centred on the glories of war – victorious battles with Wells as supreme commander. After unsuccessful attempts at being a draper's and then a chemist's apprentice, the 17-year-old Wells was sent off to school in Midhurst, where he earned a scholarship to the Normal School of Science in London. At 5 feet 5 inches tall (he blamed his mother for his height, claiming that she kept him in a short bed for too many years) with small hands and feet and a robust, heavy-set body, Wells was not handsome. His face sported a drooping moustache, bushy eyebrows and penetrating blue eyes. His chestnut-brown hair usually looked as if it had been glued to his head. To his chagrin, he had a very high-pitched voice, and a cockney accent. H. G. Wells was self-centred, irascible and sometimes crude. His associates in the Fabian Society, such as Shaw, and his literary peers, Conrad and Maugham for example, were sometimes exasperated, other times entranced, by his overpowering personality. As one of his biographers said, 'With all his faults, you could not help loving him. Bursting with brains, bubbling with humour, he was full of charm. Many women could have testified to this.'

Wells was obsessed with finding the ideal sex partner. As a young boy, 'Bertie' was first sexually aroused by Greek statues, and was to search for ever for their real-life equivalent – his 'Venus Urania'. The quest led him through two marriages, several passionate affairs and countless *passades* (defined by H.G. as 'a stroke of mutual attraction').

At 25, Wells married his cousin Isabel, a dark-haired virginal beauty with a slim, graceful body. Except for one unfulfilling experience with an 'unimaginative' prostitute when he was 22, Wells was also a sexual novice. His physical craving for Isabel was almost unbearable as he prepared for their wedding night and 'flame meeting flame'. Unfortunately, the flames were quickly doused by Isabel's tears as she found herself incapable of responding to H.G.'s ardour. The embittered husband embarked upon a string of affairs before the couple ended their four-year marriage in 1895. In his autobiography, Wells concludes that Isabel was not only naive, but unable to stimulate him intellectually. However, after the divorce, Wells could not shake Isabel from his mind. Her second marriage in 1904 threw Wells into fits of jealousy. He tore up her letters and photographs and refused to speak her name. Years later they became friends again.

Amy Catherine Robbins was one of H.G.'s students at the University Tutorial College in London in 1892. He was immediately attracted to her and they married as soon as Wells was divorced. Wells called his second wife 'Jane'. H.G. and Jane remained married until her death in 1927. The thirty-two-year marriage – which produced two sons – was an unusual one. Once again, Wells had paired up with a woman 'innocent and ignorant' of the physical necessities of life. The dissatisfied husband and the sympathetic wife reached an understanding in which she agreed to give him all the sexual freedom he desired. From then on, Wells was quite open about his relationships, even keeping pictures of his lovers in his room. Jane was the most stabilizing factor in H.G.'s turbulent life. She typed his books, invested his money, prepared his tax returns and kept their home in perfect order. When 42-year-old Wells became involved with 22-year-old Amber Reeves – daughter of a leading London family – Jane's friends were stunned and appalled. Jane – the sensible wife – went out and bought clothes for the forthcoming baby.

In 1912, Wells finally met the Venus Urania of his dreams. Rebecca West was to become one of England's foremost journalists and novelists. Writing in a small feminist magazine, West reviewed – and panned – H.G.'s book *Marriage*. Wells, usually thin-skinned about bad reviews, was intrigued by her humour and style. A year later Wells, then 46, and West, 20, began an affair that was to last for ten years. Wells had found the perfect mate. In addition to her beauty and sensuality, she was his equal in wit, imagination and intelligence. On many of his love letters Wells sketched a 'picshua' of a panther and a jaguar (Rebecca was the panther; Wells was the jaguar). They shared intense happiness and had a son, Anthony. The break with Rebecca came after an incident involving Wells and one of his lovers, Austrian journalist Hedwig Verena Gatternigg. Following a row with Wells, the Austrian woman tried to kill herself in H.G.'s London flat. Wells wasn't there at the time, but Jane – who often visited her husband's home-from-home – discovered the woman and got her to a hospital. Rebecca's name appeared in the ensuing publicity. Although the episode was covered up, scandal had come too close to Rebecca's doorstep. That wasn't her only reason for ending the affair. She had become increasingly intolerant of H.G.'s disregard for her career ('He never read more than a page or two of my books') and his restless, irritable moods. His continuing *passades* (which included birth-control advocate Margaret Sanger) and Rebecca's social isolation were also precipitating factors. At one time Wells even moved his ailing first wife Isabel into his home so that his second wife Jane could care for her – while he continued to see Rebecca.

After Rebecca, Wells sought comfort in the arms of Odette Keun – a Dutch woman born and raised in Constantinople – who was then living in France. A former nun turned writer, Odette had sent Wells a copy of her book *Sous Lenin* which he favourably reviewed. They exchanged letters and finally met in Geneva in 1924. Their rendezvous took place in her hotel room. She turned off the lights before her Prince Charming arrived and led him right into bed. Odette later recalled, 'I did not know whether he was a giant or a gnome.' The lovers built a house in the south of France where they spent all their time together – making Jane's life less complicated. H. G. remained a part of Odette's life for the next nine years.

In 1934, the 68-year-old writer began a full-time relationship with an old acquaintance, Moura Budberg – former mistress and secretary to Maxim Gorki. She refused to marry him and they kept separate homes in London, but remained friends and confidants until his death in 1946.

Throughout his adult life, Wells was rarely without a woman. Despite poor health (tuberculosis, diabetes and kidney afflictions), Wells was sexually active almost to the end of his eighty years. According to Somerset Maugham, 'H. G. had strong sexual instincts and he said to me more than once that the need to satisfy them had nothing to do with love. It was purely a physiological matter.'

C.O. (Lists 8, 10, 17, 20, 22, 25, 26, 40)

❧ Alma Mahler Werfel
1879 to 11 December 1964

A classical composer who received scant recognition, Alma Mahler Werfel gained prominence through her association with famous men. Described by her admirers as the 'most beautiful femme fatale of turn-of-the-century Vienna', Alma was married in succession to the composer Mahler, noted architect Walter Gropius and the Austrian writer Franz Werfel. A complete list of her lovers would read like a history of the intelligentsia of Eastern Europe. 'What I really loved in a man was his achievement,' Alma Werfel wrote in her autobiography, *And the Bridge is Love*. 'The greater the achievement, the more I must love him.'

Born in Vienna to the landscape painter Emil J. Schindler, Alma had wit and intelligence sharpened by the many intellectuals and artists who flocked to the family home. She received a formal education in music and composition from Vienna's finest musicians and composers. When she blossomed into a classical beauty with high cheekbones, sensual eyes and a full figure, her teachers avidly courted her. At 17 she was aggressively pursued by 37-year-old artist Gustav Klimt. But Alma held her admirers at bay because she 'believed in a virginal purity in need of preservation'. She changed her mind at the age of 21 and began chasing artistic men, involving herself in three marriages and innumerable affairs. Initially attracted to genius father figures, she married Gustav Mahler when he was 41 and she was 23. Later, she reversed roles and married poet and novelist Franz Werfel, twelve years her junior.

A 'small, repugnant, chinless, toothless and unwashed gnome' was Alma's description of her teacher, Alexander von Zemlinsky. The Viennese musician and composer attracted her anyway: 'I long so madly for his embraces. I shall never be able to forget how his touch stirred me to the depths of my soul . . . such a feeling of ecstasy filled my being . . . I want to kneel down in front of him and kiss his open thighs – kiss everything, everything! Amen!'

During her affair with Zemlinsky, Alma met Gustav Mahler at a party. He was a handsome but austere man, prone to attacks of nervous tension. His fame as a composer was based on his romantic symphonies, particularly the *Symphony of a Thousand*. Alma was in awe of Mahler's musical genius, but had doubts about accepting his marriage proposal. She finally agreed to marry him because, 'I am filled to the brim with my mission of smoothing the path of this genius.' Mahler confessed that he was a virgin and was worried about his ability to consummate their marriage. She agreed to participate in a premarital rehearsal. After engaging in several sessions of lovemaking, she wrote, 'Joy, beyond all joy,' in her diary, and soon she was suffering the 'dreadful torment' of pregnancy. But, on their wedding night a few months later, Mahler was impotent. When this continued, a frustrated Alma suggested that he consult their friend Sigmund Freud, who recommended that Mahler, who adored his mother, call his wife by his mother's name, Marie. This seemed to work, and the couple had another child, a daughter who became a sculptress. However, their marriage still wasn't satisfactory to Alma. Mahler had insisted that she give up her musical career when they married: 'You. . .have only *one* profession from now on: *to make me happy!*' She hated being a traditional wife and mother, 'I often feel as though my wings have been clipped. Gustav, why did you tie me to yourself – me, a soaring glittering bird – when you'd be so much better off with a grey, lumbering one?'

During their marriage, Alma flirted with Mahler's rival, composer Hans Pfitzner, and after Mahler's death in 1911 Alma was courted by her late husband's physician, Dr Joseph Fraenkel. In turning down Fraenkel's marriage proposal, she wrote 'My watchword is: amo ... ergo sum. Yours: cognito ... ergo sum.' Next, Alma became involved with Austrian painter and playwright Oskar Kokoschka, whom she described as a 'handsome figure but disturbingly coarse'. Beginning his career as a portrait painter, Kokoschka became famous for the daring use of colour and form in his landscapes. When he asked to paint her portrait, Alma wrote in her diary, 'We hardly spoke – and yet he seemed unable to draw. We got up. Suddenly, tempestuously, he swept me into his arms. To me it was a strange, almost shocking kind of embrace.' She enjoyed that embrace for three years, which she called 'one fierce battle of love. Never before had I tasted so much tension, so much hell, so much paradise.' Kokoschka wanted to marry her but, when she had an abortion in 1913, it was the end of the affair.

In 1915, Alma married architect Walter Gropius, whose advances she had spurned when married to Mahler. Their marriage lasted four years and produced one child. Meanwhile, Alma became enchanted with the poetry of Franz Werfel, whose first prose piece, *Not the Murderer* (1920), was a landmark of the expressionist movement in German literature. A stocky man with burning eyes and elegant features, Werfel achieved his greatest popularity as a result of his book, *The Song of Bernadette*, later made into a highly successful film. In 1917, Alma and Werfel began an affair. 'It was inevitable ... that our lips would find each other ... I am out of my mind. And so is Werfel,' Alma wrote. The poet agreed. 'We made love,' he said of their first sexual encounter. 'I did not spare her. At dawn I went back to my room.... There is something suicidal in her climactic surrender.' Alma became pregnant with Werfel's child while still married to Gropius. The child, a boy, was born in 1918, but soon died. After the birth, however, Gropius agreed to a divorce. Alma moved in with Werfel and they were eventually married in 1929 when she was 50. She remained passionate throughout their sixteen-

467

year marriage. An admirer, the German dramatist Gerhart Hauptmann, once said to Alma, 'In another life, we two must be lovers. I make my reservation now.' His wife overheard this request and quickly replied, 'I'm sure Alma will be booked up for there, too.'

R.S.F. (Lists 8, 22, 26)

♣ James Abbott McNeill Whistler
10 July 1834 to 17 July 1903

Whistler's paintings sought essences of mood and harmony, and the adjective 'Whistlerian' describes his mastery of twilight shadings and bare suggestions of form in the canvases he called Nocturnes. But he is probably best remembered for the profile portrait in the Louvre entitled *Arrangement in Grey and Black No.1* – popularly known as *Whistler's Mother*.

A small, tense man who seemed perpetually spoiling for a fight, Whistler created a raffish, outrageous façade even though he courted the patronage of bourgeois Victorian society. His typical costume was a wide-brimmed hat, white duck trousers, black velveteen jacket, yellow gloves, slim baton and monocle. Ringlets of dyed black hair set off by one white forelock teased to perfection, heavy black eyebrows and a large drooping moustache accented his savage grin. He could be exquisitely charming or thoroughly obnoxious. His fastidious mannerisms, rehearsed rudenesses, and furious tempests in jade teapots were meticulous bids for attention. Only his art betrayed sensitivity and genius beneath the peevishness of his brittle, foppish exterior. Whistler arrived in left-bank Paris in 1855 as a restless loser from a cosmopolitan background. Born in Lowell, Massachusetts, he was raised in Russia where his civil engineer father built a railway for the czar. Back in America, he enrolled at West Point Military Academy in 1851 but failed chemistry ('Had silicon been a gas, I would have been a major general'). He drew government maps for a while, then went to Europe and never returned to the USA. In France, he absorbed the techniques of Impressionism and oriental art, and his own artistic signature became a scorpion-tailed butterfly. His 1878 lawsuit against Ruskin (who had accused Whistler of 'flinging a pot of paint in the public's face') won him much notoriety and the award of one farthing. He wore the coin thereafter on his watch chain. Later, he wrote an expert's account of *The Gentle Art of Making Enemies*. For years impoverished, he bounced between Paris and London waiting for his fortunes to improve. 'I have just eaten my washstand,' he once informed a visitor. He idolized his widowed mother and Anna Whistler came to live with her son in London, wisely ignoring those things she didn't want to know. She stayed twelve years and Whistler did not marry until after her death. Whistler himself died in his London studio where he spent the lonely years after the death of his wife Trixie.

Despite the mincing image he cultivated, Whistler was entirely heterosexual with a special weakness for red-haired women – an aesthetic as well as sexual attraction. His mistresses had to be good models, and he probably slept with few women who didn't pose for him. His 'brief, half-gallant, half-uneasy affairs' were numerous even for a young bohemian, but three longer ones, with mistresses who 'wifed' and mothered him with far more loyalty than he usually deserved, were marriages in all but the legal sense.

His earliest Parisian mistress was probably Héloise – surname unknown – a tiny, pretty milliner's assistant whom Whistler called 'Fumette' and his friends named 'La Tigresse' because of her temper tantrums. On one occasion she ripped and scattered his drawings, reducing the artist to whimpering tears – the only time he was ever known to cry. She also sang, recited poetry, and modelled for his etchings. They lived together for about three years.

In 1859, she was replaced by 'Finette', a worldy-wise Creole dancer who performed the cancan. But soon there entered professional model Jo Heffernan, a lithe, sensuous Irish girl with red-gold hair. The model for such masterpieces as *Wapping* and *The White Girl*, she also managed Whistler's household and helped sell his work. She adopted his middle name, presenting herself as 'Mrs Joanna Abbott'. Whistler found an excuse to end the relationship after six years, when he learned that in his absence she had posed nude for his former mentor Courbet. She continued to be called 'Mrs Abbott', however, and raised Whistler's son John, whom the artist once described as 'an infidelity to Jo'. The boy's natural mother was Louisa Fanny Hanson, about whom nothing is known.

Then came English model Maud Franklin, who stayed with him for over fourteen years. She was quick-tempered, had prominent teeth – and red hair. Though she called herself 'Mrs

Whistler', the artist scrupulously introduced her as 'Madame' or 'my pupil'. They lived together only after Anna Whistler left London, but even then occupied separate bedrooms. Their daughter Ione was born in 1877. Maud posed for him and, like her predecessor, efficiently managed his business affairs.

During this time, Whistler enjoyed a semi-platonic love that lasted for a decade with Mrs Frances Leyland, the beautiful red-haired wife of a London patron. Whistler often escorted her about town, and was even engaged to her sister at one time – all behind Maud's back.

After architect E. W. Godwin died in 1886, his widow Beatrice ('Trixie') frequently visited Whistler's studio, provoking Maud Franklin into a shrieking rage. One scene between the two women ended only when Maud burst a blood vessel. 'Whistler did his best to avoid unpleasant scenes with women', wrote Horace Gregory. 'If he failed to dominate them, he did his best to charm them in the fashion he had charmed his mother. If both efforts failed, he walked away.' Jealous Maud was finally no match for cheerful Trixie Godwin, who instinctively knew how to deal with artistic temperaments. 'If I died before Jimmy,' she only half-humorously stated, 'he would not have a friend left in a week.' She was probably the first genuine love of his life. A plump brunette with a 'tea-rose complexion', she was taller – and twenty-one years younger – than Whistler. In 1888 he was 54, his mother was dead, and a friend bantered the couple into getting married. Trixie announced she would buy 'a new toothbrush and a new sponge, because one should have new ones when one gets married'. Whistler ducked furtively into the building where the ceremony was to be performed because he feared another scene with the still-livid Maud Franklin. When she learned about the marriage from the London papers, Maud collapsed. She raised their daughter Ione and continued to call herself 'Mrs Whistler' until the mid-1890s. At that time she married extremely well and spoke no more of the artist.

'The Butterfly chained at last,' said the *Pall Mall Gazette* in a headline. Whistler's marriage lasted until Trixie's lingering death from cancer in 1896. Whistler, a faithful, devoted, and at last respectable, husband, was devastated with grief and never again entered into a serious relationship. Suddenly old, he half-heartedly sought adolescent girls from London back alleys as his models, but his productive career was over.

J.E. (List 25)

❧ Oscar Wilde
16 October 1854 to 30 November 1900

Wilde was born in Dublin, to eccentric parents. His mother badly wanted a daughter, so, when a second son, Oscar Fingal O'Flahertie Wills Wilde, was born, she dressed the child like a girl. As a youth, Oscar was tall, almost overgrown, yet graceful and, in any case, always striking in appearance and dress. Leaving Dublin for Oxford, he began to develop his unique style of manners, garb and wit. After leaving university he was soon the rage of London society. Oscar was the ultimate party entertainment, and was in great demand. A contemporary wrote, 'He was, without exception, the most brilliant talker I have ever come across. . . . Nobody could pretend to outshine him, or even shine at all in his company.' Wilde supported himself writing art and book reviews and lecturing in England and America. He eventually moved on to writing comedy, with huge success. He was extravagant, generous, outrageous and, above all, happy. The story of his ruin sounds incredible today, but remains one of the most celebrated literary disasters.

As a young man, Wilde was decidedly heterosexual, despite his affectations. In fact, he was mildly shocked at the idea of homosexuality. His earliest love was Florrie Balcombe, whom he met when he was 21. He was heartbroken when she decided to marry Bram Stoker, the author of *Dracula*. Some years later, Wilde unsuccessfully courted society beauty and actress Lillie Langtry, who was married. In addition to a few youthful affairs, Wilde occasionally used prostitutes. One evening he announced to his friend Robert Sherard that 'Priapus was calling', and went out and picked up a high-class whore. Meeting Sherard the next morning, Wilde said, 'What animals we are, Robert.' Sherard expressed his concern that Wilde might have been robbed, to which Wilde replied, 'One gives them all in one's pockets.'

In 1881, Oscar met Constance Lloyd, a sweet, pretty girl whom he courted with passionate, poetic letters. Madly in love, the two were married in 1884. They honeymooned in Paris and, the morning after the wedding night, while Wilde strolled with Sherard, he described so vividly the joys of the previous evening that Sherard was embarrassed. Indeed, for the first few years, Oscar and Constance were deeply in love. They had two sons, Cyril and Vyvyan. Though Oscar adored his children, he was unsuited for domesticity.

471

The story of how Wilde drifted from heterosexuality to homosexuality is open to some debate. It is probable that while at Oxford he had contracted syphilis from a prostitute. The treatment at that time was mercury. (This caused severe discoloration of the teeth, which Oscar certainly suffered from.) Before proposing to Constance, he consulted a doctor who assured him that he had been cured of the disease. Two years later, he discovered that the dormant spirochetes had broken out again, and so he gave up sex with Constance and began to indulge his interest in boys. Robert Ross, a lively, cultivated young man who remained Oscar's lifelong devotee, boasted that he was Oscar's 'first boy', when he was 17 and Wilde was 32. However, it was not until 1891 that Wilde met the great love of his life, a handsome, aristocratic 22-year-old Lord Alfred Douglas, called 'Bosie' by his friends and family. The attraction was immediate – Bosie was sixteen years Oscar's junior, a poet from a prominent family, extraordinarily good-looking; passionate, impulsive, and proud. In short, everything Wilde admired. They both adored luxury and began a whirlwind friendship, dining daily at the best restaurants in England, completely inseparable. Even Constance liked Bosie.

According to Bosie's later confessions, he kept his sexual relations with Wilde to a minimum. He did not respond to Oscar's overtures for six months and, when he did, the extent of it was probably oral sex. Bosie insisted that no sodomy had taken place, and that 'Wilde treated me as an older boy treats a young man at school'. (Bosie had had relations with both sexes before meeting Oscar). Bosie's reticence was probably due to the fact that he too preferred boys – well illustrated in the story of their adventures on a trip to Algiers. By sheer coincidence, their hotel in the small town of Blidah was occupied by an acquaintance of Wilde's – the younger writer André Gide. Gide had been struggling against his homosexuality for five years and, when he realized that Oscar and Bosie were guests at the hotel, he almost left. Preparing for an evening out, Bosie took Gide by the arm and said, 'I hope you are like me. I have a horror of women. I only like boys. As you are coming with us this evening, I think it's better if you say so at once.' A nervous Gide accompanied them on a tour of the Casbah, finally winding up in a homosexual brothel/bath-house, where men danced together to the sounds of exotic music. Wilde gleefully pronounced the sentence that sealed Gide's fate: 'Dear, do you want the little musician?' Gide's downfall was complete. As the holiday neared its end, Bosie was making arrangements to run

472

off with an Arab youth he had purchased from the boy's family, but the lad left him for a woman.

In London, Wilde and Douglas were introduced to Alfred Taylor, a semi-professional procurer, who enjoyed wearing ladies' clothing and burning incense in his dimly lit apartment. He acquired for Wilde a number of young boys – out-of-work clerks, grooms and newsboys who were willing to sell their favours, and in addition unexpectedly found themselves dining in the best restaurants in London with Wilde, drinking champagne and receiving expensive gifts. Aubrey Beardsley said Wilde boasted of having had five messenger boys in one night, saying, 'I kissed each of them in every part of their bodies; they were all dirty and appealed to me just for that reason.' Although there was gossip surrounding Wilde and Bosie, all would probably have gone on happily had it not been for Bosie's father. The Eighth Marquis of Queensberry's rage was vented in abusive letters to his son, finally culminated when he delivered the famous card to Wilde's club, which read, 'For Oscar Wilde posing as a somdomite [sic].' Enraged by the Marquis's harassment, Wilde took reckless action. With Bosie's encouragement, he pressed charges against Queensberry for criminal libel, having assured his lawyer that there was no basis whatsoever for the Marquis's accusation. But, to the prosecution's immense surprise, Queensberry had prepared his case well. Hiring a team of private detectives and paid informers, he had bought the testimony of many young boys Wilde had met through Taylor. When it was clear that the boys would be produced, the prosecution withdrew, and the Marquis was acquitted. Oscar's friends begged him to leave the country while he could – even his wife hoped he would flee – but he refused. Within a month Wilde had been arrested, charged by Queensberry with committing acts of gross indecency with various boys. The procurer Taylor had also been arrested, having refused to turn state's evidence against Wilde.

During the second trial, one of the most sensational in English history, Wilde handled himself with great poise and wit – but it was not enough. One by one the boys testified. 'I was asked by Wilde to imagine that I was a woman and that he was my lover. . . . I used to sit on his knees and he used to play with my privates as a man might amuse himself with a girl. . . . He suggested two or three times that I would permit him to insert "it" in my mouth, but I never allowed that,' and so on. Hotel chambermaids even testified that they had found curious stains on the hotel sheets, though that evidence proved dubious. From these proceedings it emerged that the preferred forms of lovemaking were mutual masturbation and fellatio, with Wilde as the active agent. (He told a friend it gave him inspiration.) Sodomy was seldom, if ever, performed. Wilde was also forced to defend his published writings, such as *Dorian Gray*, and his personal letters, which were accused of having homosexual overtones. In this context he gave his famous speech on the 'Love that dare not speak its name' (a line from one of Bosie's poems), which was so moving that it brought spontaneous applause from the gallery. In the end, the jury could not reach a decision, and a third trial was called. Between trials, Wilde again refused to attempt to escape. The outcome of the third trial was grim: Wilde and Taylor each received the maximum sentence – two years' hard labour. Prison conditions in England at that time were hard and the horror of the experience drove Wilde slightly mad – he wrote *De Profundis*, a long, scathing denunciation of Bosie, accusing him of having led him to his ruin. But, despite all, Bosie remained completely loyal (unlike most of Wilde's other friends), writing, 'Though he is in prison he is still the court the jury the judge of my life.'

After Wilde's release he lived, broken and exiled – and using the name Sebastian Melmoth – in France and Italy. Constance Wilde, Bosie's family and numerous friends plotted to keep the two men apart, but their friendship and love prevailed. The last three years of Wilde's life were spent on and off with Bosie, both having returned to consorting with young boys.

While living in France, Oscar succumbed to an attempt to reform him. The poet Ernest Dowson took him to a brothel, hoping he might acquire 'a more wholesome taste'. When Wilde emerged, he remarked, 'The first these ten years – and it will be the last. It was like cold mutton.' But he asked Dowson to 'tell it in England, for it will entirely restore my character'.

A.W. (Lists 12, 14, 17, 18, 20, 25, 27, 46, 48)

♧ Harriette Wilson
2 February 1786 to 1846

Harriette Wilson drew her lovers and protectors from the most famous and fashionable men of London society during the Regency. Born in Mayfair to a Swiss mathematician and his English wife, Harriette was one of seven daughters, four of whom were fashionable courtesans for a time. John Dubochet, her father, was tyrannical but oblivious to his daughter's profession; her mother Amelia was sympathetic. Harriette adopted Wilson as her professional name when she became a courtesan at 15. Accomplished linguists and musicians who could also discuss literature and politics, the Dubochet sisters were considered scintillating company and their after-theatre soirées became famous.

With rich dark hair and flashing hazel eyes, Harriette was alluring but not beautiful, vivacious but not stunningly attractive. Bright, passionate and witty, she offered more than sex; her personality commanded independence and respect. Because of these attributes, Harriette was successful and the male élite of London aspired to love her for a night or protect her for longer. Her success as a 'Fashionable Impure' was evident in her life-style – she always owned the best that money could buy (though she once settled a debt of £1,100 with half an hour of her professional services). However, Harriette's sentimentality doomed her to die in poverty and obscurity. She would not enter into a marriage of convenience, as her sisters did, and in 1815, when she became too old for first-rate lovers, she moved to Paris and found a boyish secretary of the embassy to pluck out her grey hairs. On a return trip to London, the sinister Colonel William Rochfort picked her up on the street. Perhaps recognizing the bogus colonel as her last chance at love, Harriette paid his debts, married him, and moved back to Paris, where she wrote her memoirs. In 1832, a decayed and decrepit Harriette Wilson surfaced one last time in London before being swallowed up by the new, ruthless times of the Industrial Revolution.

Pleasure was her business, but romance was an art for Harriette. She believed virtue 'was such as my heart and conscience dictated'. Although she truly enjoyed the demands of her occupation, Harriette selected only those partners who met her standards. She esteemed breeding above beauty, despised middle-class men, preferred military men and intellectuals, and believed that indolent men made the best lovers. She was lusty, vain, elegant and amoral. Rival courtesan Julia Johnstone maintained that Harriette's first lover was a boatman on the Thames, and that his successor was a recruiting sergeant who robbed her after they had eloped. Harriette's memoirs begin: 'I shall not say why and how I became, at the age of 15, the mistress of the Earl of Craven.' He was in the military, and liked to boast of his adventures late at night. Finding him 'a dead bore', Harriette started flirting with another army man, Frederick Lamb (Caroline Lamb's brother-in-law), whom she followed to Hull, where his regiment was stationed.

While still with Craven, Harriette had written to the Prince of Wales (later King George IV) in an attempt to solicit royal patronage. He suggested she come to London for a meeting. Harriette impertinently replied, 'To travel fifty-two miles in this bad weather, merely to see a man, with only the given number of legs, arms, fingers, etc., would, you must admit, be madness.... If you can do anything better, in the way of pleasing a lady, than ordinary men, write directly: if not, adieu, Monsieur le Prince.'

After three months in Hull, Lamb and Harriette moved to London, where Lamb's parsimony annoyed her. He enjoyed himself and she was forced to stay at home. When he left town for a few weeks leaving Harriette 'without money, or at any rate, with very little', she decided to see for herself whether the Marquis of Lorne, the keeper of the great seal and vice-admiral of Scotland's west coast, was as handsome as she had heard. After an exchange of letters, he requested a meeting at his London house. She replied, 'No! our first meeting must be on the high road, in order that I may have room to run away, in case I don't like you.' After a two-hour walk (which Harriette found to be an excellent audition for her lovers, reasoning that a man who could not keep pace with her in a park certainly couldn't in bed), her curiosity was favourably satisfied and soon she moved into her own house and started sleeping with Lorne. She told the infuriated Lamb, 'I will be the mere instrument of pleasure to no man. He must make a friend and companion of me, or he will lose me.' When Lorne left London to visit his estates in Scotland, Harriette refused to accompany him. Shortly after Lorne's departure, the Duke of Wellington requested an introduction to her. Harriette was in need of 'a steady sort of friend', and Wellington became a frequent caller. Although impressed by his achievements on the battlefield, Harriette found the duke to be unmannered and 'most unentertaining', but his intermittent visits were one of the few constants in her life for years.

A man she saw horse riding daily captured Harriette's attention with his 'pale expressive beauty'. She encouraged dandy Beau Brummell to walk with her, hoping she might meet this man, Lord Ponsonby, later to distinguish himself as an ambassador. The interest was mutual; after five months of contriving 'chance' encounters, Harriette received a letter from Ponsonby and they began an affectionate correspondence. A month later, a chaste meeting started an affair which lasted nearly three years before Lady Ponsonby called a halt to it. Ponsonby was the one true love of Harriette's life; her grief over losing him almost proved fatal.

Her next lover was another military man, the tall, pale, 19-year-old Marquis of Worcester. Although his love was not returned, he would have married Harriette if his parents, the Duke and Duchess of Beaufort, had given their permission. Worcester and Harriette lived together during the next two years, waiting for his 21st birthday when they could marry, despite his parents' objections. His father arranged to have Worcester transferred to Wellington's staff in Spain. After his son's departure, Beaufort promised Harriette a £500 annuity if she would forget his son. Concerned by reports of Worcester's attachment to a camp follower, she accepted the offer. Beaufort knocked the annuity down to £200, and then attempted to nullify the agreement on the grounds that Harriette had written to his son. Harriette, exasperated by the 'paltry conduct', finally took the matter to court and won a £1,200 settlement.

Ironically, Harriette's final professional liaison of note was with Richard Meyler, who had been Lady Beaufort's lover. Meyler, a wealthy sugar merchant, proved difficult after persuading Harriette to live with him, but agreed to support her when they parted. Not all men succumbed to Harriette. Lord Byron – ever the romantic – rebuked her because he did not believe in loveless relationships, but they remained faithful correspondents until his death.

At her husband's prompting, Harriette began writing her memoirs in the early 1820s. Desperate for money and fearful of losing Rochfort, Harriette jotted matter-of-fact blackmail notes to her former lovers advising them that £200 was the price of omission from her book. Many paid up, others ignored her, and the Duke of Wellington was provoked to make his celebrated reply: 'Publish and be damned.' *Harriette Wilson's Memoirs of Herself and Others* became an instant bestseller – each instalment brought such a mob to publisher John J. Stockdale's shop that he had to have barriers installed. Thirty-one editions sold out in one year, making a £10,000 profit.

A feud erupted between Harriette and her old friend and rival Julia Johnstone, who retaliated within three months with a book of her own, *Confessions of Julia Johnstone, Written By Herself, in Contradiction to the Fables of Harriette Wilson*. Harriette's portraits were accurate, but Julia claimed much of the truth had been distorted to conceal Harriette's scandalous behaviour.

A.S.M. (Lists 1, 19, 22, 46)

♣ Thomas Wolfe
3 October 1900 to 15 September 1938

The youngest of eight children, Wolfe could talk well at the age of 1 and do simple reading at 2. His father was a stonecutter, and his mother kept a boarding house in Asheville, North Carolina, where Wolfe was born and raised. Mama nursed him until he was 3½, and they slept together until he was 9 – at which time he was allowed to cut off his curly, shoulder-length hair. Once, when two older boys began calling him a girl, Wolfe protested vigorously, then whipped out his penis to dispel all doubts. He entered the University of North Carolina at 15 and after graduation enrolled at Harvard, with the intention of becoming a playwright. In 1923, with an MA, he went to New York, where he taught English at Washington Square College. In 1930, when royalties from *Look Homeward, Angel* started rolling in and a Guggenheim Fellowship came through, Wolfe quit teaching and from then on devoted himself to writing. He made seven trips to Europe and also travelled through the US but lived primarily in New York for the rest of his life. The powerful Wolfe was 6 feet 5 inches tall and had a mop of unruly black hair and dark, penetrating eyes. His giant appetite for food, sex and alcohol was well known. He drank especially heavily when his writing was not going well. Normally, he would write for days on end, supported by nothing more than coffee, canned beans and endless cigarettes. He died in Baltimore from tubercular lesions on his brain.

With a combination of boyish good looks, masculinity and fame, Wolfe appealed to a wide variety of women. Some were publicity seekers, some were sycophants, and some wanted to mother him. One of the women said, 'He was intolerable and wonderful and talked like an angel and was a real son-of-a-bitch.' '[Wolfe] loved women and was somewhat oversexed,' wrote Elizabeth Nowell, his agent and one of his biographers. At a party, for example, Wolfe would take a receptive girl into another room and make love to her. Later that night, when someone pointed to the girl, he would shoot back, 'Who's she?'

Wolfe lost his virginity and first experienced 'the coarse

appeasement of the brothel,' as he put it, at 16. With two fellow students from the university, Wolfe went to a Durham, North Carolina, whorehouse, where a prostitute, Mamie Smith, took him. She ignited 'all the passion and fire,' Wolfe said afterwards. He soon made another visit to Mamie and was a steady customer for the next four years. During Christmas holidays back in Asheville that first year, he slipped away from a family gathering to be with a 'red-haired woman' at a cheap hotel.

In summer 1917, Wolfe fell in love. 'A nice young boy, here, the son of my landlady, has a crush on me,' wrote 21-year-old Clara Paul to her sister. Since she was engaged, nothing came of it but, writing to a friend years later, Wolfe confessed that, although he had forgotten what the girl looked like, he had never quite got over the love affair.

On Wolfe's 25th birthday, Aline Bernstein, then 44, became his mistress. A highly successful theatrical designer, she was attractive and tiny, with greying hair. They had met one month before on a liner returning from Europe and fell madly in love. That Aline was married and the mother of two grown children did not matter. Their often stormy relationship continued for six years without protest from her husband, Theo, who remained devoted and compassionate throughout. At first, the pair would meet in Wolfe's New York apartment, then she rented a loft for them to share at 13 East Eighth Street. They made love often, and Wolfe referred to her as his 'plum-skinned wench', his 'dear Jew', and his 'grey-haired, wide-hipped, timeless mother'. Aline would write, 'He called me a lecherous old woman and cursed me that he could not get me out of his soul.' He was insanely jealous, sometimes calling her at two in the morning to see if she was out on some 'bawdy mission'. Wolfe's compulsive whoring and his mother's anti-Semitic hostility toward Aline eventually diminished his sexual desire for her. Aline knew he was bringing girls into their loft. 'You've gone with dirty, rotten women all your life,' she would say, 'and that's the only kind you understand!' Once Wolfe proposed marriage but she refused. Before one of his European trips, Aline made him promise not to fool around. 'By God, I kept the faith,' he noted in his diary. At another time, however, both were in Paris. As soon as she left for New York, Wolfe headed for the nearest brothel. Aline mothered him and fostered his career, and when, at the urging of his editor, Maxwell Perkins, Wolfe finally broke away in 1931, she attempted suicide with sleeping pills. To console her, Wolfe wrote, 'I shall love you all the days of my life, and when I die, if they cut me open, they will find one name written on my brain and in my heart. It will be yours.'

Besides Aline and countless one-night stands, there were at least three other women who briefly came into Wolfe's life. One was the actress Jean Harlow, whom he met on a Hollywood set one day in 1935. That evening both left in Jean's limousine, and they returned to the studio together the next morning. What happened in between is not recorded. The other woman was Thea Voelcker, a 30-year-old German artist, whom Wolfe met just before the 1936 Berlin Olympics. He persuaded the tall, shapely divorcée to accompany him to the Austrian Alps, where they enjoyed themselves briefly. She was deeply in love with Wolfe and wrote affectionate letters to him after his return to New York. Wolfe, however, would have nothing more to do with her. While in Germany, Wolfe was also in the company of Martha Dodd, the American ambassador's daughter. He was a bit in love with her, but there is no indication that sex was involved.

Although a sexual athlete, Wolfe longed for family life and would often ask friends if they knew a nice girl he could marry. 'I can always find plenty of women to sleep with, but the kind of woman that is really hard for me to find is a typist who can read my writing,' he once said. To Wolfe, the ability to cook well indicated a sensuous personality. He would often surprise women he was interested in by asking, 'Are you a good cook?' Wolfe kept a list of women he had not yet slept with but intended to. He did not plan to marry until he was around 35, 'after possessing hundreds of women all over the globe'. In the end, still unmarried, his last thoughts were of his greatest love. Just before he died, Wolfe whispered, 'Where's Aline. . .? I want Aline . . . I want my Jew.'

R.J.R. (Lists 2, 20, 22, 24, 38, 48)

♣ Mary Wollstonecraft
27 April 1759 to 10 September 1797

This British author was an advocate of women's rights in an era when women were kept, as she said 'in silken fetters'. She wrote novels, children's stories and, among other 'miscellaneous' works, *A Vindication of the Rights of Women*, which has been a continuing inspiration to feminists of the nineteenth and twentieth centuries.

'The first of a new genius,' she called herself, and she was. She supported herself as a writer, belonged to an influential intellectual circle in London, lived openly with two men and, also openly, bore a child out of wedlock – at a time when a respectable woman was supposed to marry and hold her tongue. As a child, she stood between her parents to protect her mother from the blows of an alcoholic husband (he once hanged a dog in a drunken rage), and Mary had slept outside her parents' door at night when it was likely that violence might erupt and she would be needed. She also nursed her mother during her last illness and rescued her sister Eliza from an unhappy marriage. At 15 she vowed 'never...to endure a life of dependence'. To earn a living, she spent two years as a companion to a wealthy woman, ran a day school, and was governess for the daughters of an Irish lord. In 1787, her first book was published by Joseph Johnson of London, who became her good friend and introduced her to Tom Paine, William Blake and others. Her *Vindication of the Rights of Men* (1790) made her reputation; *Vindication of the Rights of Women* (1792) brought her notoriety. The views she espoused – for example, social and sexual equality with men, full educational rights for women – shocked many, including Horace Walpole, who dubbed her a 'hyena in petticoats'. But her manner was charming, her voice soft. Though she considered anger her worst fault, self-pity probably was. She was fervent, proud and prone to melancholy and depression. Twice she attempted suicide, and at least once considered herself on the brink of madness. Tallish, with a good body, she had fair skin, long eyelashes, auburn hair and almond-shaped hazel eyes.

She lived in France for two years during the Reign of Terror. As a member of the Girondin circle, she was also the lover of the American Gilbert Imlay. Back in London, she ended up living with, and then marrying, William Godwin. Mary died from complications following childbirth. When Fanny, Mary's daughter by Imlay, killed herself at 22, she was wearing her mother's corset, monogrammed 'M.W.' Mary's daughter by Godwin, named for her mother, was to become Mary Shelley, author of *Frankenstein*. Before eloping, young Mary and her lover, Percy Bysshe Shelley, paid final tribute to Mary Wollstonecraft by joining hands over her grave.

Early in her life, Mary had passionate, though probably nonsexual, relationships with women. She was essentially modest, shocked by the 'jokes and hoyden tricks young women indulged themselves in', and she felt that 'women are in general too familiar with each other'. However, she wrote possessive, loving, jealous letters to Jane Arden, a childhood friend, and her relationship with Fanny Blood, whom she met when she was 16 and Fanny 18, was 'a friendship so fervent, as for years to have constituted the ruling passion of her mind,' according to William Godwin. Though Mary and Fanny lived in the home of Fanny's parents, and they ran a school together, Fanny was in love with Hugh Skeys. He finally married her in 1785, took her to Lisbon, and she died there during childbirth. Her death threw Mary into a long depression.

Mary tended to like young romantic men and middle-aged geniuses like painter Henry Fuseli, a member of Johnson's circle who was short, melodramatic, married and bisexual. It is unlikely that Mary slept with Fuseli, though she was obsessed with him. When she asked his wife Sophia if she might live with them as 'an inmate of the family', Sophia threw her out. Meanwhile Mary turned down a number of marriage proposals – it was she who coined the phrase 'legalized prostitution' as a synonym for marriage.

Gilbert Imlay, one of the two major loves of her life, was an American frontiersman and writer; somewhat shady, tall and lean, with a 'steady, bold step'. It was probably in a Left Bank hotel room that Mary first had sexual intercourse at 33 or 34. 'I don't want to be loved like a goddess, but I wish to be necessary to you,' she told Imlay. When he was off on business, she wrote him love letters rhapsodizing on his glistening eyes and the 'suffusion that creeps over your relaxing features'. In May 1794, Fanny was born, and their passion faded. Mary followed Imlay back to London, where he was having an affair with an actress. Mary proposed a ménage à trois, but the other woman would have none of it. Twice Mary tried suicide, once by jumping into the Thames from Putney Bridge in the rain. 'I would encounter a thousand deaths, rather than a night like the last,' her suicide note to Imlay read. 'May you never know by experience what you have made me endure.' She was rescued by boatmen.

On 14 April 1796, she boldly paid a call on William Godwin, the radical philosopher whom she had met at an intellectual gathering five years before. (At that first meeting he had disliked her for talking too much – Thomas Paine couldn't get a word in.) A genius with a head too large for his body, Godwin was known for his integrity and kind heart. It was a case of 'friendship melting into love,' he later said. That summer, they became lovers and, although after their first night together she felt that he had acted 'injudiciously', he convinced her to continue the affair. It was domestic and joyous; they sent notes to each other constantly. That November she missed her period. (She probably knew of no method of birth control other than Godwin's 'chance-medley system' – a kind of rhythm method he may have introduced her to.)

Against their basic principles (neither was religious), they were quietly married in church on 29 March 1797. They did not live together. Mary wanted her husband 'riveted in my heart' but not 'always at my elbow', yet she was jealous when a Miss Pinkerton flirted with him. Their child, Mary, was born on 30 August with the help of a midwife. (Mary gave the job to a midwife rather than a male doctor as a form of feminist protest.) The placenta was not expelled and a male physician was called. He tore the placenta in pieces from her uterus with his hands, a procedure which caused her great agony and probably gave her puerperal fever. Puppies were brought in to suck off her excess milk, because she was too ill to breast-feed her child. When she was given opium for pain, she said, 'Oh, Godwin, I am in heaven,' and he, who had been tenderly nursing her, replied, 'You mean, my dear, that your physical symptoms are somewhat easier.' She died on 10 September.

A.E. (Lists 1, 9, 14)

♣ Virginia Woolf
25 January 1882 to 28 March 1941

Born of beauty (her mother, Julia Duckworth, was famous for it) and brains (Sir Leslie Stephen was one of England's leading literary figures), Virginia inherited both. Tall and thin, she was elegant and fragile, with deep-set eyes and a classic, ethereal beauty. Writing was her passion in childhood, and remained the reigning passion of her life. Virginia had a quality of other-worldliness which alienated her from other people. This was compounded by periodic bouts of insanity – when she would hear voices and hallucinate – which forced her to retreat from society for months on end. She had four major breakdowns, and was on the verge of one each time she completed a novel. At 25, she began meeting with her brothers' Cambridge friends (the circle later known as Bloomsbury), where she became famous for her wit and flights of imagination. Though Virginia had many suitors, she did not marry until she was 30. The following year she completed her first novel and had her most severe breakdown, lasting almost two years. Afterwards she remained relatively stable for a while and quite productive, writing at least one book every two years. A well-respected writer from the beginning, she became a best-selling novelist in her forties. At the height of the Second World War, having just completed another novel, Virginia felt herself going mad once more. Unable to face another breakdown, she filled her pockets with stones and drowned herself in the River Ouse. She was 59.

Two half brothers, Gerald and George Duckworth, provided Virginia's unfortunate introduction to sexuality. When she was 6 Gerald, then in his twenties, stood her on a ledge and explored her genitals with his hand, an incident she never forgot. During adolescence George would come into her room at night, fling himself down on her bed and kiss, fondle and caress her. Virginia, a young Victorian, endured his habits in mortified silence until she was 22.

Not surprisingly, though Virginia flirted with men, she fell in love with women. At 16, the object of her affection was Madge Vaughan, a beautiful, dark, romantic woman who shared Virginia's literary tastes. They had an intimate friendship, but Madge soon married. At 20, Virginia began a passionate correspondence with 37-year-old Violet Dickinson, an old friend of the family. Her letters to Violet sound like those to a lover in a physical sense, addressed to 'My Violet' or 'My Woman', signed 'Yr. Lover'. They are full of endearments, demands and longings, and such sentiments as, 'When you wake in the night, I suppose you feel my arms around you.' The sexual element, however, was missing, as it was from most of Virginia's relationships. Her ten-year intimacy with Violet remained a purely emotional affair. Lytton Strachey, called 'the arch-bugger of Bloomsbury' by Virginia's nephew Quentin Bell, proposed to Virginia in 1909. She was well aware of his homosexuality but accepted him anyway, perhaps because of his wit and reputation as an intellect. However, he retracted the proposal the next day. 'I was in terror lest she would kiss me,' he said. Their friendship was salvaged, and it was Strachey who suggested to political activist and writer Leonard Woolf that he court Virginia.

484

At 30, Virginia married Woolf, himself one of the Bloomsbury group, only to discover that she was frigid. 'I find the climax immensely exaggerated,' she said. Sexual relations ceased shortly after the honeymoon, though they remained in many ways happily married for twenty-eight years. Virginia loved Leonard more than anyone, except perhaps her sister Vanessa, whose womanliness she also envied. (Of herself, she once said that she was 'not one thing or another, not a man or a woman'). After her marriage, she settled into a life of asexuality and writing. At first Virginia yearned for the motherhood and passion embodied by Vanessa, but her adolescent attitudes toward sex and passion remained with her for the rest of her life: 'This vague and dream-like world [of writing], without love, or heart, or passion, or sex, is the world I really care about, and find really interesting.'

Still, there were always affairs. The 30-year-old Vita Sackville-West fell in love with 40-year-old Virginia, and the feeling was soon mutual. Vita was a beautiful writer whose aristocratic lineage went back four hundred years. Her affair with Virginia lasted five years, and they slept together about a dozen times. This was Virginia's only physical homosexual affair. It was also her longest lasting sexual relationship. Remarkably, the sexual aspect of their affair was not cause for shock, guilt or any particular elation. Nor did Leonard mind, since their marriage was not threatened. As Vita wrote to a friend concerning Virginia's sexuality, 'She is not the sort of person one thinks of in that way. There is something incongruous and almost indecent in the idea.' And as Virginia wrote to Vita, ' . . . It's a great thing being a eunuch as I am'.

Whatever sexuality Virginia possessed was channelled into her writing. During her affair and subsequent close friendship with Vita, she produced her best novels. After their affair, composer Ethel Smyth fell violently in love with Virginia, but the pursuit was largely unsuccessful. Virginia wrote two more novels. In her suicide note to Leonard, she said, 'I don't think two people could have been happier than we have been.'

J.H. (Lists 1, 14, 16)

♣ Brigham Young
1 June 1801 to 29 August 1877

Quickly taking command as the second president of the Mormon Church upon the death of Joseph Smith, Young held the post for thirty-three years. He was instrumental in leading the church to Utah, where it established enduring roots, and in making polygamy an official Mormon doctrine. Born into a Puritan New England household, Young spent an impoverished childhood which instilled in him respect for physical labour – and an austere morality that his father reinforced with whippings whenever the motherless boy (Abigail Young had died when Brigham was 14) broke even minor rules. A self-taught reader (by 16 he had attended only eleven days of school), Young discovered the *Book of Mormon* in 1830 and embraced the religion founded by Joseph Smith. Commissioned to preach, Young zealously fulfilled his missionary assignments as he rapidly climbed in the church's hierarchy. When anti-Mormon feelings culminated in the 1844 murder of Smith in an Illinois jail, Young succeeded him as president – a position he held until dying from natural causes – and his authority soon pervaded all aspects of life in the flourishing Mormon communities and industries he helped found in the Utah desert to which he and his followers had fled. Young was a strict disciplinarian and only once was his will widely ignored: Mormon women united in opposing his proposal that they dress in a 'desert costume' of his own design (an ungainly ensemble that combined an 8 inch top-hat, a baggy calf-length skirt over trousers and an antelope skin jacket). Otherwise no Mormon disobeyed the 'Lion of the Lord'.

Many of the Mormon Church's troubles in Illinois and points east stemmed from polygamy, a principle Joseph Smith claimed was 'revealed' to him as a divine truth. Young insisted that, upon learning 'plural' marriages were necessary for salvation, 'it was the first time in my life that I had desired the grave . . . knowing the toil and labour that my body would have to undergo'. None the less, it was Young himself who in 1852 officially incorporated polygamy into the church's canon, leading some members to resign since the *Book of Mormon* itself forbids plural marriages. It was also Young who most fervently practised what he preached. No Mormon had more wives than Young. The precise number is not known; conservative counts give him nineteen wives, possibly twenty-seven. The Mormon Genealogical Society credits him with fifty-three wives. Others estimate the total at seventy or higher. Anyhow, Young indisputably and enthusiastically fulfilled his 'duty' to marry often.

Nor had Young waited until 1852 to begin. His first wife, whom he married when he was 23, died soon after the pair of them joined the church. In 1834, Young married again – and waited until 1842 to take his initial 'plural' wife. By the time he issued his official blessing on polygamy in 1852, Young had married at least twenty-two times. Many of the older women were not his mates – he merely wanted to give them his name and financial support.

One of Young's daughters-in-law suggested polygamy was merely to satisfy male lust when she said, 'If Salt Lake City were roofed over, it would be the biggest whorehouse in the world.' But, for Young, lust had nothing to do with it. Polygamy, he proclaimed, was a divinely sanctioned way to enhance the church's population and to eliminate prostitution, spinsterhood and adultery. Yet, when a pretty girl caught Brigham Young's eye, he was quick to invoke his orthodoxy. Few women resisted the potent advances of the barrel-chested, 5 foot 10 inch, blue-eyed and robust Young. Only one, the beautiful actress Julia Dean Hayne, whom he unembarrassedly pursued, is known to have spurned him. But, even with Hayne, Young had the last word: after the death of this woman, he had a 'proxy' marriage performed so that they could be together eternally in heaven. Young also had no aversion to fleeting temporal weddings – while staying with the Sioux in 1847, for instance, he happily accepted the company of two young squaws who, at least for the length of his visit, were married to him.

His other marriages proved more lasting. One home held most of Brigham Young's wives, who usually had their own private, monogamous-type residences scattered throughout the city, as well. The Lion House (as it was called) was the heart of Brigham Young's harem. The second floor was divided between a central parlour for prayers and entertainment and a series of bedroom suites for wives with children. The third floor contained twenty smaller bedrooms for the childless wives and older children. When Young decided upon a bed partner for the night, he made a chalk mark on the selected wife's door. He fortified himself for each amorous visit by eating large numbers of eggs which, he believed, enhanced virility. Later, he would quietly go down the row of doors, find the one with the chalk mark, and slip inside. Afterwards, Young invariably returned to his own bedroom.

His virility was never in doubt. He fathered fifty-six children. He had his first child, a daughter, when he was 24, and his last, also a daughter, when 69. In a single month of his 62nd year, three of his wives gave him three children, and he had long sexual relationships with a number of his wives.

'I love my wives . . . but to make a queen of one and peasants of the rest I have no such disposition,' Young claimed. But many of his wives 'whined' about his lack of attention – and Young responded by offering to divorce any of them that so wished. None did at that time. Certainly Young had his favourites – for nearly two decades Emmeline Free was his chief lover. They married when she was 19 (and he 44) and over the years Emmeline bore him ten children. She was, the other wives whispered, awarded the best quarters – a room that featured a private stairway Young could use secretly.

But Emmeline's reign ended soon after 1860 at Young's first sight of Amelia Folsom, a 22-year-old who stubbornly resisted his advances and announced her love for another man. However, that rival stepped aside when threatened with a lengthy church mission and Amelia surrendered to Brigham. But Amelia relished her role as Young's favourite. When he gave her a sewing machine, she pushed it down the stairs, complaining it was the wrong brand. Young bought her the right brand. When he lectured her on her sins, she scoffed, on one occasion punctuating his sermon by pouring a pitcher of milk and a hot urn of tea on his lap. Not usually tolerant of disobedience, Young suffered it from Amelia until his death.

Troublesome as Amelia proved, it was Ann Eliza (wife number twenty-seven by some counts; fifty-one by others) who proved the most rebellious. This wife, too, rejected the ageing Young's advances but underestimated Young's determination; in 1869, a year after the courtship commenced, the 24-year-old bowed to family pressure and married him. Young got more than he bargained for. Ann Eliza complained about his inattention; castigated him for his frugality (despite his riches, Young doled out slender provisions to his wives); and, in 1873, listing neglect and cruelty among the causes, she filed for divorce. Young found himself forced to contest her claim strenuously – only a year earlier federal charges of polygamy had been dropped because of a technicality. By conceding that Ann Eliza could sue for a divorce,

Young would be admitting that he was a polygamist – and the federal government, he was sure, would pounce on him again. After years of bitter legal wrangling, Young won his case: he told the court that he was legally married to Mary Ann Angell (his second wife and his senior living spouse) and he could not, therefore, have legally married Ann Eliza. But, in splitting this legal hair, Young had in effect repudiated his cherished doctrine of polygamy – a practice that after his death was soon formally abandoned by the Mormon Church.

R.M. (Lists 8, 9, 17, 21, 25, 26, 32, 39, 52)

♣ Émile Zola
2 April 1840 to 28 September 1902

Zola's father, an Italian engineer, died suddenly, leaving his French wife and their six-year-old son penniless in Aix-en-Provence. When he was 7, Zola was sexually molested by a servant named Mustapha, and the experience left him with a lifelong loathing of homosexuals. In 1858, he joined his mother, who had moved to Paris. During the next two years Zola failed his baccalauréat examination twice at the Lycée Saint-Louis. As an adolescent, Zola was a romantic who read and wrote poetry. After failing his graduation exams, the shy country poet lost his naiveté when unemployment forced him to live in a 'louse-infested lodging-house packed with thieves and prostitutes'. The story that he avoided starvation by trapping sparrows on the roof and pawning his trousers is an exaggeration, but it is indicative of his poverty.

In 1871, he published the first of his novels which illustrated his theory of naturalism – which postulated that man's actions are determined by heredity and environment. One of his 'obscene' (but bestselling) books, *La Terre,* even provoked a 'manifesto' which suggested that the depravity in the novel was caused by 'an illness of the loins' that had made the author impotent. Zola was extremely nervous, a hypochondriac, and so sensitive that a pinprick would send shooting pains up his arm. He possessed 'delicate, mobile, astonishingly expressive hands' and a similarly expressive nose with a highly developed sense of smell. He was short sighted and lisped – but had a beautiful tenor voice. A solid man, 5 feet 6 inches tall, with brown hair and beard, Zola's face perpetually wore a melancholy expression. A gourmand, by middle age he tipped the scales at 16 stone, but after 1887 he lost much weight by following a low-liquid, no-wine diet.

As a youth, Zola was infatuated with Louise Solari, a friend's younger sister, but because she was only 12 when he left for Paris a romantic attachment seems doubtful. Years later, a story surfaced that Zola had courted a young girl called Jeanne (supposedly a pseudonym for Louise) by picking bunches of grapes because he was too shy to express himself verbally. She ate as many as she could, then thanked him and returned home.

During the years he lived in red-light districts, Zola no doubt learned much about sex from his noisy neighbours, and might have had first-hand experience as well. Some biographers contend he lived with a prostitute who left the starving writer for more comfortable circumstances.

At 25, Zola began courting Alexandrine Meley, a striking brunette a year older than him who worked as a seamstress. One story says they were introduced by Cézanne, who had been Alexandrine's lover. In another version, she attracted Zola's attention because she was weeping hysterically over her previous lover's desertion. Alexandrine became his mistress and, four years later – in May 1870 – they married.

The marriage was not sexually successful. Five years later, Zola confided to male friends that they had intercourse only every ten days. Even this periodic passion was soon spent. Zola's repressed sexuality twisted him with guilt, and his conflict was augmented by his belief that sex without procreation was reprehensible. He and Alexandrine never had children, though both desperately wanted a family, and this surely contributed to marital coldness and discord.

Physically faithful to Alexandrine, Zola poured his repressed passion into work, producing over twenty books, such as *Nana* and *Pot-Bouille*, where vivid descriptions of nakedness and copulation aroused the critics if not Zola himself. After eighteen years of a marriage that provided little sex or love, Zola at 48 was fat, unhappy and aged. He confessed he was 'plagued by the desire to go to bed with a very young girl ... who had not yet reached puberty'.

Beginning in 1887, his life changed incredibly. He started losing weight and, the following year, he met Jeanne Rozerot. She was just 20 years old, tall, dark-eyed, and modestly surprised that Zola noticed her. He rapidly fell in love and moved her into an apartment. Jeanne bore Zola two children, Denise and Jacques.

490

He was as devoted to them as he was to their mother, who gave him a happiness he had never known and, presumably, a satisfactory sex life. Zola was very protective and loving towards Jeanne. He disliked the fact that she was forced to live as a recluse because of him, but Jeanne seems to have been content, calling him her 'Prince Charming'.

After years of juggling two households successfully, Zola was aghast when an anonymous letter informed Alexandrine of his mistress and children. Alexandrine raged and threatened separation, but eventually her tirades subsided. She met the children, and after Jeanne's death she watched over them, legally gave them Zola's name, and made them her heirs.

Zola's affair ended when he died accidentally (although some suggested it was murder by political enemies) as the result of carbon monoxide poisoning.

P.A.R. (Lists 8, 16, 17, 25, 35)